Wolves and the Wolf Myth in American Literature

Wolves and the Wolf Myth
in American Literature

S. K. ROBISCH

UNIVERSITY OF NEVADA PRESS
RENO & LAS VEGAS

University of Nevada Press, Reno, Nevada 89557 USA

Copyright © 2009 by University of Nevada Press

All rights reserved

Manufactured in the United States of America

Design by Kathleen Szawiola

Library of Congress Cataloging-in-Publication Data

Robisch, S. K., 1964–

Wolves and the wolf myth in American literature / S.K. Robisch.

p. cm.

Includes bibliographical references and index.

ISBN 978-0-87417-772-5 (hardcover : alk. paper) —

ISBN 978-0-87417-773-2 (pbk. : alk. paper)

1. American literature—History and criticism. 2. Myth in
literature. 3. Wolves in literature. 4. Animals in literature. 5. Human-
animal relationships in literature. I. Title.

PS169.M88R63 2009

810.9'3629773—dc22   2008050299

The paper used in this book is a recycled stock made from 30 percent
post-consumer waste materials and meets the requirements of American
National Standard for Information Sciences—Permanence of Paper
for Printed Library Materials, ANSI/NISO Z39.48-1992 (R2002). Binding
materials were selected for strength and durability.

First Printing

18   17   16   15   14   13   12   11   10   09

5   4   3   2   1

for Patricia

and

for Bob

Contents

At dawn on a February morning in 2004 I stood in the Lamar Valley watching wolves. Ten years earlier I had visited Yellowstone National Park for the first time in my life. There had been no wolves. I am becoming an amateur naturalist; having spent time with trained biologists and ecologists in the field, I have no delusions about the limits of my knowledge regarding the natural world. The writers of wolf books might whip their excursions to Baffin Island or the Boundary Waters beyond exhaustion in order to build their own ethos, but like Jay Robert Elhard in *Wolf Tourist,* I wave the flag of the wolf-watching novice. After spending a decade in libraries and conducting interviews, after the sight of wolves behind fences and perhaps a few months of man-hours in wolf country, I offer only ecocriticism. I'm anxious to find out what wolves might gain from a book written by an English professor too often stuck inside the ivory tower.

A drama had unfolded over the prior three days that February, one that seems appropriate to a book that examines how the nonhuman world is constantly correcting our assumptions and fantasies about it. An interloper tried to gain access to the Druid Peak Pack in the valley. He was chased until he intruded upon the Rose Creek Pack's territory, where he was beaten and chased again, back into a neutral space between the zones of control. The day before I arrived, the lone wolf, likely a wanderer from Mollie's Pack down near Pelican Lake, had found the alpha female of the Druids. She was the successor to the famous #42, the Cinderella Wolf, the last of the first wolves introduced to Yellowstone National Park in 1996, and this black wolf wanted to mate with her. This was during the breeding season, and territorial margins were a little less flexible. But they turned out to be more flexible, as biologists have learned over the past decade, than that old adage about wolves being monogamous.

After his dalliance, the interloper was beaten badly again, this time by the

Druids, whose pack that season was made up mostly of lean, tough yearlings, the Druids having thinned and dispersed considerably since I saw them in the summer of 2000. For some months they'd been thirty-eight strong, but now their dispersers had founded several new and smaller packs. Regardless of his opposition's decreased numbers, though, for the second time in two days that lone wolf was whipped. He limped severely, resting often. By midmorning he gingerly sidled up to the alpha female and they mated. Three times. An incredible feat of fortitude on his part, and I admire him for his energy, although he may not have lived long after his three-day flurry of sex and violence. So much for lupine monogamy. So much for eugenics. I wasn't there for the violence, only the mating, which I chose not to watch.

At the roadside: a cluster of onlookers, biologists, and cinematographers. They, we, are always there, and I realized especially at that moment of intimacy between the two coupling wolves that the pack has no privacy except when it finds its way into the spaces that aren't under surveillance. The wolves are the source and constancy of story for these wolf-watchers, a kind of soap opera to some. Even when the pack manages to slip into a sheltered alcove of the park where it used to live in myth—the deep, dark forest or a clearing at the foot of the great mountain—many of its members are radio-collared. This is partly for their own safety until their reestablishment in the greater Yellowstone ecosystem is complete and well documented, partly just to satisfy biologists' curiosities and ensure their paychecks, and partly to keep the good citizens of privatized America from surreptitiously shooting, trapping, crowding, feeding, or do-gooding the wolves away.

In refusing to watch the mating through the spotting scopes, I suppose I drew an ethical boundary for myself as a wolf-watcher. When I heard over the radios from one park biologist to a volunteer, "Yes, they're definitely in a tie. That's their second one today," I was repelled. I'm not sure a biologist is justified in this voyeurism, but I'm certain that I'm not. I've worked hard trying to transcend the tourist mentality about the natural world, particularly about wolves. I watched a red fox mousing. He stood briefly on his hind legs, front paws out as if casting a spell, *renald statant,* then plunged into the snow in a quick arc, buried to his midriff, tail in the wind. I felt I could better justify looking through the kitchen window than the bedroom window.

During that winter in the Lamar I took several courses at the Yellowstone Association Institute, including one with Norman Bishop, one of the park's most highly respected biologists, who retired in 1997 and still teaches for the YAI. His class was called "The Ripple Effect" and covered some of the finer points of trophic cascades, elk and wolf relationships, the history of Yellowstone Park man-agement and mismanagement, the progress of scientific learning about ecosys-temic complexity, and the plasticity of wolf behavior, especially along Yellow-stone's Northern Range. Bishop's an excellent teacher, full of stories as well as data.

Another drama there. A few years before taking his class, I had met with Norm Bishop in Bozeman. He demonstrates all the qualities of both the general-ist and the specialist. He addresses with cool reason the utopianist notions of the wolf as angelic and benign, "easy for people removed from the necessity of mak-ing a living with livestock." He is able to use the same measured approach to stockgrowers associations' rejections of science in favor of a "science" excusing exploitation and destruction. At one point I asked Bishop how he came to study wolves, what drew him. He related two incidents that weigh significantly on how I formed the goals I have for this book.

Bishop grew up near a railroad track at a stopping point for steam engines. His mother had read him *Little Red Riding Hood* and *The Three Pigs* several times, and when an engine would stop and release steam, he would imagine the sound as the breathing of The Wolf. It kept him awake and afraid. In time, his parents did two things that changed both his emotional and intellectual responses. They got him a dog. They burned a copy of *Little Red Riding Hood* in front of him. It is the only incident of book burning I can think of that I support, not because of anything to do with *Little Red Riding Hood,* but because of the power of a ritual of fire used to open a mind rather than to close it.

The second incident is this: Later in life, Bishop visited a zoo that kept a lone wolf in a small enclosure. He approached the cage, and the wolf also approached. It sniffed his hand. Many people would have found the experience quaint or exhilarating, assumed that wolves were indeed very like dogs. This is precisely what saddened Bishop—that this was not the way a wolf should live—caged, lonely, socialized, bored to death. I thought of a sliver from Ted Hughes's melan-choly poem "Wolfwatching," about a wolf in a zoo:

. . . He's run a long way
Now to find nothing and be patient.
Patience is suffocating in all those folds
Of deep fur. The fairy tales
Grow stale all around him
And go back into pebbles. His eyes
Keep telling him all this is real
And that he's a wolf—of all things

> To be in the middle of London, of all
> Futile, hopeless things. (17–18)

After decades as an educator, after helping carry one of the crates containing one of the first wolves brought into Yellowstone during the remarkable recovery project, Norm Bishop has more than confronted the mythic wolf of his childhood. In a copy of Ewan Clarkson's *Wolf Country* that he gave me, Bishop wrote this note: *Old myths die hard; new ones may be in the throes of birth as we speak. Keep up the search.*

This book is the fruit of that search. It is not, however, a book about wolves. It's a book about wolf books. I am concerned with the study of mythic and scientific approaches in literature that have put imaginary wolves into the minds of the most seasoned, clinical thinkers. Many of these images are possessed of a power equal to the scapegoat, the minotaur, or the phoenix, and some are as ancient. They prompt the most and least responsible actions human beings take toward predatory animals, preservation efforts, and the politics of habitat. The focus of this book, wherever it goes, whatever disciplines it mines, is on literature. The way we read and write about an animal will affect our behavior toward that animal, as the way we read and write about anything else does. It had better, or the study of literature is a trivial pursuit. To this end, the ghost wolves that I am examining—the wolves of the imagination—must be weighed against real wolves. We don't want fantasies about race, class, or gender dictating ethical and political decisions; why, then, have even scholars been content for fantasies to govern our behavior toward the nonhuman world?

When I began writing this book, I lived in Battle Ground, Indiana, within a light afternoon's walk of Wolf Park, a captive-wolf facility where the biologists keep a "pack" they select from wolves they allow to breed. The others are "retired." Tourists, mostly local, come in to see the wolves and listen to the presentations. Their children sit on the front row of the bleachers, the wolves lined up at the fence watching the little ones, the easy prey. It's a running joke at the evening public "wolf howls." The staff there, under the direction of Erich Klinghammer and Pat Goodman, socialize wolf pups to people through a program in which disciplined enthusiasts, mostly wildlife biology students, live with the wolves, sleep with them, nurse them with bottles, and raise them until they are old enough to join the rest in the pen, should they make the cut (several wolf biologists, such as Renée Askins and Doug Smith, were "puppy moms" at the beginnings of their careers).

Wolf Park workers trot out a bison every week or so to "activate" the wolves to go into predatory behavior, then pull the bison (which costs money to replace and might hurt a wolf) before the pack gets too involved. Then they toss road-killed deer into the enclosure. Most midwesterners who visit likely only ever see wolves there, in a place just specific and big enough to assuage our consciences about zoo wolves (which these really are) and easy enough to keep us from having to go to where wolves live like wolves. I took my time with my hesitancy about the park's assertions of scientific value, read and visited, asked questions, until I finally reached a point of fundamental disagreement. Then, after a few trips to Yellowstone, I had to struggle again with the roadside-attraction dilemma. I can more soundly resolve the dilemma there, where the space and ecosystemic health is sufficient to merit several populations living closer to their own terms, and the fence is gone, and the behaviorists have to share.

The diffidence doesn't come from some vision of all wolves and people living free on the great green meadow. That's not going to happen, largely because Americans are too bloodthirsty for cheap beef and hell-bent on running the world. The Wolf Park dilemma comes from a realistic concern over whether we need to be putting more wolves into captivity, even for the best of reasons, and what really can be studied beyond basic biology in that condition. Vitus Dröscher's *The Friendly Beast*, for instance, valorizes research from the Brookfield Zoo that could not be taken seriously today except as a blip in science history. The answers I've received to these questions have told me more about people than about wolves. Askins and Smith resorted to the "Park" for their training, as they reveal in their books, out of the romantic wellspring one finds in many wildlife biologists, including Adolph Murie, and nature writers, including Barry Lopez. They wanted to "bond" with a wild animal as well as to learn wildness. What they learned was certainly more than they could learn from books, but less than they could from wolves. They finally had to go to where wolves live. The dubious value of training like that at Wolf Park can be gauged by the combination of initial romantic appeal with the retrospective reminiscence and doubt that it produces.

Sometimes in the twilight of an Indiana summer I would hear the Wolf Park wolves howling and wonder why travelers in wild lands, including many quite recently, thought of that sound as forlorn or haunting, and why now the tendency is to think of it as celebratory. The howl can go to the human soul, certainly, but has always seemed to me possessed of its own varied emotions, a register and quality of its own kind. There is forlorn; there is celebratory; there is howl. The call of a great horned owl and the trumpeting of an elk go to my soul just about as effectively, and in their own voices. What a howl means or with what emotion it resonates to a given wolf, we just don't know. We seem discontented with listening.

Over the decade spanning 1996 to 2006, the wolf recovered to an impressive number of healthy populations in the northern Rocky Mountain regions of the United States, which also resulted in remarkable recoveries of those biomes in which the wolf was always supposed to live. This phenomenon is still one of the greatest successes of park management and environmental policy in our nation's history. Recently, the wolf's proliferation has resulted in its delisting from the "endangered" designation of the Endangered Species Act, which might be seen as a success story if not for the mismanagement practices of several state governments such as Idaho, Wyoming, and Alaska, as well as several federal agencies under the Bush administration. As soon as the wolf returned, wildcatter antiwolf laws justifying another extermination campaign were written as quickly and poorly as possible. Even with proper federal oversight, a "viable population" is still pathetically defined as low as fifteen breeding pairs in some fairly large ecosystems.

Profiteers on the wolf's death continue to fill their pockets, but the progress made during the 1990s, particularly in environmental law and public knowledge, might have built a bulwark strong enough to fight off the trigger-happy yahoos bent on destroying their own ecosystems, all the way up to the vice presidential candidate famously exuberant over her aerial wolf hunting experience. I am therefore sadly aware of the continued relevance of this study on wolf literature.

A constellation of events spawned my interest in wolves, an interest only equal to what I have in many other animals. However, in experiencing a long arc of reading and analyzing their stories, and just occasionally seeing them live as wolves, I've been humbled by them, silenced in their presences, and feel something between a filial pull and an apprentice's mesmerism. People, on the other hand, haven't exactly shown themselves in the best light, and what I've learned about them through wolves has confirmed many of their worst traits, especially in mass behavior. It's been tough not to fall into a comprehensive misanthropy. I focus my disappointment, therefore, on myself, in the hopes that I will come to live a life more connected to the world and contribute something needed. If I'm eternally faulted in the academy for this failure to give humans the proper supremacy over the earth and cosmos, then so be it.

Acknowledgments

For their friendship, and for the way they live with the planet: Jeff King and Molly Siddoway-King, Steve Edwards, and Stu and Bev Knapp. For his great heart and equal mind: Dick Thompson. For their constant support and ribbing, the gang: Dan Gaines; Tim Reynolds; Mark Pendleton; Russ Clark; John Trench; Jay Morris; and Jeff Neimeyer. And for the gear: Shane Priddy. For their humor, insight, and knowledge: Charley Henley and John Kirby.

For early reading, editing, instruction, and encouragement: Vernard Foley, especially regarding the Lakota and American Indian history; Leonard Neufeldt, for his brilliance about the logic and line of argument, for his close editing during recovery from back surgery, and for his poetry and love of Thoreau; Myrdene Anderson, for her experience among the Saami and their dogs and for her friendship; and Barbara Ras for her early interest in the work. For her faith in this book, and her willingness to accept it at its most ponderous weight and see it through to its fighting trim, Joanne O'Hare. My gratitude and respect goes to Gerry Anders for his thorough editing and insightful suggestions.

For sympathetic ears and needed perspectives, and for their generosity with limited time: Barry Lopez; Jim Halfpenny on tracking; Paul Schullery, who was charitable with Yellowstone's historic resources, including his own astonishing memory; Hank Fischer of Defenders of Wildlife; David Abram; Thomas Parkhill regarding the Kluskap-Malsum legend; Cheryll Glotfelty; and A. G. Rudd for his notes and conversation and his continued interest in the book. For readings: Glen A. Love, Barton Levy St. Armand, John Price, Ian Marshall, Mark Allister, and Scott Slovic. For the education: the Yellowstone Association Institute.

For their file of journalism on the wolves of the Southwest: the staff at the Southwest Room of the State Library of New Mexico. For discussion in the Internet newsgroup I visited: Donald Ferry; Kelly Taylor; Brent Brock, and especially Ralph Maughan, whose Web site tracking the news of wolves around the continent is the most impressive I have seen. For insights into children's literature: Gail Melson. For the *Duchess of Malfi* reference: Trish Henley. For the inspiring music to which I often worked: Gabrielle Roth and the Mirrors and Mickey Hart. For insights into canid biology and ethology: Kathleen Salisbury, especially for her permission to view a canid exploratory surgery.

For making life in a big university worth living: my undergraduates in Ecological Literature and American Literature and my graduate students in Ecocriticism, especially Jason Meyer, Jill Janikowski, Sarah Eddy, Tom Hertweck, Mark Bousquet, Brian McCammack, Ellen Bayer, Neal Gill, Simone Caroti, and Maria Windell.

For being the animals I know well: the miniature horses Fanny and Tucker and their larger friends Gabby and Cowboy; Spike and Luke the cats; Ruby the dog; and especially our own cats, Annie Leroux and Cricket, and our dogs, Jack and Alice. For thriving: the wildlife of the Lamar Valley. I have also learned during the writing of this book at least one specific lesson from each of the following animals of the Wabash/Little Vermillion watershed: the coyote, great blue heron, red-tail hawk, great horned owl, kestrel, crow, blue jay, grackle, Canada goose, plover, coot, toad, raccoon, possum, skunk, shrew, mole, mouse, cicada, moth, spider, little brown bat, whitetail deer, gray and red squirrels, rabbit, Japanese lady beetle, mud dauber, hornet, and paper wasp. I have been grateful for their company.

For their knowledge of animals big and small, I thank especially the biologists Norm Bishop, Diane Boyd, Dave Parsons, Phil Gipson, and Erin Clear.

For teaching me, more than anyone has, how to be a scholar and a teacher, for his great friendship and indefatigable efforts toward making this a better book, and for his love of animals: Bob Lamb. Most of all, for being the most wonderful person I've ever known and the person who put me on a higher path to the great outdoors: my wife, Patricia Henley.

Wolves and the Wolf Myth in American Literature

Introduction

This is the book of the folio wolf, as Melville might put it. My goal is to contribute a scope-oriented study of a single animal's importance to literature. In addition, I hope to inspire the creation of more works that integrate the fundamental principles of the life sciences with literary criticism. For as much ground as I try to cover, some material is necessarily missing, material that I hope is sufficiently lurking at the edges of what is included, tempting a reader to venture farther out or deeper down. Slight treatments of comparative mythology, animal cognition, and psychoanalysis were the best this book could accommodate in favor of my incorporating as thoroughly as possible into a literary study the basics of wolf biology and ecology.[1]

There are several tip-of-the-iceberg moments. For instance, I refer to Denise Casey and Tim W. Clark's anthology *Tales of the Wolf,* the subtitle of which, *Fifty-One Stories of Wolf Encounters in the Wild,* should indicate how selective I have to be about unpacking and analyzing in depth. I do sometimes write the précis (for example, in the annotation of Brian Frost's work on werewolf stories) when it would save pages better left to be read in the original work. In several cases, the provision of a simple list of readings to substantiate and demonstrate scope is the objective. There are also, inevitably, a few books missing. Wolf books keep on coming, although not now at the rate of the 1980s–1990s, and such books as Seth Kantner's fine novel *Ordinary Wolves* appeared too recently for me to include them. The chronology of my study reaches from roughly the prehistoric (and so pretaxonomic) dispersal of the wolf to the beginning of the twenty-first century.

In order to make the management of volume easier, I have tried to structure the book in subject-oriented chapters. However, this is not an episodic project, in which each chapter is the result of an article from a journal and so stands alone. Chapter 2, for instance, isn't designed only to provide a summary of wolf biology for the novice's interest; many nonfiction books on wolves provide that. It works to serve as an empirical touchstone or litmus for other chapters, providing the healthy dose of hard biological fact that should inform the textual analyses of any respectable ecological literary criticism.

Wolf books are given to repeating both the information and the politics of other wolf books. For example, Hampton (123), Lopez (*Of Wolves and Men*. 191), Steinhart (33, 47), McIntyre (*War against the Wolf,* 246–47), and Leopold (129–30) all write about the guilt or remorse a man might feel after killing a wolf. Each writer provides an example a little different in degree and kind—ranging from a vague apprehension to a full-blown conversion—but their subject matter is the same. Such repeated use of an image or adage, as any student of literature knows, establishes a motif. It also functions as a kind of chant, the mantra of a community trying to be heard. Because one of the major goals of *Wolves and the Wolf Myth in American Literature* is to demonstrate the wolf's ubiquity as both a being on the planet and a figure in literature, I sometimes reiterate. That list of writers I just mentioned covers forty-six years of wolf literature, and the subject of guilt over killing wolves is just one among many that seemed important enough for each writer to recite. I make claims early in the text the support for which stretches over hundreds of pages, largely because of that support's multiple applications to additional and subsequent claims. Repetition should help us keep track. One doesn't break out a map and compass once, but periodically along the way.

This book examines many European myths, anthropological observations, children's stories, and bouts of cultural criticism. It includes close readings of some prominent wolf stories. It considers the material of oral narrative, particularly of recorded stories from the Micmac, Pawnee, Lakota, Kwakiutl, Nunamiut, and other tribes that have generated legends and myths influencing consequent American literatures. It accounts for novels, short stories, zoological and ecological reports, popular and scholarly criticism, print journalism, natural history, and government documents—as well as tracks, scat, urine curtains, howls, pheromones, and pack protocols.

Diane Boyd-Heger writes, "Objectivity and passion about study animals are not mutually exclusive; I wouldn't have devoted my life to studying wolves if I didn't love them" ("Living with Wolves," 96). Having come to understand this myself, I hope that, at the end of slightly less than a decade of labor and accumulation of evidence toward the writing of this book, I am able to honor another animal through a sound argument that prompts a vigorous activity among students of both literature and nature. I hope that in some way more wolves live longer in wilder places, even that academics in the humanities might have something to do with such a recovery, for all this expenditure of thought and paper and ink.

The wolf does not serve my purposes as a symbol in literature. To the contrary, I mean for wolves to be exonerated from having to present us with their purpose at all in order for us to accept their active agency in the books written about them. They deserve at least the same respect and attention from literary critics and scholars that is given to entirely fictional characters.

Most of us still have to imagine wolves. Their return to the North American regions they once inhabited, especially in the conterminous United States, is celebrated more often by city-dwellers who have only seen them in zoos than by those who live in the places likely to be populated by breeding packs. And why not? Wolves, like most wild animals, ought to be left alone, given space. Edward Abbey wrote that it is sometimes enough just to know the animal is out there (*Desert Solitaire*, 129–30). Folks who occasionally see a wolf might wear this experience as a badge of honor, their speech suddenly taking on an authority assumed from a single transformative moment. Information Age "expertise" about wolves also seems easy to come by, what with up-to-the-hour Web sites giving us every kind of information except what comes from our own presence and experience.

The wolf we imagine, what I label in this study the "ghost wolf," wrestled with the real wolf for dominance of our American thoughts three hundred years ago, and they wrestle now. The struggle between the two has been articulated as a contest between myth and fact. It is not. It is a struggle between a healthy mythology and a toxic one, because the wolf is an archetypal figure in America no matter what discipline is brought to bear on our understanding of it. Science's contribution to the myth, its remythologizing mistakenly promoted as "demythologizing," has been profound and necessary in ensuring the wolf's return to a nation historically hostile to its existence.[2]

A darkly comical example of this supposed demythologizing is recorded by Peter Steinhart in *The Company of Wolves*. Steinhart consults the wolf trapper Dan Gish, who purports to appreciate "the qualities of the wolf as he really was," then summarily dispenses with the literary work of Barry Lopez as "bunk" and the scientific work of David Mech as "misinformation" (44–45). David Brown's study *The Wolf in the Southwest* includes Gish as a contributor, a generous offer to a man "sick and tired of these new biologists making up a biology which doesn't exist" (45). Gish's choices might be thought of as spot-on, though; perhaps the two strongest works of nonfiction on the wolf are Barry Lopez's *Of Wolves and Men* and David Mech and Luigi Boitani's *Wolves: Behavior, Ecology, and Conservation;* and Brown's is still the best book-length report written for a lay audience on wolves in the American Southwest. Steinhart proves by example that *how* we fruitlessly attempt to demythologize this nature-culture relationship, and toward what degree of health, is important to consider.

Careful, progressive approaches to the role of science in the human/nonhuman negotiation are found in Hall and Sharp's preface to *Wolf and Man: Evolution in Parallel* and in Bruce Hampton's *Great American Wolf.* Hampton writes, "Today, the symbolic power of the wolf remains while our perception of the animal, as well as ourselves, has vastly changed" (255). The wolf myth's residence in our minds for so long, with so little corrective control by the animal's presence, has invested it with a strong but poorly defined function in the American consciousness. The academic humanities have furthered an anemic discourse on matters of the natural world, despite literature's being full to the brim with represented life, place, and personality beyond the human. Literature scholars have as a group treated the wolf only a modicum better than have the wolf hunters of history.

The mythic wolf is as powerful a force in the making of American thought as is the cowboy or Plymouth Rock—in part because of its pervasiveness in both Indo-European and Native American cultures beyond white colonial legends. Its power has been derived from that cumulative scintilla that is story—first told, then written. Much of the fiction using wolves either as symbols or as prominent characters is articulated in unfortunate prose marketed to a broad and mildly base reading level—derivative, clichéd, exploitive, and/or prurient. It also *sells,* multiplying quietly and pervasively, one paperback at a time. Writing about wolves that is solidly researched, clearly constructed, critically sound—this feeds the myth with enough fact to protect it from desecration, what Mircea Eliade called "profanement." A mythic structure woven of fact may take us to a healthy, if hard, knowledge. For instance, we are as a species going to find out just how sick we'll become when tigers disappear, although we'll probably still be too collectively dim-witted to see the relationship between our own decrease in health and their absence. We nearly came to this point with wolves in America. At a collective low, we knew of about five hundred left in the lower United States, all in Minnesota (Smith & Ferguson, 4).

Generally speaking, responses to my having written a book on wolves in literature have balanced between fascinated curiosity and a kind of snobbish skepticism or bafflement. The subject, especially treated in terms of its connection to physical reality, doesn't have much of a voice in my academic community. On some occasions, however—at a party or in a classroom—when someone asked about my work and I explained that I was writing a book about wolves in literature, the reaction was brief surprise, fast on the heels of which came amusement and interest, followed by some flash of memory. This metonymic moment then might lead to the recitation of an anecdote or adage, a personal story, perhaps a factoid, either about wolves in general or about one in particular (whether that animal turned out to be a wolf, a hybrid, or, by the end of the story, a coyote or husky). Sometimes the person would end in a kind of breathless satisfaction, as though I'd snagged a cathartic tripwire. I felt honored to be handed these perceptions of wolves so passionately, confessionally, and often fantastically, perceptions sometimes utterly inaccurate but delivered with firm certainty. We often articulate our ignorance in the language of expertise and conviction, maybe because of the abiding and true fear that we don't, in general, wolf biologist and television-watcher alike, know what we're talking about.

Jay Robert Elhard, in his book *Wolf Tourist,* articulates this experience by reporting the questions friends and strangers "curious to know what it's really like to gaze upon wolves in the wild" asked him after his summer in wolf country:

> How close do they let you get? Can they really vanish into thin air? Does fear for life and limb ever cross your mind? Or are they really as gentle and friendly as people say? Does the sound of their howling at night really make your hair stand on end? What about the eyes, those piercing yellow eyes? Do they really cut right through you? Do you really get a sense that there's a whole, ancient soul reaching out to you from the other side? (197)

These strike me as questions from another age, asked of Marco Polo or Magellan. They are colonial questions in a postcolonial era, the same ones asked with equal naïveté about captured Africans or about monsters like the cynocephali, the purported dog-men of the uncharted regions of the globe. Here we are among the educated and urbane, who want to know about ghosts and savages and ancient souls that vanish into thin air, who expect that a wolf would need any reason or impulse beyond curiosity to "reach out to us."

The most widely recognized biologist in the field, L. David Mech, has often spent about half of each year, half of his life, around wolves in the wilderness. Metaphorically speaking, the man lives as half wolf.[3] This might be why, like Mech's, many such biologists' efforts to better understand wolf-human cohabitation have paid off, not only because they have learned more about wolves but also because they have changed themselves, minimized their attachments to civilization's artificial infrastructure. Consequently, they have altered the direction of stories being told all over the world through a demonstrated respect for, in this case, the lupine.

There are so many imagined wolves in the literatures of North America, taking so many shapes, that they may be the perfect species from which to begin exploring our ideas of wilderness and wildness. While I bristle at a wolf being called "the spirit of the wild" or "a symbol of wilderness"—both lexical cages—we have to acknowledge this deep need we have for animal symbols. Wolves, generally speaking, have strong voices. They tend to have complicated personalities and social enclaves. They inscribe, exchange, travel, nurture, kill, consume, enjoy, question, resist, anger, expel, prefer, copulate, play, deceive, perform rituals, and die, among the other things they do that we are gripped with trying to name. As the wilderness in which they live is increasingly virtualized, relegated to shopping malls that resemble parks and parks that resemble shopping malls, a human price is also paid. It's easy for us to grow willing to accept facsimiles that replace with sterile, self-congratulatory representations the potentially life-changing truths found in physical reality. Also, unlike big cats or bears, wolves are the progenitors of a favored pet, which places them in a curious position vis-à-vis wilderness myth and domestic culture formation. They're unfortunately conducive to symbolic figuring in the human mind. We can point to our dogs and say that we molded them out of lupine clay.

The Wolves of Earth and Story

Wolves and the Wolf Myth in American Literature offers a case for the wolf's importance as a figure in literature because of its importance as an animal in the real world. First, it demonstrates that literature does not realize its importance only in terms of human race, class, and gender, however important those issues are. Literature also depends upon nonhuman subject matter that authors have always tried to articulate. Second, the argument proves with a preponderance of evidence the connection between a literature about at least one animal and our behavior regarding that animal's place in the world. The story of wolves in the conterminous United States is a representative epic, a cultural and historic narrative of a greater force than has been examined in even the best of wolf books. Perhaps a book about wolf books will amalgamate the many efforts to understand, represent, and imagine the wolf, and so clarify in some way the relationship between its reality and its mythology. This book makes seven major claims to that end.

Part I offers a model that accounts for the wolf as it appears both in the world and in books. This is the rubric for the entire study. Given its most detailed attention in the first chapter, it adds up to the first claim: that the wolf as a mystical force in the human mind merits status as a major literary figure—infusive, corrective, allegorical, and ill used—that must be considered, along with other animals, in view of its physical reality.

The next claim of Part I is that considerations of wolves take on *regional* distinction, color, language, and form, especially regarding colonial and imperial human ideas about territorialism and law. This regional influence means that the behavior of wolves is zone-specific as much as, if not more than, it is biologically essential. It also means that *individual* behavior, including anomaly, must be negotiated with both regional and biological influences. Regional thinking must be brought to bear when we read, beyond the academy's sequestering it in the attic of late-nineteenth-century New England women's fiction.[4] In a vacuum our reading suffocates and implodes. We live in regions, ecosystems, biomes. The behavior of real wolves in their biomes is the raw material—a required, if basic, knowledge—for any approach to a wolf story that could be considered at all thorough. The *eco* must be in the criticism.

Part II is a mythic historiography. It asserts the ubiquity of the wolf, especially in the Northern Hemisphere, and considers the means by which the image of the wolf in the Indo-European mind was transported across the Atlantic and collided as violently as any military event with the native nations of North America. The third of my claims is as follows: The American wolf myth is typical of most other American myths in that it is largely borrowed and reified from other cultures, rather than untraceable or original. Because it is cobbled together from prior geopolitically disseminated myths, it displays the United States' youth and immaturity as a mass culture. However, it is atypical in that it demonstrates a remarkable ambivalence over time that has actually led to the remythologizing of the wolf image and a move toward greater bioregional health, therefore catalyzing a national maturation. The mythic historiography is a map of the world drawn over time charting the real wolf's relationship with attempts to accurately represent it (what I will call the "corporeal wolf") and with imaginings that disintegrate it into shadow (what I will call the "ghost wolf").

Part II also concerns the bioregional and mythic syntheses that result in several kinds of elemental wolf stories. Wolf myths incorporate a vast land range of the species over time that is rivaled among megafauna only by humans (chapter 9), but they also are connected in literature to the expanse of the sea (chapter 7), the sky through astrocartography (chapter 8), and the symbolic landscape of our dreams in sleep and fantasy (chapter 10). And so, the fourth major claim of this book is that the alchemical mixture of such stories should stand by itself as proof of the wolf's iconic power, its role as an archetype in the collective unconscious, and its importance to literature by way of its import in the world. Consequently, the accrual of such expansive and powerful myths as those of Fenris, Lycaon, the sea wolf, and the Freudian dream-wolf all demonstrate our need to reconcile what is in our minds about an animal with the animals themselves, and with our behavior toward them.

My attempt is to shape into some more realizable form the ghost wolves carried like another disease by colonists arriving in North America and to demonstrate, largely by example, how those phantasms of the colonizing mind came to meet the spiritualized wolves of indigenous cultures already living there. Most importantly, I refer to the recurrent depictions in wolf books of what happened to wolves during this conflict of symbolic images.

Part III takes a position that might be uncomfortable at first, but I hope will result in a change of thought about where place and animal life reside in the discourse of literary study. The fifth major claim I make is that race, class, and gender are subcategories under the enveloping limits of the biosphere, which precedes and dictates the terms of those three cultural designators. This means that ecological thought is the greater category within which cultural thought resides. The theologian Thomas Berry has said that nothing but the universe is self-referential. Everything else is universe-referential (14). Race is a culturally delinquent classification following from and perverting genetics.[5] Class is the cultural phenomenon resultant from labor and production, which are themselves entirely dependent upon the raw material mined, felled, burned, processed, and measured from the world to be hammered into the artifact of civilization. We might say that class is the perversion ensuing from assumptions of ownership. Gender is the politics of adopting or altering (and so is ineluctably dependent upon) biological sex and genetic inheritance—a choice made within highly limited bounds.

In Part III we see werewolves as a race, children as a class, and the she-wolf as a gender construct. This is less to showcase these anthropocentric categories than to examine how they have bearing on our understanding of nonhuman categories, of course with the wolf in focus. One way I examine these constructs is through a particular brand of myth that presents itself again and again in the wolf story: the myth of the twins. I have found in wolf books an obsession with twinning and splitting. It should be obvious that this theme would stand grand in a chapter on the werewolf, a highly irresolute entity at once changing on the surface and changing, sometimes literally, the interior—the blood, bone, flesh, and heart. I do not favor ethnic metaphors in my examination of the werewolf but stay close to the idea of the doppelgänger or changeling. This limits my inspection regarding how the werewolf appears in literature and what makes it tick, but it also keeps me from having to write an entire book about werewolves within this book.[6]

Shape-shifting, twin gods, hybridization, and wolf brothers all run through wolf stories in a leitmotif of doubling. Twinning or splitting is a trait of many other archetypal figures as well, so I do not claim it to be specific to the wolf story. Neither does all bifurcation assume opposition or define itself by mere difference. There is also reference, cooperation, symbiosis, even parasitic relationship. The image of the twins is significant because, first, it is perhaps more readily recognizable as a myth or archetype than is the wolf. Through the werewolf it serves as a catalyst to the wolf myth's own accrual of energy. In some ways the wolf myth rides the coattails of the twins into the broader mythology. The twins motif is also significant because its empowerment of the wolf myth more sharply defines the psyche's ambivalent responses to wolves.[7]

In chapter 14 (on children's literature) I present the lives of hypothetical fraternal twins in Minnesota, named Paul and Minnie, in order to consider how children in America might grow up to form the ideas they have about wolves. Children constitute the second-lowest class in America; they are without capital, without standing except by the laws of care and welfare that only anticipate their rights, and subject to the whims of a world built for a different size of people with brains farther from the ground. In this way, they are as close as a group gets to the most oppressed class on the planet: other animals.

Further proof of the wolf's force as a foundational mythic image appears in its gendered symbolism, in this case the figure of the she-wolf, the mother of warriors and wolf packs. Modern reconfigurations of this figure now include werewolf stories in which women are the central, transformative figures (the genre was given to male werewolves for centuries). I consider both the psychology of the woman warrior who runs with the wolves, and, in a physical manifestation, the woman wolf biologist (the discipline was given to male scientists for decades).

During Part III, I interrupt the race/class/gender chapters with a close reading that ecocritically subsumes and synthesizes all three of these categories. Using Jack London's *White Fang,* in the context of his many dog and wolf stories, I provide an example of what happens when we think a story toward only our supremacy and comfort. I assert that a significant reading of the book, perhaps most important in terms of understanding London's oeuvre, has been missing from criticism. *White Fang* consistently and sharply indicates matters of race (especially white-vs.-proto-Indian stereotypes), young adult literature (that is, a literature appealing to a certain class's sensibilities about nature), and gender politics (for example, London's own masculinity as well as his character construction), all in the context of colonization (the mining of gold and building of empire by dogsled in the far north). The big three subject matter can be found throughout scholarship on London, but I hope to change how we read such scholarship as well as how we read London's work.

The resultant claim is that *White Fang*'s condition as an "opposite" of *The Call of the Wild* is easily and mistakenly coupled with the assumption that it has a happy ending. I offer that it is more convincingly a quintessential example of hard literary naturalism, in which the book ends with White Fang's demise, not his ascendance. I don't consider this to be one of the major claims of the book, but a proof that pulls together my first three claims (regarding the wolf model, regional influence on the craft of the story, and wolf behavior's direct relevance) with matters of race, class, and gender. The plot of decline in *White Fang* therefore synthesizes four of my major claims toward the greater argument about the wolf's significance as a figure both real and literary, not exclusively metaphoric, in the formation of American reading, behavior, and policy. It also serves as an example of close reading, a reminder of ecocriticism's specific purpose.

The seventh and final major claim that runs throughout this book (and is emphasized in Part III) is as follows: All of the components used in framing an argument are affected by that argument, and this must include any ecological components. For instance, if we frame an argument about gender in terms of violence—say, that male forms of dominance are often violent forms and that female roles have been regularly cast as submissive to that violence—then our thinking about gender, the ostensible focus of the argument, is affected in some proportion and relationship to our thinking *about violence*. When we use an animal as a metaphoric or iconic figure for an argument, however, too often the concerns in liberal arts studies have been with the argument's "forward" focus or anthropocentric goal, and those concerns usually dismiss or diminish the animal quite literally being used. Therefore, when the she-wolf of Rome suckles Romulus and Remus, in one "gendering" of our reading, we might focus on the role of mother to the conquerors, the feminine being used merely as life support for a long-term imperialistic male rule. This certainly will affect the way we take into account the myth's cultural context (for instance, the Latin conflation of the lupus "mother" with "harlot" in the myth), how we might reread and remythologize it today, or whether or not our culture will in time (with the slow and arduous accrual required) revise that myth as operant to our own collective identity. But we'd also better be aware that the story and our reading of it both affect how we think *of wolves*.

Any "scientific" effort at "demythologizing" is certainly doomed to, if not failure, then to that self-correction for which the sciences are famous. To the traditional patriarchy of university and industrial scientific cultures over the eras, myth has been a kind of thorn in the analytical side, a powerful proof of the separated Two Cultures. However, as Mircea Eliade has noted, myth "adapts itself to the new social conditions and new cultural fashions—but it resists extirpation" (*Myth and Reality*, 176). We don't, critic, poet, and biologist alike, demythologize. Myths follow a more complicated life cycle. Because we remythologize, some myths might fade in their energy, fold into other myths, or morph into new shapes with which our names have to catch up, but when we put a wolf in a story, that story no longer belongs exclusively to us, neither to our science nor to our humanities personae.[8]

The Claims in Brief

We should have a list here, because there are many claims, and the project of tying them together as proof of a larger point requires our keeping track.

1. The wolf as a mystical force in the human mind merits status in literary study as a major figure that must be considered in view of its physical materiality.

2. Considerations of wolves take on regional and biological distinctions during our reading, so that region must be an active agent in our reading of both wolf and human character. The behavior of real and individual wolves in their ecosystems is a required basic knowledge for an ecocritical approach to a wolf story.

3. The American wolf myth is typical of most other American myths in that it is largely borrowed, which exhibits the United States' youth and immaturity as a culture. However, it is atypical in that it demonstrates a remarkable ambivalence developing over time, one remythologizing the wolf image and exhibiting a myth defining America's national maturation.

4. The number and range of wolf stories should stand by itself as proof of the wolf's iconic power, its role as an archetype in the collective unconscious, and its import to literature vis-à-vis its ecological significance in the world's biomes.

5. Race, class, and gender are subcategories under the category of the biosphere, which precedes and dictates the terms of those three subcategories. This means that ecological thought contextualizes cultural thought.

6. The myth of the twins is conspicuous in the wolf story, at once revealing the symbolic image of the wolf as reaching beyond image and into archetype, and concealing that archetype by potentially upstaging it in our analysis of shapeshifter or doppelgänger stories. A close reading of Jack London's *White Fang* serves as an example.

7. All of the components used in framing an argument are both proactively and retroactively affected by the argument, including any ecological components. This means that when we put a wolf in a story, the story at that point must be responsible to the wolf.

The Crossing

Part IV is a one-chapter section with another close reading, here of Cormac McCarthy's novel *The Crossing*. The chapter applies six of my seven major claims and so is representative of my position on how to read a wolf story. First, the model describing the wolf of world and mind is useful and adheres. Second, the regional influence of the American Southwest has crucial bearing on the story's craft and the depiction of the wolf in that story, including a verisimilitude and mimesis that take the book toward the real through a heightened degree of corporeality. Third, the pathos inherent to the presentation of the wolf in *The Crossing* demonstrates the novel's contribution to a cultural maturation through the revision of the wolf myth. Fourth, the novel uses powerful and obvious invocations of the wolf's *crossings*—of land, sea, sky, the dream landscape, metaphoric shape-shifting, and of her crucifixion—in acknowledgment of her global ubiquity and her power in the unconscious. Fifth, the werewolf figure (the trapper) as a representative of race, the child figure (Billy) as a representative of class, and the pregnant she-wolf as a representative of gender all pertain. And finally, how we think of wolves—in this particular novel regarding both cruelty to animals and the realities of the Mexican wolf's endangered status in the American Southwest—is directly and significantly affected by our reading the story. My sixth claim, regarding twinning, is not an explicit point in this novel; it is only implicit in the werewolf imagery and in the policies facing each other between Old and New Mexico.

I hope that, in its synthesis of these many points, the resultant close reading will serve both as a convincing composite and as a final reminder of the focus of *Wolves and the Wolf Myth in American Literature* on the importance of the wolf book to the configuration of American ecological consciousness, and vice versa.

PART I

The Wolf Book

CHAPTER ONE

The Real, the Corporeal, and the Ghost Wolf

Wolves and the Wolf Myth in American Literature operates according to a model that synthesizes writings on wolves and charts their connections to human consciousness and action about these animals. It provides as well some basis for analyzing human consciousness of and action toward the nonhuman world. This model could be applied to other species that have been mythified from their real-world lives, such as the bear, eagle, horse, snake, bee, spider, whale, lion, or rat—but it is specifically oriented to the wolf book and the imaginings, here particularly American ones, that have given real wolves archetypal and/or mythic composition. The model is made of the following components:

The Real Wolf. There is, indeed, such a being as a wild wolf. He is not a social construct. She is not a figment of the human imagination. Neither are they mere progenitors of the dog, nor is their collective life reducible to a selective and solipsistic riffing about whether or not wilderness, wildness, animals, or authors *exist*. The idolization of idealism over materialism has done them no good, idealism being no more defensible a position than materialism; in situations of ecological reference versus anthropocentric reference, materialism is almost always the more practicable philosophical mode. Although wolves have coexisted with humans throughout epochal history, they were not humanly designed. This simple fact directly confronts the anthropocentric assumptions that have driven, especially, romantic and postmodern literary criticisms.

The real wolf is both an individual and part of a species of similar individuals taxonomically recognizable in relation to their biotic and abiotic environments. This animal cannot be rendered in text but only represented to better or worse effect. When I use the term *the wolf,* I do not use it reductively, but as a term sufficient to the recognizable boundaries of a species, like the term *human*. The recognition of singular behaviors within and against categorical ones is also vital to this project. We should not use subjectivity to rebut biology or ecology; on the contrary, we must look at the connections among various kinds of writing about wolves to see how they handle both individually oriented and species-level claims. Real wolves are not texts; they are the corrective entities to the texts attempting to depict them.

The World-Wolf. This is the form that embodies all the various representations of wolves in literature. I am borrowing the name from the myth of Fenris in the Icelandic story of the end of the world and the dawn of a new humanity, as well as from the concept of the *anima mundi*. The World-Wolf is therefore not the real or earthly wolf, but the "wolf" of a world of our invention, a symbolic figure shaped according to our own desires—for prowess, material, nurture, conquest, or identity, our placement in the cosmos. Here is the idealist component in relation to the materialist component. In text we are codifying imagination, and symbolic language becomes part of the assemblage of our thought. This World-Wolf may be configured as the Nietzschean überwolf, the Emersonian transcendental Over-Wolf, or the Platonic form of Wolf—including their potential misuses (respectively Aryanism, metaphysical mystification, and ontological idealism). Each position becomes useful (like pragmatism itself) when we see its evidence presented in a writer's manifestation of the World-Wolf in his or her work: Jack London's dog books quite obviously show us the überwolf, Jim Harrison's *Wolf: A False Memoir* is an example of the Emersonian Wolf, and Catharine Feher-Elston's *Wolfsong* indicates the Platonic Wolf as a rubric for her choices of essay and legend.

The World-Wolf part of the model is itself made of the following components:

1. *The Corporeal Wolf.* This is the attempt of a writer to represent the biological, morphological, ethological, and ecological facts of wolves insofar as these may be known. Over time it revises itself through a greater accrual of fact (science's foremost self-corrective practice), through rhetorical debate (the humanities' foremost self-corrective practice), and through changes in the environment (such as the behavior, number, ecological biomass, and other aspects of wolves). The life sciences, especially to the degree that they are able to uncover verifiable fact, are the principal source of the corporeal part of the World-Wolf, followed by nature essays that attempt verisimilitude and mimesis. Think of corporeality as the attempt of an author to "get it right." Its pinnacle achievement is to reach the threshold of real wolves and their plausible behaviors. Semiotics teaches us that

since a book can't be a wolf, the best it can provide is the codification of a thought, translatable by a reader, that may be very like a wolf. In realist fiction, this would be the mimetic wolf written according to, as William Dean Howells put it, "fidelity to experience" and "probability of motive."

2. *The Ghost Wolf.* I use the term *ghost* as an indicator of two historical phenomena. The first is the overwhelming presence in human culture of myth and its totemic, ethereal, unconscious, and symbolic images, including the undeniable presence of imaginary animals in our mythologies; the second is the effort in both Europe and America to eradicate the wolf from the face of the earth, leaving its revenant shade in its former regions. I could call this "the imaginary wolf," but "ghost" offers a more appropriate frisson, given what's happened to wolves in America and in its literature. A better synonym might be "the shadow wolf," one that will have especial application in the more Jungian moments of this study.

Next to the real wolf, the ghost wolf is perhaps the most important element to our study of wolf literature. I won't always point boldly at this figure; the reader might consider reading any work in this book with the ghost wolf lens always at the ready. Metaphors using apparitional language abound in writing on wolves—from incidents of mistaken identity (such as when a hunter mistakes a wet wolf for an antelope or, more obviously, a coyote for a wolf), through a mystification of the wolf's abilities (as in Roger Caras's *The Custer Wolf* or Gary Svee's *Spirit Wolf*), to symbolic spiritualizations of the wolf (such as the figures in Lewis Owens's *Wolfsong*, Clarissa Pinkola Estés's *Women Who Run with the Wolves,* or the premodern works of a Shakespeare or a Webster, on back through the alchemists and into the Icelandic Eddas or Sumerian myths). The ghost wolf is the human imagination making of the wolf what the mind wants or needs for its own comfort, reassurance, or even recreational challenge.

The ghost wolf has its own divided nature, which manifests itself with great moral complexity in literature.

a. *The Malevolent Ghost* is the half of the ghost wolf that casts the animal as a demon, a scourge. What Theodore Roosevelt called "the beast of waste and desolation" and "the archtype of ravin" had been its most powerful aspect for hundreds of years in Europe. That aspect was carried to the North American continent. It dominated the collective American consciousness, to the point of affecting some purportedly scientific premises for the study and alteration of entire ecological zones, even to the point of eliminating species. It is still present in certain political and emotional traps of thought, such as agribusiness or state-level fish–and-wildlife "management" policies.

b. *The Benevolent Ghost* has of late won a collective psychic battle with the malevolent ghost in America. This victory, however, is akin to the noble-savage or ecotopian design, which casts the wolf as a savior, not merely oppressed but transcendent. This aspect of the ghost wolf is the mythic wolf god depicted either primarily or exclusively as nurturing, calm, sociable, intelligent, and even wise, and is responsible for its own damage to the human psyche's ability to confront reality. Think of the person who tries to pet a bison, who domesticates a lion in his New York apartment, or who follows a quasi-pagan doctrine of animal appropriation. Consider the opening of Ted Andrews's entry on the Wolf totem in *Animal Speak: The Spiritual and Magical Powers of Creatures Great and Small:*

> Keynote: Guardianship, Ritual, Loyalty, and Spirit.
>
> Cycle of Power: Year Round—Full Moons—Twilight. Wolves are probably the most misunderstood of the wild animals. Tales of terror and their cold-bloodedness abound. Although many stories tell otherwise, there has never been any confirmed attack and killing of a human by a healthy wolf. In spite of the negative press, wolves are almost the exact opposite of how they are portrayed. They are friendly, social, and highly intelligent. Their sense of family is strong and loyal, and they live by carefully defined rituals. (323)

As a commentary on totems, this is very useful. As a commentary on wolves, it is a risky strategy of transposing the malevolent to the benevolent for purposes of fitting the wolf's rituals with our own. Here I will be explicit about the ghost language. Notice Andrews's use of "Spirit," "Full Moons" (an icon of transformation and an invocation of the mistake that wolves howl particularly at the moon), "misunderstood" (the wolf is not the wolf we think and so is a ghost wolf), and "rituals" (the doctrinal element of the wolf's religiosity). The "press" has presented wolves from various moral perspectives over time; there is no "opposite" for this multivalence. Regarding the "rituals": Wolves may indeed perform rituals, as we will see in chapter 6, but how carefully defined these are is questionable. And the link between wolves' rituals and their assumed loyalty or basic nature is as impossible to prove as it is to prove that our own rituals are linked to such fundamental traits. Writers prone to mystify a physical encounter beyond what the animal in the encounter can himself or herself justify, what is often thought of as a "New Age" approach to encounters with the wild, are common, and they are dangerous.[1]

One more important component of this model must be included:

3. *The Lines* demarking the divided nature of the World-Wolf are themselves part of the model. They are the points of collision, cooperation, and question. When a wolf of the mind meets a wolf of the world, what occurs is no less than a

psychological as well as intellectual education in reconciliation. These lines of separation are therefore permeable. Any World-Wolf may tend more toward its corporeal or ghost-wolf component; there is no static balance. As the representative in a piece of writing of the totality of the wolf (corporeal and ghostly, mimetic and imaginary, persona and shadow), the World-Wolf could be a mere buoy of corporeality glimmering in an apparitional sea. A story might also emphasize the very line dividing two or more *textual* forms. Nordic mythology, for instance, depicts the wolf with a knotty ambivalence, a composition at least equally malevolent and benevolent, perhaps calling into question the usefulness of such a Manichean distinction. We may say that such a story simply has balanced the halves of the ghost wolf, but where such supposed balance occurs the line between the elements becomes most permeable. As a result, we are seeing less a duality that needs to be symmetrically "fair" than we are seeing a third thing, a synthesis of many parts that creates its own whole. Solidity in the line, the cause of our inability to cross it, can be indicative of breakage, imbalance, and myopia. At times the malevolent and benevolent ghosts are in a relationship less bifurcated and more in keeping with the trickster myths, the ouroboros, or the yin and yang.

We are participants with this animal and all others in the project of harmonizing one mind with all minds, and one and all minds with that which constitutes no mind (what we might call our abiotic environment). And harmony is quite obviously not always synonymous with balance. Our lack of skill at reconciling with the real is also responsible for the general frivolity of the humanities (for example, architecture, rhetoric and composition, theater, literature, communications, advertising, compartmentalized history, even sociology and psychology) regarding the nonhuman world.

It seems worthwhile to compose a list of some literary phenomena that exhibit our inability to balance the real wolf with the World-Wolf. At various moments throughout this book I will discuss each of these with greater specificity.

There is the Freudian wolf, found from depth psychology through Jung and into Hesse, in which the iconic wolf is insufficiently known in the real world to function properly as anything but a malevolent psychological symbol. Jung came closest to redemption here, with his definition of the shadow and the role a wolf might play as a critical force rather than a merely demonic one, but he still fell short because of his lack of ecological knowledge. Jung's most succinct explanation of the shadow is found in *Aion* (8–10), and its connection to the wolf through literature is most vividly expressed in the chapter of *Archetypes and the Collective Unconscious* called "The Phenomenology of the Spirit in Fairy Tales" (especially 231–37). Here he provides some of the material for my formation of the benevolent and malevolent ghost wolves, rooting them in both the realm of spirit and the phenomenological realm of history through the fairy tale, priming them for archetypal status.

There is the character a number of people who work with wolves like to call *Canis lupus irregardless,* the figure that offers us problems in evolutionary biology and taxonomy. That is, we have a wolf population that started the taxonomy of wolves, disappeared, and resulted in wolves variously defined by lumpers (biologists favoring a broad and simplified taxonomy) versus splitters (biologists favoring a narrow and complexified taxonomy), as well as variously erased by both lumpers and splitters whenever the taxonomy was revised toward greater accuracy.

There is the devil wolf of Puritan America transformed over three centuries to the sacred wolf of environmentalist America. We find the alpha wolf, beta wolf, and, although this term seems to have waned for wolf biologists, the omega wolf or scapegoat. These designations of pack rank, long subject to exaggeration, have revealed themselves to be a result of a "debate" remarkably like the one between evolutionary biologists and social Darwinists. The abuse of Darwin by Herbert Spencer to justify what persists as an American mythology of self-reliance, divine design, and economic apologetics is at the heart of the assumptions made about wolf ethology, especially in terms of what wolf ethology might teach us about human behavior, and vice versa.[2]

There are the She-Wolves: the wolf mother, the lupine whore, the woman who runs with the wolves, and all of the attendant metaphors, both sexist and progressive, that impel the gendering of the mythic wolf. Next we see the powerful epiphenomenon of the lycanthrope, the werewolf, the shape-shifter—respectively, projects of the modern psychological imagination, the cultural imagination, and the primordial imagination. I group them as a single epiphenomenon because they are all three projects of bifurcation, of twinning the human and lupine. There are the named wolves or feral hybrids such as Kiche, White Fang, Kazan, Baree. These indicate an invented primitivism, atavism, and the inclination on our part to name an animal that already has a name we do not know, one spoken through pheromone or howl or scent mark. Finally (in this list), we find the real wolves whose biographies are written (as corporeal wolves) in order to raise the human consciousness about their lives—for instance, the Custer Wolf or wolf #9 in Yellowstone.

How much material do we need, really, before we recognize the force of this animal in our art? How much do we have to learn about how to approach the reality of wolves, when we have written so much for so long about something more representative of ourselves than of them? It sometimes amazes me that scholars of literature in America have spent so little time on the raw and living world from which we originate, even as its material for story accrues under our very noses over the centuries. The biota gives writers the content of their craft.

Binary 1: Corporeal Wolf and Ghost Wolf

We apply the World-Wolf when we read a wolf story or even the mention of a wolf in a story not ostensibly about wolves, such as Willa Cather's *My Ántonia*. A wolf in some form triggers in us the impulse to square what we have been taught to imagine with what is a real and active wolf in the world. There might be a wolf character, usually named and fitted with four basic methods of characterization—action, speech, thought, and appearance. We may see only the mention of a wolf, not explicitly characterized but presented through exposition. Exposition might give us an idea about a wolf or wolves essentialized. The writer may not be talking about a wolf present in the story but about The Wolf as the writer sees the species (that is, the writer's World-Wolf). At the appearance of any or all of these cues, a negotiation begins between the corporeal wolf and the ghost wolf.

For instance, in *My Ántonia* the wolf story belongs to two immigrant laborers on the Shimerda farm, "Russian Peter" and his brother, Pavel. Pavel is sick throughout, likely with tuberculosis, and one windy night during a gathering in the kitchen, seated by the kitchen stove in order to keep warm during a bad bout, he is frightened by the clamor of coyotes. "He is scared of wolves," Ántonia tells Jim. "In his country there are very many, and they eat men and women" (46). Jim, our focalizer, thinks of the coyotes (and, by proxy, as we will see, of wolves) as "defeated armies, retreating; or . . . ghosts who were trying desperately to get in for shelter, and then went moaning on" (46). This passage is prelude to Pavel's story that Ántonia recounts to Jim after the Shimerda kitchen gathering. It is a story that Pavel has told to Mr. Shimerda:

A wedding in Russia is followed by a midnight ride of six sledges full of revelers, including the bride and groom, lighted only by the stars. Pavel drives one, with Peter seated beside him. In the flat declarative diction so recognizable in Russian novels, Ántonia intones, "The wolves were bad that winter, and everyone knew it, yet when they heard the first wolf-cry, the drivers were not much alarmed" (48). The pack communicates and assembles using howls, and crests the hill behind the convoy as "a black drove" running "like streaks of shadow." There are "hundreds of them" (48). The pack attacks the convoy until there are only three sledges left, the hindmost one containing the groom's father. It is overturned by the pack, and the groom considers jumping out to save his father, which gives Pavel the idea that will leave him with lifelong shame.

When only his sledge is left after the wolves attack the horses, Pavel tells the groom that they are moving too slowly and must lighten the load. He then points to the bride. The groom and Pavel struggle; he knocks the groom out of the sledge, then throws the bride out after him, to the wolves. On gothic cue comes "the bell of the monastery of their own village, ringing for early prayers" (49).

We find that "Pavel died a few days after unburdening his mind to Mr. Shimerda" (50), so we may easily read as metaphoric the connection between his tubercular consumption and his consumption by guilt. Jim confesses that they did not retell the story to anyone "but guarded it jealously—as if the wolves of the Ukraine had gathered that night long ago, and the wedding party been sacrificed, to give us a painful and peculiar pleasure" (51). Later he states that "on bitter, starlit nights, as we sat around the old stove," the coyotes "reminded the boys of wonderful animal stories; about gray wolves and bears in the Rockies, wildcats and panthers in the Virginia mountains" (56).

We might consider that Cather gives the story to Pavel perhaps to avoid telling a story that would have to be called "Peter and the Wolves." We have here a tale that immigrates to the United States, adopted and amalgamated with native "wonderful animal stories." Indeed, one of the principal themes of *My Ántonia* is Jim Burden's deliberations comparing and contrasting Nebraska and Virginia in the context of eastern European history, as a way of trying to understand, literally, his place. The coyotes serve as a trigger. Not their own howling but their symbolic proxy for wolf howling is what creates the fear.

Jim's interpretation of the coyote's howls as "ghostly" touches the first chord. Someone familiar with both wolf and coyote yammering will usually be able to pick up a characteristic vibrato, a "talkiness," about the coyote. Wolves will oscillate their howling, but it is often deeper and more mellifluous than the caterwaul of coyotes. So we have, first, the telling of two tales at once—one of the Russian brothers who know the difference and are nevertheless frightened, and one of novices to the wolf (down to Jim, the rank beginner) who find the coyote's voice sufficiently synonymous with the wolf's. The wolves are molded in the gothic form, as a "drove" and as "shadow," their carnage and Pavel's guilt intoned by a church bell, and Jim incants the very definition of the gothic sublime in that "painful and peculiar pleasure." Hundreds of wolves acting at once is a highly implausible event in any era or region (wolf packs just don't get that big, nor do multiple packs tend to glom together). So, too, is their attacking healthy horses all thundering along amidst the commotion of sledge runners and harnesses. Even pulling someone out of a moving sledge, no matter how many wolves and how hungry or rabid they might be, is implausible, better suited to the romance of *The Wolves of Willoughby Chase* or Robert Browning's "Ivàn Ivànovitch":

> 'Tis the regular pad of the wolves in pursuit of the life in the sledge!
> An army they are: close-packed they press like the thrust of a wedge:
> They increase as they hunt: for I see, through the pine-trunks ranged each side,
> Slip forth new fiend and fiend, make wider and still more wide
> The four-footed steady advance. The foremost—none may pass:
> They are elders and lead the line, eye and eye—green glowing brass![3]

Pedagogically speaking, we are asked to suspend disbelief for Cather and Browning only if we know something of wolves. The average classroom moment will reach its apex at a *question* about wolf behavior, not necessarily an answer, unless some interested student does a little interdisciplinary research for the term paper, but all of the criticism on Cather leaves the wolf intact as a symbolic construct. If we accept that Pavel is telling a tall tale, then the narrative suffers because we have no indication (through Ántonia's retelling) that he believes otherwise. His hundreds of wolves must be accepted as real in order for the severity of his shame to be accepted as well. The "real point," we will say out of our indoctrination by traditional literary criticism, is about Pavel's guilt, about the moral dilemmas posed by rough life brought to symbolic ferment when wilderness encroaches, red in tooth and claw, upon the paradise of young love, sleigh bells, and starlit snowfall. Pavel, we might say, becomes wolf to man in order to save himself. Such is the conflict we must face between our ghost wolves and our corporeal ones in literature: Neither Pavel nor Pavel's wolves act like wolves, so redefining reality, as if we could, becomes more convenient for the student of literature than simply learning about wolves.

Because the corporeal wolf represents a writer's impossible quest for perfect mimesis of *Canis lupus*, its share of the World-Wolf composite will sometimes be infinitesimal as compared with the ghost wolf's share. But literary results that give the corporeal wolf a more sizable fraction of the World-Wolf may be found. They are found in scientific reports when the language of the report so carefully designates as to mythify (for example, naming a constellation "Orion" helps us remember and find the constellation, which confirms its position, and its reality, but through the art of mnemonic metaphor). Essays attempting to be consistent with data-driven reports may give us statistical, factual, verifiable, observed, and "lupocentric" articulations of wolf behavior, anatomy, or ability. These essays are at the foundation of much of the nature writing that isn't taught in colleges all over the nation except as a diversionary elective. By connecting the rules and data gained by scientific observation with the cultural devices that make reading important to us, a book about wolves (or any species) will exert considerable influence on our ecological consciousness. The wolf of the earth will inevitably meet the wolf of the imagination. We are still, even at the highest scholarly levels, in the position for the former to regularly correct the latter.

Let's say someone reads a passage written by a field biologist in which a female wolf suckles the orphaned pup of a neighboring pack, all the adults of which have died. The reader may have once believed that such behavior was impossible, that wolves of "rival" packs would never care for each other. The reader has here experienced a friction between the ghost wolf and the corporeal wolf, an assumption disproved by a report of behavior. Perhaps the reader would suspect the passage and examine carefully the proof and the biologist's credibility. If this reader *believes* that the reality of lupine nurture is divinely determined, then no amount of corroboration may convince. We are up against a fallacy of prejudicial judgment: God made wolves mean. Or, perhaps, the benevolent ghost wolf believed to be kind, generous, and nonterritorial bleeds through the line into the corporeal wolf. Now the plausibility of a wolf suckling a foundling pup, corroborated by a biologist's direct observations qualified by her training, creates perhaps too little friction with the reader's beliefs. What often ensues is a fallacy of generalization: wolves are inherently kind. When reading a short story about wolves in which a writer asserts firmly, for instance, the nonnegotiable territoriality of wolves, we may be better equipped as critical thinkers after having read biological and ethological studies, but the point here is that we still must attend to several pressing logical fallacies beyond only the pathetic fallacy.[4]

One reason that wolf books often depict the wolves of imagination and reality in a mystifying relationship is that humanity has almost no working knowledge of potential interspecies moral universes. True, we can only speculate about the moral and ethical conditions of wolves because of their inability to abstract and analyze consciousness, conduct, or good and evil. But why do we value abstraction and conceptualization so highly, given their track record of justifying evil as often as erasing it? We have not as yet been able to interpret the codes by which other species practice ethics, at least not beyond superficial and often biased hypotheses. The actions we perpetuate as a result present us with their own ethical consequences, and in the history of North America those consequences have created as many ghost wolves as they have destroyed real ones.

I can think of worse ways of learning than trying sincerely to live for a time as a wolf and failing. When a reader, having put down Edward Hoagland's "Lament the Red Wolf," sees that same day a red wolf crossing a glade in North Carolina and disappearing into the brush, then follows the wolf's tracks in order to watch her live her life, Hoagland's book is transformed for the reader by those tracks. The mental diagram is refigured to make the track the text, or—to the pure semiotician—to make that wolf the object. This kind of textualization is easily abused, since the wolf is neither a "text" nor an "object," but an active agent alive on the earth, not to be diminished by the cleverness of language worshippers. What can be defended is a reader with muddy boots and an eye better trained to recognize representation, a reader as participant with the wolf printing its tracks.

Caveat Lector. Cave Canem.

One potential problem with the World-Wolf model is the temptation to quantify each element of it and attempt a purely empirical application. Simply by devising a diagram I risk the model's being received in a classroom as an insult to literary study—something like the J. Evans Pritchard introduction ripped from the textbooks in *Dead Poets Society*. We could determine how much ghost or corporeal material appears on the page, verify every fact, even count the number of words, and draw the pie chart of the wolf's silhouette down to the exact percentages of each area. Then we could take the writer's indicated ratios and the reader's perceived ratios, add them to the text ratio, and arithmetically determine the average areas for each category on the chart. As a structuralist, I have no problem with this approach and the testing of its results. As a pragmatist, I have to consider the arbitrariness of the divisions, the frictions generated from text to reader and writer to text, that undermine imposing a strict template on the changing form of myth over time.

Another possible problem is that some readers of this study might resist so Jungian a design. We see the claim of archetype. We see unitary selves (the World-Wolf, the writer, the reader); dyads of opposition that paradoxically hold the self together (corporeal versus ghost; benevolent versus malevolent); the allusion to a "definite structure" (the corporeal as the World-Wolf's gesture to reality and vantage point for perfection); and the Stoic pneuma (conduits of connection, the lines dividing the fractional areas of the World-Wolf).[5] It would be easy for me to defend the model as Jungian and let my audience parse it appropriately. Instead, I hope the reader will test the model's viability regardless of whatever the current fashion of thought regarding analytical psychology might be. If it's useful, then use it; perhaps this will even quell some resistance to Jungian thought, which certainly has its caveats. The emerging field of ecopsychology, for instance, attempts to refine psychoanalysis by offering the thesis of intrinsic value to external conditions; provided it increases its rigor and staves off the fluff to which it is often subject, ecopsychology could take us to a next great step in a theory of mind.[6]

A final caution about the logistics of the model's direct application is called for. Canid hybridization complicates the matter of the "wolf" under examination because of the presence of the dog in the wolf. When real wolves are hybridized, then domesticated and recast in narratives as wolf-dogs, we have a complicated topic demonstrating how the World-Wolf survives. I will handle this, especially during the reading of Jack London's work, with the care its confusion deserves.

While traveling in the Arctic, Barry Lopez learned that his Nunamiut mentors did not validate travelers' generalizations about "the wolf." They had acquired such a body of knowledge that they took the choices and actions of individual wolves as givens. Someone's statement about what "wolves do" therefore received the reply, "Maybe. Sometimes" (*Of Wolves and Men,* 3). Wolves' similarities to humans—Hampton calls them "haunting" (22)—is a frequent point of examination in wolf books. Because of our own individualism in the midst of social commerce, ritual transformations are inevitable and necessary. This means they must be carefully chosen, and the issue becomes even more intricate when we are brought to the knowledge of individualism in a nonhuman species.

When the question is raised of what difference it makes that a species is lost, driven away, or carved down to a few survivors in prison cells, the answer might be found in the epiphenomenon of the ghost wolf. When wolves nearly disappeared from within the nation's borders, the ability even to *think* of wolves was threatened. We are left with only pictures of passenger pigeons and dodos, and seem too often content to let the word or the picture serve as "presence." Even the close call, the near loss, leaves a society with a horrific absence. The ghost wolf fills that dearth, and haunts subtly: a profusion of deer, more hunters clamoring for more tags, government intervention and the reliance on fickle laws, human organizations trying to play the role of wild predators and proving their ineptitude, more calendars rhapsodizing the vanishing breed, fewer wolves and more pictures of wolves. Our assessment of the world based on its beauty is too easily determined by the absence of predators. Also, a confluence forms between Augustinian obsessions with utility and Freudian phobias of victimization, and so the stockgrowers' associations stampede. Environmentalist slogans such as "Save the Wolf" and "Save the Planet" confess as much as they implore: that our own health and sanity are endangered when we are forced to live with interspecies relationships dictated solely by the marketplace, by abstracting raw material and calling it money. Noah's flood has changed from a myth about how to save animals to a myth about how to become the rising water. We either collapse into crisis language or simply brush off as "alarmist" any consideration of environmental degradation.

This is the monster we're up against, the World-Wolf. Our first corrective should come from those who strive to write the corporeal wolf, so that we are better prepared to consider the global soul of the mythic figure after we have read it in language designed to articulate its flesh and blood.

CHAPTER TWO

Basic Corporeality

The writers of wolf accounts generally cite the significance of three periods in American literary history. The first is European settlement of the late sixteen to early seventeen hundreds, following the invasions of North America (see, among others, Earle; McIntyre, *War;* Coleman, Audubon, Lackey, Hampton, and Steinhart). Next is the late nineteenth century—especially the 1880s—when the war against the wolf reached its zenith (for example, McIntyre, *War;* Lutts, *Nature Fakers;* Lackey; Coleman; Hampton; Steinhart; Lopez, *Of Wolves and Men*). The third period is contemporary with most of the wolf books written—one wave in the 1970s spurred by the environmental movement and the appearance of Barry Lopez's *Of Wolves and Men* in 1978, and one wave in the 1990s swelling to the 1995 reintroduction of wolves into Yellowstone National Park.[1] But not much has been done to track the history of wolf biology and the periods of scientific discovery that brought us to this extensive catalog of American wolf books.

In 1994 Mike Link and Kate Crowley produced the only book I have found that focuses directly on wolf biologists as a professional subculture. *Following the Pack: The World of Wolf Research* briefly summarizes the careers of twenty-seven scientists who have conducted fieldwork on wolves. Except for one chapter devoted entirely to David Mech, the book is organized either bioregionally ("Wolves of the American Rockies") or geopolitically ("Wolves of Scandinavia," "Wolves of Poland"). It includes anecdotes, brief context-driven histories, and examples of the biologists' written work, often quoting from their original studies. Link and Crowley do not focus on statistical results so much as on an introductory history of wolf research.

Because the first empirical and field studies of wolves weren't conducted until the late 1930s, after most of the wolves in the United States had been wiped out, America (like most nations) may cite a disproportionately imaginative history for the wolf. Link and Crowley include in a brief section entitled "Wolf of Legend, Wolf of Fact" this statement: "To go beyond the anthropological and sociological symbolism of wolves we must rely on the fieldwork of the researcher, for it is the researcher who confronts the questions in the minds and on the lips of the public, and who tries to sort out, in a systematic way, the factors that induce a wolf to behave as it does" (17). Let's assume that Link and Crowley are using the word *anthropological* loosely, to mean "by logic driven according to human study," rather than implying that anthropology is less than a research-based discipline. Anthropology and sociology are certainly subject to anthropocentric abuses, and both disciplines have grown increasingly quantified. Hard science of any form is considerably softened by the individual behavior of a wolf, which often forces biology and ethology into revision and always exists beyond hard science's attempts at a generalized causality. In other words, what induces a wolf to do anything is as psychological and social, therefore as variable, as it is biological and ecological. The wolf of legend is anthropological; the wolf of fact is real and may be better (though not fully) understood through science. Link and Crowley's project is about people who stopped simply believing in wolves as some phlogistonic phenomenon and started paying attention to them. It should be among the first books considered on an introductory reading list to the subject of wolves in literature.

Nature Fakers

The continuing debate over veracity in wolf stories runs as a thread from Mark Twain's *Roughing It* to Farley Mowat's *Never Cry Wolf* and continues today in the many factions of environmentalism. According to Ralph Lutts, who has written the definitive book on the topic, the Nature Fakers debate began in earnest when in 1903 John Burroughs responded to what he saw as "counterfeit" nature writing (*Nature Fakers*, 3). In an *Atlantic Monthly* article he expressed his outrage that only a handful of purported nature-writing books approached the topic with acceptable standards. For Burroughs, from what we can glean from his own work, these standards were two: an adherence to biological fact, and an inclusion of personal rumination regarding that fact (the latter giving the writer some room to reflect, debate, and envision). Burroughs, for all his purity, was still subject to the narrow view of wildlife management that prevailed, joining in the idea that fewer wolves would mean more "useful and beautiful game" (Burroughs, *Camping,* 4; also cited in Hampton, 128).

This is the sportsman's paradise notion that Aldo Leopold corrected in *A Sand County Almanac* in 1949; in fact, the passage in which Leopold explains this view as a utopian fallacy is the one leading up to his killing of the she-wolf, the fierce green fire dying in her eyes, and his missive that we should learn more to "think like a mountain" (129). In this way Leopold settles a fifty-year debate with a page straight out of John Muir, who was throughout the late nineteenth century the wisest voice on the matter of wilderness. But at the turn of the century the consummate "sportsman," Theodore Roosevelt, quickly joined with Burroughs and coined the label "Nature Fakers" for those rising as nature authorities through bad books. The chief targets of Burroughs and Roosevelt were Charles G. D. Roberts, Ernest Thompson Seton, Jack London, and William J. Long.

The lines were drawn swiftly in *Atlantic* letters and editorials and through Roosevelt's proclivity for waging furious debate. While Lutts accepts 1903–1907 as the key period of the Nature Fakers controversy, he devotes considerable time to demonstrating that the storm did not have a clear beginning or end; Burroughs had loved Muir's *Stickeen,* and Roosevelt had declared Kipling's work "acceptable" because it claimed to be no more than fiction—although a few years later he would declare London's work to be preposterous (Lutts, *Nature Fakers,* 42). The debate was also marked by its share of inconsistencies. London responded to Roosevelt's attacks by delineating a list of expository comments in his stories that he felt may have interfered with the value of his prose but were necessary for the sake of credibility. He defended the "simple reason" of his canid heroes as well as their "instinct," while Burroughs and Roosevelt held court on the matter of instinct alone as the limit of animal consciousness.

During a time when the nation was widely and intensely interested in the nonhuman world, when a national parks system was being entertained (and would be saved from the congressional ax by Roosevelt himself), the debate had great cultural currency. Lutts provides a strong working definition for the phrase "nature faker," one that draws our attention to the inevitable difficulties involved in the pursuit of authenticity and artistic skill: "Perhaps the term is best applied to people whose sentiments about nature blind them to the real living animal in the wild—people whose deeply held personal beliefs lead them to spin fanciful visions of nature. Animals go on being animals despite what we think of them. What we think of them, though, affects our ability to live together within this natural world" (176). Note Lutts's emphasis on sentiment, which is the ghost wolf, the imaginary construct taking shape in the mind of someone either unexposed or selectively exposed to the real animal. And those "fanciful visions" have manifestations called consequences.

During his first trip westward, as told in *Roughing It,* Mark Twain sees a coyote, calls it "the first wolf" about an hour west of Fort Kearney, then later calls it "the regular cayote," offering a pronunciation and proceeding with a long paragraph of insults against the coyote's appearance and manner (568). The designa-

tion of the coyote as a wolf is consistent with the parlance of his time and specifically consistent with one of Twain's influences, Richard Irving Dodge, whose
Plains of North America and Their Inhabitants appears in pieces throughout
Roughing It, particularly in Twain's sporadically meticulous attention to facts. "At
2 P.M.," Twain writes, "the belt of timber that fringes the North Platte and marks
its windings through the vast level floor of the Plains came in sight. At 4 P.M. we
crossed a branch of the river, and at 5 P.M. we crossed the Platte itself" (566).
Such careful attention to detail both echoes Dodge's style and girds the tall tales
that make up most of *Roughing It.*

Twain often employed a little truth to tell a better lie; in fact he finessed this
tactic into a general theory about storytelling in such pieces as "A True Story:
Word for Word as I Heard It," "How to Tell a Story," and "Fenimore Cooper's
Literary Offenses." The coyote classification is "common sense" for Dodge, who
explains convolutedly that the prairie wolf is "miscalled coyote on the middle
and northern plains" and that "the coyote proper I have never seen except in
Texas and Mexico." Then Dodge takes his own opportunity to curse the animal
(202). In addition to further confusing colloquial taxonomy, Dodge's labels provide the kind of plastic material that Twain loved; *The Plains of North America* is
full of anecdotes, moral dilemmas, and contradictory solutions to those dilemmas, racist statements in the midst of a decrying of racism, and a romancing of
the West while preaching factuality at all cost. For the consummate con man like
Twain, such material would prove invaluable in shaping an imaginary West for
the reader.[2]

When in 1963 Farley Mowat decided to employ much the same approach, the
controversy over both *The People of the Deer* and *Never Cry Wolf* was reminiscent
of the debates at the turn of the century concerning the Nature Fakers, although
the real indictment of Mowat didn't surface until many years after his books
appeared. Twain, it was understood, was so obviously spinning yarns in *Roughing It* that veracity was of little importance. The autobiographical nature of his
mining misadventures and his tenure as a reporter are overshadowed by the tale,
material for scholars and biographers rather than for a more general audience.
For Mowat, the same techniques worked well commercially, but not to the same
effect. *Never Cry Wolf* is an interesting combination of Twainian craft elements
and the environmental enlightenment of the 1960s. It is also the exact opposite
of London's dog book strategy. Whereas London attempted to fill his fiction
with plausibilities in wolf behavior and consciousness, Mowat laced a nonfiction
work with suspect embellishment.

Never Cry Wolf is probably the book most responsible for turning the American public away from its near total assumption of the wolf as malevolent. It likely

steered wolf writing, and several subcultures, toward the benevolent ghost-wolf gestalt. We mark "renaissances" in literature with a handful of key determining texts. *Never Cry Wolf* is one such text for the environmental movement—because of, as well as despite, its many flaws. I will return to this matter of Mowat's accuracy in more detail. First, I'd like to follow through on the Nature Fakers phenomenon.

Rick Bass walks the corporeality line in *The Ninemile Wolves,* a 1992 best seller. He approaches the story of the Ninemile Pack in an essay combining research and what he calls "my poet thing" (151). By stating that he is writing from a position of belief, rather than from a detached perspective, Bass risks a skeptical response to his essay's factuality. "I can say what I want to say," he writes. "I gave up my science badge a long time ago . . . The story's so rich. I can begin anywhere" (4). Within that ellipsis he claims to have "interviewed about a hundred people" (a rather magic number) before making his declarations. He has been to the region and has observed the wolves there. "They say not to anthropomorphize—and I'm learning not to—but in some respects, it seems bend-over-backwards ridiculous not to, for if a wolf does not have a spirit, then what animal, ourselves included, can be said to have one?" (131). Bass is often able to juggle the necessities of evidence with the generosity of artistic prose, partly because he defends more the right to make a mistake than the right to grift. This invites the reader to begin with data but to proceed with it into culture—to judge, to act—a characteristic goal of any writer. And his resistance to declaring some implicit law against anthropomorphism is rightly echoed by Onno Dag Oerlemans later, as we will see in chapter 15. However, there really isn't much reason either to "give up the science badge" or to anthropomorphize. If any animal can be said to have a spirit (and Bass takes some risk in implying that both wolves and humans are more likely than other creatures), then why not avoid anthropomorphizing off the page, and *then* write? Where there is rigor there seems little need for poetic freedoms that are self-declared as dangerous to the credibility of one's essay. A healthy anthropomorphism might result from the mere hint of its influence rather than its obvious application, like the vermouth of a dry martini.[3]

The accuracy problem is important to discussions of the wolf because it influences the political actions that will be taken, actions under pressure from beliefs as well as observations. Source credibility (from the isolated incident to, for instance, the multigenerational experiences of the Nunamiut living among wolves); the logic of philosophical determinations (such as the difference between rights and welfare, or consciousness and instinct); the function of scientific inquiry; and the assumptions of storytellers, not only about what is "true" but also about the crafting of truth—all of these factors influence the telling of a tale and the course of wildlife governance. When Vicki Hearne's essay "What's Wrong with Animal Rights" declares, with spurious logic and thin support, that an animal's rights are only determined by that animal's human ownership and subjection to "proper" training, it may be easily rebutted, but when Susan Sontag selects it for *Best American Essays,* a bigger problem develops, one mired in the politics of editorial selection and public legitimization.

Fictional Forays in the Essay

The issue of nature faking only became more complicated as nature writers became better informed. Wolf books went through a second wave of popularity during the 1970s, an era given to both metaphysical investigation, as with Barry Lopez or Annie Dillard, and confrontational activism, as with Ed Abbey. Rather than purporting to be entirely factual and then confronting the scrutiny of skeptics, wolf essays became more confessionally subjective, speculative, including fact but not committing to it. The hard factual mode was handed over to scientific reportage. At times what came from this was the accessible lay science of a Lewis Thomas, and there were those few exceptions who preceded the 1970s environmental movement, such as Rachel Carson. In the wolf book, the result of subjectivity's ascendance has been two decades of repetition of content, with some experimentation in the genre. In Bass's *The Ninemile Wolves* and *The New Wolves* small doses of hard fact combine with large doses of political ideology; in R. D. Lawrence's *Secret Go the Wolves,* Peter Steinhart's *Company of Wolves,* and Bruce Hampton's *Great American Wolf* the writer's interest in the possibility and plausibility of a wolf's behavior is often juxtaposed with material from biologists' works. Many novels in which wolves appear, especially pulp or genre work, contain in their acknowledgments the writer's indebtedness to biologists, wolf parks, zoos, and lay science books about wolves.[4] Through the freedom of subjectivity, the 1970s wolf book took on the activist's assertion of his or her right to "guess well."

This assertion appeared not necessarily as a justification of laziness or grandstanding so much as an effort toward finding a space between the two most often employed methods of writing wolves into books. The first method was scientific reportage, the lack of creativity and accessibility in which resulted in the crippling of the life sciences' capability to influence social change toward healthier ecosystems and environmental responsibility. The second method was the tall tale of the great white hunter of *Field and Stream,* which resulted in extirpation campaigns, poor habitat management, and the absence of preservationism. Writing about wolves, as evidenced by the constant comparisons of them to both humans and dogs, became a kind of self-expression that tried to keep the real wolf in view but just as deeply desired it as an icon or totem. Two ready examples are Roger Peters and Jim Harrison. Peters constructs an observational essay (*Dance of the Wolves*) that speculates often about the wolf's mind; Harrison composes a "false memoir" (*Wolf*) in which the search for the wolf is metaphoric, its physical absence from the text marking the psychological quest for a presence of self.

For his thesis—a personal essay driven by his desire to know what he assumes to be "an elusive animal"—Peters relies on a rough model comparing "naked wolves to real ones," similar in this one regard to the World-Wolf model. He also too enthusiastically employs zoo encounters, the debate over territoriality popularized by Robert Ardrey, and the speculation characteristic of the 1970s and '80s in wolf writing (see, for example, pp. 2–6). Peters includes some hero worship of the pseudonymic wolf biologist Thomas Hunt and his great (also pseudonymic) study *The Northland Wolf*—omitting the real names in an odd effort "to preserve the privacy of individuals and protect the integrity of scientific research" (Preface, unnumbered). Peters names most of the prominent wolf biologists, such as Mech, when he refers to their work, and instead of simply letting us know that, say, one biologist didn't want to be named, he invents both the names and the necessity for him to protect scientific integrity. He uses fictional italicized sections of purplish prose written in the tradition of Seton and Curwood (but not quite up to the standard of London). The italicized sections also serve a connective function; they link a nonfiction biographical essay similar to Elhard's *Wolf Tourist* with the roman à clef, incorporating facts in order to give their narratives plausibility (I will later compare, for instance, Rick Bass's *Where the Sea Used to Be* and Nicholas Evans's pulpy *The Loop*). All of this messy and frustrated effort (which marks most creative nonfiction on the wolf) serves as evidence of not only the ghost wolf's totemic power, but also of that power's evident increase as a writer begins to approach corporeality. Writers may well refer to the wolf as "elusive" ("shy" is probably the more accurate term, though not for all wolves, and it's complicated by wolves being called "gregarious" just as often); otherwise these writers' spiritual quests, which usually encompass their factual quests, would be reduced to something too easily achieved. In Harrison's case the wolf he *doesn't* see is quite simply the result of there being few wolves in the region of Michigan lakes where he wanders. The hunting down of wolves in America, Canadian wolf populations themselves wandering southward, and the prospect of the wolf's return to the eastern Great Lakes regions are all invoked most strongly by the wolf's absence.

That Harrison's memoir is not at all about wolves but is titled *Wolf: A False Memoir* reveals the meeting point of Londonesque fetishism (adopting the wolf's name as one's own), regional fact (there were once wolves to be seen in the central Great Lakes regions), and an inevitable Freudian reference to sexual identity and memory being found in the totem. Add to this Harrison's writing of the screenplay for the werewolf movie *Wolf*—an examination of male comportment and purity with the wolf as analog appearing during the late men's movement— and we see the need for the wolf's presence to establish (in this case male) identity quite literally projected.

The long line of creative nonfiction on the wolf, with all its slippage of subjectivity, ranges from Elhard—who confesses his tourism and writes with clarity and distance based on observation, rumination, journalistic interview, and gathered fact—to an appallingly pithy and exploitive business consultation book by Twyman L. Towery, PHD, called *The Wisdom of Wolves: Nature's Way to Organizational Success.* The use of a little fact in purported nonfiction can create its own fiction, one based on a profane symbolism and opportunism even more speculative and fabricated than a novel or short story. Corporeality's major competitor is not unfounded fantasy. As we will see in chapter 15 on Jack London's work, a writer's attempt to "identify with" an animal, especially through the method of adopting the animal as totem, may result in the totem overwhelming the writer. This may activate certain tricks, conventions, narrative forms, or speculative moments that reveal themselves as confessional more than investigative. That is, the totem always threatens to identify the writer, rather than being assimilated into the writer's identity. Hence the wolf co-opted as CEO.

This is, perhaps, why so many book-length essays on wolves have been written: it could be less that the material needs to be said again so much as that many writers feel the urge to say it for their own cathartic sakes. The wolf essayist often seems compelled to chant the material of those who've gone before. Barry Lopez crafted the contemporary subgenre of the wolf book as a personal inquiry mixed with historical influences. That technique continues in Bass, Hampton, and Steinhart, with Coleman simply reversing the shares by writing as an academic historian while revealing certain personal interests. So far, after two hundred years of wolf books, we have about a four-song hymnal. Where three thousand years ago we might have chanted a chorus honoring the wolf's spirit enough times for children to memorize—enough times for ritual to rest in the soul and for that soul to be transformed—today our wolf chants are just more voluminous, written in books and sold on the marketplace to reach a fragmented and exploding assortment of societies. Negotiating the individuality of each wolf with his or her species demands something more than our written attempts have been able to muster, making these literary failures all the more interesting to examine.

The effort to consider individuality has often appeared as the outlaw wolf story, in which the wolf is fitted with a name and personality only after he or she has inflicted enough monetary damage to gain infamy (see, for example, McIntyre, *War;* Caras). In the 1940s Aldo Leopold launched his "land ethic," a call to see the more-than-human world not only as intrinsically valuable but also as a lesson for human behavior. The wolf then emerged as a martyr rather than an outlaw. The famous passage of the green fire dying in the wolf's eyes, quoted in almost every general nonfiction book about wolves written in the last fifteen years, called for a paradigm shift on the order of God's voice to Job.[5] "Only the mountain," Leopold writes, "has lived long enough to listen objectively to the howl of the wolf" (137).

Between Seton's *Wild Animals I Have Known* and Leopold's *Sand County Almanac* a great change took place in the imaginary view of the wolf, brought on by experiences that did not exactly corroborate the stories of the trinity of wolf extirpation: the Stockgrowers Association, the U.S. Biological Survey, and horrific folklore converted to instructive children's literature. Quietly, away from the new fictions and parafictions of the marketplace, data-oriented studies of wolf behavior were being conducted by Sigurd Olson, Adolph Murie, and Milt Stenlund. These continued, especially following the populating of Lake Superior's Isle Royale by wolves and moose, in the works of Durward Allen, L. David Mech, and Rolf Peterson. Most of this work occurred in Minnesota, the only state besides Alaska with a viable wolf population outside of national park protection after two hundred years of violence. Eventually, through the 1960s and 1970s and the advent of environmental policies that literally reversed the extirpation thinking of the prior decades (with the exceptions of a few such politically retrograde states as Wyoming and Idaho), nonfiction about wolves became as important as fiction. Even the trapping and hunting of wolves—from traps with teeth to traps without, from bullets to tranquilizer darts—has now become associated more with their preservation than with their extermination.

The rise of Allen's prodigies Mech and Peterson and the work of such writers as Lois Crisler, Loren Eiseley, and Barry Lopez finally allowed biologists to communicate with the general public about a reevaluation of the wolf. Its extermination was to be seen not only as a tragic submission to expansion but also as symptomatic of dangerous human projection onto the natural world.

Following the Corporeal Scent

Although ecology was designated a specialized science in 1866, applied knowledge regarding ecological systems was much slower to coalesce. Roosevelt's views on predators as hindrances to the health of an ecosystem was representative of the conservationist ethic operant up to Leopold's 1949 epiphany. Therefore, much of the writing on wolves that preceded the formal studies of Sigurd Olson and Adolph Murie in the late 1930s, while at times biologically progressive, is ecologically stunted. It sometimes includes the wildlife adventure prose of the amateur naturalist, in the vein of Roosevelt's *Wilderness Hunter*—including an enthusiasm about the prospects of ecosystemic knowledge that has still not been realized.

Olson's books are popular essay collections, mostly ruminative pieces about the Quetico-Superior region; his more scientific work appeared in papers.[6] He died snowshoeing near Ely, Minnesota, now the home of the International Wolf Center, at age eighty-two and was widely known by then as the first American scientist to understand *Canis lupus* outside the context of economics. Adolph Murie's book-length work, however, was considered the first empirical field study of wolves, examining the wolf of the north beyond species biology and according to an ecological rubric in observable wilderness conditions. *The Wolves of Mount McKinley* is to nonfiction on the wolf what *The Decameron* is to the novel. Prototypical in form and substance, it provided a template for monographic treatments to follow. The power of Murie's book is found in its combination of accessible writing and statistical rigor. It is structured according to species with which the wolf in Alaska has close connections: the Dall sheep, caribou, moose, grizzly bear, red fox, and golden eagle.

Ravens and crows are conspicuously absent from Murie's study, but many more species are given attention as prey animals and participants in the ecological system he observes. Corvids would in time appear in most ecosystemic reports on wolves, especially as evidence of the trophic importance of predators to biomes, since corvids fulfill the role of scavenger and, in narrative terms, the role of supporting character. Among its other educational characteristics, the wolf-raven relationship, perhaps even more than the wolf-wolf relationship, has provided evidence of lupine idle play.[7] Murie's work combines ethology, morphology, ecology, history, and anecdote. It is what today's biologists would call the work of a true naturalist—the apex of holistic achievement for a life scientist. Murie makes no grand statements about demythologizing. His goal is self-evident: to count, catalog, observe, and quantify predator-prey relationships without losing sight of field knowledge gained from those who had been in the region prior and longer.

At one point, however, Murie and his team remove a pup from a wolf den "for the purpose of checking on the development of the pups at the den and familiarizing myself with wolf character" (45). Murie records details of the little wolf's behavior exhaustively, down to her drinking "8½ ounces of milk on May 19 and 13 ounces on May 23" (45). His project of learning wolf character lasts, unfortunately, for the duration of the wolf's life. "Wags," as they call her because of her quick and frequent tail wagging, grows up domestically, for stretches "chained near the kitchen door" (47), kenneled (48), and finally attached to a dog run (49). There are frequent mentions of how "gentle and playful" she is, a few anecdotes on her behavior that include her developing a relationship with a malamute, and a quiet transition into Murie's observations of other captive wolves. What Murie gleaned about the character of wolves is hard to sort out, but what he teaches seems to indicate the strongest lesson in what likely happened to wolves during the Pleistocene.

What I call the "campfire myth"—that wolves sidled up for meat and eventually companionship and were finally trained and bred into dogs—seems only about as plausible as the captivity narrative of forcible pup removal from dens followed by the progression of socialization to domestication. I will investigate the mythic nature of wolf domestication and the origin of the dog in chapter 17 as part of my reading of Jean Auel's *Clan of the Cave Bear*. Murie's short section on Wags is the most unfortunate in his study and is perhaps a progenitor of the captive-wolf "parks" now in existence purporting to be centers for learning about wolf behavior. It also sets a precedent for other wolf studies and their popularization: Crisler, Mech, Lopez, the Dutchers, and several other students of the wolf have "owned" one or more. They write with misgiving, often apology, about "ownership," looking back on their experiences as a stopgap for their overwhelming love or curiosity. The Dutchers are an exception; like the wolf parks dotting the United States, their project is something of a cottage industry used to sell photographs and films, to the extent of tacitly implying that their "Sawtooth Pack" is actually wild. In the end, we can count Murie's method as one of those errors in judgment to be refined over time and the accrual of a better land ethic.

Otherwise, *The Wolves of Mount McKinley* is a trove of charts and comparisons conducted in the field, citations of historical works, photographs (the frontispiece is a remarkably similar image to the cover of Barry Lopez's *Of Wolves and Men*), and interviews with rangers and outdoorsmen. His epilogue, "Conclusions," lists with humility and understatement a few of Murie's positions and ends with a proclamation as much on wildlife and park management as on wolves: "In considering the wolf and the general ecological picture in Mount McKinley National Park it must be emphasized that national parks are a specialized type of land use. Wildlife policies suitable to national parks—areas dedicated to preserving samples of primitive America—obviously may differ from those applicable to lands devoted to other uses" (232).

There's been a lot of crowing about "what wilderness really is" during the decades following Roderick Nash's brilliant but frequently misused *Wilderness and the American Mind*. Adolph Murie's work demonstrates a basic difference between wilderness and civilization too powerful to ignore. Out of a national park system that sought to preserve the ratio of wolves to the Dall sheep Murie was studying, we learned more about the wolf's reality than we had previously known. For all the effort put into diminishing the significance of wilderness, we learn the most about it from its irresistible presence, as Murie knew. The "primitive America" we preserve is certainly in the psyche as well as in the land, but this is largely because the psyche is as much a product of the land as it is of anything else. Murie stands out among a list of biologists of his time not only because he conducted such a thorough study but also because he understood in some way that its significance would reach beyond its statistical analysis.

Two contemporaries of Murie's, Stanley P. Young and Edward A. Goldman, produced *The Wolves of North America* in two volumes in 1944, the same year that *The Wolves of Mount McKinley* appeared. Part 1 is a set of essays on large predatory species that includes fundamental information on wolves. Part 2 contains both a long chapter cataloging the byzantine system of wolf taxonomy as it was in the 1940s and the best bibliography of wolf literature of its time. In *The Wolves of North America* we find evidence of the state of wolf study prior to the work of Olson, Murie, Young and Goldman. The list is loaded with such titles as "Catch 'em Alive, Jack" (508), "American Cattle" and "Coyote Coursing" (509), "How a Den of Wolves Was Exterminated" (516), and "How Shall We Destroy the Wolves?" (516), along with an impressive array of anonymous sources on "Children Suckled by Wolves," "Wolf Nurses in India," and "Wolf-hunting in Chicago" (511). More than two-thirds of the entries are on trapping, hunting, ranching, zoos, and folklore, limiting such clinical entries as "Summary of the Large Wolves of Canada" or "Utah Mammals" to a stark minority.

I have not found any evidence that proves the social contract with wilderness to have been much different in the 1940s than it is now. We awaken to some atrocity we've committed against the environment, learn a new fact, take on a new concern, then discard or offset each of these with some version of novelty that we seem to prefer, the one that costs resources and leaves no room for wilderness. When utility gains enough force of money and ignorance, wilderness disappears. When beauty gains enough of the same, wilderness often disappears as well, but in a more subtle and puzzling way. We transform ecologically sound forests into mere sacred groves, healthy canyonlands into reservoirs that pose as "lakes." As John Daniel has written, these are "the cults of beauty and utility" designed to cast luxuries as needs (36). The biologists writing the first rigorous wolf studies stepped away from the interests of agribusiness and tourism. They were looking for a wolf that many people did not want them to find. Once found and revealed, defended, explained, that wolf had a chance to participate in the national argument. And so, wolves appeared to human culture through literature more like the complex beings they actually are: alive and cognizant as well as wondrous to human beings and archetypally bound to our consciousness. They looked sufficiently like us to slow our accelerating national ego, sufficiently different to accelerate our dulled ecological consciousness. What did we do next? We wrote more books, awakened a bit more to wilderness and to the murderous destruction of the real that we'd wrought for a century.

Land Ethics

A Sand County Almanac contains the most oft-cited passage about a wolf encounter in American literature, beginning with the statement "Only the mountain has lived long enough to listen objectively to the howl of a wolf":

> My own conviction on this score dates from the day I saw a wolf die. We were eating lunch on a high rimrock, at the foot of which a turbulent river elbowed its way. We saw what we thought was a doe fording the torrent, her breast awash in white water. When she climbed the bank toward us and shook out her tail, we realized our error: it was a wolf. A half-dozen others, evidently grown pups, sprang from the willows and all joined in a welcoming mêlée of wagging tails and playful maulings. What was literally a pile of wolves writhed and tumbled in the center of an open flat at the foot of our rimrock.
>
> In those days we had never heard of passing up a chance to kill a wolf. In a second we were pumping lead into the pack, but with more excitement than accuracy: how to aim a steep downhill shot is always confusing. When our rifles were empty, the old wolf was down, and a pup was dragging a leg into impassable slide-rocks.
>
> We reached the old wolf in time in time to watch a fierce green fire dying in her eyes. I realized then, and have known ever since, that there was something new to me in those eyes—something known only to her and the mountain. I was young then, and full of trigger-itch; I thought that because fewer wolves meant more deer, that no wolves would mean hunters' paradise. But after seeing the green fire die, I sensed that neither the wolf nor the mountain agreed with such a view. (129–30)

The quoted part of this passage usually begins in wolf books with "We reached the old wolf," but I think Leopold's last paragraph is diminished if it is isolated.[8] The more complete passage contains all the necessary elements to our developing a conscience about the wolf and its role in America. After placing us, through specific detail, Leopold recounts a moment of mistaken identity. The sight of a doe wouldn't interrupt the party's lunch, but it sets us up for the surprise to follow. During the Nature Fakers account we saw the possibility of mistaking coyotes for wolves among western pioneers; here the wet animal is seen as a basic and obscured four-legged genus. In the same moment at which the assumption is challenged, by the wolf shaking out its tail, the pups appear. What we see next is like the "Grand Armada" chapter of *Moby-Dick,* in which the whalers come upon a family of whales and kill the mother of a baby whale still connected by the umbilical cord. Like the Leopold incident here, the sorrow and effrontery of "The Grand Armada" follows "The Honor and Glory of Whaling," a chapter exalting the qualities of hunters and declaring the great planetary connection of the provider. This contrast augments the pathos of conscience that emerges. How different Leopold's ethic and understanding are from, say, Francis Parkman's, whose own moment of encounter with the dying fire yields less progressive results: "When I stood by his side, the antelope turned his expiring eye upward. It was like a beautiful woman's, dark and rich. 'Fortunate that I am in a hurry,' thought I; 'I might be troubled with remorse if I had time for it'" (Parkman, 187). The eye-to-eye incident is almost identical to Leopold's; the sentiment is precisely opposite.

Leopold provides some exposition that also heightens the dramatic effect of the moment. In one short paragraph he moves swiftly from the rationale of the "sportsman's" ethos ("In those day we had never heard of passing up a chance to kill a wolf") to a graphic depiction of what even wolf hunters would deplore— bad shooting. This is the moment on which too many arguments over nature hinge. A hunter might be tempted to limit the critique of this incident to a moment of bad hunting practice, where the only fault is that Leopold didn't follow his own "one bullet one buck" (or wolf) credo. Such a hunter would have to face the irony that such a credo didn't apply to wolves for western hunters or ranchers, who would torture wolves rather than kill them "cleanly," peppering them with small-caliber shot or using them for target practice, wasting plenty of material and energy in the process (see Coleman; McIntyre, *War;* Lopez, *Of Wolves and Men*). It would be easy to reduce Leopold's third paragraph to mere guilt over having wounded and lost the wolf pup ("it" drags its leg into impassable slide rocks, meaning that the hunters can't get to it to finish the job), if only the purported ethic of the hunter as an efficient and merciful participant in the ecosystem were true.

Leopold, however, reflects. His connection to the wolf is personal before it becomes political. Once more he offers a chance for the reader to write off the incident to Leopold's youth and "trigger-itch." But he calls us back to the hard reality of ecosystemic thought. An absence of wolves does not mean to the ecosystem what Leopold had been taught, had himself assumed up to that point. No wolves came to mean genocide and ecosystemic upheaval, human-induced alteration of the fabric of a design we did not create. "Paradise" is what Leopold finally questions and reconfigures, and this is the personal epiphany made political, indeed, the realization as it is used to lead to reason, rather than to some fluffy ideological sentiment. It is based on knowledge of the natural world acquired firsthand, and the ability to change even a deep-seated position in favor of the realities of the nonhuman world, which includes its breakage at the hands and guns of men.

The "green fire dying" is not merely poetic license taken with a moment of regret and realization. It is literally the loss of life unnecessarily—the taking of something real without giving something real in return, the acknowledgment that some life taken cannot be bought or bartered for anything. This may account for it being the most frequently cited passage from *A Sand County Almanac*. When a symbol is created out of death, there is still death to be paid, and too much of literary study absolves itself of the responsibility for absence and, by overemphasizing symbolic language, celebrates what it should lament. The lesson in Leopold is ecological at base, and this makes it all the more important as a lesson in literature, and in being more fully human.

A real wolf cannot be made. He or she can be destroyed, bred, imagined as what she is not, forced into socialized or domestic situations that defy what he is. Cloned, perhaps. This is not creation; it is reification, and the province of delusion. If one thing defines ecology as a necessary discipline to ecocriticism, it is that what we are able to make is not always conducive to the health of our ecological systems. Therefore it is not always what we *should* make. This calls into question the justification of all technology, social constructs, and states of denial as "natural." As Aldo Leopold writes, "Wilderness is a resource which can shrink but not grow" (199), and he includes, in the same chapter:

> One of the most insidious invasions of wilderness is via predator control. It works thus: wolves and lions are cleaned out of a wilderness area in the interest of big-game management. The big-game herds (usually deer or elk) then increase to the point of over-browsing the range. Hunters must then be encouraged to harvest the surplus, but modern hunters refuse to operate far from a car; hence a road must be built to provide access to the surplus game. Again and again, wilderness areas have been split by this process, but it still continues. (191)

If only on the basis of the ethos generated by such observations, Leopold's (or any) epiphanic moment in a confrontation with nature is not to be lightly dismissed as bathos. The revelation encouraged him to understand the complexity of ecosystems that he had previously ignored, to the detriment of the predator population. Once realized, the land ethic he developed anticipated the beneficial trophic cascades that have occurred in regions of wolf recovery. Such is the healthy relationship of awareness and verisimilitude that a trained ecological consciousness brings to literature.

Vicious

Jon Coleman's final chapter of his history of the wolf begins with and returns to the Leopold incident (191, 220). Coleman refers to the "cultural extinction" of wolves—a phrase that would normally take me up short with skepticism of yet another anthropocentric reality-in-quotes. Instead, in *Vicious* Coleman constructs a sound argument that empowers such a phrase with the best of its qualities: He first maps out how the fame of the outlaw wolves or "last wolves" was in part the act of "bureaucrats" who mounted a campaign to incite that fame. U.S. political powers against wolves and for ranchers wrote the story of the famous last wolves, trumped up the so-called statistics of their size, predation rates on livestock, and ages (statistics that wolf biologist Phil Gipson has spent decades researching and correcting, as I will explain in chapter 6). This way, American culture was able to seize "upon the death of animals as an opportunity for reflection." Coleman then provides a historical narrative: "Standing over the bodies of the last wolves, the bureaucrats could do nothing but ruminate. The inexorable forces of private property, territorial expansion, and human progress had cornered the wolves. Their fate was inescapable. Freed from the responsibility to act on their sentiments, the wolf killers expressed tender feelings that would have shocked their forebearers [*sic*]. They saluted the last wolves" (195).

This narrative is corroborated by the histories of wolf "sentiments," some of which Coleman lists. He unfortunately includes Leopold on the list, implying that Leopold's sentiments came as cheap as any wolf killer's, but Coleman later redeems him (220). Coleman at least reveals (though without stating this) that Leopold's epiphany would also constitute a language fit to encourage the recovery of the wolf in the lower United States. "The cultural logic that guided the birth and the spread of the last-wolf folktales" shaped the rhetoric, the profound rebuttal, that would bring the wolf back to some of its former range (196).

Coleman's book raises some questions that historical study simply can't answer, such as the psychological origin of human cruelty toward wolves (a topic I will explore throughout this book). But it tracks the New England history of wolf extirpation with depth and insight; others tend to be pithy or quote-driven, making fine repositories but not as fine histories. And it connects human viciousness (hence the title's weight of reversal), differentiating the brand cultivated in eastern states from that of western states, to the practices of the frontier as it moved and expanded. Coleman conducts all of this within the structure of "the violent interaction of three timeframes—historical, folkloric, and biological," a well-balanced and well-argued structure (4). The weakest of these three time-frames, however, is the biological, the book's main flaw being some of Coleman's assumptions about, and essentialism of, wolves.

These are mostly established early in the book, with few later mishaps. Off to a good start, and quoting Mech and Lopez, Coleman begins to distinguish between human and wolf behavior, including the "wolves don't attack people" thesis I will address specifically in chapter 5. He lists what wolves can do, itself a risky prospect (3). He also claims, "In the wolf books, people are the irrational wasters and despoilers" (3) and, "Despite their attempts to challenge the way readers think about wolves, wolf studies preserved the rigid dichotomy of good and evil that always characterized people's opinions of the animals" (3–4). I have not found this to be an accurate generalization. What I have seen in "the wolf books" is both a long-standing blame of the wolf as despoiler and a savior complex about the wolf; that is, a confusion over the wolf's mythic moral role because of its triple depiction as devil, god, and wolf. Some of the wolf books, such as those by Mech, Peterson, and Murie, are at times plainly emotional even during their best efforts at objectivity. The attempt to depict the wolf as a wolf, rather than as a human projection, generates a high ethical imperative and so a paradoxical passion for cool reason. We might interpret Coleman's statements as meaning that wolf books "reveal humans to be" despoilers, and that the good and evil distinction is in wolf books written only during early American colonization and discounting native accounts, but the implication is otherwise. Coleman doesn't quite address the increasing ambivalence in wolf books from the seventeenth to the twentieth centuries.

A few other assumptions slip into the work, such as, "Unlike wolves, people also sought to pass on their possessions" (6). I understand the thinking about consciousness and ownership here, but I wonder where returning to a den for several generations might fit in. Another assumption is that wolves "accomplished these nifty adaptations as a species, not as individuals" (7). I would assert that there is no such event, in any species. Species are made of individuals, and genetics and culture cooperate or collide in them in ways we often haven't bothered to consider, even in our own species. This includes individual invention; that is, some wolf had to do it first, and may have taught that behavior to others, whatever the collective unconscious may have produced at once in different regions (as with human beings making masks or building dugouts). These certainly aren't egregious errors Coleman is making, but they do affect his following contemplations. When he opens a section with the hook that "Lois Crisler first joined a wolf pack in the early 1950s," we're obliged to wince at the baggage that this statement carries, depending on how it is qualified and contextualized (in this case, it isn't).

Coleman commits at least three other important errors: "Wolves communicate through basic dichotomies"; they "have no talent for nuance or novelty"; and their "minimal vocabulary exposes the fallacy of some people's Doolittleian yearning to talk to the animals" (29). These errors lead Coleman to speculate, without foundation, that "If wolves could speak, they would say next to nothing," a projection against projection. When he declares that humans "drove wolves to the edge of worldwide extinction" he simply blows a fact (8). Wolves have long flourished in vast regions within Canada, Alaska (though perhaps these are the next regions in which they will suffer most), Siberia, and the Arctic. Other statements essentialize, again inaccurately, wolves' hunting prowess (74), predation behavior (79), and social dynamics (159).

I'm being hard only on the parts that need correction here. Fortunately, Coleman doesn't spend too much time on wolf biology and ethology, and he salvages folklore, often a difficult topic to cover in a history. The book is a good resource if the reader doesn't quite step into rank and file behind Coleman in regard to wolves so much as in regard to cultural history, which he handles deftly. We have to acknowledge that writing about what wolves do is often simply harder than writing about human behavior, even as essentialisms go.

Even Audubon's 1835 *Ornithological Biography,* supposedly one of the most impartial wildlife texts of the early nineteenth century, contributed to the very sentiments it purported to be combating. Audubon begins his discussion of wolves with what might be considered a clinical perspective: "There seems to be a universal feeling of hostility among men against the Wolf, whose strength, agility, and cunning . . . tend to render him an object of hatred" (137). His speculation is not about why the wolf is hated, but about a matter of offhand anthropological interest—whether or not that hatred is truly universal. Inadvertently, he contributes to its potential universality by including two stories in sequence. The first is the unconfirmed account of two slaves ripped to shreds by a wolf pack while trying to visit their lovers on another plantation; the second of a farmer who tortures three trapped wolves because he is on a vendetta against the animals who "killed nearly all his sheep and one colt" and whom he is " 'paying off in full' " (137–39). Although Audubon's second story could be interpreted as an indictment of the farmer's revenge, no indictment, direct or implied, finally materializes. Audubon's account risks a gothic and melodramatic support for horrific legends regarding wolves, since only these two stories, rather than any zoological or ethical assessments, appear. In this respect, it's understandable that a good historian like Coleman would set out to account for the violence done by men alleging a distanced objectivity.

Never Cry Wolf

Ethos can sell a wolf book, sink it, or in one particular case, both. *Never Cry Wolf* appeared in 1963, almost twenty years after *The Wolves of Mount McKinley*. Both books are considered seminal, Murie's for its ecological empiricism, Mowat's for—if we might call it this—the opposite. Mowat chose to reach a wide audience with humor and the personal essay, which choice of genre alone would have been enough to raise the eyebrows of ecologists. Raising those eyebrows was part of Mowat's goal, however, as a full third of the book is composed of diatribes against the Canadian government's mismanagement of wilderness areas and ineptitude at supplying its workers in the field. The decreasing credibility of *Never Cry Wolf* among scientists, especially after an exposé article by John Goddard, met with a two-pronged response: the first from reviewers digging into Mowat's possible nature faking (reviewers who at times seem a bit too much like paparazzi); the second from the filmmakers at Disney Studios, a group as famous for its evisceration of myth and fable as for its making myth and fable accessible (see Welsh; Lutts, "Realistic Wild Animal Story"; Burgess).

The full list of Mowat's literary offenses appeared in Goddard's 1996 piece for *Saturday Night,* amalgamating the skeptical buzz about the book that had been floating around since the Disney movie. In the preface to the thirtieth-anniversary paperback edition of *Never Cry Wolf,* Mowat defends his work, sticking by his version of the story despite documented contradictions and stating that "almost every facet of wolf behavior described by me has since been rediscovered by the selfsame scientists who called my studies a work of the imagination" (vii). One is tempted to let Mowat employ his strategy of "not letting facts get in the way of the truth," since artistic license often makes the difference between merely adequate and great storytelling. Mowat defended himself as a writer of a subgenre he called "subjective nonfiction," a kind of rebuttal to the New Journalism that flourished around the same time Mowat wrote his wolf book.

For many environmentalists and critics, the defense fell flat. As Goddard wrote, "by selling fiction as nonfiction, [Mowat] has broken a trust with his public. By treating facts as arbitrary and subject to whim, he has not so much served a high purpose as muddied public debate on Inuit and wildlife issues for decades" (64). The Mowat case is now hackneyed for environmentalist readers, the smoking gun by which we convict the huckster as truth killer. Despite his stylistic similarities to Twain, especially his use of humor and exaggeration, Mowat stepped over a line. Twain is the one who regularly protests too much, in good con-artist fashion, "This is the truth." Mowat, affecting the purity of stated fact, doesn't tip his hand. Some of his observations were accurately recorded and have indeed been confirmed by scientists. Ironically, his observations of behavioral anomalies add weight to Barry Lopez's repeated argument in his 1978 *Of Wolves and Men* that isolated individual behavior needs to be given as much credence as repeated, essentializing behavior—that field biology needs to allow for behavior that doesn't fit neatly into its expectations and assumptions.

Mowat's grossest falsifications are actually his political denouncements of Ottawan federal officials—who were far more competent than Mowat himself—and statements about the duration of his observations, which were more cursory and less intimate than he describes. Unlike Twain's allegiance to Dodge, Mowat is not true to the observations of the wildlife authorities of his day. He presumes to have discovered incidents of behavior on which writers had already published in accessible journals, and he refers to no particular scientists as having provided him with the material to which he should have been educated before arriving at his field site.

What could look like splitting hairs looks more significant when we consider the widespread consequences of Mowat's very popular work. For example, the wolves Mowat saw may have napped periodically for a time as part of their sleep pattern that season, but when in a later essay Vicki Hearne bases on Mowat's book her assertion that this is "wolf behavior," we see the cost of equating nature writing with corroborated fieldwork (143). I've napped my way through both a week of the flu and a week of vacation; that doesn't establish those sleep patterns as either universal human behavior or my own consistent behavior.

Understanding such distinctions is crucial to how we understand corporeality in a wolf book. Plausible behavior does not equal general behavior, but both must be acknowledged.

To dismiss Mowat entirely would be a mistake. Konrad Lorenz, for instance, the Nobel Prize–winning guru of modern ethology, incorrectly determined certain patterns of aggression in animals and errantly split the origin of the dog between jackals and wolves (Lorenz 128), which idea he probably recycled from Darwin's *Expression of the Emotions in Man and Animals* (45). Occasional lapses in scientific rigor even by such an eminent biologist as Lorenz put a new spin on truth, but not on fact, and for such reasons, Mowat deserves some room in which to write a story. His injustice to the wolf derives from his political enthusiasm outstripping his scientific discipline. In *Never Cry Wolf* Mowat found the most uncomfortable mix of reportage and opinion that has yet been achieved in wolf literature.

This stylistic event, especially because of Mowat's own heavy protest that his work is accurate, serves as a quintessential example of the World-Wolf in operation. As Steve Burgess points out in his essay "Northern Exposure," the FOF (Fans of Farley) protested the Goddard article with the kind of fervor reserved for zealots. On the other hand, Mowat's work isn't to be found cited in wolf books geared toward corporeality except as those works mention cultural conceptions of wolves.[9] At the same time, Mowat's Canadian story brought a public voice to wolf management in the United States. It was the kind of voice without which the Yellowstone reintroduction project, a model of scientific and cultural rigor, might never have succeeded, because Mowat steered that necessary element of policy change—public opinion—toward sympathy for and preservation of the wolf.

The *Never Cry Wolf* phenomenon also presents us with a grave matter still affecting the American ecological consciousness. Ecology is a life science, versus environmentalism, which is a political movement. These words are, however, indistinguishable even to many scholars in the humanities, in a puzzling relationship for ecologists, and indentured as a great opportunity for greenwashing businesses and exploitive government programs. Mowat was both critiquing and committing this error of conflation between environmentalism and ecological study. Such a distinction was simply not articulated in public discourse during the environmental movement of the 1970s. Fortunately, rather than the worst of environmentalism and empiricism (respectively, romantic delusions and engineered solutions) governing the discussion, wolf writing's two most important and best-written books emerge in the 1970s to represent the ecological naturalist and politico-spiritual environmentalist positions. The first is L. David Mech's *The Wolf: Ecology and Behavior of an Endangered Species*. The second is Barry Lopez's *Of Wolves and Men*.

The Wolf was the modern reference guide to wolves for thirty years, until Mech and Boitani's *Wolves: Behavior, Ecology, and Conservation* updated it, and is still the definitive work written by a single biologist. Clinical and instructive, thoroughly researched both in the field and against prior theoretical errors, *The Wolf* also contains some elements of human rumination and the occasional hopeful missive or considerate remark. More ruminative and poetic, and compiled from the kind of library research of the creative essayist, interviewer, and field observer, *Of Wolves and Men* includes a biological and ethological primer within the scope of its often dark and eulogistic cogitation, and meets while it questions the criteria of science.

Both books—Mech's in the foreword and Lopez's in the epilogue—contain apologies to captive wolves raised by the authors, whose intent in making wolves live with them was identical: to imagine living with wolves. The attempt to learn the animal, to know it, brought each man to an awareness of what methods might actually keep one from knowing the wolf by allowing one to know the wolf too well. The distinctions among habituation, socialization, and domestication could become finally trivial in light of the effort to preserve wildness. (I explain the distinctions among habituation, socialization, and domestication in later chapters, defining the terms most directly in chapter 18.) Within the eight-year frame of Mech's foreword and Lopez's epilogue, American thought and action toward the wolf put to rights the arts and sciences, the spirit and the mind, in a way we seldom ever see. We find the yin in the yang within both writers' efforts to present a corporeal wolf that would lay to rest the ghost wolf of the ancient human imagination.

The Wolf is dedicated to Adolph Murie, whom Mech acknowledges as "the first biologist to conduct an intensive and objective ecological study of the wolf." The epigraph, however, focuses on two common obstacles to intensive and objective study: "Of all the native biological constituents of a northern wilderness scene, I should say that the wolves present the greatest test of human wisdom and good intentions." The quotation is from the naturalist Paul Errington, from a book on predation. It reads remarkably like Mahatma Gandhi's declaration that the health of a nation can be judged by the way it treats its animals.

One thing worth marking in *The Wolf* is its frequent use of captive wolves as examples. Lois Crisler, the Brookfield Zoo, and Mech's own manipulations of captive wolves appear regularly in the work. Thirty years later, in Mech and Boitani's *Wolves,* we do not see such credence given to research originating in zoos or "wolf parks." This is a mark of how the progress of environmental thought in America, spurred by the rigor of ecological thought, has made it possible to gather more reliable examples for assessment, more wild experience, more wolves.

The structure of these books is another study in parallels. The first two-thirds of the Mech work is dedicated to the wolf as a biological and ecological being, its opening chapter covering what Mech first calls "The Wolf Itself." Subsequent chapters cover population and pack dynamics, communication, reproduction, range, and food, and there are three chapters on predation. The last third is about the wolf's relationship to nonprey species (including humans) and the possibilities of the species's future. The first third of Lopez's book covers the same subjects as the bulk of Mech's book, almost in the same order. But the writing, the voice, is so obviously different that the one could not be said to be a direct influence on the other. Lopez's last two-thirds is on cultural mores, myth and psychological projection, on violence and the sacred, and while there is the epilogue pointing briefly toward a better future for the wolf, Lopez's subject matter is pointedly the past. He moves from the ancient through the medieval to his own recent past, employing the creative writer's freedom to compress time and fit the grand narrative into close quarters. Lopez's is the literary project, but Mech's corpus, beyond *The Wolf,* has included more than the scores of field reports and consultation he has produced over the past several decades.

Three coffee-table books, two written by Mech (with forewords by Roger Caras and Robert Batemen) and one edited by him, depict the regions in which he has concentrated his study. *The Arctic Wolf: Living with the Pack* is about Mech's extensive work on Ellesmere Island observing a wolf pack there. The project began in 1986 for *National Geographic,* and since then Mech has catalogued the behavior, biology, and systemic effects of wolves in a high arctic island ecology. In 1991 he produced *The Way of the Wolf,* an introduction to wolves. The glossy photos in *The Arctic Wolf* are Mech's, the ones in *The Way of the Wolf* Tom Brakefield's. Their composition attests to Mech's combined clinical interest in and passion for the animal. The photographs are not the perfectly chosen, postured studies in rich light that we see in Jim Brandenburg's books. Mech's are sometimes progressions, slightly blurry examples of the behavior about which he writes, like upper-deck photographs of a team's formations, an authenticating method that appears as well in Rolf Peterson's works.

An odd phenomenon of the wolf book is that while pulp werewolf stories or sentimental essays far outnumber the credible work, and while much of the credible work repeats its forebears, some of the richest material to be found on wolves is in coffee-table books. The third, published in 2000, contains essays by several undersung biologists, including Steven Fritts and Fred Harrington (with mention of Milt Stenlund, another name well known among wolf biologists), along with an essay by Roger Peters. *The Wolves of Minnesota* is the book from Mech's principal region of study over his forty-five years of wolf work. *The Arctic Wolf* and *The Wolves of Minnesota* fit in the regionalist wolf work that splits its focus between the general state of wolves and the specific behavior and concerns of their respective territories. What we have in Mech's work is an intergenre approach ranging from lay science combined with beauty (geared to those who might first buy coffee-table books for pictures of wolves) to hard science combined with data (for those who might want to know more about "the wolf itself").

The wilderness coffee-table book might be said to have started after the 1889 Harriman expedition to Alaska, or more mildly with *Picturesque America* a decade or so earlier, but the wolf coffee-table book exploded during the 1970s. The recent photo essay *Wolf: Legend, Enemy, Icon* by Rebecca Grambo with photography by Daniel Cox is indicative of the World-Wolf project, the attempt to account for the conflicted responses to wolves through both image and language. This kind of work on the wolf, fact in the context of art and vice versa, emanated from and proliferated a cult of beauty romance and has continued to reach a public wanting to "see" animals as much as read them. That romance likely saved a number of species, made habitat protection possible, and challenged the breakneck economic mindset that dammed Glen Canyon or ruined the Alaskan coastline. The time of the wolf coffee-table book boom is also the era when the Sierra Club, founded at the turn of the century by John Muir (who was on the Harriman expedition), grew toward becoming a megalithic environmental organization. In this environment of the environment, such traveler-writers as Peter Matthiessen and Barry Lopez found their paths.

Of Wolves and Men

A mark of great literature is that it is confrontational rather than escapist; therefore a mark of quality in a wolf book is that it awakens in us the capacity and desire for the real wolf's condition, our own encounters with wilderness and wildness, a better understanding of ecosystems in their inclusion of predatory animals, and our ethical systems for dealing with these phenomena. Pulp appropriates the wolf for our convenience and prurient interest, often equating wolves with either the destructive, macabre, and haunting or the ethereally beautiful, indulgently spiritual, and easily domesticatable. Just as trash writing makes pornography of sex, pleasure of violence, and plainness of emotional depth, it makes ghosts of wolves.

For decades now, well-conceived books on wolves have shared the opinion that the principal reason for the wars waged against the wolf is the projection of the human psyche onto an imaginary enemy. A related opinion is that such wars are economically motivated.[10] Leopold repented of the projection tendency—the possibility of "thinking like a mountain"—after his conscience was suddenly pricked by the death of a wolf (*Sand Creek Almanac*, 129–33). Nineteen years after that book appeared in 1949, Farley Mowat ended *Never Cry Wolf* by explaining that his exclusion from the world of wolves had long been self-induced, colored by the predilections with which he had arrived both as a representative of his government and as a subversive of it (163). Fifteen years later Barry Lopez wrote *Of Wolves and Men*, elaborating on the projection thesis and critiquing globally significant incidents of hypocrisy, spurious logic, and legendary atrocities.

Although much writing about wolves is about loss and death, of which there is plenty in *Of Wolves and Men*, Lopez concludes that while the imagination "gives shape to the universe," or "creates" animals, it does so only within its own highly constrained bounds. That is, it can only create ghost wolves. After raising a wolf in captivity and learning that he would never do it again, Lopez states: "I valued him as a creature, but he did not have to be what I imagined he was" (285). Other works on wolves, such as Burbank's *Vanishing Lobo* and Coleman's *Vicious,* have since continued to state the projection thesis as a kind of adage.

Of Wolves and Men appeared in 1978 and won the John Burroughs Medal for natural history. During the earlier development of his ecological consciousness, Lopez had studied briefly at the Abbey of Gethsemane toward becoming a Trappist monk, a discipline he finally exchanged for his life as a spiritual writer free of institutionalization. His work is infused with ethical concerns, and the numinous quality of his craft may be seen as the ruminations of a Gnostic Saint Francis, whose doctrinal training served him best as a tool toward his more personally developed ecological consciousness. Too often, nature writing is seen as the cathartic repository of a vague mysticism. Lopez, however, approaches his study of wolf stories from the adoption of mythology as a spiritual, rather than doctrinal, discipline (77). In this respect he is understandably as skeptical of the scientific restrictions on subjectivity as on the doctrinal constraints on objectivity; it is a skepticism reserved for institutional forms that tend to deny what they must in order to fulfill their preconceived goals.

I have been focusing on the opening material of wolf books, the epigraphs and dedications, because they tell us much about what was behind those books when they were still conceptual. Lopez's dedication page states that he wrote *Of Wolves and Men:* "For Wolves. Not for the book, for which you would have little use, but the effort at understanding. I enjoyed your company." His acknowledgments include Roger Peters, a likely choice for a project examining the psychological implications of an otherwise zoological subject of study. And Lopez includes three long epigraphs, from Henry Beston, Michel de Montaigne, and John Rodman, all of which concern the meeting point of the mystical and the physical. In this material we are invited to adopt a certain frame of mind without which we may have a difficult time accepting the interdisciplinarity of the project.

Much of the book examines the projection thesis, the methods and rationalizations by which human beings have made a scapegoat of the wolf (5, 144, 165, 270). Mostly implicitly, Lopez tracks how the scapegoat is deified—how eventually the victimized figure becomes a Christ figure.[11] Lopez speaks of our need for restitution, for apology, but he does not himself deify the animal. The very foundation of his project is data as they can be known through the wolf biology that had only recently come to be formalized—that is, mainly through the work of

Allen and Mech. The corporeal wolf precedes, then commands, the ghost wolf in *Of Wolves and Men*.

The book is also subtly framed. While the first part, "Canis Lupus Linnaeus," focuses on classifying the real wolf, the first sentence Lopez writes is, "Imagine a wolf moving through the northern woods," language signifying the ghost wolf (9). For the first couple of pages, he gives us a hypothetical and carefully plausible scene about a wolf finding its packmates. And in the epilogue, a personal narrative culminates in Lopez's apologetic decision against the raising of wolves. That is, while *Of Wolves and Men* follows a progression from the corporeal biological wolf to the mythic structure packed around it over time, the book is framed according to a narrative line finally favoring empiricism (in the Thoreauvian sense, as observation and verification, rather than only as lab science) and declaring the need for wolves to live like wolves. Boxed inserts throughout the body text range from stories about government action to indigenous cosmogony to biological fact. Lopez's accomplishment in *Of Wolves and Men* is his deference to the lives of wolves as he accounts for the stories of men.

After a section on biology and ethology (the book's corporeality), Lopez's "distrust of science" is expressed as a means of transition into the next several chapters on indigenous and historic knowledge (the book's gnosis). His time spent listening to indigenous people's assessments of wolf behavior that have been gathered over generations of apprenticeship makes the study as much an ethnography as a book about wolves, hence the title. However, his skepticism seems to be limited to the laboratory biologist's tendencies toward hypothetical convenience and obligatory reductivism. Field biology is less controlled than lab biology, more subject to the vicissitudes of the ecosystem and the attention of the naturalist. To the extent that observations, cataloging, and contextualization influence the field biologist, the discipline is closer to the kind of ethnographic knowledge gained from someone immersed in a culture rather than someone sampling for demographics. While Lopez obviously concentrates on the formation of the ghost wolf (*imagine* is an oft-used word in the book), he consistently recognizes the value of empirical study. Indeed, his own arguments are sometimes cleanly quantitative:

> Let's say there are 8,000 wolves in Alaska. Multiplying by 365, that's about 3 million wolf-days of activity a year. Researchers may see something like 75 different wolves over a period of 25 or 30 hours. That's about 90 wolf-days. Observed behavior amounts to about three one-thousandths of 1 percent of wolf behavior. The deductions made from such observations represent good guesses, and indicate how incomplete is our sense of worlds outside our own. (3)

Having shown us in the book's opening section the wolf's howl, its family practices, its predatory practices, Lopez is careful to remind us that any such assessments are general and subject to overstatement. The fourth through seventh chapters focus on wolves as "objects of interest to people" living in a world that includes, or once included, them. His considerations of hunting cultures and the attempts of people to "live like" or "act like" wolves are juxtaposed with evidence of disconnection, the loss of our affinity for real wolves as we eliminated them. By his seventh chapter, Lopez's version of the wolf myth indicates that modern extirpation efforts in the United States left us with only the imaginary wolf. Without the proper restraint on our imaginations and on the cultural/historical misconceptions of the old myths, we are left holding only tools used to profane myth.

The ecological consequences in 1978, the year *Of Wolves and Men* appeared, were obvious enough. Whole ecological systems in America were left incomplete and struggling under the weight of exotic and invasive species, the perpetuation of cruelty had been justified as "business," and species were being eliminated not only in the distant Amazon but in America's own rainforests. For all Lopez's effort to consider our possible coexistence with wolves, his sixth and seventh chapters both end in zoos.

And so the third part of the book, "The Beast of Waste and Desolation," looks at the wolf as pariah, particularly to the ranching industry. Roosevelt's "beast of waste and desolation" invokes the complex model of mythmaking that drove the nation's ecological awareness through the late nineteenth and early twentieth centuries—a morass of cattle-baron alarmism, conservationist management, and preservationist resistance. Roosevelt gave the wolf this label while holding his hand on a Bible before a North Dakota commerce delegation. He might have considered the proverb "A bad dog never sees the wolf," native to the Dakotas, but alas.

"Up to this point," Lopez opens chapter 10, on medieval legends, "I have been considering wolves from three fairly distinct viewpoints: as objects of scientific inquiry, as objects of interest to people bound up in the natural world with them, and as objects of hatred for livestock raisers. But the points of view are not quite so distinct. And the intimation that the wolf can be objectified is one that must ultimately break down, even for science" (203). From here, *Of Wolves and Men* shifts dramatically in time to the medieval period, about which Lopez speculates regarding its potential influence on Anglo-Europeans during the same centuries that had established the indigenous North American mythos he examined in prior sections of the book. His tenth chapter traces medieval wolf symbolism, the eleventh chapter medieval science. This juxtaposition produces a horrific effect, proving that the mere cooperation of science (in its role as politicized profession) and spirituality in the building of myth is not necessarily desirable. The twelfth chapter subject, the werewolf, logically follows. Built into this group of chapters is a call to both science and symbolism to regard the corporeal wolf with greater respect and caution, so that human understanding will not repeat one of its great mistakes—the creation and unleashing of a demon.

The conclusion that Lopez reaches must be realized in the context of when his book was written. Reintroduction projects up to 1978 had failed. Wolves lived in "the north," away from human communities for the most part except in the Arctic, which would not be studied formally until Mech's work on Ellesmere. Despite Leopold's prescient warning, stockgrowers' associations and most federal agencies still assumed that the wolf was not to be a part of fertile ecosystems. The modern version of the environmental movement was barely in its second decade of realization, still lacking ethos, gaining logos steadily, but relying much on pathos. So the search for the beast invented over centuries of cultural/historical accumulation ends, in Lopez's judgment, inside of the individual. *Of Wolves and Men* broadly contextualizes the individual story in terms of its cultural influences, but in his analyses of children's stories, Lopez recognizes the influence of each individual's capacity for storytelling on his or her culture. Lopez ends his twelfth chapter with the controversial wolf-child case of Amala and Kamala and devotes chapter 13 to children's fables. The later symbiosis he demonstrates between individual and culture mirrors remarkably the earlier symbiosis he demonstrates between organism and ecosystem.

Having established the consequences of profane symbolism and of scientists' professional politics too much derived from that symbolism, Lopez sharpens his focus. He provides insights that might come from a more humble recognition of the individual's small contributions to the great stories written by and working upon billions of us over time. He gives us an astronomical incident. We move by degrees toward the constellation Lupus as seen by Leif Ericsson, so that the stories he has recorded combine to assume the significance merited only by myth (277). The final section ends with a cry that pops us through the cosmic ether and back into the personal connection—an origin story. The transition that takes us back to the beginning, back to the individual consciousness so small and yet so vital to the universe story. This is the "crying out," the cosmic howl.

After his reach to the vastness of cosmic content, Lopez finally writes his confession. He explains why the wolf in captivity is too limited, too controlled to teach what an interspecies exchange could teach us were we to meet a wolf on his or her own terms. *Of Wolves and Men* seems to me, therefore, an act of restitution. Lopez uses his own experience not as a polemical against us feeling drawn to wolves on both real and imaginary orders, but as an encouragement for us to build the wolf myth on ecological terms—on the wolf's terms—as much as that might be possible. His project contests, as it tracks, the World-Wolf: "We embark then on an observation of an imaginary creature, not in the pejorative but in the enlightened sense—a wolf from which all other wolves are derived" (204). In the vein of Peter Matthiessen or Ann Zwinger, Lopez puts himself in the regions of his subjects, then lets those subjects participate to the degree of their dictating the prose, without forcing them to qualify on the basis of being human.

For being such an important text to the remythologizing of the wolf in the lower forty-eight states, *Of Wolves and Men* hardly spends a moment there. It is mostly set in Canada and Alaska when it isn't covering in fairly general terms the broader history of U.S. policy and cultural climate. Partly because of its attention to the Northern Hemisphere, Lopez's book serves as a necessary revision of Mowat. The complex frictional responses to *Never Cry Wolf* were diffused in *Of Wolves and Men*. Lopez's concerns, while possessed of a deep personal motivation, are cultural, with the paradoxical goal of delivering a well-represented corporeal wolf through the medium of a ghost-wolf critique.

The closing sentences of Lopez's introduction and his conclusion present us with the conundrum of the World-Wolf and the need for representative writing. They are: "I remember sitting in this cabin in Alaska one evening reading over the notes of all these encounters, and recalling Joseph Campbell, who wrote in the conclusion to *Primitive Mythology* that men do not discover their gods, they create them. So do they also, I thought, looking at the notes before me, create their animals" (5). And: "I learned from River that I was a human being and that he was a wolf and that we were different. I valued him as a creature, but he did not have to be what I imagined he was. It is with this freedom from dogma, I think, that the meaning of the words 'the celebration of life' becomes clear" (285).

When I first read *Of Wolves and Men,* both of these passages raised a resistance in me. About the first, I thought, "The point should be that we *can't* create animals. We can only create gods, and look where that's taken us." In time I realized that the only animals we can create (aside from our own babies) are ghost animals, and so Lopez was writing to get past that moment of appropriation and solipsism, writing to reach the wolf. To the second passage I responded with confusion, with the criticism that it seemed too metaphysical and cryptic. I thought Lopez had too easily abandoned the politics of his project by ending in a moment of personal absolution. But I was young then, and full of trigger-itch, and I was wrong. The corporeal wolf—the representative moment that seeks to bring life to real wolves rather justifying its taking—that wolf is in those passages. Lopez's epiphany can be taught and it can be known. Perhaps the nobility of the savage is found in its ability to remain pure through repeated attempts at its corruption, even the ones designed to ennoble it.

CHAPTER THREE

The Bioregional and Geopolitical Wolf Book

Bringing wolves back to regions they once inhabited may be done one of two ways. They may be captured and transported from another wilderness area, released either by a "soft" or "hard" method of acclimation to the new place, and likely radio-collared in order to monitor their survival success, their range of wandering, and whatever behavioral activity biologists happen to be studying at the time. Or they may come back on their own, after which they will eventually be spotted and likely captured, radio-collared, and monitored. By "come back" I mean cross some border that hasn't been crossed for long enough that civilization calls it a problem. Usually the name of a state will suffice. Bioregional designators don't always follow state lines, and the highways and agricultural zones and dump sites of humanity don't usually respect the necessary contiguity of ecological systems, so the wolf often has several borders to cross before it has "returned." As such, the laws of certain states governing land management, fish and game, and urban planning create lines that wolves can often learn but don't initially always recognize. The result is that we see in wolf literature a combination of several different regional designators being used in order to deny or accord wolves some place in their former space.

The reintroduction project in Yellowstone happened during, and spurred further, discussion about where the wolf could return. Actual and potential crossings into Michigan, Wisconsin, and Minnesota (the northern lakeland region running from the Great Lakes to the Boundary Waters) put the wolf in the "threatened" but not "endangered" category according to the Endangered Species Act (ESA), so reintroduction is a less likely prospect than simply continuing observation of Canadian wolf populations roaming south. Colorado's state politics have kept the wolf out of serious consideration for reintroduction to the southern Rockies, despite public desire.[1]

The Mexican wolf project in the Southwest has succeeded despite perhaps more setbacks than Yellowstone faced. The Northeast and the state of Wisconsin, to use geopolitical designations, look like strong candidates for healthy wolf populations. The appearance of books about these regions as prospects is an indicator that, as wolf populations grow in the United States, the wolf book will sufficiently categorize into its regional literatures, thus influencing the study of wolf books more bioregionally.

The Wisconsin Timber Wolf

In a thin book of interviews published by the University of Wisconsin at River Falls, Walker Wyman recounts several regional stories of wolf encounters. Three are about children being thrown to wolves in order to save a family fleeing a marauding pack (2, 3, 5), with a similar story of sacrificing a packhorse (14). Most of the stories are told by immigrant families, including one by a Russian immigrant whose tale is identical to the Pavel sledge-chase story in *My Ántonia* (Wyman, 3; Cather, 46–49). Another section covers several stories of loggers climbing trees to escape wolves (6–9). One of these is titled "Wolf Pack Drives Man Insane," in which a man is treed by wolves for three and half days without food or water, after which he is "mentally unbalanced" and "unable to give a coherent story of what had happened" (8).

Being treed by an animal is a common enough image in stories, and it could be that Freud's Wolf-Man, who had been read the requisite wolf fairy tales and who lived in a forested region, had a dream that, typical of dreams, reversed some of the terms. Instead of being treed himself, he found the wolves in the tree while he looked up at them from his window. The theme of "treed by a wild animal" is maintained, as is the anxiety of the incident, but with the dream allowing for the dreamer to be the point-of-view figure from his bedroom (the place of the dream) instead of "outside himself" and above the wolves in their natural position (as wolves don't climb trees). I will more specifically address the Freud case in chapter 10.

Wyman strangely follows these accounts with three stories he calls "Tall Tales about Wolf Packs," as if the prior ones weren't tall enough. The first is another treed-by-wolves story, in which the wolves fetch a beaver to bring down the man waiting in the tree (12–13), a version of the story told in Montana about Jim Bridger (Lopez, *Of Wolves and Men*, 177). The second is a mildly ribald joke from *Reader's Digest* with the necessary wolfish sexual connotations (13–14). The third story is about a wolf as big as a house (14). Geopolitical regionalism roots the stories in the immigrant agricultural history and timber history of Wisconsin while allowing the tall tale its necessary fantastic element—the symbol of great rapacious wolf.

Not recorded in Wyman is a factual account of a wolf swallowing a cloth work glove, after which the glove is recovered and the biologists studying the animal in the field spin their own tall-tale parody. One biologist declares, "This proves it. Wolves do eat people after all. Steve, we've got a scientific paper here. The poor old sot who got eaten will be immortalized." Richard P. Thiel was in charge of wolf recovery for the state of Wisconsin beginning during the 1980s and tells this story in *The Timber Wolf in Wisconsin* (94). Elsewhere in that work he declares that stories of wolves eating people "can be dismissed as products of imaginative minds" (40). He understands, however, where those minds begin looking for the raw material of their products: "What probably begins as a fireside tale, firmly ingrained with realistic, elemental ingredients (such as place names and third-person accounts) is readily absorbed by many a gullible listener. And so the stories circulated throughout the communities like wildfire" (40). Further complicating this phenomenon is that enough true stories sound like fables to shore up the fictional fireside tales. For instance, the "last wolf" known to inhabit the state of Wisconsin before the drifters began arriving from Canada, Minnesota, and perhaps Michigan was named Old Two Toes. He got this moniker for an escape from a trap that cut his other three toes from one paw. He was famous for his ability to elude trackers despite his distinctive print and, in a sad irony, was finally hit by a car, the phantom-maker of many a wild animal (6).

One of the differences in how the wolf is considered in the Boundary Waters regions versus most of the nation west of the hundredth meridian is that the project there is to monitor and abet a natural recovery, as opposed to planning a reintroduction. Thiel's project and his books about it therefore constitute a literature of wolf recovery qualitatively less political than the books written about, say, Yellowstone. His work also distinguishes itself from projects conducted in island ecologies such as Isle Royale or Baffin Island, as well as from Alaskan reportage on already long-established wolf populations.

Thiel's writing has the feel of environmental and political history being written as it happens. He keeps one eye on the conditions of habitat conducive to wolf livelihood and the other on the behavior of people who threaten wolves' return. In one chapter, called "Wisconsin's Secret Wolf Study," Thiel accounts for a state Conservation Department project to enumerate the deer population that turned into a more ecological than biological project once the wildlife biologist on duty discovered the presence of wolves. He howled into the darkness one night and was answered (123–24). This chapter is preceded by one titled "Deer, Wolves, and Politics," in which Thiel walks the Damascan road of Aldo Leopold. The awareness of wolves in Wisconsin began a life's work on Thiel's part to manage the restoration of wolves on their own terms. Unlike a reintroduction project, *finding* the wolves was the major part of the work, coupled with laying the proper public relations foundation and game management policy to ensure the animals' survival.

Because of need to concentrate on a public perception of wolves that would rise in the wake of a natural return, neither *The Timber Wolf in Wisconsin* nor *Keepers of the Wolves: The Early Years of Wolf Recovery in Wisconsin* has a sense of spectacle, of rollout. However, neither text remains merely clinical; this seems an impossibility when one writes a wolf book. *Keepers of the Wolves* begins with the chapter "Phantoms of the Forest," in which Thiel explains his interest in, and faith in, the presence of wolves in his home state. His story is very much like Norm Bishop's (for which see my Preface); prompted by literature and study, energized by curiosity and hope, Thiel wanted from boyhood to see wolves. But:

> Wolves disappeared from Wisconsin during my childhood in the 1950s; mine was the first generation of Wisconsinites unable to "experience" wolves. In 1966, when I was thirteen and growing up in suburban Milwaukee, I read Ernest Thompson Seton's story about Lobo. Then, while searching through several mammal books at the local library, I came across a map showing that wolves supposedly lived in Wisconsin. I learned that the state was responsible for managing its wildlife, and I wrote to the Wisconsin Conservation Department to get information about the status of rare wildlife. I found the response regarding timber wolves especially disturbing. (5)

Thiel's story combines a retrospective on his childhood (and his reading) with a hope that his home region might be complete and the knowledge that the ecosystemic inclusion of a predator is part of the natural mix. This is the thinking of a young scientist coming into his own—under the influence of myth but cognizant of that and able to apply it to the pursuit of fact. The phantoms Thiel pursues in the forest have their corporeality; he explains that it's "just a matter of knowing what to look for and when to look for it" (7).

And so the wolf of the Great Lakes region also has a resurrection story, a phoenix myth, moving from abundant to extirpated to endangered and perhaps into the health of the Minnesota populations, to the extent that state citizenship will have anything to do with it. This will, of course, depend on the other animals that Thiel studies in order to better understand the possibilities of the wolf's return: trappers, hunters, government agents, farmers, ranchers, university professors, romantics, urban and rural subgroups, and field biologists.

Boundary Wolf

The wolf's region between the Boundary Waters and Great Lakes has generated some powerful works, though not much in the way of fiction or poetry. Durward Allen and Rolf Peterson have done important work on the Isle Royale project, and Sigurd Olson is the narrative naturalist devoting attention to the ecosystemic health of the region and (in passing) its wolf country.[2] I'm going to save a closer reading of Allen's *Wolves of Minong*, an essential wolf book for any library, for a later section on the mythic wolf's relation to water, but it's worth mentioning that Peterson still works primarily in this region and produces frequent research on it.

David Mech has written two coffee-table books, in addition to his many biological reports, on wolves in Minnesota—summary accounts of their behavior based on his extensive study there. In contrast, Jim Brandenburg's photography gave the images of wolves a resurgent calendar and poster fame, frequently emphasizing, and to some degree mystifying, the wolf's beauty. Minnesota's importance to the wolf book is of a strange variety. The state has always boasted a viable population of wolves and permeability with Canada through the Boundary Waters region. It also houses the International Wolf Center, founded by Mech and standing as one of the world's largest repositories of information on wolves. What has kept the Minnesota wolf book from rising in artistic prominence in America is that the wolves just aren't very visible, ubiquitous though they may be. The couple of thousand running through the region live in forests, around waterways not easily accessible, and on the move in north country remote enough to make aerial spotting one of the only reliable ways to witness them in the wild. This paradoxical ubiquity and elusiveness pit the ghost-wolf adages that wolves are skulkers against the ones about their being the gregarious and curious progenitors of the dog. Nevertheless, no significant state-identified literature on the wolf has yet come out of Minnesota. In a way, it seems that the reality of wolves close at hand has come to rein in the fantasies of pulp—a sensibility precisely opposite those most often found in nineteenth-century American literature.

One personal essay set in Ely, Minnesota, stands out in part because it is written by Linda Hogan, who also figures in my chapter 17 on she-wolves as an editor of the collection *Intimate Nature*. The story is found in her collection *Dwellings: A Spiritual History of the Living World* and is called "Deify the Wolf." A wolf watcher's essay, it focuses on the connection between wolf and Indian (similar to Christopher Camuto's *Another Country*, an excellent book on the Cherokee and the red wolf), wolf life and human projection, and the past and future. It has the feel of a good compact essay appropriate to American Studies, and it contains a few moments uncommon to the wolf-watcher essay.

The mysticism of the essay holds it together. Its metaphysical bent is similar to Dillard's modernization of Emerson in that Hogan edges the natural world inward to the personal revelation or transcendent experience. But because Hogan's sensibilities are infused with both conscious and inevitable tribal associations, the voice is something more pagan and, perhaps, more true. I have mentioned the lines dividing the ghost wolf's malevolent and benevolent counterparts. Mysticism is at its best when it dwells on and perforates such lines, when the shamanic function of mediation is at work. As such, there could be a defensible ghost wolf—a symbolic and mystified being that serves the wolf rather than replaces it. Such a being would be difficult to realize, but every so often we see it surface, almost always through primitive knowledge, a brand hard to fish up with modern garbage clogging the channel.

Hogan begins her essay in a white silence similar to Jack London's. We are in the Boundary Waters region in February, where the "skeletal gray branches of trees define a terrain that is at the outermost limits of our knowledge and it is a shadowy world, one our bones say is the dangerous borderland between humans and wilderness" (63) and "the shadowy world of wolves" (75) whose howls are "dancing ghosts" (76). But we're also in a highly controlled environment. Hogan is with a group on a wolf-watchers' outing, so this is a tourist moment that attempts to transcend the tourist's limited vision. Quickly she invokes an Anishanabe myth of human descendance from wolves (64), which moves into a highly corporeal paragraph describing wolf sign, that "what we see of the wolves" is found in leftover bones, scat, tracks, and scavenger activity: she includes a powerful description at a moose carcass of "a coal black raven standing inside the wide arch of those ribs like a soul in a body" (65).

So the ghost wolf is in force throughout the essay, augmented by Hogan's emphasis on her being in a border region—of industry and nature, where the "dump pack" wolves have lived scavenging from humans; of the waters that divide nations (briefly); and of science and spirituality. The biologists in the essay are given the complicated position that they occupy in practice. They study, they seek to save, but they do so intrusively and with some loss, and are well aware of this. They meet the resistance of those who think biologists are there to "deify the wolf" and render it sacred (66). Hogan's take on this is noteworthy: "It doesn't matter that the tension between locals and what they think of as 'environmentalists,' or wolf-lovers, begins to wedge apart the two groups in much the way that a split has widened between so many European immigrants and the

American wilderness they have never been at home with" (67). This could be a one-sentence summation of much of American literature, at least from an eco-logical perspective, raising the important issue of how the symbolic rendering of animals toward national mythologies is fraught with danger.

After spending a couple of pages on the wolf pogrom's history, (requisite in almost any wolf essay), Hogan makes the wolf-Indian connection through that history of violence (68). She then moves from the comparative history of Indian and wolf to the transitional history of trapper-turned-biologist. The trap itself is Hogan's focus for a moment. The sentiment behind our recognition of the same weapon once used to kill wolves being used to protect them could encourage us to slip into complacent pleasure over our progress. Hogan does not quite fall into this complacency; she recognizes the trap as an instrument of intrusion and control that at one point during its benevolent use causes the death of a wolf (69–70). She cites the named outlaw wolves "Ghost Leg" and "Phantom" here, declares the "dispelling of many of the myths about wolves" as a goal, and slowly narrows her focus to a captive wolf, walked on a leash, that she saw in Colorado (71).

The language throughout these passages of trapping and capturing and keep-ing is the language of loss, punctuated by one beautiful paragraph on the human desire to touch a wild animal (72), until Hogan reaches the essay's epiphanic moment: "I realize now that I won't learn about the wolves, our ancestors from before history. They are too complex for that. I can only return to the way people wanted to touch the fawn and these wolves. Something wild must hold such sway over the imagination that we can't tear ourselves away from any part of wilderness without in some way touching it" (73). Hogan goes on an aerial view-ing (74), roots us again in the cold north (75), shows us dead wolves carried by biologists and unappealingly burbled over by tourists (72–73), and crescendoes to the end of her essay with howls (76), but her piece could just as well end on that insightful analysis, that very possible explanation of the human psyche's affinity for and rejection of wolves. The appositive phrase that assumes wolves to be "our ancestors from before history" is an invocation of the benevolent ghost and begins Hogan's slip from the mediating space into the religious mores that create ghost wolves. Unfortunately, she leaves the balance beam, and after the howling takes hold of her the insight of her epiphany collapses in the essay's final paragraph, disintegrating into cryptic ambiguity: "We have followed the wolves and are trying to speak across the boundaries of ourselves. We are here, and if no wolf ever answers, or even if no wolves remained, we'd believe they are out there. And they are" (77).

Oops. If no wolves are out there, then our belief doesn't put them "out there."

Hogan conflates the wolves out there that simply don't respond with the wolves that no longer remain, so that our imagining them gets the last word over their presence. As such, she buries wolves "in here," trapping us in the boundaries of ourselves, in contrast to Edward Abbey's understanding that the city dweller may be reassured by the actual animal living its life in a wilderness somewhere (*Desert Solitaire,* 129–30). The ghost wolf ends the essay in a way that belies Hogan's apparent thesis to contribute to the life of wolves. She doesn't seem content through most of the essay with only the spiritual remains of the real animal, the imagination and memory of what was destroyed, any more than she would be content with the same phenomenon occurring in American Indian history.

It's a great piece, and I feel compelled to point out that it finally demonstrates the incredible power of the ghost wolf to cut nonfiction from its moorings and send it adrift. If, throughout my study, I point out slippage as much as accuracy, then this is why. The most convenient act in criticism is simply to knock holes in someone else's creation; my goal in both analysis and evaluation is to corroborate in the primary texts the imposition of the World-Wolf, so that we may know better how to behave as critics, teachers, hikers, and students of both the human imagination and the physical nonhuman world. In the Boundary Waters region are many real wolves, but sadly far fewer than there are ghost wolves of the human mind.

New England, New York

The wolf's renewed colonization of the northeast United States is still an idea, and little writing on the subject exists beyond historical references to the pre-pogrom days of the wolf in America (for example, McIntyre's *War against the Wolf* and Coleman's *Vicious*). Two recent books stand out as forward-thinking regarding the project of wolf reintroduction to the Adirondacks. The first is a coedited academic work resulting from a 1998 conference at the American Museum of Natural History in New York, titled *Wolves and Human Communities: Biology, Politics, and Ethics.* The second is a collection of essays edited by John Elder, *The Return of the Wolf: Reflections on the Future of Wolves in the Northeast.* The titles themselves say much. Like previous significant pairings of the popular essay and popular science, the conference proceedings (the science) and Elder's collection (the essay) combine to prepare the ground in New England for the wolf both to return to its ecosystems and to be accepted by the public.

The former and more quantitative of the books considers carefully the concentrated population density of the eastern United States and the political difficulties of developing a wild wolf population. The editors of *Wolves and Human Communities* are from biology, philosophy, and policy backgrounds, their contributions focusing on law and public participation, ecological knowledge and consciousness, and designation of wilderness in terms of ecosystemic completion and health. One chapter, called "Thinking Like a Mountain," again after Leopold, critiques intelligently and clearly the relationship between economy and ecology in decision making. The contributors list is refreshingly interdisciplinary. The writers range from prominent wolf biologists such as Mech and Peterson to paleontological anthropologists, ecologists, philosophers, environmental law experts, and a Haudenosaunee artist connected directly to the regions in which wolves would appear. The book minimizes its treatment of the history of ecology abuses, refers to the Yellowstone reintroduction as a model, and then moves on to a proactive argument. Not mired in the repeated confrontations common to much wolf writing, the contributors are able to examine the present and future states of the wolf's presence in America by focusing bioregionally on what we geopolitically name "New England."

The Return of the Wolf is composed of four essays under the editorship of Elder, one of the pioneers of ecological literary studies in the academy. Nature-writing essays by Rick Bass and Bill McKibben are included with a field biology account by wildlife scientist John Theburge and a piece by environmental activist Kristin DeBoer. Taken together, these essays aim toward a sociopsychological study of wolf reintroduction. Theburge's essay, the most scientific, serves as an anchor to the more ruminative essays in the collection and draws from his knowledge obtained in large part from the studies he and Mary Theburge conducted in Algonquin Park, Ontario, that produced his book *Wolf Country*. Bass taps into the Yellowstone and northern Montana precedent for reintroduction and ecosystem completion. His article, first published in *Orion* magazine for July/August 2005, reports briefly on the fulfillment of the trophic cascade. (Not long after, in October of 2005, an article in the *New York Times* interviewing Doug Smith covered the same subject, indicating perhaps that not only the restoration of habitat for a single species but even the recovery of entire ecosystems is still newsworthy.) McKibben looks closely at how a human restoration might ensue from the presence of the wolf, and DeBoer constructs a personal essay about her motives for working politically to change the human environment around wolves. The collection is a study in analogic thought—a means by which a reader can see where the history of wolf destruction followed by restoration might take us next. The attention to human social health is the more striking and appropriate given the high-density human populations around Northeast reintroduction areas.

In the lower forty-eight, the three regions most significant in the return of the wolf are the northern Boundary Waters and Great Lakes regions, including Minnesota and parts of Wisconsin and Michigan; the northern Rockies, including

Yellowstone and Idaho; and the high desert Southwest between New Mexico and Arizona, where the Mexican wolf came near the end of its existence.

The Mexican Wolf

Peter Matthiessen's "The Wolves of Aguila," written in 1958 for *Harper's Bazaar* and here quoted from *On the River Styx, and Other Stories,* anticipates many of the same plot points that Cormac McCarthy follows in *The Crossing,* but it is set in a more modern Southwest. The outlaw wolves are gone and have become literal ghosts, but the main character, a wolf hunter named Miller, is hired to conduct a "last raid" for the few remaining "Aguila" wolves, whom he never finds. Instead he finds two feral children out in the intense desert heat and carries them with him for a while. At the village outside of which he meets the children, Miller encounters a man with a dried wolf hide hanging on his shack; the man claims it belongs to one of the Aguilas. The hide is blown off the wall by the desert wind, and we are shown a scene written as if to raise the wild in the human:

> Miller heard the crack of stiffened skin as the wolf hide fell. He pitched to his feet in time to see it skitter across the yard toward the open desert, in time to see the squatting boy run it down in one swift bound. He crouched on it, eyeing Miller over his left shoulder, the hair on the back of his head erect in the hot wind. At Miller's approach, he backed away a little distance, not quite cringing. Miller took the hide to the proprietor, who peered at all of them out of the shadows. The dark boy, when Miller glanced at him, smiled his wide, sudden smile. (86)

We see in this poignant passage not only the tone of the wolf story but also the regional emphasis, the feral-child story, and the dark portents invoked by the fall of a wolf hide to the ground, like the pennant of a defeated country. Miller travels on his hunting trips in a sedan rather than on horseback, the car's trunk filled with strychnine and cyanide guns. He resents that the "wolf runs which once traced the border regions of New Mexico and Arizona had become so few and faded as to no longer justify the maintenance of a saddle pony" (72). He travels the same country as McCarthy's Billy Parham, but unlike Billy, whose innocence motivates him, Miller is jaded, once having hunted the wolf with a sense of purpose, considering "the lesser animals unworthy of his experience" (71). Now he hunts mostly "coyotes and bobcats," and as the narrative continues he becomes more reluctant to destroy the last wolves in the region, the last vestige of his conscience creating the story's brilliantly subtle emotional core.

This faintly gnawing sense of right and wrong also creates the perfect narrative conditions for Miller's psychological projection: "He was uneasily aware that the persecution of the wolf was no longer justified, that each random kill he now effected contributed to the death of a wild place and a way of life that he knew was all he had" (72). His realization that the destruction of the ecosystem is self-destruction, even if only in a business sense, causes him to pathetically lament both the loss of the past and his contribution to that loss. He finally frightens away the two children and is left calling out to them to come back (90), a haunting parallel to Billy's calling for the three-legged dog at the end of *The Crossing* (425) and an evocative opposite to the man dying of his own ineptitude and visited by a wary dog at the end of London's "To Build a Fire." Like another London story, "The Law of Life," which ends with Koskoosh waiting alone to be devoured by wolves, Matthiessen's literary naturalist tale closes with Miller stranded in the heat of the desert, to die at the hand of unforgiving nature (91).

The combination of losses to both interior and exterior landscapes creates the deepest sadness. This idea of interior and exterior landscape has become commonplace in ecological writing. Lopez uses it in *Arctic Dreams* and in his essay "Landscape and the Imagination," and Gregory Bateson's work laid a suitable foundation for the concept.[3] Ecopsychology also uses the tandem to examine psychic states as they are affected by environments and, in turn, as they lead humans to affect those environments.[4] It's important, however, that we don't slide into the "wilderness as concept" model too easily. An interior landscape may be only as important as the exterior landscape dictating its formation and is likely to be at least laced with assumptive error. Where naturalistic determinism would have Nature force material loss upon the character, and postmodern determinism desperately tries to redefine material loss as merely figurative, an ecological sense of story realizes that the death of the local wolves like the Aguila Wolf is an integral component of Miller's other collected losses. In the end the wolf's hide, the wilderness or *sylvus,* hangs on the door of a tavern, the center of culture or *civis*

The worlds of London, McCarthy, and often Matthiessen are hard, dark ones. The languages of literary naturalism and Old Testament fear and wrath have over time served their purposes for wolf stories. These dictions attain particular regional color when they sound on the permafrost or the desert hardpan. Unfortunately, both the actual dearth of wolves in the Southwest and the long difficulty toward bringing them back must influence our reading of Miller's condition. The historical facts of the Mexican wolf's elimination from the wild and reintroduction to the United States (and, one hopes, to Mexico through dispersal) contribute much to the verisimilitude of Matthiessen's and McCarthy's stories. While most species become extinct through the destruction of habitat, the Apache and Gila National Forest lands have remained largely intact over many thousands of square miles in the Southwest; the Mexican wolf's near extermination was caused by the literally targeted efforts of human beings. The Mexican Wolf Recovery

Project has been a test of how wildness might survive captivity—of how a wolf might become a wolf again—and whether or not there will be a place inside the web of human cartography for that wolf.

In 1977 the government hired a man named Roy T. McBride to save the wolves he used to kill. He found a few in the Durango and Chihuahuan deserts of Mexico and wrote "The Mexican Wolf (*Canis lupus baileyi*): A Historical Review and Observations on Its Status and Distribution," a detailed and fascinating piece combining government-required statistics with the homespun phrases of the longtime trapper, the man who caught the outlaw wolf Las Margaritas.[5] McBride peppers the document with stories about encounters with chained wolves in Mexican villages and long rides through the desert looking for wolf runs. In the foreground of a photograph McBride took of a wolf den we can see the ears of his horse (18). The report was issued in 1980, after three years of trapping. The result: five wolves, the first cadre of the current Mexican wolf population's founders.

The recovery plan began in 1982 in St. Louis, and as the wolves bred, several other captivity programs signed on to help. In 1999 I visited one of these project sites, called ACRES (Audubon Center for Research on Endangered Species), guided by the chief veterinarian at the Audubon Zoo, Roberto Aguilar. The facility is located outside New Orleans and gained some fame for its crossbreeding of a wild and a domestic cat, producing a kitten the zoo named Jazz. ACRES is a compound of tigers, lions, and Mexican wolves, and its work is largely dedicated to the last-ditch effort at saving the world tiger population by freezing tiger embryos. It is not popular research, and the compound is set up with high security, rotating pass cards, and a fairly clandestine location.[6] I assumed this to be because of corporate espionage or protection of the animals from prying eyes (the Mexican wolves were particularly sensitive to any human activity, and we kept our distance). I was sadly surprised at Aguilar's response: "It's actually security against animal rights activists."

The Mexican wolf project consisted primarily of locating suitable release sites and breeding the wolves up to a substantial population without socializing them. About 175 wolves were living in captivity when the first families were released; no others had been confirmed to live in the wild.[7] By the late 1980s both goals looked reachable, reports were issued, and interested parties left their neutral corners in order to continue rewriting the literary history into which "The Wolves of Aguila" and *The Crossing* fall. On January 12, 1998, the fences holding breeding Mexican wolves in captivity for more than fifteen years came down, through the "special rule designating a nonessential experimental population" of wolves entered in the Federal Register and used three years prior for the Yellowstone reintroduction (Parsons et al., "Mexican Wolf Recovery Program Project Update," 6). The rule took more than twenty years of effort to reach, beginning with the ESA listing of the Mexican wolf in 1976.

Thirty years later, a moratorium has been enacted against the placement of any more wolves into the Southwest ecosystems they have populated. The oversight committee charged with this job, under the auspices of the governor's office of New Mexico and the state's Department of Fish and Wildlife, determined in its five-year reintroduction plan that "six breeding pairs" were sufficient to justify a population. As of February 2006 the Interagency Field Team monitoring Mexican wolves determined that "the collared population consisted of 22 wolves with functional collars dispersed among eight packs and including two lone wolves. The IFT estimates the 2005 end-of-year wolf population to be 35 to 49 animals, with five confirmed breeding pairs." If New Mexico goes the way of Idaho and Wyoming, buckling under the pressure of gun fanatics, "sport" hunters, and ranchers, the project will collapse and the wolf will be killed again, driven out to the further ruin of the world.[8]

Out of the Mexican wolf project came a few books and a contentious spate of local journalism. The best book covering the early stages of the program and the history of the Mexican wolf is David E. Brown's *The Wolf in the Southwest: The Making of an Endangered Species,* which contains information on wolf trapping that informs my reading of Cormac McCarthy in chapter 18. A more recent celebration of the Mexican wolf's return, with some attention to its living in a southwestern war zone of ranches and urban sprawl, is Bobbie Holaday's *Return of the Mexican Gray Wolf: Back to the Blue* (meaning the Blue Range Mountains, although the Big Sky invocation is implicit).

James Burbank's *Vanishing Lobo* considers the conditions of the Mexican wolf's demise, especially those conditions of people's interior landscapes. He comes to many of the same conclusions as Leopold, Mowat, and Lopez and constructs an essay critiquing psychological projection as well as looking at biological statistics. Burbank's prose sometimes tempts the ghost wolf, as in this passage: "I seek not to place blame so much as to embrace the terror of these meanings, to name this fear and hatred, and in this act of naming, to make peace with the wolf within" (20). But his goal is to locate the ghost wolf in relation to the real Mexican wolf, which animal Burbank can only imagine because, at the time of his writing, it was nearly impossible to see a Mexican wolf in the wild.

In *Vanishing Lobo*, we can see the World-Wolf function as the retreat of a nearly extinct species into the very mind that, because of the real animal's absence, cannot know it. *Vanishing Lobo* is one of the "dying breed" works that actually has some statistical foundation, as opposed to the manufactured "vanishings" that have been upbraided by, for instance, Vine Deloria, Walter Benn Michaels, or Shepard Krech III. Whatever flaws of sentiment might appear in *Vanishing Lobo,* Burbank's handling of the projection thesis is far better than the wolf-hybrid owner and propagandist Michael Belshaw.

Michael Belshaw, PHD, is a celebrity around New Mexico, partly because he has received the kindest possible treatment by newspaper journalists for his highly questionable work. He writes letters to New Mexico newspapers in which he regularly mentions his training as an anthropologist and economist, never forgetting to put the PHD after his name. He is dedicated to educating people on his secondary area of expertise—breeding, raising, and selling wolf hybrids. He has written a book, *All the Loving Wolves,* in which his personal experience with raising wolf hybrids purportedly serves as sufficient proof that this is a good idea. Like many hybrid owners, he takes the self-congratulatory position that "this isn't for everyone" and stresses the "proper" methods by which wolves should be turned into dogs. When a child is bitten or killed by a hybrid, he points out that dogs bite and kill people all the time, grieves the incident, and admonishes the bereft parent not to extrapolate on the basis of isolated and personal examples. He then proceeds to do just that for several paragraphs in any given editorial.

Articles featuring him have borne quintessential ghost-wolf headlines: "The Call of the Wild," "The Dreaded Wolf Finally Has His Day." The articles encourage hybrid owners to write to the newspaper, to write books, and to quote literature in defense of wolves (that do not exist). In turn, letters of opposition are often, again, personal anecdotes of suffering at the jaws of the hybrid. These letters are powerfully depressing and important but do not raise the level of debate. Here in print journalism was the background noise for the local reintroduction battle.[9] *All the Loving Wolves* competes only with Twyman Towery's *The Wisdom of Wolves: Nature's Way to Organizational Success* for the worst nonfiction book exploiting wolves that I have read.

Lacking the space for an analysis of the raft of journalism generated over the wolf reintroduction, I'll provide a representative example. One summer story was of Susan Schock, director of Gila Watch, who crashed a New Mexico Cattle Growers Association cookout/protest and accused ranchers of threatening to use violence against people in defending stockgrowers' "right" to kill wolves. Her comment was based on Catron County commissioner Hugh McKean's declaration that "increased government regulations in the county could result in a 'civil war' as ranchers fight back" (Pells). Buried well below one article's hot lead was McKean's statement that his comment was euphemistic. The backyard debate was summed up in an *Albuquerque Journal* piece in which Farm Bureau representative Tom McKenna said, "We're not as worried about a wolf at our door as we are our own government," in contrast to Mexican Wolf Coalition representative Susan Larsen's position: "The wolf was wrongfully eradicated and it has a right in the ecosystem" (Kimball).

Such stories appearing in newspapers contribute to the production of essays on the subject. The critical mass produced in communities that divide about wildlife issues draws the attention of nature writers. Rick Bass's *The New Wolves* is such a work, cobbled together from intuition and dream language (15, 59, 60, 107) as well as fact-checking. Many of the conclusions are abandoned or dashed off: "It has been a long drought, and it has everything, and nothing, to do with wolves" (25). "Maybe twenty-five or thirty of them still reside in Mexico, though there could just as easily be zero" (35; no source given for the speculative number). "Whether or not the tribal councils are looking forward to the return of wolves is a matter of conjecture" (59). And in one instance of perhaps awe, perhaps exhaustion at a loss of words, "*Life*" (55). There are loose uses of the words *evolution* (92) and *extinction* (for example, 94), and moments of sarcasm that undermine the issue at hand, such as Bass's quick and pithy speculation about ranches as potential wolf recovery sites—an idea worth a real argument that doesn't receive one (52).

Bass also uses metaphors of vanishing—one particularly acrobatic example is of "ghost fossils" of wolves and "the ponderous hooved weight of hundreds of thousands of cows pinning down the earth's crust and keeping the wolves trapped beneath that crust" (7). The requisite gestures to the mythic and real wolf are here, but in a strained metaphor that finally bases the case on pathos. At one point, Bass begins with a strongly written, if simplified, example, that of "the arguments going on in science in the 1850s—Louis Agassiz holding that each of the stages of evolution was presented by God, locked like an unread but already-written transcript within the earth, while Darwin was formulating that it was a much more savage affair, tooth-and-claw struggles going on in every living, breathing moment, and that the stories of life were in no way already written" (30). But he devolves quickly, backs out: "It's a dubious, circular argument—a question of scale and intricacy far beyond our understanding. The theologians could argue that evolution itself is already coded into the earth, that there can be no randomness, if you are aware of enough factors and plug them into the equation; that all the variables, infinite in number, can conspire to produce only one outcome" (30).

This "argument," what is now being proffered as "intelligent design," is neither dubious nor circular. Agassiz is revised by Darwin. The position is at its best teleology and at its worst prejudicial judgment, the latter built on a classic logical fallacy. Bass entertains this argument in the context of his fusing human cultural "evolution" with environmental politics, in only vague reference to the presence of the wolf in the mix. Unfortunately, he separates from what at first appeared in *The New Wolves* to be historical context. Directly following the intelligent-design passage is this characteristically terse paragraph: "Who cares? Surely the truth lies not at the beginning or end of the circle but, as with most things, somewhere in between" (30).

I still haven't quite figured out where "somewhere in between" lies along a circle, but this commentary on the spiritual and scientific collision Bass attempts does give *The New Wolves* some symbolic value. The politics of the range into which the Mexican wolf has been brought and recovered are, to understate the issue, chaotic and ill defined. New Mexico has the panoply of spiritual sensibilities that most highly concentrated urban regions have—one just has to walk a little farther across open land to reach them. I've hiked from a Catholic altar past a mosque and to a coven in an afternoon. Granted, the denizen of a big city could do the same, but the amount of land between temples changes the nature of the worship. This mix of sensibilities—juxtaposed with the hotheaded ranch communities packed around Santa Fe's Green Party mayor and its left-leaning warrens—appears in Bass's book, but messily. Wolf writing that skates too much toward a poetics of passionate formlessness creates some danger in the responses where there needs to be less such danger. Bass's intentions are clear, and he is likely the most prolific wolf essayist in America, but the craft is wanting in this case, unlike in his better-written *Ninemile Wolves,* and it hurts his argument.

Public Service

As in any political decision, the "public factor" looms large. Part of any Environmental Impact Statement (EIS), but especially important regarding both wolves and the places of their reintroduction, is the analysis of public opinion. The Mexican wolf's numbers were surprisingly high, including a 50 percent approval rating from rural counties in Arizona and New Mexico combined. One significant decline occurred, recorded by two separate polling agencies; in 1988, 79 percent of New Mexicans supported reintroduction, while only 60 percent did so in 1995 (Parsons, "Case Study," 7–8). Also, letters from schoolchildren to U.S. secretary of the interior Bruce Babbitt seemed to carry less weight in the local debates than letters from federally subsidized cattle outfits to New Mexico governor Gary Johnson.

In Dave Parsons's office I looked through a stack of letters from both schoolkids and cattle ranchers. The common thinking is that both urbanites and children have a collectively high romance factor about the nonhuman world that exacerbates the phenomenon of the ghost wolf. Such sentiments are certainly not

limited to these groups; indeed the history of wolf literature demonstrates peer-
less fable construction by ranchers and hunters claiming steely-eyed objectivity.
But the detached city-dweller and the impressionable child enjoy at least two
forms of great power over the wolf: pathos and market value. Public fora have
become a mainstay of environmental policy-making procedures, though they
sometimes devolve into shouting matches between the stereotypic groups gathering press, the Earth First!ers and the "welfare" ranchers. In this climate, the
ghost wolf looms ominously, overshadowing decisions made by field biologists
and the handful of ranchers supporting reintroduction. I have frequently heard
the standard overstatements: a wolf has never bitten a human being in North
America; the state's economy will be ravaged; our children are in danger; wolves
are gentle and shy.

In response to the studies conducted by federal field biologists, Governor
Johnson produced his own "study" opposing the reintroduction plan, a pathetic
scheme of insufficient research and illogical conclusions funded by Phelps-Dodge
Corp., a southwestern mining company that hired an undertrained analyst (Easthouse, "Peers Blast Study"). When the report was contested by the wolf biologists, Johnson followed up with a one-page letter of his own unfounded rantings
on the ghost wolf (Easthouse, "Johnson").

EarthFirst! staged a demonstration in 1987 to speed the reintroduction of the
wolf. It included Ron Mitchell, who "broke away from the Sierra Club," and the
activist Lone Wolf (Tafoya). At this point, there were too few wolves to even
consider a reintroduction protocol, a fact ignored by the demonstrators, who
picked up Mowat's cue by claiming that the wolves would live mostly on wild
mice and not threaten cattle, although Minnesota studies then being conducted
would prove that wolves may develop the taste for beef, include it as a search
image, and occasionally attack cattle (Fritts, 16).

At one point Bruce Babbitt, who spoke Aldo Leopold's language in calling for
"a new American land ethic," sat through a House Resources Committee meeting of flatly inane comments and accusations. A freshman Republican suggested
opening Yellowstone for hunting. Alaskan representative Dan Young, a leader in
Alaskan wolf-hunt legislation, sarcastically referred to Babbitt as "the alpha wolf
in the room." Idaho representative Helen Chenoweth vehemently demanded
what was already legally provided—that Idaho citizens be allowed to shoot
wolves "as predators." One of her comments followed the same logic as the
hacendado's in *The Crossing*'s pit-fighting scene: "I strongly believe, Mr. Secretary, that not only have your wolves trespassed onto the lands of Idaho, but you
have trespassed onto the Constitution of the United States" ("Babbitt Gets
Chewing Out"). Hank Fischer cites a similar exchange during the reintroduction

proposal, when then Wyoming congressman Dick Cheney declared to a news-paper that the government should let Wyoming "do what's best for Wyoming." On the House floor Utah representative Wayne Owens had to clarify to the sea-soned politician that Yellowstone *National* Park did not, in fact, belong to the state of Wyoming (Fischer, *Wolf Wars,* 106).

The Mexican wolf reintroduction has been far less visible, but no less impor-tant, than the Yellowstone reintroduction. The difference comes both from Yel-lowstone having set the precedent and from its status as one of the most popular parks in the nation. I have mentioned the importance of David Brown's *Wolf in the Southwest;* it receives some specific attention in my final chapter (on *The Cross-ing*), so I will reserve treatment of it until then. The phenomenon of the Mexican wolf's reintroduction is more comparable to what has happened with the red wolf in North Carolina, part of a larger package of bioregional progress restor-atively changing what will and should be written about wolves.

The Grid

When we learn to respect regional, land-crafted distinctions among wolves, we take a step away from the geopolitical proscriptions imposed on them—both as species and as individuals. *Where* matters. Absence means more than the clever stipulations of cultural criticism; it can mean extinction if bad policy extends far enough. In moving toward a better bioregional understanding, one based on substance and relationship, we begin to see a wolf that we do not define, but that is defined by his or her life in and of the world. This bioregional understanding is also based on broader categories than I have been able to cover in locating wolves around the geopolitically gridded construct of nation-burdened biomes, which are better defined by plant formations, temperature lapse rates, snowfall, altitude and latitude, and the macroecological concerns that influence adapta-tion, distinction, range, and trophic relationships. For now, I have tried merely to know the animal better in a regional literary vein based on something more than states and their laws. I have tried to place wolves in some sense for a reader of a wolf book who may be prone to repress nonhuman reality, confine it to boxes, and turn it to shadow.

CHAPTER FOUR

Druid Peak

Jay Robert Elhard's *Wolf Tourist* opens with a souvenir from his trip to Yellowstone in 1993, "a white ceramic mug with more irony than its maker probably intended" (ix). The mug has a heat-activated image of a spruce forest with YELLOWSTONE NATIONAL PARK printed on it. When the mug was hot, "this timberline turned translucent, slowly revealing sketches of two gray wolves, one sitting to the left on its haunches, howling with its nose pointed into a yellow sky, the other trotting to the right with its face turned squarely to the world." Elhard assumes "that the designer of this mug meant to mimic the elusiveness of wolves in the wild or, perhaps, to portray a recent change in the outlook for their official return to Yellowstone" (the fading image also contains the caption "Calling Home, Coming Home"). He concludes by explaining that he also sees this souvenir as "a fitting reflection of human attitudes toward wolves over the last 400 years—hot and cold mostly, rarely tepid" (ix). I would add the obvious fact that the image is one of disappearing and reappearing, those human attitudes themselves being, for all their passion, as mercurial as wolves have ever been.

The reintroduction of the wolf into Yellowstone National Park and central Idaho was not a success for having saved wolves from imminent extinction; globally speaking, as a species, they are in no such danger (yet). It was not necessarily a success on the grounds that the conterminous United States had no wolves; the roaming two thousand or so ignore those geopolitical lines we like to use around the Boundary Waters. And it didn't succeed because wildlife management (an oxymoron without peer) had a systematic, foolproof plan, or even an understanding of cause and effect, about bringing them back and making sure they survived. The Yellowstone/Idaho reintroduction succeeded—despite the ineptitude of the Idaho state government's Division of Fish and Wildlife, the crusades of Montana stockgrowers, and other forms of resistance—on two counts. First, it restored in a single decade one of the last large wilderness ecosystems in the United States to the level of health it had possessed nearly two centuries ago. Second, it brought back wolves not only where people could see them but also where wolves could live in ranges of their own choosing. Therefore, cultural values didn't continue to depend upon the trust that wolves existed *somewhere,* that their pictures would appear on *Animal Planet,* and that perhaps the United States wasn't still the same trigger-happy, tantrum-throwing, wolf-killing barbarity that it had been during the late nineteenth century. As an additional perquisite, the reintroduction produced a raft of books and articles designed to "educate the public" (to use the politician's cliché).

Nothing of great literary merit has resulted from the event, so my coverage will have to be culturally defined rather than focused on craft, but we are talking about some fifteen or more books written over a ten-year period that Doug Smith, Gary Ferguson, and others have called "the decade of the wolf." Government reports and Environmental Impact Statements, read by an impressive number of people generally not prone to poring over such documentation, were trotted out to town meetings all over the American West. The coffee-table book changed from its usual slate of photographs taken in zoos, wolf parks, and sanctuaries to the banner on James C. Halfpenny's *Yellowstone Wolves in the Wild,* which reads, "Incredible photos of wild wolves, no captive wolves."

Briefly, this is what happened in Yellowstone:

At least since the late 1970s biologists had considered Yellowstone a prime candidate for wolf restoration, but the logistics of how to make this happen required twenty years of work. False alarms about natural repopulations; reconsiderations of early wolf research that had justified predator control in the parks as both acceptable management and necessary to tourist satisfaction (the bear populations complicating this matter); leaps in wolf research—all of these influences grew in power as an Environmental Impact Statement was implemented. The EIS's were prepared, town meetings conducted, surveys taken, and hypotheses both scientific and political offered. I write all this in the passive voice to indicate both that the players were numerous and that they usually worked in obscurity; the efforts conducted through the 1980s on the reintroduction of the wolf were as unsung as even wildlife science could be.[1]

In the 1990s, under a more enlightened president, the plan to bring wolves from Canada to Yellowstone was introduced and the EIS filed. This is when the scat hit the fan. Antiwolf protesters of an ignorance and vehemence not seen since the Crusades showed up on street corners and in newspaper articles, preaching that the beast of the devil had returned and that liberal hippies and the socialist, vestigial arm of the federal government called the Department of the Interior were behind it. The most reasonable resistance came in the form of questions, most about livestock depredation and threats to pets and children. Because biologists had never undertaken such a project successfully or on this scale before, the best information they could provide came from Minnesota. That information, to the credit of Norm Bishop, Mike Phillips, Ed Bangs, and others, forthrightly included statistics of livestock deaths and the occasional dog killed in the backyard. Of course, one cow would have been enough to uncork the djinn from the bottle, and the lawsuits began.

The most complicated of the obstacles was the designation of these wolves under the ESA. If they were designated as "endangered," which would have been the logical and most justifiable label to give them for that region, then they couldn't be shot if they decided that beef was on the menu. Indeed, it would be a felony to protect one's cattle. Listing wolves as endangered, the writers of the plan and Bruce Babbitt knew, would undermine the project of bringing them back. The wolves were given an "experimental, nonessential" designation. This protected them from being "controlled" by anyone but park management but allowed for them to be shot if they threatened someone's life or livestock outside the national park. When the new waves of resistance began, the grassroots organization Defenders of Wildlife offered the solution of compensation from a private fund, maintained from donations, that would pay a rancher market value for a loss if that loss could be proved as a wolf kill. The waters calmed for a while.

In 1994 the Wyoming Farm Bureau Federation and coplaintiffs brought suit against the U.S. Department of the Interior to prevent the return of wolves into the Yellowstone ecosystem. The law on the matter of putting the wolf back where the wolf had already lived for centuries is as complicated and dangerous as any laws regarding race, labor, or gender discrimination. The lawyers for the plaintiffs built a case on thin evidence and thick ideology, claiming what could only be construed, even given a maximum inclusion of fact, as nonsense: that wolves prefer domestic livestock to all other prey; that because the gray wolf isn't in danger of extinction on a global scale, the ESA, as an American act and not a global one, need not apply to them (ironically, their listing did call the workings, though not the application, of the ESA into question); that the absence of viable wolf populations anywhere but Minnesota had nothing to do with ecosystemic preservation and the endangerment of a species in the contiguous states; that wolves were already living in Yellowstone (no viable populations were; a few dispersers were suspected); and that "the original Yellowstone subspecies of the gray wolf, *Canis lupus irremotus*," was extinct (McNamee, *Return*, 25–26). Legend and isolated anecdote ran the day for the plaintiffs, who lost to a judge following the law rather than legend and isolated anecdote.

In 1995 and 1996 two groups of wolves were transplanted in Yellowstone from Canada. Twice, injunctions brought against the project left the wolves literally confined in crates, threatened with death or deportation and waiting for freedom, for days. William Downes, the judge sitting for the important cases about the Yellowstone wolves, including some that risked being thrown out as egregious, finally decided that the reintroduction would go forth. The original plan to release five groups of wolves was curtailed to just two groups when those two groups proved to be, to coin a phrase, wildly successful. The biologists I interviewed shared a complicated emotional mix. They were exhausted, relieved, amazed, and in the frenzy of learning something new about wolves nearly monthly.

A wolf put into a park is trapped; numbered; drugged; examined; put in a crate; flown in a helicopter; drugged; examined; driven on a sleigh to a site away from human contact; monitored and guarded; radio-collared; and enclosed in a carefully devised cage. The cage bevels underground and overhead because, biologists discovered, wolves can learn to climb fences as well as dig under them. The reintroduced wolf has to adapt to a new place with other wolves that he or she doesn't know, with human beings showing up to occasionally throw dead animals into the pen. Then one day the door opens, and the elk are there, and the horizon is the boundary.

Radio collars are still bulky affairs, and in political terms, given that public opinion is a major factor in the multimillion-dollar project of moving wolves around, the collars smack of dogness. Radio tracking could even be seen by a purist as Orwellian, the monitoring of a wolf, testimony to humanity's inability to live with wilderness. However, biologists who radio-track species do so primarily in order to protect and preserve those animals from, if not Orwell's world, then Kafka's. And they want to study wolves, who take a lot of legwork to keep up with. As a corrective to earlier policies, the radio collar is probably both a necessary and a justifiable method, at least for newly introduced populations.

Technological advances that likely would be contested by Deep Ecologists as just further intrusions into the wild may sometimes constitute the most plausible solutions available in a techno-industrial society. For instance, all-terrain vehicles have given biologists and rangers a mobility that has made their studies more fruitful and bought time not only for scientists but for some of the species under their scrutiny. The isolationist position to let wolves migrate slowly southward from Canada, as they have been trying to do over the last hundred years, is actually shared by both those who would like to exert private control over wolves (from the stockgrowers' associations to Alston Chase, whose often spurious news articles and books have been dedicated to finding fault with the park system and other governmental forms of environmental management) and those such as Sipapu, an organization in Colorado, who act in the name of an environmental "purity" for wolves returning naturally to habitat, even if too slowly to reach viability over the last fifty years.

The isolationist position dooms wolves to follow a migratory and self-evolutionary timeline—growing slowly and wandering a little at a time toward their former ranges—while humans follow a course of near-instant change, obsolescence, and explosive suburbanization. The closing of formerly accessible migration corridors by expanded housing, strip malls, and highways will continue to limit the wolf's ability to "recolonize" the lower forty-eight. These all seem to be reasons for carefully chosen reintroductions that offer the safest havens for wolves, havens that growth-obsessed national governments cannot or will not currently provide without pressure from two sources: the corporeal wolf of reports, essays, and op-eds; and the ghost wolf of a mass culture still enamored of wild animal life.

One of the Yellowstone packs, the one that grew the largest and lived the most visibly, near the park road running through the Lamar Valley, was called the Druid Peak Pack, for the location at which they first denned in the park. Where once the park had experienced "bear jams" of cars full of oglers, now there were "wolf jams." Just off the road, on a low bluff overlooking the valley toward the Mirror Plateau, wolf-watchers with their scopes and binoculars and cameras with lenses funneling out like black megaphones got to see what they had wanted to see perhaps all their lives. There are stories (I heard one firsthand) of people taking early retirement and spending their days, and the last of their money, staring out into the wilderness before them. They peer into a world that, yes, has tourist access and a road and, yes, that's managed and controlled and radio-collared, but that now functions pretty close to how it once functioned without human presence. And they tell the stories.

The first time I saw wolves in the wild was in 2002, in the Lamar Valley, from below a rock promontory at five in the morning. I heard them step out behind me and above, not twenty-five yards away, a dozen of the Druids all together. They stood in silence for a moment. One howled. The rest joined. They left the promontory and emerged again, crossing the road through the valley, maybe a hundred yards from me. Two of them toward the middle of the pack, now at about twenty of the thirty-eight they were running that year, stopped periodically and looked behind them and toward the ground. They were leading small pups, teaching them where to go, showing them the way to the rendezvous site where the pack would hunt elk. They walked north as the sun came up with its dry heat and lit the valley rose and blue, glittered on the aspen leaves, and sharpened the definition of the pine-and-fir line along the mountains. The wolves disappeared over the plateau. I sat on the ground and wept.

Biologists didn't think wolves would get along very well in captivity, let alone mate. They didn't know if the wolves would socialize, or be afraid to leave the pen, or immediately aim their noses north and run for a thousand miles. They knew how the Greater Yellowstone Ecosystem worked, about the bears and huge coyote population and cats and bison and potential disease conditions. They knew that these wolves had eaten elk in Canada and would likely eat it here, but they didn't know if pack bonds would form strong and fast enough to make that happen before something bad did. Add this to the several biologists, such as Ed Bangs and Renée Askins and Norm Bishop, having to become diplomats because outside the park was a land run by the most territorial species on the planet. They wondered about cars in the park and wolf worshippers and survivalists. And they came to know those wolves. They were scientists who had to tell a public too upset or too rhapsodic to listen clearly that there was plenty they didn't know, that this was yet another reason wolves needed to be in Yellowstone—to teach biologists, and so the rest of us, how the world works, how wolves live.

Consider a person working eighteen-hour days keeping animals alive, turning them out into the wilderness to see if they'll have a future, have babies, make a home, eat freely and live in the hardship but freedom of the world. This is a person whose whole life has been about watching and asking someone who doesn't speak his or her language for answers to questions that this other being is perhaps utterly uninterested in answering. How do you not write stories about this?

The Yellowstone book I think best approaches that emotional resonance is Renée Askins's *Shadow Mountain,* which I will consider in chapter 17. Next is, perhaps, Doug Smith and Gary Ferguson's *Decade of the Wolf,* which takes us as close to the characters of the wolves in Yellowstone as to the biologists who work there. Along with Paul Schullery, Ferguson is one of the most prolific writers on the park's ecosystem. He accounts in detail for much of the story of the reintroduction in *The Yellowstone Wolves: The First Year.* The biologist Michael K. Phillips collaborated with Smith on *The Wolves of Yellowstone,* and Halfpenny's book is one among his dozens written from the perspective of one of the best professional trackers in America. There are two other writers worth noting on the Yellowstone wolf book. The first is Rick McIntyre, whose *War against the Wolf* and *A Society of Wolves* are excellent resources—the first on historical events related to wolf and human conflict, the second on the social behavior of wolves. McIntyre is indefatigable, logging man hours on wolf research rivaled by few if any other rangers. The second is Hank Fischer, whose *Wolf Wars* gives the best synopsis of the Defenders of Wildlife role during the 1990s. Children's educational guides, a staple of the national park system, also proliferate, and explain the basics of wolf biology and ethology, as well as the Yellowstone ecosystem.[2]

Paul Schullery's *Yellowstone Wolf: A Guide and Sourcebook* is the best archival project providing original resources influencing the Yellowstone plan. Schullery should be mentioned in more wolf books than he is; a historian and productive writer on Yellowstone's bears, tourism, natural history, and wolves, among other things, he is the most knowledgeable person I've encountered regarding the park's past and its political minutiae. Other writers of the region, such as Ferguson and Thomas McNamee, concentrate on a journalistic approach. Doug Smith and Mike Phillips have written books with an outreach agenda, a mainstream diction and mission to their work. But Schullery is the resident scholar, concentrating his collections on the most pertinent documents to the issues affecting the Yellowstone ecosystem. His prose in such books as *Searching for Yellowstone: Ecology and Wonder in the Last Wilderness* is of the quality found in *Smithsonian*, the *New Yorker*, or the *Atlantic Monthly*. He is a throwback in some ways to the era of Sigurd Olson or Edwin Way Teale, the public historian/naturalist. As such, his Yellowstone is a Yellowstone worth reading, and his coverage of the wolf's history and controversy in the park is a solid rebuttal to the chaotic and selective ruminations of, say, an Alston Chase.

However, in *Searching for Yellowstone* Schullery's handling of the wolf reintroduction plan during the prewolf years occasionally reveals more political interpretation than factual acumen. Claiming that the elk population was adequately controlled by extant predators without the wolf, he calls it "unfortunate" that "wolf-restoration advocates in the environmental groups" claimed elk populations to be "burgeoning" because "'we wiped out their predators'" (236). In point of fact, elk populations were well proven to be directly affected by the wolf's absence long before Schullery wrote *Searching for Yellowstone,* and he misses the point that elk biomass without wolves might be called a "ranch." He quickly hedges his bet: "Whether the newly restored wolves will add to the total elk mortality or just replace some of the present predation is one of the many interesting questions we are now waiting to have answered" (236–37). This is better said, even prescient, given that this became perhaps the most important question that was answered after the wolf population of the Greater Yellowstone Ecosystem was established.

It wasn't the question most often asked, though. When an ecosystem with a high biomass of prey animals, especially large ungulates, is left without one of what biologists call its "capstone" predators, the system as a whole is damaged. An elk herd, left to browse relatively unmolested except when the bears are awake (and unusually inclined toward the hard work of elk hunting over fishing), has stripped down young aspens so that the trees die during the winter, wounded beyond recovery and robbed of their protection. The elk still have grassland to browse down before they move on, slowly. They are more prone to disease and severe peaks and troughs of health and herd size. Scavengers have fewer carcasses, the absence of which creates grass and soil problems because the participants in decomposition have no way to participate. Fescue and other grasses suffer from trampled soil and overbrowsing (this point is contested among field biologists), so that small animals such as mice and foxes stay away for lack of cover from predatory birds, which in time don't bother to look there anymore and fly off to other areas. In short, the system fragments. Then the elk herd, big as life, shows up again in another season, self-regulating its numbers to its food supply more like a monoculture than a group of organisms in an ecosystem. In the absence of a primary regulator—the wolf—elk become something more cancerous and less cervine.

Human hunters do nothing to ameliorate the lower trophic levels, not only because they remove the entire carcass after a kill but also because they tend to take the most impressive animals (often the most genetically fit) rather than culling populations toward health. It's not just that the elk herd grows unnecessarily large; how it behaves may have the greater effect. In the typical American way of thinking, hunters and ranchers (and even some biologists) have focused on numbers as their method of considering balance in a system—overemphasizing linear depletion or proliferation. Correctives against "balance thinking" about ecosystems (which are subject to moments of catastrophic change) counter the assumption that flat comparative numbers rising and falling are how one assesses an ecosystem. Ecologists know better but don't always know how to look at what they seldom get a chance to see, and are stymied when it comes time to articulate such complexity to the public. Macroecology, an emergent field of study that considers ecological systems relationships over greater scale, has so much to see that formulae are sometimes as elusive as they are necessary.[3] The math done by wolves is often more elegantly simple and accurate than that written by ecologists.

When wolves entered the Yellowstone ecosystem, the elk started moving. The herds got leaner, healthier, and didn't stay quite as long in one spot. A predator that hunts year-round—usually as a family matter, in a fairly organized fashion involving rendezvous sites, cooperative strategies, selection of target prey from a herd, and a pretty high failure rate (so contributing to a few more tries at it)— keeps a prey animal on its hard cold toes. The aspens grow back. Certain species that made out like bandits during the trophic decline, weedy species like the coyote, diminish because competition is rougher. The predator level of the trophic system, now made complete, has had a cascading effect that many biologists did not expect. For the academic crowd that likes to wonder idly what wilderness really is, the change brought by wolves to the Greater Yellowstone Ecosystem is an example of what the words *biome* and *ecosystem* mean, and to whom that meaning matters.

The books that considered the reintroduction plan while it was in its formative stages, more than a decade before the decade of the wolf, were written by people who either knew early on or came to discover that public opinion would decide the matter of wolf survival. The wolf is a visible, interesting animal— "charismatic megafauna" is the going phrase—whatever moral stance one might take. Books about wolves aimed the attention of those who had never seen a wolf outside of a zoo to regions besides Canada or Alaska, regions a little more comfortably under the flag. The trend toward benevolent fantasies certainly must have helped, a trend addressed in articles and books and park pamphlets with facts that may never have reached the benevolent wolf fantasizer otherwise. In works better balancing celebration and calibration we might recognize a theme, and a chronological pattern: note the titles of Michael Milstein's *Wolf: Return to Yellowstone* (1995), Thomas McNamee's *The Return of the Wolf to Yellowstone* (1997), and Steve Grooms's *Return of the Wolf* (1999).

A Spectral Wolf

There is a photograph of the first chief ranger of Yellowstone, Sam Woodring, playing with eight wolf pups in the snow just outside one of the park's impressive travertine buildings in Mammoth. The pups were taken from their den and displayed to the public for one week. They were, according to the caption in Phillips and Smith's *Wolves of Yellowstone,* "often the subject of people's affection." In the photograph Woodring is squatting by the pups, smoking a pipe and smiling beneficently, like a grandfather. Two of the pups sniff his boots. The caption concludes, "They eventually were killed as part of the park's predator control program" (14).

Nobody's perfect. I speak in favor of biologists because I've found biologists to be less corruptible by ideology than are, say, English professors, but certainly the life sciences, especially in service to government, aren't to be exonerated wholesale. Through the assumption that the wolf will grow up as an essentialized predator, killing all the cows it can find, running roughshod through suburban neighborhoods, costing hunters their very livelihoods, and ruining the fabric of our great and increasingly artificial nation, you could easily ban a wolf book from a grade school reading list. You could take ecology to court and try to turn it into something other than ecology. If that doesn't work, you could drag it into an English Department and turn it into something utterly opaque, unexplainable and indefensible, and so conveniently manipulate it to fit whatever point you need to make to satisfy the current cultural trend, or to start one.

It's possible to teach entire college curricula without a single student knowing the first thing about fundamental ecological facts and their influence on myth and literature, and vice versa, even as places and animals appear in all their ubiquity in every work of art those students read. Enamored of fantasy, the graduate student achieves mastery in it, teaches it to undergraduates, then lands a job writing and teaching cultural studies divorced from the influence of the nonhuman world. He might eventually chair the department at NYU and run a journal and write material on what he thinks are these imaginary constructs called "wilderness" or "ecology"—publishing books, securing tenure, ringing up a high salary, and contributing to the loss of both life on the planet and literature about it without batting an eye or leaving the Insert Greater Metropolitan Area Here. The politics attendant to such an influential figure are no different from the anti-environmental politics of a James Watt Republican on the take from Big Oil, clear-cutters, or strip miners. This is how the wolf disappears. And at every little incrementally erosive step of the way, each act of political cleverness and denial and abuse seems not only reasonable but also intellectually titillating.

All you have to do is feed someone the right ghost wolf and you can create your own little cultural cascade. I've seen it happen in my former university, in courtrooms and town meetings, and in our national news. I've also stayed for days at thirty degrees below zero on the Blacktail Plateau looking for wolves, hearing the howls of what I think must have been the Leopold Pack. After just one long day and into the night at that temperature, reading a book on them seemed both more and less important. That moment out there where wolves live isn't a requirement for a student of this material, but it's a recommendation. Having gone also isn't some trump card one gets to play, either. My brief experiences are nothing in terms of sacrifice or effort compared with people who do it nearly every day, a Bob Landis or a Diane Boyd. But I think a scholar of literature who studies such moments as they appear in print stands to gain from being where those moments appear before and outside of print. And for that to happen, we need to preserve *where* it happens.

This is the very reason for my treatment of regional wolf literature. Region dictates certain terms of writing beyond "atmosphere" or "foreshadowing" or "setting" and, as I've mentioned, beyond the brilliant and long-unsung New England literary women of the late nineteenth century. Just as important is the damage done when some unassuming student of the life sciences wanders into a literature class and discovers that the way she's been studying actual bioregions has little to do with the assumed significance of literature. The gulf widens. Years later, everyone at the alumni dinner sits at tables separated according to their old unacquainted majors.

During the 1930s and 1940s the National Park Service published a series of bulletins, through the U.S. Government Printing Office, on the status of various flora and fauna. The reports are staple-and-glue bound, paper covered, and they sold for about twenty cents in the mid-1930s. The Fauna Series's second volume, published in 1935 and titled "Fauna of the National Parks of the United States," contains a section written by George Wright on bird life in Yellowstone, which opens: "Days with the birds in Yellowstone are tonic to him whose spirit is bruised by reiteration of the lament that wilderness is a dying gladiator. Too frequent exposure to a belief born of despair is not good for any man. To conservation, it is a poison the more deadly because the injurious effects remain unnoticed until a lethal quantity has accumulated in the system" (27).

As Wright continues, he shifts from conservationism to preservationism as the modus operandi of the park system. He explains that an understanding of wilderness was far more complicated than biologists had thought it would be in terms of a defensible preservationist argument for park management. But he also declares that through the hard labor of learning the ecosystem "a new principle was born. Henceforth, scientific, planned management would be used to perpetuate and restore primitive wildlife conditions" (27). This is incredibly progressive for the first half of the twentieth century. Sadly, the passage, already a bit rhapsodic, then takes its most dramatic turn:

> Even before the birth [of the "new principle"] a spectral wolf haunted the scene. Ever bolder, his howls now make the night one long anxiety, for he shouts to heaven that the baby lives in vain. Small wonder if the nurses whose duty it is to appreciate every hazard over which their charge must triumph and to prepare him for it, now and then grow discouraged. Their heavy task becomes quite unbearable with that added tribulation, the defeatist headshaking of the spectral wolf.
>
> Often it is but a small unnoticed shade of change which transforms the pleasant task into a burdensome duty. I do not know when the change occurred, but there came a day when the elk bull standing on a much-too-near horizon was no longer the embodiment of wild beauty, no longer a wild animal at all to me, but just next winter's great big problem, a dejected dumb brute leaning on the feed ground, its gums aflame with foxtails and suffering from necrotic stomatitis. (27–28)

This quotation is exemplary of the complicated contradictions running wildlife management, and the thinking that still sometimes flares up from its remission and metastasizes in the life sciences. Wright lives with two minds in conflict. He seems to attack the old world of wildlife management, but turns out to be equally retrograde in defending predator removal and the sportsman's paradise, where the spectral wolf won't bother the management program and ruin the new principle. He is convinced that the wolf is the disease from which the park's nurses have to save it. Then, without a breath, without even the usual requisite diversion and forgetfulness it takes for the common contradiction to surface, Wright's second mind expresses itself. He is miserable for the suffering elk, whose romance, like Twain's river, seems to have left Wright for reasons he can't explain. Somehow, the elk's nobility waned, diluted by strange ecological or psychological forces that create in him this ennui. "I do not know when the change occurred" contains the deepest and saddest irony, because it occurred when Wright and the new principle removed wolves from the system. He can't tell the disease from the cure. He has been fooled by the ghost wolf, and the consequences are severe to the ecosystem, to the elk, and to his own psyche.

The wolf was long fitted with this black collar, and too often wears it still. Poets, whose profession sometimes tilts them toward metaphors of sound over substance, have often abandoned the wolf to the gothic pyre of death and ravin. Take this example from John Lamb's "Aratus: The Phenomena and Diosemeia":

> When through the dismal night the lone wolf howls,
> Or when at eve around the house he prowls,
> And, grown familiar, seeks to make his bed,
> Careless of man, in some outlying shed,—
> Then mark: ere thrice Aurora shall arise,
> A horrid storm will sweep the blackened skies.

Or this one from Robert Louis Weeks's "Castles and Wolves":

> While I read, the fantasies were dreamed
> against dark backgrounds full of
> gloomy castles and damp passageways,
> perhaps horses, bears, and wolves.
> The woods were inhabited by Druids
> and circles far around the sacred oak,
> and people were led there screaming.
>
> To know such things was culture,
> and to move squeamishly away from them
> was civilization. To visualize them,

and fear them, was imagination.
Education held them all. Until you came
to loneliness.

My study is focused on prose, but it's important to note that poetry, with its ability to raise from language certain specters—emotional complexities, the substance of the world considered and the brilliance of symbolic language in cooperation—also runs a hard risk. Poetry, as a genre of compression, may acquiesce to the symbols the poet and reader want for effect at the expense of the part of the world mined for use. In this way it is a genre of powerful mythic force and subject to equal responsibility to its subject matter. In abandoning the gothic castles of Europe toward the creation of an American literature, we might repress rather than refine, and the gargoyles loom the darker for it.

Among the young civilized cultures of North America, the primordial image of the wolf was shaped by some combination of fear, competition (both emotional and economic), awe, reverence, tutelage, social affinity, similarity, eye contact, hunger, and whatever in mystery comes before all of these and more of our traits. It has proved to be an image of terrible error producing catastrophic results. In regional reintroduction we have taken a significant step toward saving an archetypal image from its profanement, as well as a real animal from its torture and murder.

Rick McIntyre writes about the killing of a male Yellowstone wolf by a man who claimed he thought the wolf was a dog. The dead wolf's mate waited for him to return for days, until finally it was time for her to give birth to her pups. As a result of her wait, she was unable to dig a den, and the first litter in Yellowstone in seventy years was born "in a shallow depression on the cold, hard forest floor" (*War,* 223). The poacher was found out by his possession of the head and pelt, evidence of his lie; he couldn't seem to give up the keepsakes of his crime even while he denied committing it. Who would keep the head and pelt of a dog? The wolf's own body served as a compass to the poacher, like the telltale heart.[4] An additional irony is that the hunter who didn't mean to shoot a wolf asked to be exonerated for the lesser crime of having shot man's best friend. His hope must have been that the wolf he shot just wouldn't be missed, or even recognized. But the spectral wolf has a way of changing from the ghost we command to the ghost that haunts us, whether we stand behind the sights of a rifle or the prow of a classroom lectern.

CHAPTER FIVE

Intermediate Corporeality

THE AVERAGE WOLF

Surely he has never seen a wolf in wild state or he would know that he is nothing like a dog. No one would ever mistake him for a dog and the wolf knows he [is] not a dog and he does not have to be in a pack to give him dignity or confidence. He is hunted by everyone. Everyone is against him and he is on his own as an artist is.
— ERNEST HEMINGWAY

William Faulkner had ridiculed Ernest Hemingway's assertion that writers should stick together as doctors, lawyers, and wolves do, and stated that "the sort of writers who band together willy nilly or perish, resemble the wolves who are wolves only in a pack, and, singly, are just another dog."[1] The exchange raises a number of issues pertinent to this chapter's focus on the corporeal wolf. First and most obvious is the dog/wolf distinction being used metaphorically by both writers in a way that appropriates the wolf. Second, as an outcome of the first issue, is Hemingway's use of the male pronoun (with the wonderful multivalence of the phrase "he is nothing like a dog," which could have as its referent a man, Faulkner, or the wolf). Third, also an outcome of the first, is his invocation of the hunt to victimize both wolf and writer, a loaded conflation coming from the great white hunter Hemingway, who depicts the wolf as the prey (of men, particularly those who aren't artists) rather than as the predator. Fourth is Faulkner's assumption, like Deleuze and Guattari's in *A Thousand Plateaus,* that a wolf outside of a pack is somehow not a wolf; in Faulkner's case this is a convenient working definition for *dog*. My favorite among the many powerful phrases in this exchange is the defense of the wolf's "dignity" and "confidence," neither of which is assumed to be inherently good or bad, but part of being a wolf/artist.

I feel obliged to point us to the source, to untie some of these Gordian knots that we imagine as wolves (without simply cutting them), and to clarify some of the foundational points of corporeality that come from wolf biology, ecology, and ethology. Wolf books are about wolves and, as such, bear the weight of trying to *explain* wolves. The best recourse seems to be the life sciences, particularly wildlife biology, and so nature writers gather their research from three sources—wolf biologists, observation, and each other—in a cumulative attempt to get at this impossible but necessary chore of accurately describing the wolf. Since what I'm doing qualifies as a project of ecocriticism, it seems necessary to include the ecology with the criticism, and so to add my effort to the corporeal mix. At the same time, the primer on wolves that follows is also an examination of certain images and methods writers apply during their own attempts.

For instance, take the "average behavior" oxymoron. Let me begin with an illustrative anecdote of this fallacy, which too often appears in not only nature writing but also scientific writing. An exhibit in the Indianapolis Children's Museum demonstrates the method by which archaeologists build a clay model of an Egyptian face from an unearthed skull. The demanding application of both science and art required to reconstruct missing parts of the bone structure and to form muscle mass from clay is indeed impressive. In order to choose the skin color of the represented Egyptian, the range of pigmentation among indigenous Egyptians was averaged, and that color applied to the clay composite. The result is a color very much like the orange tinge of a fake tan. In the end, the very act of trying to make this figure a recognizable individual is diminished by denying it the opportunity to be something other than the representative of a statistical average. Indeed, that choice probably had among the *lowest* odds of a successful guess. Who has the average skin color?

I'm uncomfortable with speaking of wolves or any animals in terms of averages, be they biological, ethological, morphological, or mythological. Statistical averages may certainly help us with quantitatively addressable questions; we should not pretend that all analysis is qualitative. Our job in the study of literature is to distinguish likeness and difference, individual style and collective context, and the breakthroughs in artistic craft during the course of literary history. It is not to employ these as if they are all of like value. Averaging animals, like averaging books or people, implies a context that doesn't exist, what Edward Said redefined as "Orientalism," and it diminishes adaptation. To average the number of pups in wolf litters of the Lamar Valley over a period of years gives field biologists a relative estimation of pack health during changing climatic conditions. To average it from among the packs of the Lamar Valley, the Brooks Range, and northern Minnesota—all highly divergent ecosystems subject to various degrees of biotic and abiotic influence and control—in order to declare the size of "an average wolf pack," denies as much as it asserts. Having a point of factual knowledge is always a good thing in science, and I certainly do not advocate cultural relativism as some antidote to scientific inquiry. But I would encourage considering the worth of a fact about wolves in terms of its application *by* wolves, not just *to* them.

We don't always say "the bear, the dolphin, the wolf" under an assumption that the species is represented alike by all individuals. Sometimes we mean that we are making a species-level claim in order to distinguish a wolf from, say, a bear. But biologists may be guilty of essentializing, for instance when they refer to canids as "the dog family," rather than as "the canid family." We prize human thought and study it because we know it to be more complex and self-referential than the thoughts of other species. By association we equate complexity with superiority, which is a foundational logical error. We ignore other species' capabilities, live in ignorance of them, and finally make their lives out to be greater mysteries than our own, even as we wave our hands dismissively at what we think of as their shallowness, their lack. The power we give to the imagined subject may grow even to the point of mythic import, but we too often invest it with this power at the expense of the raw material of its origin. Ironically, the mythic imaginary beast will bloat and twist into gigantic inexplicability over epochs of time, while the animal at the source may be removed entirely, its species gone from the planet, in one human generation.

We are reminded of Lopez being taught "Maybe. Sometimes." This should be our compass as readers of nature writing, lest we fall into Benjamin Franklin's trap of making such pithy metaphors of hollow facts as Poor Richard's "Wolves never prey upon wolves" or "Wolves may lose their teeth, but they never lose their nature." Franklin drew the latter of these adages from Draxe's *Bibliotheca Scholastica,* but he could as easily taken it from an Ontario proverb that says, "A wolf may change its mind but never its fur." Instead, I try when possible to use qualifying modifiers—"often," "may," "usually"—when a generalization has a high degree of likelihood and repeatability. In this chapter (as in general) I am more interested in what is possible for a wolf than what is possible for a human being to make of a wolf. What I have encountered is a tendency to declare common some of the unusual practices of wolves and to declare doubtful some of the most basic behaviors shared by the entire mammal class.

Evolution and Taxonomy

That wolves are more closely related to bears than to cats might seem obvious enough, but that they are more similar to raccoons than to hyenas would take a taxonomist to explain. The lupine evolutionary trace extends fifty-five million years to the development of carnassial teeth in the species *Miacis.* Twenty million years later, as *Cynodictus* developed, teeth again determined a morphological distinction. *Cynodictus* split, between fifteen and thirty million years ago, into *Cyno-desmus* and *Tomarctus,* the latter being the ancestor of both wolf and fox. By two million years ago, after the extinction of the dire wolf, *Canis lupus* possessed the basic features it has today.[2] There were no "dogs" in existence as far as archeologists have been able to tell, a distinction already loaded with conflicting criteria over the use of *dog* as both a cultural term and a morphological one. The taxonomic classification for the wolf runs as follows:

Kingdom: *Animalia*
Phylum: *Chordata* (animals with notochords)
Subphylum: *Vertebrata* (animals with skeletons of bone or cartilage)
Class: *Mammalia*
Subclass: *Eutheria* (placental mammals)
Order: *Carnivora*
Family: *Canidae* (called the dog family)
Genus: *Canis* (dogs)
Species: *lupus* (wolves)[3]

The complicated debate over a further division, the subspecies, is important to how we read fiction and nonfiction about wolves. Several names for subspecies of *Canis* imply the animal's mysticization. *Monstrabalis* means "unusual" or "remarkable," as well as carrying more obvious connotations. *Nubilus,* or "cloudy gray," and *variabilis,* or "changing," both refer to color (Lewis and Clark having preferred *variabilis*) but also significantly imply the illusory or the transformational. Lopez loosely translates *irremotus,* a term for what was once called the Northern Rocky Mountain wolf, as "the wolf who is always showing up here" (*Of Wolves and Men,* 14). Hank Fischer writes in *Wolf Wars* that at least one biologist jokingly refers to all wolves as *Canis lupus irregardless* (12). Fischer's remark, now common among wolf biologists, aims in at least in two directions; the typical rancher doesn't much care how many subspecies of wolf exist if one is eating his or her cattle, and the wolf biologist probably won't consider the hairsplitting of subspecificity as important as keeping all wolves alive.

In 1992 many of these subspecific names were conflated into the biologist Ron Nowak's list of five subspecies: *arctos, occidentalis, nubilus, lycaon,* and *baileyi* (Busch 6). This list not only created a more efficient taxonomic system but also properly complements Linnaeus's project of extending the *Systema Naturae.* The five labels represent, respectively, a bioregion, the Western (implying European) Hemisphere, a cloud, an Arcadian king, and wolf biologist Vernon Bailey. The very diversity of these categories demonstrates the mythic North America in which wolves live. "Timber wolf" is a colloquialism for a gray wolf living in forested land (especially midwestern, especially Minnesota or Wisconsin). Gray wolves aren't necessarily gray; *tundra wolf* and *Arctic wolf* are generally thought to be synonymous terms; and the red wolf in the southeastern United States (and perhaps Texas if the subspecies is related) went through a harsh analysis as to whether it was a wolf at all before its legal designations for reintroduction or preservation could be determined.[4]

The name game wouldn't get easier even if we clarified the taxonomic chart, because people like names, like toying with them, and are unlikely to systematize nicknames with binomial nomenclature. The gray wolf has been called the "buffalo wolf" and the "loafer." One difficulty in looking at the North American literature of wolves is that coyotes have often been called by wolf names. "Medicine wolf," for example, is one name for the coyote in the Southwest, as is "prairie wolf." The latter term is found so frequently in nineteenth-century journals and tales of the plains that it is impossible at times to determine whether the writer saw a lean wolf, a Mexican wolf (which has some coyotelike features), a Texas red wolf, a feral "coy-dog," or a legitimate member of *Canis latrans.* In the *Thwaites Travel Journals* we find the "brush wolf" and the "little wolf," which are probably not wolves but "cayotes."[5]

The dog as a taxonomic litmus is a disconcerting phenomenon. It demonstrates the ineptitude of human language and its tendency to undermine accuracy. Mech refers to the wolf as "a large wild dog" (*The Wolf,* 11), and as I've mentioned, the taxonomic family *Canidae* is unscientifically called the "dog family" even by scientists. Such incidents of linguistic influence on taxonomic assumptions tempt us to shore up the temple of cultural constructivism, but science is no mere slave to culture. Dogs did not evolve from wolves, they were bred down, to whatever degree they may have participated by choice in some incidents of their domestication.[6] Veterinary professor Alan Beck puts it this way: "In a sense, man created the dog in his own image" (Beck & Katcher, 167). Because the dog became a separate morphological species through the processes of domestication and breeding, it might be said that the dog is a "small tame wolf," a member of the wolf family. On the other hand, there's the dachshund.

Animal companionship, even pet "ownership," can be one of the great measures of human compassion because the reality of domestication (versus mere ownership) demands that humans reciprocate love and nurture with animals who have been, through whatever ancient human motives, bred to live humanized lives. This practice may honor both species in the exchange. But our opulence can lead us to confuse love with acquisition and increase, resulting in the desire to breed, sell, show, and own. Pet stores are no more morally defensible than crack houses, and hybridizing wolves now, given the ubiquity of the domestic dog (especially in "shelters"), defines irresponsibility. This is one among many reasons why the term *wilderness* is important more than as some cultural conversation piece. It is where wolves live well. Literature should not limit itself to an art of pet-making.

The Great Hunter

Certain traits of a wolf are overemphasized in literature and in popular culture. The pack hierarchy, mating practices, and the predatory role are the most common. These traits certainly do distinguish the wolf by degree from some other species, and biologists certainly employ them, but a wolf must be considered first as an individual. Being a predator is only one aspect of being a wolf. While eating is essential, predation is but a method. We might say that wolves "also eat." I don't want to be known only by my occupation, and I'd rather not foist that off on someone else. We should accept that certain premises required for study have to be accepted, but that wolves are constantly nipping at the edges of these premises, which is precisely what proves their active agency in texts written about them both as *them* and as *each*.

Although wolves have been cast among the most notorious hunters, they are not, as a species, the world's most efficient. The success rate for pack hunting has been estimated at between 8 and 12 percent (in Yellowstone's unusually high prey base it's about 20 percent). Often hunting consists of an encounter in which the prey turns on the wolves and braces for a fight. At that point, wolf packs frequently forgo the effort. Elk, moose, and deer have killed attacking wolves by kicking them, bison have trampled or gored them, and many prey animals outrun them. In thirty-two years of working on Isle Royale, Rolf Peterson has never seen a moose stand his or her ground and be killed.[7]

Wolves often hunt in silence, but not always, and when they work quietly they probably do so not because of some exceptional cunning but because stealth helps them avoid risky or taxing chases, and because they're busy. My uncle works silently; this doesn't make him preternaturally efficient. Nature programs juxtaposing images of growling, slobbering wolves with images of the same wolves pouncing on a hare are wrongly (and deliberately) conflating two kinds of behavior—aggression and predation (Kyrouac; Mech, *The Wolf*, 4; Murie, 80). Wolves eat because they like to as much as because of some carefully calibrated survival gauge. Contrary to legends of their eating anything thrown at them, they have preferences in taste. They will subsist on refuse out of both necessity and interest, which means they are capable scavengers as well as hunters, a fact often overlooked in romantic depictions and shunted onto the coyote or "park bear." Wolves' attraction to carrion was not lost on medieval societies, however, which found the scavenging packs to be graverobbers and body snatchers on battlefields, catalyzing the demonization of the lupine during the Middle Ages. Into the Renaissance, as demonstrated in *The Duchess of Malfi*, the wolf served as a symbol of death and disease, either in medicinal nomenclature—"But in our own flesh, though we bear diseases, / Which have their true names only ta'en from beasts, / As the most ulcerous wolf and swinish measles" (2:1)—or in moral iconography:

> In those that are possess'd with't there o'erflows
> Such melancholy humour they imagine
> Themselves to be transformed into wolves;
> Steal forth to church-yards in the dead of night,
> And dig dead bodies up. (5:2)

In addition to hunting the big game for which they are famous, wolves may eat fish and fowl, may subsist on rodents, and will eat grass as a purgative. In Minnesota they have caused comparable damage to sheep and turkey farms as they have caused to cattle ranches. Wolves generally consume about .15 pounds of prey per pound of wolf per day, which varies especially in winter. Like most mammals, their bodies convert calories to fat as a reserve during times of scarcity. They may travel for several days at a time without eating. Often all that will be left of a large kill is the skull, the hooves, and some hair and bone fragments. This is especially true in regions where wolves are providers for ravens, eagles, coyotes, rodents, and other scavengers who clean up the leftovers of a carcass in the classic ecosystemic "ripple effect" (Bishop, "Ripple Effect"). I have seen the remains of an elk stripped to the bone except for a skull cap of fur around the antlers and a few bands of hide around the hooves. When grizzlies run wolves off their kills, the pack must hunt again, further curbing ungulate populations. Wolves may overeat and thus digest more slowly; they often sleep long after meals, rather than regularly and systematically taking the "wolf naps" Mowat saw and claimed to have adopted as his own sleeping habit for a time (60–61). Lupine parents give every indication of taking pleasure from regurgitating meat for pups, although if a pup is too demanding in nipping at the provider's muzzle then the adult might walk away or gently bowl over the pup.

A person is more likely to "frenzy" at the sight or smell of blood than is a wolf. In fact, most wolves demonstrate an impressive discipline about prey consumption, given that their next meal may not come again for a while; they will even eat the blood-soaked snow around a kill. Reliable material on wolves had already posited that mice helped them sustain themselves until bigger game was available,[8] so the criticisms of Mowat for his casting the wolf as a "mouse-eater" are a bit misplaced (for example, Goddard, 49); a sounder criticism of Mowat might be of his implication that he discovered the fact (72). He does not say that they prefer mice or refuse other prey, and there is no evidence of wolves living long-term on mice. Wolves may cache food, especially in winter—an indication of surplus killing contrary to the romantic view of wolves as taking only what they need (although no record exists of one wolf selling meat to another or setting up networks of national distribution). On a number of occasions they have "bobtailed" domestic cattle, clipping off the tail neatly and leaving without performing a kill, the motivation for which practice is unknown.[9] I'll speculate here and say it's for the same "reason" that wolves will toss around a piece of hide and play tug-o'-war with it, the same reason that cats bat at dangling string. I'll also be glad to wager my paycheck that we're as unlikely to know why wolves do this as we are to explain why people invented the Frisbee.

Wolves have eaten unborn calves from the wombs of living cows. They have brought down prey and feasted on it while the animal was alive. A simple explanation for wolves treating their prey this way is that wolves like a hot, fresh meal as much as some folks like their lobster plucked live from the tub before them. Ranchers and politicians have used such behavior to level charges of cruelty against wolves as a means of eradicating them.[10] Three obvious ironies of such arguments surface quickly: The first is that domestic cattle were not the prey of wolves until they were offered up on the ranchland platter; the second is what happens to veal calves right after they are saved from the wolf; the third is the torture of supposedly mindless wolves by supposedly rational men who have forgotten more of torture than wolves could know.

Driving the argument may be a separate empathy for the cow that doesn't exist for the wolf. Many ranchers, especially those indoctrinated in their youth by 4-H, understand as well as anyone the emotional connection to a domestic stock animal. This is partly despite their complicity in the industrialization of predation and partly because of it. Some ranchers acknowledge the need for stable ecosystems and shared ranchland with other predators.[11] The logical extension of stockmen's pleas to put an end to the cruelty of predation on cattle is of course vegetarianism, although that argument is seldom carried very far at the local steakhouse or stockgrowers' meeting.

A wolf will sometimes drag down prey by the hindquarters, an arduous process, and the death of the prey will likely be shock and loss of blood rather than a swift, "clean" kill. There is some debate over the hamstringing method, which was once widely accepted and has become a legendary "fact" but has seldom been recorded and is not confirmed as a habitual or typical part of the hunting repertoire.[12] Barry Lopez mentions that wolves "reputedly lay low in the grass, switching their tails from side to side like metronomes" to lure antelope (*Of Wolves and Men,* 59). His bibliography is quite loose, though, and I have not been able to corroborate this incident. To his credit, Lopez qualifies this and a few other incidents as purported rather than validated and responds to the lack of clear data on wolf hunting behavior available in the late 1970s.

When hunting caribou, Arctic wolves might use one of three methods: ambush, in which the pack waits for the prey in carefully chosen territory; relay, in which the pack splits, running prey into other pack members or "passing the baton" until the prey is too tired to flee the anchor wolves; or chase, in which the pack sizes up a member of the herd, usually (but not always) from among the stumblers and the sick, cuts out that animal cowhand style, and kills it.[13] This last has been called the "sanitation method," most commonly known as culling, which can result in stronger herds as a result of weaker members being removed from the gene pool. However, wolves do not always follow an exact game plan; they eat when they want to and if they can. The average age of a wolf-killed elk is twelve, past the optimum breeding age. The average age of a human-killed elk is six, right at the prime breeding age. That is, the human being poses a greater danger to all prey access, human included, than does the wolf, because human hunters are more likely to ruin the breeding cycles that bring back healthy herds. But, again, those are average numbers. What they refute is the idea that human hunters "replace" wolves in systems lacking wolves, a misperception exploited for all it's worth in order to issue more deer tags and kill more wolves.[14]

If they find deer yards, points of high-percentage herd congregation, wolves might overhunt the deer population and cause it to drop, which then may create a condition called a "predator pit." The ratios of predator and prey are usually kept steady by wolf packs' and prey species' breeding cycles, but if the deer population is too crippled to survive the following winter, then the wolves may starve, and the predator-prey system could collapse. So many factors influence survival that a clear critical mass to this arrangement has been hard to define. Such is the nature of ecosystems, even the most isolated ones like Isle Royale.

The Wolf in Winter

The wolf has long been associated with winter, not only because of Russian sleigh-chase stories, Nordic myth, or Alaskan tales, but also because wolves function well in winter, grow those impressively thick coats, and are easier to see against snow. "No place is so apt for the origin of such widely exaggerated reports [of wolves] as the Arctic and sub-Arctic regions," wrote J. Stokely Ligon in 1926, "since in these remote sections there is little possibility of the fallacy of the stories ever being established" (Casey & Clark, xiv). Myth flourishes in the lack of corroboration, and it flourishes in schism, the collision of fact with belief. It also seems to thrive in snow.

In winters of heavy snowfall, wolves are capable of moving through whiteouts by using senses other than sight and by communicating as a pack, if they are in one. Heavy powder in severe winters might prohibit wolf movement by taxing energy and cutting travel distance, but hardpack or a frozen surface assists the wolf against ungulates, whose hooves crack through and slow them down. In short, wolves work well in snow because they have big feet. Wolves may sleep in temperatures of forty degrees below zero Fahrenheit, regulating the flow of blood to the skin to control their body temperature, even maintaining a footpad temperature just above the temperature at which the pads would normally freeze when in contact with ice. Pups are surprisingly resistant to inclement weather even when not sheltered by an adult (although they usually are, which I have always appreciated).[15]

Jack London's *White Fang* begins with an orphan, as do several other writers' wolf books (see, for example, Morey, Borchardt, Curwood). In the adolescent fantasy of dead parents, one brand of wolf story fulfills the coming-of-age plot through a romance-gothic/literary naturalist device of the child thrown into the hard world, made harder by winter. This occurrence is probably more commonly suffered by human children than by wolf pups. It is also connected to the adoption theme common to wolf stories, most famously written by Kipling, rooted in the mythos of wolves, foundlings, and the naissance of civilizations. The wolf in winter is a symbolic being in literature—the figure of survival and grim resolve in the blizzard. We will see this in more detail in chapters 13 and 14 on children's literature.

Snow will also cause a prey animal to travel farther and more often in order to forage and may increase the odds of its wandering into pack territory. The specific effects of snow depth on predator/prey relations are complex and have received considerable attention. In fact, sources on this subject are so copious as to remind us what is required of, and of interest to, biologists in the pursuit of a phenomenon.[16] Any gambler would place the bet on stories rather than on facts dominating the mind of a nineteenth-century trekker who confronts a wolf pack in the snow. If the facts—the odds of attack, for example—surfaced at all in the trekker's mind, they would most likely surface after he was first startled by the presence of wildness, then mortified by the presence of stories brought out of memory. On the other hand, the twenty-first-century hiker is also influenced by stories that prompt him or her to be carefree, even intrusive, and thus risk suffering the consequences of disregarding another set of facts—the one about differences between wild animals and tame ones.

Aggression and Affection

Wolves have attacked both human beings and each other, and will eat other wolves that have been killed (Banfield, "Notes," 120, and personal observation). The oft-repeated adage that there are no documented attacks of wolves against humans has repeatedly been proven incorrect, although the corrections haven't always found their way into activist commentary.[17] The most specific and reliable generalization would be that a healthy, wild, full-blooded wolf has never killed a Euro-North American, according to documentation confirmed by biologists qualified to recognize wolf attacks—which isn't quite pithy enough for most brochure material. A pack of "nonsocialized" captive wolves killed a researcher in Canada who had not familiarized herself with the wolves before entering the enclosure, where she most likely tripped and was attacked (Klinghammer, 3). Rabid wolves have bitten people (one source of werewolf legends, because of the physical symptoms of rabies in both the wolf and the bitten person). Nondocumented attacks are highly likely to have occurred—from early domestication attempts to later hybridization attempts, not to mention the more frequent pre-nineteenth-century encounters with wolves by both European and indigenous Americans.

Wolves have killed and been killed by black bears and grizzly bears, which are nonprey animals to them.[18] Their frequent prey choices are powerful animals in their own right; elk can be difficult especially at certain times of year, a moose cow with her calf is easily as dangerous as a black bear, and musk oxen and those tetchy bison are as tough as prey animals come. D. R. Gray records the unusual killing of a bull musk ox by a single wolf; usually such moments involve a weak or sick animal and a lone wolf desperate for food, but solo kills have been proven more numerous than was thought by field biologists working during the mid-twentieth century (Gray 197). In nineteenth-century reportage (granted not always empirical and barely formalized) the assumption of the wolf being a formidable solo killer was hyperbolic, but the high plausibility of a wolf hunting and surviving alone indicts the assumption that wolves hunt in packs and depend on them for their existence. We would more accurately say that wolves often prefer packs.

Wolves can hunt in water. Maybe. Sometimes. Captive wolves have been seen swimming after waterfowl, and in one unusual incident a wild wolf killed a deer while both were swimming.[19] They have also killed one another in territorial battles, in dominance fights, or in mobbing a subordinate wolf, although in the latter two cases deaths are often accidental (or incidental, to use the more behavioristic term).[20] In a wolf ecology course at the Yellowstone Association Institute,

I was shown footage of elk making for deep water in a river as a strategy to discourage wolf attacks (Landis, YAI). The preference for or adaptability to water therefore seems situational, and individualizes behavior enough to excite field biologists to confess that the relationship between individual action and essential behavior needs closer scrutiny.

The image of wolves as divinely or nefariously designed killers, perpetuated by most televised nature programs, especially of the 1970s, is erroneous. In Lois Crisler's words, "Wolves have what it takes to live together in peace" (xi), and they are generally cooperative with each other and with other species (although they consistently exhibit a loathing for coyotes). Wolves usually negotiate their territorial boundaries with a minimum of violence, and in bear country develop negotiating and attack strategies as complicated as national foreign policies.[21]

While assumptions about the wolf's "killer instinct" have been used to justify exterminating it, generalizations about its gregarity (as perpetuated by many post-1980s nature programs) have led to another brand of victimization. Romantic notions of the wolf have created such tragedies as "pet" wolves, hybrid breeding, and the overindulgence of captivity as a means of "education." Studies of the wolf in captivity have led to some basic points of knowledge, but captivity is a dubious way of learning as well as of teaching the wolf to others. Lopez points out that the ambassador wolf program helped both children and their teachers change their views about the wolf's inherent ferocity (*Of Wolves and Men*, 263). This may be true, but it risks introducing children only to another ghost wolf, since a wolf in a classroom pretends that the politics of nature function properly through embassies.[22]

The great paradox of the wolf in terms of its survival among human beings is that while wolves seem so wraithlike, are in fact seldom seen and commonly thought of as "shy" or "wary," they are as well known for their gregarity, curiosity, and social behavior—traits that have made them easier than coyotes both to slaughter and to domesticate. The generalization that wolves are "elusive" comes partly from their having been wiped out in the lower forty-eight states, as the outlaw wolves gained their fame from their increasing scarcity. It also comes partly from the fact that the populations of Minnesotan and Canadian wolves (estimated at thousands and tens of thousands respectively) live in timbered wilderness areas more often than near cities. Several nineteenth-century travelers wrote the word *coward* into their journals about the wolf that recognizes a gun barrel and runs—itself a questionable claim.[23] A century later the shy wolf shows up on calendars with warm photographs of yearlings peering from behind aspens in winter. We struggle to find The Wolf, then struggle to depict it.

The Pack

Generalizations about mating have changed radically over the last thirty years of wolf study. Pack status certainly contributes to mating opportunities but does not singularly determine it. The famous hierarchical and monogamous system of the wolf pack has been overstated. For example, the common assumption that only the alpha wolves mate, and for life, is more accurately assessed by biologist Rolf Peterson: "Wolves are more monogamous than people" (Terrell, 7). It is common that the alpha pair leads the wolf pack and is almost always responsible for producing the pack's annual litter. Some of the wolves in subordinate roles are considered "betas," those who might vie at some point for alpha status. But beta females have mated with alpha males and alpha females with beta males, as I mentioned in the Introduction. Alpha females have also chosen males from other packs. Mowat's "Uncle" Albert is an example of the important roles subordinate wolves play in the pack, their duties often including shared "babysitting" responsibilities and instructing the pups in hunting.[24] Stresses on the general population of wolves caused by hunting, the spread of traps and poisons, or a hard winter might increase both the necessity and the difficulty of mating. Larger litters create the need for more energy devoted to pup care.

A mother wolf is almost always immediately attentive, cleaning pups as soon as they are born, providing them with warmth, feeding them, teaching them to be wolves. The rest of the pack also usually participates, not only in the care of the pups but of the sick and old as well. Some are lazier or less interested than others. There have been cases of "adoption" of loners, the opposite of the hostility I witnessed in Yellowstone. These incidents are the inspiration for Londonesque fictions about dogs wandering off to answer the call of the wild and "become" wolves. Pack bonds are strong but not unbreakable, and if circumstances are right then wanderers looking for a pack may find one willing to take them in. Recently in Yellowstone a litter just old enough to wander was left abandoned when the parents were killed; a male wolf adopted the litter and took it to his pack (Maughan).

As far as has been observed, wolves select their dens intelligently, often finding places near trees that provide cover and windbreak, and usually near a water source. They almost always den in the early winter and, during the two-month gestation period (around the months of February, March, and April), stay close to home. Pregnant females will sometimes help dig the dens up to three weeks before giving birth and in some cases have dug out dens on their own. In the Ninemile Valley a female wolf whose mate was shot raised a litter on her own, a feat accounted for in Rick Bass's *Ninemile Wolves* and fictionalized in 'Asta

Bowen's young-adult novel *Hungry for Home*. One of the famous wolves in Yellowstone (profiled in Smith & Ferguson), #42, became an alpha female by deposing the tyrannical she-wolf formerly in charge, #40, who was killed by the pack. Another of the Yellowstone wolves whose territory I visited left her pack with her two pups, dug her own den, and started a new life, cooperating with her old pack from time to time.

Wolf dens may be found in hollow logs or tree bases, rock caves, and abandoned beaver lodges or dams. Wolves often dig dens in sandy soil or, especially on the tundra, in sand eskers, and will sometimes dig out a fox hole, badger den, or other burrow (Mech, *The Wolf*, 120). The tunnel to a den could be between six and sixteen feet long and is often angled sharply, apparently to create a cold trap. It opens into a chamber used to wean pups during the weeks when they can neither see nor hear. Bears, coyotes, wolfers, hunters, and biologists have dug out or squeezed into the tunnels, which are sometimes only two feet in diameter. Mowat writes of encountering his own fear of the wolf, after having wriggled his way into a den, as his flashlight hit the eyes of two pups and a pack member in the chamber. Mowat panicked. The wolves sat calmly (36–37).

Zones around denning areas and rendezvous sites usually determine the reaches of home territory. The wolf is not entirely nomadic and might maintain winter and summer dens of different territorial ranges. A pack might dig several dens within a mile or so of one another. They may travel back and forth from kill to den to rendezvous site, which itself may begin at a kill location. Some wolves dig new dens every year, some reuse one for several years, and as territories change hands or generations pass, more than one pack may successively use the same dwelling. David Mech discovered a den that may have been used over the course of centuries by uncountable packs (see Mech & Packard). The "dispersal range," or farthest radial point from the den to which a pack may have traveled in a single (noncontinuous) trip, has been confirmed for one pack at 550 miles, from Minnesota into Canada (Busch, *Wolf Almanac*, 62). Rick Bass reports an 829-mile stretch (*Ninemile Wolves*, 13).

Wolves have stood by and watched their pups be pulled from the den and killed.[25] John James Audubon tells a story that includes a scene called "Pitting of Wolves," in which wolves in a pit simply let themselves be hamstrung (525–27). This incident is used as the opening of Coleman's *Vicious* (1–2), appears in McIntyre's *War against the Wolf* (47–50) and in Mech (*The Wolf*, 6), and is fictionalized in Marly Youmans's novel *The Wolf Pit* (106). An Indiana farmer jumped into a pit with three wolves and easily cut the tendons of their hind legs one at a time, presumably before killing them, although why he did this is left to speculation. Audubon writes, "We were not a little surprised at the cowardice of the wolves"

(527). Why would a wolf let himself be maimed in this way? Durward Allen considers the possibility that wolves may become "out of it," drop into a state of shock, and so inaction, at the moment when such strange invasions and perplexing losses as pups pulled from a den and killed or even personal physical damage are inflicted on them (248).

Fictional or quasi-fictional works use the wolf den as both the place of nurture and the lair of the devil. Hitler's Prussian retreat was called the Wolf's Lair, a lupine metaphor sustained in other Third Reich communiqués to imply prowess. The Allies subsequently used the metaphor to demonize Hitler, revealing the assumption that the wolf was so justifiably a malevolent image as to enhance that quality in a man who hardly needed the help.[26]

Biologists still do not know exactly how, or to what degree of severity, human interference affects a pack's decision whether or not to reuse a den.[27] Wolves can be sensitive about incursion. Prey species migrate, and climatic changes are hard on the body—two factors that force social animals into a seminomadic lifestyle, including the human animals who over the millennia have opted not to participate in strictly agrarian or urban cultures. But even though wolves are famous for their "ranges" and "territories," how extensive and how clearly delineated these are varies greatly. After a forty-five-day study Mech recorded a winter range of five thousand square miles for a pack of ten wolves and another range of thirty-six square miles for a pair (*The Wolf,* 164; also see Ciucci & Mech). Wolves also adapt to smaller spaces when the prey base is sufficient and the habitat is comfortable, such as a national park. When home territories of separate packs meet at boundaries that produce more frequent incidents of aggression (usually during the mating season), the packs might negotiate the zones. "Buffers" are created—noncombat zones sometimes demarcated within overlapping territories, sometimes in stretches of unclaimed territory. Prey species such as Cous white-tailed deer, a major target of midlongitude gray wolves, have found those buffer zones and congregated in them, using the neutral territory for relatively safe grazing until the herds unwisely or necessarily expand into wolf territory. The packs often avoid potential conflicts that would waste energy or risk injury, especially in winter.[28]

Social Darwinists love wolf packs because they beg overstatements about the process of species-level participation in genetic natural selection—that the "best" wolves breed and the "weakest" are systematically and "instinctively" eliminated. In fact, dominance is achieved and maintained through a complex negotiation called agonistic behavior, which does not always involve violence. When it does, the violence is normally ritualized rather than motivated by rage.[29] Exchanges of active and passive submission and dominance among wolves almost always result in obvious consensus. The designation of an omega wolf, the pack's scapegoat—perhaps as a result of having been deposed or demoted for some sin or weakness—is more common in writing about wolves in work before the mid-1990s. I have seldom heard it used by biologists; it seems the designation is more questionable than "alpha," which is simply coming to mean "leader" more than "despot" or "parental figure," depending in part on the wolf in question.

The pack may operate as a unit, but pups raised by the pack might in their early adulthood become dispersers, either starting their own packs through mating and assertion or traveling as lone wolves on a harder, and often shorter, life path. Here are some averages that likely mean very little: Packs average fewer than eight members; the average litter is six pups. A far more interesting fact: In hard winters, female wolves will often respond to the environment by having smaller litters or none at all prior to denning.[30] Many different stressors may affect reproductive rates and litter sizes, including psychological impediments (most commonly the interference of the alpha pair with other pack members' mating attempts) and attrition to hunters. Packs may expand into the twenties or even thirties, depending on habitat. A pack may also consist of a pair of wolves—Aristotle's most basic political unit.

The regurgitated meat with which a pup is fed after weaning is the beginning of influence over the young wolf's tastes and contributes to the formation of "search images" taught for hunting purposes to young wolves by their parents. During the pup's early experience with solid food, wolf parents might carry mouthfuls of meat for miles back to the den. Pups will chase grasshoppers or mice for both practice and play, but when they graduate to small and/or wounded prey provided by the parents and, as yearlings, join in a pack hunt, they learn the looks and smells of animals for which the pack has a collective affinity.

Single wolves have successfully raised litters of pups, and members of a pack have brought meat to sick wolves at the den or at a rendezvous site, sometimes watching over them and providing companionship during sickness. These behaviors should disabuse those who think that wolves eat their own or leave the weak to die.[31] Pups are born blind and deaf and weigh about a pound each. At three weeks they can walk and play near the den entrance, and they may demonstrate an interest in dominance as early as one month old. I have been using the term *pup* for a young wolf; *cub* is a colloquial variant probably given its great modern currency through Kipling's books and the influence of the wolf's close mythic association with the bear.

Because of the behaviorism still controlling biologists' educations (and perhaps because of their own human and predominantly male biologies), there is a tendency in reportage to emphasize dominance as a reason for wolves' actions, especially for play. Hypothesis is as close as scientists have come to understanding wolf dominance behavior and distinguishing it from potential play. I get the impression that some—especially the more lab-oriented—could stand to get out of the office and play with their kids a bit more often. Little wolves live in the den for about eight weeks, all together and rolling around on top of one another, which begins their lupine socialization process toward pack behavior. They test their abilities to achieve dominance from the time they can walk, and some strict behaviorists have decided that such practice denies the possibility of idle play—which is "nonfunctional" and therefore anthropomorphic. Other biologists and zoosemioticians, however, have designated obvious behavioral patterns that indicate play separate from utilitarian survival mechanics.[32]

Ceremonial Burial

Wolf biologist Diane Boyd and her team recently discovered evidence of wolves burying dead pups. (Actually, the study team's dogs discovered six burial sites, although the dogs' names are not on the report.) Four of these sites had been excavated by a scavenger, probably a coyote. The other two, containing decomposed pup remains, offered enough evidence to indicate that the mother had buried her litter before she left their den in Glacier National Park. Boyd indicates that a food cache is possible, but storage of pup carcasses would be as unusual a wolf practice as pup burial. The mother had raised two previous litters, so "inexperience was an unlikely cause" of the deaths. Blood samples of the pack indicated that canine parvovirus or distemper were most probable (Boyd, Pletscher, & Brewster, 230–31). I would like to think of those wolves performing a ceremonial burial, of their capacity for grief and the blunt articulation of grief. I would like to think that they weren't stashing the pups to eat later. I am immediately checked, not by any fear of anthropomorphizing them, but by the realization that I would also like them not to starve and by the missive against projection.

When I asked Boyd about this incident, she explained that the season wasn't particularly hard, so the wolves had normal access to hunting, and that wolves had not been observed caching their dead young as food before. She also explained that she has received more attention over that two-page article, at times emotionally extreme, than over all of her other research (Boyd interview).

Ravenous

Wolves and ravens seem to have an understanding. The interactions between them make a case for sophisticated interspecies communicative systems. Among the smartest of birds, corvids learn to listen to wolf howls and follow wolves on the move in order to find scavengable carcasses. This relationship has been made famous in poems, paintings, and legends of the wolf and raven on burial grounds and battlefields. In Shelley's *Adonais,* for example, we read of "The herded wolves, bold only to pursue; / The obscene ravens, clamorous o'er the dead." In turn, wolves and foxes will sometimes follow corvids by sight or sound, especially in desperate times, in order to locate a dead or dying animal. Such incidents occurring along the northern Pacific coast have produced interesting biological studies, in addition to a plethora of myths and legends about Raven and Wolf more forgiving than Shelley's sentiment. The unfortunate result of wolf/raven cooperation is that in some cases the carcass scouted by the bird is old or spoiled and transmits disease to the scavenging wolf.

Since the birds generally travel by day and the pack might cover long distances overnight, ravens have learned to track wolves. They have been seen flying directly over tracks in winter to a kill (wolves generally travel single-file and may take turns breaking trail through snow).[33] If they find a carcass that has not been ripped open, the hide of which they cannot penetrate with their beaks, they may lead a predator to the kill site and wait for the meal to be "sliced" (Savage, *Bird Brains,* 108). They also "play catch-me-if-you-can" with wolves, a challenging pastime in which the birds are always at risk (71). David Mech reports this exchange, quoted in several wolf books: "Sometimes the ravens chased the wolves, flying just above their heads, and once, a raven waddled to a resting wolf, pecked its tail, and jumped aside as the wolf snapped at it. When the wolf retaliated by stalking the raven, the bird allowed it within a foot before arising. Then it landed a few feet beyond the wolf and repeated the prank" (*The Wolf,* 288; see also Heinrich, 236; Feher-Elston, 139).

One biologist, Douglas Pimlott, has recorded evidence of a wolf killing a raven. The legends of wolves and ravens seem to be born as much of observation as imagination, and Wotan's patron animals of Thought and Memory have a biological reciprocity at the base of their mythic one.[34] When the most respected biologist in the field is open to the word "prank," then the discipline should probably follow the animal, instead of expecting the animal to conform to the theory. For centuries, Raven myths have cast the figure as a trickster, likely basing this characterization on the bird's intelligent and precocious behavior. Confidence in the raven's ability to transcend the logical explanations of rationalists appears in American Indian mythology as well as in Aesop, as Reid and Bringhurst record in their recitation of *The Raven Steals the Light,* a story Candace Savage calls "The Raven and the First People": "So the Raven leaned his great head close to the shell, and with the smooth trickster's tongue that had got him into and out of so many misadventures during his troubled and troublesome existence, he coaxed and cajoled and coerced the little creatures to come out and play in his wonderful, shiny new world" (*Bird Brains,* 40–41).

Hybrids

Hybridization, as mentioned in the introduction, creates as many problems in fiction as it does in biology. Most of Jack London's famous "wolves" are hybrids, as are the characters in the novels of James Curwood, a blatant purloiner of London's themes. The debate over whether the red wolf (*Canis rufus*) is a subspecies of *Canis lupus* or a hybrid wolf-coyote (more likely) caused some trouble during the animal's reintroduction into North Carolina. Coy-dogs have occasionally been called "tweed wolves," a connection once again complicating matters (in the true spirit it seems of the mythological coyote—a kind of gremlin running around in the language machine).

The wolf-dog is the hybrid of choice for power-hungry or catalog-romantic pet owners. In 1994 the USDA and Humane Society conservatively estimated that 300,000 hybrid wolves were in the United States (Willems). Rather than entertain the inconsequential debate over whether hybrids make "good pets," I would simply offer that hybridization represents a massive act of human rationalization. It creates a quintessential ghost wolf. Despite hybrid owners and breeders passionately defending "their wolves," every wolf bred to a dog results in the loss of a litter that could be in the wild, pushing the wolf population farther away from self-determination. Neither the most intensive training nor enlightened (or convinced) owner will change this situation. Just as there need be no more pet stores or "pure" breeders, no more dog shows or obsessions over conformation, there need be no more wolves bred to dogs.

The discourse community developing around this debate is a knot, tangled with cultish and defensive hybrid owners on the Internet and sensible investigators into the consequences of wolf domestication. None of the rhetoric, however, adequately supports the assumption that wolves are pets waiting to be claimed. Unfortunately, the commercial subculture of hybridization functions by its own logic, a combination of the quest for power and the monetized value system that says such power can be bought, bred, and owned. The logic is much like that of poaching. The combination of zoo, park, and yard accounts for a quarter of a million wolves in the United States, about four times as many as live in the wild in Canada.[35]

My position on this follows what I try to use as my big red default button in similar situations: Leave the wolf alone. We have done what we have done, and perhaps the original act of domestication resulted in a wonderful thing—the love of a dog by and for a human being. I adore my dogs. But to have transcended or corrected a wrong doesn't justify repeating it. The hybrid's presence in literature forces us to confront the impossible complexity of the wild/domestic relationship that runs from wolf to dog in our individual and collective thoughts, loves, and abuses. How we think of this animal is how we'll read it when it appears, or disappears.

Anatomy and Physiology

Wolves at the top of their game can sprint at speeds of thirty-five to forty miles per hour; can course a prey animal for twenty minutes at slower speeds; and can travel a score or more miles in a day's journey through deep snow. An endearing factoid found by Dave Mech is that the wolves on Ellesmere Island traveled about eight and half miles an hour on barren ground except when they were headed back to the den, during which they traveled at about ten miles an hour (Mech, "Regular and Homeward"). One wolf, while being pursued by hunting dogs, covered 125 miles of varied terrain in twenty-four hours (Lopez, *Of Wolves and Men,* 25). A Russian proverb cited in Busch's *Almanac* says, "The wolf is kept fed by his feet," and Barry Lopez writes about a group of schoolchildren whose drawings of wolves changed from their focus on huge fangs to huge paws once they'd finally seen a wolf in the flesh (263). The wolf's front-paw print is, for a canid, enormous—up to about five by four inches. The back print is a little narrower and shorter, and the dew claw does not leave a mark. On a plaster cast I took of a wolf print in snow, the span of the raised pads is not much smaller than my hand, fingers spread.

Adult males average between 95 and 100 pounds, females between 80 and 85. Whatever that means. Wolves of warmer climates, such as Mexican wolves, tend to weigh less and have larger ears for venting heat; the average weight of the Mexican wolves trapped in the 1970s was 70 pounds (Busch, *Wolf Almanac,* 21). Stanley Young reported a 175-pound wolf from Alaska, by a considerable margin the largest on record (69).

Wolves are susceptible to disease. It's remarkable how much research is devoted to parasites, viruses, injury-related sickness, and other dangers to a wolf's health.[36] The subject is, however, conspicuously absent in fiction about wolves; I don't know of a single work of narrative fiction that features a wolf's subjection to disease rather than violence. We might say this is because disease isn't as appealing a hook for readers, but it certainly seems to be a staple of Victorian literature. In any biological study of wolves, one is likely to find a significant section devoted to what can go wrong with a lupine body. Busch cites a long list, placing the number of possible diseases at more than a hundred (*Wolf Almanac,* 33). Parasites that transmit many of these illnesses less frequently attack wolves in colder climates but can still do extensive damage. In warmer climates parasites rank up with people as wolf killers, and sometimes the two join forces. For instance, in one particularly cruel method of wolf control in 1909, wolves in Montana were trapped, deliberately infected with sarcoptic mange, and released to spread the virus, which may have been introduced to the Canadian prairies as result. As opposed to demodectic mange, the sarcoptic variety causes skin lesions, intense and painful itching, and fur loss exacerbated by scratching. In winter, a wolf without sufficient fur will freeze to death (34).

Dogs can give wolves distemper and have spread canine parvovirus to them as well (there was a 1990s proliferation of this in regions of wolf and human contact). Prey may give wolves as many as twenty-four varieties of worm, the tapeworm being the most common. Mosquitoes carry heartworm, a serious danger to red wolves. Rabies, the most common disease associated with canids in popular literature, is actually rare among wolves, especially compared with such problems as parvovirus and tapeworm. They can pick it up from foxes or skunks and may contract it from small prey animals who manage to bite them when being caught. The higher incidence of lupine rabies during the medieval period in Europe probably contributed to the reputation of wolves as being frequently rabid, as well as to the generation of stories about wolves as demonic beings. The psychological condition of lycanthropy probably finds its root in medieval werewolf legends, which were influenced by incidents of human-contracted rabies and exotic diseases that produce horrifying symptoms, synthesized with observations of ravenous wolves (Gibson, 100; see also Douglas; Baring-Gould).

From 1987 to 1995 only four rabid wolves were found in Alaska's population of six thousand (Busch, *Wolf Almanac*, 36). On the other hand, the real effects of rabies may be more severe than simply the number of contracted cases; in 1989–90, the four confirmed cases combined with seven more suspected in northwestern Alaska, and this small number was considered an epizootic incident. The reason is that seven different wolf packs lost wolves as a result, probably through attacks by the rabid wolves that weakened the general population (Ballard & Krausman, 244–45). Rabies striking one pack member will certainly inhibit the hunting and travel of the entire pack, not to mention imperiling its members. The movie classic *Old Yeller* is partly about the psychological response we have to man's best friend not "being himself," the transformation to a dangerous beast being the more heartbreaking because of what we think of as the dog's original innocence and domestic peace. We see this image troped in Zora Neale Hurston's character Tea Cake in *Their Eyes Were Watching God,* a novel that investigates Hurston's own anthropological and fictional comparisons of the human and animal (especially the mule) as a way of critiquing slavery and its aftermath.[37] We must remember, though, that this logic of the dog's purity, obedience, and innocence gone bad from disease conveniently masks that the dog was once, back in its original condition, a wolf.

Studies of pups born in the wild vary in the mortality rates they report. The lifespan of wild wolves is about five or six years, though they might live to be as old as thirteen. In captivity they live longer; the oldest on record lived to be seventeen. The age at death can be determined by examining the horizontal section of a tooth. The biologist counts the cementum annuli the same way an arborist counts tree rings (Gipson Interview; Busch, *Wolf Almanac*, 39). Indeed, prior to advances in genetics, much of what we learned about wolf morphology we learned from the wolf's bones.

CHAPTER SIX

Advanced Corporeality

Here is the closest I am willing to come to "textualizing" wolf communication: The wolf's forty-two teeth work well as inscription devices; they write the wolf's story on the bones of its prey and are also capable of delicate and affectionate touch. For example, one of Lois Crisler's captive wolves gave her "grooming nibbles" by "picking up the merest skin of my eyelid with her teeth" (Crisler, 156). In addition to the razorlike precision of "bobtailing" animals, a wolf may hold on by his or her incisors to a moose's nose while being lifted off the ground and flailed about. The incredible biting force of a wolf's teeth and jaws partly instigated Adolph Murie's pioneering study of Dall sheep on Mount McKinley (Lopez, *Of Wolves and Men,* 26; Murie, 100–21). Murie determined by the sheeps' horns, mandibles, and teeth how old they were, but he also had to distinguish the wolf-killed sheep from those who had died of other causes, which he accomplished through the presence of "bloody pieces of hide" and the "location of the remains," the former indicating the bite of the wolf and the latter indicating its hunting (and play) methods (Murie, 111). These are all marks that define the wolf's authorial technique. A macabre way of identifying lupine authors is by marks on their own bodies that tell the story of their labors. Divots in bone from hoof kicks, traps, or baling wire around the jaws; bullet holes; injuries from fights; or the sprung coil of a whalebone trap inside the ribcage of a wolf carcass may all act as the wolf's unpublished autobiography.

Philip Gipson, leader of the Kansas Cooperative Fish and Wildlife Research Unit of the U.S. National Biological Service, began a detective project about thirty years ago, when he first became interested in wolves and wolf legends. After many years of working for Animal Damage Control, Gipson decided to "set the scientific record straight about how much damage the famous outlaw wolves might actually have been responsible for" and "help eliminate some of the myths about them" (McIntyre, *War*, 350; Gipson interview). The "myths" (actually legends) to which Gipson refers regard outlaw wolves who allegedly executed ingenious escapes after long and expensive killing sprees.

In several cases the wolves were said to live as long as eighteen years, a stretch of triple their average lifespan in the wild (D. Smith, YAI). Gipson decided to determine their ages through tooth cross-sections, to see if the findings matched the reports that writers such as Stanley P. Young and Ernest Thompson Seton had gathered. Dollar figures and kill rates seemed exaggerated as well. Gipson surmised that the skull, particularly the teeth, could at least settle the question of longevity, and where one element of a legend might be discredited, the rest of it would become more open to scrutiny. Like many gunfighter legends of the Old West, the outlaw wolves gained reputations that would persist regardless of the facts. Such worries about cultural reception should never deter the responsible scientist, though, and Gipson forged ahead. Unfortunately, this was not his only obstacle.

All of the museums and private owners that let Gipson borrow the skulls refused to allow tooth cross-sections for determining the wolves' ages. He continued the case based on dental analyses of tooth wear and on the closure of skull sutures, both of which indicated that the wolves were far younger when they died than was reported, in some cases about half the reported ages. The lack of a cross-section may have undermined Gipson's study, but he built in redundancy with another laboratory and finally bought the teeth of Lobo, King of the North in Minnesota, with money out of his own pocket. This way he could perform at least one tooth section, which corroborated the information gathered through his other methods and proved the King of the North to have had less than his purported Old Testament longevity (Gipson interview). The museum preserved the artifacts over the facts, and at Gibson's expense. Why damage a tooth when you can maintain a legend?

Wolves' methods of exchanging messages, both intraspecies and interspecies, include general principles of rhetoric and various sensory means of articulation, both verbal and nonverbal. But the simple binary of verbal and nonverbal communication is inadequate to describe interspecies exchanges. In the wolf/human case, other forms of expression must be stressed; indeed, for wolves the verbal is much less significant than it is for us humans, who have clouded many of our potentially clear and empathic relationships by deifying the word. This, in addition to our resistance to other forms of animal communication, is probably why we emphasize the howl over urine marks or pheromone secretion.

Zoosemiotics is the study of communication systems among all animals, and so considers human exchanges as a subset, "anthroposemiotics," rather than as the standard for judging all other systems. Thomas A. Sebeok, who coined the term and has written extensively about it, acknowledges human language as a system unavailable to other animals, but instead of resting comfortably on this position, he spends much of his time explaining animal communication systems unavailable to human beings, for example, the bee dance, electro-stimuli, sonar, and other functions operating beyond the five senses.[1] Wolves are among the most intelligent of mammals, and as such they use sophisticated forms of communication both within and outside of their species. "Translation" is an insufficient term to describe how we must approach these forms. Sebeok states that one needs to be much more the cryptanalyst than the translator; the semiotic codes at work must be determined before they can be meaningfully converted (*Essays in Zoosemiotics,* 19).

The critical importance of zoosemiotics to our understanding of intra- and interspecies communication is that it examines specific sign systems without softening criteria used to define "communication" and "language" merely to accommodate other animals. For example, the sentence "A bird's song is musical" is a human metaphor of debatable value in describing what the bird is doing. The conditions necessary for music to exist are arguable regarding the intentions and systems of other species against the mathematical rules of music theory. However, approached from the bird's own discernment of tone, pitch, tempo, harmonics, and volume, given the choices the bird makes in songs according to the fundamental occasions of sender/message/receiver, and given the role of the listener in establishing what constitutes music, both human criteria and avian criteria for musicality may be met. Those avian criteria must be determined according to the sensory and differential capabilities of the bird, not the human. The endpoint is that we humans, compelled to pile up and redefine criteria toward our own benefit and comfort, are obligated to learn, in this case, avian communication systems as thoroughly as possible, which must include the humble willingness to change the criteria to represent the maker rather than merely the critic. This is done not to accommodate other animals out of some misguided, softhearted sense of inclusion, but to acclimate *us* to *their* realms. Ascribing limits to other animals only by virtue of human limits is based on arrogance about art's domain. Greater knowledge of their own generated systems should excite scholars and students alike to new readings of literature informed by the biosphere; this is what "ecocentricity" should mean.

The most revealing canid incident in Sebeok's work concerns foxes rather than wolves, but the nuances of his arguments—too extensive to detail here—justify my use of the example. In 1969 a biologist named Rüppell, working on an unpopulated Norwegian island called Diabasodden, observed a pair of polar foxes with four kits (Sebeok, *Animal Communication,* 91–94). Having pilfered some of Rüppell's food, the vixen returned to her lair, where she was mugged by her young. One of them finally stole the chunk of cheese she carried and ran a short distance away. He set down the cheese, posted himself by it, turned his back to his mother, and urinated in her direction. As the young fox ate, his mother sounded a "high-pitched warning cry," at which he and his siblings dashed for cover. There was no danger present. The vixen walked calmly to the cheese and ate it. Rüppell saw this event repeated several times until the young foxes "caught on and thereafter ignored the parental warning sign and refused to abandon the filched delicacy" (93). They had learned what it meant to cry wolf. Such an incident has not been recorded by another biologist, but Sebeok points out that Rüppell's reputation was unimpeachable. The incident must be seriously considered as an example of an animal telling a lie.

Wolves can deceive. They can differentiate, name, remember, and manipulate. They have neural capacities that allow them to recognize synechdoche and metonymy, the latter of which abilities extends to the domestic dog, who may associate a leash with taking a walk. Wolves perform ceremonies and rituals that function as epideictic rhetoric. For example, both rhetorical analysis and corvid ethology confirm that social conclaves reaffirm collective and individual identities, a phenomenon exhibited by several particularly social species, such as crows, who "get together to renew their 'crowness,'" as the rhetorician George A. Kennedy puts it (*Comparative Rhetoric,* 21). Therefore, when we read stories about wolves, we should always be mindful of the role their "wolfness" may have played in affecting those stories. And we should consider how little attention we have devoted to the possibility that they may have their own stories as well.

The implication of work done by George A. Kennedy; Donald Griffin; Georgina Ferry; Marc Bekoff; John T. Bonner; George Lakoff & Mark Johnson; Mark Turner; and Charles Darwin (in *The Expression of the Emotions in Man and Animals*) is that we should assume the ability of an animal to imagine a future condition—however embryonically—and subject both the imagining and the future condition to serious consideration. The animal's physical manifestations on the land expressing that imagination may then qualify as inscription. Literature scholars content to play fast and loose with subjects "as texts" have categorically ignored the more verifiable modes of other species. For a literary criticism including books about animals to function, we must not assume that animals lack any conceptual ability beyond meeting their immediate needs. We have assumed this of children, slaves, ancient civilizations, the lower classes, and women, and we have paid dearly—though considerably less than those Others.

The Senses

The wolf's sense of smell is many times as fine-tuned as a human being's. Wolves have detected baited traps buried under three feet of packed snow; David Mech once observed a wolf scenting a moose and two calves from more than a mile downwind (*The Wolf,* 15). Their olfactory capacity is also discerning. They can detect from urine markers whether or not a female wolf is in heat, distinguish the individual differences among the pack or invading wolves, and surmise when the marking was done. In designating territory, wolves often create "urine curtains" in a polygonal pattern around, for instance, a den area. This delineates a safe zone inside of which interlopers might find themselves in trouble, though the urine mark seems more of an "I'm here" message than a "Get out" message. Incredulity, anger, violence, etc., are all traits not necessarily determined by reason, but quite possibly implied in the scent and pheromones of intruders, since wolves can sense deliberation. Sebeok admonishes the practitioners of zoosemiotics to abandon the anthropocentric notion of the "five senses," a rubric that simply does not apply to the capacities of other species (*How Animals Communicate,* 120).

Scent marking can be accomplished with scat (feces) as well as urine. The scent post's placement alone may send a message: for instance, one wolf's urine mark above another's. The content of scat is studied (literally, scatology) to determine a wolf's time of visit, daily diet, menstrual condition, and general health. Wolves might scratch scent into dirt as well, for both an immediate visual effect (for example, a demonstration of dominance) and a lasting olfactory one (the residual scent from the paw).[2]

While olfactory methods constitute long-term communiqués, the most famous short-term method is the howl. Wolves often harmonize, deliberately choosing different pitches from one another to produce harmonic groupings that may at a distance indicate three times as many wolves as are actually howling. Wolves howl at the full moon. They also howl at the half moon, the first quarter, the stars, sirens, coyotes, nearby farm dogs, a fresh start to a new day, and people who howl first. For several years I lived four miles from the captive wolves of Wolf Park in Battle Ground, Indiana, who would howl at the whistles of passing trains. In one case, a wolf pack howled on cue whenever a woman called "Heeeeeere kitty kitty kitteeeee" from her kitchen door. The pack eventually stopped howling after they got used to the woman's voice, most likely because nothing interesting ever came of the exchange. But at one point the howling was so predictable that the woman was able to demonstrate it on demand for friends who doubted her story (Kyrouac lecture, June).

Below 250 cycles per second a wolf and human hear with approximately the same sensitivity; for instance, a wolf can tell changes in pitch of about one step on the chromatic scale. Above that frequency, wolves perceive canine frequencies and are capable of subtle distinctions. Some are able to separate human howling, a wolf howl played on a tape recorder, a dog's howl, and the howl of another wolf (Harrington, "Timber Wolf Howling," 1575). During the bison slaughter, wolves learned to follow gunshots in order to get a meal, sometimes sitting nearby until after the hunters had taken skins and tongues and moved on (Mech, *The Wolf*, 8; Audubon, 222). In a compound holding Mexican wolves waiting to be reintroduced, one of the biologists noticed that the wolves reacted to the sounds of the golf carts the team members drove, recognizing without seeing them which cart belonged to which team member, and reacted specifically (Link & Crowley, 137).

Apparently, a wolf can easily tell the difference between one wolf's howl and another's, which ability underscores that wolves "name," semiotically speaking, and therefore participate in sophisticated forms of individualized communication. Their howls can carry as far as eight miles, changing in pitch to indicate various signals. A howl lasts—one of those magical averages—about five seconds.[3] I have mentioned that packs howl to assemble, but those ethologists free of the myopia of behaviorism also find that wolves howl for pleasure and in mourning, and perhaps to indicate climatic conditions and caribou herd location and movement (Crisler, 151; Mech, *The Wolf*, 100). And they bark. The most common circumstance is when danger is possible; the leaders of a pack or parents of pups will issue series of short warning barks, then lead the pack away from danger.

Patricia Goodmann and Erich Klinghammer of Wolf Park have written a *Wolf Ethogram,* an annotated chart listing twenty different vocalizations observed in captive wolves, including a "hum" in greeting and several methods of howling. Probably first conceived by Konrad Lorenz and then refined by Erik Zimen (see Zimen, chap. 3), an ethogram describes individual verbal and nonverbal communication displays. Goodman and Klinghammer have identified 190, most of which work in various combinations with others. Aside from being a pleasure to read, the *Ethogram* demonstrates that human interpretation of what animals are up to when they interact is full of possibility. The principal problem with the *Ethogram* is that it was compiled with captive wolves socialized to human contact and living in a relatively small space. Such conditions put the credibility of any behavioral study in great question—again, unless one subscribes to a strict behaviorist model.

Written on the Body

Underrated in the wolf's repertoire is its flexibility and complexity of facial expressions. When submitting, wolves might roll their eyes away from a dominant wolf, whine, and "grin." A wolf showing its teeth is not necessarily angered or displaying dominance. The position of the ears and tail, the stance, the directness or indirectness of gaze, the position of the mouth, and vocalization are all involved in sending messages not only to wolves but to other species as well. Many of these gestures have been passed to the domestic dog and are well known by pet owners, gestures such as tucking the tail or folding back the ears.

In John Woodhouse Audubon's painting *White American Wolf,* the animal looks up from worrying a bone, crouching with tail tucked, gazing indirectly, its tongue out (223). The ground on which the wolf stands is strewn with burned wood, so centrally located that we can't tell if it's from a forest fire or an old campfire, the difference being a potential gesture to the domestic, and so to the domestic act of the painter working. While the snarl—immediately noticeable— might be a warning to an intruder approaching the meal, it could as easily be a submissive grin, and this distinction is nearly impossible for a portrait artist to make clear. The tucked tail and posture both indicate submission, as would the gaze. But John Woodhouse may well have used a freshly killed wolf wired up in a pose, as John James often did with his bird "specimens," in order to accomplish (ironically) the realism he sought. If so, then the wolf is not gazing at all, since gazing is an action. In this case, how different is the eye of a dead wolf from that of a taxidermied one, or from the eye of a wolf in a painting? At any rate, Woodhouse's choice is not a flattering one. His appellation "white American wolf" is, as far as I have found, exclusive to Woodhouse's painting as a categorical designation, appearing in no formal taxonomy.

In ethological studies of the wolf, similar attempts at verisimilitude are made, but through methods designed to predict the wolf's behavior, rather than simply to impress its image upon a viewer. Goodmann and Klinghammer's *Ethogram* is designed so that, presumably, I could use it to at least "listen to," if not "speak with," a wolf, because I could both interpret and approximate at least some of its codes, such as its vocalizations. Let's consider this in relation to the wolf myth. Earlier I mentioned the emotional range of effect on people of wolves howling. In fact, the wolf howl is one of the major moneymakers for places ranging in wildness from Algonquin National Park to Wolf Park. This means that even predictable behavior seems to have some numinous effect beyond behaviorism's capacity to explain.

Like the Audubon painting, the opening paragraph of the *Ethogram* is an indication of the importance of context to the interpretation of an encounter. Despite their conclusion that play is a purely functional act designed to "train" wolves for survival and dominance, the writers imply, perhaps inadvertently, that wolves possess the one thing almost universally used by other scientists to assert human difference, if not superiority: language. Behaviorists are notorious for limiting all conditions of interaction, including human ones, to stimulus-response—the so-called black box idea. Such scientists, properly excoriated in Donald Griffin's work, should be the last to attribute *language* to any animals but humans, since language is either considered a subfunction of consciousness (on the assumption that consciousness is an exclusively human condition) or more loosely equated with communication. The *Ethogram* writers should be in the former category. Yet they state that "without a common language it is exceedingly difficult, if not impossible, to fully convey all the observations that are made. One does not need a diploma to collect scientifically valuable information about a species, one only needs a common language. An ethogram such as this can provide that common language" (i).

Actually, at least two "common language" sets are attempted by the ethogram. The first would be the language set through which I mentally process Goodmann and Klinghammer's terms. For example, when I read "ritualized attack," I might correctly picture the behavior indicated by this phrase, this sign. The second language set, however, is the one through which the observer of a wolf understands, labels, and predicts the wolf's gestures or vocalizations. Hypotheses based on patterns of these actions may certainly follow; but they depend upon the acknowledgment of a communicative exchange. Goodmann and Klinghammer's choice of the word *language* to represent these communicative sets implicitly questions the assumption that humans hold the language monopoly.

As per George Kennedy's thesis that rhetoric precedes language, we need to question the assumptions of behaviorism regarding the process of information exchange.[4] According to his model, even the survival instinct generates rhetorical strategies, in that emotional reactions take place that demand communicative responses. For instance, a mother vervet monkey's alarm call is instigated by a predator's scent, presence, and behavior, then issued to little vervet monkeys still developing basic communication skills. This involves a highly complex rhetorical negotiation. Consider again Rüppell and the fox.

The evidence Kennedy provides for rhetorical processes already at work in a preverbal exchange corroborates Darwin's observations on the emotional expressions of animals.[5] The sender's style may be determined as well as the message's content, a fact observable in all nonliterate cultures. "The complexity of animal calls," Kennedy writes, "is proportional to the complexity of social organization of animal species." He finds support for this position in several separate observations by biologists (15). Individual members of these social organizations operate through a combination of learned and innate rhetorical acts. Therefore, a nonliterate, complex, social species has ready access to rhetoric, through both learned and innate behavior. We should also realize that interspecies communication follows the most basic semiotic conditions governing the exchange and interpretation of signs as these conditions have been explained by Charles Sanders Peirce and applied to zoosemiotics by Sebeok.[6] Furthermore, any degree of sophistication to nonhuman communication leads us logically to one of the products resulting from those interactions—nonhuman culture.

Lupine Culture

Wolves possess the capacities needed to articulate their culture collectively and to understand various protocols of other species. The term *culture* has been invested with almost as many meanings as its frequent antonym, *nature*. The efforts of Lakoff, Johnson, and Turner, for example, combine explorations of the aesthetics of poetry with cognitive theory to examine behavior and culture as products of both neural and social influence.[7] The biologist John T. Bonner's definition of *culture* accommodates both the social and biological sciences: "By culture I mean the transfer of information by behavioral means, most particularly by the process of teaching and learning" (9). Bonner's use of the term *behavioral* might suggest the stimulus-response doctrine, but his arguments throughout *The Evolution of Culture in Animals* are obviously inclined away from behaviorism.

In *Animal Minds* Donald Griffin challenges the behaviorist consensus that if animal consciousness exists, it does so in such a simple, elementary form as to make human consciousness the only kind worth cultural application. Furthermore, behaviorism does not limit its mechanistic hypothesis to the kind of food-chain hierarchy we might expect. It posits that all animals, including humans, are acting unconsciously most of the time. This renders nonhuman consciousness moot, even beneath scientific concern, in the matter of differentiation from other animals' consciousness (D. Griffin, 19–21). It also negates the very possibility of investigation into the unconscious mind beyond neural pattern, contradicting a century of progress in psychology.

The simplicity of the animal brain is a highly subjective matter. How "simple," for example, is it to distinguish color, or weave a web, or cut a calf out of a herd? If the bee dance is simplicity in action, then what took Frisch so long to figure it out, and why was he enshrined for having done so? The assumption of animal naïveté is also based on, well, naïveté—a lack of evidence regarding reflective versus perceptual consciousness, neural network function and potentiality, and formally encoded communication systems in other species. Where have these assumptions of other animals' inferiority taken us? As often to the labs of cosmetics manufacturers as anywhere else. In the wolf's case, the revelation of its complex thought did not seem to effectively countermand human cruelty. On the contrary, once arguments of simplicity and evil began to collapse under the weight of evidence, the wolf's very intricacy made it a pariah, refashioned from some blind force of nature to a demonic intelligence with malicious intent. It was labeled "cunning," like its cousins, the "wily" coyote and the "sly" fox.

Even the best wolf primers barely address the issues of cognition and culture that I have raised here. But the characterization of a wolf in a work of literature must be gauged according to fidelity to experience and probability of motive, if only to recognize what in the text damages denial. We must respect the real, even if only against the fad to culturally and subjectively define nearly everything. As Ewan Clarkson put it, "Before I got submerged under a tidal wave of contradiction, I decided that I would see for myself this world of the wolf" (68).

A human child, even before having learned to speak, can tell a story. She can hide things, lie, joke, nudge, cajole, and she can remember how to do these things again without prompting, even when her neural pathways aren't fully formed and are developing at a rate over which she has no control. If a preverbal child can tell a basic story, then storytelling could be an easier process for neural networks to perform, relatively speaking, than building a nest or showing someone how to find food on the tundra.[8] Lewis Thomas questions quantification as a proper means of determining human superiority by calling even the axon functions of insects "very small thoughts" (360).

Lupine Art

A beta female wolf rolls in a strange scent. She returns to the pack and lets the members sniff her body. If the scent is pleasing in some way—let's say a functional way, such as registering caribou urine that indicates a game trail toward food—then it elicits an excited reaction from the pack. Decisions follow. Will the pack sleep first in order to have strength for the hunt or press on even though they are tired? They may forgo the chase altogether and settle for nearer prey. There is, as far as we know, no mathematical ratio of efficiency that wolves instinctively calculate in such a case to decide among the options. Based upon the aptitudes and past experiences of the sniffing wolves, they might gather from the scent as much information as the caribou's age, its sex, and to some degree its health, the quality of the urine, and the interference of other scents on the female's coat.

Let's say the wolf rolled in the scent even though she *saw* the caribou, even though she could have howled to call the pack to the hunt or could have run back without scent-rolling in order to lure the pack to a line of sight, at which point they could decide what to do. She made a deliberate choice to use another means of expression. But why? I ask this because her recognition of causality is highly likely. That is:

1. She knows she is subordinate to the alpha wolves and that she may lack the authority to persuade the pack to move without physical proof. Thus her choice to attract attention is to use her body to carry such proof.

2. She has memory of caribou and their habits and determines the scent of caribou urine to be highly noticeable and informational proof (this would, incidentally, repudiate the conventional wisdom that canids possess only short-term memory).

3. She knows that howling to the pack might somehow affect the herd's behavior in a way that would increase the effort necessary to catch them.

All of this decision making is functional, and as such might be thought to preclude any indication or capability of artifice. But the beta female may well have rolled in the caribou scent at least partly in order to be *attractive* (in behaviorist terms, to be "accepted").

Kathryn Coe explains that the ornamentation of the body could be the very first demonstration of human art (218). To begrudge the wolf this potential assumes that the wolf knows less than we may prove she knows. We do not know the extent to which animals recognize the adornment of the body, and our having accomplished adornment with greater variety, technical complexity, and conceptual verification than other species in no way rules out those species' capabilities to decorate themselves. We dismiss the clear attraction of a pack of wolves to the scent of one of their members as something less complex than perfumery—when it is quite plausibly both the base and peak of perfumery, the very reason we use the word *essence*. Inclined to dismiss the notion of animal communication, we write this dismissal into our books, our laws, and our alterations of the land, emphasizing our supposed superiority by outlanguaging the rest of the world.

The stories by wolves were first written about a million years ago, mostly as they were inscribed on Eurasian ice and in the hides of ungulates while human culture was still forming, seven hundred thousand years before *Homo sapiens sapiens* began to write its stories (Lopez, *Of Wolves and Men*, 17; Busch, *Wolf Almanac*, 1; Mech, *The Wolf*, 20; see also Mech, Fritts, & Paul). We killed nearly all the wolves in two nations of North America, and for the most part the ones populating the third still howl from the tundra. Cotton Mather and the Jesuits in French

Canada used to call those howls the voice of the devil, or *ce loup infernal* (Hampton, 63n3); citizens of Harrisburg, Pennsylvania, in 1792 called them common and "numerous" (McIntyre, *War,* 16). Opportunists of the retail nature business refer in their catalogs to serenades. Sometimes I fear the howl may be the voice of judgment, were not the voice of judgment itself a human construct designed to separate humans into the saved and the damned.[9]

The Ghost Wolf

A MYTHIC HISTORIOGRAPHY

CHAPTER SEVEN

The Sea Wolf
(In Which a Wolf Crosses the Water)

Until the likely move from the traditional taxonomic methods to a taxonomy better founded on genetic information, the precise origin of the wolf in evolutionary terms is still only vaguely determinable. The best article I have found on the subject is Ronald Nowak's "Wolf Evolution and Taxonomy" (in Mech & Boitani), which includes a detailed section subtitled "Overview of Taxonomic Uncertainties" (239). Likely *Canis lupus* as we know it morphologically branched out of a population of "small, early canids" from South America, "the most probable ancestral candidate," according to Nowak, being "C. lepophagus" of North America (241). This would make the wolf between 4.5 and 9 million years old, not counting the various cousins, such as the dire wolf, that preceded it. At least during the late Pleistocene, dogs were bred in earnest. This is also the epoch during which *Canis lupus* came to know us best, through whatever combination of biological and cultural factors allowed us to domesticate some wolves and transform them into dogs.

But both the narrative of the wolf's participation in the collective human drama and the narrative of its isolation from that drama were wrested from biological fact a long time ago, and even further separated from ecological fact. The wolf's position in the material world of its biological origin was manipulated, both biologically and mythically, to satisfy human curiosity, which ironically led to the raw material of *Canis lupus* no longer being the source of that satisfaction. From the alchemical brew we call "interest" we write more stories about certain animals than about others, and we tend therefore to imbalance ecosystems in our artistic imagination toward animals that provide us with the most mythic opportunities—great bears, cute mice, anthropomorphic monkeys, creepy spiders. We imagine fantastic worlds of selected animals, then foist those worlds onto the complex ecosystems that we destroy. E. O. Wilson's *Biophilia* devotes a chapter to "The Serpent," explaining it as a figure invested with gnosis through primitive humans' practical avoidance of it. Many narratives have been written about both charismatic megafauna and venomous animals. But you don't see psychoanalytic bibliographies generated about the black-footed ferret or the red vole, despite their crucial parts in the stability of their ecosystems. It takes an Aldo Leopold or a John Muir, ever the pioneers of lay ecology, who devoted sections of their works to, respectively, draba(a low-lying ground cover) and the water ouzel. Stories have always been a way to answer the questions that science and history cannot answer—often a way to pose the questions science must try to answer or rephrase—and a politics of nations ensues in large part from those questions. Questions about the wolf's condition in America have generated hundreds of books, and at some point the very tonnage of writing, film, even merchandise demonstrates that the wolf's position in the world we know transcends the trivial, even the legendary, and achieves the mythic. It also helps us gauge the material transformation of the world we know.

However, in order to understand that scope, we need to consider its depth. The deeper an image's root in the individual and collective psyche, especially if it has its corollary in an animal, the stronger our tendency toward including that image, that being, in our stories. When the symbol is alive, sentient, social, and biologically comparable to us in some way, the very nature of symbology must change. To use *Biophilia* as an example again, many of Wilson's efforts tend toward simply declaring myth to be scientifically explainable, rather than creating a symbiotic framework for the archetype and the real animal. A more balanced synthesis of, for instance, Jung's mythopoesis and Wilson's biophilia is called for, since Wilson's remarkable attempt to understand the poet's place in the order of things still clearly subordinates and at times misrepresents poetry.[1] The wolf may be used as an image but is first part of a species, and an individual participant in what we assume to be and certainly is not the exclusive human drama of literature.

The Body-Spirit Confluence

The temptation to spiritualize the wolf has proven irresistible. In America we tend to "worship wolf" while refusing to change our behavior, often by appropriating American Indian myth and history. Lopez writes, "The possibility has yet to be realized of a synthesis between the benevolent wolf of many Native American stories and the malcontented wolf of most European fairy tales." He also explains that "wolves were not always benevolent figures in myth and legend nor strictly models for a warrior's admiration," which indicates that he is writing equally about wolves as about the romanticizing of American Indian wolf stories and the demonizing of European ones (*Of Wolves and Men,* 122). If we play the odds, we're right to think this way. The wolf did better under the populations of Native than invading Americans. But a purity of motive based on race or historical condition cannot be asserted either. Euro-American myths of wolves and Indians are woven together, each tugging the other along toward misrepresentation. Steinhart explains well the mythic layer of human confusion over the wolf:

> Our interest in wolves expresses the hunger of our imagination. For many, science is too narrow a view, and wolves are as much spiritual as biological. They say that, to understand wolves, we must go beyond what we can see into realms of spirit . . . A number of people suggest that, if we could regard the wolf as native Americans did, we would take it to our hearts, see it clearly, and recognize higher powers that stitch us to the cosmos. (320)

The tricks to such sentiment, as Steinhart clearly understands, are that Native Americans didn't all regard the wolf the same way, that those of us who do "take the wolf to heart" still have a hard time leaving it out of hand and reconciling our material American lives with our spiritual American lives. The idea of "higher powers that stitch us to the cosmos" has been behind both the saving and slaughter of wolves.

While the legendary wolves of literature built our myths, they are at least indirectly representative of real, individual, earthbound wolves—whether accurately (the corporeal wolf) or not (the ghost wolf). So the World-Wolf is to our imagination what a wolf myth is to a story: the form that has such a problematic and influential relationship with the animal from which it was imagined. The myth is not the origin but the bridge from the origin, which is wilderness, to the mind (individual and collective). It is therefore archetypal in its makeup. Ontologically speaking, behind the mythic wolf is the global population of real wolves; epistemologically speaking, behind the real wolf of an individual encounter is a mythic wolf, et cetera in a cyclical, eternal relationship. It's wolves all the way down. This is not a deconstructionist position, which would conclude that, as such, all wolves are irreferential and so inconsequentially immaterial. To the contrary, my position acknowledges the reciprocal, synthetic, parasitic, symbiotic, and/or frictional material and ideal, corporeal and ghost, physical and spiritual, objective and subjective. These may indeed be binaries, but they are not inevitably directly confrontational or inherently undermining. The issue we face ecologically was never limited to the sacred and profane. Ideology does not lead; it follows and pretends to lead. The critical issue, which is finally of change in varieties of health rather than change toward cascading disappearance and death, has always been invested with the necessity of materiality.

In his work on J. R. R. Tolkien, Tom Shippey addresses the project of synthesizing myths from several cultures into something accessible to the modern world. He writes:

> In 1937 (though not now) the world [of fairy tale] and its personnel were best known from a relatively small body of stories taken from an again relatively small corpus of classic European fairy-tale collections, those of the Grimm brothers in Germany, of Asbjørnsen and Moe in Norway, Perrault in France, or Joseph Jacobs in England, together with literary imitations like those of H. C. Andersen in Denmark, and literary collections like the "color" Fairy Books of Andrew Lang; and from the many Victorian "myth and legend" handbooks which drew on them. (12)

Shippey then argues that the works of these writers and collectors were limited by both their geographical separation and their lack of development toward more narrative depth. They were didactic, fantastic, isolated from each other, and as Shippey puts it, "when scholars began to take an interest in them and collect them, they seemed already to be in a sense in ruins" (13). What Shippey states as Tolkien's great achievement (*The Lord of the Rings* as a linguist's and mythicist's project of decisive synthesis) was something as much waiting to be realized as it was the great invention of one writer. This does not diminish Tolkien; it reminds us of the collective nature and force of myth. Like the magic ring of Tolkien's saga, it seems that myths cannot be separated for long from their origins or their users, will not remain in geographic isolation, and will, for good or ill, find their way home.

The longevity of Tolkien's own unfortunate use of the wolf as "warg," the goblin marauder's mount (especially emphasized in *The Hobbit*), can be understood through its derivations. First, the word implies the *were* or *war* of the demihuman, an ancient derivation becoming over time the anthropomorphized wolves or werewolves of Aesop's fables or Red Riding Hood. Brian Frost actually calls Tolkien's wargs "werewolves," based on their ability to speak. He also calls them "phantasms" that "become real only after dark," a telling and creative gesture to the ghost wolf (178). Tolkien uses the werewolf and Great Wolf of evil in *The Silmarillion* and *The Hobbit,* devoting significant scenes to wolves in both. But the "warg" so transmogrifies in *The Lord of the Rings* that by the time it reaches Peter Jackson's twenty-first-century cinematic version of Tolkien's epic, it is not only unable to speak but also unrecognizable as anything vaguely lupine, resembling something more like a giant razorback hog.

We didn't write the myth of the phoenix because we *didn't* believe in the possibility of ruins being rebuilt from their own material. Every one of those writers listed by Shippey knew and/or wrote a wolf story.[2] Why should we assume those stories to be too weak to find each other, to coalesce in the human mind and form again the idea of the World-Wolf, regardless of geographic separation? Therefore, the wolf in even one story has global implications. We must look at the World-Wolf, but looking at it lets it loose. So we must be cognizant of what we unleash, because in America that monster nearly killed its real counterpart.

To this end Walter Burkert devotes a chapter of his seminal *Homo Necans* to the Western classical tradition of werewolf mythology. "Werewolves around the Tripod Kettle" is constructed in the context of the ritual violence to which Burkert devotes the whole of his book, and makes some extremely important claims toward our understanding of wolf mythology in its oldest forms.

Like René Girard, Burkert focuses on historicizing the ritual violence of human beings. In so doing, he makes a few bold assumptions. The first is a paradox, made in "Primitive Man as Hunter," that "we can understand man's terrifying violence as deriving from the behavior of the predatory animal, whose characteristics he came to acquire in the course of becoming man" (17). Burkert bases this understanding on the Paleolithic evolutionary cycle of *Homo sapiens,* of which only about 5 percent has been spent in what we would call "civilization" after the development of agriculture. The paradox here is that we came to be "man," the civilized agrarian living in nature but separating ourselves from it, either *as* or *because* we adopted the violent characteristics of predation. I would not deny the influence of this history, but under the light of two particular facts this direct correlation is a little suspect. First, the move to agrarianism held all the potential for an adoption of vegetarianism across the board and constituted an initial and significant step away from hunting as the means of developing community. Second, predation and aggression are not the same traits in animals—there is obviously a kinesis to predation, an "aggression" of the generic form, and this is Burkert's focus, our misinterpretation of predation as aggression. But these behaviors are separate in the very animals that Burkert considers exemplary. The matter at hand is not animal behavior, but human interpretation even to the extreme of symbolizing, then totemizing, the animal.

In describing the communal hunt (an event Burkert sees catalyzing a shift to a violence by men against men), he writes: "At the core of this new type of male community, which is biologically analogous to a pack of wolves, are the acts of killing and eating," and, "What an experience it must have been when man, the relative of the chimpanzee, succeeded in seizing the power of his deadly enemy, the leopard, in assuming the traits of the wolf, forsaking the role of the hound for that of the hunter!" (18).

These ideas prepare us for the next chapter, in which the werewolf is seen as the manifestation of human aggression acted upon another human by one who has assumed the traits of the wolf. According to Burkert, ritual aggression shifted from the hunt to the battle, in a complicated miasma of "sexual complexes" and the simultaneous development in man of patterns "more closely analogous to beasts of prey" (19). He carries what he considers the basic biological and cultural combination of drive and craft forward through the ancient world and into Greek legend, where it would solidify into codes that would last for millennia. Burkert walks us with great erudition through the myths of Lykaion, Pelops, Thyestes and Harpagos, Aristaios and Aktaion—all werewolf stories of a sort and indicators of the paradox of Arcadia (the utopia that is actually a composition of violence). He unites "the biological, psychological, and sociological perspective" toward an understanding of ritual sacrifice (83).

The one problem seems to be in that biological premise. We have to read Burkert, and Girard, from the position that the consequences of fundamental drives are of at least equal weight to the consequences of cultural fabrication and ritual. Displaced aggression is Burkert's best argument. Biologically, there's no evidence that predation and aggression are quite so inevitably and closely linked except perhaps in humans, whose cultural mores conflate the two and so establish, quid pro quo, their relation. Burkert deftly handles the matter of cannibalism throughout his study as it exists in both the human and nonhuman worlds, but ritual is a bit harder to analyze among other species. He seems to assume that humans invented and then stipulated ritual as a mitigating influence on their sympathies for the nonhuman, and that other animals are both the material and repository for those rituals. Even if this were so, it would mean that if, by another animal, predation could be separated from the aggressions of territorialism, competition, sacrifice, and sheer anger, then we would have to revise our assumption of human aggression and ritual sacrifice as behavior learned from the nonhuman world. Because predation has indeed been separated from these other aggressions, and because it is readily apparent that animals distinguish behaviors both as they initiate them and as they respond to them, it seems we have a basic syllogistic refutation of the animal as mere repository. The animal is an actant. Where there are actants, there are highly likely to be rituals, by Burkert's and Girard's own premises.

The biologist Gary Kyrouac considers our assumptions about aggression ethology this way: Whenever you see a nature program that shows a wolf growling, baring its teeth, and raising its hackles, he says, and the program then cuts away to the wolf plunging into the herd to kill, you are watching a lie. The filmmakers are cutting from an aggression or dominance shot to a predation shot in order to add drama. This depicts the wolf in a way that perpetuates simplified thought. The equivalent, Kyrouac says, would be if when you picked up your fast food you first stabbed the burger angrily with a knife several times and screamed at it before you ate it (Kyrouac lecture, July).

I'm certainly not discounting Burkert's central argument, which was constructed when wolf biology told us about half of what it can tell us now. Using history, Burkert is able to formulate a model that looks ahead. He sees how human beings acknowledge one similarity of communal behavior (hunting) with wolves, then project other qualities onto those wolves, so that in turn the ghost wolves created may be turned back to the human mind, resulting in werewolves and rituals of violence. At that point, any rituals possessed by wolves themselves may be easily interpreted as "like humans," and the cycle may start again. From a psychological perspective it's a brilliantly conceived argument.

Here, briefly, is how we might revise the biological imperative in *Homo Necans.* If we see ritual acts of aggression as the displacement of predatory acts, then we have a pathology at work, and it must be seen not as a biological imperative but as a cultural failure needing therapeutic correction. Cannibalism fits into this position *because we are edible,* so the act of our being food to ourselves is in contention among situations of biological necessity (the common example of starving castaways on a life raft), cultural taboos (such as sexualizing the eating of flesh, as vampire and many werewolf stories), and ritual desire for spiritual appeasement (such as "black magic" or ceremonialized cannibalism). Predatory aggression is about sustenance, and agrarianism is the evidence that we are as able to take our cues from the herbivore as the carnivore. Ritual aggression is about order. Human codes of hunting combine these; as such, they run the risk of linking predation and aggression, the bow or gun of the hunt with the bow or gun of war, as Burkert acknowledges.

Another wrinkle: If there is evidence that a nonhuman animal has performed (especially in community) a ritual act, then Burkert's one paradox (of agonistic behavior) dances with another one. Now we have to cope with the possibility that our stories are being generated out of a sense of other animals' *preferences,* their sense of order, as much as from their biological sympathies with our own evolutionary upbringing. That wolf pack that we resemble is not for us to resemble; it is a wolf pack, and must, if we are to emulate it in our practice, be better understood. The paradox, as with the conflation of aggressions that may exist but cannot be assumed, is that the wolf's existence prior to human interpretation cannot be denied even though it was not seen. The wolf must now be seen.

Wolves like to howl, we say. Then we howl. So much for exclusionary, elitist essentialism.

The piece Burkert might be missing is that we don't know why the wolf howls—a matter especially enigmatic during moments when we also don't know why we do the same—and that enigma may be the inspiration for our equating various violent acts. Our interpretation of patterns in the nonhuman world does not necessarily explain them; it transforms them into story. If only for its potential to convince us of our separation from the world, this is a dangerous transformation. It may become the werewolf, which I will discuss in a later chapter.

Wolf Songs

One of the ways we rhapsodize about the body-spirit connection using wolves as symbols is by calling their howls "song." I have already briefly raised the issue of animal song, so here I'll point to us, to why we want howls to be songs. For centuries we did our best to consider those howls the devil's music—not even a Siren's song, the call of the wild designed to lure us out, and certainly nothing that hath charms to soothe the savage breast (a cliché commonly misquoted as "savage beast"). Then, in the turn from our malevolent myths to our benevolent ones, we shifted from the wolf whistle to the wolf song. At least four books invoke this symbolic device: Robert Busch's collection of essays *Wolf Songs,* Louis Owens's novel *Wolfsong,* Catherine Feher-Elston's book *Wolfsong,* and Harvey Fergusson's 1927 *Wolf Song.*

The back cover blurb for Fergusson gives us a sense of the sensibilities: "THE SURGE OF LIFE is in this novel—the reality of men and women who lived and dared and fought a wilderness to its knees. This is no 'movie' West—these are real men and women in a real world. The flesh-and-blood saga of Sam Lash, the rugged mountain man, and lovely dark-haired Lola will stay with you long." Full of sneaky Indians, willing women, rough country, and more clichés than you could fit on a travois, this misogynistic tale of conquest features two wolves: the first a noble savage named Black Wolf, who is part of the vanishing breed (the title seems a play on "swan song" as well as a note from the wild lands being conquered), and the woman-crushing tough guy Sam Lash, who ends his arduous plot line by "taking" a woman whose "face was a mask of willing pain" (118).[3]

Busch's *Wolf Songs* is a play on the testimonies of the writers in the collection: writers singing songs of the wolf. The Owens novel is set in the Pacific Northwest and invokes a wolf of magic realism, a shamanic totem of tribal value, in a book that is mostly about activism against industrialism and its devastation of the land. I will single out the Feher-Elston book for a closer read, both because it is the most recent and because it is written from the perspective of an anthropologist in her effort to present a wolf that sings to an audience more attuned to the animal's mystical nobility than to its realism.

Wolfsong: A Natural and Fabulous History of Wolves combines brief gestures to wolf biology (including a good basic bibliography of wolf research) with a number of short Native American and international indigenous wolf tales. There is far less natural history than fabulous. Feher-Elston attempts to find a cooperative relationship between science and myth and to place her book at that meeting point. The book's construction, however, contributes to its fantastic emphasis over the factual. It lacks any citation and is therefore unusable except as a primary source of low ethos. That is, Feher-Elston's declaration that "Wolf is clever, loyal, and slow to anger" (73), is given the same definitive quality as when she presents a wolf's number of teeth or average weight. In neither case do we have corroborative evidence except to assume that the information is somewhere to be found in the bibliography—perhaps in one of Mech's studies, perhaps in a book of Navajo creation myths. The point here is that in such a work stating both spiritualist credo and scientific fact, the negotiation of fact and myth is not productively accomplished. The end result may well be in wolves' favor, and Feher-Elston's heart may be in the right place, but the meeting point of the corporeal and ghost wolf is a dangerous one, and lends itself to creating this figure of "Wolf" (capital, without article) as if there is some monolithic spirit to which we should refer. It essentializes, rendering the wolf convenient and useful to human pious sensibilities that too often skate into doctrine and dogma.

It is difficult to tell in *Wolfsong* when Feher-Elston is writing about a mythic belief or asserting that belief to be a natural fact, because she writes under the premise that "scientific inquiry supports behaviors explained in old myths and sagas."[4] As a rule, scientific inquiry does no such thing, although there are important occasions of primitive or intuitive insight as science, leading to science, or anticipating science. On occasion, old myths and sagas sometimes demonstrate a crucial understanding of the natural world, for instance in the way that mnemonic devices aid in wilderness survival. Bruce Chatwin's *The Songlines,* which popularized in America the aboriginal dreamtime, is a good example of how this relationship functions. People in the field come to know certain particular things and ways of knowing those things, and they earn the symbols they use. Scientific inquiry will have to support that as consequence, not cause, because natural fact doesn't depend on cultural approval, either primitive or techno-industrial. More often, myth and saga demonstrate how fettered to natural fact they are by their herculean efforts to transcend, and those moments regard the human mind and culture more than they regard ecology. We're often talking about the difference between astrology and astronomy.

Feher-Elston also attributes her Native American stories to individual interviews. This is fine if we consider the interviews as stories in context rather than as some form of corroboration or culmination. That is, if someone were to be interviewed about the Immaculate Conception both before and after his time as a "saved and sanctified" believer, the interviews would be remarkably different. So the story the interviewee tells must be considered highly subjective until it is substantiated with the history of the Immaculate Conception as a root myth. To her credit, the stories Feher-Elston chooses are narratives, worth reading whether considered subjective or objective, and in many cases align with other interviews (as found in the works of Dorsey, Grinnell, and Vizenor).

The risks involved when the corporeal and ghost wolves are brought together in a text purporting to be nonfiction are considerable. The pass is narrow, and the tendency is to slide off—either into a reportage of fact that denies myth's connection to field knowledge and pragmatic environmental responsibility—or into an appropriation of selected trivia that supports the modern cult of the wolf-spirit at the expense of hard contextual fact. The spirituality of wolves', or our, lives is not an assumption to be made but a mystery to be considered as one source of myth. Here is a particularly egregious sample from the introduction to *Wolfsong:* "More and more people seek to understand Nature and her ways. Wolf is one of her most efficient and elegant creations. To understand Wolf, one must enter a world of primeval beauty, a world where life and death are inextricably linked . . . Wolf walks in legend between myth and reality. The call of a wolf on a clear, cold night is an invitation to enter this world" (xvii).

Actually, fewer and fewer people, at least in America, are spending time in the nonhuman world learning "her" ways. We can read the passage as a typical hook; the writer is waxing evocative, giving us a moment of poetic sentiment before getting into the stuff of the text. Such moments tell us more sometimes than the collected stories and facts that follow; they designate in advance the interpretive rubric used for those stories. They foreshadow the use to which the stories and facts gathered will be put. Here, Nature is a woman. "Wolf" is an entity, mono-lithic, a spirit, efficient and elegant, created by the mother. Entering a world of "primeval beauty" may be a prerequisite to understanding the wolf, which we must assume to mean wilderness, wolf habitat, but this phrase aestheticizes the issue romantically and (to the degree that it must be primeval) abstractly. Feher-Elston implies that the world of primeval beauty is where life and death are somehow specially linked to some degree that they aren't, for instance, on a twelve-lane freeway, which we cannot infer. This is a choice favoring a poetry of default human images over wolf images. Ghost wolf thinking.

We are also to assume that a wolf howl is an *invitation* of some kind. The benign brand of this assumption is that hearing the howl excites our curiosity and invites us into learning; the malignant one is that Wolf is actually calling to us to enter some penumbral world of our romances that we transpose with the real place where the wolf lives, so that we might actually intrude upon real wolves' lives, thinking they invited us. The howl means what it means to the wolf. Our projected desires might make meaning all right, but they highly risk making meaning detached from substance, and further risk justifying such "meaning-making" as somehow ethically neutral. When an actress on screen looks into the camera and says, "Come on over here, stud," she's not actually inviting me, much as I might like to think so. And if I continue to think so, become convinced to "enter her world" or "commune with her spirit" (perhaps as well as her body), then I unhealthily ignore context and reality in favor of my convenient interpretation at her expense. Stalkers are made from this.

Life and death are "inextricably linked" in all environments. Nature is not a woman. Inefficient wolves have been observed on many occasions; I've seen them myself. I am more impressed by their inefficiency than I would have been by predictably autonomic perfection. I'll just bet some wolves know a few dumpy louts who fall well short of elegant. A rose is not a rose is not a rose. Feher-Elston wants us to "understand Wolf." Unfortunately, that essential abstraction may be all we come to understand, and too easily. Wolves in this book are not sufficiently corporeal to counterbalance the wolf painted in the image of God. *Wolfsong* provides us with some beautiful individual stories, case examples accumulating toward the mythic patterns, the critical mass, of the wolf in the collective unconscious over time. This is important, and the book should be read if only for those subjective examples of potential cultural patterns.

If we follow the path mapped by a long list of wolf-stories-become-books, we may be able to finally draw that map. We would have to establish the literature of the wolf in America as a definable subgenre, a blueprint of works that have contributed to our conception of wolves over the last three thousand years in the Western world. Hopefully, through the combination of chapter 2's inclusion of more than fifty works determined to represent the wolf with this chapter's hundreds of years of story determined to etherealize the wolf, I am providing sufficient evidence of a leitmotif in our literature. This leitmotif is not only worthy of critical consideration but also vital to understanding American social psychology, its iconic art, and the writing of its national story. This story begins at three points—one in Europe and one in Native North America, where it comes together after spanning the third point of origin, the Atlantic.

Fenris, the World-Wolf

In the Icelandic Volsungasaga, the god Loki and the giantess Angur-boda have a son, a wolf pup they name Fenris. This offspring pleases them because they have lived well in the company of the wolves Skoll, Garm, Managarm, and Hati for some time. Loki, the god of chaos, has as his chief occupation the chastisement of the Aesir, keeping them from complacency in their reign over the earth and cosmos. The gods eventually grow tired of the necessity of chaos and seek an opportunity to contain it. When Loki murders the god Balder, the Aesir chain him with the wolf Garm at the bottom of the sea, where Loki is tormented by a caustic poison that drips onto his face continually from the mouth of Iormugandr, a serpent whom Wotan had banished long ago. Angur-boda is given custody of the other wolves, which she must keep away from the Aesir. Fenris, however, is an exception. Wotan decides to make a pet of Loki's lupine son, first valuing and then fearing Fenris for the wolf's size and strength as he grows. For his part, Fenris is peaceful and seemingly impossible to anger.

The Aesir recognize naming as a form of power; they even name the enchanted ropes and chains they create. To safeguard against a possible change in Fenris's temperament, Wotan binds Fenris to the world with a chain he names Laeding. But the Aesir doubt that this chain will hold the wolf, who by now has grown so large that none of the gods will approach him. Fenris yawns and stretches, shaking off Laeding's links as if they were beads of water. The gods then forge Droma, the strongest chain they can make, coax Fenris into its loop, and watch to their dismay as the wolf breaks Droma with a shrug. The Aesir know that Fenris will mean their doom and that by chaining him down they are merely precipitating their demise, which will come in battle. They commission the dwarves to forge a chain, but instead the dwarves weave a rope from the spittle of birds, the murmurings of fish, the anguish of bears, the footsteps of cats, a woman's beard, and the roots of a mountain. They name the rope Gleipnir.

Fenris, now suspicious of the trap, makes a deal. He will try the rope if the god of war, Tyr, will put his hand in the wolf's mouth. Tyr does so, the dwarves tie Fenris, the rope holds, and in his first rage, Fenris bites off Tyr's hand at the wrist. The free end of Gleipnir is fastened to a rock, the rock thrown into the sea, and Fenris becomes the World-Wolf, bound and anchored to the planet until the last battle is to be fought. As Jung has noted, he also becomes, in the prophetic fulfillment of his chosen name, the Sea Wolf.[5]

Fenris begins to howl—a deep rolling howl that shakes the earth violently. An Aesir drives a sword through the wolf's upper jaw, pinning it to his lower jaw. The blood pouring from the wound that silences Fenris becomes the river Von. The Aesir have put Loki the trickster and his wolves in place but know that to force order over chaos will cost them, that their reign will be short-lived. From his torture chamber Loki waits for the coming eclipse. Meanwhile, out of the necessity of her impoverishment by the gods, Angur-boda has been feeding the other wolves from the bone marrow of murderers and adulterers, on which fare they grow strong.

Angur-boda sends the wolves Skoll, Managarm, and Hati to attack the moon (Mani) and sun (Sol). Eventually the Death Wolves catch them and, with their powerful jaws, squeeze all the drops of blood from Mani and Sol. These blood drops become the stars, which fall to earth. The ensuing darkness causes Gleipnir to lose its power over Fenris, who breaks free and, with Iormugandr, rears from the depths. Loki takes Garm out of the realm of Hel, and the Death Horde is united against Wotan and the Aesir. The battle begins in blood and fire, the roar of the sea and the blast of Heimdall's horn, the Frost Giants leaping to their ships to aid Loki as he pilots Nagilfar, the Death Ship made of the nail parings of the dead. Tyr and Garm destroy each other, Loki and Heimdall destroy each other, Thor slays Iormugandr and drowns in the venom pouring from the serpent's jaws, and Fenris swallows Wotan. Finally, in the last fires of Surtur's burning blade, all but one of the forests are consumed, the seas boil, and in the midst of the flames Wotan's son Vidar plants a foot against Fenris's lower jaw, grabs his upper jaw, and tears the wolf apart to rescue Wotan. The twilight of the gods begins. Humanity and the Aesir are separated.[6]

At the beginning of this Norse myth we have a pack of anthropomorphic wolves living in peace with the gods. As it progresses, the story reveals its focus on the code for negotiating nature's own order and chaos, rather than the method by which to control them. We see the captivity of the wolves, and an avatar of *Canis lupus* as the gauge of all captivity and freedom, related to a war determining the fate of humanity. Just as humans have gods represented in our image, so too do the wolves have such a godlike figure cast in theirs. The narrative uses the water motifs of sea depth and river birth to establish the wolf's explosive counterstrike against its betrayal, an act incorporating the *Kore* into a plot of reversal. Fenris's jaws are both the source of original might and final destruction. Every image indicates that this myth positions the wolf's power at the foundation of the planet.

Despite the more obvious ambivalence toward good and evil promulgated by Loki the trickster, the parallels to Christian mythology should be obvious. These include the consumption of the spheres (the quince or apple, the sun and moon), which act separates humanity and the gods; and the parallels to Satan, or "challenger" in the Hebrew, as both wolf and serpent, using knowledge to corrupt humanity. The death of God is written with the ink of night and the characters of stars because the sky-god must dwell beyond the visible, and the stars are the farthest-reaching material we have with which to work. Wotan is literally swallowed into darkness, in parallel to the Judeo-Christian Leviathan sea myth. And so the myth finally binds the realms of sea, land, and sky to a cosmic center in which gods and wolf-gods struggle.

One thing we must notice in the tale is, sadly, its plausibility of behavior. Think of an animal tethered who shrugs off the tether as a game; the animal's realization finally, in dire need, that the game is cruelty; and the likely response of the animal out of self-preservation and anger. We are in some ways looking at a simple macrocosmic representation of a captive wolf biting a fool. Here are men who thought first to master a wolf when they couldn't master the ignorance and fear that drove them to the brutality of chains and drownings. The fools (that is, gods) then retroactively justify their fear by blaming on wolves the destruction they created themselves through that very brutality. Full of righteousness, that celebrated form of ignorance, they war against themselves, trapping the wolf in between, while imagining all the while that they are fighting wolves.

Northern European tales following the eleventh-century invasions from Scandinavia irrevocably influenced the construction of language about the animal world. They gathered cultures from the lower Celto-Germanic to the high Norse, all the while translating and metamorphosing language and stories until a mass of tales, legends, and myths were transported to the North American colonies. There could have been a kind of Franciscan turning point in Christian compassion toward animals, since the story of Noah had evidently proved insufficient. But there was not. Christianity's greatest corruption, present in the practice of its current mythic order, is its collective treatment of animals. The wolf is one of the strongest iconic representatives of this failing, leading to a more generalized and anthropocentric unpreparedness for cross-cultural adaptation.

The Mythic Water Crossing: Beringia

We come to the mythic wolf, oddly enough, through rituals of water as well as of land. Through policies obsessed with resource extraction, Spanish invaders engineered the rapid annihilation of the wolf in Mexico even as the famous Armada complained of pirates in quick sloops that harried them like packs of wolves, or the pirate sloop's tactic of worrying the bovine galleon to the point of fall.[7] The metaphor of the prairie as a great sea appears in the art of antebellum exploration, such as Bryant's "The Prairies," Cooper's *The Prairie,* George Catlin's painting *Out of Sight of Land,* or Parkman's *The Oregon Trail* (see esp. 47, 331), to name a few pieces, and continues through literary naturalism at the turn of the century. The quest myth of crossing the Atlantic fueled the Euro-American expansionist language of crossing the plains. Space was abstracted sufficiently so as to ignore the ecological conditions of habitat; the tundra could be an ocean could be a prairie could be a desert, all called "wilderness" as a pejorative at one time or another, all subjected to sea metaphors, even unto the vacuum of the cosmos as both the new frontier and the sea for fleets of starships led by Magellanistic captains (see Nash; Slotkin; Callicott & Nelson). The sea metaphor also contributed to the fallacy of limitlessness, which in turn catalyzed boosterism up to and at times beyond those disregarded limits of biomes and species.

The eradication of the wolf in the British Isles (England circa 1500, Scotland circa 1743, Ireland circa 1770) rests neatly between the colonization of North America and the populous transatlantic migrations of the 1800s, between the long argument over United States provincialism and "Indianization" and the industrial boom that, through urbanized mechanization and religious mandates, united efforts to tame the wilderness with efforts to conquer indigenous tribes. Accounts of the extermination of the wolf in the British Isles can be found in Steinhart (153) and Boitani ("Wolf Conservation and Recovery," 318–21). The bison slaughter, the barbed-wire homestead, the reservation system, and rail empires are the most famous examples of a balkanization of indigenous living space, which coincided (in both method and rationale) with the fragmentation of wolf habitat. Transmigration in America meant an increasingly transecting road system that began the end of the prairie sea, but the image and language of limitlessness persisted.

The Bering land bridge hypothesis—which imagined an original crossing that resulted not only in the human populating of North America but also the taming of the wolf into a domestic animal—is substantial enough for us to continue using it as a starting point for North American cultural history. But it is occasionally revisited and rendered questionable by archaeology and anthropology. Stone tools were discovered at Calico Hills in the Mojave Desert that date to 200,000 years ago; Santa Rosa Island and China Lake in California possess sites inhabited as early as 50,000 BCE (see Carter). R. K. Wayne's recent work has uncovered through mitochondria analysis that the domestication of the wolf into the dog may have taken place up to 138,000 years ago and certainly did not take place first in North America.[8] In addition, the later Pleistocene dating of the crossing from Beringia (10,000–12,000 years ago) does not necessarily mean that it was the first such crossing, nor that it was a single mass-migration demanding the domestication of the dog for human survival of the journey. Many crossings were probably made by both species, and preliterate historic cultural exchanges among people, including practices of interspecific interaction and multiple instances of wolf domestication, may have taken place over millennia, contrary to the thesis accepted for decades of a single crossing and beginning of domestication.[9] Some megafauna may actually have been migrating in the opposite direction, and the meeting of the two cultures of wolf and human resulted in perhaps the most profound act of domestication of an animal in human history. This entire theory has been challenged by Vine Deloria from a political perspective, in addition to Wayne's team from a scientific one.[10]

I raise this issue here because it is an excellent example of the symbiotic relationship between scientific discovery and mythmaking. Like the challenges to Frederick Jackson Turner's frontier thesis or European imperialist definitions of *primitive* and *savage,* a healthy skepticism of the assertion that human beings migrated in a monodirectional stream and domesticated the wolf in the process changes for us, at the least, the historicity of more than two hundred wolf books. At the greatest, it revises one of our foundational North American myths.

Isle Royale

In 1949 a wolf pack swam from the mainland across Lake Superior to Isle Royale National Park, which had a sizable moose population. The moose had, years earlier, crossed to the island on an ice bridge, and biologists studying the ecosystem of the park expected that a closed island ecology with an imbalance of browsing ungulates would result in the collapse of wolf and/or moose populations: "Trends of the late 40s posed the definite prospect that Isle Royale was to be another of those big game ranges, degraded by overpopulation, where the animals hang on at the limit of numbers permitted by their food supply, to be decimated periodically by hard winters that concentrate them into starvation areas" (D. Allen, 43). This was written by Durward Allen in his 1979 *Wolves of Minong,* a work of more than four hundred pages embodying research from three decades of field study, personal ruminations, and commentary on the Isle Royale ecosystem as a result of the arrival of wolves. Every so often biologists speculate about the collapse of such a closed system, but Isle Royale is the real example of the fox-and-rabbit textbook anecdote on predator-prey balance that we learn in junior high school.

"The Founders," Allen's opening chapter, is particularly well written— evidence of a biologically informed study written as a wolf story, not only for the attraction of the reader but, quite obviously from Allen's language and density of information, for the personal satisfaction of a writer passionate about wolves. Rolf Peterson and David Mech also have books on the island's wolves, and a battery of articles has been generated. A fine introductory essay is Thomas McNamee's "Trouble in Wolf Heaven, 1982" (in Murray).

While *Wolves of Minong* appeared at the end of the '70s, much of Allen's work was done in the 1950s, not long after Goldman, Young, Murie, and Olson began the work of formal wolf study. Significantly, Allen trained both David Mech and

Rolf Peterson, and his book constitutes a kind of biographical manual on wolves and on field biology. The significance of *Wolves of Minong* to the wolf canon is found not only in its global metaphor but also in its demonstration of biophilia, a resonant meeting of science and myth. The biophilic implications of the book surface in part because of the unusual quality of the ecosystem in question and the events that brought wolf and moose populations into focus. Packs of wolves swimming the frigid waters of the roughest Great Lake is a phenomenon impossible to consider without some inevitable macrocosmic gesture to the Great Crossing.

Allen, like many wolf biologists, understands this sense of ecosystems having a certain humbling, awakening effect, tilting the psyche toward the grand complexity of the planet. The result is that his book, especially as straight wolf biology goes, is a well-constructed narrative with many moments of strong, poetic prose. It includes personal commentary and regional history, and so gives us a contemporary manifestation of the myth of continental arrival.

Allen first contextualizes the Isle Royale field study with similar studies being done in Yellowstone and the Far North, as a way of explaining what tools were available to biologists at the time and what Isle Royale offered exclusively because of its being what Allen calls "an island laboratory" (44). He provides as well a political history. Given that Yellowstone had only recently stopped poisoning and hunting its wolves and begun ecosystemic conservation work, the debates over what should be done about Isle Royale's new wolf population were progressive. At one point the Park Service considered stocking the island with wolves to address the moose overbrowsing problem. At another there was talk of adding more wolves after the first dozen's journey, since inbreeding was (and still is) a danger (13–14). Finally, a "let it be" philosophy was adopted, one that continues to serve Isle Royale and is strongly defended by Peterson.

In a closed ecological system, an "island ecology" metaphorically as well as literally speaking, biologists can more easily observe how the health of the prey base is affected by a predator population. They may witness what Norm Bishop and other ecologists call "the ripple effect"—how the health of the predator-prey relationship then affects the health of grasses, certain trees, rodent populations— on a measurable scale for a whole trophic system. The boundaries of a naturally regulated closed system, here established by Lake Superior, give the ecologist some relief from more expansive influences of biospheric interconnectedness without losing ecosystemic wholeness. The disadvantages of such a system include inbreeding, natural disaster or disease affecting a significant portion of the system, and isolation from other systems that would contribute to the island ecology's health. What Allen and his team found was that the wolves and moose established their own parameters, that those parameters allowed insight into lupine ecological systems not covered by captive programs, and that the future of wolf study would be changed by both the information and the method of gathering it at Isle Royale.

Allen finds the island's "earliest historic record of wildlife. The account is in John Tanner's narrative of his 30 years captivity among the Ojibways . . . He was 13 (about 1793) when he and his 17-year-old Indian 'brother' were living and hunting in the vicinity of Grand Portage" (48). Allen includes an excerpt from Tanner's journal, using it to explain both the ecosystem's conditions (before either moose or wolves) and the national history of the region. The *Minong* in Allen's title comes from the Ojibway name for Isle Royale, which means "place of blueberries" (xvi). By using the native name, Allen elicits our response to the island as both an old place and a cultural divide, a place of stories generated before our stories, which gives us a broad enough context to establish that the arrival of moose and wolf is a major event in ecological history beyond human history. It also, of course, provides a context for the Tanner captivity narrative that gives Allen his earliest source of data on the island's ecology. Here, then, the narrative moment—one fitting into a standard category of eighteenth-century literary history (the captivity narrative)—functions cooperatively with the scientific one.

The book includes careful regional detail mixed with evocative prose: "In growing seasons after the fire the first flush of healing was mainly herbs and grasses, colorful meadows of fireweed, everlasting, and other annuals" (37). Allen describes the hard mechanics of dismantling and studying a wolf-killed deer carcass with that little trace of the macabre pleasure we often find in field writing: "we knock off one of the tooth rows; it comes away neatly with a piece of the maxillary bone when hit properly with the hatchet . . . Finally, we placed in small bags several handfuls (frozen chunks) of the rumen, which would provide information on what the animal was eating . . . All these specimens were joyfully carried back and piled into the plane" (78). And he is adept at providing concise programmatic histories of the biologists who worked at Isle Royale (see, for example, 96–97). Allen writes about the passionate concern biologists had for the pups that would follow the island's "founders," and of tireless efforts to monitor the health of the rest of the ecosystem. A constant thread running through the book is anxiety about the future, about what the island would become, whether these animals would survive in this place that produced some of the greatest wolf biologists ever to work in the field.

Wolves of Minong includes chapters on wolf ethology that act as narrative primers on what biologists were learning for two decades. The move happened fast from what they didn't know (about the ecosystemic ripple effect, about wildlife management, about wolf hunting behavior and prey health, about park system politics' effect on natural systems) to what they came to know, was thorough as only empirical study is thorough, and played one of the more overlooked roles in the "environmental movement" of the 1970s. Studies such as the one on Isle Royale redressed positions held by wildlife management agencies for as long as two centuries. It's easy to read *Wolves of Minong* as a case history of wolves and wolf biologists on one island. I read it as a case history of the changing mythology, the remythologizing, of the wolf in America.

Allen enters the book himself most prominently in the Prelude and in the last two chapters. Most of the rest of the study is written in a first-person-plural point of view about the research teams or a third-person objective description of the wolves and their ecology. Late in the text he includes some of the most powerful and politically complicated statements about the general relationship of wolves and humans in any wolf book (405–7). As a means of dispelling the notion of "many people unfamiliar with wild animals" that wolves are "senseless automatons," Allen writes this:

> Nearly anywhere one can find people who feel it no indignity to share the earth with other kinds of life. But men called primitive and others called modern have subjected the wolf to every brutish artifice their ingenuity could devise . . .
>
> A holdover from the frontier is an assumption that man is the keeper of all creation, that his is the privilege and duty to organize the chaos of nature, to sort its creatures, some to be reserved for use, others to be destroyed as vagrants and outlaws. Often enough, the old-time backwoodsman had a certain appreciation for the beauty of a pelt, but not to the extreme of leaving it on the animal it was intended to protect.
>
> It has been, and still is, an open question whether wolves in any appreciable portion of their original range, and in any majority of their remaining forms, can survive our pagan era of natural philosophy. The indigenous school of thought—more properly, attitude—has been a seminary of hostility wherever men of limited view have had the opportunity to react to the carnage of a wolf kill.
>
> The image people have of the wolf is, in degree, a product of applying moralistic standards. In my lecturing on our findings I regularly encounter persons of compassion and good will who ask, sometimes in a spirit of reluctance, Are wolves cannibalistic?
>
> I suppose the answer is that, given the right circumstances, almost anyone is. (406–7)

Earth Divers

Modern repetitions of the wolf's connection to the crossing of water are articulated in stories from all over the world. In old European stories nearly all werewolf legends that root the transformer's power in magic or in satanic selection involve the crossing of a body of water, usually a lake, in order for the change to take place (Douglas, 65–66, 269–70; Eckels, 33). Even in the legends of a werewolf from birth, a usual sign of power is the presence of the caul, a membrane over the baby's face that indicates (to the tale-teller) an incomplete passage out of the amniotic fluid, and a "mark" of supernatural powers that include clairvoyance, precognition, and/or transformation into an animal. In much of Europe, the animal into which the "veiled child" can change is the wolf. Indeed, the wolf-crossing-water motif is so prominent that in his survey of werewolf stories Brian Frost refers to the "lycanthropous brook" (87).

A curious phenomenon of American fiction and poetry is that this leitmotif has disappeared from Euro-American texts except for glancing symbolic mentions (such as London's title *The Sea-Wolf*); it remains strong only in indigenous myth. A Tlingit saying from the Pacific Coast is that a hunter by sea would become an orca (killer whale) when he died, and a hunter by land would become a wolf. Edward Curtis claimed that Lekwiltok belief prohibited the killing of wolves or killer whales because the spirits of land and sea hunters respectively were transformed into these animals after death (10:36). I should say here that even if we take the revisionist perspective regarding Curtis's sensibilities, we are still considering a legend, however and by whomever it is perpetuated—indeed one that may be more powerful and widespread among white America because of Curtis's fame. But the accomplishment of revising Curtis's reportage will require more than mere cynicism, since his work involved years of direct contact and immersion. It will also produce, more likely, a more forceful myth because of the focus required to revise it; the stories will be kept alive as they are cleaned, should that be the proper action, of their sepia tint.

"When anybody [Lekwiltok] chances to find a dead wolf in the woods," Curtis writes, "he sits down and pretends to cry, scratching his face and praying." He then provides two firsthand accounts of such an incident, one involving a wolf and one involving a whale (10:37). The wolf was also considered the orca of the woods, and the orca the wolf of the sea, so their two shamans held many of the same secrets. A fascinating account of one such group of shamans is given in volume 10 of Curtis's study (91). Further corroboration of this theme is provided in 1986 by the Nuu-chah-nulth artist Arthur Thompson, who designed a mask depicting the transformation of a wolf into a killer whale, an image representing a legend of his nation (Blackman, 37). In such legends, the role of predation was not to be championed as a human monopoly. In fact, the human hunter's true achievement was to enter the animal realm and learn from, before becoming, a true hunter.[11]

In *The Sea-Wolf* London included a similar kind of imaginary wolf of the ocean that had been carried around by European colonists three centuries before—atavistically resourceful and cruel. This wolf was not a wolf at all but was, as we see from the name of Larsen's ship—*The Ghost*—an apparition of European imagination. Thus, an imaginary wolf could be cast as a kind of sea monster, a wraith traveling the world like Cotton Mather's malevolent Indian or the Caribbean buccaneer. Such a concept was easy to perpetuate in the United States, where wolves were considered pirates of the cattle industry, villains in children's horror stories, a nuisance to the Russian fur trade prior to the United States' acquisition of Alaska in 1867, and abominations of nature.

In a few decades after the wolf had been eliminated in most of the lower forty-eight, the sea wolves would surface again, as German U-boat packs preying upon the British navy and electrifying the military and cultural sensibilities of America. Two centuries after the Caribbean pirate era had waned, sea captains were hunting down wolf packs once again, decades after wolves had been driven off of most American ranchland. By the time the American West could no longer be fully conceived as a great prairie sea, the wolf had become a sad figure, though still a villain. The western territories were charted, and by the advent of the environmental movement in the 1960s the West was becoming America's most urbanized region. Realists would find that they were now called to war against the old wolf of the imagination, the ghost wolf, because the large blank spot at northwestern North America on De Wit's map had been filled in, and no place existed on the map any longer in which one could write the warning, "Here be dragons."

The Earth Diver myth often has at its center a protohuman or theriohuman who travels through water (often upward) to find a new world or to begin human life on land.[12] As such it is connected to the cosmogonic flood myth, which is itself a biomythical puzzle for the Judeo-Christian. Noah apparently must have saved two wolves, which would have been considered categorically malevolent through the centuries from Hebraic Jews to Gutenberg Protestants. In Genesis 7:2 "clean beasts" were to be saved in sevens; the wolf would hardly qualify, so a viable gene pool for repopulation certainly was a miracle, as well as more problematic for the intelligent design cult.

The Cahuilla creation myth begins with two brothers who create the world during an argument over which one should be regarded the elder. At the center of the argument are the roles of water and darkness, and at stake as a result of the brothers' decisions toward water and darkness is the season's food. As a result of their negotiation, the creation takes on oddly integral terms, especially in the creation of animals, the first three of which become "water bear," "water cougar," and "water wolf" (Curtis, 15:111).

More than two-thirds of the earth's surface is water. We learn this in grade school. We are also taught, in a separate context, that most of our own bodies are made of water. What we are not taught until much later in life, if at all, is that the one has very much to do with the other. The stories of wolves reveal in us an inclination to connect them to the planet elementally. In the health achieved from the proper scrutiny of our myths, we may finally come to treat the wolf as a denizen of the land for whom the world of water is very much as it is for us, an element of survival, a biome of mystery and inaccessibility, and a realm of story connecting body and world.

CHAPTER EIGHT

Orion's Dogs
(In Which a Wolf Crosses the Sky)

The moon's role is, of course, related to the water crossing through its connection to cyclical transformations of, among many things, the tides and a woman's body. But in Western art, especially cinema, the aquatic connection was subsumed, with most of the moon's symbolic significance, in the popular psychology regarding "lunacy." From the 1930s through the 1960s the werewolf maintained its medieval Christian function as a minion or manifestation of Satan. From the 1950s through the 1980s this assumption competed with the rise of mass interest in both shamanism and New Age environmentalism. The shape-shifters of ancient shamanic traditions were commodified through Euro-American fascination with Ghost Indians who were "one with" ghost wolves, especially through the myth of the vanishing breed. What was missing from this derivation was a cosmological connection. Appropriated stories were stripped by New Ageism of their demand for sacrifice and ritual, participation, shamanic guidance requiring more than the effort needed to sit before a television, read a trash novel, or crack open a geode. The practice of looking inward is often profaned in America from self-awareness to mere self-celebration. The Freudian or Deleuzian wolf is always ready to displace the actual wolf through the externalization of this narcissism. Especially to the extent that it has been technologically and commercially exploited, our derivative, our ghost wolf, has created a paradoxical emptiness, an abysmal separation from the greater world that we used to find in other animals, in the land, in the sea and sky.

If narrative occurs in the space between two events, then narratives found, say, in the water between two land masses or in the vacuum between two stars will have been written in languages appropriate to the elements of their compositions, and this language will have preceded human utterance. Humanity has for epochs used narrative to help its navigators remember and track the stars.

"Storied astronomy," as Robert Garfinkle calls it, teaches us that the universe participates in, even dictates, the text; its interpreters aspire to become amanuenses.[1] The ghost wolves projected onto the stars teach us that by mythifying them we may sanctify them. However, if we enslave them in stories that leave no provision for both stars' and wolves' material existences, then we invite terrible consequences—flat earth theory, species extirpation. In the former case, we lose our way in the cosmos. In the latter, the wrath of the ancient world visits us as the guilt and finality of species having left us forever, and the ensuing life we must live without them, including our howling protests that we feel no loss.

About Leif Ericsson's exploration of the North American east coast, Lopez writes: "Out of Ericsson's sight, beneath the southern horizon, south of Libra and Scorpio, was a constellation of 159 stars," its brightest star considered by the Assyrians to be "a sacrificial offering, so that it came to be known as The Victim." One of the names of this constellation was Lupus. Lopez tells an atemporal story here:

> Had Ericsson and his men gone farther south than historians believe they did, been one evening anchored in the Florida Keys, they would have seen a midnight sun burning in the southern sky where Lupus was, the stellar fire of a supernova that took place some time in the year 1006. The chances are good that Ericsson did not see the supernova. The chances are that he regarded the Indians and the trees and the warmth of the seasons and went on his way, knowing not at all what would take place in this new world, what would die here and then be born again. (*Of Wolves and Men*, 277)

Lopez's accomplishment here is to transpose events of two time periods separated by centuries to tell a connective story. His juxtapositions are telling; Lupus is the Victim. Indians are juxtaposed with trees and the elements, the new world with death and rebirth. This arrangement is consistent with what Eliade explains as the attempt, while performing a ritual, to connect with the original cosmogonic acts of the gods in prehistory. Repetition of ritual serves as our presence at the genesis (Eliade, *Myth of the Eternal Return*, 35).

From the scores of North American wolf myths, I have chosen one recorded from among the Pawnee to synthesize with the Greek myth of Orion, a cross-cultural interpretation of an astronomical narrative. According to this reading, the wolf is a long-denied participant in the narrative's creation. The hope of such an act is in the precedent it might set toward a more ecological sense of myth generation. I'll start with some preparation for the comparative work—a brief explanation of storied astronomy.

The Illuminated Page

In *Star-Hopping* Robert Garfinkle retells stories driven by their combination of astronomical classification tables and constellation mythology. His is a dual sign-system of astronomy and myth sometimes creating translucence between one and the other. Consider such a sentence as, "North of Atlas shines his wife Pleione (28 Tau) [3:49; +24d8']." In this one line Garfinkle constructs an inter-disciplinary narrative (64). We reread the names of the Titan Atlas, the Oceanid Pleione, their genders and relationship. We also learn that Pleione is twenty-eighth of the stars in her constellation according to her combination of degree of right ascension (three hours and forty-nine minutes along the celestial equator) and declination (north of the equator at twenty-four degrees, eight minutes along the prime meridian). As stars are ranked by a Greek letter according to their brightness in the constellation, Alpha being the brightest, we know that she does not shine very brightly, being a Tau. But Pleione "shines." The verb invites us to several interpretations. If we read the sentence out of context, we would be unable to tell that Garfinkle is writing about a star except for his use of astro-nomical notation. A woman could be standing north of her husband in the story of the Titans, and the verb "to shine" could have amorous connotations.

Atlas and Pleione have seven daughters of extraordinary beauty who are pur-sued—in one telling of the constellation stories—by the great hunter Orion, who knows exactly where Pleione and her daughters are because of the astronomical notations that follow their names. Synthesizing the stories of the Titan myth, the celestial story that teaches us the positions of the stars, and the story as told in scientific code of where to find the constellation Pleione, superimposes myths upon one another to inform our experience with the raw material from which those myths are derived. The stars were once given "cumbersome Arabic names," replaced in Piccolomini's "inaccurate stellar atlas *De le Stelle Fisse*" with Roman letters, then changed by Bayer in his *Uranometria* with a combination of lower-case Greek and Roman letters and the genitive form of the constellations' Latin names (Garfinkle, 39). We could further historicize this descriptive apparatus, specifying dwarf stars, double stars, and so on, in order to reveal not only a mythic literature but a full context of examination—what theologian Thomas Berry calls the "universe story" (Swimme & Berry).

Pleione has a line of voyeuristic critics behind "her" name, all of whom have located her, gendered her, peered at her through their telescopes, labeled and designated her, ranked her among her fellows. Even in the astronomical nota-tion, she has become *someone*—a star with a story by which we can know and distinguish her from the other stars. Her story was once Arab but now in most of the West is no longer so, unless the reader speaks Arabic or hears the story from a person familiar with Arabic astronomical history. Even among scientists working in the Fertile Crescent, current astronomic designations now conform to Greek mythology, Roman taxonomy, and Italian and German catalogs with all of their cultural co-optation. They do so because of the necessity for global communication among astronomers. We must acknowledge the fecundity of mythic variety that awakens in all human beings a sense of awe, and that this variety originates as much or more significantly in the nonhuman world as in the human mind; indeed it tends to act as a leveler through the displacing nomenclatures of cultures.

Garfinkle's goal is to provide us with a mnemonic device by which we may learn astrophysical phenomena, not to provide a theological explanation of those phenomena. The former goal is storied astronomy, the latter astrology. We do not speak the language of hydrogen atoms as they are compressed into helium, so Garfinkle gives us a lexicon that will at least help us to find our way around the stars, which are dictating his text as clearly as are the ancient Greeks or, as we shall observe, the Pawnee.

Sirius and Artemis

Sirius was called the "Dog Star" because of its proximity to the sun. When in July and August Sirius and the sun were closest, the days were said to be "canicular," named so for Sirius's principality in Canis Major and for its "dogging" the sun.[2] Thus, the star and the dog shared the blame for the intense heat of summer, which during the Middle Ages also meant the season of rampant disease. It may be a hopeful sign that in the United States we now tend to sympathize with the dog on those hot days, and believe the phrase "dog days" simply indicates heat in which a dog pants and lies motionless for comfort. *Sirius* is the Latin derivation of the Greek *Sereos,* or "the scorcher," and indicates a personified source of heat, rather than The Victim. Notice the relevance of the fire persona found in the Fenris myth, which we now find in the story of Orion and his hunting dogs.

The great hunter Orion pursues Taurus, the bull. Sirius is Orion's fierce hunting dog, Procyon his timid one. Aldebaran, the red eye of Taurus, glares back at Orion out of the rage of being hunted. If Orion kills Taurus then he will reach the Pleiades, the seven maidens, and marry them. But unlike what happens with the Death Wolves of Nordic mythology, here the celestial spheres are not consumed toward the end of the world. Orion will never catch the bull, and the constellations will continue to revolve around Polaris in the eternal chase. Rather than the force of wild consumption, Sirius is domesticated, resulting in the paradoxical figures of the Fire Persona and The Victim. Through comparative mythology we may see how this fierce canid came to be tamed.

The domestication of Sirius is complicated, first of all in that the story about to be told here (as well as many another version) leaves out the constellation Lepus, the Hare. This small group of stars is positioned near Canis Major so that Sirius, or for that matter Orion himself, could as easily be chasing a rabbit as a bull. This would not exactly characterize Orion as a hunter worthy of the Pleiades, so the story is written selectively to favor the more formidable Taurus. Second, Sirius is depicted as the manifestation of ferocity—but this only changes the nature of his domestication. Though not the timid house dog chasing a rabbit (this might be Procyon's role), Sirius is still consigned to the role of hunting dog on Orion's quest.

Sirius and Procyon also have companions who have been left out of the myths but included in the astronomical narrative—Sirius B (the Pup) and Procyon B—each of which is a white dwarf operating in a binary system with its larger companion. A white dwarf is created when the gravity of a star exceeds its radiation and compresses it into an intensely hot and massive star, however small and hard to see. The binary relationship is gravitational between stars, so that Sirius is inextricably bound to Sirius B, as Procyon is to Procyon B. Therefore, if we accept the cosmic, cyclical hunt as the narrative of this astronomical story, then we have *four* canid stars traveling together, two of which are pups of the larger two. Now we must deal with the matter of whether or not these canids are *familiaris*.

Sirius's proper astronomical name is Alpha Canis Majoris. The nearby constellation Argo Navis, named for Jason's great ship (which the Arab world knew as Al Safinah, also "The Ship"), once carried the nickname "Noah's Ark." In the 1700s Nicolas Louis de Lacaille separated Argo Navis into several constellations, one of them named Puppis, located next to Canis Major (Garfinkle, 83). When in 1801 Johann Elert Bode published his *Uranographia* he tried to change the name of Puppis to "Officina Typographica" after the printing press, but the canid name won out. Astronomers evidently preferred to let the animals write the story of the cosmos rather than create a cosmic metafiction in which the printing press itself became a character.

As signifier of Sirius's brightness and prominence in the constellation, its astronomical name is self-explanatory. But the use of both "Alpha" and "Majoris" can be read as redundant. Without these titles, "Canis" becomes the chief sign by which we may separate Alpha Canis Majoris from, say, Alpha Centauri (a werebeast itself—part man, part horse). And "Canis" is subject to several sign systems:

most notably the dog (*Canis familiaris*), the wolf (*Canis lupus*), the fox (*Canis vulpes*), the jackal (variously, *Canis aureus, C. adustus, C. mesomelas*) and the coyote (*Canis latrans*). In other words, we haven't quite domesticated this dog, haven't quite made it conform to a single sign system that would limit our interpretations to dog metaphors. We have to choose by some means which canid we see. The myth of Orion dictates that Sirius is a dog or the most ancient of domesticated wolves. However, were we to find an alternative plot of equal and ancient ethos, retaining the characters, we would see a different canid entirely—perhaps the alpha wolf.

The Pawnee Star: Skiritióhuts

For the Skidi Pawnee, the first wolf's arrival on earth resulted in the human fall from grace. According to the Skidi creation legend, the gods forgot to invite the Wolf Star, the brightest star in the heavens, to a great council. The Wolf Star was deeply resentful and sent the first wolf to earth disguised as one of the gods. When the people discovered this ruse they killed the wolf, which infuriated the Wolf Star. He proclaimed that forever after the these Pawnee would be known as the "Skidi," or Wolf People. Moreover, since they had killed the first animal on earth, they had brought war, pestilence, and death upon themselves and would no longer possess immortality (Dorsey, 14; also in Lopez, *Of Wolves and Men*, 133). Lopez explains that the Wolf Star was "red," a color of respect, but a color as well indicating it as Aldebaran rather than Sirius—unless the color designates direction (a conflated function of color in several Native American mythic structures) rather than the star's actual hue; I have to declare some uncertainty here (102).

The Pawnee also called the Wolf Star Tskirixki-tiuhats or Wolf-He-Is-Deceived. They contended that the nighttime howling of wolves increased markedly just before sunrise, about the same time as the appearance of Venus, the Morning Star, and told the story that wolves were deceived into howling at the sun by Sirius's rising in the southeastern sky just before Venus, tricking the wolves into thinking that Venus had risen and the sun was next. In a variant that George Dorsey calls "Lightning Visits the Earth," he transcribes the name of the star as Skiritióhuts, closer to the spelling of the English "Skidi" and noticeably close to both the spelling and pronunciation of the name "Sirius" (14). He translates this name as "Fool-Coyote," which would connect the Skidi more directly to the Coyote figure than to the Wolf in his transcription (16).

In "Lightning Visits the Earth" Skiritióhuts's jealousy is directed toward Tcuperikata, the Bright-Star (likely Venus, though Dorsey does not specify it as such). Bright-Star is the daughter of Tirawa and Vault of the Heavens. Under her command are Wind, Cloud, Lightning, and Thunder. Bright-Star gives several items to Lightning, who is called Piwáruxti, or "The Storm That Comes out of the West" (Lopez, *Of Wolves and Men,* 133) for his journey to earth; one of these items is a sack full of people. The sack is a mist of winds that becomes both Lightning and clouds. At each cardinal direction during his journey (and at several other points), Lightning checks on the people in the sack and is happy with them. Each time Lightning opens the sack he says, "My Father, I feel lonesome. I am about to open the bundle for the people to come out," and its contents, the stars, are flung wide across the universe to make their camps and light their fires. Lightning then walks among them and leaves buffalo between each of his steps for the people to hunt.[3]

The gods all approve of the constellations and allow Lightning to remain on earth. All the stars are happy except Skiritióhuts, who is jealous of Bright-Star. The gods placed beings on the earth; why could he not do so as well, and why had he not been consulted? In this state of jealousy he creates a wolf and commands it to track Lightning.

As Lightning sleeps, the wolf sneaks up and steals the sack (serving as a pillow) from under Lightning's head. He unties the sack to see if something good to eat is inside, and the people emerge to set up their camps. They are confused at the lack of buffalo, since Lightning is not walking among them, and some of them go to see what is wrong. When they awaken Lightning, the wolf panics and runs, but he is killed by the people at the edge of their village. And so the wolf plays the roles of both Trickster and Victim. Lightning explains that they have killed the animal without his consent, and that a ritual must now be performed and a price paid. They are to skin the wolf with its head facing east, dry the skin, tan it, and place it on the sacred bundle with its head toward the north. Connected to the event are two consequences: first, the Pawnee will become mortal; and second, the creature they have killed will multiply. It will be called Thief (Skirihk), and the people known as Skiri, which means "Wolf's Hide" or "Carry-Wolf's-Hide" (Dorsey, 19).

Lightning goes to his brother, Ready-to-Give (Káuwaháru), and has him select a new wolf for the people so that they will not fight among themselves. Lightning and Ready-to-Give climb a mountain and discuss which wolf will suit the people best. A little wolf nearby overhears them and assumes they are talking about him. "You people there, what are you talking about?" he asks. "Do you want to kill me? I am as powerful as you are" (19). This frightens all three of them, and they run in opposite directions. The little wolf runs until he dies. Lightning and Ready-to-Give resolve their positions of power and the map of their residence. Lightning keeps the sack with the remaining people in it; these people are Clouds and Rain and include the daughter of Tirawa, called Rain-Girl, who is seen before the New Moon (20).

The story is similar in many ways to the trickster legends of other cultures, including those of many other North American nations and of the Norse. A kind of loose cousin to the coyote in many stories, the wolf sometimes doubles as a trickster figure, whose role is not the embodiment of sin but of chaos, a force that keeps the gods alert and refines the order of things. The rest of the stars, content with their lot, could not have brought about the origin of the Skidi.

As in the story of the Fenris wolf, it is when the gods attempt to trap chaos and force too strict an order upon the world that tragedy and extermination occur. Indeed, the implication of the name "Wolf People" is that the adoption of a totem is less the ownership of an image than the image doing the possessing. "Do you mean to kill me?" the little wolf asks, but he also anticipates any answer: "I am as powerful as you are." The overcompensation of chaos to correct the gods of order results in a force that exceeds the capacity of the world, and twilight ensues. When the wolf released by Skiritióhuts is killed at the edge of the people's village, symbolically the edge of their world, which is the cosmos, Lightning demands a ritual to restore cooperation to the people. We may be tempted to make a metaphoric Garden of Eden out of the story, but this would be inappropriate to the land ethic of the Pawnee as I understand it. For instance, the *lack* of bison alerts the people to the trick—more a deterministic image of utopia in externalized decline than an image of mere human disobedience.

One thing we may learn from the Pawnee stories is that the Skidi were as capable of generating myths of singular causation as are the descendants of European colonists. For instance, why assume the wolf to be *deceived* by Sirius? Wolves knew of the star's rising before it was named Sirius, when Venus and Earth were recognized in the languages of nonhuman species. It could as easily be assumed that wolves greet the brightest star intentionally with a chorus of howls more mature than premature, and that the day will also be greeted some time later, as will the night, a kill, and the other members of the pack. Through cosmogonic myth we are provided with the clues to the gods' masks. Rejection of those myths keeps us from understanding that a god may sometimes be reborn with a different face.

Fusion

Given the Pawnee and Greek mythology, and the absence of competition from the fox or coyote over this particular star pattern, let us settle on calling Sirius a mythic hybrid: The Dog Star is Alpha Canis Majoris is Skiritióhuts. All are ghost wolves. In the stars we find purity, and in their manifestations on earth we find fault. I'll address later the problems that result from this idea of "the wolf in every dog," but for purposes of the astronomical and cosmogonic arguments, let us accept that Orion's fierce hunting dog is a wolf-dog, a prototypical being, possibly domesticated and possibly not, leading a pack of four more (if we include Puppis) canid stars, three of them named. Sirius is the Alpha of two constellations, as a proto-canid it is a wolf, hybridized here with the dog of myth, hybridized as well between Greek and Pawnee. We might call Sirius a wolf star leading a pack of wolf stars mistaken for dog stars by sailors on the seas of culture.

Consider how, given this reading, the story of the hunt might change. Orion might now be *in the way of* the wolf pack hunting the bull. The dominance of men over the cosmos would be challenged by constellations greater than the sword drawn to kill Taurus or the phallic sword intended for the Pleiades. Indeed, a story corrective of Orion's hubris is perfectly appropriate, as eventually Artemis effects his death, as we will see. And if we read "Sereos," the scorcher, we invite the connection of the Wolf Star to Fenris, the great wolf responsible for consuming the sun and engulfing the lower world in flames before the twilight of the gods. We change the emphasis from the renewal after destruction to the destruction itself. As with the long periods of harmonic balance that continue in a bioregion until a volcano or earthquake institutes a fast and catastrophic change, so too is myth capable of periods of eruption and disequilibrium, and the American wolf myth contains these.

We domesticate the very stars: The North Star is known by a kitchen utensil; the dictation of constellations is known by "houses"; the Wolf Star, that place of creation and divine contention, becomes for sailors the Dog Star—tamed and leashed for the sake of navigation. The Milky Way never was, for the white European, the Pawnee "Wolf Road," the path of the wolf's coming and going from the spirit world (Lopez, *Of Wolves and Men,* 132). Even if we were to disregard Jung's definition of the collective unconscious, the travel of stories among cultures all over the globe should come as no surprise. Both the Babylonian and Blackfoot configured the Pleiades similarly, and both saw its seventh star more easily than can modern societies (Barnard, 46). Both Skidi and Norse *berserkir* watched the wolf pursue the sun and girded themselves as warriors in the ghost wolf's image, donning their bear shirts (from which the name "berserkir" is derived) and wolf belts to stoke their fury and stave off destruction.

Both Greek and Anglo-Saxon storytellers had the propensity to turn wolves into Orion's slaves, into the canicular days of sweat and toil. Some of our journeys and stories of journeys are about merely getting somewhere, and others are about finding our way. A number of our stories of wolves have been about getting somewhere, at which we have now arrived: places empty of anything but human beings and their acquisitions, living under the coronae of city lights that keep us from seeing the constellations.

In one sense, the bestiary of the cosmos has been attributed a kind of power in the schema of the stars; it is the language map by which we navigate. But animals are too often sequestered in such a role, notwithstanding that we have made sure to include a full share of hunters and maidens to maintain anthropic order over a kind of cosmic hunting ground (or, as in astrology, a predictable zoo). We imagine progress on the planet, but still we write stories to keep the wolf from devouring the sun, to render the cosmos static so that humanity will gain and maintain a monopoly over the grand narratives.

In one version of Orion's myth, it is his braggadocio that does him in and ends the great chase. When he announces that he will kill every beast on earth, Artemis hunts him down and commands his own pack to devour him, giving birth to our cliché of the "hunter become the hunted." The story appears in Hesiod and in a different version in Ovid's *Fasti* (v. 539). In *A View to a Death in the Morning,* Matt Cartmill makes the connection between Ovid's version and another in which Artemis kills Orion for making sexual advances (38–40). The corroboration of ecofeminism's position on environmental and sexual conquest, including the rape of the land, should not be missed. Artemis's retribution should also serve as a warning as to what may befall those who brazenly devise the policies of extirpation. Real wolves probably won't attack them. Ghost wolves most certainly will.

CHAPTER NINE

Terra Nova
(In Which the Wolf Discovers North America)

A proverb runs from Plato's *Republic* through Ambrose's *Hexaem,* Vincent of Beauvais's *Physiologus,* Pliny's dismissive interpretation of an "Italian story," Erasmus, and Ben Jonson, to the bestiaries. This proverb says that if a wolf sees you before you see it, you will lose your ability to speak (Robin, 101–2). Both Lopez's *Of Wolves and Men* and Jon Coleman's *Vicious* follow this proverb to its logical conclusion and cultural application—that for whatever reasons, we have projected our own fear, gluttony, and rapacity onto the wolf, and are left speechless to confront ourselves.

The question "What wolf was brought to the New World?" leads to many other questions about cultural dialogue. Because the real wolf was neither introduced to the New World nor humanly encouraged to populate it, neither was the corporeal wolf in literature. To the continent's fifty million human inhabitants in the sixteenth century, the world was ancient, not new, and given that no physical wolves arrived in steerage, the European wolf was rendered by colonists as abstract an invention as the New World itself. And then there they were—wolves, ready to be judged as the devil in the New World, better exorcised than known.

We teach as a basic premise of American literature the quest for a new art, a style and content that would reflect the building of a nation distinguishable from the Old World. Celebrated stories are of James Fenimore Cooper's break from the British novel or Poe's departure from the Blackwood tale. But the project of a new America was, and so is, utterly reliant upon the lore of the Old Countries. Cooper, as "the American Scott," *needed* the British novel to find his way to an American one. The indigenous stories of North American wolves had Greek, Germanic, Anglo, and Nordic forms superimposed upon them through the process of imperialism. But as Richard Slotkin points out, invaders of the New World were willing, out of either necessity or interest, to take on practices of the invaded, such as guerrilla warfare, the corn harvest, hunting techniques, and names (55, 177, and his chap. 6). What occurred between pagan Celto-Germanic and Christian British cultures is reflective of the tensions between polytheistic and Christian cultures revealed in American wolf stories.

Black Wolves

I'll begin with two tales recorded by George Bird Grinnell, one attributed to the Blackfoot and one to the Cheyenne. The Blackfoot legend, which Grinnell calls "The Wolf-Man" in his *Blackfoot Lodge Tales,* begins this way: "There was once a man who had two bad wives" (78). In order to teach his wives to "be good," the man moves their lodge far from the Blackfoot camp. After the move he climbs up to a high butte, sits on a bison skull there, and watches for both bison and enemies. But his enemies are at home. In no small part because they are lonely living apart from the camp, the wives plot to kill him. One night they dig a pit beneath the bison skull on the butte, then cover the pit and replace the skull. When the man climbs to his place and sits down, he falls into the pit. The wives pack up everything and return to the camp, whereupon they feign mourning and lament that their husband was lost on a hunting trip.

A wolf finds the wounded husband in the pit, calls the other animals to gather around, and declares, "Here is a fallen-in man. Let us dig him out, and we will have him for our brother" (79). The wolf pulls the man from the pit and takes him to live with the wolf pack. An old blind wolf heals the man's wounds and in the process turns his head and hands to those of a wolf. After living with the pack, the man tells them of the secret places where the snares guarding the food are set. He springs the snares for them, and the pack takes the meat from the camp.

After several such thefts, the people at the camp finally hide their stores and put out for the wolves "the meat of a scabby bull" (80). When the man finds this cache, he howls, and the people in camp recognize him as a "man-wolf." They catch him, and in the light of the fire they realize who it is. He tells them his wives' plot against him, and the camp lets him decide their fate. The wives are given to a spirit and never seen again.

The other tale is from Grinnell's *By Cheyenne Campfires* and appears as well in Casey and Clark's *Tales of the Wolf,* from which I will cite it, partly because of the editors' introduction to the tale, especially their observation that the "symbolic richness and depth of this story rival any traditional European legends about wolves" (35). The story is called "Black Wolf and His Fathers." In it, the father of a handsome boy decides that when the camp moves away, the family will stay where they are. The father is tired of the trouble caused by all the young girls who want to marry the boy. On the assumption that the boy thinks himself too good for them, two of these girls decide to punish him for the family's decision. Every evening the boy sits on a hill upon a buffalo robe; under this robe the girls dig a pit and trap the boy in precisely the same way as the Blackfoot wives do in "The Wolf-Man."

The boy's mother assumes that the boy has gone to catch up with the rest of the camp, which has moved on (she chastises the father for not having the sense to have done the same). The family leaves. Meanwhile, the two girls have secretly doubled back from the traveling camp to visit the hole in which the boy lies. At this point we find out that his name is Black Wolf. The girls steal his robe, pelt him with bison bones until he is wounded in several places, and leave.

Two wolves happen by, one a large white wolf who wants to adopt the boy and the other a "mad wolf" who wants to eat him. They dig down toward the bottom of the pit, racing each other to reach him. The boy knows their separate plans. Using the bison bones with which he was wounded, he begins digging himself out toward the white wolf's incoming tunnel. In this way, the white wolf wins and claims the boy. Thereafter, the two wolves continually argue about the boy, the white wolf always winning the rhetorical contest and the mad wolf (at this point in the story he is called "rabid") becoming increasingly frustrated.

The pack to which these two wolves belong is also evenly divided, black and white; four wolves look and act exactly like the white wolf and four are "cross and ugly" (38). The day before they reach the pack, the white wolf gives the boy a new robe of wolf hide, which the boy wears for the night. The competition between the white and mad wolf finally reaches a point at which the mad brother plans retribution. The white wolf predicts exactly what form this revenge will take and concocts a plan of defense with the boy named Black Wolf.

The mad wolf demands that in order to be accepted, the boy must be able to pick out his wolf father (the white wolf) from among all the other wolves in a kind of shell game both physical and intellectual. If he fails, he is to be eaten. White Wolf and Black Wolf have devised between them a signing system of winking, ear-twitching, toe-wiggling, and tail-switching that tips off the boy each time he must choose, and he passes the test. The pack accepts him as one of their own, fits him with bow and arrows, and makes him a warrior.

Eventually, a wolf of the pack is wounded by an arrow. Black Wolf heals the wounded pack member and goes to spy on the camp of the humans, who have returned (probably for the hunting season). He is seen by his human father but escapes. The next day, when the wolf pack goes to feed on the bison carcasses left by the Cheyenne hunters, Black Wolf is captured and taken to the human camp. At first he resists, but he is calmed by his father's voice. Here we have an invocation of an interspecies captivity narrative, differing from the standard captivity narrative and from the animal domestication story but gesturing to both through a third tropic tale, that of the feral child.

The wolf pack falls into mourning. One of them approaches the human camp and howls to the boy from a distance, telling him that the pack will surround the human camp, charge it, and free him. In order to stop the bloodshed, Black Wolf negotiates with both the wolves and the Cheyenne. In short, the plan is to cut in half the two girls who tormented Black Wolf and feed the four parts to the wolves (it's implied that only the mad wolves will be fed), who will then spare the camp if Black Wolf agrees to live with his wolf fathers for part of the year and with the Cheyenne for the remainder (43).

Grinnell's "Black Wolf" never presents the boy's transformation as physical. He becomes a wolf through learning how to communicate and live with the pack, not through magic. It calls to mind Kipling, whose *Jungle Books* would not be written until a quarter of a century after Grinnell's work, and about other colonized Indians. We have in the Cheyenne tale more of a wolf-child legend than a traditional shape-shifter legend, but the end is similar—the wolf's mythic status is affirmed by plausible incidents (rabies, pack activity, the captivity narrative and "going native," negotiated predation between human and wolf, migratory life based on seasonal change) toward a plotline of betrayal and retribution.

The World-Wolf transcends even the misogyny of the tales by pointing to the complexities of interspecific relationships in a way that contests sexism as a deficiency very like anthropocentrism—a deficiency of "human nature." Several elements commonly used to romanticize both wolf and Indian are also debunked; for instance, only the rabid or "mad" wolves (as opposed to all wolves) are credited with eating human flesh. One of the Cheyenne shoots an arrow into a wolf for reasons not given, and the wolves "steal" meat from the camp: There is no ecotopian notion of the share-and-share-alike policy until the plausible eco-political arrangement reached at the end. The story is both a moral tale for Cheyenne and a global myth demonstrating how difficult it is for humans to coexist with other species (and, allegorically, each other).

The global aspect is found in the remarkable similarity between the Blackfoot legend and the European "false wife's tale" (for example, the French *lai* "Bisclavret"), and both Blackfoot and Cheyenne tales share certain elements with tales from the Arthuriad. We have the healing of the man's wounds by the pack, a lupine version of the roundtable knights Sirs Alphouns, Marrok, and Urry, a tale from the collective unconscious.

In the Blackfoot tale as Grinnell tells it, the "man-wolf" is not changed back to a fully human being. He is apparently accepted by the camp in his werewolf form, an anomaly among European werewolf tales but consistent with many shamanic traditions, including the Irish Saint Ailbe, who purportedly had a wolf's claw on one hand.[1] The similarity of the two tales, and the similarities of both of them to Marrok's tale in *Le Morte Darthur* (which I analyze in chapter 11), raises the question of how much Grinnell may have told these stories under the influence of the legends of his own culture's history. Regardless, the realization of a shared mythos could have contributed to a negotiation of the European presence on the continent. Instead, the history of U.S. anti-Cheyenne policy testifies to how little valued was the commonality of narratives in the opportunity of conquest.

Even today the apologetics of such works as *The Ecological Indian,* some of the pieces in William Cronon's *Uncommon Ground,* and Callicott and Nelson's *The Great New Wilderness Debate* seek to prove what is irresponsible in the Indian and progressive in the modern European, glossing over certain fundamentals of measuring progress: that among Native American nations there were thriving populations of bison (among other species); healthier ecosystems and nomadic patterns that preserved them; cooperation as well as conflict; cleaner air and water; more *forests* (ridiculous assertions of the great number of trees we now have demonstrate the flawed ecological thought of which I speak); population control; and an understanding of the human species as one among, rather than one apart. Yes, they lacked modern dentistry. I'm glad we have it. Why, though, do we cite our benevolent modern acts in order to justify our malevolent ones and take up the sword against primitivism? Applied directly to the nation's ecosystems, this non sequitur seems to have done little good.

In his impressive compendium of literary references to animals, Rod Preece comments on the similar hostility he perceives from both the Cheyenne and European toward the wolf:

> It is notable that in the Cheyenne myth the wolf is as despised as the white man, and as despised as its traditional European counterpart too, as indicated not only by the fairy tale of *The Three Little Pigs* but by the philosopher Immanuel Kant who tells us that when we observe how great is the care animals give to their young it is difficult for us to be cruel in thought to them—and then adds: "even to a wolf." (11)

Preece's inclination to compare Cheyenne and European hostility comes from a line from George Dorsey's 1905 account of the Cheyenne creation myth: "The white people with long beards were in a class with the wolf, for both were the trickiest and most cunning creatures in that beautiful world" (Preece, 9).

Some unraveling is order. First, the classification of white people and wolves here does not strike me as hostile, but a far more complex and magnanimous consideration of the trickster's role in the cosmic order. There is no indication in either the creation myth or the trickster tales that the wolf's conflation with the white-bearded white man demonizes either. European imposition is what does this.

More importantly, Kant's reluctant acquiescence to the wolf as another animal in the grand order says as much about his transcendental idealism—and perhaps Continental philosophy's persistent tendency to fetishize it—as it does about wolves. The abstracted conundrum over existence and language's access to it has obfuscated the material referent, to the point of only reluctantly, if ever, acknowledging it. This is the perversion, at least forward from Descartes's assumptions about animals' lack of consciousness or Claude Lévi-Strauss's statement "Animals are good to think with."[2] What Preece absorbs is the collision of myths in North America that puts him in this bind of trying to puzzle out where the hostility toward the wolf actually lies.

The Winnowing Fork

Richard Hakluyt's *The Principal Navigations, Voyages, Traffiques, and Discoveries of the English Nation* and Thomas Harriot's *A Brief and True Report of the New Found Land of Virginia* (both 1600) were published almost exactly at the center of the century dividing Copernicus's defense of the heliocentric solar system and the advent of Newtonian physics. The early 1600s was an explosive period for what was then called natural philosophy. Hakluyt's and Harriot's works not only initiated those crossing the Atlantic to the language of cosmic destiny in regard to colonization but also remained influential for some time, even inspiring such ecologically complex works as *Notes on the State of Virginia* and *Moby-Dick*. They also acted as central texts toward the merging of clinical knowledge (through navigation and observation of natural phenomena) with ruminative knowledge about the wild world being domesticated and nationalized.

The New England colonists were as determined in their efforts to get rid of the wolf at the table as they had been back in England. Holinshed and Malory had made some telling decisions on how much of Merlin's sylvanism to include in their Anglicization of the French tales, and pagan legends diluted during the Reformation left puritan heretics with plenty of options for curtailing the mystic nature of their faith. By the time they carried the Arthurian and other legends over the Atlantic, they had purged their mythology of much of its wildness. Indeed, it was one of the only things the so-called Puritans of the Reformed or Calvinist persuasions could find in common with Congregationalists, Trinitarians, and those loathed Latinate Catholics. But wildness has a way of resurfacing, however submerged it may have been, because, like all mythic forces and basic natural laws, it is more powerful than we can control.

In 1600 the intrinsic value of the life of an animal was based on the supposed quality of its soul. A domestic animal was surely designed by God for human enjoyment or consumption; its malleability was the result of its more divine nature. With a very few mythified exceptions (such as the eagle), a wild animal was designed as a moral challenge, as were all things of the wilderness, the place where one went to be tested and to prevail through God's inspiring transcendence of Nature.[3] This notion in itself could have been the basis of an ecologically sustainable ethic and practice (as it had been, generally speaking and against current revisionist efforts to declare otherwise, for American Indian nations). Unfortunately, anthropocentric spiritualism, conceived by narcissists calling themselves "the godly," was still a long way from being adequately challenged by anthropocentric naturalism. For example, Descartes had not yet posited the modern self (with its attendant blind spots regarding other species), nor had Locke contributed the material for natural rights to function either apart from or in some cooperation with God-ordained law. In this respect, both northern and southern American colonists shared at least one view challenged only by the utopianists, whom they effectively pilloried: the view that wilderness was inherently evil because its inhabitants were inherently evil.

Over the generations of Winthrop, the Mathers, and the pre-Revolutionaries, given the absence of ecological sensibilities in the interest of enlightened policy making, divine right would manifest itself in confrontation with a demonized wilderness. Political and cultural thought was constructed over a religious lagoon in which swam the monsters of the pre-Enlightenment mind. Even reason, the principle tool of the natural philosopher, would subject itself to massive assumptions about wildlife and land. The colonists chose to cling to proto-Cartesian ideas without evidence in order to exploit the more-than-human world and minimize guilt over the act (Orr, 93). Many of the seventeenth century's faith-based assumptions about the nonhuman world were so powerful (and so convenient) that they persist today: in creationism or so-called intelligent design; in laws regarding the ownership and treatment of animals; in the romance of the pastoral shepherd that became the romance of the cowboy; and in attitudes about certain animals being more inherently evil than others.

When I spoke about this with Hank Fischer, the writer of *Wolf Wars* and one of the most important figures working for Defenders of Wildlife, he said, "Well, you know our myths about wolves are economically generated" (Fischer interview). It's easy to interpret this comment as influenced by Fischer's own position of negotiating the wolf's preservation through economic means. However, it might prove useful to consider that the wolves of myth were not simply brought to North America and applied to economic policy, but that New World economic policy helped in a large way to create American nature mythology. Before the European invasions of the continent, the land teemed with bison and wolves without evidence to suggest that wolves "ruined the livelihood" of the Cheyenne, Kiowa, White Mountain Apache, or any other tribe. In the 1990s one wolf-killed calf (or a calf imagined to have been killed by a wolf) might result in lawsuits against the federal government, mass mailings to stockgrowers' associations, and smear campaigns against environmentalists.

To the extent that our myths may be economically generated, they are profane. They profane such matters as race, class, gender, and certainly ecological awareness, since the nonhuman world can be neither assuaged nor assessed by money. The wheat on a penny is no longer wheat. Behind racist allusions to other species, and vice versa, is the assumption that somewhere removed from the oppressor is an animal that really exists as the oppressor envisions it. The real subject may then be forced away toward this ghost animal. Finding out that no such animal exists does not necessarily stop the process; on the contrary, a new and often more evangelical agenda emerges. The real animal in question is forced to conform to the mental image of it, then fitted with a price tag.

The early colonies operated in large part according to a barter system that relied heavily on animal pelts. Although the wolf is a "furbearer" by trade standards, its pelt value varied from luxuriously expensive to dirt cheap. In *The War against the Wolf* Rick McIntyre catalogs many of the laws governing wolf hunting (several of which laws are also cited in the works of Lopez, Mech, and Busch). One of the most telling was passed in 1638 in the Massachusetts Bay Colony. The equivalent of twenty-seven days' wage for an average laborer was paid out for one wolf pelt (29). Even as capital incentives go, this would be considered pork-barrel generosity today, and given that wolf pelts were not particularly suitable for fashion, the price tag indicates other motives. In league with the clearing of forests and massive trapping efforts for barter, policies of wolf extermination through habitat and prey depletion as well as shooting them on sight were set for many decades to come. Both companies and governments were willing to pay well in order to make themselves God's only appointed hunters.

Another facet of interspecific control that used the old British models despite the quest for an American identity was sport hunting. "In their consumate form," writes Thomas Lund, "the English game laws ensured that the poor could neither consume game, nor interfere with the beasts that ravaged their crops" (19). Sport hunting became a major debate in the colonies because of its potential to reinstate certain feudal rights of the landed gentry as to who would be allowed to hunt and where. During this debate an important and subtle shift in logic took place. The stronger motive for establishing hunting privileges in Britain (which were being considered in America) was not the preservation of an ecological system according to its rules and boundaries. It was British land law, a convoluted arrangement built on chaotic interpretations of property rights.

The sport hunting debate reached its zenith with William Blackstone and Edward Christian in 1772 and the rejection of the landowner take system in colonial America (Lund, 21). While establishing an "American" social policy, and admirably contributing in some small ways to Jefferson's revision of Locke's list of rights from "property" to "the pursuit of happiness," the work of Blackstone and Christian also provided the facade of plenty-for-all by allowing loose game hunting laws to sell themselves on the grounds of personal freedom, which was supposed to control crop depletion in deference to market concerns. In effect, these laws ravaged ecosystems. Two famous examples of environmental destruction—the passenger pigeon extinction and the Dust Bowls—can be seen as ecological ignorance rationalized through allegiance to property rights.

On the other hand, the monetary standard by itself is insufficient to gauge the wolf's mythic value, belying, for instance, the pelt's ceremonial and practical worth. Skidi Pawnee and Cheyenne hunters donned wolf hides to approach enemy camps or bison herds, as made famous in George Catlin's painting *Buffalo Hunt under the Wolf Skin Mask* (Lopez, *Of Wolves and Men*, 96). Wolf skins and tails were as important to the ceremonies of scores of North American nations as vestments and mitres have been to European ones. The fur is extremely warm as well, but too coarse and hard to manipulate easily for consumerist fashion. To wear a wolf is either a ritual act or a smug advertisement of exploitation.

Witch-Hunting in a Bountiful Land

The result of the cornucopian ideal was the much-celebrated and biblically justified domestication of land, which developed into the more problematic ownership model that vivisected land. The status given to such figures as Israel Putnam in Connecticut militarized the bounty system against wolves, which provided an economic job base generating national respect and legendary status for figures of wilderness prowess such as Daniel Boone, Davy Crockett, and Buffalo Bill. Like the cowboy, the wolfer grew into something bigger than he really was, while the wolf became the fictitious measure of economic failure for the farmer/rancher and ecological failure for bioregional systems. The wolf also became more individualized, each outlaw of the ranchlands gaining some degree of infamy and the magic of a name.

Colonial hunting systems were breakneck, unleashed according to a holy obsession to tame the wild, until the negative impact on game populations made colonists realize that laws needed to be instituted, at least seasonally, to regulate hunting so as to prevent eradication. Of course, the stated logic of this was that the wolves were to blame for the prey losses, a logic that persisted through the 1990s (Fogleman, 70, 84; Easthouse, "Johnson: Wolf Could 'Devastate,'" A1). It is ironic that the rebuttal used by economic conservatives against wolf reintroduction programs operates on precisely the opposite premise those same conservatives use against environmental "alarmism." The rebuttal is crisis language (wolves will ruin us) that declares crisis language (the environment is in danger) inappropriate and unfounded.

Early colonial writers had no shortage of fantastic ideas or boldness regarding mythic appropriation. Peter Kalm's otherwise respectable naturalism supported nonscientific colonial assumptions about the agrarian model, a model that worked only in timbered, watered, and fertile ground. It also worked insofar as the indigenous inhabitants of the land were displaced and ignored and the crop or corral was partitioned in the British style. In the western regions, as explained by Walter Prescott Webb in his 1934 *The Great Plains* (later reiterated by Wallace Stegner, Marc Reisner, and Charles Wilkinson), the model failed spectacularly. As per classic Euro–North American self-reliance, the yeoman farmer who failed in the West was picked up, dusted off, and recast as the pioneer hero, cattle baron, or rail baron (even these titles couldn't quite escape the lexicon of British feudal law). With the war versus native tribes came the usurpation of indigenous mythologies and the selective assimilation of the elements in them that Euro-Americans found most palatable or entertaining. Such appropriation then watered down the spiritual depth and complexity of native belief systems and their practice and sold it on roadsides.

Some of the methods by which the bounty laws were written, enforced, and cheated would be humorous were the cruelty and ultimate goal in their practice not so horrifying and sad. For example, Nathaniel Shurtleff's *Records of the Governor and Company of Massachusetts Bay,* an oft-cited document in histories of the North American wolf, accounts for the 1645 repeal of a law that delivered cash payments to white landowners for killing wolves and paid several tribes "one bushel of Indian corn or 3 quarts of wine" per wolf (McIntyre, *War,* 30). In 1668 eighteen tribes in the Bay Colony region were taxed in wolf heads, each tribe assigned a number of heads to be delivered according to the number of "Bowmen or hunters" in their bands; the assessment amounted to 145 wolves a year (McIntyre, *War,* 34). Rick McIntyre's *War against the Wolf* is still the best compendium of such material.

Brother Wolf

There is a way to kill a story and resurrect it so that we create a kind of monster, one continually redevouring the old story it misrepresents (as the dog returns to its vomit, so the saying goes). After a while the old story is no longer recognizable, and only the ghost wolf remains, from which we may learn, but in which learning there is tremendous risk. An example relevant to New World mythological and literary history is the story of Kluskap and his brother Malsum, the wolf. In order to account for the complex context of the story in a short space, I am forced to paraphrase both a version of it by Charles Godfrey Leland and the work on that version of Thomas Parkhill, who explains in great detail the cultural fallout of the story's treatment over time.

We cannot know precisely what version of the Kluskap-Malsum story was told among the Maliseet; Leland calls the story "Of Glooskap's Birth, and of His Brother Malsum, the Wolf" and claims it to be critically significant to the worldviews of the Abenaki and Micmac.[4] His version is roughly as follows:

Fraternal twins have a discussion in their mother's womb of how they should be born. Malsum, who is a wolf, decides not to wait for nature to take its course and bursts from his mother's side, killing her. Leland calls the second twin "Glooskap" (I will call the character Kluskap, following Parkhill's spelling, throughout), who emerges after this violent action on the part of his brother. Once born, the twins decide to trade an important piece of information: what single weapon might kill each of them. Kluskap says that he can be killed by an owl feather. Malsum says that he can be killed by a fern root. In time, overcome by evil, Malsum decides to kill his brother. He hits him with an owl feather, only to find that Kluskap lied. Although angry, Kluskap tells Malsum that a pine root is really what is needed. Malsum tries and is tricked again. Eventually, Beaver reveals Kluskap's secret, that a cattail is required, but Kluskap is listening in on the conversation. When his brother comes to kill him, Kluskap pulls out a fern root and strikes Malsum dead, then laments his death.

Leland's version of the story appeared in 1884, in his work as a folklorist on tales rooted in older traditions, and he likely took liberties with at least this legend. Parkhill's contemporary scholarship seeks to recover the legend from Leland's and subsequent writers' misinformation, including "an outrageous example" of poor scholarship that resulted from the mauling of the Kluskap-Malsum story—"a book that, using Leland's stories as a primary source, purports to prove that Kluskap was really a fourteenth-century Orkney nobleman named Henry Sinclair who overwintered in Nova Scotia" (61). Kluskap is a significant figure among several tribes in America and takes on various manifestations. The legend itself, whatever its status or structure in the Abenaki's corpus of mythology, existed at the time of colonial invasion from Europe and was stumbled into by those colonists.

The temptation for comparative analysis (for instance, to the story of Cain and Abel) is overwhelming, but Parkhill warns against this as premature, given our scant knowledge of the tale's origin. Several significant North American (actually Euro-Canadian) perspectives may be influencing this transformer twins legend, including: a story that may have had some early influence over Maliseet culture in New Brunswick and Nova Scotia and Abenaki culture into Maine; Leland's Euro-Canadian revision of that story; Parkhill's story of finding information about Leland's revision and its effects on several cultures, including those mentioned in point #1; and a kind of metanarrative of the legend's effects on a North American reader's conceptualization of the wolf.

Parkhill also uncovers an overstatement accepted by several scholars as to how much cultural influence the Kluskap-Malsum legend wielded in early cultures. His finding is that Leland's revision of an earlier Kluskap-Malsum story has detrimentally affected the last century of Abenaki, Maliseet, Micmac, Penobscot, Passamaquoddy, and Euro-Canadian cultures because some teachers within the tribes adopted the Leland version over the more reliable narratives from which the story originates (Parkhill interview).

In the Grinnell analyses noted earlier in this chapter, my point was to provide the comparative possibilities of stories perhaps similarly constructed among European and North American tribes even before their meeting. Grinnell's work was (and is still) respected cross-culturally, bolstered by his solid reputation in the communities he visited. With the Leland-Parkhill stories my goal is to demonstrate, through Parkhill's thorough analysis, consequences that may occur through the application of sifted, revised, and appropriated stories. And I am juxtaposing the Grinnell and Parkhill analyses in order to provide working examples of the ghost wolf's transcontinental, plausibly archetypal, influence on what seems to be the collective unconscious. Short of that bold a claim, we still have the significance of colliding wolf myths. Also at stake, as it always is in writing about wolves, is the issue of veracity, of what it means to tell the truth about the wolf when wolves are not allowed to tell the truth about themselves.

What Parkhill finds in Leland constitutes a study in remythologizing. In addition to a few relatively minor spelling offenses ("Malsum" instead of Malsunsis, the anglicized "Glooskap" instead of Kluskap or Glooskabe for the proper phonetics), several of Leland's mistakes are pointed out as having far-reaching effects. According to Parkhill, Leland fits the tale with nineteenth-century European morality, emphasizing a Manichean good/evil structure that did not exist in the original. Leland then ascribed far more importance to the Kluskap-Malsum story than existed in Abenaki or Micmac cultures (originally it was actually a Maliseet legend) and gave prominence to the same story in Penobscot and Passamaquoddy cultures, in which it may well have meant very little (61). In this way, Parkhill claims, Leland rewrote sacred history.

The first unfortunate result is that Leland's study was exceedingly popular during the late nineteenth century. The second is that Joseph Campbell, in reading scholarship that followed Leland's lead, wrote in his *Historical Atlas of World Mythology* that the story exhibits "the basic myth of aboriginal America: the Contending Twins" (47, 63n6). And so a new monster was unleashed in contemporary North America; a popular nineteenth-century study selectively edited to conform to Leland's moral sensibilities was endorsed and repeated by one of the most widely read mythologists in North America (reprints of the *Historical Atlas* carried the Leland version as late as 1989). This is not to discredit Campbell's work, which is formidable. And, to a degree, Campbell's linking the legend to the twins myth is utterly defensible. Parkhill's point, and mine here, is that the wolf in the story as it is read through Eurocentric eyes becomes a character in a Western bifurcation fallacy, with the emphasis on contention. Malsum is the wolf of danger that appears in all of our popular adages about sheep's clothing or being at the door or having it by the ears, the Cain or Jacob of the biblical deception story.

Parkhill cites the irony that later generations of Micmac students, wanting to connect more with their heritage, have turned to the Kluskap-Malsum legend told in its Manichean version (Parkhill, "Of Glooskap's Birth," 61). Because of its Canadian popularity in the works of such writers as Kay Hill, teachers in Canadian Indian schools have taught the stories in such a way as to raise the veracity argument at times without even knowing they are doing so. The fin-de-siècle Nature Fakers controversy affected the public reception of purportedly nonfictional works given to questionable ecological plausibility—but not much. That debate was over what strictures should be placed on art regarding verisimilitude versus the latitude given artists when making claims about verifiable, material reality. A subjective truth often won out over fact as the result of an argument in which the subjective truth *regarded* fact—a twist on the fallacy of prejudicial judgment. Here, in the Kluskap-Malsum story's cultural context, we see a similar problem. Parkhill explains that not only schoolchildren but also Abenaki and Micmac cultures have, to a point, appropriated the Leland story, although the traditionalists among them, as well as among the Penobscot and Passamaquoddy, give no real credence to the story (62). Ultimately, Leland's project managed to obfuscate scholarship, native self-understanding, and non-native understanding of native cultures.

If we are to talk about and teach "early American literature," then these discrepancies are a significant part of what we must discuss. Students who engage the complexities of historical revision and postcolonialism and the evolution of narratives over time will sell themselves short without a basic understanding of the participating land and species in those stories, because colonialism depends upon regionalized conflict and assumptions about nature. In short, we need to know when a wolf's a wolf and when it's not. Otherwise, when one appears in a narrative that we want to historicize, our ignorance of the nonhuman may ruin our work, whatever political position we seek to defend and expand.

The Howling West

In a superb brief history of the wolf in the United States, Valerie Fogleman tracks the course of misperception about wolves and supplies substantial research to account for the policies enacted against them. She states that the lack of interaction with wolves in Europe after the early 1500s was a "major reason" for the extermination campaigns in the colonies (64). This lack, according to Fogleman, encouraged fantasies about wolves in the minds of those who became colonists for the Virginia Company. Although reasonable, this assessment is perhaps a bit reductive. Killing wolves had been common practice in Europe over centuries when Europeans lived in clear and prolonged exposure to them—and in fact resulted in the following prolonged lack of exposure to them. And the move westward in America seems to have provided its share of wolf encounters. In other words, fantasies thrived even in the presence of real wolves. In New England, to reiterate Hank Fischer's assessment, even Cotton Mather acknowledged that wolves posed no more than an economic threat to human beings (Silverman, 245–47). The type and degree of profanement seem to change according to the type and degree of ecological attunement built into the environments of human systems.

Fogleman touches on the paradox of early Euro-American thinking about the wolf: that under any conditions of economic hardship or prosperity, exposure to or distance from wildlife, and/or apparent spiritual reward or punishment, Puritan ideas about wolves fundamentally maintained the constructions of the medieval bestiaries. She notes that "the animal hated and feared by generations of Americans was—and still is—merely a figment of the imagination based on countless tales and horror stories," and this fear and hatred cannot be attributed strictly to a lack of exposure to wolves (63). The fear has to do mainly with the early ghost wolf disseminated by colonial clerical and economic powers—a consistently malevolent version. Fogleman offers another indication of the World-Wolf model at work: "Real wolves," she writes, "in fact, barely resemble the popular perception of them" (64). The real and corporeal wolf—these are fundamental to Fogleman's report. Tellingly, she finds them by chasing the ghosts that outlasted real wolves in most of the United States. The wolf of literature was kept in a near-exclusively wicked position until it was revised in the 1830s with the rise of nature writers capable of reenvisioning wilderness both as and beyond the garden. Scientists affected this rescue as well, even those who sought biological predictability. These influences led to the slow rise of the corporeal wolf in literature and to the more refined examination of literature through an ecological consciousness.

Richard Slotkin devotes a significant section of *Regeneration through Violence* to Indianization, a process deeply feared by the entrenched powers of religion and government, by which a civilized human being might "go native" and leave the protective sphere of God and nation.[5] The complexities of this social dynamic are too numerous to list here, but they included the dubious elevation of trailblazers as social leaders; an empathy for tribal mores (such as practical dress) that threatened European-based codes of fashion, literally uniform; and, importantly, the conflation of the feral with the demonic in the Protestant (especially Calvinist) mind. The "state of mind that was prevalent throughout New England," writes Slotkin, "notably a belief that the Indians enjoyed a special and more-than-human relationship with nature, which gave them a demonic power," strongly fueled the debate with pioneers who were "capable of living on terms of ease with the wilderness and with Indian neighbors" (119). The wolf's role in this "Indianization" goes back to Mather's charge to make of the "howling wilderness" a "fruitful field" and to hunt down the Indians "like wolves," a comparison favored as well by Jonathan Edwards and Solomon Stoddard.[6] The fight against Indianization by every religious sect in the colonies was prototypical of the expansion strategies used to conquer the prairies when the eastern agrarian project began to fail.

Crossing Wolf Country

Had Francis Parkman abandoned law school and continued along the Oregon Trail in the fall of 1846, he probably would have left Fort Laramie to cross the Black Hills, pressed through the winter along the Snake River, over the Cascades, and into either Fort Vancouver or Portland proper, where he would have stopped at the ocean and gazed at the "swells" to which he had compared the hills of the prairies.[7] As a result, the book he published three years later from his youthful journals might have been considerably different. His first title, *The California and Oregon Trail: Being Sketches of Prairie and Rocky Mountain Life,* belies the journey he in fact undertook, which only partly covered the Oregon Trail, well short of the California's first independent spur, and angled down along the Santa Fe Trail. Indeed, his adventure to the prairies was to the ecology he liked least; he returned to cherished forests near Harvard, about which he wrote late in his life. Parkman's view of wildlife, particularly of predation, was consistent with Cooper's, a touristic fantasy that the wilderness was indeed a great place for those who were great marksmen—the same romance that anticipated Roosevelt's western adventures and his diatribes against "the beast of waste and desolation."[8]

The predator that Parkman most often mentions in his story, and for which he seems to harbor the greatest animosity, is the wolf. His reactions to wolves during his trip were so strong that they actually contribute something of use to our understanding of the Boston Brahmin histories written during the American Renaissance (Parkman, *Journals;* see also Wade, 446). Parkman's sentiments were representative of the famous cadre of Harvard adventurers; when one tree too many fell in the White Mountains he wrote to Congress and published an article about it in the *Atlantic.* But if the wolf had died out within the borders of America, it seems from his writings that Parkman would have lost no sleep. We might consider these predilections to be in part the results of a classical education.

Sojourns in the White Mountains were undertaken to rejuvenate students (on one, Parkman exhausted his hiking companion), to challenge them, and to teach them about the land around "Old Harvard," however far that land might stretch (Koelsch, 362, 365). Some students returned to their studies with the sophomoric assurance that they now understood and had conquered nature, others (usually prior to the 1840s) with the humility of having climbed Mount Washington to "contemplate the work of God in nature" (366). *The Oregon Trail* suggests the former conviction.

John J. Audubon was a staple in Francis Parkman's reading, along with Cooper, whose Leatherstocking saga Parkman claimed to have found "difficult to separate . . . distinctly from the recollections of my own past experiences" (Dekker & McWilliams, 248). He refers often in *The Oregon Trail* to his guide, Henry Chatillon, as "Leatherstocking," and clearly set out from Cambridge for the prairie in part because he wanted to see the places about which Cooper had written. As in Audubon's work, a strange ambivalence arises in Parkman's project: "Should any one of my readers ever be impelled to visit the prairies . . . I can assure him that he need not think to enter at once upon the paradise of his imagination" (68). Parkman continues in this often-cited passage to delineate the disappointments of the prairie, particularly regarding the "beautiful" and "picturesque."[9]

However, in the middle of the passage, he retreats to a neutral corner. "If he has a painter's eye," Parkman says of the plains traveler, "he may find his period of probation not wholly void of interest. The scenery, though tame, is graceful and pleasing. Here are level plains, too wide for the eye to measure; green undulations, like motionless swells of the ocean; abundance of streams, followed through all their windings by lines of woods and scattered groves" (69).

Parkman begins by qualifying his interest, but as the passage continues he lets himself deliver a little praise for the West he came in retrospect to appreciate. The language here is similar to the reserved machismo of Roosevelt, who also tried in his travel writing to simultaneously celebrate his excursions and project an air of professional detachment that would separate him from the tourist. In passages that gesture to both Bryant's poem "The Prairies" and Cooper's *The Prairie,* Parkman incorporates the sea metaphor. He places the wolves in an oceanic "vast plain" that "waved with tall rank grass, that swept our horses' bellies; it swayed to and fro in billows with the light breeze . . . the hairy backs of [wolves] alternately appearing and disappearing as they bounded awkwardly along." His reaction is hardly like Bryant's, however: "I dismounted," Parkman writes, "and amused myself with firing at the wolves" (112).

Here, as in his activities of the following day, Parkman turns away from his brief ruminations to a grim realism. He considers the youthful efforts of an eighteen-year-old immigrant traveler to dig two wolf pups out of their den not cruel but beneath him (112). He also describes two "Indian" boys (likely Dakota) chasing and shooting at a wolf (172). The incident contradicts noble-savage thinking, and for Parkman it affirms both the violent tendencies of Indians and the universal justification to fire at will at a wolf.

While it is tempting to attribute such sensibilities to the immature pen of a college student in his rite of passage, Parkman's later writing suggests otherwise. Wilbur Jacobs may be the only critic to credibly position Parkman somewhere between Mason Wade's depiction of him as the "heroic historian" and the Brahmin disappointment of Bernard DeVoto. Jacobs ultimately sides more with Wade, but at least regarding ecological consciousness, he rightly describes Parkman's attraction to forests but disdain for wildlife as a contradiction. "This preoccupation with killing presents a conundrum in appraising Parkman's role as a wilderness advocate," says Jacobs. "On the one hand, he wished to preserve and protect the wildland, and on the other, he demonstrated an intense desire to shoot almost everything in it from chickadees to buffalo" (349).

Parkman's conundrum is an obvious a forebear to Roosevelt's and to the hunter-conservationist mindset of the Wise Use Movement or Ducks Unlimited that still views the nonhuman world as a replenishable shooting gallery. Less obvious is Parkman's departure from Cooper's romance of the land. Cooper saw in wilderness a complex but ultimately Rousseauvian matrix; it held danger, but it was also made up of primal lives with which Leatherstocking empathized—for example during the bird slaughter scene of *The Pioneers* (in chapter 22) or his rhapsodies about lost wilderness delivered in *The Prairie*. Ironically, given his education as a historian and his efforts toward realism, Parkman imposes a more simplistic and harsher ethic on the wilderness, therefore one as romantic as Cooper's but with more devastating consequences, conducive to the leanings of an industrializing and divided nation.

The wildland preservation impulse to which Jacobs refers lasted late into Parkman's life. It is found in a surprising political essay Parkman wrote in an *Atlantic Monthly* column in 1885, in which he explained that because the bioregional distribution of forests crossed state boundaries, the only way to protect the purity of those forests was by federal intervention. In his call for federal protection of the eastern forests, Parkman decried the intrusion of "browsing animals," anticipating wildlife management arguments not scrutinized until Aldo Leopold in the 1940s and still dim-wittedly guarded by many hunters and outfitters who don't want the challenge of hunting in whole ecosystems. So Parkman's move toward conservationism during a popular time for conservationism was admirable, if hardly epiphanic, and included that caveat of predator eradication.

"When I turned down the buffalo path," Parkman writes in *The Oregon Trail*, "the prairie seemed changed; only a wolf or two glided past at intervals, like conscious felons, never looking to the right or left." The dismissive hatred of this remark contrasts sharply with Parkman's language for other animals: "Gaudy butterflies fluttered about my horse's head; strangely formed beetles, glittering with metallic lustre, were crawling upon plants that I had never seen before; multitudes of lizards, too, were darting like lightning over the sand" (125). Even the lizard receives a modicum of poetic representation, and Parkman would later come to know both the Latin and English names of those plants that he could not identify. But he would not come to know the wolf. For him wolves would always be "squalid, ruffian-like" animals that "sneaked through the hollows and sandy ravines" (124). He was enticed to shoot the antelope (in a passage I quoted back in chapter 2) because in the dim light he first thought it to be a wolf; once realizing it to be an antelope, he played the hunter rather than the warrior (187).

That Parkman was in Pawnee territory during his travels adds another wrinkle to his coverage of wolves in *The Oregon Trail*. As he traveled with men who could communicate with the Pawnee people, including Chatillon, he likely would have heard in the many exchanges at least a linguistic association of the Pawnee scouts to wolves. So a journal entry he makes about the Pawnee killing Swan and wolves desecrating the grave not only communicates to its readers his animosity toward both Pawnee and wolves but implies, through juxtaposition, a macabre and conspiratorial, if not biological, linkage (96, 393).

In one passage, Parkman constructs an almost Linnaean sequence that characterizes his frequent conflation of the Plains Indian and the wolf: "Here every summer pass the motley concourse; thousands of savages, men women and children, horses and mules, laden with their weapons and implements, and an innumerable multitude of unruly wolfish dogs, who have not acquired the civilized accomplishment of barking, but howl like their wild cousins of the prairie" (104). The next paragraph refers to the Pawnee as "a treacherous, cowardly banditti" and relates the story of one warrior who sneaked into a camp and killed travelers in their sleep (104). Juxtaposition is important here as well; the medieval bestiary logic that led to trials for animals who "committed crimes" operates here as a principle for depicting the Pawnee as something less than human. In a particularly interesting reaction to a story Parkman is told about a woman killing a dog because it "had a bad [that is, wicked] heart," he is puzzled by what he sees as the Pawnees' "ascribing intelligence and a power of understanding speech to the inferior animals; to whom, indeed, according to many of their traditions, they are linked in close affinity; and they even claim the honor of a lineal descent from bears, wolves, deer or tortoises" (291). In other passages he refers to "Indians dogging them, and crawling like wolves along the ridges of the hills" (127), and a band of Delaware braves who "fought like wolves" (178). Failing to understand either totemism or his own tendency toward malevolent ghost wolf metaphors, Parkman reveals himself to be an unintentional advocate of the Pawnees' spiritual descent from animals.

Falling deeper into the confessional abyss, Parkman would find himself developing his skill as a bison hunter by crawling along a hillside to approach-hunt them. The savagism prevalent in Cooper's writing exists in Parkman's during this passage, but without the Rousseauvian nobility. Instead, the image is that of the Unreformable Indian, which frontier settlers would co-opt when the occasion presented itself, and submerge into the unconscious along with whatever remorse might be felt over wholesale slaughter. In a commentary on Cooper, Gary Ashwill refers to the consolidation of "savagism by freezing its tenets into myth and freezing Native American difference into racial difference" (211). He tracks a disintegration of the reformist response, which he calls complete by the time the Leatherstocking tales were written. One of the beauties of Ashwill's argument is his coverage of Cooper's Native American xenophobic discontent with miscegenation. He compares Black Hawk to Magua, alike in their supremacist views: "Some [the Spirit that made men] made with faces paler than the ermine of the forests: and these he ordered to be traders; dogs to their women, and wolves to their slaves" (Cooper, *Last of the Mohicans,* 300–301).

The Reverie

Charles Hoffman describes a game called "prairie loo" that he played in 1834: "The game consists merely in betting on the number of wild animals seen by either party toward the side of the vehicle on which he is riding, a wolf or deer counting ten, a grouse one. The game is a hundred; and you may judge of the abundance of these animals from our getting through several games before dinner . . . my companion looing me with eleven wolves" (Hoffman, 261, and see Hampton, 82–83). One wonders how we might revise the scoring system of prairie loo today. Deer at a point. One wolf wins. Perhaps just being able to identify the animals at all would give the player bonus points.

In her 1870 history *The River of the West,* Frances Fuller Victor discusses the formation of a government in Oregon. Much of her work is devoted to the difficult political clashes that occurred in the territory among Catholic French Canadian trappers and travelers and British and American interests as the nations competed for corporate supremacy in the antebellum fur trade. She pays scant attention to the tribal interests in the debate, probably because the powers in place also neglected these interests. They were concerned with the same commercial gain that fed the nineteenth-century wave of broken treaties. The absence of native representation in the stockgrowers' and proto-Grange meetings that took place during the winter of 1843, however, proved critical to the mishandling of America's western ecology.

The first meeting, in February, was organized by settlers in the Willamette Valley, who posted notices that anyone concerned with protecting their stock from predators should attend. Victor's interpretation of this event is that "some truly long-headed politicians" had organized it as a way of creating the "Wolf Association," which was officially established in a second meeting held that March (Victor, 23; McIntyre, *War,* 79). At this second meeting, the Wolf Association set bounties for predator pelts and created a charter with the approval of French Canadian, British, and American businesses. The charter also resolved "that a committee be appointed to take into consideration the propriety of taking measures for the civil and military protection of this colony" (Victor, 60; McIntyre, *War,* 80). Thus the wolves along the Oregon Trail had some influence on the establishment of Oregon statehood, although their vote was never counted.

Besides the kinship he might have felt with these pioneers had he continued westward, Parkman's attitudes toward predation provided them with at least some support for their ongoing efforts, since his book would be published during one of the most significant wolf-extirpation campaigns of the Northwest, begun at the terminus of the Oregon Trail. The settlers northward and westward also supported vigorous American expansion southward from Santa Fe. In 1846, Bernard DeVoto's "year of decision," President James Polk determined to create the borders of Texas, New Mexico, and California, by force if necessary, and appointed Colonel Stephen Watts Kearny to accomplish this task with 1,600 regular and volunteer troops.

One text written during these explorations and military deployments received no critical attention until more than half a century later—Susan Shelby Magoffin's journal. Written in 1846 and 1847 but not published until 1924, it became *Down the Santa Fe Trail and into Mexico,* an account of her experience traveling with her new husband, the trader Samuel Magoffin, and a company of U.S. cavalry out of Bent's Fort, led by Kearny. She composed her original journal when Parkman turned south; he probably had no acquaintance with it. One of the most prominent midwestern families of the early nineteenth century, the Magoffins had married into the Shelby family, the patriarch of which, Isaac Shelby, was ranked in public funeral orations with Jefferson and Adams as one of the three most important Americans to die in the 1820s (Magoffin, xv).

During the military occupation by Kearny's forces, Parkman's turn southward along the eastern face of the Medicine Bow brought him to Bent's Fort in August, on the route back to the East along the Santa Fe Trail and on his second trip through Pawnee territory. In an August 29 journal entry, Parkman writes: "Afternoon, met a train of Santa Fe waggons, belonging to McLaughlin [likely Magoffin; no McLaughlins are mentioned in other records of the company]—news that the buffalo were within a day and a half—the Arapaho village, just this side. Also of Pawnees on the road. They killed Swan. He was buried, but they dug him up and scalped him. McL. saw his remains, mangled by the wolves, and reburied them" (Parkman, *Journals,* 475).

Susan Shelby Magoffin writes nothing of Francis Parkman in her travel journal, but at age eighteen she produced an account of frontier travel with better sensibilities about wildlife and regionalism than Parkman's, though she lacked his credentials. She wrote with a candor and curiosity not found in Parkman's trigger-happy encounters. Her journal also makes the wolf-Indian connection, though with a lighter hand. Her first mention of the wolf contains none of the common sentiment of the "howling wilderness," the romantic notion of fear and challenge contained in the howl of the wolf. Her account is, instead, laced with humor, touched with a little fear, but finally composed of wonder:

Last night I had a wolfish kind of a serenade! May Pan preserve me from the like tonight. Just as I had fixed myself for sleep after faning off to some other quarters the musquitoes, the delightful music began. Bak! ba! gnow, gnow, in such quick succession, it was almost impossible to distinguish one from the other. It was a mixture of cat, dog, sheep, wolf and the deer know what else. It was enough to frighten off sleep and everything else. Ring, my dear, good dog! was lying under my side of the bed, which was next to wolves, the instant they came up, he had been listening, he flew out with a fierce bark, and drove them away . . . Rided of our pest, I was destined to suffer from another.

The winged pestilence . . . (Magoffin, 13)

Later in the journal Magoffin attributes the same language to the Pawnee and the wolf when she imagines that "some wily savage or hungry wolf might be lurking in the thick grape vines . . . to bounce upon my shoulders." She may have heard a coyote song, perhaps mixed with wolf howls (the phonetic barking she writes, coupled with the sound as cacophony could be inferred as coyote; wolf howls, while often beginning with these barks, usually sound more rounded and melodic). Either way, Magoffin *thinks* the voices belong to wolves, and given how few of us could make the distinction today, we may accept as a premise that she is correct.

She remarks dryly on how anxious the men of her company are to kill some animal. When she mentions a body buried deeply enough to prevent its being dug up by wolves, Magoffin states the possibility of its being exhumed as a simple fact, not an act of "desecration," and spends the paragraph detailing the burial procedure (38). She invokes Pan and the serenade without any condemnation—the humor in the passage is pronounced—and through onomatopoeia anticipates Thoreau by playing along with the sounds. For a moment Magoffin seems to hear the wolf howl as horrific, but finally she counts the wolves outside of her tent as simply "pests." Indeed, she spends most of her complaints in her journal, including this entry, on what she sees as the real scourge of the Southwest—stinging insects. In this mention we even get a touch of realism; despite the great legends of wolves as killers of men, the grimmest of reapers is the mosquito. And her dog, good old Ring, chases off a fearsome wolf pack by himself.

Compare Magoffin's entry with this similar passage in *The Oregon Trail:* "That night we enjoyed a serenade from the wolves, more lively than any with which they had yet favored us; and in the morning one of the musicians appeared, not many rods from the tents, quietly seated among the horses, looking at us with a pair of large gray eyes; but perceiving a rifle levelled at him, he leaped up and made off in hot haste" (68). The nocturnal "serenade" is mentioned at other times in Parkman's tale, but in close conjunction with the wolves' "skulk[ing] around him by day," and at Parkman's repeated choice of measuring distance— "just beyond rifle-shot" (68–69). We have again the assumption that wolves recognize the significance of a rifle being aimed. I have mentioned that canids are capable of metonymy, but the difference between a dog's learning that a leash means a walk and a wolf's learning that a rifle means being shot ought to be obvious. The problem with metonymy is that it requires repetition.

As for the serenade—about halfway through Parkman's book, the howls are no longer called music, not even sarcastically. During the nights following the death of Henry Chatillon's "squaw," as Parkman calls her, the howls of the mourners are "wild and mournful cries, rising and dying away like the melancholy voice of a wolf" (209, 212). For Parkman, who traveled to the West ostensibly to "see" it, predation was a right best left to the human race, preferably the white race. For Magoffin, predation seems something to be observed without such hard judgment.

Unlike Magoffin, Parkman claims that wolf howls "need not and do not disturb one's sleep on the prairie," but his cocksure claim is undermined by other admissions. Consider, for example, this long reverie into which he slips one night while traveling the St. Joseph's Trail:

> At this instant a most whimsical variety of voices—barks, howls, yelps and whines—all mingled as it were together, sounded from the prairie, not far off, as if a whole conclave of wolves of every age and sex were assembled there. Delorier looked up from his work with a laugh, and began to imitate this curious medley of sounds with a most ludicrous accuracy. At this they were repeated with redoubled emphasis, the musician being apparently indignant at the successful efforts of a rival. They all proceeded from the throat of one little wolf, not larger than a spaniel, seated by himself at some distance. He was of the species called the prairie-wolf; a grim-visaged, but harmless little brute, whose worst propensity is creeping among horses and gnawing the ropes of raw-hide by which they are picketed around the camp. But other beasts roam the prairies, far more formidable in aspect and character. These are the large white and gray wolves, whose deep howl we heard at intervals from far and near . . . Far off, beyond the black outline of the prairie, there was a ruddy light, gradually increasing, like the glow of a conflagration; until at length the broad disk of the moon, blood-red, and vastly magnified by the vapors, rose slowly upon the darkness, flecked by one or two little clouds, and as the light poured over the gloomy plain, a fierce and stern howl, close at hand, seemed to greet it as an unwelcome intruder. There was something impressive and awful in the place and the hour; for I and the beasts were all that had consciousness for many a league around. (101–3)

Parkman is able here to distinguish between the "prairie wolf" (coyote) and the gray wolf, and even symbolically domesticates the coyote by comparing it to a spaniel. The humor and condescension sets up the drama given the "more formidable" wolves, and the tone of the passage changes markedly from the harmless coyote's yapping to the "deep howl." Parkman's ghosts suddenly come out to haunt him. He gives us the requisite connection of howling and moonrise, an anthropomorphic warning attributed to the howl (how does a "stern" howl sound?), and an allusion to the planet on fire that connects to the Sturm und Drang of the world's end. The diction is unexpectedly poetic and revelatory of a soul being challenged by another soul, the unfortunate confession of someone who first bonded with the wilderness superficially, shooting everything in sight, who now turns deeply introspective and bonds with the wilderness as if he might be judged by it. Unfortunately no indication is given of a bond that accommodates wilderness.

During the year when Parkman stood listening to the moonlight serenade, the Union Pacific's Luther North and Buffalo Bill were born. By the end of Parkman's life, such men had all but annihilated the bison and destroyed the Pawnee economy. In 1893, the year of Parkman's death and three years after the frontier was declared closed by the Census Bureau, Fredrick Jackson Turner would define for the Euro-American nation the term "frontier," a condition that had, for Turner, become a history of endings, a mythology that American writers would have to recalibrate and for which they would have to generate new enthusiasm. Such events unfolded as the writer of this passage could not have comprehended, events in which he was participating. The sky was burning in the West of the wolf, where the unwelcome intruders came to live.

CHAPTER TEN

Three Dreams
(In Which Some Wolves Cross the Mind)

Susan Snively's poem "Wolves" begins with an epigraph citing Freud's Wolf-Man case and is constructed in four sections, combining legends such as Red Riding Hood with prosaic stanzas devoted to the autobiography of the Wolf-Man. Consider this passage:

> The wolves
> are only picture-wolves
> in books. Yet they are always awake
> under the covers. He knows and fears
> what lies under the white
> sheets, snows, nightclothes. He sees the child
> looking at the tree
>
> and knows he will look until he cries, cry
> until he talks himself awake
> to begin the history of his dread.

The poet takes a Freudian/Jungian view of the wolf as an archetype closely akin to the shadow, and the poem's lack of corporeality provides some interesting tension. For instance, Snively also refers in the poem to hamstringing, a plausible behavior, but one the poet makes analogous of tension and violence. And she refers to the "steppes" at one point, which, given the poem's Freudian connection, counts as a literary allusion to Herman Hesse and his metaphysical wolf.[1] The poetic image is our path into the ghost wolves of dream literature.

Freud's Wolf-Man dreamed his; Scott Bradfield's title story in *Dream of the Wolf* gives us sleep symbols of the animal, a project he continues in his Orwellian spin-off *Animal Planet*.[2] Barry Lopez connects inner and outer landscapes in *Arc-*

tic Dreams and examines our invention of the mythic wolf, including our dreaming of it, in *Of Wolves and Men;* James Burbank includes revelations of and from his wolf-populated dreams in *Vanishing Lobo;* Jack London's wolf-dogs themselves dream—of lynxes and of trains; children's books such as *The Wolf Who Had a Wonderful Dream* provide us with cartoons of lupine dreams, apparently none of which are nightmares; such other works for children as Paul Goble's *Dream Wolf* and Neil Gaiman's *The Wolves in the Walls* cast the wolf as either a dream or a nightmare image. Even in this realm of the unconscious the ghost wolf is a ubiquitous presence. Some of this dreaming has only contributed to the unfortunate and unnecessary political schism between the sciences and humanities, and furthered unfortunate notions about the value and danger of dreams.

Through the historical accrual of myth, and through its conscious and unconscious renderings, we may readily see how the wolf image has been given significant archetypal power. The conditions of the natural world that created the cultural and psychological conditions of myth have not, under the civilizing obligation of humanity, lost their resonance. But they have been made subject to countless twisted, repressed, suppressed, altered, and bowdlerized fantasies that have contributed to the dulling of civilization's ecological sense. Scientific information alone has proven ineffective against deep psychosocial pathology, but it has affected, both positively and negatively, myth construction. Individual American knowledge of wolves has been the result (with some exceptions) of a lack of firsthand experience; surrogate experiences (such as trips to the zoo) passed off as "encounters"; essays driven to repetition of a standard list of biological facts and ethological conjecture; little scientific data from the field, especially as its methods and conclusions are refined over time; propaganda; resonant childhood stories; pulp fiction; and the occasional literary narrative still taught, from grade school through college, from a highly anthropocentric, allegorical, symbolic, and abstracted perspective. What should we expect of a culture shaped by such ecologically uninterested individuals but torture, extirpation, and—at its best—post facto recognition followed by last-ditch restoration efforts? It seems the environments we do "create" reciprocate, and sculpt us toward an artificiality of body and mind.

When the Wolf-Man of Sigmund Freud's famous case study wrote his memoirs, he referred to his childhood reading, thereby completing a map Freud followed to an imaginary place. The tone of his account bears striking resemblance to Victor Frankenstein's own cathartic monologue to Robert Walton, through which he must account for his childhood before he can explain with any clarity the course of his laboratory work and discoveries. Both Victor and the Wolf-Man have stern fathers inept at affection; both have experienced tragic deaths of women close to them (Victor's mother to scarlet fever, Sergei Pankejeff's sister to suicide); both men pursue natural science as a career path, the Wolf-Man finally changing to law and Victor to medicine; both undergo tremendous self-scrutiny of the psyche and dream state; both stories operate according to the subject's dilemma with a double life, a too-easy personality exchange with what each considers to be monstrous and haunting. Two piquant ironies surface here. The first is popular culture's kitschy conjoinment of Frankenstein and the Wolf-Man, lowering the brow of the Monster. The second is the role of empirical proof in both the fiction of Mary Shelley and the myth-text of Freud, which locates the haunting in the world outside the psyche. Neither Freud's subject nor Victor's creation becomes a monster. The creators are held in question. The appellation Freud gives Pankejeff (as he also does with the "Rat-Man") is as loose as his interpretation of the "wolves" of the dream. Common to the tales, however, is what Mary Shelley described in her famous 1831 introduction to *Frankenstein:* The writer of the fantastic is to "speak to the mysterious fears of our nature, and awaken thrilling horror" (171). She does this as a woman considering in then-unorthodox fashion an empirical root for philosophy, while Freud unempirically lays the haunting largely at the feet of women.

The Wolf-Man case begins when Pankejeff describes a recurrent dream of six or seven white wolves sitting in a walnut tree in winter. Later, during analysis, the tree becomes a "Christmas tree." The wolves look "more like foxes or sheepdogs," but the dreamer assumes them to be wolves (Gardner, 173). In his report, from the "History of an Infantile Neurosis," Freud connected the wolf (the "anxiety-animal") to the dreamer's having witnessed the primal scene around Christmas and having somehow conflated his trauma from that event with a fear of wolves. The dreamer remembers a story he read as a child and seeks to find the book, *The Wolf and the Seven Goats.* According to Freud, "the posture of the wolf" in one of the book's illustrations "might have reminded him of that of his father during the constructed primal scene" (183). Jung's departure from this narrow prognosis gives us the plausibility of the wolf's status as an archetypal image, with the ghost wolf as shadow. This in turn raises the possibility of a "wolf complex" in the human psyche, both individually and collectively realized. This complex would then be part of larger malfunction or dominating metaphor about animals that has driven human beings to treat other species as we do. The sexual metaphor is only a small component, if even an extant one, in the bigger picture of dreamt wolves.

Many cases of psychological lycanthropy involve the presence in a dream of a wolf symbolically rooted in the primal self, and so not a wolf at all but a neurotic vision possessed of traits utterly uncharacteristic of a real wolf.[3] Thus, the effectiveness of analysis is founded not only on the psychologist's understanding of the human psyche but also on his or her understanding of the nonhuman world, in this case wolves. Psychoanalysts, like literary critics and many writers, have proven insufficiently trained for such analysis. Consequently, the end result of analysis—of a book, of a mind, of a culture—may be the perpetuation of pathology, psychosis, and the failure of self-awareness through the symbolic language of a discipline given to disconnection with ecological knowledge. If the infantile neurosis conclusion that came to be associated permanently with the Wolf-Man case was untenable (see Offshe & Watters, 52–53), then what may be tenable with an inclusion of the wolf behind its imaging?

Freud's nicknaming Pankejeff the "Wolf-Man" is a bit odd, given that the subject's condition had nothing to do with lycanthropy. His analysis depended upon his interpretations of two fables: "The Wolf and the Seven Kids" and "Little Red Riding Hood." Both of Freud's interpretations of the fables themselves extend directly from his assumption of infantile neurosis and its sexual origin, which rooted the images of the tales, and the dream, in entirely symbolic terms. This allowed Freud to then symbolize the symbols. The infamy of Freud's interpretation came not from mere hyperbole but from a single missing source that would likely have changed the nature, literally, of psychoanalysis from Freud through Jung and into depth psychology today. This missing link is the nonhuman world, prefigured and natural before the arrival of the human psyche, and so before the world's arrival in the human psyche. The images of Pankejeff's dream are natural images, processed in the neural framework of sleep. The only implausible image in the dream is that the wolves sit in a walnut tree. Freud, however, transforms all images into those that match the infantile neurosis theory, and so mythifies the wolf as much as exploring the psyche's connection to the world, rendering the dream's real connections less plausible as he goes.

For instance, no consideration is given to this possibility: The image of "six or seven" white shapes arranged as if sitting on the branches of a walnut tree could quite easily be a constellation of stars. The arrangement and number, indeed, indicate the Pleiades, an influential constellation with the requisite sexual connotations to fulfill Freud, and a more plausible image than, say, transposing a walnut tree for a Christmas pine or fir with "presents on" it. The walnut tree is deciduous and denuded in winter, and its branches would give a proper pattern to white objects against a night sky for a constellation. The seventh star of the Pleiades is not easily seen, so that the "six or seven" wolves estimated by the dreamer imply the tricky seventh star and could explain their arrangement as well as the number of them in the dreamer's painting.

A dream often transforms the plausible, of course, and we must finally defer to the dreamer's own declaration that these are *wolves* in the tree. However, since real wolves don't climb real walnut trees as far as we know, the implausibility opens the transformative door, giving Freud room for even his most questionable speculations and for the ensuing double symbology (wolves are goats; goats are now in the tree; neither climb trees; wolves and goats are therefore convenient variables). A more plausible double symbology exists otherwise (wolves in a tree are arranged as stars in the sky and so appear as if in the sky themselves, a constellation). I am offering one among perhaps several more-feasible images behind the implausible dream image Freud provides. If the stuff of dreams is residual cognitive material on which our minds gnaw while we sleep, then the fairy tales imbedded (mostly from childhood) in the dreamer's unconscious could easily surface in mixture with the anxiety material made readily available to him. The combination of a deeply imbedded imaginary wolf of moral import with a hyperanalyzed wolf symbolic of anxiety cannot help but warp the real world relationship with the psyche. As a result the symbol (the stuff of dreams) is wrongly perceived as not only the more useful psychoanalytic tool than knowledge or experience (the stuff of wolves), but in the absence of physical wolves, it is finally perceived as the only tool. The apparatus becomes sicker than the mind to which it is applied.

Seven Wolves

Even though Freud's work was conducted in Europe with a European subject long after the establishment of American policy on wolves, I would like to take a closer look at one of the fairy tales to which he alludes several times but finally discounts in his analysis: "The Wolf and the Seven Kids." In chapters 13 and 14 (regarding children's literature) I will look more closely at "Red Riding Hood" and other representations of the wolf. What Freud considered obliquely in "The Wolf and the Seven Kids" is as important to my investigation as what he looks at directly, because even though the tale would have figured far less prominently in most Americans' story selection than "Red Riding Hood," it is in many ways more subtle. It also has direct bearing on both the Wolf-Man case and the significance of American wolf myths being sharply influenced by European imports. The Wolf-Man case, proffered by the most famous psychologist in the world, could have quietly rewoven the tale as a delicate but effective thread through time that makes for a strong unconscious influence.

A beautifully illustrated edition of the Grimms' "The Wolf and the Seven Kids" introduces the tale with an editor's note by Maria Tatar that compares it to "The Three Little Pigs" as a "cautionary fable" (Grimm & Grimm, 29). The fable is titled "The Wolf and the Seven Little Goats" but referred to by Tatar using instead the word *Kids,* perhaps a preference for the double entendre indicating the nickname for human children. From the beginning, therefore, goats are anthropomorphized for the story. This is typical of the allegory but raises what I believe to be the central question behind the animal fable: Why do we choose animals to represent people? This is a question for another book, but it is relevant here in the specific instance of the dreamer's conflations and transpositions, Freud's conjectures and symbolic choices, and recent efforts to reinterpret the dream, including my own.

The father of the goat family is absent, and Tatar reads the wolf as "a masculine presence who, with his desire to devour the children, stands in stark opposition to the mother" (29). Certainly the mothers of prey animals may stand in opposition to the predators, but here the representation is both anthropomorphic and highly gendered. "The wolf," Tatar writes—in keeping with the cautionary tale as it likely would have been interpreted—"can be seen as representing cunning and deceit, powers that undermine domestic serenity" (29). Yes it "can be," although cunning and deceit have little to do with a carnivore being given herds of edible animals in open pastures. Tatar is spot on with the traditional and still likely interpretation of the tale, so my position is not a refutation of hers but an application of it to the way in which fairy tale interpretation empowers the ghost wolf over the real wolf in the reader's imagination.

Two other telling editorial comments get at the psychological importance of the tale: "The wolf's gargantuan appetite turns him into a force of nature, a devouring *magnus pater* whose belly is filled with stones so heavy that he is pulled into the waters, where he is, in turn, engulfed by nature" (29). A wolf, it's true, is a force of nature, as is a cockroach, or rain, in that it is born outside of human choice and part of the world. But the context of the comment indicates that "force of nature" is something more, and more deadly, than what it may naturally be. The wolf is made monstrously unnatural. Again it is also mythically gendered, and yet again using the image of Kronos as devouring father (30). The commentary on what the wolf "is" is passively constructed, as if it were a mere happenstance of nature or cosmic symbology that the wolf's belly has been filled with stones, as if nature were the motive for someone, a "woodsman" (in my view the more effective *magnus pater*), torturing a wolf to death.

We are all "engulfed by nature." But there is a qualitative difference between our being engulfed by age or by a thunderstorm and our being murdered out of revenge. Even law reflects this difference. The method of killing the wolf by filling it with stones also appears in one version of "Red Riding Hood," linking the two tales and providing a horrifying repetition of the killing method with ramifications for the psyche. In these tales, cautions about sexuality, danger in the world, and predation are conflated with and solved by a domestic revenge killing that is also a metaphoric rebirth image—as the "kids" are replaced in the wolf's belly with the stones. The method also anticipates the inclusion of torture in the killing of real wolves during the modern era by codifying it in story. Tatar's second telling comment is an annotation in the margin, which reads:

> Maternal love, protection, and security are established from the start as a sharp contrast to the threat embodied in the wolf, who will be introduced as a predator whose gluttony knows no limits. The mother is nurturing and loving; the wolf is interested only in indulging his desires. The distinction between mother goat and wolf takes concrete form in the quality of voice and color of feet. The mother's voice is sweet, the wolf's is rough; the mother's paws are white, the wolf's are black. (30n)

By now we have a sufficient amount of evidence to reconsider not only Freud's interpretation of the "Wolf-Man's" dream but the resultant effects of a reinterpretation through Tatar's analysis of the tale. Her comment here begins with the assumption that the wolf is a fine representative of a lack of maternal love. That is, we choose the wolf as devourer because it eats goats, yes, but we also choose it based on our selective denial of its famous familial nature in a pack and its mythic Wolf Mother persona. An overstated connection itself, the wolf as a pack member by default still mythifies, at the very least, alpha females as quintessentially maternal. If Tatar is right, and I think she is, that the tale prompts such an anthropocentrically gendered interpretation, then what we see in the Freudian construct of the Wolf-Man's dream is a repression of the wolf for the sake of the dreamer. The dreamer would likely not have had the facts sorted out for him of wolves being looser in their social structures, less singularly gluttonous, and less patriarchal but would have been given both tale and interpretation as assumptions themselves generated by what Jung would later call the "shadow"—the repression of the real wolf. That is, both the dreamer in Freud's analysis and the reader in Tatar's are exposed only to the shadow wolf, the ghost wolf.

A predator does not exist whose "gluttony knows no limits." Even a weed, a cancer, or the human race will come to know the limits when the host is exhausted. Every stomach has its boundaries; culture is the province of greed. We are well aware that symbolic constructs attempt to represent beyond the real, and this is one of the functions of fairy tales. Specifically, though, the devourer myth attached to wolves is the attribution of a trait *to wolves,* beyond and behind the comment on avarice that drives the cautionary tale. The tale indicates a connection between predation, through gluttony, and carnal desire. We move from the physical to the psychological, and so to the plausibility of neurosis in the dreamer: The simultaneous repression of fact (that wolves may exhibit maternal care) and symbolic attribution (that the wolf represents a consuming psychological state) make the wolf a very plastic figure in the dream that Pankejeff will later have.

Finally, Tatar's commentary reaches long, as does Freud's, for symbolic interpretation. Goats don't have "paws." An actual mother goat's voice, at least as it is stereotypically judged, would seldom if ever be considered "sweet," and the editor gives no indication that she means the voice is sweet "to the kids." Not all wolves are black; even if they were, the color assumption is made at a psychologically symbolic level and could be ameliorated with a simple appeal to the fact that black is not evil in the nonhuman world. The psychological battle over purity and color symbolism was enough for Melville to examine over the course of five hundred pages; we can safely put stock in its force for a naive dreamer familiar with fairy tales.

Freud's own mentions of wolf tales in his analysis of Pankejeff's state of mind never include the respectful close readings he gave to many other works of literature in order to prove his points. What we have in the end is his sense that there was hard fact to be found in the roots of the dream, but where those roots were to be found was his puzzle. This may be because, outside of a zoo, neither Freud nor his patient had ever seen a wolf. We must expect that the symbol without a factual referent will have the plasticity of the unchecked imagination. Thus any repressed images connected to that symbol, coupled with basic factual ignorance, may easily engage the creative mind in the making of a dragon. Indeed, this is generally the process by which dragons are made. Consider the results of "The Wolf and the Seven Kids" worked out on a scale of hundreds of thousands of humans and wolves over the whole of a nation's territory. When the microcosm of tales in the individual psyche performs its chain reaction through the culture and results in a macrocosmic policy, our neurosis becomes a national characteristic, and is normalized. This mass repression has brought us, in regard to the wolf, collapsed ecological systems; a pathological addiction to cheap, chemically enhanced meat from abused animals; barbed wire and the land-ownership mode, which is followed by the ranch lobby and government subsidy; the slaughter of the bison; tortured wolves and the valorization of the trappers who tortured them; dog breeders, pet stores, and millions of discarded dogs in animal "shelters"; hybrid owners; and breakneck talk radio rationalizations of these events not only as normal human behavior but as marks of the greatness of our nation. Throw the interpretation of a dream into a symbolic lake at its center and wait on the banks for the actual results.

Several Wolves

Such repression of natural fact has also brought us to postmodern literary theory and cultural studies, which I am obligated to address. The assertion of subjectivity over objectivity proffered by poststructuralism could, when applied to the nonhuman world, have an effect similar to Barry Lopez's calls in *Of Wolves and Men* to understand animals as individuals. Unfortunately, postmodernism has far more often served an anthropocentric politics at least cynically diminishing, at worst utterly rejecting, the world. It has as a movement unilaterally decided on the resolution of the debate over materialism and idealism by simply choosing idealism. For the most part, postmodern writing doesn't *explicitly* declare this. Explicit declaration is at once an unfavored technique of postmodern discourse and, in the face of the laws of nature, an untenable one, as demonstrated in Alan Sokal's exposure of the journal *Social Text*.

Such diminishment more often occurs through ostensibly gentle notions of *jouissance* and affected reversals, or of "hospitality," and "otherness," which instead assert an anthropocentric political stance oddly similar to Ayn Rand's argument against altruism (cf. Derrida, "Hospitality"; Foucault, *Archaeology* and *Power/Knowledge*; Koertge; Sokal; Sokal & Bricmont; Weedon). Andrew Ross and Bruno Latour have both gone so far as to *blame* nature and claim that it owes a debt to one species (guess which) for nature's inherently constructed position (see Ross, *The Chicago Gangster Theory of Life: Nature's Debt to Society,* and Latour, 19). The affected reversals, made most famous by Jacques Derrida and Gilles Delueze, are founded on a bifurcated brand of negation (*différance*) as the *only* method of viewing the world worthy of serious consideration. For instance, because I use a binary structure for one part of this book—benevolent and malevolent ghost wolves—my own work *must* be classed as deconstruction, regardless of my own views on the matter of binary relationships, my efforts to avoid the bifurcation fallacy, and the inherently triadic structure I impose on nearly every binary I examine. Deconstruction constitutes the new hegemony, a pressure on literary study to conform to these speculations about speculation. Why this matters to a study of wolves in literature is clear enough: Through such methods poststructuralism has produced its own brand of ghost wolf.

Ecocriticism has been variously positioned in, against, or outside of the practice of what has been colloquially known as "theory" ever since Jonathan Culler (and to the chagrin of scientists working toward their own theories).[4] A recent example of such positioning is Dana Phillips's *The Truth of Ecology*. Phillips asks two major questions. The first, in two parts, is "Why is ecocriticism so hostile to literary theory" (7) and, hyperbolically, "to the intellect?" (ix). The second, ostensibly the thesis of his book, is "What can we do about it?"

The first question (let's disregard the insult to the intellect) seems naive, if not disingenuous, in that Phillips ignores the outright hostility against the nonhuman world exhibited by postmodern theory, including Foucault's revulsion (Love, 167–68n9); the many antinatural exaggerations of Jean Baudrillard (for example, in *Simulacra and Simulation*); and Andrew Ross's non sequiturs (using the word *environment* only in an urban context and red herrings about social problems taking precedent over, rather than being connected to, matters of the nonhuman world [Williams & Berube, 292–94]). The question also ignores poststructuralism's affinity for obfuscation and abstraction, which functions as if to prove through practice the assumption of language's lack of referential meaning. The style sheet of poststructuralism thus rejects the naming, mimetic efforts, and delineation of natural facts that characterize nature writing and ecologically informed criticism. This rejection could itself be considered quite hostile. Instead, Phillips posits "theory" as an undeserving victim rather than as an anthropocentric force steering a still largely ecologically uninformed community in the humanities.

To the second question, "What do we do about it," Phillips offers only this solution: more theory (240). Throughout the book he makes a list of what we shouldn't do in ecocriticism, including things that define the field: no more epiphanies (3, 171, 237); less real, more hyperreal (16, 20); less celebration (47); less analogy (57); less holism, quantification, and modeling (67); and no more pointing, representation, or mimesis (181). He provides only loyalty to theory as the replacement for these unacceptable practices (185, 192, 213, 218). In the end, he strips ecological literary criticism of any serviceable definition or function and replaces it with absence. This is appropriate to the poststructuralist agenda. It is also precisely the result we find at Superfund sites, in ecosytems destroyed by invasive exotics, and in the extinction of entire species.

Cultural constructivism is perhaps the most extreme form of "theory" that has recently and rightly been corrected, especially through the exposure of Ross during the 1990s (*The Truth of Ecology,* strangely enough, provides the best critique of Ross's "environmentalism" I have read). Cultural constructivism posits not only the delusionary tabula rasa but an external world at best subsidiary to, at worst formed entirely of, the will of mass or alternative cultures attempting to dodge or stave off those uncooperative laws of nature. "Theory" is certainly not composed entirely of cultural constructivism, and it offers some useful tools for the analysis of narrative structure (for example, Barthes's "codes" in *S/Z;* Bakhtin's "carnivalesque"; Prince's work on narratology; and the maturation of structural-ism and semiotics through Lévi-Strauss, Saussure, Peirce, and Sebeok). The work being done on Theory of Mind, by Searle and others regarding animal cognition, could also prove to be a way of branching from postmodern questions about referentiality to more serious examinations of it.

A common misreading of deconstruction is that it limits its critiques to the human *perception* of nature. This judgment is false according to the very definition of the word *deconstruction* so stridently defended by deconstructionists from Derrida to (formerly) Bloom. The very distinction of deconstruction from, for instance, phenomenology is precisely its allegiance to an absence of meaning that places *any* referential, representational, or factual articulation of the natural world outside the range of possibility (except, perhaps, the referentiality of the deconstructionist's own ideology).[5] Indeed, were a deconstructionist to read my previous sentence and say, "That's incorrect," he or she would undermine through referentiality the premise and differentiating feature of deconstruction.

Notice, for example, the following definitive statements from Herndl and Brown's *Green Culture:* "There is no objective environment in the phenomenal world, no environment separate from the words we use to represent it. We can define the environment and how it is affected by our actions only through the language we have developed to talk about these issues" (3). We might try to buoy this claim up on the phrase "the phenomenal world," as if the claim regarded only perception and language, or on the second sentence's tautological use of definition and language to qualify the original claim. But the allegation is clear: "no environment separate from the words we use." No objectivity means no object as much as no practice of knowing the object unless it means no hope for the object, which produces the same negating effect. Our perception is being questioned according to the assumed lack of existence of an "environment"—itself a highly generic, abstract term providing its user with the greatest latitude and so the most convenient argument.

Herndl and Brown's position is strangely close to the one stated by Ernst Schachtel in 1959: "Nature is to man whatever name he wants to give her. He will perceive nature according to the names he gives her, according to the relation and perspective he chooses" (Keller, 17). This statement appears, pejoratively, as an epigraph in Evelyn Fox Keller's *Reflections on Gender and Science,* a hard critique of the language used to infuse scientific study with a toxic patriarchal strain. Gender the pronoun neutral, and the postmodern position stated in *Green Culture* is both ideologically synonymous with and as oppressive as the retrograde sexist one.

If I kill an animal, then the animal is dead, whether or not I use the words *kill* or *animal*. Indeed the act is often performed in silence and left undescribed.

When did my discourse invent that animal? We didn't *make* deer or trees; we put the labels "tree" or "prey" on that which was here before. We objectified without the proper objectivity. What, precisely, stood there for those long centuries rooting and roaming from shade to light before I put my semiotic chainsaw to it, before I developed verbiage describing the act and measuring *my* history by *its* rings? We "define the environment" by how we affect it, regardless of how we describe it. Dead wolves aren't dead because we described them as such. They are so because they died, perhaps because we killed them and then played some language game to let ourselves off the hook. A profound lack of experience with a world beyond the human urban or academic, coupled with the assumption that an experience's subjectivity renders both it and objectivity unreliable, writes us a license to exploit. It also risks prejudicial judgment, creating a god-induced argument to which no one is permitted access without exhibiting the requisite faith and compliance.

Poststructuralism applies nonreferential language and semiotic reversal strategies that equate "reality" with "materiality" when convenient. It then defends such transpositions in the name of *jouissance* or "play" with the text. As a result, the nonhuman world is exiled to an unreachable, if only because imperceptible, status that renders it finally ineffectual, if not irrelevant. The very biosphere is then enthusiastically kept imperceptible through scholarly and experiential neglect, so that as it disappears beneath the spread of anthropocentrism, the theory claims to have proven itself, creating its own evidence of "absence" by contributing to loss. To the Baudrillardian, the environment is merely a consumable plaything, and ecology an oppressive warning label stuck on the product by some faceless hegemonic (and by default American) manufacturer. The nonhuman world's agency and presence may certainly be incomprehensible to us (ask an ecologist), but they exist before, outside of, and beyond our invention. They infuse us and the tools of our invention. And they not only may be but must be approached, because we can't avoid them. We are always already present, in and with them.

This is precisely why a study of the ghost wolf's role in literary discourse has to include poststructuralism's tendencies both to anthropocentrize and to render the physical apparitional. An example directly applicable to our study of the wolf in literature is Deleuze and Guattari's *A Thousand Plateaus*. The book offers a refiguring of the "Wolf-Man" case in the context of the authors' attempts to employ the natural world to serve their idea of systems theory. The result is a replacement of Freud's misinterpretation predicated on infantile neurosis with one predicated on poststructuralist misapplications of the nonhuman world. Deleuze and Guattari challenge Freud's assumptions about the fairy tale well enough, but then offer assumptions about both dreaming and about wolves that not only undermine their argument but also demonstrate an inattention to work on the tale and dream connections previously made by Jung, Eliade, Propp, and others who offered prior revisions of Freud.[6] There are also no wolves in their chapter titled "One or Several Wolves" and only thin (nearly nonexistent) research to corroborate the authors' claims about these animals, especially their essentialism of wolves as automatically belonging to packs (27–29, esp. 28).

Deleuze and Guattari first question the definition of what they call "so-called" psychosis on the basis of the word's lack of referentiality. That is, aren't we all psychotic, since "The Signifier" is "a despotic agency that substitutes itself for asignifying proper names and replaces multiplicities with the dismal unity of an object declared lost?" (28). Even if we accepted such a premise, we might still find it conducive to ecocriticism, given that it seems to favor individual distinction and acknowledgment of deviant consciousness (say, another animal's). Unfortunately, this is not where the authors take the statement. The next cryptic sentence reads: "We're not far from wolves." We've jumped quickly from being splitters to being lumpers here, I think. This comparison, of inherently nonpsychotic humans to inherently nonpsychotic wolves, is then applied to the Wolf-Man case. The method used is classic essentialism. "Who is ignorant of the fact that wolves travel in packs?" they write. "Only Freud" (28).

Only Freud? Three assumptions arise here: the first that wolves travel in packs (many do, and yes, who is ignorant of the fact that we might assume that they do?); the second, built on the first, is that this categorizes us with them (a strategic move that allows Deleuze and Guattari to then employ the "dismal unity" they just finished condemning); and the third is that Freud was exceptionally ignorant. This is actually a common tactic in poststructural discourse for abandoning (to "death") the prior thinker; de Man uses it against Locke in "The Epistemology of Metaphor," and Barthes against "the author." Deleuze and Guattari, those authors, do eventually circle around to a reasonable critique of Freud's transposition of wolves and goats, by which he constructs his more convenient scenario for interpretation. There's a wonderful bit of image work that rebuts Freud: "the wolves never had a chance to get away and save their pack: it was already decided from the very beginning that animals could serve only to represent coitus between parents, or, conversely, be represented by coitus between parents" (28). Yes. Right on the ecocritical mark.

How is it, then, that the "wolves" here ultimately come to serve Deleuze and Guattari's purpose only over Freud's, rather than serving their own purpose as wolves? First comes a hypothetical reference to one "Franny," planted in the audience to give an utterly implausible answer to the question "Would you like to be a wolf," as if to demonstrate somehow Freud's answer (29). A straw-man argument then materializes, the authors choosing to reiterate their own position on language breakage instead of taking their claim down the path on which they've set it—toward the wolves required to corroborate that position. "Wolf-multiplicity" has now been put in service of the argument and will never become wolf individuality or materiality. That is, the argument moves toward the ghost wolf rather than the corporeal one, and so proves circular and in service of the authors. Deleuze and Guattari are so attached to proving that "the unconscious itself was fundamentally a crowd," or a "pack," that they reject individuality for their own argument of convenience about multiplicity (which is actually grouping, not precisely multiplicity, and yet again displays the dismal unity we've been instructed to avoid). In short, they despotically replace Freud's "despotic" position while valorizing conformity (29).

From here, we see the final disintegration of corporeality in the piece. "The wolf, as the instantaneous apprehension of a multiplicity in a given region, is not a representative, a substitute, but an *I feel*" (30). Wait a second. Which wolf? The ghost wolf, yes. That's an *I feel*, but it doesn't inhabit an ecosystem; it can't be rendered extinct with tangible ecological consequences. The projection of human ignorance about wolves onto them in the psychoanalytic moment is, yes, certainly a *We feel* (indeed the very act that Freud, Deleuze, and Guattari all commit). But the responsibility of the author claiming to be looking in at this event, possessing the critical eye, is also to the wolves being exploited for this purpose; otherwise the entire critique of Freud and the Wolf-Man is simply an incident of the pot calling the kettle black.

Deleuze and Guattari's momentum finally just carries them away: "The wolf, wolves, are intensities, speeds, temperatures, nondecomposable variable distances. A swarming, a wolfing" (30). And abracadabra, poof, wolves disappear into a new trap, die of a new poison, disassemble in the machine made of clever, disconnected phrasings. The theorist, analyst, analysand, and reader all make this abbatoir run, perhaps none having bothered to find out anything about wolves. What in the world is a "nondecomposable variable distance"? Is this what now passes for poetry among critics and theorists? Even at the level of its own attempted *jouissance,* a "swarming" is a terrible choice of metaphor. It reveals the authors' disregard for wolves even as they declare about wolves. Where Deleuze and Guattari accuse Freud of turning wolves into goats, they seem quite happy themselves to turn wolves into insects. Or, as we will see, rhizomes.

This appropriation of the nonhuman world as a metaphoric or symbolic element used toward a spurious "proof" of the perception-to-world schism is a trait of many schools of discourse and not exclusive to postmodern theory; in this way Deleuze and Guattari are unfortunately common in their assumptions. The overemphasis of wolf packs as an essential structure is even found at times in Lopez (although he struggles with, even contradicts, his own assumption, the result of a genuine effort to learn). Their error here could simply be an example of inappropriate metaphor and a forgivable lack of research exhibited in a minor passage. However, the authors title their chapter, base a significant portion of their critique of Freudian discourse, and consequently stake their thesis regarding psychoanalysis on this use of "wolves." At that point we are looking neither at metaphor alone nor at an isolated passage but at rubric, premise, and ensuing argument. Even if we ignore Freud's errors on the basis that they are subject to the available knowledge of his time (not that Deleuze and Guattari found out from wolf biology what that was), then we still face another problem with *A Thousand Plateaus*. A key argument in its opening chapter reveals a severe flaw in the controlling logic of the entire book about the mind-world relationship, one that the authors then use to exploit wolves.

The "rhizome" chapter of *A Thousand Plateaus* contains certain fantasies stated as fact—about rivers being "without beginning or ending" (11) and about the rhizome being "always intermezzo" (25). According to the authors, rats are rhizomes (6). Animals and grasses are all grasses, or animals (7). Rhizomes are plateaus (11). Even Jung, who used the rhizome metaphorically, at least indicated clearly that he knew what a rhizome was and where it might be found (*Symbols of Transformation*, 47). Again, the banal position of Deleuze and Guattari regarding rivers without end isn't unusual. Barry Commoner, considered one of environmentalism's major figures, hyperbolically employed as one of his characteristics of "ecology" that "everything is connected to everything else."[7]

For the record: A river has a source and a mouth. Tributaries, however connected, have definable confluences. If my aunt had testicles she'd be my uncle, but indeed, a rhizome is not a plateau. A rhizome has a life and death, and both its growth and its rot are functions in the order of its ecosystem. A plateau is an abrupt geological formation of upland, and there are different kinds (for instance, some have escarpments caused by erosion). The former is biotic, the latter abiotic; that's just how different they are. If Deleuze and Guattari selectively distinguish a rhizome from a root in order to make their point, then they ought to as well know it from a grass or plateau in order to make their point effective.

For a metaphor to work, its two components need to be appropriate to each other; I don't demonstrate that my brother is fast by comparing his running speed to a tortoise's, unless I risk (and establish) the contextual reach of choosing a tortoise fast among tortoises. This concept of interconnectedness by those who would use "ecology" to justify any pastiche of thoughts (or rivers) they imagine might, as it does here, turn to exploitation. My points about this are simple, and two. First, ecology is a science, and not as soft a science as some would like to believe (it may have been Gregory Bateson who first said, "There are the hard sciences, and then there are the difficult ones"). Second, poststructuralism declares itself as a discourse of absence and apparition in human service that finally circles back on itself so that any object-called-subject disappears. As a consequence, the wolf-man dream is alive and well, and still suffers from approaches that disallow the roles of wolves, goats, and walnut trees in the integration of the human psyche dreaming them. Freud, in his own struggle with the wolf-man dream, which struggle he freely confesses (205–6), recognized the opportunity for abusive uses of his work:

> Previously it was enough to challenge the reality of the facts asserted by analysis and to this end the best technique appeared to be to avoid any kind of verification. Apparently, this procedure is gradually being exhausted and opposition now takes a different route, acknowledging the facts but disposing of the resulting conclusions by means of reinterpretation so that it is possible, after all, to fend off such offensive conclusions. (207)

The natural state of the psyche, Freud seems to know, is somehow connected to the nonhuman state of nature, which is the house of fact. He (and Jung) simply weren't equipped— either by their discipline or by the maturation of the life sciences—to take the next logical, ecological step. By making rhizomes into what are not rhizomes, wolves into essentialized and fantastic performers in a carnival, we risk doing to literary wolves what has long been done to real wolves— destroying them as pests. Even Sergei Pankejeff knew to "scream if a horse was beaten and once had to leave a circus for this reason" (214). "The Wolf and the Seven Kids" is a cautionary tale indeed, and Deleuze and Guattari's dreaming, for all its fashion and play, has still left us with only ghost wolves. We may say that no poststructuralist would categorically deny the existence of the real world, but we then have to say that its existence doesn't seem to sufficiently get in the way of assumptions about it.

One of poststructuralism's major premises is that language's role as a mediator between mind and world is problematic—fraught with assumptions, cultural influences at subtle and not-so-subtle levels, and systems of signification that are apt to break as well as to function. Indeed, much of the argument of *Wolves and the Wolf Myth in American Literature* regards the extent to which humans have failed the world (specifically the wolf) because of precisely these dysfunctional language conditions. The outright rejection of mimesis, along with the implicitly anthropocentric understanding of "the humanities," however, has not exactly presented postmodernists as either diligent or articulate advocates for the non-human world, and calls into question the pragmatic value of their relationship with language.

It's an innocent error at first to conflate ecology with environmentalism, but it's not an error worth sustaining for its initial innocence. Ecocritics such as Neil Evernden and Patrick Murphy have written in cooperation with poststructuralist ideas and incorporated them into a brand of ecocriticism that steers sharply from ecology to a kind of meta-ecology. Andrew Ross's direct hostile conflation of and sarcasm about environmentalism *as* ecology marks the poststructuralist approach that ecocriticism, which did not originate as a discipline in the poststructuralist community, once sought to refute. On the other hand, Michael Branch, offering what he calls "ecosophy," writes this:

> Like poststructuralist theory, in which meaning is seen as "scattered or dispersed along the whole chain of signifiers" (Eagleton, 128), contemporary ecosophy understands value to reside relationally, to be diffused throughout the interconnected fabric of the ecosystemic or planetary whole. On the other hand, I believe there is a perilous sense in which poststructuralism's infinite deferral of meaning is strongly at odds with an ethos of environmental concern. After all, students of nature and its representative literature are more interested in environmentalism's goal of freedom from decimation than in deconstructionism's goal of freedom from meaning. While ecosophy replaces the hierarchical anthropocentric paradigm with a vision of an ecologically decentralized natural community, few ecocritics would concede that nature ultimately has no determinate meaning, or that the natural system can adequately be described as simply the interminable "freeplay" of its "signifiers." On the contrary, normative concepts such as intrinsic value and the rights of natural objects demonstrate that contemporary ecosophy retains a genuine concern for specific loci of meaning and value. (44)

One could easily reply that we need not choose between "freedom from decimation" and "freedom from meaning," but Branch's argument here very clearly refutes the untenable assumptions of poststructuralists about meaning when the natural world adheres (and that, incidentally, is always). Branch's is a sound rebuttal. It brings to mind an inside joke among academics that ends with the punch line, "When Jacques Derrida needs directions to the bathroom, suddenly language has referential meaning." We might in this context use the phrase "when nature calls."

The danger of never having faced the raw material of the world other than, ironically, through the very language and human constructs that "theory" purports to deconstruct, is that we are permitted, even encouraged, to build a political and critical platform on clear-cut timber and the bones of extirpated species.

For the sake of those who lack human speech and have had a deaf ear turned to their own languages, practitioners of literary diversity and inclusion should refrain from turning the humanities inward upon itself. The ghost wolves of literature should be considered as narrative dreamings. What may function as "play" for us may prove the most dangerous game for those around and among us, in this case other animals, a game destructive rather than simply deconstructive.

Shadow Wolves

The third and final dream I will examine is found in Jolande Jacobi's *Complex, Archetype, Symbol in the Psychology of C. G. Jung.*[8] Although this final dream is also specifically not about wolves, it gives us the necessary material we need to take Freud's Wolf-Man, through Jung, to a point of informative and constructive application. This will also establish how I am using archetype and myth through-out my study to inform my conclusions about wolf books in American literature. Since I do not assert my approach to be precisely "Jungian" per se, it seems the more important to clarify how Jung's work, especially his definition of the arche-type, informs it.

An eight-year-old girl has the following dream, which she calls "The Dream of the Bad Animal": "I saw an animal that had lots of horns. It spiked up other little animals with them. It wriggled like a snake and that is how it lived. Then a blue fog came out of all the four corners, and it stopped eating. Then God came, but there were really four Gods in the four corners. Then the animal died, and all the animals it had eaten came out alive again" (Jacobi, 139).

Here we see again the fairy tale image of the animal that disgorges its prey in a rebirth scene. The most ready connection to Deleuze and Guattari's dream is the four Gods and the indeterminate animal, the puzzle over how many and what kind. Jacobi calls this "more like a vision than a dream" (139), and Jung quickly analyzes it as a root image of the subhuman and superhuman. From this "primordial image," of God and the animal in conflict, Jacobi states, "The stage on which this struggle has been enacted since the dawn of history is the 'inner space' of the human psyche, whose different aspects appear as the protagonists in the drama of the psyche" (141). Missing again from the analysis is a critical point of understanding—that the stage for all such struggles is not a stage at all, but the world, which was the place of enactment during prehistory and at the very in-ception of the human psyche. This is our first point of insight into the dream-world's connection to the real world, which is a resultant as well as symbiotic connection.

The next most relevant point Jacobi raises is a significant one to our under-standing of the wolf book:

The bilateral nature of fabulous animals is something characteristic of primordial times; consequently such animals always belong to the deepest realm of the unconscious and when in dreams they rise up out of its darkness they bring with them all the horror of primordial experiences. For they have their origins in the time when water was regarded as the beginning of the cosmos . . . In their symbolic language, the animals belonging to this primordial world were also symbols of the "matrix," the receptive feminine principle, of the alchemical "vas," the "krater," the "vessel," hence representative of the inexhaustible multiplicity of the Great Mother, in whom the male principle is not yet operative, of the Great Mother as symbol of the deepest realm of the unconscious, where the opposites, male and female, are not yet separate. (145–46)

This is precisely the wolf dominating American literature, this bilateral fabulous animal. As we will see in the chapter on She-Wolves, the feminine wolf archetypal images play significant roles in the full formation of the wolf archetype, in keeping with this analysis of the bilateral, androgynous animal of dreams. Our cultural divisions of it into demon and angel of wilderness; its role as both paternal threat and maternal progenitor; its twins in the realm of the imagination (such as the werewolf, a twin image itself) and the world; its position as avatar of the primordial world (especially, for instance, in Jack London); its symbolic and actual position in the health and completion of ecosystems, now kept whole for the most part in those alchemical "kraters" we call national parks—all of these features connect the macrocosmic condition of wolves on the land with the microcosmic conditions of the fabulous wolf in the individual psyche.

An important irony is that we discovered the Great Mother to be indeed exhaustible, at least in her material form, and the children of the Wolf Mother to be ungrateful. Our wolf stories, as evidenced in their repetitions, are the articulations of the psyche's full range from symbolism and complex through shadow and repression in the guises of various personae and from the depths of the archetype. What the stories articulate collectively is a great impassioned confession, a purging of souls over the tragedy that was, and the effort to repair the damage.

The Root Wolf

The archetype as conceived by Jung was adapted in literary study by such critics as Annis Pratt, Maud Bodkin, Philip Wheelwright, and Northrop Frye.[9] During the 1940s and '50s, these critics took archetypal images or patterns and applied them to literature. In so doing, they had to jettison the principle criterion of definition for the archetype, which is its inaccessibility, its inability to be observed (Jung, *Archetypes*, 79, 160–61). As a result, *archetype* attained a stipulative definition in literary study as a motif, pattern, or character template. In part, this move avoided the difficulties Jungian psychoanalysis faced in asserting primordial, inherited archetypes functioning at the level of a collective unconscious. The "death" of myth and archetypal criticism in literary study occurred partly through mere cultural change to the new mesmerisms of postmodern theory, partly through the proscriptive nature of myth criticism's structuralist bent in trying to explain or frame archetypal images in literature according to a symbolic system.[10]

The overarching goal of my study is to prove, through the wolf's ubiquity and persistence in the imagery of American literature, that its near-global roots and the policies of nations constitute a macroscope in reciprocity with individual and subjective notions and actions. More importantly, this happens not in the context of obvious cultural artifact; we aren't talking about the highway system, or entertainment technology, or fashion (themselves still subject to the raw materiality of resource extraction). The relation between culture and nature here occurs in a context that defies the totalizing claims of social construction because it involves another living being, an agent in the formation of the idea, one marginalized as severely as any human subculture ever has been. It is no matter that the wolf doesn't speak our languages or possess our same quality of consciousness. It is of great matter that we have reified these wolves out of opportunity and expediency. Behaviorism, the adherence to programmatic predetermination, offers insufficient latitude for behavior to be cognizant or chosen, while cultural constructivism rejects sufficient definition of behavior outside of situational modes (often selected by the constructivist) or by social determination. These two faiths therefore *share* the adoption of determinism, merely occupying opposing sides of the fatalist coin.

This does not mean we *invent* the form of The Wolf; adamantly to the contrary, we always find that The Wolf, if it exists, is a mystery like any other god—an encoded faith—and we inherit it. We find that the world was once and could be full of individuals within a species, and that the form of The Wolf lives unattainable in that space between intraspecies behavior and individuality. So we must go to wolves, the real animals of the biosphere's own creation. The material world is the attainable, the form the unattainable. And if we cannot go to them, or if they do not come to us, then our burden is greater to understand how the real world functions outside our manipulations and exterminations, and perhaps the more important. At the very minimum, the base of ethics, we must let them live. Otherwise the wolf we imagine is only the shadow, the repressive warping of real wolves, and a notion that will come back on us with the energy of chaos and damage. We see the evidence of such repression and the shadow's activity now in our desperate efforts to return wolves and heal the land, just as we see it in our historic cruelty to them, just as we see it in our readings and applications of literature.

The monstrous beast image is a manifestation of our inability to reconcile our inner, human selves with the outer, nonhuman world. For all of its symbolic value in Jungian analysis, the animal is not ultimately a symbol any more than a human psyche can *be* a symbol; symbols are tools of psyches, and wolves live. Indeed, Jung entertained the possibility that other animals could *have,* not just be, archetypes.[11]

What we have done to the wolf can be explained in large part through how we have handled its archetypal standing. Coleman's questions in *Vicious* about our motivations for torturing wolves are to a great degree answered when we see what we have done to the wolf in our minds in parallel relation to what we did to wolves with our hands, our guns and poisons, our traps and machines (47). The archetype explains the myriad ways we approached the real and mythic animal in such an explosion of natural and cultural chaos that we could not recover our senses for a thousand years, over the cascade of a thousand books, from the vantage points of a thousand actual plateaus.

The more wolf images we find in American literature, the more we find them to be a fluctuating combination of wolves' real biological selves and the false intellectual constructs of a highly synthetic and uncomfortable fabric. Allow me to sustain the metaphor: This fantastic cloth was woven from Scandinavian, Celtic, Germanic, British, and French thread spun out of ancient Indo-European (particularly early southern Russian) legends that were themselves tailored to suit human fantasy. The wolf transformed and transported over the Atlantic was not only draped over the shoulders of Nordic travelers, not only interlaced into the unconscious of the European mind, but also tied to those cultures' deepest collective consciousness—archetypal robes for mythic selves. After centuries of slow spellcraft and transmutation, what crossed the great sea to America was the World-Wolf, the Lupus Mundi, but only a fine thread was left of Fenris himself. The more efficacious, if more secret, symbol that crossed was Gleipnir, the rope.

PART III

Werewolf, Wolf Child, She-Wolf

RACE, CLASS, AND GENDER RECONSIDERED

CHAPTER ELEVEN

The Loophole

LYCANTHROPY, SHAPE-SHIFTING, AND THE WEREWOLF RACE

We imagine this: Maybe there's a way to change into an animal. Maybe somewhere there's an Altered State, a morphological result of a psychological invention. We know that psychosomatic manifestations are possible: blackouts, changes of the skin or physical ailments, even simply heavy sweating. Is there a way that, by looking outward intensely enough and with enough faith or the right incantation, we might suddenly find ourselves looking inward at what was outward? The film actor becomes someone else, grows fangs. This is what we imagine.

Loophole is the word for an arrow slit in a medieval wall (Sturgis, 793). It is likely derived from the medieval Dutch *lupen* meaning "to peer" or "to lie in wait." The French spelling is *loup* without the "e," although this is probably connected to the jeweler's loupe, a magnifying glass. The Greek reference to Apollo as both light and wolf (*lykos*) prompts us to think of the lupine and *lupen* as perhaps related. I'm indulging in my own language play here because of a story I was told in New Orleans that the loophole was the small, sometimes moon-shaped opening cut in the door of a privy so that, when the user was finished, he or she might peek out to see if "le loup" was lying in wait. Even without a credible etymology to back this up, even as a cocktail party moment, it's an effective Creole-flavored yarn similar to Thoreau's Latin puns on the saunterer in his essay "Walking" (Emerson & Thoreau, 72). The story gives us another ghost wolf for the list. The loophole is a kind of eye or lens, a transformation of gaze from simply looking out the window to looking out for something, or, as it has come to mean, looking for a way out. In our civilizations that try to transcend the outhouse and the wolf-populated wilderness, *loophole* has come to mean a clever discovery of language that will let us do what we weren't formerly allowed to do. We call a procedure of jurisprudence that we don't like "a loophole in the law," as if this were a means of cheating rather than a way of peering closely. We might say that the loophole is a way to adopt the gaze of the ghost wolf. We might also call it a noose.

Killing a pagan is easier than killing a myth. The comparative details of transformation legends from the Americas and Europe did not finally work to unite cultures in colonial North America but instead served as the necessary material to justify fears of spiritual corruption. Just as a pioneer could be Indianized, or a praying Indian grown, so too could a susceptible reader come to sympathize with the animism, atavism, and theriomorphism of New World cultures. Since such traits of story were already present in their own histories, it seems that Euro–North Americans attuned their stories, including their werewolf legends, partly to undermine shape-shifter mythology, not only of indigenous North Americans but also of their own prior historic civilizations. Time has repeatedly demonstrated how the repression of a deep myth in the collective unconscious erupts in violence, pathology, and—in our better moments of conscience—ensuing reform.

Large, predatory (or seemingly predatory) animals constitute one of the most intense childhood fears, one that usually lasts into adulthood. In his investigation of how we perceive and label wilderness, Roderick Nash includes Yi-Fu Tuan's *Landscapes of Fear,* in which Tuan claims that, besides darkness, "large animals are the only other subject of innate terror in very young children" (Nash, *Wilderness and the American Mind,* xvi, n.; Tuan, 133). Whether or not this is because of some biophilic impulse, fear generates images in the mind, which generates story. The stories born of animal fear or affinity appear early and often as fairy tales, folk tales, and (with sufficient force and time) myths, which Jack Zipes distinguishes from one another—and from other story categories—according to their methods and motives. They are: first, that the fairy tale is a written story, while the folk tale and myth are oral; and second, that the fairy tale originates from the "wonder story," designed to enchant, to awaken wonder, and so is built principally on transformation (Zipes, *Oxford Companion,* xv, xvii). The fairy tale's literary rise (xxvi–xxviii) against the stream of puritanical forces aligned to suppress it is in all but one way remarkable. It is unremarkable in that resistance and oppression always infuse the oppressed with a fire of new life unto the point of their total destruction or regrowth. The rise of the fairy tale is remarkable partly because that formidable stream of resistance to it united two otherwise crossed currents. The first was a religious crusade versus paganism that itself employed considerable magic (Flint, esp. 114–15; Westerkamp, 70). The second was a techno-industrial rationalist crusade against nature even as it tried to explain nature through science. Other animals living on the raw material of the earth, and so becoming totemic to pagan and especially nomadic societies, suffered greatly from the toxicity of this stream, despite all of its productive uses to eternally modernizing civilizations. Therefore, whatever degree of influence biophilia may have on the psychological formations we develop about animals, mass culture is adept at manipulating, warping, appropriating, filtering, and mediating those manifestations in practice. We can watch this happen, on page and screen, in werewolves.

We can safely say that the werewolf is a widespread figure, not exclusive to European mythology. But it is also not a generic manifestation of the global demihuman. Virgil writes in his *Eclogues* that by the power of "baneful herbs" (an alchemical mix of vervain and frankincense) "I have seen Moeris change to a wolf and hide in the forest, and often seen him conjure up souls from the depths of their tombs and move crops that have been planted to other fields" (Eclogue VIII). A specific formula is needed, a specific animal referent the result. To locate the werewolf in its American form, however, we are mostly outside of literature and into American Indian history and mythology. A few books in America, such as Alice Herndon Ernst's anthropological study *The Wolf Ritual of the Northwest Coast,* the fictions of Leslie Marmon Silko and Tony Hillerman, and Paula Underwood's *Who Speaks for Wolf* give us some insight to native ghost wolves. As with many of the myth collisions that occurred during European colonization, the werewolf mythology of Germany, France, the British Isles, and later legends imported by the British Raj or eastern European immigration found its way into a land already possessing a complicated demihuman mythology.

More animal-centered and biocentric for the most part, myths native to North America still contained their fair share of appropriation of the animal image. Among the Dineh (Navajo), the skinwalker was a malevolent force, while shamanic transformations in other tribal traditions were often horrific, traumatic.[1] A handful of examples of European and Native American myths will, I hope, sufficiently demonstrate the deep structure of transformational mythology that informs our current fascination with the werewolf. I will approach these later in the chapter.

This fascination manifests itself in America through pulp fiction and, perhaps more forcefully, through movies and television. Efforts to advance the technology used to refine the werewolf "change scene" in the movies are the focus of reviews; the werewolf genre depends heavily upon special effects.[2] But in some cases, especially on television, the makeup is so atrociously tacky and so little effort is made toward representing the werewolf in more than a vague symbolic fashion (rubber mask here, patchy tufts of hair there, something mean about the eyes, and some fangs pointing about in whatever direction) that our attention is called more to story. The mask's very inaccuracy shapes and augments its obvious symbolism. From the first *Wolfman* movies to the campy *I Was a Teenage Werewolf* and the *American Werewolf* films, through Jack Nicholson's publishing-house romance with Michelle Pfeiffer in *Wolf* to the neogothic machinations of *The Howling* or *Underworld* or the metacamp of *Buffy the Vampire Slayer*, Hollywood-budget effects and story combine to feed our fascination through image, and the quality has some range.[3] In print, as well, the result has mostly been pure pulp. Because this is a study of literary representations and not of film, and because the werewolf story in America is limited both in its indigeneity as literature and in its quality, film will have to receive cursory treatment. The werewolf is one among many tools we have used to create a wolf in our own image, an ever-present one in the bookstores and video feeds of America, and furthers the investigation into the mythic roots of our current pathological consciousness about other animals.

I will inspect some ancient stories that figure prominently in American re-mythology, then consider some of the western European material on werewolves, the British Isles having come to the fore as the enduring region of the figure. First, however, I feel the need to provide stipulative definitions of three terms that will appear in this chapter, so that we may consider the various layers of the werewolf in culture and the collective unconscious. These are *lycanthrope, shape-shifter,* and *werewolf.* Many works use these terms synonymously, which I am not necessarily opposing. But it's worthwhile to separate them for the purpose of differentiating the forms of "shifting" that define the human/wolf confluence. I'll say here that I am equally content to let the word *werewolf* suffice as the overarching term for this study, since looking at the monstrous manifestations in literature of the ghost wolf is where this road most often leads.

I would define *lycanthropy* in two forms, one the umbrella term in werewolf fiction for fantastic transformation, a subset of "werewolf," and the other a psychological condition, a taking on of certain pathological notions, neuroses, or behaviors that are inspired somehow by a ghost wolf and so are really pieces of a very human puzzle in the mind, sometimes having nothing biologically defensible to do with a wolf. The term *lycanthrope* appears in fantasy fiction as a way of legitimizing and complicating the werewolf; but it is still the id-driven side of the mythic coin, opposite clinical or ego-driven lycanthropy. That is, *lycanthrope* has a twin meaning, a double persona. I want to emphasize the second state; think of it as clinical lycanthropy. The lycanthrope may believe himself to be a wolf or werewolf but may not engage in any ritual transformation borne of a doctrine or headed toward some manifest goal. There is merely the vague notion of something "wolfish" that prompts behavior, a notion likely fueled by ignorance about real wolves.

Such behavior is often sociopathic and finally criminal, as Sabine Baring-Gould writes in *The Book of Werewolves:* "But it is very fearful to contemplate that there may still exist persons in the world filled with a morbid craving for human blood, which is ready to impel them to commit the most horrible atrocities, should they escape the vigilance of their guards, or break the bars of the madhouse which restrains them" (38). Michael Chabon picks up this theme in *Werewolves in Their Youth* in his story "Son of the Wolfman," which is about the offspring of a rape, with the rapist as (metaphorically speaking) a lycanthrope.

Shape-shifting is a ritual process by which a person tries to become, physically, an animal or some human-nonhuman interspecies aggregate. The animals of shape-shifting are myriad; the doppelgänger may change even into another human. This behavior, too, begins in the mind, but has two qualities distinguishing it from lycanthropy. The first is that it is generally communal, quest-oriented, and instigated by a sense of collective connection through ritual, often with the goal of return to the tribe and "changing back." The second is that it has faith in a physical transformation as a plausible outcome of the psychological transformation toward a wolf state of mind.[4] The depiction of the native shape-shifter to the exclusion of fuller cultural codes and mores is a high risk in fiction, criticism, and ethnography. The shape-shifting distinction may well be simply a white romantic way of framing the benevolent ghost. This strikes me as a case-by-case distinction to be made, as a shamanic moment is also too easily assumed to be New Age appropriation by default, diminishing a ritual experience by cynically "academizing" it.

While lycanthropy is privately psychological, however inevitably influenced by cultural mores, myths, and pressures, shape-shifting is communal and psychosomatic, however private the final experience of merging might be. If damage is the end, it is usually either in war (as with the *berserkir*) or toward a specific and conscious evil (as with skinwalkers). The physical possibility of a morphological transformation toward the lupine is literally immaterial to this definition. The werewolf is a belief, its manifestations all artifice.

To be possessed of a certain kind of wildness on the battlefield is perfectly acceptable; likewise of a different kind in the bedroom, and still another on the hunting ground. But a certain degree of faith is required in order to shape-shift, faith defined by stories that have conjoined into myth. I have to stress the difference in quality of the faith of the shape-shifter. It is more like the faith a weightlifter has who begins a set "to fatigue." Rather than performing a set of eight or ten repetitions, the lifter continues until the body cannot complete another rep, until the muscles reach their limit and the weight must come down. That limit isn't known at the start; indeed, the point of such conditioning is to let gravity, a law of the universe, determine the accomplishment of biology. This is the kind of faith that sets the athlete forward to an indeterminate goal, in the trust that the course is the reward. In the end, the athlete follows a faith in the body's ability to teach through action. The combination of raw talent, discipline, intelligence, and expert mentoring combine to this end.

The shape-shifter must believe in the transformation to a bear or jaguar or wolf, or the journey toward that impossibility will yield only theatrical results. The shape-shifter finds her way to a new self, but (and this is crucial) only *according to the animal as defined*. That is, how we think of a wolf determines the wolf we "become." Were it physically possible to transform, it would still, therefore, be far easier to change toward a ghost wolf than a real one. Transformation grows easier as the wolf becomes more ghostly—that is, more defined by what we make up about wolves than what wolves do and are. So we inevitably write stories about the demibeing, because it acts as the door, however dreadfully constructed, between ourselves and the selves of other animals. It is a dangerous door and more often than not results in some form of destruction, once its threshold is passed. How predictable it should be, then, that stories of transformation are usually either championed as emblematic of some violent prowess or rendered as narratives of horror. However, when the real wolf is maintained as both source and goal of the transformation, and so the corporeal wolf writes the doctrine, a certain kind of health may ensue, as through the vision quest. The shape-shifter may experience an epiphanic moment beyond simply "becoming a better hunter" and become a more fully defined human being, if only by virtue of realizing a truer nonhuman state.

The werewolf, as distinguished from the clinical lycanthrope or shape-shifter, is a monster. The werewolf is the most popular Western form to last in America out of a menagerie that includes the centaur, the minotaur, the satyr, and the mermaid (the latter's bid still alive through the manatee). Its presence permeates the vulgar literatures of horror and fantasy rooted in ancient European narratives of transformation. The frequent appearances of twins and doubles, and the invocation of crossings (of breed and border and water), in wolf mythology indicate some relationship—likely symbiotic—to the werewolf as a binary apparition. We seem obsessed with this bipartite design of the fantastic animal (we entertain a few more complicated combinations, such as the manticore), and the more intense this becomes, the more paradoxically permeable grows the separating line between the two sides. As such, the line becomes itself a powerful component, thus rendering the design tripartite, as I have explained with the World-Wolf model. There is air around the demibeing, land under its feet, water to drink. And this context explodes the isolated binary construct that the designer of the werewolf seeks to contain and control. Context classifies the organism. We have to make a werewolf fit in the world. The sheer titillation of that project, the dance with it in order to organize the world somehow and invest the environment, that realm outside our design, with our inventions—this is utterly irresistible. Indeed, it is one of the most intoxicating powers known to human beings.

What the lycanthrope, shape-shifter, and werewolf share is substantial. To say the demihuman is a person possessed of *wildness* is insufficient as an explanation of any of these forms. First, the possession may be of any moral degree and kind, so no universal motive can be located and no one pragmatic value determined. What we mean by all these terms is that someone is acting outside of social normalcy or civilized codes. The demihuman lives beyond mere transgression; it lives according to transformation. Half-animals are used in parables to teach lessons taken from the wild world and applied to the civilized world, and morals are to be found in nature as evidence of the order of God. But the demihuman may also be an indicator of demonic possession or malevolence, not so much a teacher as a challenger, and although the results may be the same from an encounter with either, the motives are necessarily different.

Multivalence is key to understanding this spiritual and religious design; crossing is not the affirmation of dichotomy but the perforation of it. Knowledge of self, each demibeast implies, is the beginning of both moral virtue and worldly wisdom. The lycanthrope demands therapeutic analysis of a mental condition of self. The shape-shifter demands repositioning the self outside the center of the universe and replacing it with another self. The werewolf is the classic id assuming control, or the shadow, the knowledge of which can only occur once the change back to human (if permitted) occurs. All forms focus on knowledge of the carnal or bestial self, with the biological self as indispensable to the equation.

This delineation of terms, including the flexibility for some interchange and the use of *werewolf* as the generic, is not a forecast for this chapter. Instead, I hope to better answer the question, "What is a werewolf?" only toward the end of better answering, "What does this mean to *wolves*?" This is so that we can learn what in us is helping or preventing the wolf's return to the world.

The Werewolf Model

Richard Preston Eckels's 1937 dissertation "Greek Wolf-lore" gives us the best available single study of the roots of occidental werewolf transformation. His four "classes of shape-shifters theoretically possible" constitute a heuristic applicable to all werewolf tales, including, but not limited to, the Greek legends on which he concentrates. The four classes are:

I.   Voluntary-congenital
II.   Voluntary-acquired
III.   Involuntary-congenital
IV.   Involuntary-acquired. (41)

These categories cover nature and culture, desire and surprise, choice and inevitability. All romance and realism is possible in them, from Ovid's great emphasis on the story of Lycaon and the Arcadians as a progenitive myth, through the medieval *lais* moralizing the gentility of transformation, to the bite of the werewolf causing a viral or genetic transfer. I have found no werewolf story that falls outside these designations. The rules having been established, the ghost wolf poured into the American mind from the great cauldron of world myth is hardly originally American and must be considered in terms of its colonialism. Eckels applies his system exclusively to Greek legends of shape-shifting, specifically werewolf stories, connecting his work to Walter Burkert's *Homo Necans,* Mircea Eliade's *Myth of the Eternal Return,* and René Girard's work on the scapegoat.

Another important compilation, this one annotating and chronologically categorizing an enormous array of werewolf writing, is Brian J. Frost's *Essential Guide to Werewolf Literature.* As a handbook to the genre, it is rivaled only by Adam Douglas's *Beast Within,* which is more concerned with the lycanthropic model of transformation, more narrative in its approach, and slightly more British in focus. Frost takes some risks declaring firsts and lasts but often demonstrates some prescience. He also corroborates thoroughly. He notes *The Satyricon* as first employing the werewolf (51) and gives us several milestones for the werewolf story. In the meantime, a précis of Frost's book should sufficiently prove the scope of the werewolf tale and its literary importance. His work is chronological; I will at times reorder it more categorically.

According to Frost, the first step the werewolf tale takes beyond its classical form is "Bisclavret," which transports the tale to England from France (51). He credits the "Lay de Melion" and "Arthur and Gorlagon" with energizing the British werewolf tale (53), and I have not found a rebuttal. I will return to these stories in a later section. "After the demise of the medieval romance," Frost writes, "interest in the werewolf motif waned almost to the point of extinction and wasn't fully revived until the early nineteenth century" (55). He calls "William and the Werewolf" the first "benevolent werewolf" story (55) and traces the benevolent werewolf from this moment through his entire chronology. Seabury Quinn's eight werewolf stories for *Weird Tales,* for instance, include "The Gentle Werewolf" in 1940, which is set in the Holy Land and resonant of the French lays (157).

Frost also has the Victorian era introducing the female werewolf (59). He tracks this as a subgenre.[5] Several of the stories he notes are not of transformations into wolves, but into other animals. This contextualizes Frost's work in terms of the transformation tale, though at times it diverts us from the agency of the werewolf in story.

A number of canonical examples pepper Frost's annotated chronology. Montague Summers perhaps barely qualifies for the literary list, but his *The Werewolf* is a seminal text in the genre, referred to as often as any other werewolf book. Algernon Blackwood's "Running Wolf" appears in Frost (102), and the combination of Blackwood and Summers gives us in part the context in which Poe worked and from which he departed to form his own fiction. Frost uses George W. M. Reynolds's *Wagner the Wehr-Wolf* as a literary example of the penny-blood (63–65), and Dumas's *Wolf-Leader* is a little-known work by the famous adventure novelist (66). Most of the stories achieving some literary value are lycanthropy stories—focused on the psychologically monstrous rather than on the gore and prurience of other werewolf fiction.

Some examples include *Hughes-le-Loup; or, The Man-Wolf,* which introduces the psychological werewolf story (68–69), Guy de Maupassant's "The Wolf" (see Frost's comment, 70), and Stevenson's *Dr. Jekyll and Mr. Hyde,* all psychological stories related to lycanthropy through a highly generic sense of the beast transformation (72–74). Frost deftly connects these to Stevenson's specifically lycanthropic story "Olalla" (75–76). Arthur Conan Doyle's "A Pastoral Horror" (79), Rudyard Kipling's "Mark of the Beast" (80), and Ambrose Bierce's "Eyes of the Panther" (which is conflated with the werewolf) are all psychological stories, and this group is capped in Frost's view by Clemence Houseman's "The Were-Wolf" (81–86). Houseman is given superlative reviews and used as transition to the Nordic interest written into other British tales. Frost cites *Steppenwolf* as the modern realization of psychological lycanthropy (102) and mentions Greye la Spina's "Wolf of the Steppes" (119) and Bernard King's *Vargr-Moon* (210) as strong modernist lycanthropy stories.

I would add Frank Norris's line in *McTeague,* when his main character is "wondering what now he was to do to fight the wolf away," to be read as a lycanthropic metaphor, bearing in mind that the assumption of the wolf's aspect in Norris's story is of both its economic referent and McTeague's own malevolence (258). As a plot-of-decline narrative, *McTeague* follows a man to a mythically bestial state. Although it is not a literal transformation, Norris's own use of the wolf image (and our knowledge that "The Wolf" was to finish his three-novel commentary on class) indicates a literary moment invoking the werewolf tale. Frost does mention Norris's *Vandover the Brute* and "The Wolf." He also adds the obscure Norris story "Crepuscularism" from *Overland Monthly* (97).

Most of Frost's list to this point covers two major categories of British werewolf fiction: the Victorian tale and the modern tale, tracked through various subgenres. The subgenre of satire (95, 183–84) includes a story called "The Beatnik Werewolf" and sets up the '60s kitsch tale.

Gothic horror, especially through the vampire connection (92, 114, 133, 137), includes a set of stories that link the werewolf and vampire via the crucifix—which gives the connection a Christian flavor beyond the mark of the beast (169). One novel combines the vampire theme and the benevolent werewolf theme: "Peaceful werewolves find themselves the target[s] of an unknown assassin in Tanya Huff's *Blood Trail* . . . , which is the second volume in a series of mystery-adventure novels featuring a crime-fighting vampire" (222). This theme is made popular in the role-playing games and spin-off novels of the World of Darkness, which seem an obvious influence on the *Underworld* movies.

The Christian connection is worth considering vis-à-vis Slotkin, Coleman, and other pogrom histories, and Frost cites it several more times.[6] The White Wolf books of The World of Darkness, which offer an environment of decidedly Catholic-versus-pagan conflict and naturalistic determinism, are briefly mentioned (227). As if this accounting of subgenres weren't sufficient, Frost even manages to find an entire thread of works using the "severed limb" theme (92–96).

Perhaps most prominent in this category of Frost's study is the relationship of the werewolf to the vampire through sex (Red Riding Hood and the bite/seduction) and cannibalism (especially the consumption of the innocent). During the 1930s, Frost notes, there was a shift to "Weird Menace" stories that included "fake werewolves" (see 141–42), among them "Werewolf of Wall Street," a story fitting the literary naturalist metaphors used by Zola, Norris, and many others to connect corporate industrialism to human violation. But the vampire and werewolf did not finally dissolve into metaphoric suggestions of transformation; on the contrary, they outlasted those. Like werewolf stories, vampire stories are now too numerous to track, part of the explosive replication that takes place in Internet culture, where stories congeal and restream like blood cells.

The body as consumed, the "little death" metaphor of orgasm, and the "beast within" are all prominent motifs in the vampire story. But what differentiates the werewolf story is its dependence upon the beast *without*. The vampire, while totemically connected to the bat, the wolf, the venomous snake, and to vapor, maintains a basic human vantage point, however hideous. The werewolf is about how bestial the human might become—more specifically, how lupine. The wolf, rather than the human, is one of two figures in the transformation, so that the binary is connected to a real animal, a living being associated with wilderness. This linkage also means that the differences between wolf and man are no more important than the similarities, the cooperative figuring into the werebeing. The vampiric binary is between life and death found in the liminal space, or the third state, of undeath. Another prominent feature in both the werewolf and vampire story is the transformed character's obsession with control, the struggle over whether to live wild or civilized that in turn becomes a struggle over fate and free will. The werewolf story's wildness is unlike the generic and anthropic form of the vampire's because its yin and yang were fully formed outside and before the mind that perceived them. Frost does not make this distinction; I offer it here because it is crucial to how we use such a bibliography to comprehend the influences on the wolf myth in America and distinguish, in this case, the gothic ones from the werewolf's characteristics that are not to be subsumed by one subgenre.

The strict murder-mystery structure casting the werewolf as killer is noted only once (102), to which I would add Tony Hillerman's *The Blessing Way* and Wayne Smith's *Thor.* We find that the werewolf murder mystery is almost always couched in the erotic horror story: "Red Riding Hood" turned slasher pulp (see esp. 141–42); Robert Bloch's twist on it vis-à-vis an affair story in "The Man Who Cried 'Wolf!'" (165–66); and a she-male fetish turned violent in "Night Drive" (176–77). Bloch's "Eena," which Frost calls his best work, includes several of the tropes of the transformation tale: a lake, raising a wolf, a she-wolf, and a beautiful woman in the romance tradition (which I find continued through to Kelley Armstrong's *Bitten*). Stephen King's *Cycle of the Werewolf,* which connects erotic and Christian themes through a werewolf priest, ranks as high-end teen market erotic pulp (209).

Frost also mentions the werewolf western (119, 167), including Max Brand's "The Werewolf," which appeared in *Western Story* magazine in 1926 (119). I'll single out this story for several reasons. First, it indicates Brand's wolf interest that he continues in his novel *White Wolf,* which is a wolf western rather than a werewolf western. Second, the preparatory short story indicating a wolf interest that later appears in a novel seems to be a pattern revealing itself in Frost— although he doesn't make this explicit—from pulp like Brand to literature like Norris. This is true of London as well and indicates a pattern of testing the werewolf character in story before trying to sustain it. Third, Frost points out that *Western Story* was one of the very few publications that ran werewolf stories besides *Weird Tales,* which controlled the genre for many years (119). To the werewolf western list I would again add *The Blessing Way,* a versatile high-pulp novel for the werewolf genre.

By the end of his third chapter Frost has covered thirty-three werewolf stories and mentioned nearly a dozen more. The numbers grow nearly exponentially, as what Frost has uncovered is the growth of the werewolf tale over time, rather than its diminishment by the supposed civilizing of Europe and America. He tracks specific works until he reaches his point of fatigue, the numbers finally proving a supply, if not inexhaustible, then beyond comprehension. As the chapters continue, both their titles and Frost's language indicate an increasing labor to keep up with the werewolf bibliography.

After treating the pulp magazines in his fourth chapter, Frost continues in the psychological vein, demonstrating how werewolf literature of the 1930s–1940s moved to a more Freudian mode even while the romance werewolf stories still continued and sold (145). He gives his closest attention to Guy Endore's *Werewolf of Paris,* which receives the most thorough treatment of any story in Frost's book (145–52). His fifth chapter is "The Beast Within," the title of Adam Douglas's book. It contains a thread of psychological lycanthropy and carries this to the fusion of mind and body popularized in 1960s treatments. Frost cites this period as a weak one for werewolf writing (campy and satirical treatments seem to have been more the norm). One odd development during this time, prophetic in a way, is the turn toward technological and biological explanations for—and instigations of—werewolf transformation. There are stories placing werewolves on other planets or transporting them from medieval Europe to the present (185, and especially Niven's "There's a Wolf in My Time Machine," 200). This techno-futurist theme continues into the 1980s, when it turns to biotech with David Robbins's *The Wrath,* a novel that depicts a transformation-inducing plague in the postapocalyptic world, and other stories connecting lycanthropy with viruses or drugs (209–10, 174–76, 178, 225).

Frost calls the 1970s the "Boom Years" (187). He notes Whitley Streiber's *The Wolfen* as a stronger realization of the theme begun in Williamson's *Darker Than You Think,* the theme of "werewolves living among us" (also see Martin's *The Skin Trade* for the secret society of werewolves theme, Frost 213). Gary Brandner's *The Howling* was the 1970s' highest-selling werewolf novel, followed by "inferior sequels" (190). Both Streiber's and Brandner's novels were made into popular movies, which themselves spawned a revival of the gothic romance in other movies, followed by commercial novelizations in a kind of vicious cycle (192–94). In one brief section of his work on the '70s, Frost lists twenty-seven stories and a half dozen poems (200–201), with eighteen novels listed in a following section on the 1980s (211), which he calls a particularly gory period for the werewolf story (201).

The medieval theme threads through Frost's study as well. He includes the

Nordic stories of Tyr (81), Sigmund (100), the Ring of the Niebelung (155), and of course, the *berserkir,* especially in Roger Elwood's "The Berserkers." A "werewolf history" theme is prominent among werewolf myths, partly as it invokes the primitivist romance of the "long ago" (which I address in chapter 12) and partly as a way of asserting a fictional corporeality—an "evolved" werewolf. Chelsea Quinn Yarbro's "The Godforsaken" places the vampire/werewolf connection in a presentist medieval court drama, a common approach to vampire stories (203) but seldom applied to the more feral werewolf until the World of Darkness phenomenon summarized in *Underworld.* The source for this courtly setting with a werewolf at the table is the story of Marrok, the werewolf knight at Arthur's Round Table. Frost gives a moment to *Moon Dance,* S. P. Somtow's two-hundred-year violent epic of werewolves fleeing Europe (205–6). H. P. Lovecraft, who had written his own werewolf verse narrative in the medieval tradition ("Psychopompous"), once called for a story from a werewolf's point of view (Frost, 141). This request would be periodically answered through the 1980s, the success of each attempt less important than the complex experiment with cognition that formed the lycanthropy story.

Frost titles one section on the 1990s "A Werewolf Bonanza" (215). After the dearth of work in the 1960s was followed by the rise of the werewolf novel over the next two decades, the 1990s produced a number that "was quite phenomenal, eclipsing the output of any previous decade by a wide margin" (216). The writing maintained a characteristically "low standard" in Frost's opinion. This means, if we accept Frost's judgment (and I am obviously inclined to do so), that the werewolf myth gained in appeal to a broader base of the reading population but held its vulgar form throughout its growth, influencing the minds of readers with material that retains a regressive and increasingly violent approach. This should come as no surprise; nearly all commercialized literature works in this way, but what the pattern here corroborates is the force of the ghost wolf over the production of image on a mass scale. It also points up the difficulty of the real wolf—given its far less ubiquitous presence—to compete. Frost here categorizes a list of 132 novels in an eighteen-page span (215–33). Mentionables include Brian Stableford's *Werewolves of London* (219) and Smith's *Thor* (224), told from a German shepherd dog's point of view.

A phenomenon of the 1990s werewolf book is what Frost calls "the paranormal romance," which he incorrectly describes as "a relatively new category of popular fiction" (230) but does a fine job analyzing nonetheless. The paranormal romance was once known by such other appellations as the "specter bridegroom" story or the "arabesque" and was a staple of the nineteenth-century marketplace, where it was perhaps best realized in the psychological experimental fiction of

Edgar Allan Poe.[7] Where Frost hits home is in this summation of the subgenre as it modernized:

> Aimed primarily at women readers, these novels [the paranormal romances] are for the most part spicy love stories in which vampires, werewolves, and other supernatural beings play a major role in the plot. There are, however, some striking differences between the supernormal protagonists of novels in this category and their counterparts in horror fiction. Werewolves of the male gender, for instance, are generally portrayed as misunderstood outsiders who regard their ability to change into a wolf as an asset rather than a curse. Dark, brooding, and slightly dangerous to know, they embody the admirable as well as the wild and unpredictable qualities of the wolf; but, most importantly, they are magnetically attractive lovers whom the heroine is unable to resist, even after she has learned their dark secret. (230)

What we see here is the benevolent ghost wolf; the connection to the gothic romance and revision of it toward the popular and pose-driven goth subculture; the resolution in the modern (especially gendered feminine) mind of the Red Riding Hood erotic frisson; the puzzle over wildness; and the standard "dark secret" of romance plotlines. In trying to reconcile the Old World werewolf and the New World obsession with newness, the plots of the paranormal romance revert to certain necessary mythic tropes. One is the ancient, the prospect of the supernatural simply being an older natural—a fantastic world that existed before, rather than away from, this one. Another is the period romance, usually the medieval romance of Britain or France or the Renaissance romance of Italy, France, or Spain; Frost spends two pages considering such representative texts as Susan Krinard's *Prince of Wolves* (232–33). The low quality of the writing in the werewolf subgenre as a whole reveals itself when Frost declares Alice Borchardt's *Silver Wolf* to be "a brilliant debut novel," one of his few points with which I disagree (233).

After spending a few pages on children's werewolf literature, Frost concludes his study with an excellent list of anthologies, along with analyses of those anthologies. The literary examples come to the fore here, primarily in Frost's edited *Book of the Werewolf* and Bill Pronzini's *Werewolf! A Chrestomathy of Lycanthropy*. The latter includes: "The Wolf" by de Maupassant, Kipling's "Mark of the Beast," Stoker's "Dracula's Guest," and "Gabriel Ernst" by Saki (Frost, 241). Peter Haining's anthology *Werewolf: Horror Stories of the Man-Beast* includes a list of science fiction and fantasy authors of note such as James Blish, Brian Aldiss, Mercedes Lackey, Fritz Leiber, Algernon Blackwood, T. H. White, and Jane Yolen (Frost, 240–43). Frost takes a few sentences to explain that the Blackwood story "The Wolves of God," rather than being a werewolf story proper, only has "a minor reference to shape-shifting, but the supernatural beings known as 'the Wolves of God' are actually a ghostly pack of wolves who, according to Native American Lore, punish malefactors" (242). The anthology he cites as the "biggest, and possibly the best" is *The Mammoth Book of Werewolves,* to which he devotes three pages of detail (246–48).

I have lingered on this several-page introduction to an annotated bibliography in large part out of respect for Brian Frost's indefatigable efforts. His stamina for reading prose that often requires more than perhaps it gives back is commendable, and his organization of *The Essential Guide to Werewolf Literature* is clear and accessible. I have also lingered in order to show how even a cursory treatment of a summary text still reveals the considerable volume needed to account for the galaxies of werewolf stories whirling about the American mind over decades of accumulation and recasting.

We have to spread out a big map that includes parallel universes in which the fantastic markers are clearer to the traveler than the real ones, a map on which there are drawn gates through which we pass and transform. The map of the real cannot become less tangible, though. We have to come back. Wolves grow easier for us to change into dogs, into human beings, into monsters of mind and body, when we travel using the wrong guidance. The reason for the fantastic map is self-analysis, which is reconciliation with the real, not subjugation of it.

The Werewolf Ships

The *Mabinogion* (eleven tales of Wales's early mythic national history), the Roman wolf mythos, and the Nordic legends of wolf totemism may have lurked even longer in the shadow of French and British minds after their classical occupations were it not for a resurgence of the werewolf tale in the 1400s, which released it in force. This occurred in no small part because of witch-hunting. The Inquisitions of the thirteenth century, especially Pope Gregory IX's crusades against shape-shifters through the *Ad Extirpanda,* combined with two forms of tract literature toward embedding the werewolf in the northern European mind. The first form was the higher, evident in the songs of France, such as the "Lay de Melion." The Holy Roman Empire's condemnation of Else of Meersburg for riding a wolf in 1440 and the conflation of Gilles de Rais's child murders with shape-shifting were among many political incidents that generated the second form of story—the medieval equivalent of tabloid journalism. In the midst of all this appeared two of the most important fictional documents in Europe, each of which contained subtle versions of the werewolf tale. The first was Sir Thomas Malory's *Le Morte Darthur* in 1469, which absorbed the French *lais* into a Celto-British tome that established a sizable portion of British identity. The second was the *Malleus Maleficarum,* or "Hammer of Witches," published in 1487—perhaps the most influential occult text of the Renaissance aside from the Bible. The "Hexenhammer," as it was called in Germany where it first appeared, tried to prove witchcraft to be both present and effective in order to provide the Holy Inquisition with greater power.

By 1550, when Johann Weir began the work of considering the werewolf as a psychological phenomenon rather than as a magical manifestation, the legend had already built sufficient momentum to become myth (Steiger, 320–21). The delusion defense did little to assuage the belief that the werewolf was at work in the world; indeed, it may have made the ghost more terrifying by abstracting it further. For a hundred years, beginning in 1575, trials against a fertility cult called the Benandanti, along with scattered stories from the prior century, brought Italian werewolf legends to the fore (see Ginzburg). In eastern Europe the legends of both gypsy trail and king's forest promoted a globalization of the tale up to the Age of Enlightenment, which then repressed what had already been adopted en masse. In this way the lycanthrope lost out for two centuries to a more polarized negotiation between the shape-shifter and the werewolf monster.

The British colonists born from the 1570s to '90s would have known (from their parents and ministers) of the French werewolf trials and of the new sophisticated ways of tracking and trapping werewolves developed from Spain to Scotland. When they boarded their ships, they carried with them more than a concept of religious freedom, the means to built trade colonies, and the rats and diseases of Europe. They carried the complexes and neuroses of minds deeply troubled about wilderness.[8]

The label G. L. Kittredge uses generically for the many stories similarly depicting transmogrification into the wolf is "The Werewolf's Tale" (2). The ghost wolf connected to the water crossing survived in popular culture as the werewolf, during the founding of the colonies very much alive as an element of witchery and as a presence in the forests surrounding the little lighted clearings of settlement, kept alive in the modern consciousness first by campfire tales and sermons, then by movies and television. The tale followed the most powerful course of story-to-myth mass regeneration and is an undeniable presence in the American unconscious.

The streams that feed major rivers are called tributaries, as are the subservient kingdoms or baronies of a feudal empire. Legends might follow this metaphor as well—a great legend fed by the tributaries of other stories may be compared to water changing colors at a confluence—and this process may be violent. The Arthurian cycle is one of the great legends influencing Euro–North American literary culture, and as such its tributaries—the *lais* and tales of the troubadours, the Latin allegories of the parish priests, the bestiaries and the märchen, *The Mabinogion*—these all feed that stream we dam into controllable reservoirs of Euro–North American power, as Herodotus or Holinshed or Monmouth would have liked. When we trace our modernizations of those stories backward, exploring how their hermeneutic puzzles have remained unsolved, we may find buried in the old texts some significant underground rivulets, some feculence of superstition and violence that poisons our supposed progress toward an easier, more convenient world. As a result, we perpetuate medieval thinking even as we attempt to transcend it through hypertechnology and jackbooted industrialism.

The accrual of some medieval legends of the werewolf should help us better understand the mythic constructs that follow over the centuries before the colonization of America and the formation of the Euro-American wolf myth. Characteristic of the tale is that the forest of adventure is juxtaposed with the court as the story's setting. Other common elements to tales in which the wolf appears include a noble as the werewolf; a false wife, often precipitating an act of deceit that causes or complicates the werewolf's transformation; the removal or misplacing of clothing; a body of water often connected to the transformation; a ring or other talisman; the werewolf trapped in wolf form and forced to communicate with humans in some clever way; and the werewolf raging at a ceremony, often a wedding involving the false wife.

In the 1189 "Bisclavret" (or the Norman "Garwaf"), a noble in Brittany named Bisclavret sometimes disappears for three-day stints until his wife fears that he has a lover. She confronts him, to which he replies that he cannot tell her why he disappears. She finally coaxes him into revealing that he travels to the forest and hunts prey as a werewolf, that he must be naked to accomplish the change, and that, should he ever lose his clothes from their hiding place, he will stay a werewolf forever. He finally reveals the hiding place—a hollow stone near a chapel. Overcome by her terror at being married to a werewolf, the wife bargains to be the mistress of a knight she does not love in exchange for his theft of her husband's clothes. The noble, trapped in wolf form, disappears, and the lady marries her paramour.

A year later, on a hunting expedition, the king comes across a wolf so noble and well behaved that the king takes him back to the palace as a pet. At a feast to which the barons of the land are all invited, the wolf tries to attack the knight. Never having seen the wolf furious, the court assumes that he must have a reason. This reason is provided in time when, during a stay at a country house after hunting with his pet wolf, the king is met by Bisclavret's wife. The wolf attacks her, tearing off her nose. Instead of killing the wolf, a man in the king's entourage offers the hypothesis that the wife must know the wolf's reason. For his part, the king tortures the wife until she confesses her betrayal. The king has the clothes brought to Bisclavret, who is too embarrassed to dress until the court provides him privacy. In the king's bedchamber the noble dresses and falls asleep, as a man, in the king's bed. The story ends with the banishment of the wife and the knight, who have several children born without noses.

Other similar Werewolf's Tales are the "Lay de Melion," "Guillaume de Palerne," the Morraha (also known as "The Story of the Sculloge's Son from Muskerry" and a story-within-a-story called "Fios Fath An Aon Sceil"), "Arthur and Gorlagon" (a redaction of the Tochmar Etaine from the Welsh *Mabinogion*), and one line from Sir Thomas Malory's famous *Le Morte Darthur* (what Eugène Vinaver published as *Works of Sir Thomas Mallory*). The "Lay de Melion" maintains the resonant images of The Werewolf's Tale (the hunting noble; the device, here a ring, of transformation; and the recognition of nobility in the animal by the king) and includes the Celto-Germanic element of the Irish princess, although the fée ethic is forgone for a political version of The False Wife's Tale.[9] It involves a noble's marriage to the virgin Irish princess, a hunt during which Melion uses a ring to change into a wolf, the wife's betrayal of Melion with a squire, and a ceremony in Arthur's court in which Melion attacks his betrayers, is vindicated, and is returned to his normal shape (Donovan, 74–75).

Kate Watkins Tibbals claims that the central figure of "Guillaume de Palerne" is not William of Palerne, but Alphouns, the werewolf (1). Another fine analysis of the story appears in Charles Dunn's *The Foundling and the Werwolf*. In this tale we see the water crossing, the juxtaposition of court and wild, and the hunting scene that mediates those spaces. There is the magic of the number seven and the significance of clothing versus nakedness as emblematic of taming the savage nature.[10] A stepmother-enchantress jealous of Alphouns's birthright over her own son's begins the trouble, which ends in a Shakespearean multiple marriage. It includes the abduction/adoption of William by Alphouns, with the werewolf raising the man who becomes, at the story's end, the emperor of Rome. It is a foundational tale and stands among those that influenced James Fenimore Cooper—full of disguise and intrigue of highly implausible but mythic value.

The work of G. L. Kittredge on the tales of Morrighan, Morraha, and Arthur and Gorlagon is indispensable to an understanding of the medieval werewolf legends and will appear as I unpack the Arthurian story of Marrok. All of these tales feed the Arthuriad, but I would like to focus on a curious line in Malory as indicative of the way the werewolf is subtly insinuated into the mythos of colonial America.

Marrok

The Arthurian cycle is possibly the most prominent late European myth transported across the Atlantic, and embedded in its text, almost smuggled over, is a very subtle but influential image of the wolf. In *Le Morte Darthur* Sir Thomas Malory writes of a brief incident regarding the healing of one Sir Urry. Malory claims to have taken this incident from the "Freynshe boke," presumably a vulgate of the Arthur saga from which he selected most of his information (Vinaver, 1145). Malory again mentions the source in his conclusion, this time referring to the great battles of Lancelot, the knight who for a time lived as *l'homme sauvage*, the Wild Man of many legends (1154). According to Malory, Urry sustained his wounds at a Spanish tournament, during which he slew an earl's son named Alpheus (in the Greek a river god, in the Germanic a derivation of "wolf"), and received seven wounds while doing so. "And thys sir Alpheus," says Malory, "had a modir [whiche] was agrete sorseras; and she, for the despyte of hir sunnes deth, wrought be her suttyle craufftis that sir Urry shulde never be hole, but ever his woundis shulde one tyme fester and another tyme blede, so that he should never be hole untyll the beste knyght of the worlde had serched his wounds" (1145).

The best knight is, of course, Lancelot, who finds Urry only after the wounded knight, carried on a horse-litter by his mother and sister, has searched for seven years over the king's lands.

The healing of Sir Urry is, in many ways, a lull before Lancelot's confrontations with the family of Aggravayne. We get a roll call of the 149 knights present at the Round Table in Lancelot's absence, which includes a Sir Severaunce, against whom Lancelot was never to fight because Sir Severaunce wished to fight only "ayenste gyauntis and ayenste dragons and wylde bestis" (1148). It also includes a Sir Melyon of the Mountayne (Urry is also "of the Mounte") and a Sir Tor "that was begotyn uppon the cowardis wyff, but he was begotyn afore Aryes wedded her," so that Tor was actually a son of the Pellynore. I mention these characters because of the topics with which each is associated, respectively: monster-slaying, a mountain (or wilderness) birthplace, the name Melion, and a false wife. Among these knights, all of whom try their hands at the healing of Urry, is one Sir Marrok, "the good knyght" whom Malory says "was betrayed with his wyff, for he made hym seven yere a warwolff" (1150). Note that by this point we have a wolf-mother (Alpheus's witch mother) cursing a knight (Urry) whose healing is attempted by a werewolf (Marrok) but can only be accomplished by a wild man (Lancelot).

In the larger context of the knights' great deeds and the sheer mass of the Arthurian *Works,* the line on Marrok may seem to be a matter-of-fact mention, one among many more significantly fantastic elements of the tale that would depict Arthur as a hero-king. Because he was using a French book of unknown origin, Malory was allowed to quote freely the fantastic as something peculiarly French, to which the readers of medieval England could respond as they wished without struggling over the correspondence between pure fantasy and propaganda (which is moderated fantasy) such as Geoffrey of Monmouth's *History of the Kings of Britain*. Despite King Arthur's traffic with the werewolf, when William Caxton's 1485 printing of Malory's version was distributed, the real wolf was already being driven from the British Isles, and the corporeal wolf was being expurgated from writing, along with legends of the fée and heresy about beasts. The wolf's image as the devil was then recast during the Enlightenment as a more utilitarian target—a pest to shepherds and cowherds. But the former devil image was not replaced; it was paired with the image of this economic pest, each image serving to bolster the other during a time when the equation of prosperity with godly favor began to mass-monetize barter economies.[11] This was the ghost wolf that would be carried to the New World.

In his *Bestiary* T. H. White writes, "The eternal enemy of the lamb is of course the wolf, and the shift toward Christ the Lamb naturally led to the growing use of lupine imagery in Satanic iconography" (115). White's comment is in response to the depiction of animals in art as representatives—for instance, that Christ is not to be painted *as* a lamb but may be painted *with* one in order to reinforce the allegory: "For what can we mean by the Wolf except the Devil, what by the man except sin, what by the stones except the apostles or other saints or Our Lord himself?" (115). Adam Douglas refers to the lamb/wolf relationship, "proverbial among pastoral cultures from time immemorial," being used by the church of the Middle Ages as a clear metaphor for the Christ/Antichrist relationship (114–15). He also refers to the verse from Isaiah in which the wolf and lamb lie together (11:6) as "apposite" to the werewolf tale (315). The common misquotation of this verse as having the lion lie down with the lamb is in keeping with the tradition of denigrating the wolf and ennobling the lion, even as a metaphor for the Adversary and even so far as bowdlerizing the very Bible. Kirby Smith states that the Norse myths, which through the Volsungasaga's concern for battle prowess were possibly the most complimentary of werewolf stories, are nevertheless fitted with a satanic persona in the Fenris wolf—the great destroyer (37), either equating the trickster (Loki, Fenris's sire) with the devil or acknowledging Satan as a trickster (challenger) figure or foil.[12]

What, then, sits across from Arthur at his table each day up to and after the healing of Urry? What did Sir Marrok see in the knight who also bore wounds for seven years until he was healed by Lancelot, a feral man and the seducer of Arthur's wife? And why would Marrok, himself once bedeviled, gain the blessing of Arthur and become one of the trusted knights of the realm? Far from an incidental mention, the line in Malory about Marrok's transformation emphasizes the motifs of infidelity, chivalry, rebirth, forgiveness, and justice that resonate throughout the Arthurian cycle and its later Christo-American versions.

Wild Men

The best work to consult for an overview of how several cultures' legends create this amalgam of European werewolf stories is Kirby F. Smith's "Historical Study of the Werwolf in Literature." The Volsungasaga of Scandinavian mythology generated a shape-shifting legend of "wolf-coats," the úlfheðnar akin to the *berserkir*, who by wearing the skins of wolves became superhumanly ferocious in battle (8–9). This is a fairly popular wolf legend to modern readers, but in the Norse and Scandinavian sagas the wolf took on a variety of pagan roles that maintained only a few vestiges in the later British and French tales. The shape-shifter could as often be female as male, both Odin and Freya having wolf totems; it could be both benevolent and malevolent, both Odin and Loki having wolf totems; and it could negotiate those binaries itself, as seen in the Fenris legend (see Wallner).

The founding of Rome by the progeny of a she-wolf is also burdened by multiple and contradictory meanings colored by the politics of ascendancy. The *lukos* borrowed by Latins from the Greeks and Etruscans in order to build Rome's image may have been conflated with the "lupa," a harlot who raised Romulus and Remus, as the Romans called prostitutes "she-wolves" and Livy entertains the idea that Acca Larentia, who may have raised the twins, was less an earth mother than an opportunistic courtesan (Livius, i:4; Hornblower, 3). The *lukos* and *lupus* connection is also of linguistic interest—linking the wolf both to light and to Apollo, who also had a wolf totem. The twins may have been further elevated by the myth of the exposed child—common in cultures all over the world from Moses to stories of the Buddha to Mowgli and the Amala and Kamala hoax in India of the 1950s—in which the abandoned child is raised by wolves and grows to some important position in his or her culture.[13] The wolf in Roman legend was also considered a god of death, and in the later *Ecbasis captivi* and *Ysengrim* of the tenth and twelfth centuries respectively, the wolf Isengrim appears as a mythic devouring wolf driven by stupidity and blind greed.

Through the Roman Empire's commerce with Scandinavian legends that resulted from both the Viking invasions and the dominating mythology of Germania, a paving of the foundational European wolf mythos occurred. On it the

Holy Roman Empire stood, directly between the gothic wolf myths and fables of eastern Europe and the western European Christianization of the bestiaries, *lais,* and allegorical moral tales.

The Germanic wolf legends grew partly out of, partly adjacent to, the Norse mythology. The wolf skin for battle becomes a wolf girdle, and the Grimm brothers collect German folktales they occasionally rewrite away from the Nordic sentiments more forgiving of wolf nature. The German tales are particularly important because they seem to provide a forked bridge to the British tales. The first fork runs to the Celts, the second to the Norman French. Charles Perrault's version of "Little Red Riding Hood," the one finally adapted in the United States to include a hunter who saves the day (as opposed to Red and Grandma simply being eaten), was probably influenced greatly by German folk versions of the story.[14]

While it is impossible to list the full panoply of wolf stories that infused the culture of the second wave of colonization of the Americas, I have tried to provide a few influential examples. Without some sense of the half millennium of Northern Hemispheric exchanges that occurred regarding wolf myths we cannot know the form and color of the invading mythos that reached North America in the fourteenth and fifteenth centuries. The attempted extermination of the wolf became analogous to the extermination of whole ecosystems and of the cultures that inhabited them, and such a scale of destruction required a mythic fuel for its fire. In order to shape a nation in the image of the colonizers' gods, which were the Holy Trinity and Money, the marriage of which produced the demigod the colonists thought of as Civilization, they needed ancient justifications. Whether they were fully conscious of these is beside the point. The embedded myth does not necessarily require full disclosure; indeed, it may be most powerful when repressed.

Finally, it is important to note that while the Northern Hemisphere produced the strongest wolf legends (because wolves lived in it), the southern legends of India, Abyssinia, and South America all carried shape-shifters. Smith mentions the Tiger-Men of India and the Abyssinian Hyena-Men (40); other sources examine the werejaguars of the Amazon and Crocodile-Men in swampbound cultures and devote some attention as well to parallel myths of transformation (see Bynum; Frost; Douglas; Eliot, Campbell, & Eliade; and Burkert). Arriving from Africa, reenchanted with powerfully ambivalent biblical imagery and a horrific Roman legacy, the lion achieved the most prominent heraldic position in all of Europe, and throughout Europe the shape-shifting myths of exotic cultures legitimized their universality. Especially with the rise of agriculture on grander scales, the wolf became one of the more popular choices for transformation stories. In all these cases, men wore the mantle, and even when advancing age forbade their transformation in war, they were yet compelled to become bestial in art.

The tapestry art and folklore of the Middle Ages made popular the legend of the Wild Man, a fictional figure who usually lived in the woods and was depicted with profuse body hair, a club, and occasionally a loincloth of vine. Richard Bernheimer provides an excellent summary of this figure, including its appearances in Arthurian literature. He includes two particularly relevant notes on the werewolf, one regarding Guillaume de Palerne and the other Monmouth's *Vita Merlini*. Bernheimer's discussion of Guillaume, corroborated by Smith, identifies the story as a cousin of the Wild Man legend. The lovers in Guillaume depend for their survival on the help of a werewolf, a sylvan creature who before his transformation was human. But Bernheimer rightly separates the legends; the Wild Man may keep the company of wolves (*Gawain and the Green Knight* contains an example) but is in fact not a shape-shifter. He is human, though feral (Bernheimer, 164).

Bernheimer's notes explain more deeply the Wild Man's relationship to wolves, and he adequately covers this relationship without assuming all connections to be through the *versipellis* (Latin werewolf) story (213). The wolf and werewolf material is cited primarily in the chapter "Erotic Connotations," less so in the chapter "Natural History" (10). Lust as lupine is an allegory launched far forward from antiquity, such as the Greco-Roman connections of the lupine and female prostitution. These extend even to the womanizer's "wolf whistle" and revisions of the Big Bad Wolf as a potentially or actually violent lecher and/or pedophile, with the latter likely the allegorical motivation for Perrault's version of "Little Redcap."

While Marrok, a knight and former wolf, could qualify as a Wild Man figure simply on the basis of his experiences and his humanity, he might be disqualified by his transformation. Although his change is couched in the language of cuckoldry ("betrayal" implying more than simply the trickery of transforming him into a wolf), Marrok's own potency is not the focus of the embedded tale. Also, Malory gives no indication that Marrok is still wild; for example, Arthur allows him the opportunity to touch and smell blood during the healing of Sir Urry. Were the king to assume a wild nature in one of his knights, he would certainly assume that the feral beast was unable to control itself at the sight of blood. Moreover, since Arthur had more than a hundred knights to perform the task and probably knew that the exercise would result in Lancelot's success, the slightest doubt as to Marrok's nature would disqualify him as a potential healer. By Ambrose Bierce's definition of a werewolf, Marrok could only be "as humane as is consistent with an acquired taste for human flesh" (193). Bernheimer also points out that Malory's use of *wylde* is synonymous with *insane* (12, 190n). Thus, were Marrok still considered wild, he would also have been marginalized. Here too we see the lycanthrope, the psychological werewolf, submerged, waiting for psychology to catch up.

Le Morte du Loup

A significant connection of the Wild Man to Marrok's status as an ex-werewolf might also be found in Malory's choice to invoke Merlin sparingly. Both Kittredge and Carol Harding attribute the decreasing use of Merlin to the Christianization of the Arthurian cycle (and most other legends), which increased from the twelfth through the sixteenth centuries. Adam Douglas connects Merlin's diminishment in legends with seventeenth-century witch hunts that included the persecution of werewolves (155–83, 193). Merlin is obviously a pagan representative in Arthurian legend, and a reduction of his role would help establish a chivalry built on Monmouth's *Historie* rather than on his *Vita Merlini* or *Prophetiae Merlini*.[15] The *Vita*, as explained by J. S. Tatlock (280) and Bernheimer (165, 213n), connects Merlin directly to the forces of nature above and beyond government, including his fond address to the wolf that begins, "Tu, lupe, care comes."

Harding explains in detail how during the Middle Ages paganism was worked into romances via the use of marvels. Some of these writings on marvels were then claimed as "histories," quasi-factual accounts that often functioned as moral and political allegories (Harding, 29, 39–40, 55). For instance, British redactions of French texts cast God as a displeased feudal lord, rather than a more languid participant with the earthly or pagan or folk. Harding's mention of shape-changing as one of Merlin's controversial abilities during the Christianization of his story points directly to the relevance of Malory's mentions of "the Freynshe boke."[16] The separation of wilderness and civilization as theaters of simultaneous conquest and loss is popularized centuries later in the Arthurian fiction of Sir Walter Scott. Scott's romantic schism is then Americanized by James Fenimore Cooper, parodied by Mark Twain, and analyzed extensively by such historians and ecocritics as Roderick Nash, Annette Kolodny, Max Oelschlager, and Richard Slotkin. We might therefore view Malory's conservative use of Merlin as a literary winnowing of wilderness from civilization that catalyzed, if not began, a trend in the Western canon: When the wild figure is rejected from the imagination, the language and function of wilderness are lost as well.

Vinaver's complete edition of Malory's *Works* is a "civilized" text in that it favors the predilections of a growing urban population, even mimetically so, since Caxton's printing house and the advent of the press gave the Arthurian cycle the power of wide distribution. It also favors a civic piety over more rural and superstitious tale-telling. The civilized text often (retrospectively) laments these very phenomena of urbanization and centralized authority, and in this respect, Malory's story is no exception. Less of Merlin from the French vulgate to the *Works* means less of the fantastic, and to the extent that the fantastic survives, it does so with emphasis on the beast fable and the magical forest. But Malory (like Monmouth) strongly implies that the purpose of telling of human or social history is to confirm the authority of kings and nobles over a Christian civilization. In this way we may see the Arthurian romance in Euro-American literature as a contentious text. In American literature, Leatherstocking's continual struggle with the cutting of trees is offset by his role as one of the vanguard of expansion. The characters of John Steinbeck pursue their prairie grail quests only to find that civilization has abandoned them to the forces of the land. Jack London's wild men and dogs become like tempered steel as a result of hard labor but are finally hammered down by the forces of both the savage and the civilized worlds. The friction between the wild and the civilized in all of these texts has its precedent in the medieval romances with which many American writers were well acquainted.

Harding explains Chrétien de Troyes's romances as distinguished from Roland's by, in large part, Chrétien's position on evil (5). Where Roland always makes evil an outside force, Chrétien allows evil to dwell within, both within the realm of good and within the heart of the hero. This important distinction fits with bestiary representations of the wolf as Satan, whose original sin in heaven was greed for power within the kingdom. The wolf as a cunning and rapacious beast found in the fold (sometimes wearing sheep's clothing), complete with connotations of both eroticism and usurpation, overtly symbolized the corruption that lay within the good human heart.

Marrok's presence at the Round Table, as well as his chief identifying feature being a marvel, implies Malory's acceptance of any or all of the following narrative elements:

a)   that Marrok could be changed to a wolf by magic;

b)   that an original French writer of the *lai*, and the French as a society, may have believed that he could be changed;

c)   that in the course of compiling the material of the "Freynshe boke"—surely influenced by other cyclic texts both Latin and French—there was no need to omit the reference (as he had with many Merlin passages);

d)   that his audience in Britain could reconcile Marrok's transformation with the history of Arthur and his knights.

Malory's willingness to employ these marvels pulls the text back toward an early–Middle Ages pagan consensus even while he writes the *Works* to support the ascendancy of Christian kings as the proper force against paganism. This presence of the pagan in the Christian is training for the colonial mind, preparation of the recognition, Protestant disintegration, and Catholic entertainment of indigenous mythopoesis.

Marrok has been a wolf for seven years, and he sits across the table from Arthur as a portent of Lancelot and Guinevere's sin against the king. Rather than horns, fur and fangs seem to be the marks of cuckoldry here. If the Wild Man appears in this story, then he does so in the form of Lancelot, who turns feral after his affair with Guinevere, while the truer representative of wilderness, a man who was once actually an animal, has escaped punishment by Christian society by sitting in the court of Camelot.

The misogyny of the tales in which a false wife is the cause for the valiant husband's suffering took the form of witch crazes during the late sixteenth century and throughout the seventeenth in Europe and, in the latter century, in North America as well. Women were especially subject to accusations of witchcraft, and although accused werewolves were often men, werewolf trials were by-products of the greater frenzy against "magic," a term often used to mean simply cultural deviance or nonconformity. The confessions of werewolves, manipulated by the selective questioning of the torturer, predictably corroborated one another and assured the church that it had an epidemic of satanism on its hands (Douglas, 195–98; Westerkamp, 111). One weapon of persecution was the famous *Malleus Maleficarum;* printed for the first time one year after Caxton printed *Le Morte Darthur* and used primarily to try witches, it was another cultural horror that would inspire the Mathers in Salem and the werewolf mythos in America.

If the werewolf is associated with the devil, then why would Marrok be chosen as a knight of the Round Table? From the narrator's point of view, two things about Arthur's selection are consistent: He will choose a knight flawed or familiar with the warping of the Infernal on the basis of political necessity, such as the need for a region to be represented or for a faction to be either confronted or appeased; and he is influenced in his decisions by God directly, who sometimes chooses the most unlikely candidates for service. Reconciling the malevolent ghost wolf with Marrok's knighthood might also be as simple as the pagan root of the wolf as a war symbol, granting Marrok a brand of battle prowess traceable to the berserkirs or the house of Scipii.

This is where the German and Scandinavian influences on Marrok's and Arthur's stories may be inferred, especially to the extent that elements of the Celto-

Germanic fables appear in stories of Merlin and Arthur. Douglas's summary of the berserkirs, what he calls "wolf-coats" as a close enough cousin to the literal "bear-shirts," explains well the connection of the wolf to war rather than to erotic force or cuckoldry (94). He writes, "Although the Celtic-Germanic figure of the werewolf had a violent, aggressive, even murderous aspect, he had a specific social utility in the Heroic Age—to put it at its simplest, the berserk rages of the wolf-coats helped to win battles" (102). This relationship between the demonization and "social utility" of the beast becomes a dominant thread in the wolf literature of the United States, a classical redux inevitably used by those doomed to repeat history.

Et in Arcadia Ego

From Shakespeare, whose Macbeth cast the wolf as the sentinel of "wither'd Murther / . . . whose howl's his watch," and who "moves like a ghost" (2.1), to Milton, who wrote in *Lycidas* of "what the grim wolf with privy paw / Daily devours apace, and nothing said" (lines 128–29), the European ghost wolf found reception in the most highly educated minds in the American colonies. Shakespeare has a number of lupine moments scattered throughout his corpus of plays. In *A Midsummer Night's Dream* Puck connects wolf to moon: "Now the hungry lion roars, / And the wolf behowls the moon; / Whilst the heavy ploughman snores, / All with weary task fordone" (5.2). In *Henry V,* equally appropriate to the ghost wolf that occupies Shakespeare's works, the wolf is a battle icon also associated with a justifiable malevolence: "Give them great meals of beef and iron and steel, they will eat like wolves and fight like devils" (3.7). And in *Much Ado about Nothing,* one of the many attempted reconciliations casts the wolf as twilight envoy of past problems: "Good morrow, masters: put your torches out, / The wolves have prey'd; and look, the gentle day, / Before the wheels of Phoebus, round about / Dapples the drowsy east with spots of gray" (5.3).

A set of assumptions that would control politico-religious thinking for more than two hundred years was built in part on fables and legends more easily wrought in the absence of the real animal they characterized, and Augustinian assumptions that another species's worth was to be found in what it "meant" symbolically undermined the rigor of science until the mid-nineteenth century. As a result of several centuries of faith in a wolf better left unseen, the ghost wolf as demon, angelic guide, pinup, and economic obstacle has gained increasing currency over its corporeal and real counterparts.

In the modern era a kind of resurrection of the Arthurian legend in its most romantic form occurred. Outlaw wolves, including the Custer Wolf immortalized in Roger Caras's book, serve as proof of our allegiance to mythos rather than logos as the scheme for where wolves belong in the order of things. The Custer Wolf was said to have eaten over one hundred sheep in one night, in keeping with the exaggerations of wolf attacks discussed in chapter 2 that made the wolf into the American Questing Beast. A telling interstitial instance in which twelfth-century fable reached twentieth-century zoology is found in T. H. White's *Bestiary:* "Solinus, who has much to say about the nature of things, reports that on the backside of this animal there is a small patch of aphrodisiac hair, which it plucks off with its teeth if it happens to be afraid of being caught, nor is this aphrodisiac hair for which people are trying to catch it of any use unless taken off alive" (58). Wolves and other canids do, in fact, have a patch of hair above the tail, often darker than the rest of the fur, marking the precaudal gland, which is present in all canids, visible in many. For wolves this would certainly be an aphrodisiac in the right season, and indeed would only work if the wolf were alive, though its amorous powers for the rest of us have yet to be proven.

The material sent east to the major population zones of the American colonies would have accumulated slowly from coastal cultures retaining and insinuating their mores. As America grew into more literate eras than the colonial sermon or Federalist political tract ever produced, a mythos of the United States was allowed to root deeper than even didacticism could manage. Eventually, modernism and the rise of anthropology as interdisciplinary with literature provided studies of cultures that survived closer to their precolonial conditions, such as Alice Herndon Ernst's magnificent *Wolf Ritual of the Northwest Coast.* The cultural iconography supplied by interdisciplinary work produced an accrual of evidence toward the way the wolf was perceived, imagined, and allegorized conjunctively throughout the nation. One tool for shape-shifting has long been the mask, both a prime subject of anthropology and a dominant metaphoric image in literature. It is the door between human and other. The mask is also a way to understand the postcolonial condition in which the ghost wolf inhabits the regions of real wolves, because it demonstrates the difference between the shape-shifter dominant among native cultures and the werewolf dominant among colonizing ones.

CHAPTER TWELVE

Wolf Channel

Now, lest they choose his head,
Under severe moons he sits making
Wolf-masks, mouths clamped well onto the world.

— TED HUGHES, "FEBRUARY"

Among the Nootka, Kwakiutl, Quillayute, Makah, and Haida of the Northwest Coast, among the Yup'ik of the Far North, and among the Iroquois in the False Face ceremonies, the mask is an eloquent form of "projection" slightly different from the psychoanalytic use of the term.[1] Psychological projection defines the image of subjective experience as iconic but imaginary. In order to physically project the voice of the mask-wearer in ritual, projection is more often an attempt to render and respect the voice of the actual animal whose face is carved onto the mask, so that the medium of ceremony reiterates the myth's importance. It is theatrical, so it reconnects with the psychologically projected and finally completes the collective social order of both physical and metaphysical projection and reception in mythmaking. This is what it means to re-member, to join again the unit to the whole. It may also be what prompted Margaret Blackman to call the Northwest Coast masks "visual literature" (27).

The mask ritual may offer an opportunity to look at the sometimes permeable lines of the World-Wolf. Spiritual instruction may be an aid rather than an obstacle to, or a substitute for, ecological consciousness. Barry Lopez writes, "We embark then on an observation of an imaginary creature, not in the pejorative sense but in the enlightened sense—a wolf from which all other wolves are derived" (*Of Wolves and Men,* 204). Rather than reading this as a social constructivist position, I have to see Lopez's comment on Platonic enlightenment in the context of his larger project in *Of Wolves and Men,* which is about the way we think of the wolf in dissonance and/or harmony with the way wolves really live. "The truth is we know little about the wolf," he writes. "What we know a good deal more about is what we imagine the wolf to be."[2] A real wolf simply hasn't been seen by most people in America and isn't understood in any defensible way by more than a handful who have. Physical participation in the alteration of human consciousness through such methods as dance, quest, sojourn, or field biology trains us to be both rigorous in discipline and imaginatively supple when we read. We may also have a wolf that triggers our imagination, not merely a projected anthropomorphized wolf, although we cannot *have* a real wolf. Myths are great stories often because they are about what we cannot have.

Klukwana

From 1932 to 1940 Alice Herndon Ernst conducted her brilliant ethnographic study of a ritual called the Klukwana when conducted by the Nootka, and the Klukwalle when conducted by the Makah. According to Ernst, it consists of the "active dramatization of a legend which enacts the capture of a number of people (initiates) by Wolves, their recovery by certain other people already initiated (members of the secret society or fraternity known as Klukwalle) after they have received certain powers or instructions from the Wolves, and the exorcising of the Wolf spirit that possessed them" (2).

Her introductory chapter emphasizes ethnographic diplomacy in the face of an imperialism threatening a culture with which she feels some affiliation. She determines that the people of the Northwest Coast are "innately silent," and she is compelled to gather her data before the rites disappear "in the rapidly flowing wash of time" (1).

After initiation by the wolf spirit, one gains the right to participate in the rituals of the winter season. The Klukwalle may have originated from the Kwakiutl word *tlu'gwala,* meaning "to find a treasure," specifically from a spirit. Directly following ceremonies dedicated to the Wolf, the initiate must compose an individual song, construct a mask, and create a dance to fit the mask, which often represents a spirit or "mythical-animal ancestor." The mask sometimes indicates the initiate's hereditary tribal status by using elements from the first song of the initiate's eldest brother or sister.[3]

Among the Makah and Nootka the ritual included a phase similar to the Coyote admonishments among many Plains and southwestern Pueblo nations in which members who had stepped out of line (Ernst cites quarrelsome husbands and wives as examples) were ridiculed or harshly disciplined by a wolf dancer. The wolf may have been chosen for the Klukwana because it was considered the fiercest and bravest of animals, coloring the ritual as a warrior-connected one, but this is speculative, and Ernst does not cite her informants. In addition to her loose terminology about primitive theater, Ernst is given to touches of forgivable melodrama and reveals in her writing both the poetic style and ethnocentric biases of her mentor, Franz Boas (4). The wolf's connection to a "cosmic symbolism" does not escape Ernst as a fine opportunity for developing, in good form, her own primitive theater. She ends her introduction:

> By even the most complete realists among informants, it is stated that, when the lonely whistles and cries of the Wolf initiates began to sound in the sacred winter ceremonial, the wolves of the night, the living wolves in the wood beyond the villages, would join in the long-drawn-out chorus. Mysterious and aloof, the wolf, dark warrior of forest and plain, takes over his own ritual everywhere in the dim fastnesses of the region (5).

This beautifully written passage is an example of the ghost wolf's insinuation of itself into a work of clinical prose, just as the initiates experience the wolf's presence at the ceremony. It is a literary moment in an anthropological work, replete with fruitful misstatements (wolf as warrior, "of the night") and poetic turns ("sacred winter ceremonial," "dim fastness"). After several pages on the Makah ritual, Ernst adds a significant fact. She writes, "The potent communal long house has given way to the modern picture show . . . For good or ill, the fastnesses have succumbed to the leveling hand of civilization; and, like the wolf himself, his ritual is stranger in his old haunts" (10). What Ernst sees, then, is not so much the loss of ritual to "time," as she had previously stated, as one civilization's progress through time being had at the expense of another's.

The postcolonial condition here is found in the replacement of ritual masks, devices of participatory ecological consciousness, with the simulacra of escapist entertainment. More and more stories change to increasingly disposable forms that are less interspecific, certainly less human and less attentive, cool media. This has happened in Alaska, Vancouver, and the Olympic Peninsula; one need only walk by either a trailer or a mansion and see the blue flicker in the windows. When at one time a mask was carved in order to tell a story, to translate a language of the animal world, now it is projected two-dimensionally to a crowd that is not a crowd at all, to a marketplace that is no longer a community. And insofar as these legends are disposable, celluloid simulacra, so will our thinking be. As a consequence, both our myths and individual psyches will separate from the raw material of the world to the point of pretending that the synthetic or abstract is the world. Such masks disappear like money, leaving other cultures to pay for the witchery used against them by those whose faces are hidden, who rationalize through their economically generated myths the annihilation of animals, until the only animal faces left are carvings. These are hollow masks, cold and profane, inside of which are only the Abstractors. "In any present-day record of a vanishing belief," writes Ernst, "much detail is lost, part of its meaning forgotten; time lays rough hands on the folkways of a people. The relation of this study to the field of primitive theater will no doubt be obvious. If, in addition, it aids in understanding today's less vocal neighbors on the American continent, the intent of the writer will be well served" (52).

Many variants of the Klukwana exist. In such Northwest Coast tribes as the Makah and Nootka, masks of ravens and thunderbirds are made with moving parts, mouths open to reveal Fish inside, or Raven, or a human being. Elaborate wolf masks four feet long require the help of another dancer, extending coopera-tion in the ritual. Where there is a benevolent ghost the malevolent one is always present, according to the liturgical dictates of fear and respect as well as admira-tion or attraction. Ceremony tries to transcend what is human while attaining as respectful a position as possible for what is not, and therefore it need not be diminished as an activity merely for the superstitious or childish. Indeed, there is a need for activity as well as abstraction; then correctives to both have realizable effects. Boas collected songs from the Kwakiutl that propitiated the Wolf Chiefs, said to be the oldest on earth, in order to calm them so that Wolf would not "unexpectedly shorten our lives and kill us all by moving its tail" (82n). The re-turn for their genuflection was, according to the Kwakiutl storytellers, as material as it was spiritual. "In these early days," writes Ernst, "the wolves really helped the people of the village by bringing deer to them, after they had learned to fol-low the precepts of the woman not to harm or shoot the wolves. In times of famine [the wolves] would bring a deer to the edge of the village and leave it, or lie down beside it to guard it. But when they saw man approaching, they would go away" (90).

Notice this as a "long ago" myth, the powerful primeval invocation. Whether we read it as an ancient rationale for stealing a wolf kill or as the primitive shar-ing of a meal with a wolf, its efficacy is found in the tangible connection made between story and lived experience. That connection generates in turn a new ver-sion of an old story each time a ritual is performed. The story is most complete when the wolf participates in its writing.

While Ernst attributes the forest wolves' attendant howls during the Kluk-wana to the realism of the initiates' howls, an event that regularly happens in wolf country today, we know that wolves might howl at whatever they find inter-esting. This fact in no way detracts from the event of the ceremonial howl. On the contrary, the wolf's "response" constitutes an interspecific exchange inviting conjecture, demonstration, storytelling—all the elements that raise both indi-vidual and cultural appreciation of language.[4] It is important to consider, there-fore, that there are at least two categories of mask in question. One is a tool through which to examine the material world, in order to provide intellectual and spiritual insight through role-playing, mimicry, and shape-shifting. The other is a tool by which to escape reality. This latter should be seen as a profanement, neither an inevitability nor a subject of equal literary merit.

Wearing the proper mask should be, ultimately, a compassionate act, as the theologian Frederick Buechner has defined compassion: "the sometimes fatal capacity for living inside someone else's skin" (15). Hyperreality and the simulacrum are serviceable critiques of *exploitation* of the natural world; they are examples neither of nature's lack of materiality nor of representation's inevitable demise. Not all masks necessarily substantiate the simulacratic rush toward meaninglessness. They may also be constructed to empower what already exists in threads as yet unwoven into cord. The hope of a wolf mask dancer is that, aided by the mask, the exchange with a wolf will be somehow more on the wolf's terms, *and to the wolf's benefit.* In this way, ritually raised ecological consciousness demands confrontation with an observable reality, and the donning of a mask of rite may provide a means to that end better than a retreat into the abstract. Recreations of the visage in both Egyptian and Blackduck burial masks provided meticulous genuflective representations of the departed for purposes that looked more toward the future than to the past (Torbenson, 83). This is a qualitatively different form of thought from either a museum's averaging skin types for a three-thousand-year-old Egyptian skull (which generalizes the past) or the morphological change of a wolf's skull into a bulldog's (which "looks toward the future" by denying the past).

Whenever we read a story about any animal, we should question the method used to re-create that animal. Is the skull preserved in order to maintain the illusion of Lobo, King of the North, as an American legend? Is it examined, as in Phil Gipson's work, to consider who Lobo may have actually been during his lifetime? Is the real wolf taxidermied and fitted with glass eyes—ostensibly an attempt at corporeality—in order to convince children visiting an exhibit that wolves should be "saved," and if so, then does such a method work? When an extinction occurs, the collective story of a species and the myriad stories of its individuals can only be molded from the clay of human memory and conjecture. Such a horrible mask, which we have created for so many species, we have nearly created for the wolf. But the messages of the remaining wolves contain more stories than bleached skulls can provide.

From a pedagogical point of view the construction of masks can be a great step toward an education of interspecies dialogue. The artist Tim Panjabi-Trelease assigns his high school students library and behavioral research on an animal, then has them make a mask of the animal, about which they finally tell a story connected to the mask. It has been a highly successful assignment, in no small part due to the tangibility of its reward. It also catalyzes young students' interests in three fields at once. But children, artists, and scientists are often easier to reach with reality than are literary critics.[5]

Tuunraq

Rick Bass's story "Swamp Boy" is told from the point of view of a man remembering that during his youth he was complicit with his friends in the torment of another boy unaffectionately called Swamp Boy. The main character doesn't actually hurt Swamp Boy, the green character so named for his walks through the woods near a bayou, but remains safely on the side of the vicious group, afraid to break from it. In a plain of tall grass prairie on the other side of the woods, as the main character is feeling his guilt swell, he feels as well the "magic" of the place, and imagines wolves cutting bison from their herd. He takes to going for walks himself, "as if summoned," in empathy for Swamp Boy (26). He begins to be healed by watching the frogs jump and thinking of the place as, in some pure way, belonging to this victimized child. The group of tormentors spies on Swamp Boy, and we learn more about him through our narrator's voyeurism as he remains with the group. They continue to abuse him, the main character watching him return home to solace. A dyad of conflicting plotlines emerges for the narrator, one in which he is "a devil" and one in which he finds what Swamp Boy finds by immersing himself in the nonhuman world (27).

At one point the group puts on "wolf masks" and makes "spiked collars by driving nails through leather dog collars . . . We spoke to one another in snarling laughs, our voices muffled through the wolf masks" (33). They chase Swamp Boy to see how far he will run. He runs to a bluff and dives into the bayou, then swims away. The story takes another and sudden turn. The narrator calls the whole tale "a lie" and claims to *be* Swamp Boy, rather than one of the boys chasing him. In the story's resolution, he finally claims to be both tormented and tormentor, "at the edge of fear, the edge of hesitancy," and considers what he "would have done" (34). It is a striking story with a cryptic ending. It is a literary ritual.

The story also fits into a literature of disfigurement, as in the stories of Edgar Allan Poe, Paul Bowles, or Robert E. Howard. Howard's "Black Hound of Death," for example, is about a white man captured by Inner Mongolian devil worshippers, his face disfigured to look like a wolf's. His torture causes him to lose his sanity, and his madness, marked by an obsession with revenge, completes the man's transformation to a werewolf. Its Orientalist intolerance and malevolence are apropos of the werewolf genre (see Frost, 126–27).

We see in these stories one kind of wolf mask. Here is another: The Yup'ik of

Nunivak Island used the verb *agayu* to indicate a request for plentiful plants and animals in the coming year, and this request was articulated through the construction of masks. They held a ceremony of dancing, family gathering, and courtship, many of them making arduous journeys to attend. According to Ann Fienup-Riordan, "As Christian missionaries' suppression of masked dancing began at the end of the nineteenth century, the verb base *agayu-* evolved to mean 'to pray' or 'to worship'" (xiv). That both the Yup'ik and Catholic religions are monotheistic may have contributed to the survival and reflourishing of certain traditions under priestly scrutiny. Priests instructed the Yup'ik in varying and contradictory degrees as to which parts of their ceremonies to eliminate—some seeing more Christian value in some elements of the ceremony than in others (xvi). One priest eliminated the masks but participated in the dancing, while others labeled the entirety of the ceremonial festivals evil. However, an enlightenment of the priests who now reside with the Yup'ik has recently begun.

Mary Mike, of the Anagcirmiut people, explained to Fienup-Riordan: "Since last year [Father Astruc] has been telling us to renew some of our traditions." Fienup-Riordan's contribution to the revival was to find Yup'ik masks from museums around the lower forty-eight states and collect them in an exhibit called "Agayuliyararput: Our Way of Making Prayer," in Toksook Bay, Anchorage, where the ancestors of their makers gathered and told the stories of the ritual dances (xvii). Her book is printed in both English and Yup'ik.

By looking into the faces of the masks, the people Fienup-Riordan interviewed would remember the stories they had inherited, the dances they had sometimes seen as children. Their accounts often ended with brief disclaimers such as "I am telling part of the story as I remember it," or "That is as much as I know of the story." Lopez, Underwood, and Estés all adopt this disclaimer as well, a mark of both the storyteller's humility and the generous flux of oral narrative. The interviewees were taught by dancers who removed the masks, stepped forward to the guests at the ceremony, and told the stories of those masks, many of which regard hunting or *angalkut* (shamans), with several involving an animal called an *amikuk,* which Fienup-Riordan explains as a "legendary creature, usually depicted as one difficult to capture, and often described as quite changeable" (229).

Mary Mike distinguishes the amikuk mask from a wolf mask and tells two separate stories but points out that she cannot remember what an amikuk is. Barry Lopez's interviews with Nunamiut hunters, however, reveal that the amikuk (or amiguk, as Lopez spells it), may also be the wolf, as this is the word the hunters use when referring to it in their accounts. Mowat anglicized the word to *amorak* (85), which has been used in other stories as well, and a phonetic description may suffice as circumstantial evidence for a connection. The pronunciation of the last syllable is a glottal, as with the French "r." In both Yup'ik and Inuktitut, the glottal is severe, to the point of the "r" sounding much like a velar "g"—hence "amorak" and "amaguk" or "-kuk." On the other hand, if Mary Mike distinguishes the pronunciation of the first "k" in *amikuk* from the guttural "r," then the connection, if there is one, may be distant. The point here is that the wolf in form lurks in the language and may be found in glyphs that change slightly, hiding in translation—but the wolf of substance speaks his or her own language and lives, requiring no mask. Our terms are masks we wear not to confess the nonexistence of amikuk but to approach the existence of that real animal, right there.

The totem spirit, or *tuunraq,* that sometimes entered the dancer did not always offer its instruction in celebratory terms. In Mary Mike's Yukon account of a ceremony involving a pair of wolf masks, she recalls closely several bloody parts to the dance, that the masks were frightening, as were the howls of the dancers and the violence of their attacks on one another. However, at the end of their fighting dance, "Unexpectedly, neither had received cuts from the fight. Yet we had seen blood on them while they were fighting" (141). Whether the sight of blood is hallucinatory, staged, or real, the fact of the violence connected with the wolf, the fear of its visage and howl, should act as a caution against commercial outfits selling passive ritual "heartstones" and "totem spirits" under the pacifist Indian "way of life" that dominates advertising. A child on All Hallows' Eve dressed as a wolf (that is, a werewolf) better understands the value of ritual invested in the mask: that fear might be more beneficial to the human spirit than commodity.[6]

One of the purposes of carving a mask is to realize the effects of eye-hand labor on the mental condition; the mask's surface must be observed and shaped on the inside as well as the outside in order to make the face of the represented being adhere to the face inside the artifact. The result hoped for is a deeper-than-physical connection, spurred by but not limited by the touch of the mask, between the wearer and whoever is represented by the outer image. The writing and telling of stories is this same act, performed by an author and presented to an audience in the language of a character. Art provides a conduit between worlds—a channel of communication.

The *nepcetaq* examined in Ernst's work is said to adhere to the wearer's face by some unknown means. Several of the Yup'ik concur that the nepcetaq is the most powerful of masks. "You see, long ago when the temainaunelnguut [ones disembodied in some sense] used these nepcetat, sometimes the mask [placed on the floor, inside facing up] would fuse with a shaman's face and adhere to it after he bent his head to bring his face down into it" (Fienup-Riordan, 49). However this molding works, its purpose is the conformity of the shaman to the animal or ancestor of the mask, his or her submission to it. Note here that the role of the disembodied one is consistent with psychoanalytic terms of projection; in fact, the disembodied one both shapes and is shaped by the physical mask. Corporeal and apparitional beings thus share a highly permeable boundary. Such a condition is not as prevalent in the modernization of masks by the invading cultures of North America, who have used them more often as monumental self-representations during the founding of colonizing cultural identities, white hoods of subjugation.

Nepcetaq

Ted Hughes's "February," which provides this chapter's epigraph, appears in *Lupercal*. Although a modern British writer and thus tangential to this study, Hughes raises an important point of lore by the title of his collection. The Luperci were priests in ancient Rome who had power over wolves, although as Leonard M. Scigaj writes, "there is no regular Latin derivation of Lupercus from lupus" (62). The etymological problem manifests itself in Greek as well, in the connection of Apollo to both light (*leukos*) and the wolf (*lykos*), which may be an inadvertent, but eventually became a mythic, lexical fusion. This shows us what human language can do to skew the defining features of wolves that distinguish them from, say, priests. Or ghosts. Scigaj cites Jane Harrison as discussing "the Lupercalia and the Greek Anthesterion as both being exclusively concerned with purification of the dead and the placation of ghosts—for the purpose of acquiring 'freedom from bad spirits and their maleficent influence'" (63).

Hughes uses the wolf in several poems beyond *Lupercal*—for instance, in another collection's title poem, "Wolfwatching," a powerful work about seeing a wolf in a zoo—as a way of looking at specific characteristics of a nonhuman animal, at the investiture of divinity in animal avatars, and at both of these as reflecting human consciousness about the self and animal self, almost always toward a poetics of idol and totem.

The olfactory senses are the quickest route to the brain, and one of the strongest prompters of memory. If I were to put on that child's Halloween mask, smell the cheap plastic, feel the bite of the elastic band over my ears and in my hair, I would more easily imagine myself as a child, more easily stand with that child on a doorstep, waiting to have candy drop into my pillowcase. This could be an intrinsically traumatic ritual, although it is usually a mild and highly controlled one (the far greater trauma comes with the profane moment of warning, inherent to civilization, against razor blades, poison, and psychopaths and pedophiles). From outside a four-foot wooden wolf mask come the hollow drafts of

sound from the wooden whistles of the secret Klukwana society, the pulse of feet
against the road through the village. Inside smells of cedar, human sweat rubbed
into the skin with salt water and fish oil and juniper like a coarse salve; the angles
of the carving against the cheek and ear, the refraction of breath through the
mask's nostrils and the tunneling of vision through its eye sockets, its weight on
the skull, an itch on the scalp where the hair is rubbed and damp. Maybe the
mask won't come off. Maybe this is what I am.

Both incident and degree of trauma are subjective, even during the rawest
rituals of the earth. Some of us are "tougher" than others, and this is what determines the truths to be had through ritual for an individual. But those rules that
make an experience a ritual are collectively, hegemonically codified. To the extent
that such codes are influenced by conditions of the raw physical world, the active
participation of the nonhuman in a ritual is essential to its success in transcending, critiquing, or changing human power structures poised to destroy individuation. Subjectivity and individuality thus gather strength from social systems far
less than (or even in antithesis of) the ecological systems preceding and subsuming society, indeed constituting the very matter on which a society depends. Such
success of a ritual is possible because the world constitutes the objective reference
point for the subjective experience. Generic animals make for ineffectual rituals.

When the wolf dance begins there are scars to be had, there is the stamina of
five days' concentration. The transformation is not only auditory but olfactory
and tactile—it is taxing. When we speak through a mask, we use a voice synaes-
thetically altered by the image we have taken on. In order to speak like a wolf, we
must learn to speak through its apparatus, the original of which is made of the
bone and cavities of its skull. So we try to reconstruct that skull (in vain, yes, but
also in the wonder that possesses its own reward). This is the first step toward
shape-shifting, possibly the first step toward acknowledging a narrative born in
the body, married to the material born in the body of another species. The human
being who once stood in the place of the mask-bearer is, for the purpose of
narrative, somewhere else. The hollows of the skull awaken the ghost wolves in
their house, invite them to travel into the cranial vault of the shaman under the
mask. As with Max Beerbohm's happy hypocrite, the mask worn long enough
may finally change through practice the face, and then the soul, of the person
beneath.

For Shakespeare the world is a stage and we merely players; for biological
determinists the genetic code dooms us to a patterned response to the world; for
literary naturalists that biological pattern must be fate negotiated by atavism and
nihilism; and for the Captain Ahabs of the existential seas, the pasteboard mask

must be punched through, even to the void. For the ecologically conscious myth-maker the mask is the door beyond which transformation to a more biotically and abiotically aware self waits. We may even, over time, reach the point at which we become less intrusive into the animal world, less prone to alter it, and so reverse the current ten-thousand-year trend. Our temporary efforts at connection might then become more benign than malignant. Samuel Hearne writes:

> Few of the Northern Indians chuse to kill either the wolf or the quiquehatch (wolver-ine), under a notion that they are something more than common animals . . . I have frequently seen the Indians go to their dens, and take out the young ones and play with them. I never knew a Northern Indian to hurt one of them: on the contrary, they always put them carefully into the den again; and I have sometimes seen them paint the faces of the young Wolves with vermillion, or red ochre. (224; see also Curtis, 18:51)

"Foul!" we cry. "Sentimentalism!" Is this not the Ecological Indian, that noble savage whose intrusion here now justifies the cascade of colonialism? Pull the pups from their homes and make them into dogs! Build condominiums over the dens, for wilderness is now trammeled and can only be defined by its absence!

The touching of those wolves, let alone the painting of them, may indeed amount to a violation of privacy, even a moment uncomfortably close to habitu-ation. I wonder if the vermilion or ochre was in any way harmful to the wolf pups. Let's also wonder what these Ecological Indians might have done after-ward, since we know that there were more wolves in the world when those In-dians we can't figure out how to handle were in charge of the human role in the land.[7] If the vermilion didn't hurt the pup, then something about this act seems to me to *draw* a line rather than to cross it. Some moments that seem to grate against our civilized sensibilities might finally change our behavior from an abu-sive distance to a permissible intimacy. What if once upon a time a little habitua-tion went a long way toward health? A mark of our current condition is that such an act can't be defended anymore.

In the end, I am tempted to celebrate the masks on the faces of those little wolves, provided the act didn't physically or emotionally harm them. I am tempted to set it against all the times some wolf hunter closed down his con-science while a mother wolf stood nearby watching him pull pups out of a den to kill them. Given the overwhelming number of urban intellectuals who appar-ently haven't the slightest idea what a transformative experience in the non-human world is, this moment of painting wolves' faces must seem like a great opportunity to shore up the ivory tower and its obsessive schooling in abstrac-tion and separation. For Samuel Hearne, and for the person he saw commit this act, it may have felt like an earned experience, one that the wolf pups might have even enjoyed without their being domesticated. It looks, from this narrative, like an act of tenderness.

Still, I'm ambivalent, nervous to say that removing these pups isn't a step in the wrong direction. What might qualify the act is if it's not a step in any particular direction. I could be wrong, am willing to be so, and so could Samuel Hearne about what he saw. I am generally of the "Leave them alone" persuasion about wild animals because of the high pile of evidence that human intrusion into their lives has done far more harm than good. But we just can't seem to tell the difference anymore between conscionable and unconscionable behavior toward another species, and we'd better learn this distinction fast. Our stories too often take the place of our experiences, instead of expressing them. I'll probably never paint a wolf pup's face and don't want anyone else to try, but this in part means that I'll never live when the act might be considered in the context of all that wide and populated wolf country, with all those lupine eyes watching and indicating their own judgment of few enough and smart enough people around for them to remain safe from transformation.

Skinwalkers

Those who would commodify either Indian or wolf as a way of "getting in touch with its spirit" may just get what they wish—a return on their self-centered investment—and enter a world for which they are not prepared. To the characters in Leslie Marmon Silko's *Ceremony,* white people and their mythos are merely by-products of a great evil, one perpetuated against all people and animals. The shaman Betonie teaches Tayo that creation is not always a good thing, that some discoveries are meant to be left alone, unsaid, denied the power of the myth. This lesson is not limited to race, however. It is extended to the racism of the Laguna themselves. Throughout the book, Silko interposes older stories of witchery and quests to defeat malevolent magic, including skinwalkers.

"Long time ago," Betonie tells Tayo, "in the beginning / there were no white people in this world / there was nothing European" (133). The story that follows regards the creation of white people, which is performed by a powerful witch. Some allusion to the cosmogonic trickster is implied when Betonie says, "This world was already complete . . . There was everything / including witchery," but he makes clear the difference between witchery and trickery. Witchery produces "dark things." In Betonie's story a contest takes place, during which all of the witches ("some had slanty eyes / others had black skin") impress one another with their shape-shifting. They wear animal skins of the fox, badger, bobcat, and wolf. The contest crescendoes, witches cooking babies over pots and committing other mutilations. One witch waits in silence before winning the contest with a story, cast as a powerful spell of destruction (135). This witch's condescension to the others is founded on their reliance on "their stinking animal skins" for power (138). The storytelling witch is a force ungendered, abstracted, and it uses the weapon of abstraction—language—to affect an annihilation. Here, the wolf skin is a source of malevolent power, but it is also subordinated to story. The morality of this tale both diminishes totemism and declares its force.

Tony Hillerman's *The Blessing Way* puts a dime-fiction spin on this issue of Navajo identity and history in connection to witchcraft. The plot is driven by a colorful combination of Dineh lore and the hard-boiled detective novel, with the noir replaced by bright southwestern sunlight. The criminal is a Navajo Wolf, a skinwalker who has murdered witnesses to his witchery. Combining another literary tradition with the dark detective novel—the empirical gothic—Hillerman reveals by the novel's denouement that the skinwalker is actually "from Los Angeles . . . a 'Relocation Navajo'—a child of one of those unfortunate families moved off the drought-stricken Reservation to urban centers during the 1930s. It had been one of the most disastrous experiments of the Bureau of Indian Affairs, turning hungry sheepherders into hungry city alcoholics" (260). There's no indication that this skinwalker is a "city alcoholic"; as it turns out, this Wolf is a clever thief using the legends of the skinwalker to scare people away from his salvage of equipment lost by the American military in a canyon in witch country.

The protagonists of Hillerman's novel realize that the L.A. witch learned Navajo ways from books. Through one character, a professor of anthropology brought in to aid detective Joe Leaphorn, Hillerman creates some interesting friction between the benefits and drawbacks of both academic outsider knowledge and tribal knowledge. The book bears many situational similarities to Silko's better-crafted novel: Military hardware is the real heart of the witchcraft; mythic tradition is neither written off as superstition nor declared as gospel; the integration of old stories and mainstream modern plotlines is brought together both didactically in reminders of injustice and lyrically in the ruminations of the main character.

In both novels the wolf is cast in a poor light, though in Hillerman's the revelation of the trickery implies an exoneration of wolves as exploited while it simultaneously invokes them as horrific images. The first appearance of the Navajo Wolf is of "a big man with his wolf skin draped across his shoulders. The forepaws hung limply down the front of his black shirt and the empty skull of the beast was pushed back on his forehead, its snout pointed upward" (11). During his crimes he lowers the skull over his face. The image of the Wolf in this passage could as easily be written of the berserkirs. The full knowledge of the skinwalker or berserkir being human is always at the surface, but the circumstances of its appearance empower the malevolent ghost Wolf until it is reconfigured by other powerful stories. One of the last uses of the wolf skin in *The Blessing Way,* after the villain has been killed, is the anthropologist's consideration to hang it on his office wall (270). The gothic horror has been explained away, souveniered, no need for the appearance of any real wolves.

Transcendence is not found in tearing away the mask and shouting *Aha!* It is not found in believing that the mask's visage is the only one present in the pageant, but that each mask represents at least two personae and a boundary separating them, the permeability of which makes poetry, shapes narrative. This seems a necessary understanding if we are even to begin considering the interspecific possibilities of art, literature, language, and the ecological position of human artifice.

When we stand on the rimrock, cup our hands around our mouths, and howl, we do more than employ the laws of acoustics, even more than hope that wolves out of sight are within earshot. We chant belief. It would be just great if wolves could tell by the pitch and timbre of the human howl whether the motives behind it are pure, but that wish tempts the kind of sensibilities that do more harm than good. We have to hope instead that the stories told by their bones become less important than those told by their voices. What we write in our literatures from here forward bears the responsibility of protecting wolves from ourselves and from what we do to them, just as a literature of quality has always taught us how to share a country. We are at no risk of being exterminated, or diminished, by wolves, and we never were. Exactly how our efforts to become them fail, and at what expense—this is the difference between a culture that is childlike and one that is childish.

CHAPTER THIRTEEN

Raised by Wolves

When he was sixteen years old Ernest Hemingway wrote one of his first efforts at fiction, "Judgment of Manitou," obviously inspired by his adolescent wilderness readings. In this short story an act of revenge backfires and two men wind up catching themselves in their own traps, to be devoured by wolves. One of the trappers, a caricature French Canadian named Pierre, decides to kill himself and save the wolves the trouble, realizing that his fate has been sealed by the "judgment of Manitou" (Hemingway, 96–97).

In Paul Bowles's "The Frozen Fields," a young boy, psychologically abused by his family, lies in bed at Christmas. "On the borderlands of consciousness he had a fantasy," writes Bowles. It is of a wolf entering the house and killing the adults (Bowles, "Frozen Fields," 144–45). At the end of the story boy and wolf run away together across the frozen fields that lie along both the landscape outside the house and the horizon of the boy's imagination.[1]

These two wolf stories—one treating adolescence in terms of the writer's own coming of age through adventure, the other with the adolescent as main character and arrested by a rending of the heart—both have significant biographical underpinnings. The first could be read as an early indicator of Hemingway's later outdoor affinity (and of the dormant desire in many young boys who live in the suburbs to try their hands at both fiction and wilderness). The second is difficult to read outside the context of Bowles's own troubled childhood and tortured retrospect on that childhood.[2] The contrast of a wilderness environment and a domestic setting, along with the stories' respectively malevolent and benevolent figures (the wolf seems benevolent to the boy in the Bowles story, if not to the parents), demonstrates the ghost wolf's fictional range as a retributive force of nature in an adolescent context. Hemingway's apprenticeship to writing and literature occurred during the late period of literary naturalism and the advent of the Jack London brand of nature adventure story geared to boys. Bowles's depiction of the wolf as a phantasm with some corporeal root indicates his stylistic tendencies toward the high modern, the surreal, and primal images that reveal the collective human unconscious (see, for instance, many of the stories in *A Distant Episode*). Both Hemingway's and Bowles's stories chime atavism, beast myth, ghost wolf.

As the World-Wolf is to the world story, so is the individual corpus of wolf stories to the individual mind's development. A child learns ancient stories through local and accessible versions, which germinate and grow and develop as the child does. Maturation may connect or separate that child-become-adult from the images in those stories, may connect or separate him from his own mythic past. When the time comes for ethics, for policy to be made, the wolf in the mind cultivated by certain stories and manipulated during maturation will be the Wolf used to write that policy and enforce it. In such works as *The Jungle Books* wolves have raised children. Children in stories have lived like wolves or joined wolves, have been carried on their backs, have been terrorized by them. In such books and movies as *The Suburban Werewolf,* the Teenage Werewolf subgenre, and a popular shape-shifter series of 1990s youth novels called *Animorphs,* children also become wolves. Wolves also have been turned into people by the writers of children's stories, by transformation, domestication, or anthropomorphism. We have raised children to think with factual irresponsibility about animals, raised a national citizenship to think like children about animals into its adulthood. Adults who are the products of such thought are actually less fit to meet the nonhuman world on its terms than are uneducated children, who are closer to their animal selves, whose fears are more honest and immediate, and whose capacities for wonder and connection are unpolluted, if not greater.

Since the inception, in 1938, of the Caldecott Medal for illustration of books for children, a substantial proportion of the medals and honors have gone to books about animals, including several versions of monster-animal tales, such as *Saint George and the Dragon, Goldilocks and the Three Bears,* and *Little Red Riding Hood*. This is not to say that the judges tilted toward animal books (they may have), only that animals constitute an enormous share of literary figures offered to children. The wolf is among the most popular, as evidenced in such European and Russian staples as "The Three Little Pigs," "Peter and the Wolf," and "Little Red Riding Hood." But from the Endangered Species Act to the recent wolf reintroduction successes and failures, the benevolent counterpart to the Big Bad Wolf has begun feeding at the kill. To complicate matters further, the romance of the wolf in children's literature may vacillate between scientifically informed considerations and bathetic depictions, depending on the wind of culture, the school curriculum, and the knowledge of teachers.

Misunderstandings

One of the most common comments about the wolf is that it is "misunderstood," a term that pervades wolf literature.[3] In 1982 Constance and Roger Powell attempted to correct at least one form of misunderstanding by conducting a study on children's literature designed to discover how the subject of predation might best be approached in the classroom. They combined sets of interviews that tested students and teachers on their knowledge of and attitudes toward predators. They also examined five hundred children's books, sixty-eight of which met the study's criteria for "books with mammalian predators as main or subordinate characters" in "stories, picture books, and poetry," not including "folk and fairy tales and scientific or descriptive books lacking a plot" (238). The Powells then divided depictions of predators in these books into three categories:

> 1) "animal role with animal characteristics" (the predator has a role feasible for a real predator)
>
> 2) "animal role with human characteristics" (the predator carries out activities feasible for a real predator but is also endowed with such human capabilities as speech and emotion)
>
> 3) "animal role with possible substitution by a human role" (the predator carries out human activities not feasible for a real predator, rather human activities such as keeping house, going to work, and driving a car). (238–39)

The Powells organized these categories according to the books' positive and negative characterizations of predators: "positive" included not only predation as "good" but also "a realistic view of predation without judging it good or bad" (239). In the study's quantitative analysis, however, the Powells separated "positive" from "neutral," creating a third category. They list 79 percent of the predators as positively presented; 13 percent as "picture reference only" (that is, inherently neutral, according to the Powells); and 8 percent as negatively presented (241). The Powells' project cross-references factors that the World-Wolf model treats as more symbiotic, but it obviously corroborates the rubric. The study is designed to test not simply what people know about real wolves but also the moral positions included in the ways they learn and the ways they categorize their animals.

The Powell model (which found the wolf to be the third most often presented predator) sometimes blurs the line of division with examples of purportedly human qualities that may easily be attributable to other species. For example, the Powells assume "speech and emotion" to be absent from nonhuman predators and base their classification of categories partly on this assumption, although without providing a clear definition of which communicative forms besides speech do qualify. "Keeping house," too, is considered anthropomorphic, even though this behavior could reasonably be credited to the fastidious pica, the eagle's selection and maintenance of an aerie, or the systematic division of turf used by pigs to separate their sleeping, eating, and defecation spaces. When the classification is based on architectural rather than behavioral criteria, qualification is based on the definition of a house, rather than on the definition of "keeping" it. The maintenance of a dwelling is not nearly so humanly exclusive an act as, say, driving a car, another category on the study's list. The study's problematic systemization of what is uniquely human and what is not complicates as well the Powells' designation of "descriptive books lacking plots." Without providing narratological criteria for when, exactly, a plot is missing, the Powells' index leaves us unable to apply their model reliably. Nevertheless, it helps us examine how projections of human psychological predilections (for example, phobias, affinities, totemic propensities, and biophilia) are given wolf-shapes early on in children's lives and passed on to subsequent generations by adults, who sometimes allay fears and sometimes enhance them.

Sarah Greenleaf skillfully tracks a macroscopic "evolution" (although I'm often uncomfortable with the metaphoric use of this word) of the wolf in Western children's literature. The article's thesis testifies perfectly to the complex nature of the ghost wolf when the author states that "the wolf has been branded with the most devastating stereotype in all of literature, even when the merciless image is often used with tongue-in-cheek" (1). Greenleaf looks at the development of sign systems, in keeping with Thomas Sebeok's zoosemiotics but more sharply focused on the development of those systems in children (Sebeok's focus, and mine, is on the development of such systems through the lives of individuals—wolves as well as humans). A reader pursuing the wolf in literature while being extensively exposed to other media will have quite a task to perform in sorting out the sign system "Wolf."

How does the canon of wolf books learned by a person, from the first bedtime story to the moment of initiation into adulthood, shape the image of the wolf in that person's mind? An "initiation experience" in this case might be a wilderness excursion following the typical pattern of the quest myth, such as a vision quest, or a "blooding" on a hunting trip. Second, how does a mind so shaped respond when finally faced with both the possibility and actuality of a wolf's presence? Constrained both by this being a literary study and by a lack of sufficient familiarity with neuroscience, I am approaching the problem through extrinsic instruments of influence—specific books and cultural media—rather than from intrinsic neurological or psychological ones.

Anatomy of an Imaginary Wolf

Rebecca Lukens presents "in children's terms" the general questions she believes literature should answer about the human condition:. "What are people like? Why are they like that? What do they need? What makes them do what they do?" (10). Rather than examine a broad scope of handbooks, I will look closely at Lukens's thorough and practical *Critical Handbook of Children's Literature* as exemplary. Providing "glimpses of answers" to these questions is a goal of children's literature. Like many of the writers Lukens cites, she uses *Charlotte's Web* as her touchstone. The novel features animals in communication with one another and in interaction with humans, resolving in a confrontation with death that provides only glimpses of answers to one of the Big Questions we begin asking as children.

Heightening a child's interest is at constant risk from what resides between the proverbial lines—such concerns as truth-telling, inadvertent emotional effect, potential disillusionment, and, Lukens emphasizes, boredom (xi).[4] In the long process of maturation through reading fiction, a child, say a little boy, may live many years between *Charlotte's Web* and *Animal Farm*. He may read the stories again as an adult, to himself or to his own children, and realize that the political lessons of *Animal Farm* were just beginning to surface for him when he read it at fourteen, that Charlotte's lessons of loss and compassionate service to another person have embedded themselves deeply within his adult consciousness. When he chokes up as he reads *Charlotte's Web* to his daughter it is for a different reason than when he was seven. He cried then at the finality of death, but now he cries as well in response to all the intervening experiences he has had with suffering, the knowledge of his daughter's maturation, even his own possible misgivings about the lives and deaths of "livestock." He witnesses her tears as she hears the story. She is being taught by these barnyard animals of her imagination, and the next time she sees an animal on a farm, she will have these stories in her mind, bolstered by the filial emotions that come from having been told them by her father. She will compare them to what she sees, and this is when the animal of story and the animal of the physical world produce a strange charge in the human psyche. Determining the quality of that charge and evaluating what action it instigates are what make literary study important to interspecific coexistence.

To those suspicious of any form of anthropomorphism, emotional responses to talking animals press all kinds of alarm buttons. The regular practice of attributing human traits to animals may interfere with the quality of discussion rather than aid it, and the wolf has been done no real favors by its depictions in children's stories. How far apart are the child who believes that the spider in her garden talks to young pigs and the grown woman who believes that her fox terrier is trying to speak a human sentence when it yowls and whimpers at her? Lukens's response is that "to fail to apply critical standards to children's literature is to imply that children's literature is inferior to adult literature, that children will not benefit from good literature or be harmed by poor literature" (xiii). Therefore, if children can be helped or harmed by the content of what they read, then the effect of anthropomorphism in a book must be weighed as carefully as any other criteria, especially given the number of animals appearing in children's books. Unfortunately, the debate is too often over the mere *presence* of anthropomorphism rather than over its effects.[5]

Lukens takes a nuanced position: "In [nonfiction] books about animals condescension often takes the form of anthropomorphism, an attitude that suggests a lack of interesting qualities in the animals themselves and a need to jazz up their lives by making them more nearly human" (283). This is a quintessential case of an ecocritical tenet—intrinsic value. That animal lives are important to literary study because they are, not because they are symbolic, is the result when we correct the condescension and appropriation Lukens condemns. She cites this case of a fox's thoughts as presented in Alice Goudey's *Here Come the Wild Dogs:*

What a fine morning for racing with the dogs!
    Excitement!
    Adventure!
    And yes, even danger!

Lukens asserts that "these may be reasonable emotions for people" but that the child may be "led to believe that foxes relish the danger and adventure of being hunted . . . It is important that when the child expects a factual report, a factual report is given" (283). This claim raises once again the issues of truth and fact that apparently begin some time before readers move into mature writing, another manifestation of the Nature Fakers problem. Does the child expect a factual report? Do we? Perhaps this is less the issue than the matter of duplicity when nothing in particular is expected, when of all the tools available for educating, a writer chooses nonsense, especially a nonsense prone to justifying such a horrific and indefensible act as fox hunting. Lukens further says, "Wild animals' lives are filled with serious battles with hunters, blizzards, mountain lions, wolves, and starvation; books should show far more convincingly than the fox book how an animal responds physically to its natural enemies" (283). I'll add "or unnatural ones." Foxhounds are ex-wolves bred down and trained to kill foxes. The conditions of agonistic behavior between wolves and foxes in the wild are significantly different in quality and kind.

In the absence of clear criteria about animal cognition, children's nonfiction apparently emphasizes the struggle for survival (even Lukens's own choice of corrective resorts to the language of "battles"). Thus she argues that insofar as it speculates, nonfiction must be "convincing," unlike fiction, which must be interesting. As belief has merely to do with interest in fiction, it may be suspended. It is as potentially dangerous to assume that veracity might be found in the stereotypical depiction of an animal "battling for survival," as to essentialize the force against which the animal struggles. A wolf is not a blizzard.

Jean Craighead George's *Julie of the Wolves* is an excellent example of fiction that understands sufficiently the ecosystemic functions of the world from which it draws. George specifies and differentiates the forces of nature with as careful judgment as we might expect writers to use when differentiating characters, and she presents wolves as more than mechanistic predatory abstractions acting against prey animals. The reader of a George novel, Lukens explains, "while absorbing detailed information about the gray wolves, acquires at the same time an admiration for their grace and intelligence" (284). The choices of words here risk both cult-of-beauty ("grace") and cult-of-utility ("intelligence") thinking, especially because we don't know whether these qualities are to be assessed by lupine or human standards. Yet Lukens avoids a direct declaration of a good/evil distinction in these passages. Therefore, her warning us against anthropomorphism while potentially committing it should be read as an example of linguistic, rather than ethical, incongruity. Even human beings may be considered, as a species, both graceful and intelligent. Indeed, lupine intelligence is a far more complex and less subjective and aesthetic matter than is lupine "grace."

Children's literature is an epicenter of moral and ethical instruction. Therefore, from an ecocritical perspective, no writer may absolve himself or herself of the possibilities of animal emotions, communication, and individual distinction from other animals in order to present credibly a moral universe. Good and bad may indeed be applied to a nonhuman culture as long as we stipulate the conditions. If a female northern wolf crosses the territory of a male southern wolf and the southerner sinks his teeth into the ear of the northerner, then by the southern wolf's standards the northern wolf has committed a transgressive act by crossing the line. She was an invader, a foreign power, a threat to the pack system inside the southerner's territory, and her "trespass" had to be confronted. And the pain of a wounded ear may be sufficiently "bad" in the wandering wolf's ethos as to affect her future behavior.

In a pack, hierarchy and individuality are recognized; what is "good," if we apply a Darwinian principle, is what the pack decides, highly influenced by the alpha pair. The criteria for the wolf's distinctions may simply make "evil" synonymous with "invasive" or "weak." If this seems too anthropomorphic, then consider this: The speculation about the "mind of the hunter" in a children's nonfiction book about a Paleolithic tribe, while risky, could under tightly controlled circumstances help the child understand what we do know of Paleolithic tribes. One of those controls would be for the writer to make clear that the hunter character thinking in the text is subjectified, that one hunter is not the same as another, and this criterion would logically extend to other characters. Hence, a wolf should not be presented as "an essential predator." The writer, certainly the reader, must concentrate on what one wolf might do, rather than on what all wolves do, as the potential measure of truth. After all, both character and individuality are to some extent factually representable. This attention to a combined aesthetic and scientific ethic in writing seems to me of crucial importance in determining what the wolf's role in literature both has been and should be.

Autographed Photos

One of the major subcategories of wolf books is "illustrated." Although the Powell study considers photographs a "neutral" medium of presentation, that medium actually represents a number of choices by the photographer that do not occur in an ideologically free zone. While providing an image of a wolf may save us from having to imagine what it looks like, we must imagine many other things about it; the wolf we're given smells like ink, feels like paper, sounds like the glue of a binding cracking. When the image is linked with print, as in a caption, we also have the potential for dissonance in the semiotic system.

The wolf image, the wolf imagined because of the image, and the wolf we are told about in the caption may all be in contention. For instance, captions may instruct the reader to place the wolf in some habitat that must be imagined beyond the borders of the photograph. The choices and quality of visual art in a book may inhibit or enhance the viewer's ability to take an imprinted image into a wolf's habitat and function in accordance with reality—that is, to function with ecological and environmental responsibility. Wolf images have power to supplant the word, especially with an audience desperate to see wolves. The images of the coffee-table-book or children's-book cover tend to repeat certain tropes and shapes: the howl, the pack feeding, running, misty and half-hidden poses, aerial shots, pup close-ups, growls, the flat close-up stare. Such tropes create categories to which we're prone in literary study, the motifs and patterns that collect to shape assumptions about the being represented by the images, especially if the actual being in question is entirely absent from the imaginative act.

Marilyn Janovitz's *Is It Time?* shows two canids, the species of which could only be known by the summary printed under the Library of Congress description, which calls them wolves (13–14). At no point during the book are they labeled as such. They discuss bath and bedtime. They smile throughout. The parental wolf, the larger one providing the answers to the smaller one's questions, wears a watch. The smaller wolf uses a bathtub, wears pajamas, has a stuffed bear named, appropriately, Ted. There are mentions of canid (implicitly lupine) traits, one in which the little wolf brushes his (or her) "fangs" and the other in which the little wolf "gives a howl" after bathing. Here is an obvious allegorical use of an utterly humanized wolf, in which the references to canid traits are inconsequential and easily converted to a child's performance and obedience (apparently the book's goal). I have not been able to find a corresponding example in which a children's book depicts two wolves deciding on disobedience or rebellion at home or in society. This seems to be the province of the lone wolf, although Neil Gaiman's *Wolves in the Walls* alludes to the horror of a ghost pack.

The names given to canids often say a great deal about what sort of characters we are reading. White Fang is primarily wolf, while Buck is primarily dog, and Diable is the demon canid. In *Julie of the Wolves* Miyax names the alpha male Amaroq, which is the word both for wolf and for wolf essence or spirit; she names the other wolves after her family and gives the pups more generic names (15–18). The omega wolf, the least powerful in the pack, she calls Jello, the only reference to Euro–North America, a commercial world that both attracts Miyax and makes her wary. In addition to the book's other merits, *Julie of the Wolves* can teach children about the human need to name and the drawbacks of such naming. Miyax herself becomes Julie in order to enter the Euro-American world, but her story ends with the loss of both wolf and Inuit to acts of war and assimilation. London and his imitators—particularly James Curwood and Walt Morey—named wolves after Canadian and Alaskan rivers or chose names that had some vague and essentialist "primitive" or indigenous phonetics, such as Kata, Kazan, or Baree. Their attempts at investing the wolf with native ecosystemic and native cultural élan pale in comparison with George's realism and detail.

'Asta Bowen's young adult novel *Hungry for Home* is billed on its dust jacket as containing "no anthropomorphism or sentimentality," a cue to us that it will certainly contain some, given the consistently bad choices made in dust jacket copy. Sure enough, Bowen fits the wolves with such monikers as Marta and Oldtooth (11). However, to her credit, she does a good job of flirting with anthropomorphism without often committing it, prompting us to consider how hard our definition of the term is. Anthropomorphic moments should be defined not by behavior that simply "seems human" but that *must* be projected—behavior implausible for a wolf. In Bowen, wolves "have their own arithmetic" (17), are assumed to be monogamous (18), and are conscious of their dignity (25). None of these are entirely implausible choices. Bowen's care demonstrates the risks of language and its tendency to humanize, even with a writer making a concerted effort against this tendency.

Bowen's story is a fictionalization of the Pleasant Valley and Ninemile packs' experiences as they were covered in newspaper journalism—a kind of roman à clef involving real animals. Some of these wolves were named by biologists or the public, and Bowen uses those names, so that we have the name invented out of sentimentality being both the author's choice and a cultural choice the author represents; we have the split of anthropomorphic names (Marta) and an attempt at wolf-consciousness through names that indicate a condition by which a wolf might be known under some vaguely animal rubric (Oldtooth). The pattern also includes the naming of a wolf after a location; in Bowen's novel—borrowed from the real wolf named by biologists—it is Tenino.

Dennis Nolan combines speculation about language and high-adventure fantasy elements with names from an imaginary Pleistocene. His technique anticipates later texts for adults, such as Jean M. Auel's *Clan of the Cave Bear* and Elizabeth Marshall Thomas's *Reindeer Moon*. To people, Auel and Thomas give "prehistoric names"—those hard monosyllabics that inevitably seem comical— but they refer to animals in capitalized generic terms, ones commonly used in American Indian protohuman tales, such as Bear, Crow, and Otter. Especially because Nolan's book is written for children, and Thomas and Auel have made strident cases for the rigor of their research to satisfy adult readers, suspension of disbelief becomes more about audience maturity than a matter of flipping some readerly toggle switch.

The fictional/nonfictional distinction in regard to names also affects how parents and children might consider promotional materials designed to protect wolves. Wolf Haven, Algonquin, and Wood Buffalo national parks have offered various marketing packages employing named wolves. Wolf Haven and other organizations put together "Adopt a Wolf" packets, ads for which often appear in mail-order catalogs such as *Wireless* or *Coldwater Creek* alongside gauche tokens for the upper middle class. These packets may be bought for $20–25, and the money is generally dedicated to facility maintenance and wolf medical care. In the packet comes a glossy photo and, printed on the back, the wolf's name, pack status, date of entry into the sanctuary or park pack, and age, along with other information about wolves and the park. Other perquisites of membership clubs are included in the tradition of the old wilderness magazine clubs often marketed to boys over the last century. The parks sometimes allow schoolchildren to name new captive wolves. "Adopted" wolves receive dog names such as Hambone and Lightning, New Age tags such as Windsong, and mythic and historic names such as Nimrod, Apollo, and Socrates.[6]

Celebrity certainly has its dangers, but some recognition of individuality, however clumsy and amateurish, may be a necessary step toward our better understanding other animals. The Taoist belief that naming diminishes power should be taken seriously. Perhaps the power relinquished by the named, the ambassador or representative, might be used to empower the unnamed remainder being represented. Sanctuaries such as Wolf Haven that give celebrity status to individual wolves forced into captivity help us understand victimization. They make visible to us the invisible, an encouraged practice in nature writing.

Gender and ethnicity studies have struggled to correct generalizing (often conflated with essentialism), but generalization is still the foundation of literary study in regard to other species. Analysis that ignores or wholly symbolizes an animal is often so remedial that it has many steps to take before any comprehension of animal individuality is possible. Children exposed to such figurative symbology are thrust immediately into a complicated form of thought that may actually affect less the integrity and purity of their child minds than their later adult minds, which may have failed to process such formative moments over the decades. When the residual image becomes the resonant one, this is food for the shadow. It also drives academic abstraction of the world in literary study. One irony here is that children are often more exposed to facts about animals than are humanities scholars. A staple of children's reading is the scientific primer on bugs, or marine life, or wolves. It is possible, scholars beware, that a ten-year-old and an associate professor of transatlantic cultural studies have precisely the same knowledge of the nonhuman world when they approach texts chock full of representations of that world.

Let's say a child's book (1) influences a phobia that appears in a dream (2) that is recounted (3) to a therapist who writes a version interpreting it, after which (4) the therapist's story is analyzed by critics, each of whom has a particular narrative explaining its relevance (5+), which is read by readers who talk about each narrative (6∞). Throughout the entire process not a single real wolf has appeared; in fact, wolves may be deemed unnecessary to these narratives. This is perhaps the strongest case against both Deleuzian exploitation of the nonhuman world and the reader-response method of literary criticism. While a reader may complete a kind of circuit with the writer (and/or "discourse community") through the text, the reader's and writer's disparate bodies of knowledge about the subject

will moderate whatever other influences, in this case animals, affect the formation of story. The process is presumed to follow too closed a system. For instance,
Derrida's brief and affected empathy with his domestic cat in *L'Animal que donc je
suis* devolves quickly into a set of unsupportable assumptions about otherness
used to justify compassionate Cartesianism—an anthropocentric philosophy
built on an absence of even basic biological or ecological influences. The dyad of
human/nonhuman, like the dyad of author/reader, needs to be contested and
corrected, not employed toward the erasure of one or the other. Such is the rhetorical necessity when faced with the bifurcation fallacy.

Twinning

In chapter 9, discussing the World-Wolf, I mentioned Joseph Campbell's attribution of the Kluskap-Malsum story to the important Contending Twins myth
found in many tribal mythologies. This myth raises an interesting paradox in
regard to binary relation: It is so pervasive as to serve an archetypal function, one
especially fit to challenge our dualistic ideas of good and evil. The trickster role of
Kluskap and the related but culturally separate role of Nanabozho in the Great
Lakes region are two examples of the complex relationship, the permeable lines,
between twins.[7] For so common a literary image, the actual birth of twins is a
rarity, and as such has been considered auspicious for much of human history.
Claude Lévi-Strauss's *Story of Lynx* contains a chapter called "Twins: Salmon,
Bears, and Wolves," in which he considers the power of twins in several Northwest Coast tribes. The Kwakiutl, writes Lévi-Strauss, developed rituals by which
twins in their community were used to control the weather. In fact, he notes that
all over the Northwest up to Alaska, the association of twins with meteorological
phenomena has been prominent (119). Other tribes feared twins; the poor, who
could not raise them, killed them to "send them home" where they could be
cared for. Some peoples referred to twins as "wolves" (126); the Twana considered this a pejorative, while the Quinault used it to replace the pejorative (the
word *twins*) and give the children dignity. Lévi-Strauss mentions that in Siberia
the association of twins and wolves was a common mythic configuration (126).
Finally, he links the hunting of wolves to near extinction (during ancient times)
with the twin. When the great hunters of the Coast Salish tried to kill the wolf,
they merely split it into living halves, one-half of which escaped to the mountains
(127).

   We have already seen the application of binaries in the World-Wolf model,
which includes varied degrees of permeability among its various pairs. The most
complicated example is probably the hybrid, but there are many others: the trickster's split personality; the role of meteorological phenomena as demonstrated by

Lévi-Strauss, among others; and cultural parodies, such as Ishmael Reed's *Yellow Back Radio Broke-Down*. In Reed's novel a Creole gunslinger playing the counter-culture trickster calls himself the Loop-Garoo Kid (a play on the French *loup-garou*, or werewolf). The corrective to noble savage ideology is found in the split forms of power—benevolent and malevolent (including the combination of the two forms in ambivalence or covalence)—attributed to the wolf in several indigenous and invading North American societies. The complication of the observed wolf's purity as both image and species resulting from hybridization, especially breeding, is not only a matter of narrative corporeality but also of mythicization.

Now consider the powerful force of this construct when placed in the mind of a child open to tales of transformation, identity complexity, likeness and difference, the Manichean self. The ghost wolf's protean form, augmented with the specifity of twinning power, is a commanding primitive myth affecting cultures close to the land. The augmentation occurs not only through the werewolf phenomena I have already addressed but also through feral child stories, wolf brother and mother stories, and wolf domestication stories. The symbolic value of wolf images in stories that follow the Wolf that is Like Me, or My Brother or Mother, the Wolf that Might Have Been Me or Raised Me had I been left in the wilderness by my lost parents—think of this as emanating from that wolf twin of our collective and individual interior landscapes. That particular ghost wolf, the doppelgänger, must be reconciled with the wolves of reality to some degree when we are children, or we will have to learn our ecological maturity in our adulthood with the same degree of difficulty as learning a language, or the piano, or our own confidence, during a period when the skein of life has already been let out to some place a long way from home.

CHAPTER FOURTEEN

The Twins and the Timber Wolves

A CASE STUDY

At this point I want to offer a hypothetical case, in which the human beings are imagined and the wolves rendered as accurately as possible. This will, I hope, demonstrate several of the World-Wolf's possible influences. We will see how children are ecologically educated through stories, and how powerful a force the wolf has become in various human interpretations of those stories.

Our subjects for the study are fraternal twins named Paul and Minnie, born and raised in Babbitt, Minnesota, a town surrounded by Superior National Forest and near Birch Lake. They live in a ranchette with their parents and maternal grandmother, a family born of four generations of lifelong Minnesotans, originally Norwegian immigrants to Chicago who moved to Babbitt as soon as they could afford a wagon. Paul and Minnie's parents each remember being told about their own fathers' wolf experiences. Dad's father

> was hunting and trapping in the territory around Thief Lake . . . and one day had shot a deer, which he hung up on the spot, intending to return for it the next day. When he arrived he found that the carcass had been pulled down and much of it devoured by what he judged from the tracks to have been a lone wolf. Distributing some poisoned bait about the carcass, which he left untouched, he came back the next day and found a very large timber wolf lying dead nearby.

Mom's father,

> at a logging camp near Red Lake . . . saw the carcass of a large buck that had been killed by timber wolves. The dead animal lay in the sleigh tracks within about fifty feet of the door of the camp horse stable and had been killed just before the teamsters came out to feed their horses at about four o'clock in the morning.[1]

The latter story is corroborated by Grandmother, who has memories of wolf hunts before The War, when men would travel to the Boundary, to Wisconsin, and to North Dakota, filling a pickup bed with Newhouse traps and buckskin-wrapped mason jars filled with an overpowering concoction. She tells other stories about wolves as well, some of the same ones W. P. Kinsella's Yugoslavian grandmother told him: "Everything was at peace, the world unfolding as it should. 'And then,' Baba Drobney would say, springing the trap, 'knocks at the door a stranger'" (Kinsella, 1).

Paul and Minnie's parents remember being told these stories as young children and have since mulled over their own preservationist politics in the context of the harrowing experiences the grandparents had. The parents have seen wolves only in zoos and at the International Wolf Center in Ely. In 1972, before they became Mom and Dad, they participated in a survey at the State Fair designed to measure the effects of stories on children's attitudes about wolves (Roger T. Johnson, 37). They were among 1,692 people who answered questions at a fairly primitive computer terminal, next to which sat a taxidermied wolf. The questions were oriented to measure the extent, if any, to which adults had "moderated their views about the wolf" from their likely confusion "between the prejudices of childhood and the more objective adult information" (37). Most of the participants were from the Twin Cities; the rural population that included Mom and Dad was in the minority.

The survey determined that the group most likely to view wolves negatively was composed of children less than ten years old; and the group least likely to view them as such was aged nineteen to thirty-five. The latter group included the parents of our Minnesota twins. The greatest contrast in data was between young children and teenagers in their considerations of whether the wolf was a danger: 70 percent of children under ten said yes, as compared with 14 percent of those aged ten to eighteen, including those living in rural areas (38). Finally, 55 percent of the total sample "reported they had encountered no information about wolves recently, 34 percent had read or seen information favorable to wolves, and 11 percent had encountered unfavorable material recently" (39). The parents, then in their early twenties, marked that they had seen both favorable and unfavorable information.

In his assessment of the data, Roger Johnson asserts that more important than getting rid of the stories in which wolves are villains—any character may be a villain, and villains make interesting stories—"is that another side of the wolf should be presented to children in a relevant way that they understand" (39). He suggests asking children such questions as, "What is the wolf's side of the story?"

He points out that the State Fair setting was "safe" because no real wolves were around and wonders what might happen "if [the respondents] were placed in a lonely night campsite in northern Minnesota and heard the *plaintive* and *disquieting* call of the wolf nearby" (39, emphasis mine). Johnson's own predilections seep into the study here, but at least one—the "who speaks for wolf" approach popularized by Paula Underwood—indicates perhaps a predilection at the level of the collective unconscious, as well as simply a logical argument.[2] Perhaps the presence of real wolves would have a negligible influence on the level of safety. Perhaps a night alone camping is not "lonely," and the wolf call is not "disquieting," or is so for reasons beyond this study's gauge. I have heard the call of wolves from a lonely campsite; it struck me as a sound more celebratory and exuberant than plaintive and disquieting. But what it was for the wolves may have been something else, and likely was something slightly different for each wolf, whatever the biological imperative. Johnson is right to demand a study conducted more on the wolf's turf and terms—highly progressive especially for a 1972 analysis.

Some time before they begin reading, Paul and Minnie are told the same stories at the same time. They have felt secure with parents who make careful selections—no scary stories at bedtime, no violent stories, often stories that "teach something." In the wolf stories this latter criterion is particularly important, as it reflects the parents' own education about wolves and the educational goals they set for their children.

The children hear the version of "The Three Little Pigs" in which the wolf gets tuckered out and leaves all three pigs singing and dancing in the brick house, rather than the version in which the little mason builds a roaring fire and cooks the wolf when he comes down the chimney. Among the music that their parents play at nap time the children hear Prokofiev's orchestral *Peter and the Wolf.* They are read "Little Red Riding Hood," but the parents are in disagreement about the ending. The mother shops for a book, preferably illustrated, to resolve their difference and discovers not only that most children's books consist of animal stories in one form or another but also that a large pack of wolf books occupies the shelves. She finds Jack Zipes's collection *The Trials and Tribulations of Little Red Riding Hood* and discovers as well the mythic resonance of the story through thirty-eight of its versions.

Back at the ranchette, the kids look with their mother at Janovitz's *Is It Time?* and see the pup happily taking a bath and preparing for bed. After dozens of trips through this book, Mom is driven to find a different one. In *Isn't It Nice to Have a Wolf around the House?* they read a story of a very old man and his very old pets who hire a wolf to cook, clean house, and entertain them. The wolf does a bang-up job, but tragedy strikes when the newspaper headline reveals that he is wanted for bank robbery. When confronted by the very old man, the wolf, wearing an apron and chef's hat, suffers a nervous collapse and has to be nursed back to health by the man and his pets, who find that their own vigor is renewed by taking care of the convalescing wolf. They testify on the wolf's behalf, he is granted clemency, and the clan retires to Arizona.

Since the kids seem most taken by the wolf stories from among their repertoire of reading, Dad gets in on the act and picks up two wolf books to add to the A. A. Milne and Maurice Sendak. The first, *The Story of the Kind Wolf,* which really seems to be a parody of psychoanalysis, is about a wolf counseled by an owl on being nicer and not terrorizing the forest creatures anymore. The wolf takes the owl's advice and goes south to practice being nice, which he rather enjoys. This leaves the animals with a new freedom, to which the fox responds by eating one of the birds. "The fierce animals," writes Peter Nickl, "enjoyed themselves, but the timid and gentle ones were terrified" (8). The fox becomes the subtle foil to the owl's clinical analyses throughout the book. During a hard winter, when the animals are starving and sick, the wolf returns and decides to hang out his shingle as a doctor. The owl convinces the other animals not to visit the wolf, however, with the *Poor Richard's* proverb: "A wolf may lose his teeth, but never his nature" (12). Finally, in an isolated clearing in the forest, the wolf is able to nurse a small rabbit back to health. This impresses all the animals except the owl, who thinks it a trick. Meanwhile the fox, sick from eating forest animals, ignores the owl's advice and is healed by Dr. Wolf, who converts the fox to vegetarianism. The wolf builds a thriving practice, takes in another wolf to help, and at the conclusion of the story stands in a field picking flowers and herbs for homeopathic remedies.

Dad's second choice is a fractured fairy tale called *The True Story of the 3 Little Pigs: By A. Wolf.* The wolf gets to tell "his side of the story," which is that the pigs are obnoxious neighbors who refuse to give A. Wolf a cup of sugar when he comes calling. He has a terrible cold, and his sneezes knock down the first two pigs' houses; Wolf observes that they aren't very smart builders either. At the brick house the pig inside taunts A. Wolf into a fury, and while he is pounding on the front door the police (also pigs) arrest and jail him. "I was framed," says Wolf, and ends the story by holding his prison cup through the bars, asking the reader for a cup of sugar.

Big Red Riding Hood

"The Tale of Little Red Riding Hood" is a bridge story to the ancient myths, like the strongest fairy tales, and its Euro–North American revisions of older European tales give it at least occidental scope.[3] Children are likely told or have read to them "Red Riding Hood" before their reading primer period. In Paul and Minnie's case the story is told to them as one of many bedtime stories early on. But which version is told? Perhaps in no other children's wolf story is this question as important, because the adaptations and revisions have at stake more than mere cultural nuance. In "Red Riding Hood" the effects of reversal, a common device in children's literature, are as immediate, relevant, and powerfully allegorical to Euro-American children as in "Peter and the Wolf" or "The Three Little Pigs," but "Red Riding Hood" also employs the powerful combination of filial loyalty and sexual temptation, depicted through the doppelgänger, the figure of disguise and transformational twinning. Unlike "The Wolf and the Seven Kids" or "The Three Little Pigs," in which the wolf is instantly recognized as a predatory figure of danger, "Red Riding Hood" gains much of its energy from the wolf's duplicity and humanization, even to its predatory hunger being metaphorically sexual.

Zipes's anthology covers the story's literary history and scope and includes examples of its modernizations, the two most famous versions being those of Perrault and of the Grimm brothers. Perrault ends the story, "And upon saying these words, the wicked wolf threw himself upon Little Red Riding Hood, and ate her up" (93). The Grimms' version concludes, "Then Little Red Cap went merrily on her way home" (138), the wicked wolf bested by a hunter who comes to the rescue. In variants of this latter version, the hunter either shoots the wolf outright or catches him, cuts him open to free Red and Granny, and fills the wolf's belly with stones in order to kill him, as per "The Wolf and the Seven Kids." This last variant seems to me more rightly European and American, a western sort of yarn in which the hunter gets to torture the wolf to death to "teach it a lesson." Note again the symbolic act of killing the wolf by making it eat and the mythic import of forcing it to swallow the earth.

Perhaps Dad tells the Perrault version. If this is the children's introduction to the wolf, then they are introduced to the malevolent ghost. But Zipes includes thirty-eight versions of the tale, and our twins may be exposed to some of them—perhaps versions told at school or by a babysitter—different from the one chosen by Mom and Dad. Ten of the renditions Zipes includes are classified as "American," ranging from an anonymous 1796 tale that ends with the moral lesson, "And was not he a very naughty wolf, to kill such a pretty little creature?" (98) to stories written in 1990 by Gwen Strauss ("The Waiting Wolf") and Sally Miller Gearhardt ("Roja and Leopold"). Gearhardt's tale begins, "Once upon a time, in a bedroom community of Silicon Valley . . ." Chronologically, the first five American tales after 1796 were written by men, while the last four, beginning with

Anne Sexton's 1971 poem "Red Riding Hood," are by women—a telling example of the entrance of women writers, and of second-wave feminism, into the wolf story.

During the next few years the children recognize the "Red Riding Hood" stories as a multivalent moral tale about sexuality, as both they and their parents must contend with their awakenings to their bodies and the world around their bodies. Zipes takes the position that the tale, through its traditional editing and revision by men, serves as a male projection of fantasy, and both Géza Róheim and Bruno Bettelheim have used it for extensive psychoanalytic readings.[4] But as Minnie grows older she finds Anne Sexton. One day, as a young adult digging through old library books and journals, she giggles at Gearhardt or at a wonderful parody of Bobbie Ann Mason written by Jim Wayne Miller, but Sexton retains the resonance of literature. In Miller's version, called "Lambs and Wolves," the country bumpkin Leroy Wolf is flirting with Red, who is home from college and trying to change her grandmother's diet to health food. "The Wolfs," Miller writes in his Mason persona,

> a whole pack of them, all intermarried, some people claimed—lived out near the lake, in shanties, tarpaper shacks, and lately in rusted-out mobile homes, junked campers and old schoolbuses. The Wolfs had a reputation for living off the land—running trotlines, digging herbs, trapping. From time to time they were accused of stealing cattle and sheep. Leroy, true to the Wolf pattern, never finished school. He had hung around all these years, doing occasional odd jobs. Now he lived in his pickup truck with a camper shell mounted on it. Everybody said he sold dope. (50)

Minnie might walk a hiking path along Birch Lake with her family one evening and hear the howling of a pack in the distance. Will she think of the wolf-encounter scenes she has read in Laura Ingalls Wilder's *Little House on the Prairie* and *By the Shores of Silver Lake*? Will she think the wolves are howling at the moon? Will she interpret through poetry and self-analysis? Maybe she will expect to meet a wolf on the trail. Maybe her father will turn to her with a good-natured grin and say it's a good thing she's not wearing red. She has matured to the point of understanding parody and recognizing that symbolic language can produce all kinds of squirmy little side effects in human thought. She has also matured into the cold world of ghost wolves transposed with real men that prey on young girls. Whether she matures to the point of understanding the difference between actual prey and sexual prey is an element of her ecological education, which in turn is a measure of her cultural clarity or entrapment by metaphor, symbolism, and the abstracting power of culture. Much of this will happen unconsciously and in the context of all her other reading. Other animals and their myths will accrue quietly, sinking silently and deep until they rise from the sediment as gods or monsters.

Our hypothetical case shouldn't be narrowly defined as a story of children obsessed with wolves (itself a common enough occurrence); on the contrary, Paul and Minnie often hardly notice what living in wolf country and reading stories is feeding their developing psyches. Twenty years later, when she returns home from college, perhaps calling herself Minerva, Minnie walks the trail along Birch Lake again. By this time, the wolf population in Minnesota will have exceeded two thousand. Editorials in the papers will call for sport hunting to manage the population; the timber wolf will be under consideration as the name of a basketball team, as the state animal, and as having its "endangered" status changed to "threatened." What will happen now in her mind if Minnie sees a wolf? Her focus on animals will likely have gone through the typical phases of childlike fascination and love or fear to adolescent indifference or conditioned distance, to the political and intellectualized responses of the adult for whom animals are others falling down the list from more pressing concerns. But somewhere during those phases she might return to the world.

She sees a wolf trot along the path ahead of her, turn into the woods, and become only the sound of paws in leaves. She considers that the wolf might be female, with her den nearby, with pups being taught every day how to live in a land crisscrossed by roads to grandmother's house.

Encyclopediae Lupinae

After the kids have learned to read they begin making their own choices. They stumble across such tales as Jim Murphy's *Call of the Wolves,* in which a wolf is chased by an aerial hunter and manages to escape and return to the pack, the illustrations airbrushed efforts at realism rather than cartoons. Paul finds Esther Baskin's *Creatures of Darkness* and reads the entry on the wolf, which begins, "The wolf, a terror to animal and man alike, walks about in night forests and isolated villages," and ends with a peasant killing a woman with an ax because she saved herself and let the wolves take her children (12). Something doesn't seem right here, so Paul and his father go to the library and find *Wonders of Nature,* a book published by *Parents'* magazine. The entry for "Wolf" reads:

> The Wolf is a form of wild dog. Some people think it is the original ancestor of all our domestic dogs. Others think it is an altogether different breed. But we do know that Wolves can be tamed, and then they become as affectionate as the most affectionate

domestic dog. Since they are very powerful, they are sometimes mated with sled-dogs, to make a stronger stock. In the wild state, Wolves can be terribly vicious and destructive. They hunt in packs and will attack sheep and cattle. They make their homes in caves and hollow tree trunks (96).

This entry is so poorly constructed, partly outright nonsense, that Dad has to face Paul's increasing interest in facts, and when his son asks about getting a wolf as a pet, Dad turns to the encyclopedia.

Paul and Minnie are growing up in the early 1990s, so the Internet encyclopedia listings, the various compendia that always indicate their ephemeral nature and dubious points of origin, are only just forming. The family instead consults some established encyclopedias, old-school stuff printed on paper. The 1996 *Encyclopedia Americana* entry on the wolf is written by "a Professor Emeritus of Zoology at the University of California at Davis." The first half of the entry is primarily statistical, mentioning only once in several paragraphs that the wolf is "clever." It cites that the wolf is a night hunter (actually, wolves are more often crepuscular) and ends the statistical section with the statements that "domestic livestock brought them an added food supply" and that wolves still kill horses and livestock "in remote areas." The next half of the entry is more editorial. "Since civilization began," it reads, "wolves have been a menace to man, his herds, and large game animals." The wolf is given a "crafty character," which the article attributes to its mythic and legendary depictions. It cites wolves as "somewhat uncertain" pets, and it mentions the old adage of no documented human kills in North America by healthy wolves, though the entry is more accurately equivocal—"few or no authenticated deaths." It includes in the same paragraph that over the millennia wolf pelts have been worn by humans and that "wolf flesh is a human food in extremity"—a selective set of details as much about people as about wolves (94).

Paul and his father work back through a few other encyclopedias. George C. Goodwin's entry validates the wolf as one of the intelligent mammals. He lists anatomical statistics, as well as range of distribution and the politics affecting it. He notes as a "belief" that wolves mate for life—his phrasing a prescient anticipation of the revision of that position (see Terrell, 7, which I also cited in chapter 5; and McIntyre, informal talk). He calls their howl "memorable." This entry also refers to Russian sleigh stories, the Romulus and Remus legend, Kipling's stories, and sled dogs' similarities and cross-breeding with wolves. Goodwin's last sentence, from which Paul grows more attached to the idea of a wolf as a pet, states that wolves raised in captivity can be quite tame (556–57). *The Columbia*

268 | *Werewolf, Wolf-Child, She-Wolf*

Encyclopedia of 1993 is more statistically oriented and includes sources as well as the occasional adverb-adorned fact ("Because of their raids on livestock, gray wolves have been hunted ruthlessly" [2992]).

Surprisingly, the 1948 Funk and Wagnall's *New Standard Encyclopedia of Universal Knowledge* is no more editorial than the 1996 *Americana* entry. One mention of "great ravages among sheep" is countered by the claim of "experienced hunters that wolves never attack man" and the description of wolves as "cautious," rather than "clever" or "cunning" (262). Several encyclopedias of the 1930s generally attempt to resolve the debate by offering binary classifications. The pairs of taxa are often different among the different encyclopedias. One commonly used pair is "coyote/wolf." Another is "black wolf/white wolf," which is sometimes used synonymously with "timber/Arctic" and which contributes to the chaotic colloquial and regional taxonomic inventions that still crop up. Elizabeth Marshall Thomas, for instance, uses "buffalo wolf" and "tundra wolf," colloquialisms implying but not exactly indicating the gray wolf and Arctic wolf, as if they were precise designations (45). These pairs indicate earlier methods of distinction, when pelage was of greater influence. They also indicate the revision of designation methods over the decades, revision to which Paul and his father have access through just one trip to the public library. Importantly they indicate the human propensity toward bifurcation. It seems appropriate here to note that bifurcation is a logical fallacy—the either/or supposition too commonly made in argumentation. Even the phrase "lumpers and splitters" implies a tendency to divide rather than to constellate. At the level of language and method, at the archaic level of distinction, all disciplines have been seduced by the simplification of the world into blackness and whiteness.

The entry in the 1920 volume *American Animals,* apropos of its era, is almost straight propaganda. It contains such words and phrases as *dreaded, menace,* and *unsettled beasts,* inaccuracies on wolf behavior, and legendary tales employed not to separate the ghost from the corporeal wolf but to connect them. Pictures included are of wolves in zoos, the cages visible and sadly consistent with the encyclopedia's definition (277–78).

Among the generic pen-and-ink drawings of other canids in the 1910 *New International Encyclopedia,* the wolf appears almost Rubenesque, languidly recumbent in a pastoral setting and howling with a soulful (as opposed to vicious) look on its face. The text of the 1910 edition belies the illustration, referring to the "peculiarly vicious expression to the countenance" given by the wolf's "oblique" eyes, with an implicit Orientalism. The wolf is characterized as "cowardly" and "stealthy," and the debate over its proper taxonomic designations is mentioned.

Finally, Paul and his father reach the oldest encyclopedia the library has in stock, the 1897 edition of *Johnson's Universal Cyclopaedia*. Paul is enamored of the "w" volume itself, the binding cracking and chipping, the smell of the old pages, its heft and faded gold letters on the cover. He expects to read a magic spell from it. The editors write that "wolf" is "the common name for the larger wild species of the family Canidae and genus Canis which most resemble the dog, and which agree with the ordinary types of that animal in the possession of circular pupils to the eyes and a somewhat bushy tail" (815). Paul sees some consistency with the newer encyclopedias, such as the division into two categories (wolf/coyote), but wonders how much has changed in learning in one hundred years.

For instance, he is used to hearing about how the eyes of wolves and dogs are different—in fact how one can use that trait as a means to tell them apart. He reads that the members of *Canis lupus* are "properly called wolves, although more generally designated as wild dogs or foxes" (815). He is thoroughly confused by the entry "Wolf-dog," which reads: "a large variety of the domestic dog, allied to the shepherd's dog, now found almost exclusively in Spain, though formerly common in Ireland and Scandinavia. The name is also applied to a dog of any kind that is trained to protect sheep, etc., against wolves" (816). His father reminds him of breeds he already knows—the Irish and Russian wolfhounds, and Paul thinks of dogs he has seen staring at him from certain yards, dogs he has seen in movies, dogs bred to protect and bred to kill.

Minnie's Path

Minnie has taken a slightly different course. She reads Dennis Nolan's *Wolf Child*, in which supposedly prehistoric people look decidedly WASPish, at the end of which Teo and Nyac, human child and wolf child respectively, sleep together by a fire. What appeals to her is the experience of the outdoors, the possibilities of learning from the animal directly. She and her brother share the sadness they feel when reading *The Yearling, Born Free,* or *Old Yeller,* but their interests separate over time, and as she discovers that the Girl Scouts are a little too institutional and conventional to suit her, she turns her reading attention toward preparation for her own outings.

When she advances to chapter books, she finds *Animorphs,* a narrative in which a group of teenagers is given the power by an alien to borrow the DNA from an animal through touch, then transmogrify into that animal. One volume, the cover of which shows a teenage girl changing into a wolf, uses a kineograph at the bottom corners of the pages that shows her transformation taking place.[5] The teenagers have been chosen to save the planet from aliens who intend to conquer it. The Animorphs learn to work as a team, handle youthful romances, and contend with the difficulties of their double lives (having to lie to the parents after transformations is one of their ongoing moral dilemmas). The books are full of point-of-view exercises in physical shape-shifting (which is painless) and altered perception. Minnie also finds a subculture of fans devoted to *Animorphs* books, clubs, Web pages, and contests. She tells a teacher that she is interested in wolves and might like to learn more about them by going to see them. She also wants to know what to read on the subject. The teacher mentions Jean Craighead George to her, and Minnie's mother remembers *Julie of the Wolves.* They read the books together: *Moon of the Gray Wolves, Julie, Snow Tracks, Julie's Wolf Pack.*

George's work might be the best of children's literature on wildlife, especially on wolves, produced to date. The books range from a kind of Arctic pastoral—"That night the bright November moon shone down upon the wolves of Toklat, running free and playfully across their white domain" (*Moon of the Gray Wolves,* 38)—to a hard determinism: "The oil drum she had seen when the skua flew over marked the beginning of civilization and the end of the wilderness" (*Julie of the Wolves,* 134). George names wildlife specifically rather than generically, and places her characters and her readers. What makes these stories particularly powerful is the deftness with which George weaves ecological lessons into the narrative. Didacticism works subtly with fine prose, as in this passage from *Julie:*

> Not a tree grew anywhere to break the monotony of the gold-green plain, for the soils of the tundra are permanently frozen. Only moss, grass, lichens, and a few hardy flowers take root in the thin upper layer that thaws briefly in summer. Nor do many species of animals live in this rigorous land, but those creatures that do dwell there exist in bountiful numbers. Amaroq watched a large cloud of Lapland longspurs wheel up into the sky, then alight in the grasses. Swarms of crane flies, one of the few insects that can survive the cold, darkened the tips of the mosses. Birds wheeled, turned, and called. Thousands sprang up from the ground like leaves in a wind. (9)

The story has a potent effect on Minnie. Miyax transforms into Julie in order to assimilate, but she remains resourceful, kind, and resilient rather than passive and compliant. She navigates her worlds. Only thirteen, she has left her abusive husband in Barrow, Alaska, and is trying to reach San Francisco, where she has a friend. She gets lost on the tundra. Although her cooperation with the wolves saves her, Miyax's story ends in elegy:

> The seals are scarce and the whales are almost gone.
> The spirits of the animals are passing away.
> Amaroq, Amaroq, you are my adopted father.
> My feet dance because of you.

My eyes see because of you.

My mind thinks because of you.

And it thinks, on this thundering night,

That the hour of the wolf and the Eskimo is over. (170)

Whether or not we see this as noble savagery or the vanishing breed fallacy is inconsequential to Miyax's own observations in the narrative. George and her main character have built sufficient credibility for this position. By now Minnie's decision is made. She will study animals. She will go to the wilderness.

Teen Wolves

Edward Topsell believed that rubbing an infant's gums with a wolf's tooth helped the child to cut its teeth (Topsell, 1071; also in Lopez, *Of Wolves and Men*, 222). Metaphorically speaking, he may have been onto something. The ghost wolf often proved a powerful mentor in the bildungsromans of Euro-American authors. The result is an impressive collection of contradictory notions about "wolf power." A wolf's portrait might be airbrushed on the side of a van with a BSA bumper sticker, a van carrying someone of voting age to a wolf howl, someone who also believes that after a giant flood the animals he hunts were brought back to genetic viability from pairs four thousand years ago and that the wolf's demise in his home state is simply the result of evolution. He votes for whichever candidate lets him keep his guns, because he desires a kind of power provided by the magical wolf he would love to shoot, up there in the mountains somewhere, since his city killed that wolf a hundred years ago, since his suburb captured that wolf twenty-five years ago and put her in a zoo. He would love to rub his child's gums with the wolf's tooth and hang the tooth around his neck.

During the late cold war, with its highly public and sometimes hastily gathered statistics on global disaster, the subgenre of ecological fiction set in a post-catastrophe Eden flourished. Novels such as Ernest Callenbach's *Ecotopia,* which combined the sexual revolution with a treatment of the United States as a Babylon of the Apocalypse, were very much products of their time. But Cynthia Deitering points out that a large group of novels in the 1980s acted as a gauge of cultural awareness of the biosphere's condition, an awareness she calls "toxic consciousness" (196). Predictably, such fictional influences mean new projections of the imagined natural world (such as Bill McKibben's problematic term *postnatural*).

Thus the manipulation of the wolf into a salable iconic Euro–North American figure has affected teenagers' ideas of what wolves are and why their existence matters. Joel Chandler Harris borrowed the wolf and rabbit from the plantation slave narrative, in which these function in pedagogical allegory toward a warped end perpetuated by the Disney Empire: slave tales removed from their contexts and reduced to young childhood bedtime yarns that deny the very history they declare. For Kipling the wolf remained an allegorical figure that functioned to champion order in the empire. The Disneyfication of Kipling as well soft-pedaled the colonial allegory in favor of the coming-of-age plotline, in which Mowgli learns to cope with death and human love, is told by the animals (and seems secretly to "know") that he cannot remain in the jungle, and walks into the setting sun toward a civilization only his by virtue of his species and the lure of an Oriental girl. His only future, it seems, is to live under the British Raj and those forces more dangerous than even Shere Khan.

I remember seeing the Disney *Jungle Book* at the drive-in. I sat in the back seat of my parents' car in the cooling night, past my bedtime and wearing footie pajamas, listening to the crackling speaker hooked on the window. When Mowgli looked over his shoulder tearfully at Bagheera and Baloo and turned toward the village, I felt an emotion more complicated and stronger than mere parting. I thought, "You don't *have* to go. Stay with them." The logic of the message—that one must live with his "own kind"—just didn't work for me. The myth of the hero's journey through the wild and back to civilization was in strong competition with the myth of the wild child who remains, transforms, and disappears into the new world that adopts him, saves him, and changes the very meaning of "his own kind." I felt a strong desire to leave the car and run to the woods that surrounded the dusty gravel lot of the drive-in. I was simply too afraid to do so, afraid to leave not only my parents but also the *car*, and too young to know that this particular brand of fear is the core of the civilized soul, the soul with which I contend now at the age of forty—softened, adept at arguments of comfort and convenience, less likely to cross the threshold into the wild having accumulated more (or the semblance of more) to lose. My very profession is governed by such a tame heart and seated rump.

Jack London's popularity depended in part on his persona as a man's man, in part on how he finessed Kipling's Law, and the naturalist tradition provided him the means to both. His work, as will be discussed at length in the next chapter, made palatable the hard determinism of the "law of life" with an appeal to the reader's desire to understand, and conquer, the wolf's world. London's apparent verisimilitude and the novelty of the wolf's point of view distinguished his work from Kipling's. He "Americanized" the Euro-wolf tale through a new mode of domesticating the wild, a tradition continued by the Boy Scouts (which appropriated Kipling in order to create young Londons and Roosevelts), *Boys' Life* magazine, and the golden age of the American pulp western (the 1930s through the 1950s). Cinematic versions of London's work varied, but Disney's dismissed the literary naturalist view for the sake of a boy-and-his-dog "nature tale" about the gold rush. This slick presentation carried *White Fang* all the way through the 1990s.[6]

However, another side of the adolescent wolf story surfaced near the end of the cold war. Whitley Streiber's novel *Wolf of Shadows* and the role-playing game *Werewolf: The Apocalypse* are both popular-culture examples of how and where the determinism and nihilism of the literary naturalists has been kept alive. The Jules Verne age of science fiction was not postapocalyptic but optimistically futuristic, however politically allegorical. The détente-era fear of devastation by war and the present fears about environmental devastation both figure into narratives that in past centuries would have concentrated on Industrial Age factory disasters or financial collapse.

To continue on Paul and Minnie's paths: We see them open *Wolf of Shadows* as soon as they finish *Julie of the Wolves*. Both books operate according to survivalist plots in which wolves teach and nurture the main character, who in turn does what she can to help them. The character is then marginally accepted as a kind of ad hoc member of the pack. Like Jean Craighead George, who has Miyax and Amaroq resist Euro-American destruction of Inuit and lupine cultures, Streiber makes the wolf a participant in a quest for both lupine and human survival. His story is set during the aftermath of a thermonuclear war and the onset of nuclear winter.

One of the main characters in Streiber's novella is a wolf biologist, a choice made as well by Rick Bass in *Where the Sea Used to Be* (here the character is an amateur student of wolves) and Dennis Danvers in *Wilderness*.[7] Streiber's scientist is caught in Minnesota with her daughter as the sun is blotted out by ash and the summer temperatures drop below freezing. They must travel south while avoiding radiation fallout, looters, starvation, and frostbite. The story's point of view shifts between his unnamed biologist with a child and a black "timberwolf" that Streiber presents as "a disaffected adolescent" named "Wolf of Shadows" (3). He is the largest of his pack yet lives on its fringes, as he comes to terms with the forces of stratification and sexuality and his own reluctance to challenge the alpha male of the pack. But when he sees that he is the only wolf to recognize the danger of the frozen summer, he uses his intelligence, along with his great size and strength, to assume leadership.

Streiber occasionally uses unfortunate euphemisms to affect point-of-view experiments; rifles are "death-sticks" (8), traps "agony-jaws" (22). The point of view is also sometimes problematic—blurred by changes from third-person exposition to the internal point of view of a wolf (and the nagging discomfort we feel at the combination of both the pathetic and intentional fallacies). The human mother is accepted by the wolves and socialized to the pack (53), which saves her from starvation and from a pair of looters threatening her and her child (88–90). In turn, she finds a bridge unknown to the wolves and builds fires to keep the pack warm. The latter detail is incredible in that no wolf but one suffering from severe mange would need a fire until a human would have already frozen to death, although the wolves certainly might like the warmth. The fire-builder role is also a crucial element in the tale's mythic foundation, evoking the Pleistocene campfire myth of lupine domestication on the heels of, again, the Fenris myth and the great wolf of Earth's burning, especially given that this is a novel of world-ending fire. In the cold war tradition of the postnuclear gothic, the novel ends with a cliffhanger—we do not know if the characters ever find "the warm valley" and survive.

A map is printed on both the front and back cover leaves, arranged so that south is at the top of the map, ground zeroes depicted in terms of megatons surrounded by overlapping rings of fallout. The route of Wolf of Shadows's pack, including its human members, is drawn from "Wolf Territory" to the Ozark Plateau and just into the mountain range. To Streiber's credit, no state borders are marked; the map is bioregional and geopolitically superimposed only with the template of war. The verso of the title page contains a blurb about the Sierra Club, and the book is "dedicated to the hope that children and wolves have a future." Each chapter opens with an epigraph from an American Indian. The subtext to these techniques seems to imply strongly a sacramental approach to the post-Armageddon landscape, in the way that Mircea Eliade explains in *The Myth of the Eternal Return,* that "when possession is taken of a territory—that is, when its exploitation begins—rites are performed that symbolically repeat the act of Creation: the uncultivated zone is first 'cosmicized,' then inhabited" (9–10). The manner by which wolves and humans territorialize has been sufficiently similar to justify direct comparison, as by Robert Ardrey in *The Territorial Imperative,* but this similarity has been overstated. In Streiber's survivalist scenario the territorial imperative is dictated according to a global and utterly artificial violence far different from that of the ancient rites.

An "Afterword" explains that following his postapocalyptic novel *Warday,* Streiber felt compelled to respond to a letter that asked the question, "What about the animals?" and wrote *Wolf of Shadows* as an answer. He tells the reader that the wolf/human relationship he depicts is "conjectural, based on research, my own personal experience of wolves, and knowledge of Native American ways of viewing the wolf, which are so different from the modern image of wolves as vicious enemies of man" (105). He speculates about how humans and animals might live together, about animal consciousness, and about the open ending of the novel. The biographical note on the final page mentions that Streiber "has studied and tracked wild wolves in northern Minnesota, the lake country described in *Wolf of Shadows.*" "Studied" implies a bit more than novice outings, and there's no evidence that Streiber has done more than confer with biologists in the field, as any good writer might. The wording to the biographical note grants him the ethos that perhaps would have been better stated if the biologists that taught him were credited instead. Coupled with his generalizations about Native Americans, the "Afterword" and note seem a bit adamant in their assertions of Streiber's expertise beyond his considerable skill at writing for adolescents.

None of this defensive metatext is included in Jean Craighead George's realist work of adolescent fiction *Julie of the Wolves.* George proves her depth of insight, her knowledge of wilderness, and her lack of anxiety about her indigeneity through the book's fabula. A key reason for George's credibility may be that the point-of-view character is a human being who identifies with the pack through close observation and exercising her own resourcefulness, which requires details gleaned from a combination of research and experience, with a focus on plausibility rather than generality. To have attempted an animal's point of view would have presented a number of problems resulting from the ineptitude of human language, problems that surface in Streiber's narrative and burden him with their awkward weight. Partly through the genre distinction between fantasy (romance) and realism determined by elements of craft, George's approach gives us a wolf of a different color than Streiber's, even though the two stories share much subject matter. The miniature science lessons incorporated into George's fiction are simply better crafted than are Streiber's attempts to portray a canid point of view, depictions of the wolf-human relationship, and implications of Euro/Native American romantic history. Both are high-quality adolescent literature, better than but similar to Gordon Dickson's turgid *Wolf and Iron.*

Paul's Game

Let's say the twins' reading habits drop sharply during their adolescence, a safe enough speculation in the Information Age. They are already computer savvy in the early nineties. Their school has just begun teach them to conduct research on the Internet, their classes use some interactive video and early HTML Web site study guides, and some of their rainy-day time is spent online or playing the new computer games. Our young Minnesotans are halfway through junior high school and have been initiated on their thirteenth birthdays: Paul has been given a rifle and taken hunting, and Minnie has received a plane ticket to go to her aunt and uncle's in Alaska, her first trip alone. He likes *Wolf of Shadows;* she likes *Julie of the Wolves.* They return from their outdoor experiences with money from Paul's first sale of venison and Minnie's snow chores in Alaska, and having gotten on the "wolf kick," they pick up a CD-ROM game by Sanctuary Woods and Wolf Haven International, called *Wolf.* The cover shows a close-up of a pair of eyes, the left human, the right lupine. It comes with a "survival guide," the rule book explaining that they will choose pack members from the list of Wolf Haven residents, take that pack out to forage for food, fight for dominance, dodge hunters, sleep, den and mate, and otherwise live out their simulated lives.

The game is an educational exercise offered by Wolf Haven to teach the players about how a wolf pack might live, from one day to an entire lifetime. The senses of hearing and smell are represented by pop-up icons that tell the player what his/her wolf perceives. Aerial and ground hunters are ever-present dangers; the wolf must den, mate, find food (including domestic cattle), make successful and dangerous kills, and obey (and/or rise up through) the strata of the pack. If the players don't want simply to "exist" as wolves, they may choose from a long list of scenarios, such as "Find a Missing Cub" or "Kill a Mighty Musk Ox." Paul grows bored with the game (too quiet), whereas Minnie likes the idea of playing out a lifetime of the pack (which could last, in real time, indefinitely) and saves the game to come back and see periodically how her wolves are doing. Occasionally Paul sits beside her when he has nothing better to do.

The twins begin to consider what it might "really" be like to live as a wolf, and that somewhere near them real wolves are doing so. Minnie saw wild wolves in Alaska during cross-country ski trips with her aunt, and she likes the idea of pretending to live with them. When a wolf is shot by an aerial hunter in the first five minutes of a scenario, the game feels to her like a puzzle to be solved. When one of "her wolves" is shot during a lifelong pack scenario into which Minnie has invested several weeks of real time, she is upset. The ghost wolf of the computer screen spurs some concern for real wolves, some desire to learn more about them and eventually to see them again. It taps into an understanding of invested time, of labor for no commercial gain, and of labor for loss. She turns once again to books, and the computer game sits unused for some months, until it loses its novelty and is replaced by other games. When the twins stopped playing, Minnie's pack had established a mating pair. She played the alpha female and was searching for food during the pack's fourth winter, in preparation for denning. At any time, years later, given the correct hardware, Minnie could begin the game exactly where she left off and her wolf would be standing precisely where it was on the screen when she "saved" it, frozen in code and existing only in her memory and in the cryogenesis of virtual preservation.

Paul has quickly forgotten the life of his sister's digital pack and found another game to play. *Werewolf: The Apocalypse* is a paper-and-pencil role-playing game for a group of people who want to act out being werewolves. Its world is highly complex, mapped out in a three-hundred-page rule book and a score of supplements that provide character profiles, submerged population groups, and adventures. Paul realizes the social stigma of role-playing games but has found a group of friends who negotiate the problems well enough to suit him, one of whom is an imaginative Storyteller (or referee of the game). Fortunately, Paul was raised by parents who read to him and has developed a flair for telling stories himself, despite his softening media habits. He spends hours every weekend fleshing out his character, considering the Storyteller's plot twists, and conversing with his friends in the pack.

The game is constructed on the premise that the Garou are being wiped out and that Gaia, the earth, will eventually be destroyed.[8] In the face of this doom the Garou have decided to go down fighting. They resist the incursions of forces both preternatural and supernatural. One great power of the Garou is the ability to Rage, which is brought on by the rise of blood and gnosis given to them by the moon. The game spawns a collection of stories called *When Will You Rage*, published by White Wolf Games and set in the role-playing World of Darkness, a neogothic pulp atmosphere of deterministic naturalism laced with the requisite existential angst, from which *The Crow* and *Underworld* movies draw their tone.

The explanation for why human beings do not know about the existence of this vast society of Gaia's chosen is called "The Delirium," a condition of madness induced by the sight of a Garou in its horrific werewolf form. Having seen this form, the person represses the incident. The Delirium is one indication of the game's modus operandi, as is the rule book's epigraph, taken from Malcolm South's *Mythical and Fabulous Creatures*: "In reality, the werewolf and other human-animal combinations are basic archetypes of the psyche" (Rein-Hagen, Hatch, & Bridges, 24). Knowing that role-playing games are about testing the imagination in community, the writers of *Werewolf* metatextually involve the players by having them analyze even the imaginations of the game's fictional characters. The use of "archetypes" (often the term used in RPGs to indicate character templates) and an implicit appeal to the collective unconscious give the game great role-playing potential.

The World of Darkness games merit a book-length popular-culture study. *Werewolf* borrows from a long list of mythic literary sources to create stereotypes of "tribes" by race and geographic location. It often employs typical adolescent male sexism and ethnic stereotypes, although the writers try to use gender-inclusive language. In an effort to create a race of Garou to appeal to women playing the game, the writers have invented such tribes as the Black Furies, loosely borrowed from the Greek maenad legends and depicted in the rule book as a group of second-wave-feminist lesbian bikers. The twelve tribes of Israel are implied, along with the American Indian tribes of North America, the latter highly romanticized in their ethnotypes. The "vanishing breed" idea fits perfectly here, connected to a catholic history of assault against the Indian, the Garou, and Gaia and the grim fatalism of Nordic and Germanic myth. The World of Darkness's spiritual order includes the holy trinity of "Wyld" (the force of nature and chaos), "Weaver" (the force of balance and systems), and "Wyrm" (the force of evil, especially as industrial pollution and the corruption of wilderness). Liturgies are used by the various tribes to express their interpretations of the "triat." There is a global record of war and loss that accounts for the existence of werewolves in the world, who once themselves conducted a pogrom against humanity called The Impergium.

The game uses a symbolic lexicon of glyphs for the Garou, a "litany" or set of rules for being a werewolf, a system by which the transformation takes place, a combat system, a chapter on the basic elements of narrative structure and role-playing, and a magical element that includes the Umbra, or spirit world. Throughout the game puzzling questions are inevitably raised by the players about how a wolf (one of the achievable shapes of transformation for a Garou) might act, prompting both research and the distinction between fact and fabrication. Unfortunately, the writers do not include their literary sources, presenting the game as if it were entirely invented. In a passage of "Suggested Books and Films" they cite a brief and eclectic list that does not do justice to the mythic and literary references from which most of the material has been drawn.

Paul has created a character for the game, one of the Glass Walker tribe (urban werewolves) who works for an oil company with the goal of subverting and sabotaging its operations. One of the game's book-length supplements, *Monkeywrench Pentex!* calls for the werewolves to act as ecosaboteurs against the Wyrm's corporate "banes." A clever handout for the players parodies the greenwashed oil company, prophetically named Endron, with a brochure that includes some exposition on the tragedy of one of its tankers, called the *Pequod,* that sank off the Great Barrier Reef. The rules to the adventure explain that Pentex and Endron are, of course, front companies housing both evil humans and evil spirits who are at work for the Wyrm against Gaia.

The ghost wolf of the 1990s, like the Glass Walker, had added to its myriad forms the cybernetic image on the World Wide Web. During the early decade of the Web such newsgroups as "alt.wolves" exchanged daily information about the current legal, environmental, biological, and reintroductory status of wolves all over North America. Web pages for such places as the International Wolf Center and Ralph Maughan's impressive site still provide voluminous bibliographies of research and daily activity. Other sites are less concerned with corporeal and real wolves, including hybrid breeder advertisements; computer games and listserves turned into MUSHes become chat rooms become blogs; photo galleries; cathartic poetry; Wolfman Jack shrines; and antivegetarian environmentalists calling themselves werewolves. The early newsgroup "alt.werewolves" was composed of participants who called themselves a "cyberpack" and considered their postings a form of shape-shifting. Many of the members shared with one another what they were reading—often a mix of New Age appropriations of Cheyenne or Blackfoot spirituality, pulp fiction, Joseph Campbell, David Mech, Barry Lopez, and material on psychology and medieval history. They discussed their various knowledge of real wolves and ethology, preservation and endangerment, all the while trying to create permeable membranes both between one another and between themselves and the animal world. This was, and is still, albeit in slicker forms, attempted through a medium itself inconducive to experience, devoid of touch or smell, sterile and encased, but fast with a riptide of information.

In the absence of physical wolves and the near omnipresence of McLuhan's "cool media" (despite the advent of such "interactive" media as the Internet and video games that replace experience with vicariousness), from where do the experiences that shape an adolescent's ecological consciousness come? From adults, most of whom have settled into identifiable and usually consensual roles vis-à-vis their culture. Adults have spread the tales of demonic wolves: They have experienced psychotraumatic lycanthropy, nearly annihilated the wolves of the lower forty-eight states, and done so partly on the basis of the childhood stories with which they were raised. We have been, collectively speaking, poor teachers of the real world that exists before and beyond what we are sold, guiding minds still close to the vicissitudes of nature down a path that leads from found to lost.

Signs of Life

Minnie decides to learn orienteering. While her brother reads London and Stephen King, she plots her reading to augment her hiking trips, excursions to the International Wolf Center, and interest in biology. Sometime after reading George's *Snow Tracks* she picks up Colby's *First Book of Animal Signs* and learns about beaver cuttings, squirrel nests, otter dens, scats, and tracks. She takes the book outside with her and watches for the illustrations to appear on the earth. The entry for the wolf tells her, "The first time that you look down and see a wolf track beside your own boot, it may seem too huge to be real" (55). When she reads Johnson and Aamodt's *Wolf Pack,* she finds that Jean Craighead George is not the only woman out there who understands wolves. Through Johnson she learns more about the study of both wolves and human social power. She learns about endangerment, that the wolf's "threatened" status in her home state is considered a badge of honor in comparison with the rest of the lower forty-eight.[9] She reads *Looking at the Wolf,* the Teton Science School's wolf primer, and commits it to memory, reciting to herself the parts of the skull and taking the short quiz on the last page. It gives two options ("Humans" and "Wolves") to check for such choices as "They display information with signs," "They are opportunists," and "They inflict pain upon taking prey" (Thompson, 12).

Minnie thinks about the quiz during a walk after school. She hikes with her family through wolf territories, talking about the differences between Alaska and Minnesota, but she does not see a wolf in the wild for many years. Every evening before going to sleep she reads about extrinsic sign systems, about ways of learning that exist outside of print, beyond iconography, signs left by other species that can be understood, if barely. She knows that the signs are out in the world, that some are meant to be found, that her language is not the only sign system, and that those signs belong to what has been observable for many centuries before she arrived. She has slept outdoors many times, learned to pitch a tent and start both a camp stove and a wood fire, and felt the flush of a day in the wind before drifting off to sleep.

Minnie will never expect to dream about seven wolves in a generic tree, although she might have a vision. The form and substance of her thought is developing antithetically to the virtual world of planned obsolescence, commercial fad, and simulation. A lecher by the trail will undoubtedly be human, so she will most likely be more disgusted than surprised by what she finds in place of the wolf she seeks. She walks the trails as cautious of the civilized as of the wild, hopeful that she will find a track, recognize the sign, follow it to within sight of a wolf that she will then leave as undisturbed as possible after her brief encounter, what she hopes will be seen as a visit, or a game, something reciprocal. She begins to find beauty in toughness rather than mere shape, finds that porcelain skin and smooth heels are not for her, and at times impresses her brother with what has come to be the long clear gaze of someone at home in the real world.

Mowgli's Children

In a Salishan story of northern Washington State a Nuwíls villager determines to outsmart the wolves. Edward Curtis calls the story, told by a Shoalwater Bay man, "Conflict with the Wolf People." The human/animal clans of this tale are both distinguished and conjoined in the style of the shape-shifter narrative. A woman gives birth to both a wolf and a human child, the latter of whom the Wolves decide to kill if it is a boy. The woman shows them the human boy, "holding him in such a way that he seemed to be a girl" (9:159). In this way the human boy is preserved, and he grows dedicated to avenge deaths of his ancestors sacrificed to the Wolves. However, he has become friends with his Wolf brother and therefore vows to spare the Wolf boy when he takes revenge on the other Wolves. Eventually he tricks the Wolves into the belly of a whale, who carries them out to sea.[10] In the end, through the help of Condor, the human becomes the progenitor of the race of condors and, blowing on the tail fur of his brother, scatters the strands to become wolves, thus also fathering, in mythic resonance with the great flood myths, the present race of wolves (9:159–60). While revenge and dominion over an offending race are certainly part of "Conflict with the Wolf People," we must acknowledge at least the coincidence of a narrative that reverses the depletion of both wolf and condor during a time when such depletion was occurring in reality, making the story more complex a creation myth than a story of human dominion.

Feral-child legends are found in both antiquity and the modern world—including the wolf-child legends from British colonial India that inspired Kipling. But many other tales, from medieval Wild Man legends to Rousseau's account of the wolf child of the town of Hesse, indicate a global scope and recent history of their telling. The best summary is probably J. H. Hutton's presidential address to the London Folk-Lore Society in 1940, which covers dozens of wolf-child stories from all over the world. In reference to "the New World" he mentions one Chippewa story but emphasizes the lack of North American stories of children raised by wolves. Hutton's assessment of this dearth is noteworthy: "If there really is a complete absence from the American continent of any stories of children nurtured by wild animals, such a fact would tend to suggest that stories of that kind from the Old World are based more upon some deep-rooted tradition or belief than upon genuine experience" (30). By using the lack of North American wolf-child stories to question the veracity of European ones, Hutton emphasizes experience over reportage, especially as that experience produces fantastic traditions. One of his goals has been to find out whether any wolf-child stories are verifiable. "It is with no little reluctance that I find myself unable to conclude on a note of finality," he concedes (30). His address anticipates the Reverend J. A. L. Singe's purported discovery of Amala and Kamala in 1956. Singe's analyses were discounted by proof that the twins were not, in fact, wolf-children, and debate ensued over whether Singe's effort was an intentional hoax (Douglas, 246–48).

The feral-child legend can be divided into stories of exposure, in which a child reverts and dies, and stories of human rescue after the child has been raised by another species for a time. The latter subgenre divides further into whether or not the child is then taken back into human society and assimilated (as in most captivity narratives), as well as whether or not the child survives the experience. Two folktales from Wisconsin describe chases in which the families throw their youngest children to the wolves in order to save themselves. In one tale the wolves eventually pull down the mother. The next day, the father, guilty over having saved himself, "heard what he thought to be his wife's voice calling to him from out of doors." He runs out of the cabin only to be eaten by the wolf pack, which has tricked him. The storyteller also involves the Chippewa, thus presuming to give the tale primitive credibility: "two of my Chippewa friends watched the whole occurrence from a distance. After the carnage the lead wolf came over to them and spoke in a woman's voice, saying, 'vengeance is satisfied, don't interfere in the settling of accounts,' after which she disappeared" (Wyman, 6). Curiously, no wolf speaks for the infant the family offers; only the mother is spoken for, by the she-wolf.

Lopez records "a Texas story" he titles "Wolf Girl," in which a young girl, whose mother died in childbirth and father died in a storm trying to get help, disappears and is assumed to have been eaten by wolves. Ten years later sightings and wolf sign are reported by Apaches and whites alike of a young woman running with wolves and attacking domestic sheep. Eventually a hunting party captures her and confines her to a locked room. "That evening," Lopez writes, "a large number of wolves, apparently attracted by the girl's loud, mournful, and incessant howling, came around the ranch, the domestic stock panicked, and in the mélée the girl escaped." After one more sighting, in which she appears with two pups, she is never seen again. Lopez ends his account by writing, "That is the story they tell," a resolution in good form, honoring the tradition of the storyteller, who must remind the listener that the story has been passed along by other people from other places and times and has aged into wisdom (*Of Wolves and Men*, 243).

Freud's case study of the Wolf-Man fits here as well because it is directly germane to the connection of literature and child development. Whereas in Freud the primitive is individual, seen as the basic function of a childhood fantasy and reality collision, Jung's macroscopic departure from this doctrine defines the primitive as a collective human condition, a deep-rooted influence on individuation in part because of its archetypal form (Jung, *Archetypes,* 5–42). The feral child as the noble savage has for centuries been sophisticated adulthood's safety valve, the primitive fantasy providing a release from the hardships of modern technological living, progress, and responsibility—driven in part by the pathos of the "imperiled child" story. Humanity's fascination with the captivity narrative of the half-wild child reaches from this mythic source of human narrative.

American captivity narratives often bear remarkable resemblances to the wolf-child stories. The basic steps of both genres are: the loss or capture of the subject through exposure, accident, or invasion; the raising of the child to adolescence or adulthood; the sighting of the child and renewed hope in the colonial community of rescue; the return of the child, either through an organized search, the subject's escape from captivity, delivery by the tribe, or according to the child's free will and journey; the reeducation through both religious and political instruction; and the results of culture shock, either in the subject's sickness and death or in epiphanic conversion and recital of tales.[11]

From Rowlandson's narrative to *Little Big Man* and *Dances with Wolves,* many North American cultural representations of Indians and of whites "going native" closely resemble fictional narratives of feral children. The Indian's role as both "bad" (capturing the child, perhaps killing the family) and "good" (caring for the child, converting the child to better cultural conventions, providing the child's original family with stories upon his or her safe return, teaching the child useful skills) confirms a broader ambivalence felt over not only the pioneer's wilderness experience but also the fundamental animal conditions of both purity and what has come to be called "Otherness." The greatest similarity between captivity narratives and feral-child stories may be the juxtaposition of war's dystopia with nature's utopia, in order to raise the dilemma of shared land versus conquered land in terms of species and ecological zones rather than merely nations.

The projections of savagery in fiction are inextricably linked to attitudes about nature, particularly about other animals. Linnaeus understood *Homo ferus* to indicate a biological human unable to function as a social human, to adapt to the ways of humanity.[12] In this light we might think of one kind of feral child as someone who *imagines* wolf-children, someone acting out of a fear that prompts him to project the demonic onto the wild—a child of the feral phantasm, who lacks the means by which to cope with what is not civilized. It is all irony, in the context of our study, that the daughter of a Scotsman serving as a British general in an American novel derivative of a European romance would be threatened by a Huron that her head might become "a plaything for wolves" (Cooper, *Last of the Mohicans,* 108).

Mowgli Revisited

The European colonialist mentality in Kipling's wolf pack found its American home in *The Wolf Cub Scout Handbook.* In those pages we see noble savagery and appropriated *Jungle Book* tales, which the framers combine to create a paramilitary American Jungle Law. Furthermore, the handbook attributes this primitive law to "Indians" (the North American stereotype, conflated with Kipling's own subcontinental natives). The 1969 handbook contains a nine-page introduction entitled "Akela," illustrated with a howling wolf pack. The caption begins, "Many moons before the palefaces came to America in their big ships with sky-wings, the red men lived and hunted in the great woods . . ." and concludes, "Akela and the Webelos is a fable you may want to read with your parents" (vi–vii). After a bathetic primer about The Indian, a series of short episodes begins, starring Mowgli, who is presented as an American Indian boy living in a tepee. In the *Wolf Cub Scout Handbook* the wolves send Mowgli out of the wilderness with a farewell howl so that he may become a man. Although the chief of the "Webelos" is named Akela, no mention is made that he is connected to wolves, let alone that he is named after the *Jungle Book* alpha wolf; the focus remains on the young boy coming of age. The introduction ends with a set of glyphs drawn in sequence and provided with a key by which the Scouts (all Caucasian in the illustrations) can decode and "understand the speech and signs and calls of the Webelos" (xiii–ix).

True to the spirit of Kipling's own imperialistic age, the young Cub Scout is first taught to render American Indians both generic and manifestly colonized. He is then to transform himself into both an "Indian" and, through an appropriated and unthreatening quasi-shamanism, a "wolf." In the Arrow of Light ceremony, the older Scout playing Akela wears Plains Indian accoutrements and makes a stilted and euphemistic speech to induct the Wolf Cub. When he leaves the Wolf Cubs, he is to have matured beyond the Akela story into a Boy Scout, and eventually into a man, by which time he should have "outgrown" the Akela story. This supposed mythic tradition is entirely derivative, appropriating several traditions without honoring any one of them, and the assumption that maturation will sort all this out is both costly and absurd. The Scouts are certainly a representative American tribe—cobbled together and reified to fit such myths as the New World and the American Dream. The Eagle Scout is modeled after the hero of U.S. legend who bears the standard of the nation. Yet by the time a Scout has grown into this position, his honor code is severely influenced by the falsification of Native America and the glorification of uniformed hunter-conservationism. Wilderness education, community service, and a sense of self-discipline, the higher attributes of Scouting, were institutionalized during one of the most ecologically oblivious periods in American history, and regardless of the powerful value of ritual experiences, such contextual influence can't be simply glossed over.

An Echo

Jim Goldberg's ten-year photojournalistic project presented in the Corcoran Gallery in 1997 depicts several homeless adolescents living under bridges and in alleys, primarily around Hollywood. Many of them have been sexually abused by their parents, some have been shot, most are drug-addicted and involved in petty crime, and some are prostitutes. Their discourse is mostly cynical, scatological, and alienated, but full of the surprisingly revelatory information one tends to find in such ethnographies. Goldberg's project combines dialogues from tape transcripts and is written as a dramatic script laced with graffiti-style quips from the kids in the study. Two characteristic samples: "I wanna piss on the moon put quaters [*sic*] in the juke box and bitch about the music" (150–51); and "Born a wicked child / raised by wolves / A screamin kamakazi / I will never crash" (166). The title of Goldberg's study, *Raised by Wolves,* is derived from the latter quotation, which is derived from ten thousand years of wolf stories. It refers at once to an urban-jungle ferality adopted by the teenagers, the cruelty of their parents or guardians, and their own roles as metaphoric prey and predators. In this respect it indicates an urban use of the rapacious malevolent ghost wolf. But the study has a moment of true mythic connection, an episode from the lives of two of Goldberg's chief characters, Dave and Echo. The episode is printed in white type on black pages and titled "The same 'ol story, Romulus and Remus, Griffith Park, LA." Dave reveals his history to Echo:

> Here's the truth. I just appeared one day in an alley of La Brea. That's where Lupé, this wild chick, found me. She was on a tweek with the rest of her crew and there I was, screamin' my brains out, wrapped in a bloody blanket, bleeding at the stomach. She didn't know me from shit, but she took me in her arms and I didn't come down for another twelve years. Me and 'bout eight others. I swear, this bitch must have been knocked-up permanent. Seemed like there was always some kid planted on those tits of hers . . . From when I was about four 'til I was seven, we crashed up here in the rocks and bushes. Called ourselves "The Pack." We had a hell of a good squat going. (156–57)

Eventually Dave picks up the story by going back in time to the incidents that lead up to Lupé's finding and raising him. A politician impregnated a prostitute and offered to pay her to have an abortion, which she refused. In the seventh or eighth month of her pregnancy, he had her kidnapped and sent to a clinic, where he paid a doctor to perform the operation. Upon discovering that she was carrying twins, a boy and a girl, and refusing to perform what Dave calls in his story "the two-for-one special," the doctor delivers the children. The boy, Dave, is born with half a stomach. A nurse's aide is bribed to drown the children but takes the bribe money and disappears with the girl, Dave's sister, whom he has never seen. Dave is "exposed" as per the old feral-child stories—left for dead—and found by Lupé. "I've found it easier to tell everyone what they expect to hear," he says, "that I'm a low rent welfare number's junkie son, you know. No one would believe who I really am." The last image in the episode is of Dave, his arm around Echo as she sleeps, talking "to the moon" (158–59). It is easily the most eloquent passage of the book, horribly plausible, and proof that ancient stories survive in precisely the places where they are most needed. From the point of mythic resonance, it simply doesn't matter whether or not Dave's story is factual.

However unfortunate the view of the wolf projected by Goldberg's title, and the possibility that Goldberg himself is nature faking, Dave's self-identification as a modern Romulus is one more product of the literary history of the wolf and its migration to North America. His story engulfs everything about the wolf in literary representation except its physical reality. The politician's tryst with a prostitute named Lupé (whom Dave calls a "bitch") refers directly to the legends of Rome's foundation by either a wolf or a harlot. The rocks and bushes outside the Griffith Observatory overlook both the place where movie werewolves are fabricated and the constellations depicting the most ancient of journeys. There is a reference to the exposed child, born to a wealthy and heartless patriarch, saved by a compassionate "peasant" and raised to tell the story of his abandonment. There is a speech made to the moon. To whatever degree any such ethnographic project risks calling attention to its effort as art at the expense of the exploitation of these teenagers' existences, and whatever knowledge the kids have of the stories they are appropriating, Goldberg presents these mythic elements without irony. In some unpredictable and tremendously risky way, such a story might somehow benefit the real wolf even as it perpetuates the malevolent ghost wolf, if only because the story begs the reader for a compassionate response to these wolf-children and a reeducation to the resonance of the wolf in continuing mythology. Or it could just be a lie told for money.

CHAPTER FIFTEEN

The Fall of the Wild

JACK LONDON'S DOG STORIES

In his introduction to the Modern Library's combined edition of Theodore Roosevelt's *Hunting Trips of a Ranchman* and *The Wilderness Hunter,* Stephen Ambrose writes:

> Throughout his life, TR was obsessed by manliness, which sometimes got him into trouble but far more often was beneficial to him and the nation. He was no male chauvinist, incidentally: he advocated changing the marriage ceremony to have the word 'obey' eliminated; he supported equal rights for women; and nothing disgusted him more than 'male sexual viciousness' or the Victorian conceit that a wife is the servant of her husband's lusts. (Roosevelt, xvii)

I mention this because Ambrose's defense of Theodore Roosevelt directly follows a comment in the same paragraph on TR's attachment to hunting and "the chase." Ambrose's choice to emphasize, and juxtapose, these two particular subjects inevitably contextualizes both gender politics and the politics of hunting as, if not conjoined, then cooperative toward our better understanding Roosevelt. His life as a "man's man" while being among America's greatest scholar-presidents should not be written off as simpleminded machismo with the gentleman's "C." Roosevelt's complexities, as much as the singular tenacity for which he was famous, made him a very public president on a list of issues, one of the most important of which was catalyzing a national level of understanding about wilderness. He is, therefore, a perfect starting point for our investigations into the masculine outdoor adventure fictions of Jack London. Firm in his resolution and resolute in his pursuit of natural fact, Roosevelt was perhaps even more subject therefore to his blind spots, and one of his positions during the Nature Fakers debate, in which both London and the wolf were among his adversaries, demonstrates this in a way germane to our study.

Roosevelt called the wolf "the archtype of ravin, the beast of waste and desolation" (699). Boosted by Roosevelt's reputation as an outdoorsman and by the interests of cattlemen, that statement from *The Wilderness Hunter* was given a high degree of ethos. It begins in the memoir a delineation of good versus poor hunting according to TR's own experiences, written with his characteristic intensity of emotion. He devotes several pages to stating clinically the methods and motives for the wolf's extirpation, then puzzles over their demise, in the contradictory bewilderment symptomatic of "sportsmen" writing on wolves. After mentioning the "tens of thousands" killed by hunters, ranchers, and government agents, Roosevelt writes, "Yet even the slaughter of wolves wrought by man in certain localities does not seem adequate to explain the scarcity or extinction of wolves, throughout the country at large" (701).

What could this other phenomenon be, competing with those numbers racked up by a rather efficient human system? Wolves had "learned caution," Roosevelt thought, and he incorrectly declared them "the shyest and hardest to slay," so that by his logic either both or neither their timidity and gregarity wiped them out (701–2). He seems finally to decide upon natural selection, although he never quite follows through with his line of thought. Instead he delivers a dispensation of pure Spencerianism. He moves first through a loose taxonomy of different sizes and kinds of wolves, laced with occasional tangents of prurience: "Yet I doubt if an unarmed man would be entirely safe should he, while alone in the forest in midwinter, encounter a fair-sized pack of ravenously hungry timber wolves" (704). After a handful of anecdotes that leave his original question behind, Roosevelt finally plays his hand for the chapter. He reluctantly and regretfully confesses that he has shot at and missed wolves on his ranch, which leads him to the firm and solipsistic projection that the wolf "can only be hunted successfully with dogs" and that "the true way" is "with greyhounds on the open prairie" (710).

The paragraph is a knot of non sequiturs. How did we go from a question about human extermination of the nonhuman through a brief and erroneous lecture on morphology to a confession of failed marksmanship and a discussion of the man-versus-nature pleasures of hunting wolves with dogs? This kind of chaotic, desperate grasping for reasons actually characterizes much writing on wolves. For the next several pages, Roosevelt regales readers with accounts of his dog hunts, and the reason for the wolf's disappearance disappears itself in the smoke of hunt-club stories. But a reason is strongly implied. The wolf, for all its apparent savvy, was somehow in Roosevelt's discourse not *meant* to live here, not designed to proliferate as a species among the superior race. In a sublime and gothic irony, the superior race includes a figure of the transmogrified wolf turned against itself—the wolfhound, the dog bred to kill wolves. Roosevelt was right to invoke the wolf as an "archtype," meaning an archetypal image, but ill prepared for confronting that image and reconciling it with its origin and actualization. If his hard comments against wolves revealed anything close to fact, it is the degree to which human beings chock full of hubris tend to become what they hate and fear.

Roosevelt's social Darwinism is cited often enough in relation to his presidential policies; I am considering here the progression of an egocentric logic alive not just in him but in much of U.S. population in his time. This logic spawns the same violence against nature that has always existed when what facts as can be gathered are proven inconvenient and consequently ignored rather than pursued. Paradoxically, as was Roosevelt's mode, his policies included some of the most radical, laudable efforts toward conservation and preservation the nation has ever seen. Never before did America have a president so aware of the health of a nation being dependent upon the preservation of at least some significant portion of its raw and wild lands, and perhaps it never has had one since. This strange phenomenon in Roosevelt's thought, this incompleteness in both the scientific study and the faith-based bowdlerization of ecological systems, should seem to us all too human. In the context of this study it only points up more sharply the establishment of the ghost wolf versus the corporeal wolf in the American mind. Like Roosevelt's individual consciousness, the societal consciousness of America did not know how to handle the completion and sustained health of an entire ecological system being dependent upon the "archtype of ravin," that denizen of the collective unconscious.

The Wilderness Hunter appeared in 1893, the year of Frederick Jackson Turner's frontier thesis and in the midst of increasingly popular nature writing that appealed to America's wonder, ignorance, and desire for titillation. Plant two hundred years of flawed logic and projection into the American mind from a man soon to become the leader of the land, widely known for his nature excursions, and scientific study will have both a necessary and a difficult row to hoe.

Roosevelt was therefore both representative of the cultural context in which Jack London became the highest-grossing writer in the United States and a whip for that context's pervasion. It was in part because of the Nature Fakers controversy and its high national profile that London's writing gained its fame beyond the children's shelves, at the heart of which was an argument not only over scientific accuracy but also over male identity. Out of his concentration on both wilderness adventure and nationalist expansion during the boosterism decades that loudly championed these strange bedfellows, London crafted about half of his corpus of work. And despite a concerted effort to discredit that work, Roosevelt

helped to sell it, through the valorization of the rough-and-tumble man of aptitude and strength in the face of a cruel environment that became the most popular brand of fiction in the nation.[1]

The Wolf-Dog as an Archetypal Image

Pairing the great wilderness adventure with the animal allegory creates a powerful blend, and certainly it brought both the youth market and mainstream
readers to London's work. But the social and intellectual substance of his Yukon
writings was given little attention, submerged beneath high school treatments
focusing on his adventure fiction, brief (if any) mentions in undergraduate surveys about his minor and all-too-accessible position in the canon as a literary
naturalist, or a few assorted considerations of the social commentary (however
didactic) found in his other works, such as *Martin Eden* or *The Iron Heel*.[2] There
seem to be two Jack Londons in literary study—a Yukon Jack and former oyster
pirate of self-reliance and capitalist obsession and the socialist London of the
streets, who once spent time in a brutal jail for vagrancy while researching his
populist novels. However, we have here no early and late Wittgenstein, no man
whose body of work inexorably changed, as with Twain's late fatalism or even
Wharton's or Cather's moves toward modernism. We have instead a writer tormented by something besides his drink or ambition—the fastening of several
forms of thought that were at once brand new to his era and as old as the political foundations of Europe and the Americas.

In *The Call of the Wild* and *White Fang*, as among several other of his works,
London attempted to synthesize no less than Darwinism, atavism, early Marxist
socialism, the Nietzschean concept of the over-man, and the tricky relationship
between deterministic naturalism and survivalist self-reliance. The fallout of his
and others' efforts toward such synthesis is a list of problematic pedagogical exercises: the conflation of Spencerian social Darwinism with evolutionary theory
(especially in the oft-corrected use of the phrase "survival of the fittest"); animals
diminished to the role of mere symbolic value while given subtle but unexamined intrinsic and emotional capacities; consequently, the attribution of anthropocentric symbolic value to animal social behavior (such as a wolf pack); the
misnomer "superman" and its connected baggage for Nietzsche's concept of the
transcendent psyche and the cultivation of consciousness; and the simplified
code one learns in high school while reading *The Old Man and the Sea* of "man
versus nature, man versus man, man versus himself." What lies beneath a London "dog book" is actually some of the most powerful and complicated social
psychology of the last two centuries.

London's literary position is a telling one in relation to his subject matter.

While bridging pulp and literary fiction—the raconteur's macho western story and the naturalist's humiliation of man in the wilderness—London's work was the inspiration for writers of a wide quality spectrum telling the male adventure story, nature tale, or wilderness bildungsroman: Ernest Thompson Seton, James Curwood, Walt Morey, Sterling North, Jim Harrison, Michael Jenkinson, Rick Bass, Nicholas Evans, Stephen King, and Ernest Hemingway. Like Hemingway, London has been sacrificed on the altar of revisionism because of his oeuvre's high testosterone count, even though much of his work shows some strong currents of early, at the very least call it latent, feminism. He has been postscripted to a position unworthy of his contribution to literature also because the urbane sensibilities of the academy have relegated "stories with trees in them" to a second-tier status.[3]

On the other hand, and unlike Hemingway, London wrote too much, too fast, and his work suffers from his process exposing itself on the page unpolished—a form of didacticism adopted as well by such nature writers as Rick Bass. This raw technique sometimes compromises the quality and integrity of the craft to a nature writer's shorthand. The force of emotion behind an environmental argument often results in a purpling of the prose, a groping to clarify what is more easily treated as, for instance, a "representative of the wilderness" than as a wolf. Wolves (and ghost wolves) seem to have a qualitatively exceptional power to excite such activism, especially if the writer makes an effort to incorporate the difficult principles of ecology and ethology in the context of a profound history of violence against the wolf.

A literary figure becomes totemic according to its tendency to overwhelm a writer. However it might serve as a key to the totemic door, metaphor is insufficient to account for totemism, because metaphor may be both selected and, to some recognizable degree, controlled. Writers must rely on their command of the craft to survive the pitch and yaw of forces old and large as a planet. Totemism differs from mere metaphor or analogy in that the totem lives symbiotically with the rules; it both requires a code to be followed (in order to differentiate and sanctify the image) and itself dictates the behavior ensuing from exposure to it, thus defining sanctity. It does so in part to ensure that future codes are spiritually, rather than dogmatically, proscribed; in this way it also differs from an icon.

That is, a writer doesn't "make" a totem; indeed, the effort to control one simply results over time in its reactive eruption. A totem *becomes* according to the force it has prior to our arrival, a force that is then translated and transformed so that the writer may even begin to approach it, carve it onto a log, chisel its petroglyph, write it down. We often call such a thing "a force of nature." To say, "You don't choose the totem; the totem chooses you" would be reductive as well as

hackneyed. Choice has little to do with totemism at all. Craft, however, has much
to do with it. In the case of totems from the nonhuman world, woodcraft is as
useful a skill as literary craft. In the case of animal totems, the individuality and
mind of the animal, which seem to the civilized mind to complicate the issue,
quite sharply define the issue. Our lack of aptitude in and knowledge of the animal world has warped our animal totems over time into objects more revelatory
of our conflicted, unnatural selves. This is one of the grand struggles running
through Jack London's work, made most obvious by his personal relationship
with the (ghost) wolf as his totem.

The Man's Wolf

There is one more grinding of the lens through which I would like us to look at
London's material. In chapter 2 we saw how the Nature Fakers controversy fac-
tionalized and clarified the debate between two groups: writers demanding exac-
titude in representation of the nonhuman world (through realism's veracity, verisimilitude, and mimesis), and writers championing the liberties of story (ensured
by romanticism's employment of symbol, elevation, and analogy) at the expense
and/or in question of the accuracy of natural facts. Both the modern hunter-
conservationist credo and the preservationist manifesto developed out of this
very friction. It is no light irony that declarations of the glory and honor of hunting, at least when made in the industrial context of the white man's world, belied
a practice remarkably unhealthy for ecosystems. This irony is especially obvious
regarding the hunter's allegiance to wolf extermination. The conflation of predation and aggression probably finds its greatest plausibility when applied to men
rather than to any other animal. Once aggression, including bravado, in the
hunter displaces the cooler sensibility of filling the larder, the motive, method,
and outcomes of totemization must take on the characteristics of that aggression,
since the totem is symbiotic with what is found within. When *Canis lupus* shifted
in the modern American mind from competitor to enemy, it was a move of one
square.

So, too, did hunting change quickly and easily from primitive subsistence to
two cultural phenomena that appropriated and abstracted the eating of meat:
sport hunting and commercial animal killing. The former took the most appealing mythic aspects of hunting and removed them from the context of need,
under the pretense that what is done when an animal is shot and killed, whatever
the context, can be justified as a spiritual enterprise. The latter, with the help of
the increasing abstraction of money and the development of inappropriately
monetized value systems, made commercial gain, rather than survival, the goal of
the hunter. I raise this issue because London's struggle with overhunting can be

seen throughout his Klondike fiction, particularly in the surprising fact of his near-total omission of the wolf hunter/trapper.

While accepting hunting as a given and asserting certain rules to maintain the semblance of purity in it, London's stories regularly compare the primitive life of "the red gods" with the increasing reliance on money of "the white gods" throughout both *The Call of the Wild* and *White Fang*. The primitive/civilized negotiation takes place through (and often on) the dogsled. The dogs live in a space between the feral and domestic; they haul their gods to the golden staircase or to panning sites on rivers; they carry the gear of civilization out to the wilderness and back; and, in London's two most widely known dog stories, they either begin or end in San Francisco as pets. Indeed, as I will explain later in this chapter, the opposite issues of Buck's desire to be free of his domestic conscription and White Fang's desire for love and domestication to save him from the hard and short life of the wild are actually the two sides of the same totemic coin.

From out of the context of the hunter-conservationist ethic emerged a new male model for nature stories. Its precedents are found in the mid- to late-nineteenth-century western memoir, the early naturalist novel, and the pioneer adventure story dating all the way back to John Filson. But the new model also applied both a national and a personal sense of sequestered ownership, through a division of land that did not exist as sharply during the era of the territories and free grazing, and so took a hard look at social values, particularly the concept of freedom. The new male nature writer often specialized in the increasingly factory-oriented model of agriculture, in sojourns to rough country that tested his mettle, and in the natural sciences. Such pursuits, along with the creation of the cowboy as the American icon, define him as heroic in nature and *in nature*. The new male nature writer's approach departed from the mystical ordination of romanticism's heroes, but it still included divine right when the occasion demanded, emphasized physical toughness over emotional acuity, and posited an overarching force that was merely antitheistic rather than entirely amoral in its composition. Masculinist nature fiction interpreted the rugged events taking place across the American West while gradually sculpting conventions of literary style to fit the lands in which it was usually set—alpine regions, open deserts, and the tundra. Even at its most verbose and florid, both brands of naturalism used their focus on experience and language in cooperation to tug fiction toward the muscular and often minimalist prose of later writers, from Hemingway to Cormac McCarthy. In this way literary naturalist fiction and the scientific (or amateur) naturalist essay helped define certain regions, in London's case the modern American West and the Far North, in a mythic back-formation.

I am establishing a position here neither in favor of a feminist revision nor in favor of a masculinist canon. And I am most certainly not justifying, through a critique of the inconsistencies found in experiential versus language-based forms of knowledge, an opportunity to simply render the natural world "imaginary" or "constructed," as has too often been done. I am instead emphasizing that the gendered mode is often an outcome of, and subsidiary to, the environmental mode—without doubt to the biological and ecological material—from which both fiction and nonfiction are made. What we see in the typical story of and by the great white male calls out to be critiqued, revised, and placed. Its prose can be brilliant, its story defensible, its contribution to the structure and quality of fiction in America immeasurable, and its cultural significance pronounced. The totemic narratives of the white male hunter, explorer, and imperialist certainly produce more pulp than work of literary merit, but their tendency to do so must not be allowed—by presentism, revisionism, or any other flawed cultural rubric for study—to categorically nullify the work that emerges. The wilderness story is always in danger of being ignored because of anthropocentrically politicized definitions, not only of wilderness or ecology, but even of such seemingly obvious critical conventions as regionalism, naturalism, realism, and feminism.

London adopted frontier booster content as often as pure hunter-conservationist content, but his work was perhaps the most momentous contribution to the hunter narrative's *structure* since Cooper's. The survivalist mode of his writing inspired teenage boys for generations to join the Scouts, read *Boys' Life* and *Field and Stream,* and try their hands at animal and adventure stories, some of which boys went on to become writers of some degree of fame. Most of them, such as James Curwood and Walt Morey, simply wrote London stories, shamelessly cribbing every technique, including his plotlines, hooks, resolutions, and regions, to capitalize on the profits from a public hungry for even watered-down sequels to London's Yukon wolf-dog tales.[4]

London may have been easy to copy, but he was hard to match, because the formula he concocted did not include the cheaply bought totemism of a writer who built his plots like Longfellow from the comfort of a study. I have mentioned the lack of wolf hunters and trappers in London's stories. He did not write about quests to kill wolves for money or for God, nor to kill all wolves for the betterment of civilization. Indeed, the wolves that breed with dogs to form the great sled teams, the vehicles that allow men to use the Far North (though not to conquer it), and the wolves that come to seduce those dogs away from domesticity seem to materialize out of wind and powder, and no matter how many writers revived those characters, they would always belong to London, who before he invented them met their real counterparts in the world. Nature is both competitor and provider in London's world, both wolf and dog, which makes him all the more representative of a pure literary naturalism, the copies of which could only turn out to be silvered romances by the inherency of their reflective nature.[5]

The absence of the privateer wolf trapper in a London story also differentiates his work from another branch of wolf story that depends upon such a figure. We have in London a "northern" rather than a "western"; that is, a set of conventions that create an adventure story qualitatively different from the lower-forty-eight westerns that feature wolf trappers. As we will see later, Cormac McCarthy finds the red-hot center of the trapper story and gives it literary value. But while McCarthy's westerns always seem to use the past to harken forward, to needle us with the present, London brings the ancient campfire myth of domestication to fruition and uses the past (his recent past) to throw us further back. The campfire myth is copied often, certainly troped in the wolf trapper western and obviously inspired by Kipling's tales, but its naturalist sensibilities are unique and undeniable in London's work. And it is well suited to the far northern climes in which fire is of paramount value, in which *Canis lupus* has never been endangered, and in which ancient reference to the Bering crossings has a ten-thousand-year resonance.

A significant accomplishment of London's, therefore—largely unexamined in criticism and perhaps the driving force behind his international success—is that with his work we have the categorical division of the wolf story into different types. There is the northern-wild versus southern-domestic (or wolf versus dog) Nietzschean naturalist story; the prairie horse-and-gun wolf encounter story; the western wolf trapper story (remarkable in its absence from London's choices); and the eastern transatlantic allegorical tale derivative of Europe. In short, Jack London's popularization of the Yukon and Klondike adventure nationalized the American wolf tale's literary taxonomy. It did so both by bringing attention to the canid story itself and by distinguishing U.S. annexes (in this case Alaska) from the connected bioregions of the contiguous states while simultaneously appealing to the reading sensibilities of other cultures and nations at deep archetypal and ecological levels, Russia being the best example. He also set his work where wolves were plentiful, yet minimized their appearance—rather than setting it where wolves were under siege and emphasizing their appearance (the more common approach to the modern wolf story). In this way we can assess wolf stories written after London by what they keep or reject from his dog stories.

The first four story collections London wrote are not about wolves and are barely about dogs. They focus on men and women of base manners living in primitive conditions; the woman as breeder and possession, but a stronger being than the city-bred men sick with gold fever. As the stories progress, they expand their gendered focus to include racial collision. Kipling's imperialism and a proto-eugenics approach surface as London's more gendered subject matter wanes. We see James Fenimore Cooper's influence as well, in several stories from *Children of the Frost,* such as "The Sickness of Lone Chief," and from *The Faith of Men,* such as "The One Thousand Dozen." There is sexism and brutality, as part of both the camp story in the hard environment and the sensibilities of a twenty-four-year-old man writing at the turn of the century. And we see London's place in the literary canon take shape between Cooper and Hemingway.

Some examples of the wolf sentiment in the most famous of the Leatherstocking tales, *The Last of the Mohicans,* include the Hurons being called (35) and compared to (39) wolves—in the pejorative, of course; wolves being said to "hover about an Indian ambushment, craving the offal of the deer," then fantastically that wolves howl for hunger and that Indians can recognize this (51); and references to wolves as surreptitious (64, 192, 194), insatiable (67, 192), gruesome (108), alert (258), false (296), and raging (324), assessments made by Cooper's European and Indian alike. That is, in the selective symbolic romance of Cooper we find an early version of the hard, unforgiving world that would dominate the symbolism of the literary naturalist.

Of Hemingway's reading influences, Michael Reynolds writes, "Other than Jack London's stories and *Call of the Wild,* he had read nothing that could be called modern" (*Young Hemingway,* 49).[6] As in Hemingway, London far more often reveals men's ineptitude with women, including their brutish, pathetic attempts at domination, while demonstrating their equal ineptitude at coping with the nonhuman world, again according to a rubric of faith-based domination that in hard literary naturalism is always doomed to fail. We should not assume, however, that London is positing a simple equation of woman and nature as objects gendered feminine, a position rightly scrutinized in ecofeminist criticism.[7] To the contrary, London's recognition of the difference between nature and culture is entirely the point of his naturalistic approach (and of an ecocritical view of his work), and the world of his fiction is most decidedly not Mother Nature. Certainly in tone we are reading a masculine voice out of the nineteenth century, but when London begins crafting his dog stories the wolf's position as totemic is not constructed only in terms of its position in a man's world. Even if we read London's she-wolves as projections of a sexist psyche, he always ultimately takes us to the relationship between humanity and the nonhuman world, to the she-wolves as wolves, insofar as his ability allows him to approach corporeality. London more often asserts that the wolf is some essential representative of wilderness superior to other animals, rather than a representative of men superior to women, and he does so without the sustained metaphor of woman/nature, given that his wilderness is a force transcending gender.

"The Son of the Wolf" is about white men and the Sticks Indians along the Tanana River, the latter of whom use the wolf as a symbol, first for white men in general as thieves (31), then for Scruff McKenzie specifically as a tough white man who receives several names (32), and finally as the only name for McKenzie, who asserts himself as an outsider stealing a woman from the tribe. The appellation "Son of the Wolf" is a metaphor connecting man and ghost; there is not a single wolf in the story.

The animal's allure for London in his real life would draw him toward his own adoption of the ghost wolf totem. It would also prompt his efforts to demonstrate and explain his atavism in both *The Call of the Wild* and *White Fang*. Wolf-dogs (in London this almost always translates to "huskies") appear a handful of times in all four collections combined, and most of the material does not regard the dogsled drama. The sled-dog stories (for example, "To the Man on Trail," "The Wisdom of the Trail," "Where the Trail Forks") all converge in "An Odyssey of the North." This story is the great journey taken by the character London uses to connect many of his stories, Malemute Kid, and is a gesture to the sea epic here told on tundra and ice.

"The League of the Old Men" examines atavism through the prehistoric theme. The sentiment of *when the men were men and our dogs were wolves* throughout the story anticipates White Fang's decline into domesticity, which I will soon consider in more detail. But finally four short pieces most evidently break ground for *The Call of the Wild* and *White Fang*. The first three are the short stories "The God of His Fathers" and "A Daughter of the Aurora" and the *Harper's* essay "Husky: Wolf-Dog of the North." The fourth piece, "Bâtard," was first published in 1902 as "Diable—A Dog"; the 1902 story was retitled, revised, and published in 1904 as "Bâtard." The two versions of "Bâtard" bracket *The Call of the Wild* and so alternate with the converse novels *Call* and *White Fang*. "Bâtard" therefore works as a prototype for *White Fang*, part of a more complicated process through which London was working out his use of atavism as an element of craft, and most importantly a bridge—a third piece that highly problematizes the supposed binary opposition of the two novels. If we include "Bâtard" with the novels, then we learn better what the "wolf-dog" is to London, that it runs the whole range of the tame, domesticated dog ("Husky: Wolf-Dog of the North" in 1900) to the wild demon wolf ("Diable" and "Bâtard" in 1902 and 1904 respectively), and what its function is in his mythos of the white silence, the venue of the Yukon and Klondike in which he sets his naturalist stories.

I'll begin with a story that focuses at once on gender roles and power as it reveals itself to be a prototype of the wolf-dog novels. At the outset of "A Daughter of the Aurora," London establishes the context of men trying to win women and women subverting the effort (224–25). Joy Molineau pits two men against each other in a sled race for an abandoned claim and her hand as the prizes. One of her suitors, Harrington, has "been broken in" by her, grown used to being driven by her beauty, which carries with it a primeval strength: "And very enticing she was just then, her lips parted, her color heightened by the sharp kiss of the frost, her eyes vibrant with the lure which is the greatest of all lures and which may be seen nowhere save in woman's eyes. Her sled-dogs clustered about her in hirsute masses, and the leader, Wolf Fang, laid his long snout softly on her lap" (225).

We see Molineau as the ice queen, the daughter of the aurora borealis, and the woman of the major arcanum "Strength" in the tarot, wreathed here in the fur of her wolf-dogs. She is accompanied in this archetypal portrait by her favorite, Wolf Fang, the prototype for both Buck and White Fang not only in name but also in occupation (lead sled dog, like Buck) and origin (wolf/dog hybrid like White Fang). The race for the gold claim hinges on the strength and speed of the relay dog teams, especially the anchor team, and Joy's Wolf Fang "has no equal" (226). In this quasi-medieval romance, the arranged marriage by right of land is dependent upon the lady's choice of her champion and the champion's possession of the right steed. It is also, of course, the model for Buck's great sled-pull contest in *The Call of the Wild*.

Joy gives Wolf Fang to Harrington to lead his anchor team. Up to that point she and many others seem confident in the rival suitor, Savoy, winning the race, and London withholds her motive for giving Harrington the dog. It could be a bump of the odds for betting purposes, an expression of preference for Harrington, a sporting lack of confidence in his ability, or mere caprice (this is, after all, a naturalist story). In any case, her decision is made with the clear indication that her greater romantic interest is in Savoy (225, 227).

In the race for the abandoned claim, London creates a situation that demands the best dog, a competition for supremacy resolved through a combination of nature and nurture, natural law and human law exhibited in the genetics of the sled team leader and the politics of the gold rush, the training of the team, and the running of the sled (226). The human law London employs for narrative structure is that an abandoned claim has a sixty-day grace period before a new claimant can file to assume ownership. This puts a specific time on the legal takeover, and results in a rush, which is the perfect circumstance for a race. The natural laws of temperature, snowfall, and pockets of gold create the situation, which is then put into action using the written human laws about claims and racing rules. Property law takes over the story briefly, and London is quick to connect it to natural law, then to connect natural law to ancient archetype:

> The command had gone forth that no man should place a stake till the last second of the day had ticked itself into the past. In the northland such commands are equal to Jehovah's in the matter of potency; the dum-dum as rapid and effective as the thunderbolt. It was clear and cold. The aurora borealis painted palpitating color revels on the sky. Rosy waves of cold brilliancy swept across the zenith, while great coruscating bars of greenish white blotted out the stars, or a Titan's hand reared mighty arches above the Pole. And at this mighty display the wolf-dogs howled as had their ancestors of old time. (228)

Joy, made representative of women, is also rendered as a force of both nature and intellect, of a brand as dangerous as she is alluring (230). She is a type in the naturalist mode in prelude to the hard-boiled femme fatale. Through description alone London attaches Joy Molineau and Wolf Fang, setting up the story's resolving device from its inception (when London withholds Molineau's motive for giving Harrington Wolf Fang). Only at the story's end does her plan become clear, first when she places a big bet on Savoy, then when she calls out Wolf Fang's name during the race's last leg (231). At first, her call seems to be one of encouragement, but when Wolf Fang responds he leads the sled off the path, running Harrington into a snow bank. In the last line we learn that she has used Wolf Fang as an accomplice against Harrington.

The device of the false call is used again in "Bâtard" to different effect, when Leclère first explains to a judge that when he says "keel," Bâtard will attack (633). While in the noose, Leclère growls at Bâtard, "I will keel you," prompting Bâtard to attack him out of conditioning to the command word, ironically rather than to be warned off by the threat (638). Both incidents are moments of betrayal, but blame for the act is hard to place clearly; the animals are acting on their training, so they seem blameless. A further complication is that Bâtard is cognizant of his actions, just as Wolf Fang is conflated with Molineau in several ways that implicate him (though far more vaguely). That is, London casts betrayal itself in the naturalist mode—as something that sooner demonstrates the inevitability of nature than it requires clear and human motive or reason—while using devices unique to an animal story. This is at once a departure from the realist mode back to the romance and an advanced realist gesture to human/animal cognition. We will see later that the betrayal device is also used in both *The Call of the Wild* and *White Fang*.

Loyalty versus treachery is a theme of London's, a problematic one in that it must be meted out in a world governed by the basic, unmotivated drive, the ostensibly amoral impulse. Joy Molineau, for instance, betrays Harrington despite our never having seen him wrong her and gives the race to Savoy without our having seen Savoy prove himself a better choice. Like Iago's treachery, Molineau's seems intrinsic, fundamental. The name "Wolf Fang" here becomes linked to that treachery not because of the dog's evil nature coupled with an evil master (as in "Bâtard") but strictly through the dog's loyalty. Wolf Fang is a tool, manipulated according to his domestication. London is also obviously conscious of the effect such a name would have on a reader; before the benevolent ghost wolf's arrival in full on the literary scene, the name "Wolf Fang" would certainly be assumed to have some malevolence attached to it. London's completion of the Great Dog narrative—in no small part through the invocation of the wolf or some wolf blood—occurs in the novels, when he finally deepens the canine point of view as can only be accomplished through a novel's longer narrative arc.

Perhaps the most important short piece that London wrote giving us insight to the creation of the Great Dog novels is the essay "Husky: The Wolf-Dog of the North," published in *Harper's* in June of 1900. As mentioned earlier, for London "wolf-dog" signifies the husky breed, what would then have been called interchangeably the Alaskan or Siberian husky. London's idea, and a correct one, behind this phrase was that the husky was closer to its lupine morphology than most other dogs—an opportunity to examine atavism that would not be lost on him. Men don't keep wolves in London's works; they keep huskies and the occasional hybrid. The wolf is the denizen of wilderness, motivated entirely by the nature that is alive in (but only partly driving) the wolf-dog. In his description of the husky London does reveal an essentialism that still pervades the language of the breed-obsessed. The breed, rather than the individual, determines thought and action: "They are far from humble, as their wild ancestry attests. They may be beaten into submission, but that will not prevent them still snarling their hatred. They may be starved into apparent docility, and then die, suddenly, with teeth fast locked in a brother's throat, torn to pieces by their comrades" (682). This first tenet of the breed is itself an unintended ironic comment on the nature of the human being instead. It's difficult to tell here whether London's comment is a declaration about the breed or a declaration about the perception of cruel and ignorant human beings trying to train huskies by torturing them. It seems, unfortunately, that he is of the former disposition. He writes, "Rather, has little attention been accorded them because the interest of man has gravitated inexorably toward the natural, mineral, and social features of that far-northerly land" (682). Huskies are possessions, tools, commodities, features of the civilizing impulse. This tells us something about the narrator's (if not the author's) relationship to his focalizers in the novels. His next tenets of the breed include the following:

1. "No white man" ever figured out how to tie up a husky, but the Indians learned to tie with a stick through the collar to keep them from chewing the thong. The rope is then staked to the ground at the other end (683). The husky's close connection to its wolf origin is indicated here, wolves being notorious escapees and runners when kept as pets.

2. "In the summer-time . . . the huskies are thrown on their own resources" (683). That is, when the winter work is through and the sleds are no longer running, the wolf-dogs are left to go feral. The assumption is that this toughens them and drives them back into their primal selves, to reestablish order as (it is generalized) a wolf pack would.

3. "They are superb travelers . . . making runs of seventy or eighty miles" (683). This would be the most lupine of their characteristics, but not in London's preferred universe:

4. "It is in fighting that they reveal their most wolfish trait." The assumed "trait" is that the pack of huskies lets two huskies fight without interference until one falls, at which point "the whole band pitches upon him" (684). As a "wolfish trait" this is utter fabrication, but as a human-influenced mechanism of torture and starvation in a culture of violent behavior (the pit fight, for instance) it has a sad plausibility. London's assertion should be read as more a lesson about the wolf of the human mind, the ghost wolf, than one of consistent wolf-dog behavior. This is the animal inhabiting the ultimate symbolic space of human evil and perversion—the cockfighting pit.

5. "A peculiarity they are remarkable for is their howling. It can be likened to nothing on land or sea. When the frost grows bitter and the aurora-borealis trails its cold fires across the heavens, they voice their misery to the night" (684). The mythic invocations here are obvious and several. Worth noting is that London imposes misery on the howl; perhaps a safe enough assumption, given the dogs' apparent condition, but a projection nonetheless. He sustains the mythic metaphor in ghostly language, comparing the howls to "a wail of lost and tortured souls" and "as though the roof had tumbled in and hell stood naked to the stars" (684).

While *wolf-dog* means "husky" in most contexts for London, it has some flexibility. In tenets two and four above, *wolf-dog* is used more in reference to a behavioral state than as a synonym for the breed. Leaving huskies to go feral, for instance, becomes a kind of ethical tract on the hard wild, in particular vis-à-vis stealing food. A man is shot for such behavior; a dog is not only exonerated but also quietly respected for it (683).

In this treatise on the husky we see most of the foundational assumptions behind *The Call of the Wild* and *White Fang*. In writing the piece as an essay, London writes premises, rather than possibilities to be examined as they are in fiction. Although in the comment on the "interest of man" away from wolf-dog behavior London subverts some of his credibility, he is also critiquing that interest as misplaced (682). Modern man, according to London, drifted away from the dogs so responsible for giving him access to "that frigid El Dorado" of the Klondike. The most obvious indicators of the essay as a progenitor for the novels include these statements: "In the annals of the country may be found the history of one dog-driver who wagered a thousand dollars that his favorite husky could start a thousand pounds on a level trail," and, "Of course it was an exceptional dog, but creatures are often measured by their extremes" (684).

The emergence of his process through the stories and essay leads us to *The Call of the Wild,* but London would have to take one further step in order to complete his reconciliation of Darwin, Spencer, Marx, and Nietzsche. He needed the twin. He needed the opposing but related figure in his mythic construct to achieve his totemic structure of the wolf-dog and the individual-versus-social being. The novel long purported (including by London himself) to contain this figure is *White Fang,* but without "Bâtard" in the mix, London's creative process is left to a simple contrasting pair of novels that does not do that process justice.

Russ Kingman considered "Bâtard" to be a contrast to *The Call of the Wild* that followed a similar structure (9), but Jack London finally gave this role to *White Fang,* calling it an "antithesis" and ensuring that the two novels would often be published in the same volume as companion pieces. The distinctions among "Bâtard," *Call,* and *White Fang* indicate that London's process toward establishing the binary between wild and domestic was as much a complicated study of the psyche as it was a knowledgeable treatment of biological imperatives. In my view, such psychological discomfort over the nonhuman world is what spawned the Nature Fakers controversy more than anything else, and still spawns such controversies today. Andrew Ross's ideological allegiances, for instance, far outstrip his knowledge of ecological facts, and the vitriol in responses by Sokal and Gross and Levitt indicate something beyond an objective disagreement over those facts. Concern over the nature of nature has lost none of its power to incite arguments about good and evil, and the literature of the wolf is brimming with such incidents. In the character Bâtard we see the full structure of London's wolf-to-dog idea, which discloses as well London's struggle with atavism and the primal self in several ways.

First, *The Call of the Wild*'s main character, Buck, is made free and feral. This is called good, a return to or realization of his fundamental self resulting in an anthem to freedom despite the hardness of the world. It's hard to tell if, according to London's worldview, all dogs possess this wolf self or if some are fundamentally bred to weakness and have lost the wild soul. One problem in London's thinking here is that a feral dog is not a wolf, and the degree of lupine blood's presence has only morphological bearing on fitness for life in the wild. London also makes an assumption about "the ancestral" in that the shepherd/Saint Bernard mix in Buck is somehow a ready conduit to a Platonic, ancient wolf beyond morphology. Implicit as well is the idea of Buck's potential acceptance by a pack, which is highly unlikely, indeed barely plausible.[8]

Next, the title hero of *White Fang* is tamed and domesticated through love.[9] This too is considered good, an earned retirement and an acceptable transference of the dominance model to civilization. According to London's system, White Fang's hybridization (one-quarter dog) renders him more justifiably, if not easily, tamed than a pure wolf. The problem is that the matter of domesticating his wolf blood has to be fitted into the same system that celebrates Buck's freedom. London's precedent is his construct of the "wolf-dog" (the husky) of the sled teams, which is at once tamed enough to work for humanity but wild enough to tough out the hard conditions of the white silence. It is a brilliantly and errantly fabricated ghost wolf.

Finally, as the linchpin between the novels, the title antihero of "Bâtard" possesses a symbiotic evil, the naturally cruel made also humanly cruel by way of directly applied human cruelty—an approach representative of naturalism's pessimistic determinism and class commentary. The friction here is *within* the malevolence model—that Bâtard is not simply called a devil because of his response to a cruel owner but has actually become or has always been inherently demonic, possessed of a soul and cunning that our narrator asserts to be born of his evil.

Which, then, is the "antithesis" to *The Call of the Wild—White Fang* or "Diable/Bâtard"? It seems that the binary London was trying to construct has become at least a triad: good, natural evil (which tends toward the amorality of nature), and constructed evil (which mediates the wolf and dog through both their blood and the morality projected upon them). All three stories suffer from certain assumptions of what is good for the dog or wolf, but the primordial image of Wolf that surfaces in *White Fang* is not nearly the image of evil that the hybrid Bâtard becomes. London is negotiating (intuitively, it seems) the nature and nurture argument according to highly Jungian methods that correct Manichean thought. He is negotiating as well the role that the biological wolf plays in the moral universe of his fiction.

Bâtard's father is a "great gray timber wolf," his mother "snarling, bickering, obscene, husky, full-fronted and heavy-chested, with a malign eye, a cat-like grip on life, and a genius for trickery and evil" (627). We see first a gender proscription giving power to the father and evil to the mother, next the mother's evil as a partial explanation for Bâtard's capacity to become devilish (rather than, say, submitting or dying) when mistreated. We are also given the premise that the cunning is only as genetically inherited as the evil, foretelling the implausible act Bâtard performs at the story's end. This is a Spencerian concept borrowed from Lamarck—that genetic tendencies include moral ones and are linear, one-generational transferences.[10] It is also a Nietzschean concept in its invocation of purity and an individual's basic motive as both arbiter and goal (see Moore, esp. 21–33).

The role of Leclère, Bâtard's owner, is to balance nurture (including the lack thereof) with nature. London works out the relationship between culture and genetics in this situation of human cruelty to an animal, a situation that will un-fold with more nuance in the novels. His negotiation of the various philosophies and sophistries he was absorbing prompted London to depict canids as test subjects only as pure and obtuse as humans proved to be. He offers the position that an original genetic configuration requires simply the proper hand both to bring it out and to "mold" it back into the self it was at the root, especially against its pollution by the softening influence of civilization (628). The "proper master" idea is not investigated in "A Daughter of the Aurora," as it is in the novels, mainly because we have no insight into Wolf Fang's point of view. In "Bâtard," however, the "proper" master is the one appropriate to the individual dog's ge-netic material, not necessarily the one either morally sound or socially acceptable. Leclère the devil is the proper master for Bâtard, indicating the Spencerian idea of a fated genetics and a determined culture as manifest evolution.

When others witness Leclère's abuse of Bâtard, he declares the act to be his "own business" and anticipates the matter London will call "lordship" in the novels (629). The animal is property, which either supersedes cruelty or nullifies even the possibility of cruelty. In both *The Call of the Wild* and *White Fang* London establishes a more omniscient narrator, removed enough to question the assumption of ownership as an amoral model. In that way he is able to reconcile his evolutionary ideas with his socialist ones. We also see overturned the domi-nance/loyalty assumption about dogs and wolves, that *no one but my owner beats me*. Bâtard defends himself against both a stranger and Leclère and later carefully *plans* Leclère's death (629).

Throughout London's works, dominance of an animal is emblematic of a taxonomic superiority, but it always results in a highly moralized position, a morality often pathologically twisted and therefore constituting evidence of the ghost wolf's effects on the human psyche. After a contest with Bâtard that severely wounds both the dog and Leclère, he demands of the doctor that Bâtard be healed first, only so that he may have the chance to return to his program of finally breaking the animal's will (632). As Leclère demonstrates to the doctor the nature of his contest of wills with the dog, we are given that image common to many wolf stories of a wolf recognizing a pistol and avoiding it, even though never having been shot at (632). A missionary who asks how their relationship works, particularly why Leclère wants Bâtard healed rather than killed, is given this answer: "De taim is not yet. He is one beeg devil. Some taim Ah break heem, so, an' so, all to leetle bits. Hey? Some taim. *Bon!*" (633).

Bâtard, "like the rest of his kind," doesn't like music (633). We can't tell if "the rest of his kind" means all canids, only evil canids, or wolf-dogs. His response is to howl, the howl now given the intrinsic aspects of anger and loathing. Of course, Leclère therefore plays music constantly in order to "break" the dog. The howl is therefore marked in this story with an internal device. In wolf stories, howls almost always fall into one of three categories: They are described as representative of some general horror, danger, or sadness—that is, they are externalized for the purpose of mood; they are internalized, attributed (usually through cause and effect) to a specific emotional condition of the wolf or dog or hybrid howling; or they are interpreted as dialogue. Of course, combinations of these three categories are common. Bâtard adds the internalization of the howl to London's repertoire. The novels employ all three of the categories.

The Jim Hall episode in *White Fang*, which I will discuss, is also anticipated in "Bâtard," in the murder trial of Leclère. Maintaining the story's dark irony, London uses the moment to have Leclère offer up all of his gold claim and a confession to his judges so long as Bâtard is hanged before he is. This also invokes the ancient animal trial, in which an animal is held culpable for the owner's offenses (see Noyes, 29; Wise, 39). That, too, is immediately and ironically reversed; Bâtard kills Leclère by knocking the block out from under his feet after his exoneration but while his head is still in the noose. Bâtard is shot dead, still clinging to Leclère's hanging corpse (639). The macabre image is a reminder of naturalism's connection to the romance, in particular to the gothic images found in "The Hound of the Baskervilles" and in later pulp horror stories such as *Cujo*.

The Primordial Howl

The Call of the Wild put Jack London on the map. The "dog story" writer grew in parallel popularity to the writer of *The Sea-Wolf* and novels of social commentary until, in time, the writer of the dog story won out, even at some expense to his reputation as a naturalist. *The Sea-Wolf* also acts as a bridge between the dog stories and sea adventures, linking them through the mythic connection of water and wolf analyzed in chapter 7, and is the only other canonized work of London's (*Martin Eden* and *The Iron Heel* are considered minor canonical works but are seldom cited and rarely if ever taught). The device driving *The Call of the Wild* is the "white silence" established in his earlier stories and that set the hard determinist tone of his Yukon corpus.

"The White Silence" is both a story and a label for the naturalist theme found, for instance, in "The Law of Life" through the wolves that devour Koskoosh. Within this model of a massive and enveloping world without its spiritual sphere, the wolf is no more a conscious agent than is a blizzard. "It" is a force of nature certainly red in tooth and claw in its imagery but appropriate to naturalism only in its *indifference*. Cruelty is usually a nonissue, a matter of casual default in London's naturalism, except in terms of human domestication of an animal, when cruelty is critiqued from the point of view of another character or, more clinically, by a third-person narrator. The word indicates for his characters either the natural state of things or an all-too-human response to that state. But his real puzzle, which he began piecing together in his short fiction, was how to depict this force of nature as a being he knew to be possessed of life and thought, even free will.

Although he never said so directly, Jack London's work demonstrates a focused effort to understand the Fenris myth through a combination of naturalistic determinism and atavism. He dropped into the northern white silence a super-wolf, a hybrid whose dog blood would reconcile him with human culture and whose wolf blood would equip him for survival. By Zarathustra's way of thinking, the dog might fit the ignorant and docile condition of humanity, domesticated far from its morphological state as a wolf. In this way, according to the prophet, the wolf instructs the dog (Nietzsche, 79, 135). In the Norse context, the stakes of a wolf-dog reconciliation were no less than the end of the world. And so London is now faced with another conundrum—how transcendence must work, how the soul might exist and function in a deterministic existentialism. What he decides upon as the vehicle for this apotheosis is the nonhuman psyche, and he chooses the wolf-dog event, the human manipulation of evolutionary biology, as his departure point.

It's worth noting that the iconic status of the wolf as a totem of many indigenous Siberians and as both demonic man-eater and vermin to czarist Russians contributed to London's popularity there, which was augmented later by his socialist writings.[11] And London's more symbolic wolf moments would be corroborated by the Freudian/Jungian interpretation that Hermann Hesse made internationally famous and linked directly to the eastern European landscape. Hesse employed the wolf as a harrier of the questing character, replacing the monkey on the back. This shadow, the *Steppenwolf,* assembles itself from the range of northeastern Europe to the Far East, bearing connotations of the Golden Horde and the Khans' lupine lineage, the German political division of Hesse's time, and the individual's own psychological territorial conflict. The steppenwolf was cast by Hesse as that which needed to be subdued, denied, in order for a person to have a complete and stable self. Such repression, however, paradoxically empowers the ghost wolf, makes it grow and run, hungry and hard and around the world.

This is the context in which *The Call of the Wild* came to be, and through which the primordial image of the wolf gained greater fame in America. The chapter titles in *The Call of the Wild* are enough to indicate its deeply atavistic and archetypal structure; such chapters as "Into the Primitive," "The Dominant Primordial Beast," and "The Sounding of the Call" are interspersed with chapters on "law," "mastership," and "toil." London's exaggeration of the hardship in nature, the struggle for survival, clarified naturalism through Spencerianism. By careful juxtaposition, the world of human cruelty simply looks "natural," determined, fated, automatic. The little latitude allowed for choice is dwarfed by images of violence and suffering. When elements of romance arise through the few people capable of demonstrating tenderness and through the basic innocence of the dog's heart, they are the more powerful for their appearance in the white silence. The combination of nature red in fang and claw with purity and self-realization added to the education in ambivalence of later generations, amounting to both the deification and the demonization of wolves.

The best edition of *The Call of the Wild* I have found is Daniel Dyer's, with its annotations and "Illustrated Reader's Companion." Dyer combines a useful and well-presented collection of photographs with a number of literary and biographical facts about London's craft (for example, that he considered the title "The Wolf" for *The Call of the Wild;* that he is credited with coining the phrase "call of the wild"; and that he used several sources on sled dogs, which Dyer lists). Dyer cites Barry Lopez and Desmond Morris, rather than scientific sources, for wolf information, and he includes *The Hidden Life of Dogs,* but the bulk of the annotations tip toward place specificity and zoological history (for example, dog breeds and how they were known at the turn of the century). I have little to add to Dyer's commentary beyond recommending it and will forgo too much analysis of *The Call of the Wild,* as ultimately it is a novel about a dog. *White Fang,* however, regards a hybrid more closely related to and surrounded by wolves, and takes London's dog and wolf stories to a telling conclusion.

White in Fang and Claw

In the December 1906 issue of the *Dial,* May Estelle Cook wrote an essay on twelve books that she characterized as "Nature-Books for the Holidays." Although she included the biologist C. William Beebe's *Log of the Sun,* Cook's list consisted mostly of books such as *Briar-Patch Philosophy, by Peter Rabbit; Shaggycoat* (the "biography" of a beaver); a handful of quaint, illustrated observations of wildlife; and Jack London's *White Fang.* During the previous eleven months London had written three books, one of which, *The Game,* had received significant attention. But 1905 had been as important a year as any for London; the label "best seller" had been coined to describe the *Bookman*'s lists of recommendations that began in 1895, a label with which Jack London would regularly be associated. In the fall of 1904 Macmillan published *The Sea-Wolf,* about a year after *The Call of the Wild,* and *White Fang* was certainly poised for the trifecta. Cook wrote one of the first recommendations for how to collate London's "dog stories," declaring that London was a writer of children's (particularly boys') gift books:

> In "White Fang," Mr. Jack London has given us a book that probably will be more read than anything else he has written. It is a remarkable story for its own sake, and is further remarkable for being the converse of "The Call of the Wild." There is as much that goes against the reader's sympathy in one book as in the other; but because the story of White Fang ends happily, much of the cruelty in it will be forgiven and forgotten. The early life of White Fang is narrated with an understanding of animal psychology which seems almost uncanny, yet shows Mr. London's power in one of its best phases . . . The book will be judged inferior to "The Call of the Wild" by sticklers for "strong" endings; nevertheless it will be more enjoyed by the mass of readers. (389)

Book reviews are easy targets, but the choice of language here is exemplary of the language in many of the reviews of London's dog books and provides some gauge of public perception. Not only does Cook interpret the ending of *White Fang* as "happy," but she also strongly implies that it is weak. She then tries to convert that weakness into the key characteristic that will make *White Fang* a success with the mass readership. The gratitude for a happy ending implicates London's work as escapist, its supposedly celebratory finish allowing us to brush off the cruelty practiced in the novel by both humans and animals. White Fang has been psychologically vivisected by London's "uncanny understanding" then diagnosed, if not as "well" in the structural sense by sticklers for strong endings, then at least as "good" by the Christmastime moralist. The kids may now read Nietzsche. This common interpretation of the ending is perhaps the sharpest and most widespread misinterpretation of the book. It denies the wolf as it posits an "opposite" plotline to *The Call of the Wild* by way of assimilation.

In his essay "Cuteness," Daniel Harris indicts "the aesthetic of cuteness" for invoking sadistic power plays in a consumerist public that wants to buy cute, then impose cuteness on children to the point of abuse. "Advertisers have learned," he writes, "that consumers will 'adopt' products that create . . . an aura of motherlessness, ostracism, and melancholy, the silent desperation of the lost puppy dog clamoring to be befriended—namely to be bought." Harris unfortunately indicts cuteness on the principal charge that is it "dehumanizing," which is reasonable but misses a point worth making about his essay's many animal examples (134). His critique is entirely appropriate to the very market techniques that contributed to the popularity of London's dog books, particularly in the case of the character White Fang, who takes his place in the novel as a helpless, bumbling, and adorable puppy. London is quick to divest his narrative of the language of cuteness, but the introduction to *White Fang* in the chapter titled "The Gray Cub" certainly follows the pattern Harris describes as a strategy to elicit the consumerist response. The hard world of the white silence is the more dramatic through its contrast with an adorable little wolf pup.

Literary scholarship has for the most part supported Cook's reading that *White Fang* ends in a Dickensian distribution of Christmas-morning rewards. A century's dearth of critical commentary on White Fang's decline into domestic sloth indicates that Cook's naive reading was never adequately contested. A close reading of the text will disclose conventions of coming-of-age stories that are incommensurate with the stronger naturalist/determinist endings of both *The Call of the Wild* and *White Fang*.

The Apprenticeship

Best sellers run for the most part on three basic plots: the revenge plot, the mystery puzzle plot, and the coming-of-age plot. Since *White Fang* bears all the appropriate marks of a bildungsroman, it would appear to be a novel about the apprenticeship of the character whom Mrs. Scott calls the Blessed Wolf (that is, the benevolent ghost wolf). As a bildungsroman, the novel divides neatly into five acts. London structures it with five "Parts," but I would suggest as well that we might read it as a four-act structure with prologue and epilogue, in which Part I, "The Wild" is actually the prologue, the three following parts are Acts 1–3, and Part V "The Tame," is divided into its first four chapters and its last two as the epilogue. Respecting the five-act structure London gives the novel:

Act 1 is a three-chapter self-contained short story about Kiche, during which several men are transporting a body for burial. It resolves with the men becoming casualties themselves, to wolves. Kiche is given special status through the following exchange by the wary men:

> "An' right here I want to remark," Bill went on, "that that animal's familyarity with campfires is suspicious and immoral."
>
> "It knows for certain more'n a self-respectin' wolf ought to know," Henry agreed. "A wolf that knows enough to come in with the dogs at feedin' time has had experiences."
>
> "Ol' Villan had a dog once that run away with the wolves," Bill cogitated aloud. "I ought to know. I shot it out of the pack in a moose pasture over on Little Stick. An' Ol' Villan cried like a baby. Hadn't seen it for three years, he said. Ben with the wolves all that time." (89)

The act gives us a wolf passing for a husky to be fed, the ghostly harrowing of the men by the pack each day until their nightly attacks, and an implicit reference to Buck's condition in *The Call of the Wild*. There is also the allusion to habituation, that Kiche's knowledge indicates a degree of either expert cunning (strongly implied) or potential domestication (realized later in her pup White Fang). This is how London has it in the novel proper, and calls this section "The Wild."

In act 2 (chapters 4 to 8) White Fang is born to a half-wolf, Kiche, and an old one-eyed wolf sire. The pup begins life dependent and blind in the darkness of a den during a time of prey scarcity. Were it not for his mother, the pup would become one of the casualties of an indifferent natural system, but the narrator tells us that food is supplied in precisely the minimum rations that allow a strong pup to survive (122). That White Fang lives through a famine while the rest of the litter dies, and that he is born to a seasoned one-eyed father, are obvious signals that he is on the hero's journey.

But the novel proves to be more concerned with White Fang's victimization and resilience than with a narrative that follows the steps of the hero; it is more a Dickensian orphan's story than an ascension of the pioneer or warrior. Indeed, White Fang's only heroism for three-fourths of the novel is his ability to suffer "civilization's" brutality and its determination to exceed the brutality of the wild. The novel's late reversal is the more powerful for this narrative of abuse, and the very structure of the book calls into question its supposedly happy ending.

Act 3 (chapters 9 to 14) follows White Fang's life in the Indian camp of Gray Beaver with an alcoholic who beats the young wolf-dog relentlessly, never shows him affection, and breaks him to the sled. Kiche, White Fang's mother, has been taken into the camp as well, in the only incident of wolf trapping I have found in

London's work—although it is not given the full arc of the common trapper-story plotline. She escapes eventually, and White Fang's first howl is recorded as a lament over both the loss of his mother and the miserable condition of his world (147). During his captivity with the Indians he learns that the other sled dogs hate him, and he begins to establish his dominance (but also to live as an outcast, politicizing the "pack mentality" while he endures violence at human hands).

In act 4 (chapters 15 to 20) White Fang is educated to the ways of white men when Gray Beaver sells him to the "Mad God," Beauty Smith, a grotesque and quintessentially naturalist figure whose physical ugliness corresponds to his lack of compassion. The violence finds its bottom in act 4. In addition to beatings and humiliation, the forces at work on White Fang wrought by the "gods," who in London's world are all human beings, propel him toward becoming a "demon." This transformation follows the logic London began while crafting White Fang's prototypes—Bâtard, who was originally the demon dog Diable, and Buck in *The Call of the Wild,* who answers the Call to become the "Ghost Dog of Yeehat legend" (74). Among his companion references in the margins, Dyer mentions Lawrence Clayton's claim that the Eskimos of the Bering Strait had a tale about the "'shades' of dogs." Dyer also cites an instance from London's little-known novel *Michael, Brother of Jerry,* in which one of the characters speculates as to whether a dog so ferocious as the dog Michael could be real. The man concludes, "The dog was not real" (*Call of the Wild,* 226 and 53n).

In all of his wolf-dog stories London plays with the definition of corruption; he does so primarily through his use of atavism but also views corruption in terms of certain social hierarchies. For instance, the wolf-dog's transformation into a "demon" has its human parallel: Beauty Smith traps Gray Beaver by addicting the Indian to alcohol, thus establishing himself as both the stronger god and a demonic force. He then molds White Fang in his own image. Biblical metaphors abound in London's language, especially of the potter and clay, which point will soon be addressed. Here we have the transformation of benevolent to malevolent ghost wolf, both in constant negotiation with the domestic elements associated with the dog.

In act 5 (chapters 21–25) we follow White Fang's socialization into domesticity. He first experiences human kindness twenty chapters into a twenty-five-chapter novel. By the denouement in act 5, "The God's Domain," he finds peace in the Scotts' San Francisco household and, importantly, in its attendant rules of domestication. These chapters serve to demonstrate that in civilization certain "laws of the pack" apply as well. White Fang learns to dominate other dogs of the neighborhood, and throughout act 5 the social Darwinism of the human city surfaces in London's language. In San Francisco White Fang meets his mate, named Collie, who is labeled generically as a "sheep-dog" (238).

The novel takes an odd turn in the last two chapters, which constitute a shorter contained narrative than the first three chapters of act 1 and loosely serve as an epilogue, even though London contains them within his last act. This is the "Jim Hall" episode. Having accepted his domestication, White Fang is now dedicated to protecting not only Weedon Scott but also Weedon's father (a judge) and mother (a homemaker), the representatives of law and order. An escaped convict, Jim Hall, once sentenced by Judge Scott, comes to the Scotts' to kill the judge, and White Fang thwarts the would-be murderer, suffering injuries in the process. This final portion of the narrative is split into chapter 24, "The Call of Kind," in which White Fang rejects the temptation to run away, and chapter 25, "The Sleeping Wolf," in which White Fang convalesces with his and Collie's puppies after his heroic fight against the threat to the family.

As per a Freytagian plot structure, *White Fang*'s rising action is long and increasingly arduous.[12] The climactic moment, which is White Fang's realization that love can exist between humans and canids, is written in obviously religious terms, implying that the wolf-dog has experienced an epiphany. And the denouement takes up little of the novel, so as not to risk anticlimax, ending happily in a reclined White Fang. A perfect bildungsroman.

The chapter titles of *White Fang* emphasize this standard plot structure. The climax occurs in "The Love Master" with the return of Weedon Scott, whose alliance with White Fang prepares the wolf-dog for his later encounter with the murderer Jim Hall. Love of the dog pacifies the evil wolf within, and the epiphany for White Fang occurs upon his surrender to Scott (234–48). The novel then turns south toward its denouement, to warmer climates both emotionally and geographically. After "The Long Trail," White Fang reaches "The Southland," which is "The God's Domain." By the time he hears "The Call of Kind," White Fang has "learned to laugh" (270). This transformative result of having entered the loving god's presence is at once the Hero Quest and the anthropocentrism upon which London's critics focused during the Nature Fakers controversy (Lutts, 143). When White Fang accepts "The Call of Kind," what he accepts is Collie's offer to mate. This union allows London to pursue psychoanalytic connections that apparently supersede Scott's ownership of White Fang. London's strategy only emphasizes that in order to domesticate an animal, one must own the animal and defy the transcendent principle of love, which is wildness: "But there was that in him deeper than all the law he had learned, than the customs that had molded him, than his love for the master, than the very will to live of himself . . . The master rode alone that day; and in the woods, side by side, White Fang ran with Collie, as his mother, Kiche, and old One Eye had run long years before in the silent Northland forest" (145).

London's name for the dog, "Collie" (which is not her breed), is fitting for the gentleness and domesticity of the love White Fang has found, à la Lassie. It is also suggestive of the predominantly dog-blooded pups he will sire. In comparing Kiche and Collie, London implicates them both in a kind of sexist and Aryan conspiratorial miscegenation. White Fang's domestication has tainted his bloodline, domesticating (in another Aryan metaphor) the "pure blood" in him. This point is ironic in that London tries to construct a superwolf but chooses a hybrid as his raw material and drives the novel toward that very domesticity he abstractly condemns as narrator. Who can blame May Estelle Cook for missing what apparently almost every scholar since has missed in the story—that the standard plotline presents us with the literary naturalism of London and Norris, a Nietzschean disintegration rather than an epiphanic triumph?

We might also consider the possibility of classical tragedy at work here. Act 4 in the five-act structure is often the reversal, the moment at which things look as though they will turn out well in a tragedy or poorly in a comedy. If we read *White Fang* as a bildungsroman, then the wolf-dog ends well and follows the comedic structure. But the key element affecting our interpretation is the point-of-view character. Although the story is told by a third-person narrator, its focalizer is the wolf-dog. This is precisely the characteristic of the book that made it popular, spawned a raft of copycat writers, and came to constitute a taboo (the animal point of view and attendant assumptions of the pathetic fallacy) in the serious novel. Ironically, in the case of *White Fang* that point of view actually establishes the novel as a deterministic tragedy rather than a coming-of-age comedy.

The final chapter title, "The Sleeping Wolf," is crucial to our understanding both the ambivalence of the novel and the plotlines at work to create that ambivalence. In this melodramatic last chapter White Fang's reward for doing justice—that is, for taking on the exact human role of Judge Scott by putting Jim Hall away—is to sire pups and lie in a sunny place (282). This seems to be a fine reward for either wolf or dog, and the coming-of-age story supports it as such. *White Fang*'s categorization as a young adult novel is probably the best evidence we have of the critical assumption that it is a bildungsroman. Palatable and instructive to children, the book is easily marketed and simplified in the same terms that have diminished *Adventures of Huckleberry Finn,* a story about an abused runaway, to an idyll on a raft.[13] Consequently London's deeper concerns with determinism and the "superwolf," obvious throughout the novel, are all but ignored.

The dilemma is then how to approach London's novel, which, like White Fang himself, is a hybrid mating palatable pulp with naturalist convictions.

After being beaten into submission by both Gray Beaver and Beauty Smith, White Fang gains the knowledge that he is beaten because "it was his god's will": "This faithfulness was a quality of the clay that composed him. It was the quality that was peculiarly the possession of his kind; the quality that set apart his species from all other species; the quality that had enabled the wolf and the wild dog to come in from the open and be the companions of man" (96). What seems to function merely as inexorable and indifferent fate for White Fang is really presented in terms of his being educated to that fate. This thinking is in direct opposition to the "campfire myth" I have mentioned, in which the wolf's domestication is assumed to have been benign and cooperative. Forces are powerfully at work beyond White Fang's ability to control them, in accordance with the oft-quoted Nietzschean adage that "that which does not kill us makes us stronger." His knowledge of those forces not only secures his survival but also educates him socially and morally: "They were his environment, these men, and they were molding the clay of him into a more ferocious thing than had been intended by Nature. Nevertheless, Nature had given him plasticity. Where many another animal would have died or had its spirit broken, he adjusted himself and lived, and at no expense of the spirit" (228).

This approach is called an *erziehungsroman,* a novel of education, and is indicative of London's attempt to reconcile Spencer, Nietzsche, and a socialist political agenda. Within a few pages London has created an anthropocentric hierarchy consisting of Personified Nature, Man (tiered as white over red), and anthropomorphized Beasts, just as Kipling (to whom London is often compared) had done in his "jungle law." London's term *plasticity* accounts for not only the wolf but also the dog (White Fang is both) and refers to an adaptability to the hardships of the wild that allows for development and growth. Perhaps now the hybrid state of the canid is a tool for its adaptation, rather than a foil to purity.

White Fang tempers his body and retains his spirit, even though that spirit is steadily being converted to evil by Gray Beaver and Beauty Smith, according to the pattern London designed in "Bâtard," until the last possible melodramatic instant of rescue accomplished by Weedon Scott. Scott is the white male force who challenges the stratified privilege of Nature over Man and, as a result of his success, seems to take White Fang to a higher stratum as well. The irony is that, in so doing, he separates "Nature" from other animals even as he transcends it, because he removes nature (the wolf our narrator calls White Fang) from Nature. The stratification of Nature/Man/Beast implies that the deterministic forces of Nature dominate all species, yet "Man's" dominance over animals is supposed to provide hope for human transcendence. This approach, through the personification of nature as an entity that "molds" White Fang, fits with the *entwicklungsroman,* or novel of development, and is one of the points at which anthropocentrism (hierarchy) and anthropomorphism (projection) meet to build the coming-of-age story. Once again, the definition of "development" in this case, especially vis-à-vis its dependence upon the personification of Nature (capitalized by London) as a hardening force, is typical of literary naturalism. Transcendence through domesticity is, at best, a paradox.

In *The Call of the Wild*, it is the *künstlerroman,* a form of bildungsroman specific to the development of an artist, that London most explicitly employs. In the following passage, London writes of the artist's coming of age, but in terms of the "paradox of living," by which London seems to mean strength gained through independent growth but also determined by a natural and limited order: "There is an ecstasy that marks the summit of life, and beyond which life cannot rise . . . This ecstasy, this forgetfulness of living, comes to the artist, caught up and out of himself in a sheet of flame; it comes to the soldier, war-mad on a stricken field and refusing quarter; and it came to Buck, leading the pack, sounding the old wolf-cry, straining after the food that was alive and that fled swiftly before him in the moonlight" (49).

Such expository moments reveal the epiphanic designs that London has for both Buck and White Fang. London asserted in correspondence that *White Fang* was "a companion to *The Call of the Wild*. Beginning at the very opposite end— evolution instead of devolution; civilization instead of decivilization. It is distinctly NOT to be a sequel. Merely same length, dog-story, and companion story. I shall not call it 'Call of the Tame,' but shall have title quite dissimilar to Call of Wild" (Labor, Leitz, & Shepard, 455; Dickey 7–16). An odd term, *decivilization,* and a clue to London's definition of *antithesis.* His formula of "evolution" for an animal being equal to "civilization" violates the principles of both literary and scientific naturalism in order to affect opposing lines of thought between his two novels (only Spencerianism proposes that civilization has anything to do with evolution). The künstlerroman passage of Buck's artistic and soldierly ecstasy is so similar to White Fang's initiation into the world as to distract us from recognizing the plotline of White Fang's tragic decline into blissful enslavement. Buck is not a wolf, yet sounds a wolf-cry. He is the artist/soldier preparing, not his literal progeny, but his literary progeny—White Fang—to perfect the art of war. Buck's ecstasy is the warrior madness by which White Fang will survive, and the "summit," the achievement of a more perfect state, is the resonant image carried from *The Call of the Wild* to *White Fang.*

Since *Call* ends with Buck's charge (flight?) into the moonlight, the "antithetical" ending of *White Fang* seems obvious enough: White Fang falls asleep in the bright sunlight, a legend in his own mind. But the language of White Fang's obedience subtly reveals the tragic element of the plot, as it is so laden with images positive to human beings that are not necessarily positive to a wolf:

> Hand-clapping and pleased cries from the gods greeted the performance. He was sur-
> prised, and looked at them in a puzzled way. Then his weakness asserted itself, and he
> lay down, his ears cocked, his head on one side, as he watched the puppy. The other
> puppies came sprawling toward him, to Collie's great disgust; and he gravely permitted
> them to clamber and tumble over him. At first, amid the applause of the gods, he
> betrayed a trifle of his old self-consciousness and awkwardness. This passed away as the
> puppies' antics and mauling continued, and he lay with half-shut, patient eyes, drows-
> ing in the sun. (152)

It's not the sleeping in the sun among pups to which I am objecting. This certainly seems to give plenty of animals plenty of pleasure. It's the applause. The gods who applaud White Fang do so as directors for whom White Fang's life is now a performance. He is a puzzled spectator of his own life, which had once depended upon keeping his feet during a pit fight, a battle designed by this same pantheon. Now the language describing his last days includes "sprawling," "disgust," "tumble," and "awkwardness." The collective effect of these words indicates that if White Fang is at all genetically compelled toward wildness, then wildness must include this controlled state of repose and largess—a direct contradiction unsupported in the rest of London's writings. The words certainly do not leave any doubt as to the purgation from White Fang's spirit of the "fighting wolf" he had been for many chapters. Whereas *The Call of the Wild* ends with "straining after the food that was alive," White Fang ends with his surrender to death. His weakness "asserts itself" both in the paragraph and in the larger argument of his fated devolution, despite the Jim Hall incident's straining effort to assert that White Fang's wildness has simply been channeled to ethical use in the human world.

According to Philip Fisher, the formal devices of literary naturalism often include a plot of decline, during which one main character "falls" while another one "rises," as in *Sister Carrie,* or the main character experiences a simultaneous rise and fall, as in *The Rise of Silas Lapham* (Fisher, 171). If anthropomorphism and zoomorphism are employed to affect the plot of decline, then they usually act as metaphoric masks designed to change the faces of characters who decline into brutishness. I should note here as well that in addition to Fisher's "plot of decline" the plot also follows a pattern of colonization, in that it contains the following steps: violation of the indigenous bloodline; inducement to fight followed by demonization for fighting; then sequestering the colonized culture in domestic spaces that serve the controlling god. Not only does Buck become the "Ghost Dog of Yeehat legend," terrorizing the tribe and breeding hybrid pups throughout the timber wolf population, but "the tale grows worse." London writes: "Each fall, when the Yeehats follow the movement of the moose, there is a certain valley which they never enter. And women there are who become sad when the word goes over the fire of how the Evil Spirit came to select that valley for an abiding-place" (*Call of the Wild*, 101). If Buck is an Evil Spirit, then turning feral means going bad. At the least, he has taken on the traits of the supernatural rather than the preternatural. In the climax of *The Call of the Wild* Buck's conversion to "evil" reaches beyond the bestial state even while the bestial state is valorized as pure. Unlike Norris's McTeague or Dreiser's Hurstwood, who devolve into metaphorically bestial states, Buck begins as a corporeal beast, and so paradoxically *devolves* into something both extra- and super-natural, something existing beyond the brutish material condition—a symbol. This is why, when a book declares a wolf to be a "symbol of wilderness" or the "spirit of the wild," it casts an evil spell, whatever its intentions. The signs of London's foundational ambivalence, his struggle to reconcile complex metaphysical positions into some defensible practice, indicate a mythic struggle.

The conversion of the wolf in popular North American culture from the ravenous devil of the nineteenth century to the nature saint of the twentieth might prompt the present-day reader to infer that Buck's "demonization" is actually a neopagan happy ending. Buck is free, and a demon only in terms of the Christian morality imposed upon him. While such a reading only underscores White Fang's collapse, it must be understood in the context of real feral dogs, millions of which are "put to sleep" every year in America. The condition of the feral dog in America is only symptomatic of the condition of the nation, which has such a population of animals bred, grown, owned, warped, threatened, tried for their retaliation or adaptation, imprisoned, and then killed. Simplifying Buck's freedom is akin to the postslavery dilemma that America created for itself. And although *White Fang*'s melodramatic ending and the convenient use of "fate" to drive the plot are both low artifice, fate is at least a means by which London tries, perhaps fails, to unite the atavistic tale with the political treatise. Thus White Fang's decline into passivity is given an importance that stretches beyond the novel. A deus ex machina in realist readings, Fate is a necessary character in mythic ones (Kermode, 1055).

The White Silence

The friction between the ostensible bildungsroman and what I am positing as the plot of decline in *White Fang* should provide us with some ways to examine how an animal focalizer in a narrative affects our responses to that narrative. If the protagonist's role as a canid is critical to interpreting the plot, then an informed human artifice has the potential to depict animals as personae rather than merely as anthropomorphic props. Our approach to animal voice is thus refined by writers in pursuit of more sophisticated fictions representing animals. The level of sophistication is gauged by readers in pursuit of the information from wildlife biology that will allow them to recognize the exactness and usefulness of those fictions, even as all of this information itself improves.

A good example of the double plotline of bildungsroman/decline in a naturalist novel contemporary with London's work is Theodore Dreiser's *Sister Carrie*. Fisher sees a chiasmus between Carrie's bildungsroman and Hurstwood's devolution. He calls Carrie "the one dynamic, unsettled figure in a world where everyone else represents terminal points, places and levels at which she might arrive and stabilize herself" (170). Hurstwood begins at one of those points, but he loses his footing, at which moment Dreiser takes control of his slide downward to a literally "terminal" point. Fisher explains that Hurstwood's theft of the money from a vault, "which might be viewed as the cause of his destiny in New York, and so it would be if the order of Dreiser's world were a moral rather than a Darwinian and economic order, is in fact only a notation in compressed form of the inevitability, at some point, in his life of a balanced moment at which he teeters unaware that he is no longer rising but beginning to fall" (173).

Note that Fisher does not consider this a dynamic characterization of Hurstwood, even though Hurstwood's plotline in the novel follows a Freytagian path. Instead, Fisher's strategy is to define Dreiser's design of the deterministic forces acting upon Hurstwood. Fisher's reading also reveals two important possibilities in a naturalist text: first, that the bildungsroman and the plot of decline may function simultaneously in the same narrative, one continually vying with the other; and second, that the world of natural order, as opposed the world of moral order, allows for fate (mistakenly labeled "Darwinian") to play a part in the outcome of the plot.

In "The 'Lure' of the Naturalist Text" David Baguley compares naturalist literature to "the popular genres, which work upon and transmute many of the latent fears, repressed desires, and fundamental taboos of a society; however, instead of veiling these dreads in literary conventions, naturalist texts draw them starkly to the reader's attention with shocking distress" (276). While London's work supports Baguley's definition, one way in which he does not comply is the way he treats the domestication of the hybrid canid. By using anthropomorphism and by positing that human love may finally justify ownership of the wolf, London veils several dreads and directs the reader away from any shocking distress. Whether or not London was writing potboilers and intended to veil the dreads, *White Fang* has been read so often as a canine bildungsroman that we might judge the book, as Teddy Roosevelt judged it, to be as much a naturalist failure as a commercial success. But this judgment oversimplifies the argument as well, limiting the book to a competition between literary craft and monetary gain.

For all its polemical assertions, London's "dog writing" provides literary scholarship with ghost animals to be studied—animals depicted in the terms of the literary naturalist, if not the ecological naturalist. Nineteenth-century literary naturalism's invocation of verisimilitude cooperated with ecological naturalism toward the latter's credibility and popularity between the late nineteenth century and World War I. By teaching the reader of the suffering brought on through unchecked industrialism, the literary naturalists were indeed environmental naturalists by impulse (for example, *The Jungle* and the ensuing regulation of the meatpacking industry). London's hybrids are to the Yukon as Crane's soldiers are to the Civil War—beasts struggling under the clouds of either "white silence" (London's term for the overwhelming force of the cold) or cannon smoke (Crane's image of the overwhelming force of machinery). And what has happened to London has happened to Crane: A superficial reading of *The Red Badge of Courage* ends with Henry as a decorated hero instead of a deluded pawn of the corporate death machine. Like Wilhelm Meister in Goethe's exemplary künstlerroman, White Fang performs for his owners the tasks of an apprentice, which strengthen his insight and resolve, prepare him for the moment of revelation, and secure his retirement.

Good Dog

Lynn DeVore's 1974 essay "The Descent of White Fang" is the only other critical work seriously, if briefly, addressing the possibility that *White Fang* does not end happily. After the nicely chosen double entendre for her title, she opens with London's declaration that in *White Fang* he would "give the evolution, the civilization of a dog—development of domesticity, faithfulness, love, morality, and all the amenities and virtues" (122; see also *The Unabridged Jack London*, 382, which uses this quotation as an epigraph to *White Fang*). Having pointed out London's failure to accomplish his stated aim, a failure she links to weaknesses in the novel's structure, she turns to an extended metaphor of the Old Testament Covenant. DeVore demonstrates that biblical allusions in the novel affirm diabolical temptation as preparing White Fang for his epiphany (123).

The novel, she declares, "assumes a downward course" (124). She adds that "the movement from *Call* to *White Fang* is less aptly described, as some have done, as one from Nietzschean superman to melioristic humanism than one from romance to progressive disillusionment" (126). As the wolf becomes more "evil" and increasingly resistant to redemption, the drama of conversion is intensified in a fashion similar to the American captivity narratives. White Fang's naturalistic experience makes him seem beyond saving from the hardness of natural law; his "superwolf" experience makes him seem unsavable because there is no God but himself. But the force of biblical myth that DeVore finds London to emphasize makes White Fang's redemption possible, and in fact creates a subtly powerful coming-of-age plot. I think DeVore overemphasizes the Covenant metaphor, but her recognition of White Fang's fall is unusual and thoroughly logical—particularly notable in that, since its appearance, no one has followed up on her observation. What the biblical read does provide is, once again, the ubiquity of ancient and mythic sources for the wolf book.

DeVore's article also appeared during an explosive time in wolf research, but she uses no information from wolf studies in her reading. Her recognition of a biological decline seems coincidental rather than scientifically informed, although it works for her purposes (125). Her choices of biblical analogies in the text are sound, and although her article is not concerned with biological or ecological matters, her acknowledgment of some kind of "descent" at least raises the question of how we distinguish the difference between wolf and dog in a story.

White Fang's physical ascent overlaps his spiritual/social descent in the Indian camp; the rest of the book is devoted to his degeneration under the force of oppression. When Weedon Scott arrives we may be prompted to forget or deny the plot of decline, yet at this point the narrative actually pitches sharply downward. When White Fang is in his worst physical condition he is held in the vise-jaws of Cherokee, the bulldog, and the hand of Fate (anthropomorphized in Weedon Scott) appears. The "love master" tempts us to believe that we may own a better world than the writer has shown us for the last hundred and fifty pages. Were White Fang to die in Cherokee's grip, the plot of decline would be obvious to any reader and London would be innocent of the charge of melodrama in the form Scott's intervention. One complexity here is that Scott does the ethical thing by intervening, the dogfight being one of the cruelest and most incriminating of human indulgences. The ethics attached to the disgusting euphemism of "putting the dog out of his misery" are in effect in Cormac McCarthy's *The Cross-*

ing, which perfects the pit-fight intervention that serves as a plot point in every London spin-off, even in the best emulations.[14] They are not, however, a part of the puzzle in London. "Up from the bottom" seems to be the sentiment in this scene for *White Fang,* and we can only respect the decision to pull White Fang from the pit, even though it will lead to his final domestication and the symbolic erasure of the wolf.

In saving White Fang's physical life, Scott also breaks what London has articulated as the wolf's behavioral essence—its wildness, its spirit. Such a moment characterizes literary naturalism, yes, but it is also the poetic side of ethological domestication, or breeding, and because it calls on us to both essentialize and ethicize, it is a moment of mythic fantasy. The manipulation of genetic proclivities into assimilative behaviors is the modus operandi of domestication; breeding is only its most extreme form.

London blurs White Fang's wolf self with his dog self at the writer's convenience. In moments when it seems important to reestablish White Fang's potential domestication, the dog blood is assumed dominant. For instance, Scott's long absence results in White Fang's sickness of heart, and when Scott returns, White Fang greets him by "snuggling" (*White Fang,* 120). The plausibility of a wolf's response is not so much the key issue here (that is, wolves certainly sometimes "snuggle" among themselves) as Scott's assertion that follows: "I always insisted that wolf was a dog. Look at 'm!" (122). The next scene is one of surrender, of the final domestication of White Fang, and it is written in biblical prose: "I put myself into thy hands. Work thou thy will with me" (123). The passage seems to say: He is, after all, a dog at heart. He's just had a hard life. The cultural fallout from London's allegorical applications of hybridity is found in current rationalizations of many wolf-dog owners—it's a dog when you want it to be, a wolf when a wolf serves.

One Spring in Missoula, Montana, I walked out of a coffee shop to find a short flatbed with a white cab parked along the curb. It was cool out, cloud-heavy and gray, and the coniferous wall of the Bob Marshall wilderness was spread below a fog that was partly the smoke of the paper mill by the Clark Fork. On the flatbed stood a wolf. It wore a thick collar studded with blunt chrome and fitted with two bolt rings, one to each side of the collar. From each ring stretched a length of heavy chain down to larger eyebolts on the flatbed. Little slack in either chain. I sat on the curb and waited for the owner, who explained that wolves were runners, you couldn't keep 'em behind a fence, and that he had to "keep my wolf still" while he did his business. Had a stray hunter's bullet found its way into that man at that moment I wouldn't have shed a tear. For his part, the wolf stared at both of us, long-legged and apparently whipped, and didn't seem to care any more about my anger than the other guy's idiocy, although I remain oblivious as to what was going on inside that wolf's head. I'll lay my paycheck on it being nothing good. This is what happens to Fenris in the reality of a culture that won't learn from its mistakes, and it generates a profound and lasting body of literature. Unfortunately, the academic humanities have traditionally treated that moment, and whatever attendant emotions are connected to it, as a "wolf encounter" like any other, all abstracted so that a wolf chained on a flatbed is the same as any other wolf—a symbolic device serving the greater human drama, and not worth our attention as anything more real than that. Literary critics tend not to carry bolt cutters.

A writer's use of anthropomorphism for any purpose might invite an ecologically conscious audience to judge negatively not only the author's purpose but especially the method. In "The Meanest Thing That Feels," Onno Dag Oerlemans examines anthropomorphism in romantic poetry and art, stating that "the concept of anthropomorphism, and the consequent prohibition of it, are inherently a feature of anthropocentrism" (4). While I disagree with the asserted inherency and totalization here, I support where Oerlemans takes it. He separates anthropomorphism from anthropocentrism in terms of practice. He asks if there can be a legitimate, reasonable anthropomorphism—a practice that, while attributing supposedly human characteristics to animals, does not automatically result either in their subjugation or in the falsification of characteristics that may actually exist, characteristics not to be denied simply because they are uncomfortably similar to human ones. In the case of White Fang, we witness the anthropocentrism that the ecologically conscious audience justifiably fears: that we must shape White Fang into a dog (or a simulated human) in order to see his peace at the end as a blessing. Otherwise we would have to grapple with the truth of the wolf's demise at the hands of "civilization," a fact that literary naturalists near the turn of the century were hoping to impress upon their readers (Howard, 11–12).

In "The Other Animals" London writes that his books on other species are "a protest against the 'humanizing' of animals, of which it seemed to me several 'animal writers' had been profoundly guilty" (108). While instructive about his agenda, this is an unconvincing essay for a number of reasons, not the least of which is London's interesting but convoluted speculation on the "simple reason" (109) and psychology of animals.[15] Literary naturalists were concerned with the proliferation of industrial forces more powerful than the most noble powers of humans or other animals; they demonstrated their concerns by rendering not only the animate machine but also the human brute. This position contradictorily equated beasts with machines and ennobled beasts by casting human beings as automatons—slaves both to machines and to other human beings who lack psychic and organic freedom. The result of this complicated negotiation is a set of characters, writers, and readers, all subject to their own comparisons of beast to machine, demon, or mind. Literary criticism regarding the nonhuman world will mature in a way that it thus far has not if we can just give up our addiction to analogically truncating other species' lives.

Jim Hall

Read as a bildungsroman, *White Fang*'s plot ends with the hero's realization of his strength, his maturation to protecting the domestic sphere. What seems to be the strangest and least congruent turn of the plot is the Jim Hall scene (see Giles). We know that only his wild nature and the conditioning of his atrocious life make him fit to defeat the evil Hall, who is depicted as another kind of "antithesis," a figure brutalized in many ways similarly to White Fang but who emerges without the adaptability and station, though he possesses the same toughness and strong fight instinct. London refers to him as more beast than man, which is not itself a condemnation coming from London (146–47). In London's world other beasts also have moral selves, so Hall's evil is not a moral feature exclusive to humanity. What makes him a formidable force for White Fang is that Hall is both in his environment (the city) and one of the greater gods (white and human-brained). Our hero's realization of his power is therefore cast in his defeat of a being at once beast, human, and god. In the pit White Fang fought out of his feral nature and for his life; in the house he employs but transcends his feral nature and fights for someone else's life. The role of his feral nature becomes so complicated as to make the Jim Hall chapter, ostensibly incongruous, crucial to our understanding of what London is tackling in terms of the natural-versus-civilizing forces that constitute being and behavior. The range of conflict from tundra to fighting pit to bourgeois household is itself a comment on London's attempt to negotiate the raw material of the world with the artificial constructs we fabricate from it. This range, these places, themselves become shaping environments that negotiate with biology the kind of feral or civilized qualities that form identity and dictate appropriate action.

If anthropocentrism may facilitate the bildungsroman, for instance through the assumption that White Fang's domestication constitutes a rising plotline, then it may also facilitate the plot of decline. We could compare White Fang to devolving human characters in naturalist novels (I have already gestured to McTeague, Hurstwood, and the materialist half of Silas Lapham). We could also consider how the constellation of environment, psyche, and biology pattern the narrative of decline in terms of both nature and culture. Jim Hall provides us with an intratextual example of this logic, especially if we consider London's use of zoomorphism in opposition to the novel's anthropomorphic final image.

Hall is dropped into the novel more abruptly than are the caged fighting dogs in the story's middle chapters. He is first depicted as "a human beast" when he escapes from prison. "Two other dead guards marked his trail through the prison to the outer walls, and he had killed with his hands to avoid noise." He is pursued by a pack of bloodhounds, "the sleuth-hounds of the law, the paid fighting animals of society" (146–47). The line between animal and human (as well as the one between law and violence) is blurred here, not only in reference to the criminal but also to his pursuers: London zoomorphizes humans involved in the chase, who are purported to devolve as they participate in what London assumes to be a brutish practice. The converse, that evolution follows a civilizing progression, is articulated when Hall breaks into the Scott house: "White Fang burst into no furious outcry. It was not his way. The strange god walked softly, but more softly walked White Fang, for he had not clothes to rub against the flesh of his body. He followed silently. In the Wild he had hunted live meat that was infinitely timid, and he knew the advantage of surprise" (148).

Here we see that White Fang is not quite entirely civilized. He retains some vestige of his "way." Not until he has grown sedentary in domestication will he "evolve" as he learns the last great civilizing practice, which is to father a family and settle down. Also, if White Fang hunted in the Wild, then his prey would certainly not have been "infinitely timid." London's assertion of the wolf-dog's "way" is again suspect when he endows the animal with a human consciousness of tactics, rather than an acknowledgment of whatever tactics (as I examined in chapter 5) animals might possess without an anthropomorphic and expositional self-referentiality.

My point is that White Fang has acted out of fealty to humanity, out of a conditioning away from his lupine inclinations, which may themselves include fealty to other wolves—the very inclinations that, ironically, make him trainable. The attack on Jim Hall is a by-product of domestication and occurs inside the house. The prisoner here is White Fang; Jim Hall has escaped, because he dies a free man inside domestic human confines. White Fang kills "the bad guy," another way of framing the novel, given that in the opening chapters wolves kill one of "the good guys," men trying to give a fellow a decent burial. By the time Hall appears, White Fang has learned the difference between good and evil. His attack is pure iconoclasm, but from it he earns a title and the blessing of the Scotts, the inevitably iconic outcome of iconoclasm. Of course, the killing of a god indicates that White Fang has violated the hierarchy to which he is subject, but that he does so through his own fitness to live, and within the bounds of human law, apparently exonerates him in the views of London, Sartre, Baudrillard, and Judge Scott (less so Nietzsche)—all proponents of killing certain gods at certain convenient times.

Weedon allows White Fang the freedom to kill under "the right circumstances" during the chapter "The Southland" (268–69). When White Fang turns against the neighborhood dogs and places himself at the top of the hierarchy, Scott watches him do so. Now that he has been removed from the wild North, White Fang's behavior occurs entirely within the necessary boundaries of the human family and city structure. And although it is common for writers to compare an essentialized wolf pack structure to human communities, the analogy is usually unsound. Not all wolf packs are the same. Not all wolves live in packs. Wolves do not build prisons, zoos, colleges, arenas, or cities; these are institutions of civilization to which real wolves must be brought and broken, at which point they become ghost wolves.

CHAPTER SIXTEEN

The Big North Draw

While London's worldview in *White Fang* is clearly both ethnocentric and at times (despite his famous effort) anthropocentric, a summary rejection of the novel on that basis teaches us nothing and dismisses as well some important ideas with which he was working. If we first accept White Fang as the point-of-view character and then accept that the limitations of human language will prevent us from completely determining the plausibility of his point of view, we are free to examine the metaphors London uses to attempt that point of view, even if only through suspended disbelief. These moments may in fact be the most telling to an ecological reading, providing some indication of a writer's strong suit being interspecies events beyond their mere symbolic connection to human (usually race, class, gender) events.[1] If readers of *White Fang* fail to look beyond the human to the nonhuman, then they will miss much of the significance of White Fang's being three-fourths wolf, one-fourth dog, and about half human—a sum of parts made possible by the ghost wolf. Likewise, the ecological critic who reads London's metaphors as a mere anthropocentric characterization will miss the importance of the plot of decline, the wolf enslaved psychologically as well as physically.

In Plato's *Symposium* Aristophanes provides an allegorical figure for Love in which the back and sides of the primeval human form a sphere with four hands and feet, topped with a Janus head of two faces. At some point in prehistory the sphere is divided, and the two halves, separated by a great distance, seek one another. When they meet again, the two parts of the primeval human, "each desiring his other half," throw their arms around each other, "eager to grow into one" (22). For Aristophanes love needs no authority figures, no manifestation in a master. Love exists when the life of one being is fully composed and arranged by the life of the other into what eventually becomes an identity of connection more than separation. This story of the primeval human reinforces London's ideas about atavism, particularly about there being a Call of the Wild, and about love, particularly through domestication. Atavism, Aryanism, and domesticating the animal become for London the means to imagine some pure but malleable bloodline wrought by Nature and found in the anatomy. London's romanticism of animals is found not only in his obsessions with pedigree but also in the vision of a "chain of being" rather than a "web of life." Stratification and heritage go hand in hand as justification of the notion that animals are dealt their lots by fate alone, rather than in significant measure by human schemes. Those concerned with heritage alone also lose sight of Aristophenes's spheric primeval human in favor of a linear hierarchy of species, and erroneously conflate descent with ascent. This is an impasse between realism and romanticism.

Because we humans are, generally speaking, classifiers, we are prone to this fault even after we divide ourselves into lumpers and splitters. Out of our need to distinguish dogs from wolves we reveal the deeper fear that our civilized readings may only be rationalizations for a Spirit we have already declared either evil (and thus have condemned) or good (and thus have confused). When we close a novel we take with us some intangible but resonant image. Even if we may say that White Fang's one-quarter-dog blood qualifies him as a subject to be domesticated, the more important point is that the novel constitutes a justification for domesticating the wild, and therefore domesticating wolves. To the extent that the image we take from *White Fang* is the one familiar to us since May Estelle Cook's interpretation, our closing of the book implicates us as complicitors in the domestication, which is the elimination, of wildness. We incorporate it, assimilate it, colonize it, and descend into such cleverly self-serving arguments, made quite popular of late in such works as Simon Schama's *Landscape and Memory*, that because we "make landscape" we therefore "create wilderness" and that a nature of our invention is "all the nature we have" (8, 56). Frost tells us "the land was ours before we were the land's," or Dickinson declares "the Brain is Wider than the Sky," and we take those lines and run with them. This brand of exploitation is to literature what clear-cutting or poaching is to ecosystems.

White Fang ends his story asleep in the sun, and London wants him to feel the human comfort of his position in the yard, surrounded by puppy dogs. But White Fang is not a human being and is barely a dog. Culture didn't make him a wolf; it merely bred him down to dogness and then took credit, page after page, for both his wildness and its decrease. For White Fang that sun of human comfort is a falling star, the yard an Orwellian captivity, and he is, after all, put to sleep.

The Wolf-Watcher Novel

The wolf story written today (with the exception of the hyperhybridized and more mercurial werewolf story) is more often a paean to nature, a celebration of the wolf in its reality and renewed presence, and contends less with a deep mythic hostility than a superficial economic hostility. Pulp, however, is a weedy species, and has some comparative effect on how we read the wolf story. Rick Bass's *Where the Sea Used to Be* is more literary than Nicholas Evans's cliché-infected *The Loop,* but the books are remarkably similar in many ways and demonstrate how the wolf in the white silence has changed its image in literature, giving us a historical range from the London novel and its creation during the conservation era to our current marketplace environmental sensibilities.

The hunter-conservationist mode finds in Bass its most recent literary spokesman, among whose many works are several books on wolves. *The Ninemile Wolves* is his best and the one gaining the most attention. *The New Wolves* is an essay on the Mexican wolf reintroduction in the American Southwest and reads like leftover journal notes. His novel, expanded from a short story also called "Where the Sea Used to Be," has a wolf biologist as one of its main characters. He has also written essays in John Elder's collection on the wolf's future in the Northeast and, for *Orion* magazine, on the trophic cascade created by the reintroduction of the wolf to Yellowstone. I consolidate this list here not only to give Bass the position he's due in the literature on the wolf but also to consider him as comparable to Jack London in a few relevant respects and as a direct descendant of the hunter-conservationist ethic of the nineteenth century.

Bass writes often about hunting, and his language for it borders on the obsessive, hailing hunting in the romantic vein of what makes a man, what balances the world, and what constitutes a ritual of right behavior. Take these examples: "I really believe the tradition is as important as the venison" (31) in *The Deer Pasture,* a book in the Leopoldian vein. *Colter,* in the tradition of Muir's *Stickeen,* is an ode to Bass's dog, the difference being that Bass's is a bird hunting dog. In a story revisited in *Brown Dog of the Yaak* he writes, "Hunting with Colter: I needed him like an addict needs opium, or a drowning person needs a rope. Beyond my loving the essence of what he was, and what he did, hunting with Colter was a time when I did not think about the environment, and did not think about writing, or craft" (*Brown Dog of the Yaak,* 14-15). *Caribou Rising* regards the Arctic National Wildlife Refuge through the lens of Bass's hunt with the Gwich-'in tribe, a sacred-game moment. And consider this rose-tinted moment from "Why I Hunt" in *Sierra* magazine:

It astounds me sometimes to step back, particularly at the end of autumn, the end of the hunting season, and take both mental and physical inventory of all that was hunted and all that was gathered from this life in the mountains. And most precious of all, the flesh of the wild things that share with us these mountains and the plains to the east— the elk, the whitetail and mule deer; the ducks and geese, grouse and pheasant and Hungarian partridge and dove and chukar and wild turkey; the trout and whitefish. Each year the cumulative bounty seems unbelievable. What heaven is this into which we've fallen? (1).

I'd like to let Pattiann Rogers offer a possibility of what heaven it is:

Some of us give thanks
and bless those we kill and eat,
and ask for pardon,
and this is beautiful as long as they are the ones dying
and we are the ones eating. (34)

There is in Bass a heavy dose of the Roosevelt who never met an animal he didn't shoot, although Bass has certainly adopted the more enlightened position not to sport-hunt predators. This stance makes his prose inviting to the hunter-conservationist but limited in its ability to express an ecological consciousness outside that mode, especially given that Bass is also polemical and at times loose with his arguments. Such an approach is common to essays written in the spirit of Cactus Ed Abbey, whose approach of hyperbole and paradox worked better in the 1970s, especially with Abbey's understanding of philosophy and art behind it, than it does for Bass. So when, in *The Ninemile Wolves,* Bass writes, "I can say what I want to say. I gave up my science badge a long time ago," and estimates his interviews at "maybe a hundred" (4), we might wince a little and ask for more substantive positions, rather than applaud the mere freedom of rumination that governed romantic arcadianism and now has ecological literature in something of a bind.

In addition to the hunting fixation, Bass inherits from the nineteenth-century struggle over the wolf's place in the world an interest in the friction between scientific fact and narrative romance. He has done as much as any recent writer to turn American sentiment in favor of the wolf's return and protection, especially through *The Ninemile Wolves* and his own active, outspoken advocacy. This activism has to be reconciled with some of the prose, which tends to ignore one hard fact of hunting: that it is neither a necessary nor a necessarily redeemable occupation. We don't *need* to eat meat; we *like* to eat it. We don't hunt because it makes us part of the great chain of being; we do it for the same reasons that we eat

Krispy Kremes or roll and smoke Insert Plant Here, which acts we also ritualize. It's certainly a better thing to hunt for what one eats than to think that meat grows in a grocery store; Aldo Leopold perfectly explained that modernization of the hunter's ethic. But this nuance only means that it's therefore a better thing not to eat meat at all, if we're talking about better things. We've got vegetarians in the NFL; meat's not a requirement for health. And the ritual of hunting, as often as it expresses some pure state of the noble savage in the modern man, also expresses the glorification of violence in the modern man. For every Rick Bass trying to Find the Balance we have several Ted Nugents, and in between we find organizations of men learning how to use the language of balance to greenwash an addiction.

For starters, the "sacred-game" idea needs to go, whether it originates in indigenous myth or modern denial. This is the notion that "the prey gives itself to the hunter" in some fulfillment of a sacred pact in the cycle of life. It raises this question for me: Then why do they run? Why do we have to sneak up on them? I've never met an elk, sacred or otherwise, ready to pitch in the ultimate loss in order to fulfill some human god's plan.[2]

The particular mix of Bass's strengths and flaws of argument and prose style is what draws my attention to him in the context of the wolf book in America. Bass rises above the mere iconization of the symbolic animal in that he has earned his stripes through a land-connected life and achieves some literary quality in his work. He has the awareness that has saved the wolf from the nineteenth-century model of his hunter-conservationist forebears even as he embraces the continuance of that outdated mode. Bass's corpus of work represents well the conflicted condition of the wolf in America.

Bathos on Ice

In contradistinction to Bass, Nicholas Evans mines environmental sentimentalism to full effect and without the burden of depth or nuance to his craft. Horse whisperers, smoke jumpers, and wolf lovers are his subjects. His theme is the transplanted city denizen falling in love with the wilderness and its representatives, having an epiphanic experience, then returning home with the fond memories and bittersweet embrace of life, Aaron Copland fading in her head. It's a magic formula in the marketplace; for the last two decades or so, and given the utter provinciality of the Manhattan publishing monopoly, if you set a book in both New York and a Big Western State, then you've got a stand-and-deliver moneymaker.[3]

In *The Loop* Evans acknowledges Lopez, McIntyre, Fischer, Mech, Steinhart, Thisted, Bangs, Mike Jimenez, and "Koani, the only wolf I can possibly call a friend." Black Elk gets the epigraph, using the "loop" of the title as a metaphor for the circle of life. The loop also indicates the trap used to snare one of the story's wolves (84), might be a play on *loup* (although that never quite surfaces), and refers to the seasons, which divide the book and chronologically govern its plot. At one point, the main character declares that his dream is a circle of wolves "like the picture he used to love in that old copy of *The Jungle Book* he'd had as a kid" (165).

Evans does his homework; every trope of the wolf book is in here. He often avoids anthropomorphism and maintains a humble speculative position as to wolf cognition and behavior: "some believe" (1); "as if deer and insect were of equal consequence to a wolf" (4); biologists guessing at the wolf's motivations (18). Indeed, his wolves are better written than his people, who are all carica- tures. We also have the "yellow flash of [the wolf's] eyes" and the wolf's essential animosity toward dogs (10), both generalizations, the latter safer than the for- mer. And the ghost-wolf stealth tropes abound: "vanished into the shadow of the forest" (11); wolves at a den site "simply vanished . . . leaving Luke to wonder if he'd dreamed the whole episode" (22); "Indian folklore had it that the spirit of America's slaughtered wolves lived on" (86). At one point a resident of the town runs out with a gun after wolves and "couldn't even find their tracks" (158). Helen's dreams of trapping wolves are reliable indicators that she actually has one in a trap she's set (195).

We get the mention of healthy wolves never killing people (25). We get a blow-by-blow description of a moose hunt (178–82) that refers to predation as being understood by both prey and predator, a "bloody compact," and a quota- tion from Lopez (182). The Thisted ranch, *The Ninemile Wolves,* and Defenders of Wildlife are mentioned (224). We have the requisite references to the alchemical wolfbait, a concoction of "putrified bobcat and fermented coyote anal glands," and to Newhouse traps (138), as well as to "shoot, shovel, and shut up" (238). One outlaw wolf has a missing toe (246). There is a wedding scene disrupted by wolves attacking cattle, slightly reminiscent of *My Ántonia* (405), and another scene nearly identical to the opening of *White Fang:* "The white wolf paused in the mouth of the den while the two biggest and bravest of her pups tottered between her legs and out into the moonlit world" (409).

The wolf biologists of the story follow a plotline of negotiating the wolf's return to the region with the hard-nosed conservative ranch community in the town called Hope, Montana: fictionalized Rick Bass country. One of the conser- vatives is Buck Calder, the father of our sympathetic leading man, Luke. Luke is a teenager with the gift of wildness, a love for animals, and a heavy stammer, and he falls for our main character, Helen Ross, a wolf biologist fighting for the wolves. He distrusts radio-collaring because he sees it as making it easier to get rid of wolves, ironically adapting to a preservationist end the same political line against government surveillance that his conservative counterparts would advance (174). On Luke's bookshelf are London, McCarthy, and Leopold (94). An interesting characterization in the book is of wolf biologists, who live lives of "divorce, nervous breakdown, and suicide" (14), which has no sound statistical bearing beyond the rest of our tendencies toward these states. Their job seems to take on all the intensity of air traffic control. We meet Ruth Michaels, the requisite New Yorker, who opens a cappuccino bar (15), and Bill Rimmer, the Animal Damage Control field agent who plays good cop with the ranchers and loggers to Dan Prior's desk-jockey bad cop.

History is mythified in the novel. Evans tells the legend of the "wolf skull road," a half-mile stretch built by wolf hunters as a monument to the extirpation of the wolf, apparently paved with skulls (77). There is a preacher named Josiah King, called the Reverend Lobo, who was also a wolfer and Indian fighter and who delivers a Matheresque sermon on the wolf as evil (82). Evans himself waxes poetic here, as when he refers to an 1886 freeze that killed cattle, after which the depredations were blamed on wolves instead: "So the wolf became Hope's scapegoat" (82). He refers to Roosevelt's rant against "the beast of waste and desolation" (83), and he pairs Indians and wolves in the vanishing breed mythos (297).

Evans brings us to the present with the offspring of Joshua Lovelace, his son J.J., a throwback from the early days of wolf hunting. Joshua was the wolfer hired to take out the "last few," the inventor of the "Lovelace Loop," the trap that will take them out (84). J.J. will now set out to kill the pack that Luke and Helen observe. Pages 257–79 give us his profile, including one description of him as a "ghost" (271). He kills a pup on Christmas Day, but in a nearly direct quote from Leopold he hesitates about it because his heart's not in it (331). He reads only the Bible (338). At the novel's end, "no trace of the old man himself was ever found" (432).

Someone loses a dog. Luke knows of the wolf pack before anyone else does, and knows that the big black alpha killed the dog. The chase begins, with the love story girding it up as we go. All the while, the Calders are metaphorically cast as a kind of wolf pack, Buck's supercharged hormones and the "Calder gene pool" qualifying him as the alpha male (27). Calder refers to the wolf as a "killing machine" (36), while casting himself as a sex machine. Hunting is sacred to him, profane to his son (98–104).

The wolf den site is Shangri-La, a return to the primitive past of Montana's history, and a haven for Luke, who doesn't fit in with the world of the bold and eloquent and civilized (22, 60, 97). Helen is the college-educated liberal activist who falls for the young Luke while, of course, she is in a relationship with a biologist named Joel, whose work studying horseshoe crabs keeps him a convenient distance from Montana. She is, along with every other human being in the novel, pretty. She is working on her thesis that cattle depredation among wolves is "more learned than inherited" (48). Her "longest relationship with a male" is with her dog, Buzz, who was, typical of the novel's superlatives, "the ugliest dog in the pound" (51).

As the plot continues, Luke secretly subverts the efforts to prove the existence of the wolves, moving carcasses and running various forms of interference to protect them. Helen comes to participate, develops friendships with Prior and Rimmer, and is eventually referred to in town as "the wolf lady" (124). The widowed alpha female, now radio-collared, takes over the remains of her pack (259). Luke begins studying to become a wolf biologist. The "call of the wild" happens for Buzz the dog (330–31). Everyone has affairs. Here's the way they work: "Luke? Hold me. Please hold me" (301). In a wincer of juxtaposition, Evans follows a sex scene between Helen and Luke with Luke going into the field, "slithering down into the hole" of a wolf den and thinking it a fine place to die (347). He does nearly die, and the novel also has a false death and the bathos of return (432). At one point, someone is kneed in the groin (356). You get the picture. In time some wolves are killed, but the Montagues and Capulets lose to the lovers, who drive to Minnesota as sunlight shines through the bullet holes in the road sign that reads "Hope (population 519)" (434).

I cite these many examples of the pulp romance because I have mentioned several times the tendency for the wolf book to submit to them. *The Loop* is perhaps the best example of a book that nearly succeeds, but is overwhelmed by its own dedication to the conventions of the Harlequin romance in its effort to capture the tremendous force of mythic wolf images. The most impressive thing about this novel is the amazing thoroughness of its wolf symbol shopping list. A near précis of the ghost wolf is planted into the heads of hundreds of thousands of readers in an accessible and powerful script. It's not that the brow is low so much as that the heart is pure at the end of each cliché. All the wolf we want to know is here on the page, and that might strangely do more for the wolf we *don't* want to know than long treatises on hegemony or the subaltern or discourse communities. A heavy degree of deprogramming still needs to happen, but pulp fiction using the ghost wolf to this effect may finally save more wolves than ecocritics can.

Hunter's Paradise

A step up from Evans's book is Rick Bass's *Where the Sea Used to Be.* I'll give it less treatment because it's less about wolves, because it doesn't contain the catalog of sources that Evans does, and because it didn't reach quite the audience that Evans did, so its effect in terms of articulating the myth to America isn't quite as powerful. While the prose is better, *Where the Sea Used to Be* suffers from the opposite problem of Evans's novel. Rather than pithy and light, the book bogs down under the weight of overtly sustained metaphors, long expository passages on geological history, and a plot that worked well in its short-story version (published in *The Sky, the Stars, the Wilderness*) but is grown ponderous with meat in its novelization.

Bass's novel is remarkably like *The Loop:* In Old Dudley we see another larger-than-life patriarch with an unquenchable libido, compared repeatedly to both a falconer and a continent (though, thankfully, to neither a rhizome nor a plateau). The novel is about a family of conflicted politics, people torn between ethical systems that value the land according to its yield for human beings (Dudley) or its intrinsic value (Dudley's daughter, Mel). Bass's strength is in writing about place, so the Swann Valley is the strongest active agent in the book. Like Evans, Bass supplies the novel with a love triangle that runs parallel to Old Dudley's plotlines of lust and oil drilling and his long geological soliloquies. Bass has an understanding of the craft of fiction and has written some well-received short stories, but in the novel, the implausible devolutions into bad love-writing (see especially 361–62) and the sledgehammer metaphors finally cost him. One example relevant to an ecological reading is Bass's overt juxtaposition of birds' mating songs with the love interest between Mel and a geologist named Wallis. The comparison risks being corny enough on its own, but the metaphor then turns inappropriate to the sentiment. Wallis, Bass writes, had heard that birds would sing so vigorously "that their vocal cords would burst" and they then "sang blood" (288–89). In addition to the metaphor poorly serving Bass even if he were trying to get across the notion that Wallis's love was self-destructive (which is not the context), it misses the fact that birds don't use vocal cords to sing, but sing through the use of the syrinx.

Comparable to Evans's Luke Calder, there is an innocent young boy primitive named Colter (a favorite name of Bass's), who "hitched his power to the rising springtime as if in lockstep and harness with it" (290). Colter develops an intimate relationship with Mel and trades tricks with her about the natural world. All of the characters in Bass's book are field types, but on the line of lab to field, with Wallis being lab, Colter is fully field, seeking his knowledge in the untamed places (181) and refusing to essentialize animals (106).

The falconer metaphor refers to Dudley's ability to both train and wear out the workers who come to help him on a fruitless quest to find oil in the valley, and to the predatory destruction of the land they perform to fulfill that quest. In Dudley we have a more complicated character than Buck Calder, who is a cartoon, but Bass certainly isn't constrained by verisimilitude either. The book contains, for instance, an immaculate conception (312) but without fully adopting magical realism. The Swann Valley's active agency flirts with the phantasmic moral center of one of Gabriel García Márquez's novels but doesn't finally take the plunge, so the fantastic and rhapsodic elements simply seem out of step with the novel's many passages of heavy verisimilitude rather than in harmonic cooperation with them (as we would find in magical realism).

Bass writes a voice for Old Dudley so disjunctive as to border on a multiple personality disorder, and there are occasional lapses in point of view so that we can't tell if the cryptic rationalisms that punctuate the book are a character's or the narrator's. A particularly disturbing example of this last craft element is one in which someone botches the killing of a deer on a hunt:

> For a moment, Wallis saw it all with clarity, as with a sudden gust of wind that brings new scents—an understanding, where before there had not even been a question. He saw how the long, sleepy moments of things lie in calm stretches, eddies, which we continue to believe are peaceful, serene moments—nothing more than slow passages of time—but which are really only a coiling and deepening in preparation for the sudden, near-frantic weaves and pursuits—the lusts. He saw how in the hunt, it all falls into place—how all the elements that seemed previously to be meaningless become now spurred into action: how every element, every atom, has meaning—and how this is the perfect desire of nature, the moment toward which all waiting, which is not really waiting, moves. (26)

This is indeed a novel of lusts, and the big one, vying only with Dudley's satyrlike libido, is hunting. A corpse reposes nearly every five pages. The above passage, at first acceptable enough as Wallis's observation, stands on a foundation of free indirect discourse, didactic truth-telling about the order of things. The metaphysical consciousness of Ahab, for whom "every atom has its cunning duplicate in mind," is here in the consciousness of Wallis, but presented as a sermon inseparable from the narrator's "objective" position. The "perfect desire of nature" is declared perhaps ironically, given that the deer in the hunt is made a mess of, but we can't really tell if the irony is deliberate, because the prose doesn't distinguish the surface from the depth. The abstractions of "waiting which is not really waiting" or "near-frantic weaves and pursuits" are red herrings, dodgy constructs of a quasi-philosophy that confuse how *this* lesson was gotten from *that* moment.

If two people sit down to tell a story in *Where the Sea Used to Be,* it will be about either oil or hunting, briefly interrupted by either sex or wolves. Not a bad set of subjects, but these characters are, to a person, monofocal, driven, obsessed. And they are certain. As with Mel's notion of the truth about death or Wallis's epiphanic clarity on hunting, none but a few tertiary characters in the novel are ever more than briefly unsure. The deeper layer of this book, perhaps intuited by the author, is that we see a conflict of relentless truths colliding in an environment of fact; but neither the exposition nor the necessary scenic cues reveal that such knowledge influences the narrative. Indeed, hunting is declared as the glue that binds the universe, and by page 223, a little more than halfway through, the wolves have to some extent been co-opted as representative hunters, symbols for the great truth that Wallis has ostensibly reached about all of it falling into place.

The wolves rise in visibility, but not necessarily in corporeality, as the novel progresses (the first sighting is on page 199). Indeed, they take on increasing totemic value as well as economic value in conflict with the land ethic of the oil drillers (again, similarly to Evans's conflict between ranchers and wolves). There are some moments of poetry in Bass: A map painted on hide used to pinpoint potential oil sites is transformed into a map to locate and protect the valley's wolves, for instance (culminating on 333), or a passage describing a bear searching for ants powerfully invokes the ancient world (326). Evans simply isn't up to this level of craft, but then Bass is spotty, so when the prose slips (as in Dudley's characterization or the didactic missives on hunting), the breakage is more severe. Bass's wolves are largely peripheral to the plot, as they are often peripheral to the plot in the human world, and when the brief verisimilitude of their world works best it adds a great deal to the story, offsetting the hyperbole that seems to govern the human plotlines.

Mel studies wolves, as an amateur, and spends her time tormented by her affections. She teaches schoolchildren about wolves and ecosystems (for example, 215) and so gives us part of the corporeality of the novel (the rest being the narrator's own provided glimpses into wolf behavior, for example, 200). She does this, however, with a dose of Emersonian Over-Soul metaphysics (104) and, outside the classroom, reveals a New Age sensibility that runs some risk, again because of a fuzzy point-of-view moment. About a deer being shot and crawling "a hundred yards or farther to die under the cedars," she says: "Scientists will give you some mumbo-jumbo about physiological responses, that the cedars are darker and cooler. They'll talk about thermal regulation and reduced fucking phototropism. The truth is simpler. The deer are leaving this layer of earth and are going to the next kingdom, and the cedars are a bridge between those two worlds" (36). These sensibilities come to make her the catalyst for the ghost-wolf element in the novel, a woman running with ghost wolves. This passage is perfectly representative of the Scylla and Charybdis facing academics—the behaviorism and quasi-philosophical assumption that tend to govern, respectively, the sciences and humanities.

Mel is described as a "green woman" (17) whose infertility (240, 267), is at one point given a lunar context (240–41). She follows wolf tracks backward through snow, so as to find patterns in their travels without disturbing them, which also means that she spends years tracking wolves "never knowing even the color of the animals she was following," imagining one of them to be "the color of smoke," and "not seeing the real thing" (94). In her need for open space to think and heal, she wonders if "the wolves were not but an excuse to be drawn out across the landscape" and follows them "almost dreamily" (96). A wolf shows up in town, disappears, and appears later; it is, at one point, conflated with Mel in her partings with love and society (298). Another wolf appears chasing a horse, then disappears (240–47). These are representative ghost images; that is, the corporeality in them is in the way the images of the novel are true to many experiences people have viewing wild animals. The animal appears briefly and disappears, moves into its own spaces and away from us—a cougar's tail disappearing into the rocks, or a reflection of light off a fox's eyes—one of the reasons we use the word *elusive*. Wolf passages that are most surreal in Bass are often most representative. Dudley has a wolf hallucination followed by his hearing the howls of "real wolves" (277–78).

One evening at a typical feast, after the villagers "ate until the meat was gone—and then they carried all the bones and carcasses off into the woods for the ravens and coyotes to help themselves to," the "villagers disappeared like wolves into the smoke." Mel thinks "how even if one day the wolves were gone from the valley there would still for some short time afterward be the echo or shape of a thing like wolves" (386). The juxtaposition shouldn't be missed here. Taken at face value, what's left of the wolf is the rationalization of humans eating meat and sharing it beneficently with the rest of nature; that is, whatever the position on hunting as sacred or gluttonous and whatever the cooperative spin on the sacred-game concept, the village hunter is finally the arbiter of the wild wolf's rights to land and livelihood in the so-called circle of life. If we get rid of them, at least their ghosts will survive, which is beautiful as long as they are the ones dying and we are the ones eating.

The Wolves behind the Wolves

Except for Peter Matthiessen's "The Wolves of Aguila," Wallace Stegner's "The Wolfer," the first third of Cormac McCarthy's *The Crossing,* and a few moments of brilliance in otherwise unremarkable stories, modern wolf books don't show many signs of literary merit. But they're loaded with anima and animus, thunderous invocation of earth archetypes, and (the prerequisite for both) biological and ecological referentiality. The legacy of Jack London is a mandala composed of his own subjective struggle over the wolf, husky, and hybrid in relation. That he also struggled over most of the major strands of political and psychological thought that completely reconfigured human culture during the nineteenth century only augments this dog/wolf struggle. But his first concern of dog to wolf and back does not function as merely symbolic or metaphoric of his second set of concerns. These struggles are integral for London, which implies the possibility of their being integral at base. The wolf as a political animal, in the London tradition, appears in each one of the writers I have just mentioned.

It may not be impossible to write a wolf book today without instigating thoughts of Jack London in a reader, but as we can see in Evans and Bass it is certainly difficult, evidence of an antiquarian artifact source that supplies our future relationship with wolves. For all the assumptions that London's dog books fit into a testosterone-driven adventure model, we can see by now that they are every bit as much about domesticity, particularly through subjugation. The juxtaposition of the wild and domestic in his dog books, prepared in the early story collections, is the prime mover of their plots. In writing the domestic novel's codes of household, tameness, convention, comfort, and etiquette into a novel presenting on its surface the codes of hard determinism in the wilderness, London accomplishes a dual feat. First, he marries naturalism to the romance by applying stereotypically feminine codes to a masculine cultural environment (less skillfully than, but similar to, Melville's men at sea or Whitman's body politics). Second, he raises an important issue in the shaping of American attitudes toward wolves and dogs—the knotty problem of distinguishing wild from tame.

However, in London's brand of atavism is found the greatest obstacle to his fiction's connecting us to the world—more specifically, to his wolf's connecting us to real wolves. Atavism is an inward-focused symbolism prone to high levels of, perhaps paradoxically, both narcissism and essentialism. We should see a circular relationship here: The essence of the beast to be found in the depths of the human psyche, mined and brought up from those depths to influence our behavior, is the invocation of a god within. To define this essence, to name it, we engage in symbolic thought. The wild man in me is the wild man before me but also the wild man of my making; it must take the shape, the archetypal image, that I give the raw essential form of the Wild Man archetype. My shaping of the Wild Man archetypal image leads to the incorrect postmodern assumptions that we cannot "see naturally"; that our shaping of the image is by necessity a collective invention; that our shaping of the image is the same as the shaping of the archetype itself; and that nature is an undefinable thing of our making. But the archetype itself is shaped *from* the realm of nature—the world preceding and superseding my design. It's not that I don't see naturally, it's that I don't write, or paint, or build violins "naturally." Those are artifacts, shapings of the archetypal image, not of the original form. We didn't invent the eye or its neural connection to the brain, any more than we invented the wolf at which we're looking. Whether I do or do not acknowledge and include the intrinsic necessity of this natural origin is the difference between a healthy archetypal image and an anemic one.

Once I accept an intrinsic image, I will tend as well to adopt, to accrue, a symbolism that supports that image's original condition before and beyond my conception, one that sustains it, gives it muscle and force to be carried outside of me and applied back to its own world. I may do this whether or not I have gathered a single natural fact about it. To the extent that I make the world conform to my preconceived ideas about it—especially about its value to my psyche—I will engage in that paradoxical interdependence of narcissism and essentialism. In the ultimate civilized reversion to infantile thought, the world becomes a sphere designed by a god for me or, if undesigned, then a thing for me by virtue of god's absence and my own clever self-service, whirling around me and funneling its resources to me, manna from heaven, gold in them thar hills, bricolage.

And so, in this metaphoric realm, the Saussurian "tree," that symbol of symbol making for semioticians, loses its viability, not because language lacks referential meaning but precisely because it possesses that quality. Perhaps his "tree" remains an oak to service the needs of oak symbolism I and my culture craft (for example, an oak "is" strength, endurance, the acorn a child developing, the old oak a geriatric wise man); perhaps it remains *that* oak, in my yard, as an individual, so long as it services my individuality. My connection to the oak through archetypal symbolism disconnected from the world of the oak is narcissism, because it denies the hard fact that I may be responsible for an oak's use but not its origin and asserts that I am its arbiter, creator, steward (but without a lord), that its soul is mine. Meanwhile, an actual oak of the world that has grown and lives according to systems I did not design and with which I can only interfere, its own lord, might teach me lessons I can neither comprehend nor would want to incorporate into my sense of self.

So a wolf becomes a representative of wilderness, or power of some various forms, or family values, or of hunger, death, demonic possession, depending on the convenience of both individuals with vested interests and cultures that institute and influence, even reshape, those interests. Through our attachment to symbolism as a mechanism of writing, we at once engage the highest form of language and (perhaps because of having done so) flirt with natural disaster on the grandest scale. Metaphors that essentialize any aspect of the nonhuman world create a shockwave of influence on the psyches of those who are taught the metaphors, one that provides the means to eliminate that aspect—even to love it to death.

CHAPTER SEVENTEEN

She-Wolves

Ecofeminism has likely done more important and consistent work in the political theater than it has in literary study, but one thing it does provide in criticism is a chance to radically revise how we read animal fictions.[1] Especially when coupled with the close attention to oppressive language and essentialism found in studies of ethnicity and feminism proper, ecofeminism provides a rubric that helps us conceive of consequences resulting from our misguided assumptions about animal cognition and behavior. When the connections are examined as thoroughly as in, say, Carol J. Adams's *Neither Man nor Beast* (one of the best works available covering the similarly oppressive systems affecting both gender and species), Marina Warner's or Annis Pratt's insightful essays on myth, or the work of Karen Warren and Nisvan Erkal, then widely accepted conventions regarding the subjugation of animals meet a thoughtful and powerful opposition. When the connections are run through retrograde and romantic counterattacks against science or narrative as *essentially* patriarchal and oppressive regimes—conflating the politics of those in a discipline with the raw material studied by the discipline—they are of far less worth.[2]

From the writer's perspective, the anthropological language employed by Jean Auel and Elizabeth Marshall Thomas, the animal ethology adopted by both Thomas and Vicki Hearne, and the psychological appliances of Clarissa Pinkola Estés all offer us some useful ways of considering our own histories and cultural mores. They too often do so by committing the very sin they wish to purge from the patriarchy, which is the essentialism and domination of women compared (in such ecofeminist works as Kolodny's and Merchant's) to the domination of nature. They do so by romanticizing, thus essentializing and dominating, animals.

Vicki Hearne's work is certainly not feminist per se, but her comments on animal behavior have been adopted by Thomas in fiction and essay work with the empowerment of women as a major theme, and spread in such venues as Susan Sontag's edited annual of *Best American Essays*. In the latter, a Hearne essay appears that justifies wild-animal captivity on the grounds that an animal who lives longer in the compulsory domestication of a zoo lives better (206). This assertion runs contrary to the politics espoused by, say, Renée Askins, who writes, "Caged animals are not wild, any more than a Hopi vase decorating a restaurant is sacred" ("Shades of Gray," 375). Hearne's essay "Justice in Venice Beach," appearing in *Intimate Nature* (Hogan, Metzger, & Peterson, 187–88), also implicates her as an opportunist on several counts, including her allegiance to the American Kennel Club and her tendency toward a sexist didacticism.

The primer material in some wolf books seems to be written less with the goal of our understanding wolves than with the goal of understanding human tendencies, assumptions, affinities, and (emphasized in wolf books) myriad forms of cruelty. Elementary information about wolf ethology, ecology, ritual, symbology, and cognition always addresses and often generalizes the same two themes: domesticity (for humans, domestication for wolves) and wildness (internalized for the human, externalized for the wolf). When we are disabused of the essentialist notions that "wolves mate for life," that "only the alpha pair mates," that "a wolf has never killed a person in North America," and that "they only hunt the sick and old"—let alone that they freeze the blood with their gaze or never stop eating or guard sleeping vampires—then we are forced to ask why we ascribed such referents to wolves in the first place. The accrual of wolf stories over time seems to indicate that they raise quite sharply the question "Why did I think that?" as often as "What should I do?"

When we gender an animal story, the question of domestication becomes the more bewildering, because we now infuse nonhuman systems with human gender issues. Domesticity is a fundamental biological proclivity in many species, an uncomfortably hard fact for certain political animals to handle.[3] Its fortunate trait is that the domestic sphere of much of the nonhuman world isn't gendered female but is a condition transcending gender. However anthropomorphically or allegorically an animal character may be written and its domestication cast in human terms, to some important degree all characters are crafted from real figures in the world, some of whom may be highly domestic in practice. They may also be highly androgynous, follow codes utterly foreign to us, and adapt to cultural influences. We tend to leave ourselves with symbols transformed by symbols, where the real referents—both the wolf and the woman—are impossible to recognize. Finally the structure is so worn, so molded into a nondescript shape, that we can't tell goats from wolves, men from women, wilderness from civilization. What is to be celebrated about those conflations must be carefully specified, and the method by which we break down the boundaries of gender must contribute to our transcendence of gender, rather than limiting itself to the violence of the breakage, in the forms of mere redress or vindication. Otherwise, we tend to claim both our constructs and their destruction as reality, rather than as the fabrications and manipulations they are.

Wolf biologists try to distinguish "domestication" from "socialization." The distinction seems obvious when the contrast is between a dachshund (domesticated) and a captive wolf in Wolf Park (socialized), less obvious with the wolf in Wolf Park and the wolf in Yellowstone National Park, and a little less obvious still between the Yellowstone wolf and one in the Northwest Territories that no human has ever seen, let alone "habituated" (another tricky term in the mix). There is the question raised by such writers as David Quammen about zoo animals: Is a wolf in the zoo or research park really a wolf? The question is predicated on behavior as an effect as much as a cause: To what extent is a wolf defined by his or her actions, his or her life? What vestige of the lupine endures in a zoo wolf? It is difficult, if not impossible, to see the domestication of the wolf into the dog without invoking certain gender codes of subjugation as well—right down to the soubriquet "bitch."

The domestic novel was long the province of women in America, often denied the merit of craft, as in Nathaniel Hawthorne's frequently cited attack against the "damned mob of scribbling women" outselling him (see Baym, 21; Matthiessen, x; Pattee, 110; Myerson, xiv; Hawthorne's original letter in Charvat et al., 17:304). Far more threatening, however, to the patriarchal construction of gender codes than the woman writing from the domestic sphere is the woman warrior, the woman who breaches this sphere. She has not often enough been examined in the context of wilderness, and when the connection is made, it is perhaps too often in terms of Earth Mother or Mother Nature.[4]

The protofeminist totemization of the wolf is a qualitatively different archetypal incarnation from the wolf mother of ancient patriarchal (even if matrilineal) myths. The powerful global network of militaristic leaders descended from, adopting or adopted by, or being suckled by wolves was a domestication of the wolf symbol. It assumed a sex that was then gendered: The wolf mother could not be *owned* but had to be positioned to establish the patriarchy, and separately from the dog. The descent of a great leader from a lupine material lineage occurs all the way back to Odysseus, whose grandmother was a werewolf, who felt quite deeply for his dog back home, and whose own epic inspired the later saga designed to mythically shore up Roman culture. It occurs as well in Aeschylus's *Agamemnon*; in the Median-Persian Cyrus, whose story is similar to that of Romulus and Remus; and in Herodotus (Burkert, 109). When the wolf mother transforms *herself*, however, what we see is the completion of the wolf myth in the fullness of its gendering, a power greater than the controllable separation of the archetypal mother and warrior images. Conducted with an acknowledgment of the real wolf behind the myth, the revision of the male model (which historically denies wolves their factual existence, demonizing them and destroying them) completes itself in a lasting and fundamental form. By avoiding the tendency to abstract and essentialize The Wolf toward a feminist political end, instead letting the reality of wolves influence the social construct so that it can live with the world, the feminist political end is better served.

Through to the late 1990s, books by American women that featured the wolf as a prominent figure were, for the most part, popular gothic romances (for example, Ann Arensberg's *Sister Wolf* and such werewolf novels as Alice Borchardt's *Silver Wolf* and *Night of the Wolf* and Kelley Armstrong's *Bitten*). The major exception is Lois Crisler and her field reportage in both wild and semidomestic spaces (for example, *Captive Wild* and *Arctic Wild*). The romances emphasize erotic and sublime elements recontextualizing the Victorianism still influencing modern societal gender codes and reading predilections. Crisler's essays break into a world of field study dominated by men and by masculinist prose and represent those studies even as they revise them—around the same time that Rachel Carson's work would do the same in pesticide use and, better but less famously, in oceanography. Through Arensberg's subtle craft the wolf is alluded to but seldom employed, as opposed to the prose in Borchardt, which combines high affectation with the exploitation of the wolf as a purely imaginative figure to produce a gothic romance of the werewolf that is aesthetically almost unbearable. In Clarissa Pinkola Estés and Diane di Prima, "the wolf" is twisted conveniently into what it needs to be in order to empower women through a psychotherapeutic model too often having very little to do with wolves but nonetheless referring to them with the semblance of authority and fact, a subtler form of exploitation than the purple romance, but equally anthropocentric.

Wolf writing by women has produced four literary events, all regarding the wild/domestic schism. The first is the rendering of a feminist prehistory and the application of a feminist primitivism in fiction, handled most popularly and adeptly by Jean Auel and Elizabeth Marshall Thomas. The next is a feminist psychology in the woman-warrior mode, popularized by Clarissa Pinkola Estés (but also having some roots in earlier Jungian myth criticism by such writers as Pratt and Nor Hall or Wiccan writers such as Starhawk) and in Diane di Prima's book-length poem *Loba*. The third is the rise of the woman wolf biologist, a polymath who has to an important degree remythologized both the wolf and field biology without sacrificing scientific rigor; three prominent figures are Lois

Crisler, Renée Askins, and Diane Boyd. To this third section I add an excellent essay by the literary scholar Jody Emel called "Are You Man Enough, Big and Bad Enough?" which I will discuss at length later in this chapter. Finally, through Kelley Armstrong's novel *Bitten,* the she-wolf as a female werewolf constitutes the fourth event. It should be seen from the variety and foundational significance of these four gates into the subject that the matter of gender is as multivalent and influential on the craft and consequence of the ubiquitous wolf book as it is anywhere else. The wolf book is not merely the province of adventurous and atavistic men.

Nor are Askins and Boyd the only women currently working in wolf biology; Jane Packard's and Cheryl Asa's works appear in Mech and Boitani's *Wolves: Behavior, Ecology, and Conservation,* which cites several women in wolf biology. Mollie Beattie, who worked many years in Yellowstone prior to the reintroduction, is the woman for whom the Mollie's Pack is named, and a number of the young biologists working in the park system are women (Erin Clear was a great help to me during the summer of 2002). Crisler is perhaps the earliest of women biologists to popularize the wolf against its malevolent ghost persona, and I recommend her, along with Askins and Boyd, because of their publications outside of scientific writing. Through their work, several arguments about the gendering of science, assumptions about essentialism, and the contributions of women to field biology are addressed.

In the Pleistocene adventures of Auel and Thomas the difficulty of depicting prehistoric thought, language, and relationships links with totemism toward a highly symbolic application of animals to gender politics, which we can readily accept in the context of light fiction. These writings are influenced perhaps too strongly by anthropology over ecology; they also rely too heavily on the ethos of bibliography over the logos of fictional craft to accomplish their goals. However, Auel's and Thomas's efforts to re-create, to represent, finally count toward the importance of their work at least in its influence on readers to learn more about origin, prehistory, and wolves. That is, their anthropology is sound.

A conclusion reached by these literary events of women's wolf writing seems to be that the *science*—the found fact, the realizable research articulated in an accessible prose, especially a prose bent on something other than conquest or opportunism—produces the needed corrective work that should influence fiction, but that genre fiction provides opportunities for a new gender politics to emerge from stories by using science loosely. This is a gendered craft technique visible at least since Mary Shelley's *Frankenstein.* In addition, the scientific approach, particularly in Askins and Boyd, is in flagrant opposition to the sexist characterization of women's writing as somehow "intuitive" to the detriment of its credibility. Strengths and weaknesses in the prose style and in the tendency to assume on the basis of little experience or sparse data seem to be the same for both male and female writers of wolf books, further indicating that the ghost wolf as a totemic image transcends gender. Therefore, the gendering of wolves in literature should be considered as an effect and manipulation of the real wolf akin to any other such effect. To what end that manipulation is conducted will determine the work's efficacy, not only according to its articulation of the non-human world but also according to what that articulation reveals about the credibility of its gender politics.

The Long Ago

During the 1980s a handful of best-selling novels set in the Pleistocene combined a realist approach to the ancient world populated by Ice Age megafauna with a once-upon-a-time tone of high fable. This subgenre served as a corrective to the typically romantic and sexist treatments prior, from Edgar Rice Burroughs's *Lost World* to Michael Crichton's *Jurassic Park* or *Congo,* the latter writer bringing up to date only the gee-whiz technology of the era while maintaining the pablum of the prose. The advent of the new Lost World fiction would turn to anthropology and revisionist history for its sensibilities and rethink the homogeneity of other approaches. Meanwhile, the wane of myth criticism in American universities was supplanted by a methodology that curtailed the pursuit of cultural and intellectual history under myth's influence.

In this context a popular conjuration became the new Earth Mother figure, who was then liberated from her spherical roles of incubation, birth, and envelopment into the freedom of muscle and adrenaline that also retained the best of the Earth Mother's traits: the compassionate intellect, the Arcadian lore, the clarity to circumvent war with ritual. Jean Auel's novels in particular gained the attention of both academy and marketplace for a time, offering a feminist revision of perhaps the most testosterone-saturated of worlds. The woman *of* men became a woman *among* them, experimenting with plausible behavioral and political options for historicizing prehistoric societies. In adopting the male totems and transmogrifying them, regendering them, both Auel and Thomas tapped the language of a growing Wiccan subculture, the resurgent interest in primitive psychology, and a carefully selected mythology that helped them construct fantastic worlds rooted in research.

Primitivism moved from the favored experiment of artists in the essentialist Rousseauvian mold of the 1920s to a favorite context for the trinket-art, mass-produced opportunism of New Age sensibilities. The animal totem suffers from at least two kinds of appropriation: It is assumed to be fully codified and systematized as a way of forming tribal identities (as in a dream dictionary or symbol encyclopedia); or it is considered so fluid and subjective that it lacks any ritual criteria and is simply for sale (like much realist wildlife painting or assembly-line abstract soapstone sculpture by the imitators of "native" styles). Auel and Thomas fall prey to the former approach too often in their craft, but their efforts toward an anthropologically informed fiction based largely on archaeology makes the reading worth the energy.

The Long Ago—both for London in his obsession with the dominant primordial beast and for Auel and Thomas in their revisionist atavism—is not also the Far Away. It is not a fantastic world set on an invented land or in outer space. "Once upon a time" is asserted as a study in prehistory, a story in time before recorded time, in this world, on this land. The long ago's animal analogies to human society, gender roles, need versus greed, language, and cultural development are muscle on the bones of fact—whether metareferenced or bibliographically appended—the fantasy made more effective for its connection to the raw material of prehistory. This approach—especially when coupled with clichéd prose, recognizable tropes (such as euphemisms and phonetic, monosyllabic names), and romantic plot structures—has not only sold millions of such books but also packaged the subgenre of Pleistocene fiction with the essays of Thomas, Estés, and Jeffrey Moussaieff Masson. It is strange bedfellows with survivalist postapocalyptic primitivism, such as Streiber's *Wolf of Shadows* and Dickson's *Wolf and Iron,* and Jack Williamson's *Darker Than You Think,* a novel built on the premise that *Homo lycanthropus,* the werewolf, was an archaic (and magical) species (see Frost, 161–64). The Streiber and Dickson novels also feature women cooperating with wolves in order to survive the brutalities of desperate men and ravaged nature.

Importantly, Auel and Thomas do not contest or revise the aspects of primitivism, atavism, determinism, or symbolism present in the male wilderness adventure story. Rather, they cleverly employ those devices toward historical revisionist ends. Their work instigated a body of spin-off prehistoric fantasies that at once maintain and contest the feminine-gendered narrative (for example, W. Michael Gear, *People of the Wolf,* 1992, first in a series of seven). If we accept Joan Bamberger's thesis that there is no proof of an ancient or prehistoric matriarchal society (though there are matrilinear ones), then the works of Auel and Thomas classify themselves more strictly as fantasies. The wolf's totemic role is shaped by a compression of epochal time: speculation on the Long Ago story of the Pleistocene with the presentism of environmental and cultural politics, anthropology, and historicity. The wolf of such a story, certainly in Auel's work, becomes a thirty-thousand-year totem, an avatar, in this case of a feminine strength. The domestication of animals, a major subject in these works, thus puts the wolf in a highly volatile position as a fictional character, at once wild and domestic, masculinized and feminized, adopted and adapted, progenitor and property. What a writer says "happened" in that long ago, the generalizations made about comparative behavior, evolution, and domestication, especially in a gendered context, once more infuse the wolf myth in America with a layer of cultural assumption and belief.

Clan of the Cave Bear is more a bear story than a wolf story, and had Auel stopped there we would have had the Pleistocene epic of the Great Bear myth with some mentions of comparative hunting behavior. There are five massive books in the series, however, covering a long arc of the woman warrior Ayla's development. In *The Plains of Passage* she domesticates a wolf, whom she calls Wolf, implying the invention of the word. This ontological moment is typical of fantasy, since the genre is often built on unknown worlds that are renamed after their authors reassemble the raw material inspired by the known one. Here the temporal world is the unknown, and the naming is, ostensibly, the first naming of the material of the found world.

Ayla is a Cro-Magnon among Neanderthals, dropped into a dim society from her more enlightened background, and the ensuing story—including birth rites, hunting rites, ritual protection, and issues of political participation and ascendancy—reflects the importance of this developmental divide. "Many ages before," Auel writes, "men and women, far more primitive than Brun and his five hunters, learned to compete for game with four-legged predators by watching and copying their methods. They saw, for example, how wolves, working together, could bring down prey many times larger and more powerful than themselves" (*Clan of the Cave Bear,* 69). As important is where she takes this statement: By developing tools "rather than claws and fangs," human beings found that cooperation "prodded them along their evolutionary journey" (69). Like the campfire myth that wolves were fed and companioned little by little into a benign domestication, the tool-as-claw myth surfaces here as a singular evolutionary development and constitutes an adoption of the evolutionary biological origin for culture. This loose Darwinism (inspired by *The Descent of Man*) gives us a fictive situation that allows nature and culture to coexist in the book as parts of the same puzzle. Whether we have a representative moment of the natural origins of culture or a kind of feminist Spencerianism in the making is unclear in Auel's work, but it also isn't the province of fiction to settle such an issue.

Nurture, one of the Earth Mother traits retained by Ayla as over-woman, is placed as at once a biological imperative and a cultural divide. In a passage of several pages Ayla takes a rabbit into the cave to raise and care for him. She is berated by the patriarchy of the tribe, which has set up strict codes against caring for animals in the domestic space, in order to maintain the divide between the hunter and hunted (117–22). *Clan of the Cave Bear* also begins with a London-esque situation problematizing nature and nurture. Ayla is a "Child of the Earth" emerging from a "hide-covered lean-to" (1) and soon encountering a "cave lion" (8), her first totemic moment that will later affect her choice of mates in the clan (59). Her ability to combine hunting skill (of both prey and predator) with attractiveness as a mate also causes her to be seen by some of the men as transgendered; they wonder if she might be "part male" (257).

The Craft of the Canid

There are, with variations, two basic stories of the domestication of the wolf. The first I have called the "campfire myth," which goes something like this: During a hard winter, a tribe sits around the campfire eating meat; the wolves are starving and come near the fire; someone decides that rather than driving them off with brands or killing them, he will "make a friend," and offers some of the meat (a variation is that the wolves come around after the feast, eat scraps, and grow more languidly familiar until one is captured). In measures the wolf is tamed; over time wolves are variously bred for certain traits and become the breeds of dogs, on a par with the development of, say, cuisine or apparel.[5]

The second story is a bit harder and more direct: the wolf is trapped, caged, beaten into submission, put to work, bred for its optimum traits, and killed or abandoned to "turn feral" if the effort doesn't pay off. The liminal space between these mythogenic explanations, the one component they share that unites them, is that the wolf's offspring will be raised (or disposed of) in captivity. Here, it seems, is a pretty solid line between socialization and domestication. Our wild tribe may "get along" with wolves, but once we raise them and breed them over generations into deformity, conformity, and pathology (with all the attendant love, loyalty, familial affinity that we may comfortably extend), then we have dogs. In time, we use some of those dogs to hunt down wolves.

Ayla's domestication of Wolf is slightly more of the second order than the first, excluding the typical masculine cast of cruelty found in London. The patriarchal dominance model (still favored in nature programs that emphasize dominance, predation, mating, and aggression in wolves) is forgone for a nurturing, though still subjugating, approach. The original circumstances are characteristically masculinized, however. Ayla kills a mother wolf and takes the pelt, considering it in terms of both trophy and domestic gift (a scene we will see faintly repeated in McCarthy). What ensues from this act becomes a feminist plot thread when the codes of the tribe—the assumed lesser hunting prowess of women, the complex totemic codes about killing a predator, the taboo against bringing a predator into the cave (the household)—are all subverted in favor of Ayla's bildungsroman. The next three books of the series suffer from some repetition and decline in craft (a common flaw in fantasy series) and track Ayla's adventures as a tamer, healer, and warrior over miles of rough country and a few thousand pages with two horses, Wolf, and a human mate clearly her inferior. Ayla has become the Londonesque Love Master.

Her reputation is, finally, as a domesticator of animals; she is the apparent matriarch of the human race's claims to ownership of the broken horse and the pet wolf. Her approach is more of the whisperer, the nurturer, the empath—progressive, no doubt, so that we can't say that either the methods or the results are the same as in a masculinist dominating mode. The method of domestication, the level of cruelty versus compassion, certainly makes a significant difference in the text's message. In an ecocritical read, however, the celebration of Ayla's strength and independence is a bit suspect, given that the feminist accomplishment occurs ultimately at the expense of the nonhuman wild as much as in an embrace of it. We shouldn't play kill the messenger here; the animal domestication plot fulfills the historicity Auel constructs for her prehistoric story. But it provides us with the complexity of adopting the male model to subvert it while accepting that human accomplishment begins and ends with human comfort and conquest. It raises as well the inherent flaws of the utopian vision, giving the Earth Mother model the complicated internal dialogue it deserves. The result of Ayla's woman-warrior quest is, like White Fang's, still finally the questionable reward of the human domestic sphere and separation from the wild.

Where London tried to find the fundamental primitive in the modern world, Auel and Thomas try to find the fundamental primitive over and beyond presentist obstacles. This makes their limited uses of wolves in their fiction worth noting. Auel writes:

> The land was unbelievably rich, and man only an insignificant fraction of the multifarious life that lived and died in that cold, ancient Eden. Born too raw, without superior natural endowments for it—save one, his oversize brain—he was the weakest of the hunters. But for all his apparent vulnerability, lacking fang or claw or swift leg or leaping strength, the two-legged hunter had gained the respect of his four-legged competitors. His scent alone was enough to veer a far more powerful creature from a chosen path wherever the two lived in close proximity for very long. The capable, experienced hunters of the clan were as skilled in defense as they were in offense, and when the safety or security of the clan was threatened, or if they wanted a warm winter coat decorated by nature, they stalked the unsuspecting stalker. (*Clan of the Cave Bear,* 98)

Auel's project here is to cover at once all of the following: the myriad issues of an only vaguely realized ecological system; utopianism and the noble savage; the human's position in a larger, rawer world; and the development of culture and art. This is one of many paragraphs employing multiple narrative devices to sustain all of these threads in the building of this Lost World. She both ennobles and diminishes other animals in the developing human system, anthropomorphizing their "respect" for men (her default pronoun) under the assumption of cultural (especially violent) superiority as the determinant.

It is difficult for me to read the passage without irony, however. Grizzly bears, for example, certainly seem not to want human beings in close proximity in most cases, but "respect" has little to do with it. The conventional wisdom among rangers and biologists is that grizzlies just typically hate the smell of us; we reek of chemicals and synthetics and car. They come to us once they get that first toxic and addictive taste of processed food, and in short order subject themselves to being shot as "trash bears," habituated to humans in the ultimate profanement of the campfire myth.

Auel's narrator introduces us to two principal reasons for hunting predators: first, protection of the clan; next, fashion. In such a depiction we see where the wolf fits in the moral universe of her primitive society; it is at once a threat, a symbol of prowess, and (when dead) an object of art. Because hunting for fashion is sport hunting versus subsistence hunting, Auel's fictive prehistory indicates that the ghost wolf was alive in the primitive mind in other ways than purely spiritualized totemization. She pursues this thesis as she genders the wolf myth through a fashion that differentiates male and female adornment and power.

Lone Wolves, Women, and Wolf Packs

Elizabeth Marshall Thomas's *The Hidden Life of Dogs* was a best seller, praised by both George Schaller and Maxine Kumin (a combination of eminent scientist and renowned poet obviously chosen for the book's dust jacket). It focuses on canid behavior, especially canid-human behavior in the domestic realm, and gives us some insight into Thomas's prehistoric fiction as well, a body of work built on certain devices and assumptions conducive to anthropology but, despite Schaller's praise, at times overstated and proscriptive in a way that violates its purported realism. At base, both this book and *The Social Life of Dogs* are examinations of wildness tamed, and an effort to examine what translates from the wild life of the wolf to the domestic life of the dog.

"Why does a dog need high rank?" (30). This question follows the closing phrases of a preceding chapter partly about an abused dog in which Thomas refers to "dogs more fortunate than he, dogs who were wanted by their owners"

(29). We have a tricky juxtaposition, perhaps a contradiction, typical of *The Hidden Life of Dogs:* compassionate treatment of a pet is married to the assumptions that dogs need rank, that ownership is justified by this need, and that, apparently, the highest rank belongs to us. "Among dogs as among people," Thomas answers her own question, "there are many reasons" (30). Now we see that people need high rank as well, meaning that we need someone enthroned, since the nature of rank is that everyone can't have the same one. The conflation of what *is* with what is *needed* renders Thomas's assumptions about wolf and dog behavior subject to other overstatements. She tends toward a loose phraseology: "Among the wild canids and even among free-ranging domestic dogs, males of high rank are more likely than not to be selected for mating by females, while the rank of a female can make the difference between life and death for her children. Wolves know this, and dogs who are free to make their own choices show that they know it too" (30–31).

The label "free-ranging domestic dogs" is a troublesome one. The continuum of dogs from those living in confined spaces to those living feral lives has merited closer examination as civilizations continue to urbanize and expand and wilderness continues to shrink. But this is not quite what Thomas is saying. I think of the notorious stories of people leaving their dogs in closed cars in hundred-degree heat, or the feral dog who certainly roams widely but is, after all, bred to domesticity. These are two hard stories of cultural determinism more than of differences in a dog's "freedom of choice" or the Call of the Wild. The rank of a female wolf "can" make the difference for her pups, yes, but what difference it makes is still too much a mystery for Thomas to build a case on it. For the lone female in Yellowstone who dispersed from her pack with her two pups and lived separately but cooperatively near that pack, "rank" was largely a nonissue. Her behavior wasn't necessarily an exception to some rule; it seems to indicate that there aren't as often such hard rules as we'd like to assume for our comfortable arguments, and certainly that those rules aren't very easily converted either to domestic dogs or to domestic humans. We have to consider that these dogs who seem to need high rank universally lack it—they're all either owned or on death row. The idea offered, of "high rank among other dogs" (47), is a projection of one essentialist approach (the pack order) to another (that wild order translates to domestic order).

I am not arguing here with training methods. In order to have a dog as a pet, the consensus among those who have had the most, and most compassionate, success is that a "pack" order is necessary with the pet owner as alpha. Pragmatically speaking, this works, and it works far better than beating dogs into submission. I am arguing with the conflation of a wild state with a domestic one, especially to the extent that the former is used to justify the latter so much that the domestication of wild animals starts itself to look like a wild (that is, the extension of a rationalized "natural") state. Dogs are already dogs when we start training them. They aren't wild, though they may be unruly. They may turn feral, but the wolf as correlative creates all kinds of ethical problems in human thought and action regarding canids.

Thomas's fiction follows the campfire-myth pattern, including a moment in *Reindeer Moon* when her primitives tie a domesticated wolf within a "ring of thick brush" around the campfire so as to prevent her mates from coming in to free her (362). The assumption that the pack would do so is built into the act, so that the actuality of tying the wolf naturalizes the assumption of the pack coming to the rescue. The domestication fantasy, certainly one full of emotional resonance, permeates this book as it does the Auel books, negotiating the images of the woman warrior with the domestic sphere as it is articulated through the taming of animals. In both Auel and Thomas, the woman as animal tamer asserts both the assumptions of female biological earth connection and political dominance. From either perspective, the potential for contradiction runs high, as does a very loose interpretation of evolution that incorrectly conflates it with breeding.[6]

Animal Wives

One important thing that the she-wolf book has produced is a transcendence of the mother/whore bifurcation of both wolves and women that was used to legitimize the city-state. No longer is the woman-wolf myth merely of the mother either suckling or exposing her children—as in the stories of Lycastus and Parhassius, Romulus and Remus, or Ataturk. Nor is she the harlot cast off by men seeking more virgins to turn to harlots, nor the wolf mother inheriting the bastard sons of absent parents (for example, Genghis Khan's mythic ancestor Borte Cino, "Gray Wolf," raised by a wolf mother). The warrior role has been adopted by the modern woman, in a mythic revision of an economic and political wave, rather than necessarily the other way around, and historical fiction is being rewritten to populate the mythic world with more sympathy for Medea, and with more Artemises than Aphrodites and Heras.

If a reader to this point in our study should still doubt the ghost wolf as a fundamental mythic archetype in the formation of American sensibilities about wilderness and literature, then now would be a good time to take stock. We have seen the wolf child, wolf mother, wolf warrior, wolf devourer or destroyer, and wolf mentor perform as archetypal images crafted in our own psychic image. We have seen the ensuing gender construction that is then always anthropomorphized and, as we have seen, frequently hermaphroditic, hybridized, at least androgynous. We find as well the theme of atavism, the pattern of the ancient given a combination of historic and presentist treatment (the balance between these influencing the story's vulgarization and popularization). This interest in the story of the ancient world in which humans were young and wolves already old is different from, though related to, the noble-savage story, contextualizing the wolf myth beyond ancient to modern Western thought. From our realization that there are such ancient stories, from the possibilities of prehistoric cultures as the founders of our mythology, come the later noble-savage stories that in turn usually lead to New Age appropriation and commodification of the primitive world. This pattern of appropriated atavistic primitivism gives birth to the anthropological/psychological collusion that we find in examinations of cultural rites and individual dreams, the sacred ground of the ghost wolf.

Diane di Prima's book-length poem *Loba* is a second-wave feminist effort at invocation of the wolf goddess, an effort that demonstrates the dangers of image appropriation and symbolism without the requisite respect for the real. Another problem is the second-wave argument asserted during an era ready for a more progressive diplomacy in art. As in Ann Arensberg's *Sister Wolf*, men in *Loba* are characterized as *inherently* weak, fragile, worthy mainly of condescension—Zeuses in their stomping childishness, at their very best merely gentle, to be fed to the destroyer persona that primarily characterizes the wolf goddess. In di Prima we read, "If he did not come apart in her hands / he fell like flint on her ribs / there was no middle way" (11). We read: "Is he in bondage? Does he bow / to her embrace? Her velvet claws / skid on his tender skin" (53). And: "for what else is man / but to span, like a wrought-iron bridge / what but to bind / the sky, unto the sky." Throw in the later pejorative use of "Animus" (264), and this goddess constructed of a cultural grudge is perhaps a fitting antithesis to London's apparent masculinism.

The publisher's blurb for *Loba* declares that it was "hailed by many when it first appeared in 1978 as the great female counterpart to Allen Ginsberg's *Howl*." Although one *Publishers Weekly* reviewer employs this blurb, I have not as yet been able to find the "many" that made the comparison to Ginsberg nor, in fact, any plausible comparison in subject matter, line, or tone. The blurb seems merely an effort to make *Howl* seem to have something to do with wolves as well, and to find a comparison within the beats for di Prima's literary identity. In terms of content and approach (though not construction), *Loba* is far closer to the work of Ted Hughes, whose mythic animals range widely in their verisimilitude and are as opportunistically gendered and anthropomorphized as di Prima's. Hughes is the more narrative poet, and his allusions are clear enough to connect that mythic thread to the wolves or crows that spawned his work. "Wolfwatching" is a titular realist poem that reverses Hughes's romances of *Lupercal* or *Crow;* it starts from the literal and refers to the mythic. Di Prima's howls invoke the myths with little regard for the physicality beyond the human woman necessary to pay the myths respect.

For a few stretches di Prima abandons the violent mannerisms that hold *Loba* together, and over the course of the book's sixteen parts she eventually covers several wolf myths: The Loba (an oddly chosen Spanish locution for a figure not at all Spanish) is a destroyer goddess (18, 25, 52, dormant for a time and returning in book XV as Kali); a mother and daughter (30, 33, 60), in which roles she is abused (69) and in which she is original mother Eve (139); a feminist pantheon of goddesses, including a roll call of 120 of them into which Loba is constellated, with special attention given to Lilith, Ishtar, Shiva, and Kali-Ma; heroines such as Helen, Guinevere, and Persephone—whose reprise poem ends the book; a dream (67, 82); and an urban denizen in the beat tradition (3, 12, 43, 90, 126, 219) who becomes more abstract, more galactic, over the book's second half. Loba in any of these incarnations is always, however, a ghost wolf. Not a corporeal wolf appears or is considered in the poem as having any connection to the goddess; to the contrary, cats consistently appear as conflated with canids (3, 48, 210, and in frequent uses of "hissing" by the wolf goddess). The Loba goddess is placed in Latin American venues both farther south than the range of wolves and in territory the cultures of which would be highly unlikely to invoke the wolf rather than the jaguar. Perhaps this is the hissing cat connection, which would be a powerful metaphoric device, but di Prima offers us no means by which to form that connection, not even a discernible pattern of juxtaposition.

Di Prima's poem is a holdover from the beat generation's style that she honed over two decades and more than thirty books. *Loba* was twenty-eight years in the making, generated first from a dream that spawned a few poems, then transformed into a poetic saga employing what di Prima calls "a wolf" or "wolves" but which is instead an entirely psychic construct of an amorphous goddess.[7] A characteristic of the beat style is justification of an image based on its globalization; that everything is connected to everything else makes it possible to simply call something everything else. The fallout of an otherwise admirable ecumenism is that it sometimes diminishes the systems it claims to empower. The same has happened with the loose use of *ecology* as a term indicating systems that prove interconnection and so relativism, which is no more ecology than a wolf goddess is a wolf if disconnected from the progenitrix. Di Prima asserts that metaphor is not a direct relationship but an amorphous, intuitive, "many-layered" one—thus defining something wonderful and fascinating to use for the generation of poetry, but which is simply not metaphor. She also employs the technique of direct contradition to allow herself total freedom with the image. In "Some Lies about the Loba" she lists:

> that she is eternal, that she sings
> that she is star-born, that she gathers crystal
> that she can be confused with Isis
> that she is the goal . . .
>
> that she is black, that she is white . . .
> that there is anything about her
> which cannot be said
> that she relishes tombstones (62)

An excellent potential critique of the ghost wolf, except that the Loba goddess of this saga does or is nearly all these things. She is eternal on page 33, connected to stars and crystal on 158 and 226, conflated with Isis on 54, and black on 123. The lie that there is anything about her that cannot be said is found in omission, or else Loba claims to have said it all; and a set of images on page 276 of the poem are grave ones indeed.

I may be risking a literalist reading that interferes with poetic license, but this is a necessary risk when bringing an ecological consciousness to bear on a work of art—similar to the risks associated with sussing out sexism, racism, or elitism that were taken in the process of radically altering the literary canon. With all structuralist/new critical (that is, potentially "literalist") dangers in mind, we have to ask a few questions of di Prima's application of the lie. If the lies told about Loba are being revealed and condemned as defamatory, then the fundamental traits (not merely anomalous actions) of Loba that make those lies true create a clever but artificial and unstable meaning that does nothing for the wolf but everything for the mythmaking human, mainly because nothing else in the poem's narrative aims us toward a meta-meaning that frees the wolf from the poet's own use. If the lies constitute poetic license, and Loba is having her fun with us by turning the lies true as a trickster strategem, or if this is an Ars Poetica that points to art (especially poetry) as a set of "true lies," then which lies are we to honor and which to beware? Lies about gendered inferiority are, it seems, to be fought. Lies of poetic opportunism seem to be permissible if only animals are appropriated. The Loba is what the woman warrior wishes her to be. I think we have to be aware that such freedom comes at the expense of the wolf that di Prima did *not* imagine, the unacknowledged source of her work finally and simply employed from and caged in a dream.

Di Prima's technique would be justifiable if it weren't for the position in which it puts the women united with a goddess that unmakes the wolf. I am not accusing di Prima of an absence of acceptable logic, which a poem is not obligated to employ. I am accusing the goddess of anthropocentrism, and the narrative voice of *Loba* as being in collusion with that exploitive goddess. To the extent that the poem is gendered (a considerable extent here), anthropocentrism poses an extra danger, because the logic that does adhere—the argument against images favoring the power of prejudice over the freedom from that power—may undermine the gender politics with the politics of human domination and appropriation of the animal.

I mentioned in the critique of poststructuralist theory that the free play with an image that has its counterpart as a living being in the physical universe is no less exploitive, however different in its brand of management, than hunting or breeding that animal. The possible benefit we gain from di Prima's approach is the contextualization of the wolf goddess legends in the greater goddess mythos—the attention brought to our dream thinking and to the issue of feminine power beyond its traditionally gendered constraints. This attention is most beneficial when it serves the corrective function of remythologizing beyond reactionary impulse. Di Prima gives us one half of a metaphor—the symbolic and therefore more dangerous half. She invokes the primal dream, the atavism of the ancient, but cannot control it sufficiently to include the wolf in the ritual that uses it. In *Loba* the voice for woman is strong enough, but no one speaks for wolf.

Women in the Field

The first appearance of wolves in Ann Arensberg's *Sister Wolf* is of a pack being released into a homemade wildlife preserve. Our main character, Marit, is a New England version of an old English character and lives in the world of the revived gothic. She rescues wolves from the Dangerfield Zoo and gives them sanctuary on her property (23–29). Eventually the wolves play an important part in the story, and during the denouement the narrator takes the opportunity to sum them up:

> Wolves are frauds, and the language abets them. A lewd man is a wolf; greedy followers have wolfish appetites. The wolf at the door is poverty, cold and starvation. Liars cry wolf; lone wolves are unsocial and ominous. A famous murderer was nicknamed the Wolf of Buxton. The popular image of a wolf is a false face painted with bloody fangs and pointed ears, and a ring of black outlining its slanting eyes.
>
> There is also no one around to puncture their bad reputation, although a man in Colorado once taught some wolves to sing, and another man claimed that they subsisted entirely on mice. Marit Deym never tried to defend them. She locked them up

and appointed herself their guardian. An optimistic person might have handed out leaflets explaining the place of the wolf in the ecological scheme, or the ability of wolves to form emotional attachments. Marit knew that her neighbors preferred the homicidal image, the way the people of Salem preferred to believe in witches. (183)

This is one of the finest assessments of American culture regarding the wolf to be found in fiction. It also raises the issue of women living in a world predominantly designed and managed according to male politics and explains the thick skin Marit finds it necessary to grow in order to take the realistic and critical position she takes. Her knowledge of folklore feeds her politics as much as does her pessimism. The forms of activism in question in *Sister Wolf* connect the sentence-level craft with a political environment that strengthens the corporeality of an otherwise highly romantic work. The book serves as a bridge from the arts to the sciences, to those later women wolf biologists whose "leaflets explaining the place of the wolf" are backed by lifetimes of research. It is through Marit's exposure of the ghost wolf, the "fraud" wolf, that some work of practical, applicable value may occur.

In the works of Crisler, Askins, and Boyd we see the conversion of biology to spiritually informed and accessible writing that combines the requisite corporeality with an understanding of symbolic and mythic thought. It is highly unusual for memoir or the naturalist essay to accomplish this task, and more such work should continue to improve itself, refine its language to a level of literary proficiency that pushes the gendering of the wolf book toward the transcendence of gender that wolves seem already to have achieved in their own societies.

In 1998 the writers Linda Hogan, Deena Metzger, and Brenda Peterson edited *Intimate Nature,* an anthology of essays on the theme enunciated in the book's subtitle, *The Bond between Women and Animals.* Six of the selections are on wolves and women. They include the Mary Tall Mountain poem "The Last Wolf" (which is noted during my analysis of Cormac McCarthy's *The Crossing*), Hogan's "First People," and Paula Underwood's "Who Speaks for Wolf." The book also contains tales invoking the native and ancient mythic codes of conduct with animals, a selection by Diane Boyd-Heger in a section called "Deep Science: Living in the Field," and selections by Peterson and Renée Askins in a final section titled "Bringing Back the Animals." The first three selections (Leslie Silko's "Story from Bear Country," Hogan's "First People," and Underwood's "Who Speaks for Wolf") are Native American creative pieces, the last three (Tess Gallagher's "Venison Pie," Ann Daum's "Coyote," and Brenda Peterson's "Apprenticeship to Animal Play") all invoke the role of science and fact in the potential for restoration— of wilderness, species health, and human spiritual growth.

Boyd-Heger begins her essay, "Living with Wolves," by explaining that for two decades she has "attempted to unravel the secrets of one of North America's most elusive carnivores, and in the process I have discovered many truths about wolves and myself" (90). Like Askins, she tracks her training, her confrontations with the ranch and other antiwolf communities, and her arrival on the site where she would spend most of her time at work—Glacier National Park and lower Canada. "During the early years of my research," she writes, "I was told it was not OK to have feelings for your study animals" (94). At this point the essay takes its best turn, as Boyd-Heger begins to question some of the assumptions about the culture of the profession. "I find that most 'tough guys' are somewhat disarmed by a forthright woman seeking an honest discussion," she writes, and explains that her credibility had to be earned among biologists as well as among those who would challenge inconvenient finds in biology by whichever sex (95). She then gives herself license to have those feelings (as in the earlier example on her loving wolves as the motive for her studying them), to rhapsodize on wolves a bit, and to do so with no loss of scientific rigor.

This is one of her great accomplishments—not just nearly three decades in the field and the long list of publications, team contributions, and knowledge of hard science, but the language of encouragement for women to offer "another perspective" to the field, through different problem-solving strategies and observations. One woman hired by Paul Paquet in Canada to conduct research on a pack "was unfamiliar with traditional beliefs about wolf pack social structure." She reported, to Paquet's surprise, that "the dominant female led the pack in behavioral interactions. It had been preconceived and previously reported by many researchers that the alpha male directs a pack's behavior" (95). One thing that should strike us about this account is that the phrase "traditional beliefs" does not refer to ancient tribal reference points but to the assumptions of scientists at times unprepared for what their discipline might do to correct itself, given the proper lens through which to look. Boyd-Heger is less concerned here with a science-studies approach that extrapolates from the politics of science a universal gender bias or a sharp drop in credibility than she is with something more . . . well, logical and scientific. She is examining the study in question and the revision of procedure to the benefit of scientific fact and data analysis. It is now quite common for observers of wolf packs to recognize that alpha females may sometimes be calling the shots, and there is a far lower tendency on the part of biologists (besides behaviorists) to essentialize wolf behavior. The failure of field biologists to recognize for decades the actual roles of female wolves both alone and in their packs may certainly be because of a gender bias in the profession, but that failure is finally rectified not by someone's differing politics so much as someone's clarity in understanding the referential language of wolves.

Perhaps the most important piece Boyd has contributed to the field is a page-and-a-half-long article on the possibility of ceremonial burial among wolves, which I have previously mentioned in the section "Ceremonial Burial" in chapter 5. I could quote nearly the entire article here, which makes it the more remarkable for its brevity. It requires a career spanning a quarter century to write such a piece, a boldness to report it and back it with the profession's rigor in the field. It imbues science with the right kind of magic, the kind born of myth and the revision of myth, part of its inheritance from such women as Crisler, Diane Fosse, and Jane Goodall, who worked against the sexism of their fields to enter the actual field. Boyd shares this inheritance with Renée Askins.

Crisler's *Arctic Wild* and Askins's *Shadow Mountain* have much in common. Both are memoirs of a woman's experience observing, caring for, and trying to save wolves. Both also reveal the language of their eras regarding these animals, the assumptions, latitudes, and scientific facts apropos of when they were written—Crisler's in 1958, Askins's in 2002. Comparatively, they demonstrate the arc of accomplishment and the progress of scientific knowledge over half a century, but they share the cooperative language of feeling and fact, and they pioneer for their times the woman writing from a "man's profession." The biggest difference is that the Crislers (Lois with her husband, Chris) in Alaska are far more hands-on in their interaction, coming to "own" wolves and socializing them (especially in *Captive Wild*). Askins, in Yellowstone, has the opposite goal, of seeing wolves run from her rather than to her, out of their transport crates and into the wilderness. She begins with wolves in captivity (in Wolf Park, Indiana) and ends as one of the Yellowstone team's point people for influencing public opinion.

Shadow Mountain is also the more literary of the projects. Askins's essay for *Intimate Nature* serves as a prologue to the memoir, which covers her life as a lover and researcher of animals. Her dogs and her work with captive wolves figure big in the first fourth of the memoir, but as she nears the Yellowstone assignment and the chance to reintroduce wolves to their former range, the book's language of advocacy takes on greater power. The case for wildness and wilderness as necessary and instructive conditions to a human life give the memoir its depth. The memoir is a genre prone by its very nature to solipsism. Like Thoreau, Askins solves the problem by placing the Self in the context of the raw material of an Other far beyond what the academic humanities have as yet been willing to confront. The wilderness is not some artificial designation for Askins, as much as she plays with the language used to define and control it. She examines as well the language of gender. Much of her memoir consists of Askins contending with the testosterone factor of both the science and antiscience communities, and her narrative is carried not so much by the content—an inspirational story about wilderness empathy common to young girls' coming-of-age essays—as by its enthusiasm and energy.

Askins's enthusiasm is contagious. Her memoir balances her (literally) public relations with humans and her more personal ruminations about wolves. Her ending encapsulates several issues I have raised in this study. Radio-collaring is one. The intrusion and surveillance of radio-collaring is tempered only by a loose rule that when the battery goes dead on a collar (about a six-year life), then the wolf might not be recollared (292–93). Natasha, a wolf we follow through Askins's story almost as closely as we follow the author's own life, has long worn a collar, which goes dead. By the time this happens, Natasha is also nearing the end of her hard life. Askins writes:

> Her dense silver gray coat has now turned snow white except for a hint of black on her tail . . . This is an earned white. From that fated day in Alberta—January 10, 1995—she has passed through all the complicated shades of gray, through death and grief in all of its manifestations, through the utter heart of darkness, and now she will at last be able to slip back into mystery, into the light and shadow from which she came, free of the meddling of our race, free from our good intentions. When the mother of the Yellowstone wolves dies, where she dies, and how, I hope we will never know; it should be that way. The wild's grace and mercy. (293)

This benediction is similar to Linda Hogan's "Deify the Wolf," but more direct and plainspoken. I have said throughout this study that the ghost wolf is split between its benevolent and malevolent forms, and that each of these does its own kind of damage. But there are the lines between, and Askins finds a permeable point in *Shadow Mountain*.

The writer invokes the ghost wolf (of death, of light and shadow, of a gray that is at once vividly real aging yet also symbolic of vanishing and memory). But she does so toward the healing of both the ecosystem in which Natasha lives and the ecological consciousness of those who affect her and other wolves' lives. Askins understands that the benevolent ghost wolf given our "good intentions" is a fiction, and a harmful one, just as Hogan points out in her essay that biologists are often cognizant of how close they are to the old trappers. And we understand, after two-hundred-plus pages of what Askins has faced—in hate mail, threats, sexist belligerence, wolf-hating fanaticism, bureaucratic resistance, and personal tragedy—that the malevolent ghost wolf is still a part of the human psyche and capable of doing harm (a particularly difficult passage is on 168). This balance she negotiates, along with an overwhelming energy of involvement, carries the memoir forward to its realized goal, a positive if temporary resolution.

The importance of this book as a feminist text is that it is the only one we have in which the writer's life as a woman as well as a biologist is brought to bear on our understanding of the Yellowstone project in particular, wolf study in general. Whereas Crisler worked alongside her husband and encountered mainly the difficulties of life in a tough environment in Alaska, Askins's greatest obstacles are, in large part, men. She looks at this fact with hard-eyed realism, rather than reverting to strategies of any particular wave of feminism, and presents the arguments in the manner of an enlightened pragmatist even while she regularly adopts the language of the romantic.

The book also contains a number of literary allusions. Askins quotes Peter Matthiessen (134) and Gary Snyder (32), uses the Mary Tall Mountain poem (132), and places literary epigraphs at the beginnings of her chapters. Her reading and her strategies of reaching people with the message of wolf recovery are hand-in-glove, in that she articulates herself as a person with art and its influences at her disposal—a better realization of E. O. Wilson's *Biophilia* than perhaps Wilson's own book accomplished. In a passage about her creation and application of an exhibit now famous among wolf-watchers, she writes this:

> One of the truly remarkable aspects of the exhibit is that it used the power of the wolf's mythological role through history to examine how we relate to the animal today. Too often science is isolated from myth; both [the exhibit's developer Kurt] Hadland's and Lopez's genius was in seeing that each dimension deeply informs the other, and that allowing the imagination of the viewer or reader to range between the scientific and the mythical helped create an intimacy with the real animal. The exhibit explored myth and fable, biology and ecology, and the social and political dimensions of issues such as wolves' predation on livestock, purported attacks on humans, etc. Its primary goal was to penetrate and integrate the superficial dichotomy between what wolves have been to humans culturally and what their presence could mean today, biologically. Mech's intuition was astute—the exhibit could be a perfect vehicle for gently forwarding the discussion of Yellowstone wolf recovery. (111)

The exhibit—"Wolves and Humans: Competition, Coexistence, and Conflict"—was placed in Yellowstone at the beginning of the EIS work on the program in order to elicit public opinion. Through interviews with Hank Fischer, Norm Bishop, and Paul Schullery and from a presentation given by Doug Smith, I learned that it is widely thought among the biologists involved in the reintroduction program that this exhibit is one of the major reasons for that program's success. Askins's memoir is also such a vehicle in retrospect—the best book to read of a personal involvement in the Yellowstone project, certainly the book with the strongest narrative. Askins is exceptional among wolf writers; there's no "demythologizing" here. In her work, Dave Mech's intuition, not his data collection, is emphasized. Askins and the biologists working at Yellowstone learned that the success of reintroduction depended upon myth reconciled with science and that the life sciences would either understand this or wind up embroiled in a contest of ideology that would undermine the pursuit of knowledge. In time, it seems that such knowledge of myth as it has bearing on the disciplines of science is gathered a little less begrudgingly. Now the problem is what happens when the interdisciplinary knowledge gained conflicts with the myopia of, for instance, the retrograde state-level politics of Alaska, Wyoming, and Idaho or the hostility to science of certain factions in the academy.

Askins was made a liaison because she had ideas, methods, and a language that wasn't the common language of the men of science around her; she also had the guidance and aid of men who understood her language, had some of it in themselves, some anima waiting to be expressed perhaps, and they participated. The hate messages Askins received weren't the garden-variety psychos calling to complain about the Nazi government and lambaste the tree-hugging environmentalists. They were often and apparently sexual in their violence, as driven against woman as they were driven against wolf. In that unity of intuitive men and logical women is hard evidence for the necessary gendering of the profession of biology toward a healthier mix of fact and feeling, knowledge and sense, intimacy and empiricism beyond their stereotypically gendered limits. These are anima and animus issues, not male and female ones. Far from precluding the furthering of gender equality in the sciences, this work toward a unified understanding of how and by whom knowledge is processed requires voices of different registers.

Of Wolves and Women

Jody Emel's excellent chapter appearing in her coedited *Animal Geographies* is titled "Are You Man Enough, Big and Bad Enough? Wolf Eradication in the U.S.," its title alone indicating several layers of gendering to the wolf myth. Her dual orientation (and sustained metaphor) is between the male wolf-hunter and the Big Bad Wolf and continues throughout personal essay sections of the article. She begins with a story about her best friend's father as a hunter and about the hunter subculture she knew in Nebraska. This experience "gave birth to a nascent radical ecofeminism that I could only name many years later" (91). The scholarship that follows heavily cites Barry Lopez and David Brown and includes other staple works by Mech, Ligon, Young and Goldman, Mowat, and an interview with Luigi Boitani. For some crucial points, however, she uses two sources that are not so strong. I find Jane Tompkins's *West of Everything* to be at times overstated and poorly argued, using a diction indicating the author's too-distant relation to her subject (see, for instance, page 59 on the essentialism of western men as "silent"), and Donna Haraway's *Simians, Cyborgs, and Women,* especially the essay "A Cyborg Manifesto," is largely hyperbolic cleverness.[8] Fortunately, the bulk of Emel's sources are books on wolves, and the directly ecofeminist articles she cites are staples in the discipline. Other selections in *Animal Geographies* stray at times into shaky speculation and performance language and praise the movement a bit too much for its achievements without holding it responsible for its more general capitulation to typical, detached, anthropocentric political positions regarding the environment.

Emel links the wolf-eradication programs to various other environmental oppressions and, in the ecofeminist vein, sensibly and convincingly parallels those with sexism and hypermasculinism. She includes a photograph from Young and Goldman of a female wolf and a litter of at least ten pups, all laid out for the camera after being killed by strychnine (98). The article is a combination of the standard historical primer on wolf eradication and the puzzling over human, particularly male, violence (105–7). Gendering and ethnicizing identification with prey, the language of machismo and sport, the outlaw/wolf connection, and the first-person essay are all employed as techniques to plumb the psyche of violence against wolves.

In the end, the article takes a political stand on the side of "sentiment," and Emel explains that the loss of emotional defenses to seemingly rational arguments about taking animal life results in a greater systemic loss (112). The lack of wolves in Nebraska, for instance, is positioned among her own cultural experience, western U.S. history, and the masculine models so heavily influencing both toward the disappearance of the wolf. This assertion of the wolf's absence as akin to a loss in the human soul is rooted in Lopez, who asks what the wolf hunter is "really trying to kill" (Emel, 112; Lopez, *Of Wolves and Men,* 138). By gendering her approach, Emel allows the inclusion of a language distinguishable from much other wolf writing and opens another angle on the "Why" question regarding the historic attempt at the animal's eradication. Without blaming the male order she rightly implicates it, and so rounds out the probable determinants for the war against the wolf.

In the context of Askins and Boyd, Emel's article also legitimizes through scholarship the necessity and power of a gendered approach to the wolf book. It is, in short, impossible to approach the body of wolf literature in America without considering that literature's assumptions about a gendered domesticity; the long-standing tradition of men almost exclusively handling management, eradication, and scientific inquiry; the androgyny and transgendering of wolf fairy tales sustained from their Old World origins; and the emergence, in both fiction and nonfiction, of the woman's voice, body, and politics in the creation of that literature. We must be better prepared to address wolf literature on terms that transcend any one school or approach and that more properly constellate the episodes we have used to build an American wolf mythos.

The final analysis here is that the wolf of the wolf book cannot be used conveniently as a means to forward a politics of gender. Gender is a made thing, an artificiality, and its role in establishing the wolf as a literary figure, however defensible its politics in the human sphere, hasn't done the wolf as much good as it might with a less anthropocentric set of metaphors, the methodology of which would not so directly contradict the very gender politics being proposed. The gendered wolf prompts us to consider an environmental politics that envelops sex and gender in the larger concerns of ecology and its systemics, its epochal evolution and biological necessities. These *enrich* the gendered text—which I am certainly not suggesting we ignore or diminish. They subsume (perhaps even more than explain) any masculinist or feminist assertions of cultural power and render a gendered anthropological or literary study effectual only to the extent of its biological and ecological awareness. The wolf is too often used to serve a symbolic function by scholars ostensibly motivated to contest exploitation or the essentialism of the Other; those concerned with the politics of gendered language face quite the challenge when they must examine their own language about animals, because other animals are as aware of and dependent upon sex, if not gender, as are we. This brand of exploitation—the fitting of an animal with the symbol collar—is particularly tricky when we are presented with the animal in a text purporting corporeal representation.

When Elizabeth Marshall Thomas or Vicki Hearne tells us how "wolves are" or "dogs are" in the interest of a better understanding, their arguments don't suffer because they are made by women in a traditionally male field of study; they suffer from the recourse common to race/class/gender essentialism because they are equally as opportunistic. Using the language of corporeality, they depend on the ghost wolf to keep the real wolf under control. Essential wolves can provide us with remarkable anthropological fantasies and humanistic power. In the politics of gender this is called sexism; in environmental politics it is called greenwashing.

Bitten

There is one more type of she-wolf as yet unexamined in this chapter: the woman who becomes a wolf. The final and most profound stage of totemism is transformation, and so the woman who runs with the wolves and wants to keep up must finally change her very morphology. This happens in the realm of fantasy and romance, and as it has been modernized, the werewolf story has developed more obviously as social commentary. Also, shape-shifting is another form of twinning or crossing, inviting commentary on other such forms as gendering or transgendering. I could use Estés's *Women Who Run with the Wolves* to investigate this type, but another text, at once more literary and better representative, should better serve.

I'm briefly going to hop the boundary north. While built on European wolf history, *Wolves and the Wolf Myth in American Literature* has been necessarily limited to literature of the United States, but the Ontario writer Kelley Armstrong's novel *Bitten,* set in Toronto, contributes certain features of both the werewolf novel and protoecological feminism in an urban environment relevant to our considerations of the American wolf book. Armstrong tells the story of Elena Michaels, an upwardly mobile city werewolf who tries to balance her romantic relationships with her lunar transformations. Subtle feminine connections (starting with allusions to the lunar transformation) course through the book, and Armstrong's writing in the romance genre is proficient enough to handle the tropes of shape-shifting, especially at the novel's outset. Elena turns into a wolf when she changes, rather than into a monstrous demibeing. Armstrong understands the wolf myth and makes decisions about her character that invoke it at every turn, giving an otherwise superficial romance (for example, the characters of the book are all moneyed and beautiful) some of the depth and substance of deeper stories. *Bitten* is built on a sexual politics that are at least glancingly concerned about where wolves and women belong in a masculinist urban society.

The first ten pages of the book are of Elena's change to wolf form, told in first person. The sentences are short and declarative but sufficiently explanatory and unencumbered by primitivism ("I can hear people inside, a room full of people, grunting and whistling in sleep. I want to see them . . . My nails click against the pavement . . . A wind gusts from the south."). In the first paragraph, her change is compared to childbirth: "My battle is as futile as a woman feeling the first pangs of labor and deciding it's an inconvenient time to give birth. Nature wins out" (1). Armstrong has decided that her version of transformation involves both consciousness-changing agony (she capitalizes the word *Change*—since the lower-case implies changing only clothes) and an environment inconducive to being a wolf: "In the alley I Change then yank my clothes on and scurry to the sidewalk like a junkie caught shooting up in the shadows. Frustration fills me. It shouldn't end like this, dirty and furtive, amidst the garbage and filth of the city. It should end in a clearing in the forest, clothes abandoned in some thicket, stretched out naked, feeling the coolness of the earth beneath me and the night breeze tickling my bare skin" (8).

This prelude contains the werewolf elements that determine what sort of she-wolf we will be following through the novel, establishing the premises of the writer's chosen werewolf myth. "I am a wolf," Elena confesses, "a 130-pound wolf with pale blond fur. The only part of me that remains are my eyes, sparking with a cold intelligence and a simmering ferocity that could never be mistaken for anything but human" (3). In addition to her choice of a painful transformation for her main character, Armstrong's decisions about how human the werewolf will be include having Elena becoming fully wolf in morphology but retaining several human traits: her own consciousness, though with heightened senses; her own hair color; and her human size (130 pounds is abnormally large for any wolf, especially a female). She also retains the demihuman eyes common to wolf myth and romance. In a gratuitous battle scene involving some city coyotes, Armstrong dips a bit more deeply into how the eyes of the werewolf function: "Animals don't know what to make of me. They smell human, but see wolf and, just when they decide their nose is tricking them, they look into my eyes and see human" (6).

After an engaging beginning the book devolves into the gothic fantasy trope of a woman caught between the subterranean world of monsters (who are less monstrous for their fantastic transformations than for their internal politics) and the daylight world of zoomorphized humans. The vampire story has altered over time from tales of individual stalkers to sagas of high-drama vampire societies that function like a combination of Renaissance courtiers, fraternities, and *haute couture* fashion models, to the point at which their goth World of Darkness has been parodied and metaparodied in movies and on television.⁹ Armstrong's she-wolf travels in such a world, a conflation of the vampire story with the werewolf genre—the latter usually having that requisite "clearing in the forest" environment and a politics of either noble or ignoble savagery. The dilemmas are contrived at times, there's a great deal of posing, and the prose doesn't always sustain itself, but through *Bitten* are scattered a number of graceful sentences and descriptions of werewolf transformation that constantly (and often effectively) gender the story's politics, which are almost always a politics of subjugation. Both Octavia Butler's *Fledgling* and the *Underworld* movies examine this issue as well, by casting werewolves as the once indentured guardians of vampires as they slept, now liberated and, in *Underworld,* in conflict with their former masters.

The matters of subjugation, victimization, and imprisonment have been revised and revisited by women writers for the lifespan of literature, and writing about wolves includes this strain of concerns crucial to our development as readers, whether or not the motive and modus has been overtly ecofeminist. This literature has developed in resistance to the sentiment found in Mariève Rugo's poem "In the Season of Wolves and Names":

> How they crouch at my door, pelts glinting
> in the shadow. How tall their tongues,
> flaring out of the darkness. They know me well.
> I always submit, let them chase me
> across the margins between my seasons
> into this soundless cavern, stripped
> of all names but the one they are hunting.
> They have me where they want me—hamstrung, belly-up.
> They ransack my body to find that last,
> merciless name, the one I can never say
> for fear the children might hear me. (31)

Rugo uses the hamstringing image as does Susan Snively in "Wolves," although more pointedly toward the metaphor of rapine, and in both the violence is a profoundly physical analogue for the implied psychological state. Whether the development of the wolf as a totem of empowerment rather than as Rugo's image of violation has also empowered the wolf is a question that will determine the effect and defense of an ecological feminism. It is not enough to save the fiction of the ghost wolf from the masculinisms, perceived and real, of a Jack London and his ilk and era, perhaps not even enough to recognize the complexity of gender and environmental politics in the revisionist impulse of literature and criticism toward the reconstruction of the canon. It must finally be said that in the nonhuman world gender is less important than is sex, and that this fact doesn't make gender construction a point of evidence in favor of civilization's superiority.

PART IV

Big Sky Wolf

CHAPTER EIGHTEEN

The Skull That Wakes the Spirits

CORMAC MCCARTHY'S *THE CROSSING*

Let me risk a set of anecdotal connections here that may at first look like a perusal of tea leaves but should end up as a simple and plausible synthesis.

First: In *Drumming at the Edge of Magic,* the autobiography of his life as a percussionist, Mickey Hart tells the story of a Tibetan instrument he received as a gift, a consecrated ritual clapper drum called a damaru, fashioned from a human skull. At a party for Vietnam veterans held in the barn that houses Hart's drums, an ethnomusicologist picks up the damaru and shakes it. Since this is a drummer's story, Hart phonetically transcribes the sounds the damaru makes: "Binnnngggg . . . Gunnnngggg . . . Gunnnngggg . . . Binnnngggg!" Some days later Hart attributes a violent sickness he has come down with to the playing of that drum, which prompts him to hand it over to a Tibetan lama, the drum's "rightful owner." The lama tells him that the damaru possesses great power: "It wakes the dead, you know" (21). The academic's comment at the party had been more detached: "It's a damaru from Tibet, though not a particularly unusual one" (181).

Caught between mentors, Hart finally rests on the personal transformation he experiences in playing his drums, when "my body awareness starts to fade, time disappears, instead of blood it feels like some other juice is pumping through my veins" (22). However, he revises a prior opinion—"Drums give up their true secrets only to players, not PH.D.s"—and willingly pursues the unity of knowledge between mind and body catalyzed in him by several teachers: the previous owner of the drum; the ethnomusicologist; and the damaru itself, the voice of which Hart tries to teach us through his transcription. It is narrowly categorized by inscribed sound as bitonal (a *bing,* a *gung*), consonant (the percussive *b-* and *g-* of the clapper on the bone), exclamatory (he punctuates it dramatically), and symmetrical (four *n*'s, four *g*'s in each shake) (22). Without such a voice, the story would deflate considerably; the observations of a "different juice" pumping through his veins, of shamanic secrets found in the drum's vault, would become abstract and self-referential, a pervasive problem in academic writing, which could use a few more Binnnngggggs and Gunnnnggggg in its vocabulary.

Next: Melanie Acevedo's sepia-tinted photograph on the cover of Cormac McCarthy's *The Crossing* depicts an arrangement of cattle skulls on snow-patched dirt. From the foreground skulls to the background skulls, the details of sutures, pits, and teeth become less distinguishable as they blend in with the mass of bone and snow around them. The photograph invites the viewer to look into the contrasting blackness of eye sockets, of nasal cavities shaped like bat wings against the jagged remains of mandible and rostrum. The skulls call the viewer to imagine not only the hide and lashes and lips that once covered them, but also the contents of them, the gray-pink slabs of tongue and coils of brain now absent. We might consider what emptied those chambers of bone, what horrible event arranged the skulls in near rank and file on what is presumably the desert. Part of our question is answered in the cover's lower left corner, where we see the thin perforated hem of a tarpaulin, its seam running like the margin of a page, and the tarp's uniform mesh belying the primeval material of scattered dirt, snow, and bone that cover the plastic. The blackness of those cavities once contained the answers to another part of our question, about what the cattle last saw, about what preyed upon them: the predator that arranges cows on a tarp for a picture.

Finally: The lines dividing *Canis lupus* subspecies designations in the Southwest, challenged by Ronald Nowak's 1983 study but still generally applied until his 1995 study, make a certain h shape at one point of a map depicting wolf distribution (see Nowak, 1983, 1995, 2003; Carbyn et al., *Wolves, Bison*; Busch, 7; Steinhart, 358–59). We see this same shape in the sutures of a wolf skull around the optic canal and the h- or k-forms of the pterion region sutures in a human skull (Evans, 159; Rogers, 43). We know well enough the atlas as a representation of the globe; *atlas* is also the term used in craniometry to map the suture patterns of the skull. Shaped like Hamlet's, our symbolizing mind prompts us to see the skull, shaped like Yorick's, *as* the world (and vice versa). Such thinking persuades us to alter both the world and the body with similar tools. We mark, or carve, or breed artificially what already has been marked or carved or reproduced naturally, then we say that the map we've made is the world just as much as is the map we've altered or destroyed. We draw geopolitical borders that do not follow the bioregional borders predetermined by rivers, aridity, timberline, and we are equally reluctant to let our borders shift as those do. Likewise we breed down the wolf and alter its morphology. We make countries into nations, wolves into dogs,

the corporeally absorbing the infinity of death into the mere self-absorbed fini-
tude of memory.

The memento mori, that powerful device of the artist, is an appropriate
enough image for the collective thought about wolves in America, and a nexus
for the three anecdotes of the damaru, the cover of *The Crossing,* and the border-
lines of the two atlases. Wolves are indeed alive, even thriving in some regions.
But to *want* them dead; to assume them dead before they are; to resurrect the
dead ones; to reify them to our ends; beyond the fact of actually killing them in
droves—such a world of thought is a world of loss and absence, totemic nihilism. A sizable faction of human beings has tried to construct this world for the
wolf, the world in which Cormac McCarthy's writing is placed and on which he
turns a hard eye.

McCarthy's novel is set in the land of the Mexican wolf, *Canis lupus baileyi,*
and that species and its region must be examined in order for us to have an ecocritically informed lens through which to view that book. A Mexican wolf physically differs from a northern gray wolf in large part because of necessary adaptations of biology to ecology. Subspecies regions immediately prior to Ron
Nowak's studies were designated primarily as a result of craniometrically based
taxonomy. Back of that, they were built on methods of decreasing reliability,
including pelage, as we recede historically.[1] Gray predominates in the wolf's
pelage, although Arctic wolves are usually white, and red wolves are aptly named,
all generally speaking. Black wolves are not always so for life; black is also a
"phase" of pelage through which many wolves pass before taking on their adult
set of markings.[2] Truly black wolves gray as they age; if they live long, they may
turn a peppered white. The white of an Arctic wolf's fur is a result of pigmentation being replaced by air, so that each follicle contains a pocket of insulation
(which phenomenon is not an evolutionary universal for all white animals). I
have mentioned the dark patch of hair commonly found around the precaudal
gland, located on the top of the tail near the body, a trait found in all canids, but
pronounced in wolves and certain breeds of dogs. These facts, and the rise of
information on morphology and genetics, displaced pelage as a gauge of subspecies. Today the surest method of division is through the study of mitochondrial DNA, a method possessed of its own limitations.[3] Despite all this, there
persists a tendency in public discourse to name wolves according to the colors of
their coats.

The biological information indicates that the lines drawn on the land by wolf
populations adapting to their regions are symbiotic with their morphologies;
wolves go where they're fit to go, and they adapt physically to where they've long

been. They, and we, draw lines demarking their positions as groups or cultures. Because taxonomy itself is subject to the lumper-and-splitter debate, taxonomic separation is not entirely built on ecology and morphology, but for all its impurity it has served better than either the divinations of the medieval augur or the sophistry of the poststructuralist. During a more splitter-driven taxonomy in the 1920s–1940s, the Southwest was the most intricately distinguished set of wolf subspecies regions in North America, subject to many frictions and fusions. Nowak's lumping of wolves into five subspecies designations allowed for at once more individuality of wolves and greater acknowledgment of wolfness, its less transected design shifting our attention away from the logistics of our own splitting and toward wolf packs as they might determine their own territories.

The Crossing, a novel very much about blood and bone, is set in this Southwest. The book depends upon our ability to perceive a Mexican wolf in the context of this metaphor of skull and land, written in a gothic mode that consistently invokes the memento mori in order to achieve its force of narrative and image. I've mentioned the crossing of a body of water as a motif woven into the wolf myth—one of transformation and travel between worlds by the ghost wolf, migration and adaptation by the real wolf. Crossing is also of metaphoric value when considering human political borders, wolf runs and pack territories, or mountain passes.

A "wolf run" is a corridor of migration or frequent travel. Snaring as a method of trapping often depended upon finding a strategically narrow and camouflaged place on the path. Wolf runs can be wide and open, however, and are not just found through mountain passes (Mech, *The Wolf,* 327–28). I've seldom seen the phrase used in recent publications, and it seems to be a colloquial label as often as a clinical one for wherever wolves have traveled between two landmarks. I use it here as a likely saying for a trapper in the early to mid-twentieth century strategizing how to catch a wolf.

Of course, "crossing" refers to hybrid breeding and invokes the miscegenation theme. Far too much is made of "crossing borders" and the language of boundaries in cultural studies; I do not intend simply to use the phrase as an eccentric exercise in metaphoric leaps. An actual, physical crossing of border or blood can have a cascade of effects that are resultantly psychological and sociological; the conceptual crossing depends upon it for efficacy. Myths involving a border transgression are, like all other myths, built on the combination of a physical phenomenon (for instance, of terrain) and a psychological dilemma that invites a response of law, doctrine, or rule. Edwin Arnold demonstrates the power of this understanding when he includes in his excellent analysis of Mc-

Carthy's novel the interpretation of *crossing* as a verb synonymous with *crucifying* (216).

If the she-wolf in the novel were considered to be of the subspecies *Canis lupus monstrabalis,* then her kind would have been obliterated by 1935; if *Canis lupus mogollensis,* then by 1942. Both subspecies are now part of *Canis lupus baileyi,* the Mexican wolf, an animal recently restored to the American Southwest under extremely hostile conditions, which I will address in greater detail. *The Crossing*'s present-time ending in the late 1930s stands between these two dates of subspecies "extinction" and precedes the first two Border Trilogy novels (*All the Pretty Horses* takes place between 1949 and 1950; most of *Cities of the Plain* in the 1950s.

In McCarthy's work the vanishing breed is not only the Mexican wolf or the American Indian. It includes the romance-novel cowboy and the notion of American innocence between the wars—both leitmotifs of American fiction. The wolf's actual eradication from the region anticipates Billy's microcosmic condition in *Cities of the Plain* (289) as an out-of-work movie extra sleeping in a section of highway culvert pipe in the year 2002. But the wolf isn't used simply as an emblem of a greater human loss or vanishing. To the contrary, *The Crossing* devotes a third of its volume to a wolf's story, and without didactic intrusion, implying that the wolf's demise is easily as historically and literally significant as anyone else's. McCarthy achieves his verisimilitude through an unusual attention to the corporeal wolf in a novel that includes, quite consciously, the ghost wolf.

The Pit

The she-wolf in *The Crossing* does not see Billy Parham pull the trigger as she stands battered in a dogfighting pit. He shoots her in the head and then trades his rifle to the claimant of the pelt so that Billy may carry the wolf's body out and bury it (122–29). To the accompaniment of coyotes howling along the Pilares, he touches her fur, her teeth. His imagination and grief are galvanized when he places his hand on the she-wolf's head, and he progresses from sympathy to empathy:

> He took up her stiff head out of the leaves and held it or he reached to hold what cannot be held, what already ran among the mountains at once terrible and of a great beauty, like flowers that feed on flesh. What blood and bone are made of but can themselves not make on any altar nor by any wound of war. What we may well believe has power to cut and shape and hollow out the dark form of the world surely if wind can, if rain can. But which cannot be held never be held and is no flower but is swift and a huntress and the wind itself is in terror of it and the world cannot lose it. (127)

Holding the wolf's head lets Billy imagine her alive again, and the color of his imagination indicts the wolf's tormentors, forces us to confront the act we commit when we imagine in a profane fashion rather than in a sacred one. Rather than, like Hamlet, conflating death and memory, Billy recognizes the power of the real world to teach, to render the present in greater detail rather than foggier abstraction and self-concern. As with the famous epiphany Aldo Leopold had from watching a wolf die, here we bear witness not only to grief but also to the griever's ability to generate story, and so influence our own capacity for both grief and action.

Although the subject is death, and inside the cavities of those skulls on the cover are secrets, the *Crossing* passage is not automatically a candidate for a mere metaphysics of absence. The hollows are encased in the corporeality of bone. When tempted to focus on "what cannot be held," we must consider that Billy does indeed hold: the stiff skull. He "reaches to hold" what cannot be held. Rhapsodies on what blood and bone cannot make are inconceivable without the blood and the bone, without their physicality in Billy's hands, which are the origins of his imagination and the correlatives of his grief. The complexities of Billy's doomed effort to save the wolf and his apocalyptic encounter with her world should be understood in the context of both ecology and symbology, of the literal systemic as well as the figurative systemic, of the awe at creation as well as the awe at death. What escapes from the wolf's open skull into Billy's hand travels to his imagination and is the mythic moment, not a mere idea of the primordial, but an experience of the primordial shared with and largely responsible for that idea.

From the Yukon to Oaxaca: The Christ and the Lady of Guadalupe

No work of fiction to date has better represented the wolf than has *The Crossing*. This is not only because of the author's attention to the integrity of the sentence but also because of the careful treatment, more sophisticated than any preceding wolf book's, that he gives a lupine character. The first section of the novel articulates the very threshold between the corporeal and ghost wolf. It also stands alone as the strongest part of the novel itself, which over its next two-thirds slips at times into cryptic abstraction and biblical grandiosity. The wolf story, like Jack London's opening chapters in *White Fang*, is its own contained narrative and is evidence of its own power in that it controls the narrative, not just in its occupation of nearly a third of the book's volume but in the foundation that it lays for the human drama that follows. The images of both London's prelude and McCarthy's resolved first section are elemental, deep-rooted, legendary. They threaten the rest of their novels with their own resolutions even while they act as quintessential preludes to prepare the remainders of those novels. The wolf preludes challenge even the profound abilities of each writer to find an ensuing narrative up to the standard of each opening wolf story.

The Crossing begins with two typical characteristics of a wolf novel: First, it is a bildungsroman set in the great outdoors; second, the initial contact is made by hearing a wolf's howl. Hidalgo County is brand new, and Billy is teaching his younger brother, Boyd, both the "spanish and english" names of "features of the landscape and birds and animals." That landscape also holds beneath its surface a memento mori common to both the gothic romance and the naturalist novel: "the bones of a sister and the bones of [Billy's] maternal grandmother" (3). While the education of a child to the natural world remains a tenet of the romance, the birds and animals of McCarthy's world are not mere props on a stage. For example, while horses transport cowboys, move cows, and make the whole business look good for photographs, they are also given a kind of domestic individuality and a mystical as well as corporeal presence (especially, of course, in *All the Pretty Horses*).

With the appearance of the wolf, the wild animal will obtain a separate kind of individuality and a separate shamanic role deeper than a mere pose in a tableau landscape. The world in which these characters live is a paradox—a "New" Mexico but an ancient world—governed by the ethic of death and blood that McCarthy employed to great effectiveness before the Border Trilogy began, in *Blood Meridian*. This world to which we are introduced also appears at first to be teeming with wolves. It is the howling wilderness, the Old World notion of North America so easily translated into the myth of the West.

After hearing the howls that begin his story, Billy Parham takes the next communicative step. He tracks the wolves through the snow. He crawls stealthily to the edge of a juniper forest and witnesses seven wolves hunting antelope. The antelope look to Billy "like phantoms in the snow," and McCarthy writes, "the wolves twisted and turned and leapt in a silence such that they seemed of another world entire." The wolves walk down toward the valley "until they were the smallest of figures in that dim whiteness and then they disappeared" (4). Just before they vanish, and as Billy is about to head home, the wolves stop and stare at him, an invocation of another common wolf-story image—the wolf's gaze. He tells no one of his first encounter with the tribe of the novel's Christ figure. This fantastic gothic introduction is one of the most poetic and misleading passages of the book, an anachronism fit for Billy's beginning struggle over the vanishing-breed myth, through both the real and ghost wolf.

Something similar happens in *White Fang*. The first two chapters are about Kiche's wolf pack attacking two men transporting by dogsled a body in a coffin.

When it is resolved, the long scene seems disjointed from the novel that follows; it reads much like one of London's complete short stories. But it prepares us for his concept of the "White Silence"—the determinism that will come to govern White Fang's existence. The wolf-antelope connection is made in a similarly haunting way in Leopold, whose hunting party sees an animal emerge from a river and think at first that it is a small doe. It turns out to be the wolf of the famous epiphanic passage. This is not a poetic stretch or inapt comparison: From a distance a wet wolf takes on a kind of generic four-leggedness and shrinks considerably in size. The shape of its limbs and muzzle, with its ears sticking up off of a much sleeker body, can indeed resemble some small ungulate. I made this error once, thinking a wolf emerging from a creek to be some other animal I couldn't quite name, until the wolf shook off the creek water and these passages of literature sprang to life for me. The poetry, in other words, of the predator-prey connection or the perception of men with guns is in the reality at least before, if not more than, it is found in the language.

Wolves are nearly gone from the Southwest by 1939, and the she-wolf crosses the international border for the first time "not because the game was gone but because the wolves were and she needed them" (25). She has been separated from her pack. She is alone and, we later discover, pregnant. When she finds a kill but "no traces of wolves," we are left with her as the only lupine character for the novel's duration, with no explanation but our knowledge of history for the disappearance of the rest of her kind (25). Within a few pages Billy, remembering his encounter with the wolf pack (made ethereal to the reader but corporeal to Billy within the narrative), closes his eyes and imagines the she-wolf "and others of her kind," an act he will repeat throughout the novel. His efforts to understand her and to connect her with a pack do not achieve the scope of Ishmael's attempts to understand the whale, but they are comparably obsessive and tragic. The pack he first saw will increasingly have to find its place in his mind—"wolves and ghosts of wolves running in the whiteness of that high world as perfect to their use as if their counsel had been sought in the devising of it"—because their place in the world is shrinking (31). Notice that both our narrator and Billy are cognizant of the difference between wolves and ghosts of wolves, their comprehension of a wolves' counsel beyond the fanciful ceremonial councils of a Kipling or a C. S. Lewis.

Just as Kipling's imperialistic jungle law resonates in London's "Law of Life," so too does London's "White Silence" appear in McCarthy's story, transposed to a Southwestern landscape. The conversion of the frozen north to the Chihuahua or Durango deserts is not such a long jump, either metaphorically or ecologically. First, much of the Arctic region is desert (Glazov & Goryachkin, 14–15).

Second, as noted in chapters 7 and 9, such conversions have long been made in literature between various deserts or prairies and the sea, with sustained metaphors of agoraphobia or biophilia: William Cullen Bryant's "The Prairies," Gretel Ehrlich's *The Solace of Open Spaces,* Paul Bowles's *The Sheltering Sky,* Michael Ondaatje's comparisons of whiteout and sandstorm in *The English Patient.* These biomes also invite solitude, in which the author may feel free to spin out the philosophies and ruminations of the lone figure on open ground. "One could wish that McCarthy more often provided [Billy] with someone to talk to," writes one reviewer (Shepherd, 172). The point is that even remedial knowledge of basic ecosystems helps us know when to compare them and when to contrast them, not just for effect but also out of responsibility.

Other passages in *The Crossing* demonstrate the long-standing marriage of literary naturalism and romance that makes McCarthy's novel as much an old-fashioned western as it is any kind of revisionist text. In one he speculates on the wolf's "Dreams of that malignant lesser god come pale and naked and alien to slaughter all his clan" (17)—in direct contrast to London's great white Love Master whom Diable, Buck, and White Fang all know to be the ruler of the cosmos, superior to the Red God Indian. Both the narrator's voice and the characters romanticize the Indian and his closeness to the wild wolf (14). We hear a surrogate for London's deterministic narrative voice, an old man who tells Billy about places at which "God sits and conspires in the destruction of that which he has been at such pains to create" (47). There is the repeated assertion that the power to create and destroy is always located in some other world beyond the physical one. Importantly, the she-wolf's resistance to the human touch never falters throughout *The Crossing,* as opposed to so many adolescent wolf books in which the loving caresses of a human being "naturally" awaken the wolf's supposed yearning for domestication (60). We see the capture of the wolf and her transport to town (105). We see a pit fight and the wolf defending herself in absolute silence (114). The naturalist/romance connection here expands the application over time of the story and does so specifically through the negotiation of the wolf's corporeality both with her resonance as a mother/daughter figure for Billy and with her mythic power. The number of wolf tropes in the novel creates a leitmotif and affirms again the consistency of the World-Wolf model and its workings in our efforts to articulate, and at unfortunate times to control, this figure.

While Billy Parham and Weedon Scott play roughly the same roles in their respective stories, Scott's mastery over White Fang is established in only a few pages; the development of Billy's uneasy alliance with the she-wolf requires more than a hundred. Billy meets her as a trapper, not a savior, long before the pit-fighting scene. He comes to the vaqueros' fire "for no reason at all" and sets the trap when he spots a wolf track in the ashes, though "his heart was not in it." After doing so, he sits his horse for "a long time" (49). His contemplation is decidedly deeper within McCarthy's spartan exposition than are Scott's musings during his argument with Matt over whether to kill or keep White Fang. As hard as London tries, through thick expositional passages at times purple, he does not achieve a complex internal struggle within Scott. In McCarthy's dearth is his depth. We find this in Billy's silent hesitation to set the trap. The obvious reason for Billy's sitting the horse is that they've been working hard and he is resting the horse (whose name is Bird), but we can easily infer another reason: He has not yet decided to catch the wolf. His heart has to be in it. He looks "back toward the pass" then "out over the valley again" before finally riding away (50). Later, Billy returns and sets a proper trap, knowing it to be properly prepared, and he believes—perhaps with some moral misgiving—that he will catch the wolf. This passage also marks the novel with the Hemingway brand: combining a rendered male aptitude with minimalist exposition on that aptitude.[4] Such a combination fits an animal story well, given that an animal protagonist rendered corporeally is understood by observation of his or her actions, with little translatable communication.

When he catches the wolf Billy fits her with a muzzle (after she breaks the bit he first tries), binds her, and leads her on a rope behind the horse until their encounter at the first ranch, where he holds the wolf's tether himself (63–64). When dogs come out and his horse bolts, Billy opts to stand by the wolf and hold off the dogs, actually pulling the wolf "hard up against his leg" until the dogs are called back by the owner before they reach their intended victims (64). He finds an understanding family and stays there to heal the trap wound on the wolf's leg (70). The family fits the wolf with a dog collar "with a brass plate that had the rancher's name and RFD number and Cloverdale NM stamped into it" (72). Billy and the she-wolf drink from the same canteen several times. He offers her food, which she refuses until she is too hungry to refuse and is convinced that he will not harm her. Eventually Billy's negotiations with the wolf undergo a slow and expertly crafted change culminating in this sentence: "He and the wolf between them ate the whole bird then they sat by the fire side by side" (89). She is still bound, but a treaty has been effected, one requiring twenty-seven pages. It is an invocation of the story we have told since the Pleistocene and a rendering of the sometimes fine-lined socialization/domestication issue.

I partly support Arnold's assertion that Billy neglects his family to follow his "romantic desires" to return the wolf to the wilderness (Arnold, 224, 226–27).

This certainly seems a point of both guilt and hope for Billy himself, an element of characterization. It's at least an incomplete assessment of the action in that Billy is neither the family breadwinner nor particularly romantic in his idea of returning the wolf. While from the twentieth-century perspective of our main character we could make this judgment, from a twenty-first-century reading we have to consider that Billy Parham is the most responsible character in the book, largely because of what he sacrifices in trying his best to save something wild in an increasingly hostile human world.

To others Billy declares himself the wolf's "custodian." She is "the property of a great hacendado" who lives "there and in other places as well"—so that Billy is, if not steward *of* God, then a temporary caretaker of someone who belongs to God, the great hacendado (90). Throughout their entire journey she struggles for freedom and Billy struggles to return her to her "home," in stark contrast to Weedon Scott's taking White Fang to his own home in San Francisco. When the she-wolf is taken from him and thrown into a cart, Billy calls to her, in one of the most moving passages of the novel because it has been so painstakingly prepared. She "rose instantly and turned and stood looking at him with her ears erect" (105). The pathos is profound here because the conflict is between two acts of domestication that catch the wolf between them: the first a typical and cruel human one of the village pit fighters; the second an act of love at least recognized by the wolf as a possibility for escape. Billy's act is motivated by a desire to free the she-wolf rather than to possess her. Her acknowledgment of him, given whatever biological and behavioral explanation we choose, is an act of connection in a desperate moment of separation. It is the nexus of our collective relationship with The Wolf bound inexorably to that other great generator of emotion in fiction—the loss of a pure and innocent love. This combination has come to be known, too often pejoratively, as "environmentalism."

There is a difference between custodian and owner, as there is a difference between socialization and domestication. But such distinctions, as I have demonstrated in chapters 5 and 6 on corporeality and the real wolf, require some sorting out. By definition, socialization is the establishment of an amenable attitude in one animal toward another (connotatively, the other is a human) but is not meant to imply human ownership or lupine docility. It is a process by which a wolf is raised in some communal proximity. If the community is one of wolves, then socialization refers to one stage of early development. If the community is a human one, then socialization refers to the means by which a wolf learns to associate as much with a human as with a wolf.[5] Wolves may be trained after they are grown through a slow progression of several steps toward relating to the dominant human (Mech, *The Wolf*, 10; Packard, 64). The belief is that the wolf is not "domesticated" but "socialized," but the distinction is still contained within the wolf's being denied the freedom of wildness.

The final declaration of their alliance is made with Billy unhitching the muzzle, releasing the chain, and standing by the wolf in the fighting pit as she is finally free of any binding, although now they are both trapped. And Billy still considers "if she would bite him or not"—indicating that her socialization to him might still carry the hope of her remaining wild and returnable to the wilderness, as well as the obvious characterization of Billy's being cognizant and cautious of her as still very much a wolf (117). The Mexican handlers thwart his rescue effort, force him to return her to the fight, and acknowledge his bravery with a pathetic display of machismo. London's Weedon Scott/White Fang resolution is finally judged by McCarthy's story through Billy Parham's Medean act of love for the wolf: He shoots her in order to save her from the dogs (122). In Steinbeck the shooting of a dog is a symbolic foreshadowing of the human ignorance and cruelty that crushes the innocent; in Hurston the shooting of a man with rabies symbolically resolves the quest for a love that is wild and true, and functions as a commentary on the animal/human station so richly revealed throughout Hurston's oeuvre. But in McCarthy the wolf becomes the endpoint rather than the vehicle, to as powerful an effect on the human scale and to far greater effect on the ecological conscience.

Doomed Enterprises

After trading his rifle for the carcass, an act reminiscent of the Romantic Hero (except we must remember that this is a wolf—for whose carcass Leatherstocking never would have traded his longrifle), Billy buries the she-wolf and delivers a eulogy in his mind. It is another beautifully written passage, a two-page benediction in the language of John of Patmos, embellished with "celebrants of some sacred passion," animals "richly empaneled on the air for her delight," and Billy sleeping "with his hands palm up before him like some dozing penitent" (126–27).

But this is not the resolution. It is a false ending. The she-wolf is buried pregnant. Rather than neatly ending section 1 with her death and beginning section 2 with the more typical language of the western genre in its second paragraph ("They rode the high country for weeks and they grew thin and gaunted man and horse"), McCarthy begins section 2 with a horrifying reversal of the resurrection theme. He shatters any hope for putting the wolf's death behind us. "Doomed enterprises divide lives forever into the then and the now," he writes:

He'd carried the wolf up into the mountains in the bow of the saddle and buried her in a high pass under a cairn of scree. The little wolves in her belly felt the cold draw all about them and they cried out mutely in the dark and he buried them all and piled the rocks over them and led the horse away. He wandered on into the mountains. He whittled a bow from a holly limb, made arrows from cane. He thought to become again the child he never was. (129)

Billy will not have that chance. His wandering, like the wolf's, will take him back and forth between civilizations, and his brief experiment with wildness as the feral child will not last. McCarthy takes liberties with time and biology in having the wolf pups survive so long in their tomb; by the novel's chronology rigor mortis would have set in on the she-wolf and they would have died before their burial.[6] Billy wanders into the mountains as the last Mexican wolves are dying; and he, the last wolf trapper, will return home to discover the deaths of his own parents. McCarthy reminds us repeatedly of the world he has constructed, one that he attributes as well to the wolf—"A world burning on the shore of an unknowable void. A world construed out of blood and blood's alcahest and blood in its core and in its integument because it was that nothing save blood had power to resonate against that void which threatened hourly to devour it" (73–74). London gave us a father wolf lounging with his pups in the sun as the antithesis to the pull of wilderness and hard but true freedom. McCarthy, it seems, better realizes the naturalist project, and resolves his narrative where so many wolves have ended in America—with death in the darkness of enclosure and hopelessness.

Each archetypal character in the novel plays some role in pressing us to the threshold of the corporeal wolf and ghost wolf—oracles, skeptics, bandits, magistrates, fighting-dog handlers, and Billy's own brother—toward a realization of the World-Wolf. McCarthy shows us the verge between corporeality and spirituality in two important ways: first, through the Christ figure and the biblical roles of surprise and fear in its appearance; second, through his firm discipline against anthropomorphism while he manipulates point of view. These approaches successfully link his tale to the mythic traditions of cultures that have envisioned or could envision themselves as cooperatively spiritual and natural, or physical and metaphysical. By writing the wolf as an active figure and focalizer, he is then able to represent those visions and assume the tremendous responsibility for corporeality without resorting to didacticism.

Most significantly, McCarthy's application of the biblical myth is carefully annunciated through the she-wolf. She is fitted with iconic language, the poetry of both Messiah and Madonna. Billy Parham is cast as a disciple. That the story takes place in Mexico adds a Catholic shade to it, especially considering Mc-Carthy's omission of any Protestant language attached to the Parhams' beliefs. Billy is catechized under Mexican dons, mystics, hacendados, and a wolf. Mc-Carthy's depiction of the wolf also demonstrates his ability to contort the romance; the Madonna/Christ is contained in the ghost wolf, which is one of the traditional images of the devil—ruler of the howling wilderness and devourer of children. However, even in the biblical reference, the diabolic wolf is not always strictly delineated. We're back to the oft-misquoted passage from the book of Isaiah about the lion and lamb lying down together: "The wolf also shall dwell with the lamb, and the leopard shall lie down with the kid; and the calf and the young lion and the fatling together; and a little child shall lead them" (11:6). Arnold compares Billy to Saint Francis on three well-stated premises, that they both: "believed in the existence of the animal soul, befriended a murderous wolf, and later buried it in holy ground" (230).

McCarthy simultaneously walks the line between a wolf of carefully accurate presentation and the explosively metaphoric Christian ghost wolf. He also turns the Christian analogy into a deterministic naturalist one by denying the birth of the pups; he replaces the sacrificial lamb with the wolf; and he chooses specific moments in which Billy's clear discipleship reminds us that the novel to follow is as much like the Prophets as it is like the Law, that it is more Old Testament than New, and that the Christ of *The Crossing* is more Isaiah's than Paul's. If only by virtue of its thin connections to the collected stories of both the Bible and the wolf, as well as the Kipling/London tradition of the wolf story and the older form of the picaresque, McCarthy's narrative resonates with a full Euro-Christian mythos.

Billy's journey with the she-wolf and his identification with her is couched in a constant religious fear. In their first exchange after the wolf is trapped and roped, Billy tries to dominate her while reciting, in both direct and indirect discourse, a litany of revelations: "He was amazed at her quickness"; "It aint no use to fight it, he told her"; and "He could not believe how strong she was"; all within a few paragraphs of struggle (56–57). He wonders if the "living blood with which [the she-wolf] slaked its throat" has "a different taste to the thick iron tincture of his own. Or to the blood of God" (52). Again, we must remember that the wolf is not simply an icon of Nature corresponding to humanism in the context of the novel. She is a nonhuman conscious being and asserts her own agency.

During his "custody" of her, Billy guesses repeatedly at what goes on her mind. "I know you think I'm tryin to kill you, he said . . . He thought she'd be terrified of [the fire] but she was not . . . He already knew that she was smarter than any dog but he didn't know how much smarter . . . He thought she would very likely bite the spatula but she didn't" (81–83). In most other wolf fiction the temptation would be to subject the she-wolf's mind to the narrator's speculation as well, especially to assert that speculation as hard fact, but McCarthy focuses solidly on the wolf as an active agent in her narrative. This results in a shining example of the Lupus Mundi as a psychological limen. The she-wolf's mind is lupine in the most literal sense available to a writer—basic, guessed at by the human being seeking empathy and predicatibility—but she also functions according to a code that not Billy, the narrator, or the reader can crack; hers is the mind of God in God's own universe *because* it is the mind of both *Canis lupus* and this specific wolf.

Before the she-wolf is sacrificed to the town's greed and baseness, she is captured and held in a cart, the one from which she responds to Billy's call. A sequence of events unfolds resembling the stations of the cross: The townspeople poke her with sticks, and at one point, while being dragged on her chain and prodded with a rake handle, she tries to "keep low to the ground to protect her underbelly" (105, 112). Children spit on her (108). Drunks kick and curse her as she is dragged to the fighting pit. Her entrance to the bodega is the beginning of a descent into hell, the arrival at Golgotha: "The illumination from within seemed to bow the walls and in the apron of light before the open doors the shadows of figures inside reeled and fell away and the company entered dragging the wolf over the packed clay" (113). The cross is in the pit's center. It is surrounded by "bleachers or stands scaffolded up on poles" and a low wooden palisade "black with the dried blood of the ten thousand gamecocks that had died there and in the center of the pit was an iron pipe newly driven into the ground" (113). When I've read this passage I have often thought off the page of the men digging the hole for the pipe, pouring the concrete footing, lowering the pipe into it to set. I wonder what they talk about, how they can do this—the sheer labor of that effort by the stupid and cruel in a ritual act of profanement. I have known people, academics even, capable of achieving this color of cruelty but can't say that I understand it. In this way the language of other animals seems at times more accessible than some forms of our own.

Jon Coleman offers—directly or implicitly—several possibilities in *Vicious:* that we retain ancient and brutal rituals (5); that our stories teach us to be cruel to wolves (5); that we aren't necessarily evil but just don't play well with others (14); that, as per the ecofeminist logic regarding women and land, our conflations destroy both human and animal—for example, that we treat the Indian as we treat the wolf (31); that rancher logic prevails, an idea akin to Hank Fisher's comment to me that "our myths are economically generated" (36); that our concept of applied punishment and retribution is simply twisted (49); and that, through cooperation theory, we're involved in rectifying and negotiating such pathologies (158). It's an easy out for us to say the answer is "something of all of these." The more responsible route, it seems to me, is to consider who has tested these ideas—Burkert, Girard, Quammen, Slotkin, and here McCarthy, and to act beyond mere language.

Just before the pit fight that becomes her crucifixion is a beautiful passage of pathos without a single slip into anthropomorphism. The wolf stands chained to the iron pipe, looking at the handlers, who are themselves depicted as brutish, without language, and worse than their fighting dogs (116). "She looked small and ragged," McCarthy writes, "and she stood with her back bowed like a cat. The wrapping was gone from her leg and she favored it as she moved sideways to the end of the chain and back, her white teeth shining in the light from the tin reflectors overhead" (113–14). Dozens of dogs are prepared, brought in a group at a time, so that the pit fight is no betting contest but mere sideshow torture.

When Billy interferes the first time, holding the wolf only by the dog collar with which she has been fitted by the rancher's family, McCarthy again unites him with the she-wolf metaphorically by casting him as a martyr: "He looked like a man standing on a scaffold seeking in the crowd some likeness to his own heart" (120). After Billy shoots the wolf, the alguacil who stops the deputy from killing him speaks the benediction: "He said it was finished" (123). In exchange for his rifle, Billy then takes on the roles of both Joseph of Arimathea and the Madonna in *The Pietà*, carrying the she-wolf's body out of the bodega and wrapping it in "the remainder of the sheeting the rancher's wife had given him." He buries the body in a grave he digs himself and covers with stones (124, 129).

In this case Billy as a kind of Saint Francis has failed; there is no negotiation with the townspeople of Gubbio about coexistence with the wolf. After he receives the she-wolf's body he finds out the answer to his question about "living blood," an answer at the core of the narrator's naturalism: "He could feel the blood of the wolf against his thigh . . . and he put his hand to his leg and tasted the blood which tasted no different than his own" (125). The wolf's body is draped over Billy as he rides, and although it is her blood on his thigh, the Fisher King allusion is pronounced here, both in its euphemism for his emasculation and in its symbolism of a barren land. The Fisher King's connection to land is also revised. He is here connected with an animal—and not a lamb, not a lion.

Through a Glass Darkly

We have seen that a widely recognized icon in literature, let alone in "nature writing," is a pair of lupine eyes. In *The Crossing* the wolf's "world of blood" is

revealed to the reader through her eyes, which are depicted as glowing coals—
"intractable eyes so red in the firelight." A few sentences later McCarthy writes
that "she was always watching him. When the flames came up her eyes burned
out there like gatelamps to another world" (73). He alludes directly to the ghost
wolves of gothic romance, indirectly to London's Diable and to the ghost wolves
of many cattle ranchers, state governors, and evangelicals. He tempts us to condemn the wolf's world, to dread and fear it (as did naturalists such as Norris)
through his invocation of hard determinism and the fall of men, presented
zoomorphically.

But perhaps the passage should be read as an articulation of the benevolent
ghost wolf's ability to see into the malevolent ghost wolf's world. Who but
Christ knows hell better than Satan? The she-wolf may possess the vision of that
dark world and stare at Billy incessantly, but she may also be looking to him for
freedom. "When those eyes and the nation to which they stood witness were
gone at last with their dignity back into their origins there would perhaps be
other fires and other witnesses and other worlds otherwise beheld. But they
would not be this one" (74). Although she sees the world of blood, she cannot be
held by it, as the closing passage of the novel's first section reads; in fact the
world of blood is in terror of her, though it cannot lose her. As she is a witness to
blood and death, so is Billy a witness to her life, and he will become a disciple of
her vision.

We see the trope of the wolf's "almond eyes" appear early on, when Billy
meets the hunting pack (4), but the next mention of the wolf's gaze is a credible
description of what biologists call a "search image": "At night she would go
down onto the Animas Plains and drive the wild antelope . . . watching the precisely indexed articulation of their limbs and the rocking movements of their
heads and the slow bunching and the slow extension of their running" (25). A
search image is the imprinting of a prey animal on a young predator. Some of it
is hardwired into the young wolf, but it is also taught and includes catalysts
beyond sight. The regurgitated meat with which a pup is fed after weaning is the
beginning of influence over the young wolf's tastes and contributes to the formation of search images. Some of the methods being used to deter wolves from
killing cattle include allowing for enough wolf habitat to limit the number of
wolves stumbling into cows in their wanderings while they are teaching their
young. Wolves seem fine with convenience; if the elk are near and plentiful, then
there isn't much incentive to go looking for some other food source and imprinting young wolves on the shapes, smells, and hormones of domestic animals.[7]
However, I don't want to emphasize too strongly the search image as "the way of
the wolf." Mech and others have pointed out that wolves eat what they can, that

they are always ready to hunt, and that their adaptation to various carnivorous food sources is one of their survival strengths.[8]

McCarthy concludes the description by combining this "index" with another semiotic turn, "looking for anything at all among them that would name to her her quarry" (25). In this last phrase he combines the search image of an antelope with the ability of the wolf to select *which* antelope she will kill. Naming is given added importance in the entire novel through McCarthy's choice, rare among writers, neither to name nor to have Billy Parham name the she-wolf. The domesticated horses may have monikers, but wild animals may not, so that the codes of communication among wild animals aren't designed according to anthropomorphic (especially domesticating) systems. There are no Akelas or Kazans here, no animals that simply "have" names by virtue of the narrator's assignment, and no names provided by the human characters from their own points of view.

The dog collar the ranchers give Billy is a puzzle. We could see this episode as a brief "passing" narrative; the collar is apparently put on the wolf in order to fool others into thinking that she is a domestic dog (which mistake is never made). There is also a tag on the collar, the inscription on which is not said to include a name. We are left to wonder if a name is written on the tag. If so, then it would show the name of a dog who it seems no longer needs the collar and tag, who may no longer need even the name. The collar is an inefficient disguise and another lesson to us about cultural constructivism, since the assertion here that we can make a wolf into a dog at any moment and without consequence is a damaging falsehood. In London's novel, White Fang is named by the author (through the Indian who "finds" him), and not by Weedon Scott. London's market sense (naming domesticates and sells the ghost wolf to the reader) contends with his sense of Scott's own decision *not* to fit the dog with a name. When Scott's wife calls White Fang the "Blessed Wolf," the benevolent ghost wolf is domesticated by sacred title for both the reader and the Scotts (250). The she-wolf of *The Crossing* contends only with the names of a ghost and those names she might have chosen for herself through the pheromone, the scent-mark, the timbre of her voice, or whatever inward gaze (despite Descartes's assumptions) may identify her to herself.

Looks are exchanged throughout the novel that convey emotional communication, especially when the interspecies code seems to be otherwise unbreakable: "She looked up at him, the eye delicately aslant, the knowledge of the world it held sufficient to the day if not to the day's evil" (55). When Billy releases the she-wolf from the trap, a paragraph filled with such verbs as *twisting, fighting, gasping, scrabbling, struggling,* and *wincing* ends with the spartan sentence, "She looked toward him with her yellow eyes and closed them slowly and then looked away"

(54). Throughout the journey to the Pilares she is, McCarthy writes, "always watching him" (73, 82) so that "he felt all his motives naked to her" (78).

The evidence that McCarthy's dark world does not belong exclusively to the wolf and that her gaze is not driven only by her clairvoyance of that world is indicated in two particular passages. First, the Airedales waiting to destroy the she-wolf are clearly in possession of (or possessed by) the world of blood and death, which is revealed when lamplight "ignites" their eyes, and "the boy saw a thing that not even the pit dogs possessed in such absolute purity and he backed away mistrustful of the chains that held them" (116). One possibility found here, according to the binary in the ghost wolf, is to read the Airedales as the demonic opposition to the Madonna/Christ she-wolf. A healthier perspective may be to imagine them as such according to *Billy's* point of view, and to recognize them as abused by humans into this violence. The great fortune provided by McCarthy's language is that we have such an option. Projection—onto the wolf's eyes, the Airedales' eyes, and onto and through human eyes—is scrutinized for how it might reveal physical components of a mythic concoction.

The second passage indicating that the she-wolf is not driven exclusively by some supernatural force contains the paradoxically mythic image of the reflective pool, which demonstrates that the wolf's eyes are windows to her own soul as well as to the other world. The mythical force of the reflecting pool's symbolism is also used to material effect, which remythologizes the image rather than burdening it with merely supernatural tropes. Billy gives her water, and: "Her eyes did not leave him or cease to burn and as she lowered her head to drink the reflection of her eyes came up in the dark water like some other self of wolf that did inhere in the earth or wait in every secret place even to such false waterholes as this that the wolf would be always corroborate to herself and never wholly abandoned in the world" (79).

The passage seems to me representative of the larger wolf story in *The Crossing*. It describes the complexity of the wolf's soul and the collision of wildness and domestication, and foreshadows section 1's powerful ending. In the reflection is the subtle conflation of Billy's perception with both the narrator's and the wolf's. Billy sees her eyes reflected in the pool, and we see him see those eyes. The mirrored set shows both Billy and the reader the "other self of wolf," which the she-wolf is not considering at all, as far as we are shown. As always, she watches her captor—we want to say for an escape opportunity, but we could just as well say out of curiosity and/or fear. The image in the water, because the waterhole is "false" (that is, neither naturally occurring nor of her free choosing), is a reflection of the wolf's wildness, a demonstration of human projection, and a manifestation of the ghost wolf, the Lady of the Lake, the Self at the Abyss, our notions of power revealed through our desire to interpret to our own ends our actions against the nonhuman world. For all that is implicit to this moment, McCarthy's minimalism reminds us that the moment is, first and last, the simple drinking of water by a captured animal—a basic act of the survival finally denied her.

The Eye Pronoun

The lack of a gender-neutral third-person-singular pronoun in the English language creates a complex problem in writing about animals. In daily conversation the animal-identifying pronoun may help us assess some of a speaker's cultural assumptions. Say a woman walks a malamute past a man walking a Pekinese. The man says, "Nice husky." The woman says, "She's a malamute. Who's this little gal?" to which the man responds, "His name's Apollo." During the exchange the woman loses track of the malamute, who is wandering toward the street. A passerby yells, "You'd better watch that thing or it'll get hit." The dogs have just been fitted with a series of appellations, most wrong, and the malamute finally reduced to an object. Poetically, each dog likely knew in an instant the other's pedigree and sex.

We are witnessing a proliferation in subject/pronoun disagreement in number, as well as the use of the incorrect plural *they* for a singular subject in order to avoid the horrible *s/he, (s)he, he/she,* or *he-or-she* attempts at gender-neutrality. Culture will steer language, it's true, and one year's violation of a rule is the next's revision of the dictionary. But the effects of grammatical problems on meaning pale in comparison to the ineptitude and carelessness of the language we use in reference to other animals. Our acceptance of the objective pronoun *it* for sexed beings expresses a degree of failure at least as severe as the racist or sexist epithet. Throughout this project I have studiously tried to avoid denying wolves their sexual identities. Just as we should be conscious of how we gender an animal in conversation, one means by which we might ecologically critique a text is by applying some scrutiny to the writer's choice of pronoun for an animal subject and to how that decision affects the narrative's human subjects.

When the hacendado's son steps into the pit with Billy Parham and the wolf in order to negotiate, he uses two rhetorical techniques that establish for Billy the anthropocentric rules of the negotiation. First, he lies. He tells Billy that the wolf "had been caught in a trap in the Pilares Teras which mountains are barbarous and wild and that the deputies of Don Beto had encountered *him* crossing the river at the Colonia de Oaxaca" (118, my italics). The lie carries some historical interest, Oaxaca being the southernmost point of gray wolf territory in North America (Link & Crowley, 135). The second technique is to equate Billy with the wolf—first by referring to her as male, then by using the border crossing as an instructive metaphor for Billy's situation—thus denying him the power to negotiate further. Billy explains that the wolf "knew nothing of boundaries," with which statement the young don agrees but counters that "whatever the wolf knew or did not know was irrelevant and . . . the boundary stood without regard" (119). One bargaining chip of the don's is the spontaneous levying of a "portazgo" that Billy cannot pay, for which they have decided to accept the wolf in lieu of cash. "When the boy said that he had not known that he would be required to pay in order to pass through the country the hacendado said that then he was in much the same situation as the wolf" (119).

Billy's own empathy for the wolf begins before the hacendado fits them with the same political trespasser status, and it continues after. Several times throughout the story Billy closes his eyes and imagines what she might see or how she might look when they are apart. The first includes McCarthy's phrase "ghosts of wolves," a picture of her running with the pack that Billy saw hunting antelope; it also includes Billy's conjecture about the wolves' role in the creation of the world—the invocation of the cosmogenesis of those cultures prior to his own, "in the whiteness of that high world as perfect to their use as if their counsel had been sought in the devising of it" (31). He is in bed imagining her when he wonders (or daydreams) at the tastes of his blood, the blood of the wolf's prey, and "the world it smelled or what it tasted." This is also one of the rare moments in the novel when McCarthy uses the pronoun *it* for the wolf—in this case a representative pronoun of some being larger than the she-wolf, though *she* is also used within the passage (51). Billy's imaginings are desperate acts, born out of grief, launched by his hand on the wolf's head and by her opened, unseeing eyes. He closes them, and in so doing he steps from a sympathetic to an empathetic position. Luce (162) refers to the she-wolf as Billy's "totem" and follows a logic appropriate to both McCarthy's work and to the condition of the Mexican wolf. This is the end of the last wolf and of the last trapper, both of whom have been chased into oblivion by the border law that they learned in the fighting pit. And having been at some time both a trapper and an outlaw, Billy has learned, in the tradition of trappers and outlaws, to become a wolf in his own imagination.

The Mind's Eye

A story from the Bella Coola of British Columbia describes a shaman's attempt to change the animals into human beings. He is completely unsuccessful except for one partial transformation—the eyes of the wolf (Lopez, *Of Wolves and Men*, 4). Steinhart gives a concise description of how wolves see (133–34), as does Zimen, who includes commentary on how expressive wolves are with their eyes

(60, 66–67). When submitting, wolves might roll their eyes away from a dominant wolf, whine, and "grin." They often squint when they are contented. Goodman and Klinghammer's *Wolf Ethogram,* suspect as I find its point of origin, includes a number of observed eye expressions. Encyclopedias over the last 125 years seldom fail to note the eyes of the wolf as a defining characteristic.[9] Narrative moments that hinge on the wolf's gaze are too numerous to mention; they range from Mowat's encounter in a den to Auel's *Clan of the Cave Bear* to Svee's *Spirit Wolf* (112) to James Curwood's derivative story of Baree (1). It seems the only more frequent narrative device used to augment the wolf as a force of nature than the eye is the howl. Both London and Max Brand open chapters from a wolf's point of view that include, respectively, White Fang's first vision (119; note also that his father is named "One Eye") and a female wolf's opening one eye from a nap to see what her mate is up to (17).

We make certain judgments of character based on aesthetic preferences. A wolf's eyes have a shape, a light, an apparent intelligence that seems to inspire us to various forms of guilt, violence, rhapsody, or nobility. The World-Wolf's eyes augment this effect because our judgments are imaginative and projective, and the wolf of literature speaks to those judgments more clearly than does the wolf of reality. And so, as McCarthy uses them, a wolf's eyes are to Billy (and then to us) portals to another world. That world is obviously mythic, more specifically biblical, and takes us consequently to its language, its baggage of human history. The she-wolf's eyes serve as a point of human and animal exchange, first in communication, then in remembrance, then in transformation.

"She watched him with her yellow eyes and in them was no despair but only that same reckonless deep of loneliness that cored the world to its heart" (105). Is the feeling of loneliness in the wolf mere anthropocentric speculation? Is it anthropomorphic but without anthropocentric conceit, as Oerlemans distinguishes the two? Does it qualify as plausible, and if so, is this plausibility sufficient to exonerate the writer? These seem significant questions to ask whenever we encounter a point-of-view device employed by a narrator regarding an animal's thoughts.

The sentence beginning "She watched him with her yellow eyes" next comments on what is *not* in the wolf's eyes: there is no despair. How can the narrator tell this? If we attribute omniscience to the narrator and therefore go on trust, then we face another problem. The passage occurs right after Billy has called the wolf and she has responded to him, so Billy is the implied focalizer, looking at the wolf and reading her expression. He talks to her, making "promises that he swore to keep in the making" (105). This act of communicating with her indicates that *he sees* no despair in her eyes, implying that Billy is projecting, that he is fashioning the ghost wolf to reflect his own loneliness and sympathy for her. It implies that he is unable to see the whole world as anything but the realm of that loneliness. If we read the passage this way, then is *Billy's* projection anthropocentric, and if so, what effects might his projection produce? We may, for instance, lose the wolf. If we differentiate the main character's projection from the narrator's and parse out the rhetorical devices used by each, then it seems to me that we have encountered another facet of reading, if not exclusive to ecocriticism, then certainly integral to and defining it. This facet is defined by the third gaze, the missing point of view of the nonhuman animal that remains to a significant extent out of reach of both the character involved and the narrator depicting the animal. The very rubrics of nonhuman forms of communication drive the matter of articulating their points of view beyond the problems of human language and literally homogeneous (which implies "of the same race," in this case human) representation. These questions should point out the futility of establishing static criteria by which to measure anthropocentrism, especially that which condemns any form of anthropomorphism. But they do deserve some kind of answer.

Billy's implied focalization interferes with neither the narrator's information nor position, so the passage, while speculative, is not anthropocentric. If the narrator tells us that the wolf's eyes carry a globally analogous loneliness, then they do so in terms of the narrative, the point of view of which we may question abstractly while accepting narratively. To paraphrase Barry Lopez's lesson against essentializing the wolf—*this* wolf's eyes carry *that* loneliness, and no despair as far as *this* observer can tell. If Billy is "interpreting the wolf" as such, then any issue we have with anthropocentric thinking we also have with the fictional Billy Parham's assumptions and projections, and we may judge the fictional character accordingly. We can only judge the narrative to the extent that McCarthy has executed his donnée. We also, then, are obliged to turn the same judgment on ourselves (one of the functions of great literature).

The point of view throughout *The Crossing* is technically that of an omniscient narrator, but subtle shifts in focalization manipulate this point of view so that the narrator's, wolf's, and human characters' perceptions are all complicated by more ingenious and redeemable methods than mere anthropomorphism. For instance, McCarthy carefully uses the simile in order to qualify the human observation of the wolf's behavior, a technique Ernest Thompson Seton tried with less success. The best of Seton's uses is quite close to McCarthy's, relying on a causal juxtaposition to speculate about Lobo's thinking after the wolfers killed Blanca, his mate: "He seemed to know exactly what had taken place, for her blood had stained the place of her death" (Seton, 26). Of course, Seton is purportedly writing nonfiction. In another passage Seton equates observed causality, "he seemed to be coming toward the home cañon, for his voice sounded considerably nearer," with anthropomorphic assumptions about the howl itself—"It was no longer the loud, defiant howl, but a long, plaintive wail: 'Blanca! Blanca!' he seemed to call" (25–26). This is a more obvious indication of Seton's conscience and consciousness than of a well-founded discernment of wolves' howls. Finally Seton throws in the towel and simply anthropocentrically embellishes the legend: "the cattle had gathered about him to insult the fallen despot, without daring to approach within his reach" (27).

The she-wolf of *The Crossing* "seemed to take an interest in the country and she would raise her head and look out over the rolling meadowlands" (84). Seton's ghost wolf Lobo "seems to show [his bested captor, Joe Calone] that the big wolf simply scorned his enemies, and had absolute confidence in himself" (17). McCarthy's simile is designed to present plausible action; Seton's to assuage human humiliation. The passage from "Lobo" looks to be more about the minds of a couple of failed trappers than about the mind of a wolf. Scorn may be an emotion of a wolf; pride certainly seems to have presented itself at times in wolf behavior. But in Seton's context this is an *argumentum ad ignorantium,* not a premise of pragmatic value.

At one point the she-wolf, unable to move away from Billy because restrained, "seemed to be at odds what to do" (78). Here we have an implied focalizer, the narrator's explanation of what Billy must be observing without attributing the speculation to Billy. It is also plausible speculation, as the wolf may very well be "at odds" in circumstances foreign to her. While she "seems" this way by a human standard, the standard is used as a comparative reference, not in order to humanize her intellect, and certainly not applied sentimentally. The wolf sniffs the air "as if to make acts of abetment to the life in the world" (93), and the flapping of her wound dressing as she swims "seemed to terrify her" (94). Were it written without a simile, the first clause would invite anthropocentric interpretation; to make acts of abetment to life is abstract conceptual thinking, which is usually (if errantly) attributed solely to human beings. That the flapping bandage seemed to terrify the wolf is perfectly plausible. The wolf could easily be terrified by the motion of a bandage in the water on her leg, perhaps a perceptual distraction sufficient to frazzle her in the midst of her struggle to swim the current. Why McCarthy continues to use the simile is itself idle speculation, but the effect could be that the simile's superfluous use is an indicator of our propensity to debate the "rules" of anthropomorphism. So what, the passage implies, if her terror here *seems* to exist or actually does? Yet the writer still treads lightly around a reader's tendency toward ethological skepticism.

McCarthy also risks an attempt at the wolf's own unalloyed consciousness:

"She circled the set for the better part of an hour sorting and indexing the varied scents and ordering their sequences in an effort to reconstruct the events that had taken place here" (26). The temptation for the reader ready to cry foul at the first sign of an infinitive used to describe motive (*to reconstruct*) should be resisted here. Although the narrator speculates about a wolf's motive, this hardly violates even the most hard-line behavioristic thinking. Wolves' memories reach back many months, aside from their so-called instinctive patterns of behavior, such as hunting, and they may catalog and examine complex sets of circumstances from which they draw conclusions (Link & Crowley, 137; Mech, *The Wolf,* 8). That is, we have proof in abundance of wolves' ability and inclination to reconstruct events. The processing of information in this passage is as reasonable as the kind of information chosen.

McCarthy's dance with anthropomorphism varies even within a single short passage: "The ranchers said [wolves] brutalized the cattle in a way they did not the wild game. As if the cows invoked in them some anger" (25). The sentence fragment could be attributed to the ranchers, to the narrator commenting on the ranchers' anger over brutalization, or to the narrator stating that the brutalization itself looked sufficient to merit the simile. The ranchers assume a difference in the wolves' treatment of cattle versus wild game but more carefully speculate about the cause-effect relationship.

Otherwise, the bulk of the novel, particularly its opening section, is articulated strictly through a behavioristic paradigm. It is worth noting that in all of narratology, behaviorism provides the only model designed acceptably to accommodate an animal character (Prince, 1–3). This sad fact serves to corroborate the black-box, stimulus-response thinking that has been rightly challenged by Donald Griffin and others (Griffin, 19, 116, 234; Bekoff). The consciousness of an "actant" (that is, consciousness at both the surface and deep structural levels of a narrative) need not be exclusively human and need not demand the suspension of disbelief whenever the character is an animal. Even in a narrative that supports the tenets of behaviorism, moments of both plausible and proven animal cognition may occur.

We should consider a means by which the human and animal are united besides strictly one-way zoomorphic (naturalist) or anthropomorphic (romantic) metaphors. We should see in *The Crossing* the mythic pattern of identification and transformation, the potential to move between the canid and human worlds. McCarthy manages to accomplish this through Billy's initial identification with the she-wolf until his sympathy becomes empathy, a shamanic identification. The reader is given some basic methods by which to better understand the wolf in a situation conceivable to human beings—imprisonment. The wolf's intelligence to the ways of humanity, displayed through her adjustment to subjugation, extends the transformation process from Billy to the reader. Our emotions respond, and we take a step toward a new behavior.

Shadowfolk

So far the presence of the romance in *The Crossing*'s naturalism (and North American naturalism in general) has been insufficiently examined.[10] The best example may be the appearance in the novel of the Indian, one of the possible murderers of the Parhams (in addition to the Mexican workscouts). Boyd disturbs the Indian's hunting in a typical pulp western encounter, nearly tripping over him: "The indian squatting under a thin stand of carrizo cane and not even hidden and yet Boyd had not seen him" (5). At this point they make eye contact, and the Indian's eyes have the same reflective and apocalyptic qualities as the wolf's:

> Eyes in which the sun was setting. In which the child stood before the sun.
>
> He had not known that you could see yourself in others' eyes nor see therein such things as suns. He stood twinned in those dark wells . . . the selfsame child. As if it were some cognate child to him that had been lost who now stood windowed away in another world where the red sun sank eternally (6).

Boyd responds to this Indian in the same fashion as he and his father respond to wolves: "You don't know what a indian's liable to do" (14). His reactions are more than western clichés. They are indications of the détente conditions existing in the 1930s near Apache reservations as a result of the Wheeler-Howard, or Indian Reorganization, Act (see Deloria, *Indian Reorganization Act;* G. Taylor). The combination of fact and trope is what makes such moments clear invocations of the earliest and strongest tenets of the romance.

At the fair where the she-wolf is destroyed, McCarthy slips into the vanishing-breed myth, presenting it through yet another manipulation of the point of view. He refers to the canvas of a tent in the same way that he refers at the section's end to Billy's imagination, in which the animals are "empanelled on the air" for the she-wolf, an apt metaphor for pheromone detection. A female wolf in heat produces intense pheromones picked up by a male wolf through "tasting the air." This may be observed when wolves travel side by side, in regular contact with one another, the male's tongue darting out periodically. Wolves emit pheromones under many different conditions and have the ability to read those conditions in the chemical messages, which may carry for some distance on the wind.[11]

McCarthy describes the fairgoers in a colorful list of crowd-scene details until we come to "a row of children halted half dumbstruck before a painted canvas drop depicting garish human abnormalities and Tarahumara indians and Yaquis carrying bows and quivers of arrows and two Apache boys . . . who'd come from their camp in the sierras where the last free remnants of their tribe lived like shadowfolk of the nation they had been." The fair is then described as "the pageantry of some dread new dispensation visited upon them" (104). The surrealism of the event could as well be found in the actual fair as in the canvas drop, but the oppression of tribes is clear enough, their loss apparent in the literal impending doom at the fair. The death of the she-wolf is itself sufficient to romanticize the Indian/wolf connection in the vanishing-breed context.

The assault on the native population of America is a verifiable event and is written into the poetry and lore of those cultures in the modern era, as in Mary Tall Mountain's poem "The Last Wolf."[12] The more than three hundred tribes in what is now the conterminous United States had their numbers reduced from about 5 million in the fifteenth century to about 250,000 in the nineteenth, and the bison population upon which the Plains nations depended was reduced from about 10 million to 1,000 in about three decades (Lamb & Thompson, 1). The "vanishing-breed" theme, however, reaches beyond statistical fact into a pathological sympathy for what is not only not quite gone enough but surviving and growing in earnest. It is a nostalgia for what mostly white "forefathers" tried to destroy completely and failed, turning instead to the destruction of the national conscience. In this way, and not in some conflation of Indian with beast, is the pogrom against wolf, bear, bison, and Indian born of the same hatred.

One noteworthy omission from *The Crossing* is the hybridization of the wolf with the domestic dog, as is found in most wolf novels. McCarthy depicts not simply an icon but also a wild Mexican wolf. This fact guides the reader's possible interpretations in two important ways: First, it prevents assuming human identification with the animal as an attraction merely to its "dog side"; second, it forces the reader to confront the *existence* of wilderness and negotiate a human stance.

Like a Steel Trap

The jaws of a good-sized healthy wolf can bite at about 1,500 pounds per square inch, twice the pressure of a German shepherd, so trap similes come easy.[13] And what of the metaphor of the mind as a steel trap? A wolf dodging a hunter is said to be "smart," or acting on "instinct," or simply lucky; these things may be said of the hunter as well. When lacing the prairies with strychnine and shooting millions of bison wiped out the largest portions of wolves, the scattered few proved more difficult to get (see Caras; McIntyre, *War*, 217–52; Hampton, 58–60; Seton). Certain wolves gained infamy and were blamed for cattle deaths sometimes far beyond the capability of any strong (even rabid) predator. These wolves received names and reputations among ranchers as outlaws and rustlers, and their packs were compared to bandit gangs. Old Three Toes, Old Aguila, Las Margaritas, Lobo the King of the Currumpaw, the Custer Wolf, Rags the Digger—these are zoomorphic projections of beings living outside human law who merely inhabit the bodies of wolves.

The wolf and the trapper play a terrible game in which the trapper tries to predict the wolf's behavior based on the information he interprets from the wolf's sign and habits. The wolf survives by means no one has adequately explained, partly because too many scientists forbid guesswork about a wolf's motivation, intention, or strategy. The game is semiotic, based on finding one set of signs that determine what "set" of signs will be placed in order to lure the target into the trap. During the campaigns against wolves in the late 1800s the game developed such sophistication that the trappers had to become amateur chemists. Furthermore, they had to imagine, to the best of their ability, that they were wolves. In this way the trappers themselves were mysticized in the popular press as the bounty hunters of outlaws possessed of another mind. Some wolfers even had the opportunity to work for their government as patriotic assassins of the few wolves left.

Wolf-extermination policy transported from Europe to America traveled from Gubbio, Italy, through the king's forests of Britain and on to the town of Pomfret, Connecticut, before reaching its nationally historic status in the wild West, where it now lurks in the files of Idaho's, Wyoming's, and Alaska's governors. The denizens of Pomfret did not name the wolf that Israel Putnam killed in 1739, but the melodramatic story of his heroics before he became a major general in the Revolutionary War was one of the early outlaw wolf legends to enter the lore of the new United States (McIntyre, *War,* 41). In a century and a half, by the late 1870s, over 700,000 wolves would be killed in Montana alone. In the 1940s Stanley P. Young estimated that a hundred million dollars in bounties had been paid since the 1640s, when the wolves received no names, when "Indians" were paid for wolf pelts with corn and wine (Casey & Clark, 140, 143). Thus the definition of a "state" as America moved westward included its replacement of wolves with dogs as of bison with cows.

Books such as Roger Caras's *The Custer Wolf* and stories such as Seton's "Lobo, King of the Currumpaw," Zane Grey's "Wolf Tracker," Peter Matthiessen's "Wolves of Aguila," and Wallace Stegner's "Wolfer" have popularized and, most important, often revised the local tales told by ranchers, travelers, gold rushers, and cattle bosses for more than 150 years.

After the elimination of viable wolf populations the enemies of "lobo" or "timber wolf" adopted guerrilla tactics, and the trapper-versus-wolf stories were conflated with legends of cowboys and Indians, lawmen and bandits, captains and pirates, preachers and sinners, Allies and Axis. Because the wolf covered most of North America, nearly every state has its wolf lore, however thin, and its named lupine rustlers. The American and Canadian West, however, is the expanse over which wolf packs were so shattered as to produce a number of wandering loners or pairs. This phenomenon raised in the stalwart westerner, imagining his work to be the work of God and country, an even more fervent desire to hunt the last few wolves to death. And as so often accompanies the hubris of doing God's work, wolf hunters were prone to make their adversaries into formidable opponents, even demons, in order to establish their own reputations as effective crusaders or Inquisitors. Out of this set of influences emerged legends especially individual and violent in their construction from the arid and expansive ecosystems of the American Southwest and American-Canadian cattle ranges. From the following names one may easily see the connections to the other, human, outlaw legends that make up Euro–North American folklore:

Arizona: The Aquila (or Aguila) Wolf (or wolves); the Truxton Wolf; Old One Toe. *Arkansas:* The Traveler. *Canada:* Black Buffalorunner (Manitoba); Werewolf of Nut Lake (Saskatchewan). *Colorado:* Old Whitey; Big Foot; Rags the Digger; Old Lefty; Three Toes of the Apishapa; the Queen Wolf; the Greenhorn Wolf; (the) Spring Valley Wolf; the Spring Creek Wolf; Old Clubfoot. *Minnesota:* Lobo, the Killer Wolf of the North. *Montana:* Ghost Wolf of the Little Belts; Ghost Wolf of the Little Rockies; the Pryor Creek Wolf. *Oregon:* The Syca[n] Wolf. *New Mexico:* Lobo, King of the Currumpaw; Blanca (Lobo's mate); Las Margaritas. *North Dakota:* Shishoka; Mountain Billy; Wosca (who may also have been the Cody Wolf and/or Cody's Captive). *South Dakota:* Badlands Billy; Three Toes; (the) White Wolf; the Pine Ridge Wolf; the Custer Wolf. *Wyoming:* the Split Rock Wolf; the Gray Terror; Cody's Captive; the Snowdrift Wolf.[14]

That similar (if shorter) lists exist for bears, mountain lions, even coyotes, demonstrates that the über-animal is more pervasive in our thoughts than only in its wolf shape. We have the Leviathan strain leading to *Jaws,* Peter Benchley's vulgarization of *Moby-Dick,* and we have the dolphin fascination (which stories still primarily regard animals in captivity). But we have few persistent legends that generate contemporary stories of marine animals or of birds. Perhaps this is because we have insufficient direct encounters with animals of the air and deep seas, largely inaccessible regions to us, to generate as much invention. I am making the case that we do not simply invent stories of legendary animals out of nothing; we require just enough reality, a modicum of encounter, to warp reality and claim invention.

Many of the outlaws were named for their tracks, some of which exhibited missing toes from former trapping failures. These war wounds added to their legendary status. Snowdrift and Lady Snowdrift gave birth to a pup who became Jack Dempsey's mascot in 1923 and another who became Lady Silver, a 1920s movie star playing the lupine lead opposite a dog named Strongheart. The pups were two of eight taken from the den of the Snowdrift wolves by a trapper (Casey & Clark, 201–2). Trapper stories are full of respect for the enemy and elation over his or her death. These tales, along with the claims of ranchers that instigated painstaking hunts lasting for months or years, yielded some rules of thumb for the malevolent ghost-wolf story:

1. The wolf will be bigger than is plausible, sometimes up to two hundred pounds. Its howl freezes the blood, its gaze freezes the muscles (an adage taken from the medieval bestiaries), it is invisible by night except for its eyes. Either the howl or an enormous track will present itself first, then the wolf will appear as a shadow. Its emergence will reveal dripping fangs. Its eyes will resemble burning coals. Its longevity will be the measure of its power; great outlaws are hunted for a dozen years.

2. The outlaw wolf can kill anywhere from fifty to a hundred cows in a single night. In his short lifetime Old Lefty was reported to have killed 384 head of livestock. Tens of thousands of dollars in claims have been recorded, and bounties were issued rivaling those placed on the heads of the James Gang. Lobo, King of the Currumpaw, warranted a $1,000 bounty in 1893. The case of a wolf killing unusually high numbers of cattle only "confirmed" the prowess of the wolf outlaws. Ironically, however, the tall tales became such a regular occurrence that those inflated numbers became a sign of the whole species's basic nature to kill without restraint.

3. Its mind is cunning and without conscience. A perfect predator, a man-eater, it will kill for pleasure. I'm darkly amused that this tenet is often used to assert the ninjalike stealth of an animal genetically responsible for the endearingly goofy domestic dog.

4. The hunt for the wolf will be fraught with danger and beyond the means of mortal man, no matter what the technological age (Three Toes, for example, purportedly required 150 trappers and hunters at work for thirteen years to catch him). Any ineptitude on the part of hunters will be demonstrated, if at all, through a group of tertiary characters being eviscerated by wolves or otherwise dying in the wild in order to give the hero credibility and incorporate some gratuitous violence for marketability.

Like the reasons for trapping, the nature of the legends being generated has changed, in many cases reversed. Today whole packs, rather than individual outlaw wolves, are gaining fame, and occasionally (but less often) individuals from those packs receive attention. Rick Bass's book *The Ninemile Wolves* made a northwestern Montana pack famous. The Sawtooth Wolves captivity project run partly by the Dutchers resulted in a coffee-table book and a dubiously wilderness-oriented video presentation shown on PBS. The Dutcher wolves are sometimes confused with an Idaho pack of the same name that was wiped out through human action in the 1990s. The Soda Butte, Druid Peak, and Rose Creek packs are well known to American wolf-watchers in Yellowstone's Lamar Valley as founding packs, spoken of with the same reverence some of us reserve for golden-age baseball teams.

Given the list of ways wolves have been imagined, damaged, hunted, domesticated, tortured, rebuffed, and diseased, it's a marvel they have survived. Yet the declaration that it is "up to us to save them" is too often an inadvertent assumption, yet again, of human superiority. In many cases, saving wolves simply means that we merely stop actively killing them. The saving of *habitat,* which has as much to do with systemic integrity as with wolves per se, is a far more difficult feat.

In the 1920s two white wolves who had become famous as outlaws were trapped in Montana. One was Snowdrift (perhaps the Snowdrift Wolf mentioned previously); the other was a female called the Ghost Wolf, who supposedly killed more than $35,000 worth of livestock. Lopez places the trapping of the Ghost Wolf in the Little Rockies and of Snowdrift in the Judith Basin (*Of Wolves and Men,* 193), while Busch's *Almanac* locates the Ghost Wolf in either the Judith Basin or the Highwood Mountains (105). The Snowdrift Wolf was killed by 1923, but there could easily have been more than one Ghost Wolf. Furthermore, the Little Belt Range runs into the Highwoods, so the "Ghost Wolf" may have just been another name for the Snowdrift Wolf. Things can get confusing when suddenly *Canis lupus irregardless* is given a specific and infamous name. According to Busch, "Hunters shot [the Ghost Wolf] in the hind leg, knocked her down, tried to run her down by car, set traps all over the county . . . At one point she even outfought five imported Russian wolfhounds" (105). The Ghost Wolf may have been shot in 1930. There were so many gray outlaw wolves, however, that they sometimes blend in the apparitional habitat of ghost wolves—the human imagination.

By the 1930s, when *The Crossing* begins, the Southwest was all but rid of its wolves, and North America was divided into the Canadian region of wolf survival and the U.S. region of wolf extermination. Only Western Europe, northern

Mexico, and southeastern Asia had bested America in their clean sweep of wolves, all taking far longer to accomplish the task than America's eastern regions had. What took northern Europe centuries to accomplish the United States was on track to surpass in a matter of decades, partly out of its driving need to prove itself at once wilder and more civilized than the European powers.

The game, therefore, is conducted globally as well as individually. In a historic pissing contest, Jefferson proved to the Compte de Buffon that the woolly mammoth had lived in America and that megafauna were not a measure of European greatness (Wood, 30). The United States was then free as a great nation with a grand history to continue the colonial edict of extirpation in full force, to put the wolf down with the mammoth. Asian communities established in Canada and the U.S. only supported and intensified the mythic and economic complexities of the wolf in human dominion. The Chinese wolf of the steppes was considered a malevolent ghost (perhaps a castigation of the Mongol), yet the ancient gate to heaven was guarded by a mythically angelic wolf (Gordon, 100).

When the scattered, anonymous few wolves killed more cattle in order to survive, they took on first national infamy, then legendary proportions. I think they also killed more cattle because they were driven mad; wolves without even the possibilities of pack structures, with great distances between them, lone wolves who might not have been suited for lone wolf life, with wide ranges filled with food—this set of circumstances seems conducive to surplus killing. Consider the excesses, the fallout, of a lonely America spending mind-numbing hours in cars, on computers, in shopping malls. The stories of the outlaw wolves would be funny—quasi-biblical assurances of the dominion of man—were they not also grounded in a cruelty that obviously had nothing to do with the economics of wolf "control." Wolves were strung up with baling wire and peppered with small-caliber fire. They were dragged behind horses; they had their jaws wired shut and were turned loose to starve. This was vengeance killing in a "civil" war that continued well beyond 1865. Wolves were pulled apart between pickup trucks in the 1950s, and the ethic of some current western ranchers has gained infamy as the "Three s's"—Shoot, Shovel, and Shut Up—the vigilante code used to dodge federal fines and maintain the war effort.[15]

In New Mexico the U.S. Forest Service held a series of fourteen public fora regarding reintroduction. One, held in Santa Fe in March of 1996, was moderated by a Sierra Club director, with a panel including three of the most prominent voices in New Mexico on the politics of the project: David Parsons, the U.S Fish and Wildlife Service project director appointed in 1990 to draft a formal reintroduction plan; David Henderson of the Audubon Society; and Al Schneberger, director of the New Mexico Cattlegrowers Association.

During the question-and-answer period a woman talked about her dog being attacked by a wolf when she lived in Minnesota; someone said that wolf spirits were haunting New Mexico; several people asked specific questions about the progress of the project, and when wolves might be released, if they would proliferate, and where they would live. A handful of ranchers sat in the front two rows and said nothing. Parsons answered the questions about government and the project, Henderson about local involvement. Schneberger responded to almost every question. He said he felt outnumbered, that no one was concerned about the plight of ranchers, that "ranch welfare" was a derogatory term and he received none of it. He declared the Defenders of Wildlife reimbursement, which went national immediately after the Yellowstone reintroduction, an unsound program that wouldn't help ranchers survive.

At one point a seasoned cowboy in dress western, white hat, and handlebar mustache stood from the group up front and declared that he didn't much care what some government or state organization run by whomever wanted; if he saw a wolf he'd follow the policy of the Three s's. Parsons pointed out that he'd just admitted his intent to commit a federal offense. The man smiled back at Parsons, apparently undaunted, and sat down in silence for the rest of the meeting. Someone in the back of the room declared that ranchers were pests and that we should have licenses to shoot them if they expanded their territories too far for our liking.[16]

Trapped himself in the body of a man with a limited olfactory capacity, slow locomotion, and susceptibility to the elements, the wolf trapper must learn the wolf's habits (this is articulated as "thinking like a wolf" or "being a wolf," which phrasing certainly follows the language of transmogrification legends). Popular culture has invented the werewolf for Euro–North Americans; Dineh culture has skinwalkers; the Oneida have shape-shifters; the Kwakiutl and Inuit cultures have the Klukwana and Amaguk. Perhaps the wolfer is the true werewolf—clearly man first, bound to humanity, championing its proliferation and right of ownership, championing the champion, the man's man, a walking system of redundancies supporting the were-ness of the world. But the trapper (in the old days almost always a man) tries to imagine the mind of a wolf. He "changes back" briefly when it is time to break the neck of a wolf pup pulled from a den, since thinking like a wolf at that moment isn't to his benefit. Because eradicating wolves is ultimately, if not constantly, his job, the kind of wolf-mind he possesses is Freudian, "lunatic," a moon-howler canted toward genocide. And if the rebuttal is that money, rather than obsession, is the motive, does that redeem him? Or maybe, as in those cases when so-called hunters torture wolves before killing them, he changes into something else entirely, not quite human and not quite wolf, since torture wrought by a human is a political act, and torture wrought by wolves is still but an unproved possibility.

Ernest Seton was himself one of those trappers who, with his partner, found it wise not to waste a bullet or spoil a hide. He dropped lassos around a wolf's neck, he and his partner tying off the ropes to their saddle horns and pulling in opposite directions until the wolf was strangled. One of those wolves was Blanca, Lobo's mate, and within a few pages Seton experiences several emotional shifts difficult to respect in the context of his melodramatic salesmanship throughout the rest of the story. He "exults" over Blanca's death, then discerns in Lobo's howling afterward a sound "sadder than I could possibly have believed" (25–26). He feels "something like compunction" when he traps Lobo, keeps the wolf alive in much the same manner that Billy does when he first catches the she-wolf, delivers a victory speech to the "Grand old outlaw, hero of a thousand lawless raids," and wakes in the morning to declare (likely, to lie) that Lobo has died "of a broken heart" (28). The cattlemen deliver a one-sentence eulogy that puts Lobo back with Blanca, "together again" (30). This respect-for-the-enemy strategy allows Seton to be both conqueror and compassionate human, to exhibit a dual superiority over the wolf. He makes sure to spin a good yarn by investing his ghost wolf with a pathos that "Lobo" never needed before Seton determined to keep him alive for a while as a captive with no hope of return to the wild. This is a tactic developed by many ranchers and some biologists, this head-shaking acquiescence to necessity. Of course, the necessity is purely political, based on the greed inherent to the mass production of meat and the micromanagement of park systems, in profound opposition to Leopold's enlightenment.

In George Waggner's classic 1941 horror film *The Wolf-Man,* Larry Talbot, sweating and filthy, clothed in rags, bearing a pentagram on his hand, wearing the obvious pallor of guilt after having just mauled someone in the forest, is the werewolf. Hardly anyone in the film notices. This is one of the things that makes horror movies so enjoyable for the fans: the less logically the implausi-bilities of the film are explained, the more fun the suspension of disbelief. The audience for *The Wolf-Man* ripples with laughter at the stupidity of the movie's two-dimensional characters. They leave the theater, go to a bar, and raise their glasses to a man in boots, a ducking jacket, and a cowboy hat who reeks of lupine menstrual blood and week-old urine and meat, a local hero of the agricultural community. Mere hours prior, the man was in the midst of altered conscious-ness, thinking like a wolf as best he could until finally he was able to kill the three pups of a pair of alphas standing meekly by and howling, let's say in grief. The people in the bar call him a "man's man."

We may all safely and gamely talk about the movie—exhaust ourselves with our clever and clinically distant *jouissance*. Throughout the long and involved setting of our mind-traps over cocktails in the behavioral sink of civilization, something else is happening. Out in some mountain range we never visit, the alpha pair that escaped for one more day but lost its pups to the wolfer looks for them sometimes. Sometimes their minds wander back just enough to remember *pups,* the smells and sounds of them. However each member of the pack thinks, however limited lupine cognition might be, collective and individual behavior has been altered from what it was the day before: milk in the mother's teats is still being produced, and the father's inclination when he hunts, what we call "instinct," is to feed five. Whatever guilt the trapper at the bar might feel he can easily veil with his contempt for the academic chatter wasted on a foregone conclusion, a *necessity.* He lives in the present. Let's say we're right about other mammals' memories being short. This means that the difference between animal and human memory is that we forget selectively. We go to the movies.

The Trapper Mystic

If we knew only one fact from one wolf book about what has been done to wolves in the United States—one item that would stand as the deal-breaker of the millennium, demanding that we rethink ourselves, our literature, and our mythology in earnest—it might be this: Ben Corbin, one of the famous wolf trappers of the turn of the century and author of *Corbin's Advice; or, The Wolf Hunter's Guide,* baited fishhooks, strung them on lines, tossed them into wolf dens, waited for the pups to swallow them, then yanked the pups out of the dens and killed them (McIntyre, *War,* 20). If I had to write a pedagogical lesson on the literary criticism of the wolf book in one long, complex sentence, that would be the sentence. Literature can save our minds from becoming Ben Corbin's, but not if we're only conscious of ourselves and our own cultures. Out of ourselves and our cultures in isolation from the nonhuman world, we become Ben Corbin. I have watched for ten years the practice and organization of ecocriticism making itself more complicated, in some unfortunate effort to become somehow more "rigorous" or "interesting." Simplify, simplify. Sometimes the job is to aim someone's face at Ben Corbin's advice and hold it there until revulsion gives way to awareness.

In *The Crossing,* the master trapper is a man named Echols, based on W. C. Echols, in reality one of the best trappers in the Southwest during the 1920s (D. Brown, 67, 76, 83). An old man explaining to Billy the mystic elements of trapping considers whether "Echols es medio lobo el mismo" ("Echols is half wolf himself") and that "él conoce lo que sabe el lobo antes de que lo sepa el lobo"—that Echols knows what the wolf knows before the wolf does (45). The trap mechanism and poison matrix meet with the characters' "horse sense" of outdoor experience and knowledge of both cattle and wolves, to produce an alchemical metaphor vital to both Billy's search and to McCarthy's border cosmos. I would not go so far as to directly compare McCarthy's mysticism and use of alchemy to Gabriel García Márquez's, despite some similarities (both, for example, have close ties to Faulkner's work). But García Márquez's work seems stylistically separate enough from McCarthy's romantic naturalism to warn against close comparative assumptions.

McCarthy is as exact in his description of trapping as he is in the description of guns in *Blood Meridian* or horses in *All the Pretty Horses*. The Parhams read wolf sign for some time before setting the traps, and Billy follows the she-wolf without seeing her; he sets the right trap intuitively (32). McCarthy correctly identifies the Newhouse 4½ as the wolf trap of Billy's era and refers to the trapper's practice of reading up on other methods and engaging in the tradesman's craft of cataloging the wolf's tricks. The famous Newhouse leghold trap, first the 4½, with teeth added in the #14 version, was retooled as the #114, which could accommodate the longer foot of wolves living in the Far North. These traps have been so efficient that the toothless versions are still employed in biological study, though the injuries wolves sometimes incur from them has prompted protests against their use and aerial darting is the preferred, though more expensive, method (see Bateman; D. Brown). McCarthy includes the cowhide horse-hoof slipper and the buckskin cloth onto which the trapper dismounts, and he describes in detail the preparation, scenting, setting, and anchoring of traps. But writing a textbook on trapping is not McCarthy's method of presentation. Manipulations, both subtle and drastic, mythologize the process and take the trapping of a physical wolf into the realm of the ghost wolf.

After following the old oracle's advice (to which I will return), Billy sets the trap beneath the warm ash of the vaqueros' fire, a technique used by the actual trapper Roy T. McBride to catch the outlaw wolf Las Margaritas (D. Brown, 163). With a blackened stick he writes a note in the sand (in Spanish) to the vaqueros, in order to prevent their stepping in the trap. When he leaves he says, "You read my sign . . . if you can" (50). The comment is ambiguous; Billy could be referring either to the vaqueros or to the wolf. His father is clearer about who might find the message, ordering Billy to go back and change the set because he can't be sure the vaqueros can read (51). The semiotic game has subtly shifted, first from illiteracy (the wolf's) to translation (Spanish/English), to interspecies duplicity (the trap set), then back again through translation to literacy/illiteracy (the vaqueros'). This scene is one among several in which the reader learns the magician's tricks. The famous trappers, in *The Crossing* named Echols and Oliver, are invoked as trade wizards; Billy's father tells him that Oliver could set traps from horseback, though he doesn't know how the man accomplished the feat (23). McCarthy zoomorphizes the traps in a locution marked by Scandinavian myth, "with their jaws agape like steel trolls silent and mindless and blind" (36). Like Stephen Crane's cannons in *The Red Badge of Courage,* personified industrial monsters trumping any horror of nature (121), the traps are both mechanical tools and living beings, participants in a process beyond themselves.

Four pronounced mystical elements assure us that McCarthy is spiritualizing the trapper's occupation. The first is found in Echols's cabin—in real life located at the OK Bar Ranch in Cloverdale, New Mexico (D. Brown, 87)—an alchemical war room made to look like a friar's apothecary, "with its chemic glass a strange basilica dedicated to a practice as soon to be extinct among the trades of men as the beast to whom it owed its being" (*Crossing,* 17). In this room the wolf becomes the devil against whom the Templars wage their crusades. But the paganization of the sacred material, the Catholic root, is found as well in the "dark liquids. Dried viscera. Liver, gall, kidneys." And the god of human beings, who have taken as their mission the destruction of the wolf, is depicted as "insatiable," unable to be appeased by "any measure of blood" (17). The vials contain the relics, the matrices, scents of wolf and prey brewed to draw the wolf to the trap.

The next mystical element is found in direct conjunction with a passage in which Billy's father is teaching him how to dig and set a trap. We are witness to the process until Will Parham finishes and backs away from the device, at which point he is transformed by the narrator: "Crouched in the broken shadow with the sun at his back and holding the trap at eyelevel against the morning sky he looked to be truing some older, some subtler instrument. Astrolabe or sextant. Like a man bent at fixing himself someway in the world. Bent on trying by arc or chord the space between his being and the world that was. If there be such space. If it be knowable" (22).

Here is Ahab after the white whale, just as the trappers of the Snowdrift and Ghost Wolf were tracking white wolves somehow more malevolent for their desecration of whiteness (probably the mere result of their graying with age). It is difficult not to see the mythic hunt in place through a metaphoric empowerment of the trap itself as much as the trapper. Will Parham's apparent bent on "fixing himself" in the cosmos is Orion's quest as well, the conquest of all beasts in the race across the heavens and in the drama of the hunt. The expanses of tundra, desert, and sky meet here in the common wolf-book motif of wide open space and raise the question of who is entitled to that space.

The third mystical scene is the most powerful. Billy is led to Don Arnulfo, a dying old Mexican who himself bears the name of the wolf and knows the wolf better than anyone in the novel, although neither Billy nor the reader realizes this until the two characters speak to each other. Billy has come looking for Echols. He tells the don that he carries two of Echols's matrices and is trying to trap a wolf. Arnulfo explains to Billy "that the matrix was not so easily defined. Each hunter must have his own formula," and that "only shewolves in their season were a proper source" (45). When Billy tells him that he is after a shewolf (only in this passage does McCarthy write the word without a hyphen, as if to honor Don Arnulfo or if only to indicate that the speakers are using Spanish), the man replies that the wolves have all been trapped by Echols. Eventually he offers cryptic advice leading Billy to set a trap in a dead campfire; he says to look for "that place where the acts of God and those of man are a piece . . . Lugares donde el fiero ya está en la tierra, the old man said. Lugares donde ha quemado el fuego" (47). He does not part with this information without first dispensing some more important advice: "El lobo es una cosa incognoscible" (45).

Billy learns from Arnulfo as a questing hero from a shamanic mentor. He learns to see, through a glass darkly, the world between the acts of men and their helpless cries, but this does not save him from the experience. At the end of the novel Billy calls out apologies into the darkness to a three-legged dog who has hobbled away from his cruel rejection (425). That itself is a complicated moment psychologically; Billy rejects the dog after his experience with the wolf but is incapable of doing so with compassion for the dog's (here exaggerated) subordinate condition (see Arnold, 230-31). He learns that the wolf cannot be held and that she disappears upon being caught, that the Wolf in the Trap begins the transformation toward death, toward the ghost wolf found first in memory, then in the warping of memory, the denial of memory, and the projection of an invention that was never in fact the wolf. "Not even God can bring it back," says Don Arnulfo, whom the other villagers think is a *brujo,* the equivalent of both the Navajo skinwalker and the Puritan witch. When Billy leaves, the woman caring for the don delivers her own prophetic challenge, though she does not imply that she considers it to be prophetic. "You see this old man?" she says. "You know what a terrible thing it is to die without God? To be the one that God has cast aside? Think it over" (48). Billy does think it over, each time he imagines the she-wolf's life and when he buries her and her living pups.

The final mystification of the hunt is found in McCarthy's indication that the she-wolf is caught in Billy's trap on the day his parents are killed (52–53). On McCarthy's desert, just as on Melville's ocean, there is no mechanical trap without its astral counterpart, no body without either a soul or the argument over a soul, no world of blood without a matrix for blood behind it—no wolf without a ghost wolf.

Aside from Edwin T. Arnold's excellent "McCarthy and the Sacred," which I've cited several times here, one other critical treatment of *The Crossing* has thoroughly examined the novel's wolf story. It is Dianne C. Luce's "The Vanishing World of Cormac McCarthy's Border Trilogy," and it deserves a close look. Luce's thesis follows from the "vanishing" motif common to the literature of endangered species. She also links "the ecological vision of the Border Trilogy" with "spiritual concerns," the philosophical positions of both Billy Parham and the story's omniscient narrator (162–63). In McCarthy's nihilistic world the wolf is predictably cast as a symbol of that which is being driven out, destroyed, tortured by forces that are or pretend to be amoral.

At times Luce overstates what she calls the "evanescence" of other species and slips dangerously close to the world-will-find-a-balance approach so easily co-opted by exploitationists, although she clearly doesn't adopt this position herself. "The great terror and beauty of the world's creatures are evanescent," she writes, "while the world itself endures" (164). It's unclear whether Luce is presenting this as McCarthy's vision or following it herself; my disagreement is simply with the statement at face value. We certainly may say that an animal lives and dies within a shorter time frame than a planet, which is Luce's point, but the world's creatures also *constitute* the world and its substance in order for it to be considered a world (as opposed to a mere planet, rock, asteroid, meteor, or comet). This is not an observer-dependent position, only a catalog that includes the organism as a defining feature of ecology and of "world." Otherwise, Luce's employment of phenomenology, through which she connects sight and existence, is, again, appropriate to McCarthy's fictional environment. That is, the real in McCarthy is presented in fine enough form to permit the brand of totemism and nihilism he asserts. Luce covers the incidents of blindness, whiteout, absence, and other vanishings with sound close readings.

The article is strongest in its context. Luce applies Leopold, Lopez, Burbank, and David Brown (upon whom she relies heavily for five pages) to both the generic history of wolves in America and the Mexican wolf (in Burbank and Brown) in particular. She also includes some of the connective work between Echols and McBride that give *The Crossing* a measure of its corporeality.[17] The application of these writers succeeds and makes the article both an excellent introduction to the Mexican wolf story and a fine piece of ecocriticism. The main problem with the piece is Luce's invocation of Ortega y Gassett's *Meditations on Hunting*, which is rife with machismo and poor rationalizations of hunting as a spiritual game that includes the animal's complicity. It conflates sport hunting with subsistence hunting and seems at times far too in love with the writer's own clever poetry than with reality. Luce could have expurgated this piece; it does not

fit with the other writers she chooses, especially at one point when it is inappropriately juxtaposed with Leopold's epiphanic wolf encounter (Luce, 171–72).

A commendable feature of Luce's research is her inclusion of the Malpais
rancher group and a brief consideration of the status of the Mexican wolf. Luce
does not simply adhere to the vanishing motif but discusses the handful of ranchers, like the handful of wolves, who are surviving in some cooperative arrangement. Indeed, she ends her article on this hopeful note (188–90). The vanishing
motif tends to perpetuate both the *act* of vanishing and the errant concept of
vanishing where flourishing may be the reality. Applied to American Indian populations, the vanishing motif is an insult. Applied to wolves, it is a similar romance, a gothic frisson that may well entice us to maintain someone's vanished
status in order to keep ourselves guilt-free and entertained. Luce indirectly analyzes how wolves, cowboys, and Indians have all been diminished by story.
McCarthy's work actually has a better sense of wolves, individually and culturally, than it has of Indians, and so his contributions to solving problems of, say,
boosterism seem to serve us from the ecocritical perspective before, if not over,
anthropocentric perspectives.

The intra- and interspecific codes at work in *The Crossing* eventually expand
and combine to create a volatile mixture of border law and trespassing; reward
and punishment; global and ancient legends given localized voices; the picaresque; historical events of carnage and loss through the modern era; and the
collision of the observable world with the mystical world, of the wolf with its
own ghost. The narrator gives us a fairly specific location for the she-wolf's crossing along the international border, and although this is the first crossing, it will
not be the last. Therefore, the title of the novel might indicate that one crossing
in particular is most important. We are never told which one, though the she-
wolf's first one is most fully delineated (24). We are told that her "ancestors had
hunted camels and primitive toy horses on these grounds" (24–25). The narrator's focalization continues to exhibit the plasticity it had during its synthesis
with Billy's point of view; here it is conflated with the she-wolf's. For approximately three pages during the account of the crossing, it is difficult if not impossible to discern the relationship between what the she-wolf thinks and the narrator's external explanation. The narrator tells us the she-wolf will not now return
to a kill or cross "under a wire fence twice in the same place." She has learned.
"These were the new protocols. Strictures that had not existed before. Now they
did" (25).

One point of view revealed through the wolf's gaze is designed for the reader
alone: the glance back to the ancient world of wolf epics. As were the she-wolves
of Ataturk, Genghis Khan, and Romulus and Remus, the wolf in *The Crossing* is

pregnant, a traveling companion to a boy, and a nurturer. But she is also transformed from those other myths. Now the maternal wolf is also vulnerable; she is without fantasy or humanity or empire-building behind her actions. Instead she educates Billy as a wolf to a human, rather than as an icon to a hero. The reward Billy receives is her temporary companionship. He even learns something of ferality, the hard way. And eventually, he will participate in his own revision of an epic, when he tries to pull the chain holding the she-wolf out of the bottom of the fighting pit before the end of the world.

In the Eddas humanity originates out of the one forest that does not burn. The fires of Ragnarok purge the earth, the rivers flow, and Sol is rejuvenated. *The Crossing*'s last sentence tells us that "after a while the east did gray and after a while the right and godmade sun did rise, once again, for all and without distinction" (426). This faint image of hope declares a Whitmanesque world, if darkly, in which all are made equal by death and the living are made equal by the rising of the sun. In both Germanic and Pawnee mythology, darkness and the wolf complicate the role of light or lightning, but they are not diametrically opposed to light. In this respect, the trickster holds a more liberated post than does the devil. In the Southwest the representative canid for the trickster is Coyote. For the Wind River Shoshone, Wolf is the principal creator and lawmaker, but his role is given equal importance to Coyote's as trickster; in Greek mythology the fifty sons of Zeus Lycaeus's great disciple, King Lycaon, attempt to play the trickster's part and discover consequences similar to those for the Skidi Pawnee, but in a profanement of the trickster's role (Earhart, 288, 371). In McCarthy the Christian symbology of the wolf is backgrounded to the actuality of the wolf's corporeal self. She is purely who she is.

Wolf and Whale

In 1995 a hybrid, mostly wolf, journeyed from Montana to El Paso, where "it" (the report omits the sex) was hit by a car and killed, then picked up by El Paso animal-control officers. The animal wore "eartags and a Fish and Wildlife radio collar." The officials traced him or her back to Joe Fontaine, who had originally tagged the animal in the summer of 1994 in order to see if this was in fact a wolf. Over a couple months of tracking, Fontaine decided the animal had been socialized. The hybrid canid showed no fear of humans, "hung out in wheat and barley fields" within a five-square-mile area, and demonstrated ineptitude at hunting. Fontaine lost the signal in October and finally assumed that the animal had died, perhaps because of there having been no sightings of a socialized wolf. After it turned up in El Paso the conclusion was that someone had picked up the hybrid, driven to Texas, and possibly tried to raise him/her, dead radio collar and all. This conclusion seems, for several reasons, to be about as supportable as the animal's having traveled the distance on foot, living a life between the worlds of wolf and dog (Holmes). The distance between Livingston, Montana, and El Paso, Texas, is 987 miles.

When in the last pages of *The Crossing* Billy Parham rides his horse north back into Arizona and then New Mexico, he arrives at a "blacktop road" as a truck passes (422). He has become an anachronism, the vanishing breed appropriated by advertising agencies and novelists in his day and for years to come. He sits his horse not far from where in 1998 there would be wolves again. The first test of whether this story will survive in our own world is passed whenever a pack crosses (or avoids) an Arizona highway, when a rancher lets them escape, when a driver decides to stop. Maybe the last test will be passed when the highway itself is the vanishing breed.

It's easy to accuse ecocritics of being Luddite retrospectivists desperate to return to a primitive past. Actually, one may read my position as a look to the future. The petroleum- and macadam-based system of road building in America has proven to be more readily abused than efficiently designed, contributes to tens of thousands of deaths a year, and is overbuilt for its purpose. It cuts up the ecosystems of the continent in ways that cause inbreeding, invasive species proliferation, and breakdowns in contiguity and ecosystemic health, not to mention the ubiquity of what we so crassly call "roadkill." So I'll go to the dentist rather than back to the past, but when the present isn't quite working, I'll advocate its change toward a simple and elegant solution rather than a complex and monetized one. That might cost us our comfort, and this, it strikes me, is what we academics in the humanities join the mass in being most afraid to lose.

The Crossing, expertly rendered though it is, will never be The Story of The Wolf. It is still one story about a fictitious wolf, based on stories of dead wolves few people ever saw, used to represent living wolves fewer still have seen. If reading a book about a wolf in the context of twenty-year political imbroglios may transform the wolves of our imaginations, then we should consider what might be accomplished by our actually witnessing the track or sign, hearing the howl, seeing the long stride and ripples of fur on a wolf at full sprint, even looking into those famous eyes on their terms, in the clarity of such rules as exist outside civilization and under the wider realm of the physical universe. I can state from personal, if limited, experience that it's possible to read hundreds of written texts on wolves and have all of them only ever coalesce in the transformative, educational moment of witness.

Perhaps the great fictional experiment in North American literature regarding the link between taxonomy and story is Ishmael's project in *Moby-Dick*. Melville's epic was written during the advent of the natural sciences in the United States and in the waning days of the Nantucket whaling bonanza. By the end of his story Ishmael considers himself "omnisciently exhaustive in the enterprise" he has "undertaken to manhandle this Leviathan." He compares the whale with all other animals, asserts its superiority, and determines that while grandiosity should be staved off when describing another animal, "when Leviathan is the text, the case is altered" (378). One of the many plots running through the novel is the story of how this semiotician/naturalist comes to his learned position: we see an accumulation of epigraphs, chapters on cetology, microscopic detail on processes, and material from both science and mythology that overwhelms him through to the sinking of the *Pequod*. He realizes finally that the grandiosity he adopted in order to describe the whale may have been to some degree an attempt to screw up his own courage with knowledge in the face of his confusion and fear.

So much of McCarthy's narrative universe is similar to Melville's that it's worth a minute to gauge the later writer by his forebear. Ishmael's project of "knowing the whale" is the driving intellectual charge of *Moby-Dick* and depends utterly on the cetology chapters. He employs the gamut of possible approaches to knowledge of this "fish":

1. a pre-Darwinian scientific rigor that includes metaphor at every turn ("Cetology," in which the metaphor is the book; "Brit" and "Squid," in which the eating and agonistic traits of whales are juxtaposed with four following chapters on how the crew of the *Pequod* eats; "The Sphynx," "The Battering-Ram," "The Great Heidelburgh Tun," and "The Prairie," all obvious enough metaphors for the head; and "The Cassock," a hilariously irreverent reference to whale anatomy);

2. a direct and mythic analysis of art ("The Counter-pane"; chapters 55–57 on paintings; surmises on the doubloon's images; the combined iconic and crafts-man's language of Ahab's compass, quadrant, harpoon, peg leg, and line; and both Queequeg's and Ishmael's tattoos); and

3. an invocation of horror and fantastic revelation ("The Spirit-Spout," "The Whiteness of the Whale," "The Try-Works").

All of these are also elements of composition in McCarthy. From "The Bower of the Arsacides" onward, Ishmael's quest combines his methods in a boiling broth that leads him to the mythic three-day chase. In all, the effort toward the corporeal whale in the confusion of the ghost whale lasts from chapter 32 to chapter 105, making the novel actually framed by its "plot," which is largely handled in the two blocks of chapters 1–31 and chapters 106–35, with the chapters on the gams holding the *Pequod*'s narrative thread together throughout the middle. *Moby-Dick* is both an über-animal story and an appropriate wellspring for *The Crossing* by way of content and position as well as diction.

A final analogy is unavoidable: McCarthy had written a play called *Whales and Men* that preceded *The Crossing* and contains much of its sentiment and imagery (see Luce; Lilley). Melville's whale may have inspired McCarthy's wolf, as both throw off-kilter all the metaphysical, incorporeal rationalizations of an existence without material referent, a life not just of the inevitability of human-centered human perception but also of destructive selfishness. The whale's whiteness, the wolf's mythic position, these are both worth our consideration's resulting in something beyond solipsistic rumination. The white whale must have its whaleness. The wolf that serves us is called a carcass, or a god, or a dog.

Both Ishmael and Billy Parham hold in their hands the damaru, the skull that wakes the spirits, resonating with the energy of another animal's voice and thoughts, and with the wind in the hollows of bone. This is how they try to punch through Ahab's pasteboard mask. In the existential metaphysics of both Ahab's and *The Crossing*'s literary naturalism, on the other side is the void. In reference to an actual mask, or to the casing of bone holding the brain, on the other side is the wearer of the mask, or our own psyche and viscera. Wolf books humble us to our position in a world shared with another animal, one subject to human drama and politics. They prompt us to think on what and where and when we have done these things to these animals. They invite us to create the conditions for new and more hopeful stories.

Lupus Mundi

Before we lived, there lived a world we have chosen to call wilderness, not as the backdrop to our existence but as its *prima materia*. Something of that world clings tenaciously to the planet under the onslaught of concentrated efforts to erase it. And because once it is owned or tamed, wilderness is erased, no wolf can be owned, just as no human can be owned, just as land and water and air can never truly be owned, whatever will be done to them or by whom and under what sign or law or language. What can be possessed is only the story this one animal tells to this other, which possession begs to be shared. When one of us says, "my story," (or, for that matter, "my dog") it should mean what we mean when we say, "my grandmother," not "my car" or "my money." When an animal acts, speaks, lives in shared spaces with us, it is the gauge of our empathy and wisdom how we share the possession of that story. The heart of such ownership is therefore more cooperative than competitive, made healthy by a communal land and a mutual hope to live beyond mere survival for the rest of this day. In the stories of wolves we come up wanting, and in the critical readings of the stories of wolves and men, of the nonhuman in relation to the human, we up-stage, chewing up the scenery of our textbook "settings" in the assumption that we alone are the drama. What faint hope I have for literary criticism's practical value resides in its ability to aim a culture toward art, to say the things about art that might contribute to the enlightenment of the living, and so to honor the dead without increasing their numbers. This book is not an opportunistic puzzle to be worked for the entertainment of cultural critics. It is a plea, an entreaty for us to turn away from the ways that we abstract and so disrespect the living world that we pretend to be removed from it, as if these animals were here for our leisure.

Introduction

1. When I present Freud in this book, I present his work as a piece of writing about the ghost wolf through his symbol-centered case work and his unarguably valuable contribution to dream study, and not according to its consistency or lack thereof with current cognitive research. I encourage the reader to consult the work on cognitive theory, evolutionary psychology, and animal cognition that anchors my position on the matter of human and nonhuman participation in the making of literature: e.g., Donald Griffin's *Animal Minds,* Marc D. Hauser's *Wild Minds,* John T. Bonner's *Evolution of Culture in Animals,* Charles Darwin's *Expression of the Emotions in Man and Animals* and *Descent of Man,* Michael Bekoff's *Minding Animals,* Joseph Carroll's *Evolution and Literary Theory* and *Literary Darwinism,* Jonathan Gottschall and David Sloan Wilson's *Literary Animal,* Georgina Ferry's *Understanding of Animals,* Richard Dawkins's *Unweaving the Rainbow,* and Steven Pinker's *Blank Slate* and *Language Instinct.* Briefly, I will say here that genetic research continually proves, not isolated individual genes for every phenomenon in human behavior, but complex genetic composites that advance the *study* of human behavior. The major obstacle to cognitive study has been the life sciences' great bane—behaviorism—which vies only with the humanities' cultural constructivism for a bunk in the moldy jail of anthropocentric thought.

2. E.g., Link & Crowley, 15; Gray, 129; Busch, xiv. Coleman refers to "dispelling the myths" (3). Lopez asserts the need for field experience in *Of Wolves and Men* (284), and continues to discuss it, as he did at the conference of the Association for the Study of Literature and the Environment, Missoula, Montana, July 1997, toward science's understanding of context and meaning, so to better understand themselves as well as wolves. Raglon quotes Lopez on the matter but unfortunately uses the opportunity to cast nature writing and "the scientific method" in opposition, with "science" at fault.

3. Peters, *Dance of the Wolves,* opens with a pseudonymic wolf biologist toting research gear, whom the author calls "the wolfman" (1).

4. See most literary handbooks, including Holman & Harmon and Frye & Baker, among others, which contain definitions of regionalism (sometimes including local color as a distinctive category) that focus on the cultural vernacular and rightly emphasize the advent of these styles as rooted in women's fiction, specifically through such writers as Sarah Orne Jewett and Mary Wilkins Freeman. The plantation tradition on which Brodhead and Kaplan focus gives the South its due, and Kaplan does excellent work on regionalism on a broader scale. Discussions of Plains and western writers deemphasize the term, subsuming it in "agrarian" or "border" models. Fetterley and Pryse are most markedly responsible for rendering regionalism nearly synonymous with women in New England, to the point at which the regionalist/local-colorist distinctions defined by culture-centered character and narrator analyses far outstrip the role of place. For other treatments see Ammons, Bell, D. Campbell, Howard, and Sundquist.

5. See Gould, especially *The Mismeasure of Man*. This text also has bearing on my several mentions of craniometric measurements as taxonomic determinants.

6. I would be interested in someone of some expertise taking chapter 11 more deeply into race matters, as Cornell West would put it.

7. See Marina Warner's superb essay "Beautiful Beasts: The Call of the Wild," a chapter in *Six Myths of Our Time*. My thanks to her, as well, for reminding me in her work that Max in *Where the Wild Things Are* could be wearing a wolf suit.

8. For a kind of antithesis to this position, see two werewolf stories: James Farlow's "The Demythologized Werewolf" and James Blish's "There Shall Be No Darkness," both of which consider fantastic "scientific" explanations for and manipulations of werewolf transformation. Both stories are discussed in Brian Frost's *Essential Guide to Werewolf Literature* (174, 196).

Chapter One ■ *The Real, the Corporeal, and the Ghost Wolf*

1. See, for instance, Susan Chernak McElroy's *Heart in the Wild*. The melodrama of symbolizing an animal so personally as to change the animal into what we wish it to be is, in the end, distracting more than instructive, because it only aims inward, finally excluding the animal.

2. A telling example: Diane Boyd corrected long-standing assumptions about a male domination of wolf packs. Her clarity about scientific study versus cultural proclivity is worth examination by humanities scholars. See "Living with Wolves," 95. For the Spencerian abuse of Darwin, see Spencer's *Data of Ethics* and the critical assessment by Fieser.

3. For more on the Russian sledge-chase wolf story and its influence, see Paul Schach, "Russian Wolves in Folktales and Literature of the Plains."

4. For a list of sources from field studies on wolves being adopted by packs, see Mech & Boitani's "Wolf Social Ecology" (2) in their edited collection *Wolves: Behavior, Ecology, and Conservation,* including information on wolf dispersal from packs (12); contrast this with Robert Ardrey's popular, if dubious, *The Territorial Imperative*. Ardrey hardly men-

tions wolves, but the passage in which they appear (a dominance example) is tellingly juxtaposed with human ritual aggression (340–41).

5. See Nathan Schwartz-Salant's *Jung on Alchemy*. The selections from Jung include passages regarding projection that are in harmony with my model on wolves in literature; see particularly pp. 3, 10, 13, and 81–83. Consulting the original selections is certainly necessary, but the order Schwartz-Salant gives them is worth attention, and his own thesis is directly relevant to the World-Wolf model.

6. See Roszak, Gomes, & Kanner's *Ecopsychology*.

Chapter Two ■ *Basic Corporeality: Wolf Biologists and Nonfiction*

1. For books directly about the Yellowstone wolves, see esp. Fischer, Schullery, D. Smith, D. Smith & Ferguson, McNamee, Phillips & Smith, and McIntyre. This proliferation, however, is both result of and contributor to a swell of interest during the program's conception and after its success, such as Askins, Bass, A. Bowen, P. Bowen, Busch, Casey & Clark, Elhard, Hampton, Hogan, and Link & Crowley.

2. See Kime, Kolb, and Setterburg for details regarding Dodge's influence on Twain and for Twain's manipulation of facts toward the furtherance of a legendary American West.

3. A bit more severe than Bass in this regard is, again, McElroy's *Heart in the Wild*. I don't mean at all to diminish the animal god aspect of a spiritual path, which I adopt and support as deeply valuable to one's establishing a moral position regarding animals. The language used to articulate that position is a more difficult matter. Publicly expressing a position changes it from a moral to an ethical one, which demands that we not exploit the real animal in service to our gods.

4. E.g., Streiber, Dickson, O'Brien, Brand, North (who refers to his book as "a documentary novel"), and Elizabeth Marshall Thomas.

5. Among its many mentions, the "fierce green fire" passage is quoted in: McNamee (*Return of the Wolf*, 30–31), McIntyre (*War*, 9 [Bruce Babbitt's foreword] and 326–27), Coleman (191–92), Murray (22), Hampton (151), Link & Crowley (19–20), Fischer (32), Busch (*Wolf Songs*, 11), Nie (65–71), K. Jones (35–43), and Grooms (30).

6. Most frequently cited is "Organization and Range of the Pack" (see Mech & Boitani; Allen; and Young & Goldman's *Wolves of North America*. See as well Link & Crowley's profile of Olson, 16–19. For Olson's work in the nature essay, see *Songs of the North,* which includes "Timber Wolves" (234–41) and is a stylistic precursor to the craft of Wallace Stegner and Edward Hoagland; *Reflections from the North Country* is a Thoreauvian rumination near the end of Olson's life. Most significant of his work is the Wilderness Act of 1964, which he helped draft and which constitutes one of the most important pieces of environmental legislation in U.S. history. For the best collection of his material, see Mike Link's *Collected Works of Sigurd Olson*.

7. Lopez (*Of Wolves and Men*, 67–68); Heinrich (231–38); Kilham (227–28); Busch

(*Wolf Almanac,* 58–59); Savage (142); Mech (*The Wolf,* 287–88); Ballard, Carbyn, & Smith (in Mech & Boitani, 269–71); D. Allen (287–92); Harrington ("Ravens," 236–37); and for one cultural perspective on the relationship, see Garfield & Forrest, *The Wolf and the Raven: Totem Poles of Southeastern Alaska.*

8. E.g., McNamee, Grooms, Foreman, and Kellert & Wilson all isolate the last part of the passage. Abrams et al., Swinburne & Brandenburg, and Feher-Elston quote the passage in its fuller context.

9. Steve Burgess summarizes the court of public opinion on Mowat in "Northern Exposure" for Salon.com: http://www.salon.com/people/bc/1999/05/11/mowat/index .html.

10. In addition to the examples that directly follow in the text, I would add Hank Fischer (interview and *Wolf Wars*), Durward Allen's *Wolves of Minong,* and as a polemical counterexample, Alston Chase's "Purpose of Yellowstone's Wolf Return Circus" and *In a Dark Wood.* Fischer's work with Defenders of Wildlife is notable. The organization has been one of the most effective preservationist groups in American history.

11. See esp. René Girard's *The Scapegoat* and *Violence and the Sacred,* Walter Burkert's *Homo Necans,* and Scully's *Dominion.*

Chapter Three ■ *The Bioregional and Geopolitical Wolf Book*

1. *Santa Fe New Mexican,* November 30, 1995; *Albuquerque Journal,* January 28, 1995; and Manfredo et al.

2. See D. Allen, Wolves of Minong; R. Peterson, The Wolves of Isle Royale; and Olson, Songs of the North, The Singing Wilderness, and "The Quetico-Superior."

3. See Bateson's "Steps to an Ecology of Mind and Mind and Nature."

4. It's unfortunate that ecopsychology has not taken on the more rigorous uphill climb necessary in mainstream work to reach the hard skeptic against New Age fluff. Roszak, Gomes, & Kanner's introductory collection of essays is a great start for the field. Subsequent efforts have ranged too widely, from "sacred space" work (Lane, Roszak, Plotkin; and much of Roszak's more recent output) to the more solid, and in my view more necessary, work of Michael Cohen, Richard Louv, and Ralph Metzner. There still hasn't been enough scholarly investigation of the role of the nonhuman world as functional beyond its symbolic value to the psyche, especially as an apparatus for literary study.

5. Another wolfer participating in the project and whose story is germane to this study is Dan Gish (Steinhart, 41–48; D. Brown, 181), whom I also mention in the Introduction.

6. Besides the sad and obvious trauma to the animals, the loss of a whooping crane, and a power outage that killed some of the sea life at the zoo, the Audubon Center for Research of Endangered Species weathered Hurricane Katrina and, as of this writing, continues its cleanup.

7. See Parsons, "Case Study," 1; Parsons et al., "Mexican Wolf Recovery Program Project Update," 2. Cf. *Santa Fe New Mexican,* January 6 and May 4, 1993.

8. For continually updated information on the Mexican wolf's status, see the Wolf Recovery Program's Web site: http://www.fws.gov/ifw2es/mexicanwolf/brwrp_notes.cfm.

9. For the Belshaw coverage in New Mexico, see *Santa Fe Reporter*, March 21, 1984; *Santa Fe New Mexican*, January 14, 1985, February 12, 1987, November 16, 1993; and *Albuquerque Journal North*, December 18, 1991, February 8 and March 11, 1992.

Chapter Four ■ *Druid Peak*

1. The Environmental Impact Statement "Wolves for Yellowstone?" (Varley & Brewster) accounts for more than a decade and a half of research toward reintroduction. Schullery's *Yellowstone Wolf* includes pertinent documents, many from the EIS. A more personal history is Askins's *Shadow Mountain*. McNamee and Ferguson each provide overviews.

2. E.g., Johnson & Aamodt; Bruce Thompson; Beach-Balthis; Petersen; and Hughes, Hill, & Hughes.

3. See J. Brown; Gaston & Blackburn. The latter is focused on avifauna in Britain and so provides a macroecological study highly animal-focused. Brown's is the introduction to and definition of the field.

4. This phenomenon of the wolf's body leading to the killer appears in 'Asta Bowen's *Hungry for Home,* Rick Bass's *Where the Sea Used to Be,* and Nicholas Evans's *The Loop,* all books set in and around Montana.

Chapter Five ■ *Intermediate Corporeality: The Average Wolf*

1. Ernest Hemingway to Harvey Breit, June 29, 1952, in Baker. My thanks for this to Robert Paul Lamb.

2. Mech (*The Wolf,* 20); Roberta Hall (chap. 8 in Hall & Sharp); Zimen (chap. 2); Steinhart (19–22); Hampton (16–25); Grey (1–26); Nowak (239–58 in Mech & Boitani). Most of these (and add Fox in Hall & Sharp, 25) lead to the speculations about what I am calling the "campfire myth" of wolf-dog domestication. The wide range of these accounts and interpretations, from Grey's storybook-quality prosaic rendering to Nowak's clinical assessment, should demonstrate both the knowledge and lack that we have.

3. I have slightly modified Busch (*Wolf Almanac,* 3), who lists *Canidae* as "the dog family"; I am qualifying that label because it is a poor decision by the scientific community. Busch also lists *lupus* as "gray wolf," when it actually indicates all wolves. He rightly omits subspecies designations from a taxonomic list.

4. See Nowak (250 in Mech & Boitani); Phillips, Henry, & Kelly (274–88); and Hoagland's essay "Lament the Red Wolf" (in Hoagland, 109). For a fine book-length personal essay that includes much on the reintroduction of the red wolf, see Christopher Camuto's *Another Country.* It is similar to Peter Matthiessen's *Snow Leopard* in its insights about interior and exterior landscapes, and beautifully written. It also makes a clear and

defensible connection between Cherokee culture and myth and the red wolf—that is, connection between the ghost and real wolves.

5. See Clark & Lewis: brush wolf (1:112, 3:235), little wolf (2:19), cayote (throughout vols. 1, 3, 6, 7).

6. See Budiansky, 17, 102–4. Budiansky's work is highly questionable and tends to make facts out of either speculations or puzzles as yet unsolved. It fits in a "half-cooked" category with some of Jeffrey Moussaieff Masson's work. I offer the Budiansky references here to acknowledge that such speculation is in print.

7. Nelson & Mech, "Observation of a Swimming Wolf" and "Single Deer Stands Off"; Weaver, Arvidson, Wood, & Rausch.

8. Mowat, *Never Cry Wolf,* 108, 111. For refutations that wolves have subsisted on mice or that they can, see Banfield, "Review"; Pimlott; and Mech, "Challenge and Opportunity."

9. Bobtailing is conspicuously absent from Mech & Boitani. See "Gray Wolves" (USFWS Report); and Carbyn. The main point of interest about this is that it is among several observations (such as eating unborn calves; see note 10 below) used primarily by stockgrowers to condemn the wolf as cruel. Whether the claim is factual or the act frequent is less important to the claimant than the ghost wolf that results from its use.

10. See Bass, *Ninemile Wolves,* 5, 60; Lopez, *Of Wolves and Men,* 131; Hampton, 3; Young & Goldman; Caras, 27.

11. See Bass's chap. 5 in *The Ninemile Wolves* re: ranchers willing to cohabitate with wolves (Bass focuses on the Thisted ranch in Montana). The Malpais Borderlands Group also works with ranchers and life scientists in cooperation and has done some exemplary work in the American Southwest.

12. Busch, *Wolf Almanac,* 74; Hampton, 92, 100.

13. See Olson, "A Study in Predatory Relationship with Particular Reference to the Wolf"; Fujino & Warren; Peterson & Ciucci in Mech & Boitani.

14. See Leopold, 128; Bass, "Wolf Palette"; and Smith & Ferguson, 118–19, re the trophic cascade.

15. Mech, "Neonatal Wolves" and "Resistance of Young."

16. The following sources are a smattering of the many more available: Hillis & Mallory; Huggard; Fuller ("Effect"); Heard; McRoberts, Mech, & Peterson; Mech, Fritts, & Paul; Nelson & Mech; Peterson & Allen; Telfer & Kelsall.

17. Dusiak; Jenness. Also see Lopez's *Of Wolves and Men* regarding Inuit testimonies of wolf attacks.

18. Horejsi, Hornbeck, & Raine; Paquet & Carbyn; Ballard.

19. Nelson & Mech, "Observation of a Swimming Wolf." See also p. 79 of Stanley Young's *Wolves of North America.* The duck chasing happened at Wolf Park, Battle Ground, Indiana, in the summer of 1997, and biologists at the park said it had happened before. Wolves at the park live on road-killed deer, so moving game comes in the form of rodents getting through or under the fencing or waterfowl landing in the pond inside the enclosure.

20. See Marhenke; Van Ballenberghe & Erickson.

21. See Lent; Rogers & Mech.

22. Mission: Wolf uses the same strategy to introduce children to the "real wolf." See *Santa Fe Reporter,* August 3, 1988; *Santa Fe New Mexican,* July 1, 1990, September 14, 1992, and January 23, 1993; *High Country News,* May 2, 1994; and *Albuquerque Journal,* November 14, 1995.

23. E.g., Parkman, 401; Hendricks, 120; Audubon, 527. This alleged behavior is also mentioned in the movie *Dances with Wolves* and came up in my interviews with Norm Bishop and Phil Gipson.

24. Mech, *The Wolf,* 137–39; Packard, esp. regarding "age-graded hierarchy" (in Mech & Boitani, 53–55); and Mowat, 58–66.

25. Casey & Clark, 201–2; Parkman, 112; Curtis, 18:51; Mech, *The Wolf,* 5; Murie, 22.

26. See Roger Elwood's pulp historical *Wolf's Lair;* also Douglas's explanation of the 1920s Nazi Operation Werewolf and the resurrection of the wolf image late in the war (31–32).

27. Ciucci & Mech; Ballard, Ayres, Gardner, & Foster; Ballard & Dau; Fuller, "Denning"; Mech & Packard; Ream, Fairchild, Blakesley, & Boyd; Rausch; Stephenson.

28. Mech, "Wolf-Pack Buffer Zones" and "Buffer Zones."

29. Golani & Moran; McLeod & Fentress, "Patterns of Aggression" and "Aggressiveness."

30. D. Allen, 264–65; Busch, *Wolf Almanac,* 71.

31. Boyd & Jimenez; DelGiudice, Mech, & Seal; Malcolm.

32. Bekoff, "Social Play and Play-Soliciting by Infant Canids," "Social Play in Coyotes, Wolves, and Dogs," and "Development of Social Interaction"; also Feddersen-Petersen; Loizos.

33. See Mech, The Wolf; Heinrich, The Mind of the Raven; Savage, Wolves.

34. See Boas; Harrington, "Ravens"; Wetmore. See also D. Allen 287–92; Busch, *Wolf Almanac,* 58–59; Mech, *The Wolf,* 287–88; and Savage's *Bird Brains.*

35. Frank & Frank; Willkomm; Lawrence & Bossert; Freeman & Shaw; and Iljin. The number of wolves kept in zoos is mentioned in Busch's *Wolf Almanac,* and the "cage" should be understood to include the backyards of hybrid owners, who have taken the wolf out of wolves both by breeding and by enclosing them. Iljin provides an interesting historical perspective on genetics and the taxonomic debate.

36. As of January 2007 the popular online archive JSTOR contained 822 relevant pieces (249 on pathology); Mech's 1972 *The Wolf* and Mech & Boitani's *Wolves* both contain chapters on physiology devoting long sections to the subject; Busch's *Wolf Almanac* provides a good overview; *Biological Abstracts* carries 256 articles on pathology including wolves, with 91 on parasitology and 136 on diseases. The bulk of the research is on canine parvovirus and rabies.

37. Hurston's metaphor of the mule as the totemic figure of the burdened but resilient African American, especially of the woman in power relations both black and white, is an extended metaphor from her anthropological work through her fiction. See especially her *Mules and Men.* See also Brian R. Roberts, Leigh Anne Duck, and James E. Spears.

Chapter Six ■ *Advanced Corporeality: Wolf Sign*

1. Sebeok's work addresses the genetic/linguistic communication forms and in so doing provides interesting ideas about life versus nonlife that have been found in shamanic cultures for millennia; see "'Animal' in Biological and Semiotic Perspective," in *Essays in Zoosemiotics.* The book also provides a refreshing antidote to the deficiencies of journals such as *Social Text;* see particularly Sebeok's chapter "Zoosemiotics: At the Intersection of Nature and Culture." See also his and Jean Umiker-Sebeok's *Biosemiotics,* 111–16.

2. E.g., Peterson et al., "Leadership Behavior"; Briscoe, Lewis, & Parrish; and the fascinating article by Schultz & Wilson.

3. F. H. Harrington's "Chorus Howling" article considers the possibility of the "Beau Geste Effect"—that the wolf howl may have evolved so that chorus howling could harmonically create the impression of a larger pack. This would explain the common literary reaction to howling as a cacophony of many animals later discovered to be a mere pair, sometimes even a single virtuoso, as in Dodge, Parkman, and Magoffin. See also Servin for durations of Mexican wolf howling.

4. See Kennedy's chapter "Rhetoric among Social Animals."

5. G. Kennedy, 3–4; cf. Darwin's "principle of antithesis" in *The Expression of Emotions in Man and Animals,* esp. pp. 60–63.

6. See Peirce, esp. *Peirce on Signs;* Sebeok, esp. *Animal Communication* and *Essays in Zoosemiotics.*

7. Lakoff & Turner, *More Than Cool Reason;* Lakoff & Johnson, *Metaphors We Live By;* and Turner, *The Literary Mind.*

8. Dombrowski and "the argument from marginal cases" (AMC); cf. Porphyry's *De abstinentia* and Zeno's advocacy for vegetarianism.

9. See George Stone's *A Legend of Wolf Song,* Rick Bass's *Where the Sea Used to Be,* London's *Call of the Wild,* and Feher-Elston's *Wolfsong.* In all, the howl serves as the "voice of the wild" rather than simply the voice of a wolf.

Chapter Seven ■ *The Sea Wolf (In Which a Wolf Crosses the Water)*

1. Wilson's attempt to bridge the two cultures is made with a heavy science bias. Poetry is diminished as a singular discipline while science is a synthetic one (*Biophilia,* 62); science's new interest in the mind (versus the brain alone) is now wresting from the humanities the exclusive rights to mind that art now "sparks" for science (74, 76); and both are occurring because, according to Wilson's thesis, aesthetics is a biological function, hardwired into the human and so finally "best understood" by science (60). His assessments of art on these pages reveal a novice understanding of the making of art, and a tendency toward condescension. My thanks to my insightful former student Derek Kirk and his paper "E. O. Wilson: Empiricist and Imperialist" (a bit too severe a title for the thesis). Some of Wilson's tone also seeps into Brockman's *Third Culture.* I'm quick here to say that

these are groundbreaking efforts toward reconciling the cultures of the life sciences and the arts, and they only point out more sharply the need for clearer communication on the part of humanities scholars.

2. See Grimm & Grimm, *The Annotated Brothers Grimm;* Asbjørnsen and Moe, *Norwegian Folk Tales;* Perrault, *The Complete Fairy Tales;* Jacobs, *English Fairy Tales;* Andersen, *The Complete Fairy Tales;* and Andrew Lang (the 12 Books in 1 collection is aesthetically terrible, but an omnibus; the best way to read Lang is in the individual "color" books).

3. Fergusson may be a worthy recovery project as western writers go (see, for instance, Pilkington), but there's simply no denying the crudity of the diction and the diminishment of the subject through a rough-hewn craft in *Wolf Song,* with no evident consciousness of those craft elements (i.e., some metatextual level or turn of point-of-view that reveals an awareness of the vulgarity). Pilkington also offers an impassioned defense (in his biographical review for *A Literary History of the West*) of "Fergusson's masterful portrayal in *Wolf Song* of the rigid, tradition-bound social structure that the ricos established in the colonial Southwest" (551) and other ostensible accomplishments. Were the novel written in 1827 the defense might be more convincing; it was instead written in 1927. What *Wolf Song* has, and Pilkington correctly recognizes this, is a thick layer of detail that would certainly interest any historian reading the fiction.

4. Feher-Elston, xvi. Clarissa Pinkola Estés (14, 26) also makes this assumption. It seems a flaw almost particular (although Wilson's case in *Biophilia* is similar) to anthropological approaches, one tending toward the benevolent ghost, viz. the motive of comparative ethology with human beings.

5. In *Symbols of Transformation,* writing of Rubens's *Last Judgment,* Jung interprets the image of a serpent castrating a man as a "motif which illustrates the end of the world." This is followed by a note in which Jung symbolically connects the Midgard Serpent Jormagandr (trans. "giant serpent") to "the world-destroying Fenris wolf," which Jung explains "likewise has connections to the sea. *Fen* is found in Fensalir (Meersäle), the dwelling-place of Frigga; originally it meant 'sea' (Frobenius, Zeitalter, p. 179). In the story of Red Riding Hood, the serpent or fish is replaced by a wolf, because he is the typical destroyer." (Cf. p. 431, para. 681, including n. 87.)

6. See H. A. Guerber, *Myths of Northern Lands,* paraphrased in Lopez's *Of Wolves and Men* (75–76). The Celto-Germanic connection is also important to a fuller understanding of the myth's European radius. Celtic mythology has a wolf swallowing the sun at the close of each day. See Gibson, p. 100, and Markey's article, which asserts that the totemic nature of the dog/wolf-champion implicates it as pre–Indo-European, which icon may have been appropriated by Indo-European invaders.

7. For fiction, see esp. Parrish, also F. Scott Fitzgerald's story "The Off-Shore Pirate." For history, see Cordingly.

8. R. K. Wayne, "Molecular Evolution" and "Use of Morphological and Molecular Genetic Characters." The maps redrawn of the species ranges can be found in a number of wolf books, including Busch's *Wolf Almanac* and, together, in Steinhart, 358–59.

9. Davis; B. Lawrence ("Antiquity of Large Dogs"); Matthew; Olsen & Olsen, "The

Chinese Wolf" and "The Position"; Spiess; and Mochanov. Mochanov's article is a fascinating examination of climatic effects on human evolution and includes a number of references relevant to coevolving species study. See as well Kimberling; in 1854, near New Harmony, Indiana, Owen and Granville uncovered a fossil of what they claimed was "the first known dire wolf and thus established a new species" (2).

10. See Deloria's *Red Earth, White Lies,* chaps. 3–5, in which he contests both an "original" crossing of the land bridge and the "Pleistocene overkill hypothesis." Some unconvincing strategies appear when Deloria's diatribes against Eurocentric science fail to give scientific fact the intrinsic value it might deserve, despite the cultural myopia of the scientists at work.

11. For the mythological analysis, see Campbell's *Primitive Mythology* and Eliade's *Shamanism;* for a fictional representation, see Silko's *Ceremony.*

12. Dundes, "Earth-Diver"; Martin; Swan; and P. G. Allen.

Chapter Eight ■ *Orion's Dogs (In Which a Wolf Crosses the Sky)*

1. See Garfinkle's *Star-Hopping* and Thomas Berry's *The Dream of the Earth.* The latter must be qualified as theological thought too close to New Ageism, which often presses the limits of empirical rigor. Nevertheless, Berry's spiritual approach, closely connected with the Deep Ecology movement, offers a point of reference for cosmogonic application.

2. *The Oxford English Dictionary* tracks this allusion from Trevisa in 1398 through Disraeli in 1847, including a mention of the Egyptian canicular year of 365¼ days, "from one heliacal rising of Sirius to the next," and the canicular cycle of 1,461 years, called the Sothic period, through which, fantastically, "any given day of the year of 365 days would have passed successively through all the seasons of the natural year" (*OED,* 831).

3. *Hac urget lupus, hac canis* ("The wolf presses here, the dog there") is a reference to the dark beyond the fire's dim light in a Roman camp, again supporting the half-light metaphors, lunar light being a mythic root in Latin, that use the wolf/dark, dog/light paradigm. This also provides an obvious mythic connection between the stories through their use of campfire light (Lopez, *Of Wolves and Men,* 209).

Chapter Nine ■ *Terra Nova (In Which the Wolf Discovers North America)*

1. See Eliade (*Shamanism*) and Doniger. On Saint Ailbe, see Brown & Cory's *Book of Saints and Friendly Beasts* and Tom Cowan's *Fire in the Head.*

2. See Lévi-Strauss, *Totemism,* 89, and Preece, 364n38; see also Robert Pogue Harrison's chap. 3, "Enlightenment," for an excellent critique of Cartesian environmental ideology.

3. See, e.g., Barber's *Bestiary,* T. H. White's *Bestiary,* and Hassig's *Mark of the Beast.*

4. Parkhill, "'Of Glooskap's Birth,'" 46. See also Leland's *Algonquin Legends* and Parkhill's *Weaving Ourselves into the Land.*

5. See esp. chap. 6, called "The Hunting of the Beast: Initiation or Exorcism? (1675–1725)," and 120–29, 204–67, 327–67.

6. See McDermott (541, 544). Mather also mentions the loup-garou and werewolf in the *Magnalia* (II:VII, art. VII), and see "Nehemias Americanus," chap. 4. Mather worked the wolf metaphor to strong effect, employing it as well against the Quakers in "Little Flocks Guarded against Grievous Wolves," a sentiment sustained by Michael Wigglesworth's "God's Controversy with England." See also Heimert; Ferling; P. Miller; Lopez (*Of Wolves and Men,* 142); and Fitzpatrick's fine article linking Mather's missives about wilderness to Rowlandson's captivity narrative. Mather's language is used by Filson regarding Daniel Boone, which sentiment carries forward to Cooper's Leatherstocking.

7. See Henry Nash Smith's *Virgin Land* and Fredrick Hoxie's *Indians in American History.* Parkman refers to the prairie directly at one point as "a turbulent ocean, suddenly congealed when its waves were at the highest" (245). For other moments, one combining wolves and the ocean, see pp. 362, 399, and 413 in *The Oregon Trail.* Parkman's metaphoric treatment of open range land is very much like Cooper's prairie, an amorphous swell rolling around a theatrically located rock acting as the lodestone for the characters' interactions. Both men prided themselves on "woodcraft," to which Parkman eventually returns.

8. Roosevelt's comment is accounted for by Lopez (*Of Wolves and Men,* 142) and his views elaborated on by Lutts in *The Nature Fakers.* See as well James Fenton's "The Lobo Wolf: Beast of Waste and Desolation," Roosevelt's *Hunting the Grisly and Other Sketches,* and further coverage in McIntyre's *War against the Wolf.* Edmund Morris's biography of Roosevelt up to the beginning of his presidency, *The Rise of Theodore Roosevelt,* includes mentions of Roosevelt's equation of hunting and war, one in direct reference to the wolf: "All men who feel any power of joy in battle," Roosevelt wrote, "know what it is like when the wolf rises in the heart" (654). This is a vintage example of how Roosevelt, like many great white hunters, wanted to have the wolf both ways.

9. See Lackey. The article is dedicated to specifically defining these terms. Lackey articulately distinguishes between them as a means of explaining aesthetic responses to landscape and the political arguments that ensued out of aesthetic differences.

Chapter Ten ■ *Three Dreams (In Which Some Wolves Cross the Mind)*

1. Snively's poem is found in *Kenyon Review* 2, no. 3 (Summer 1980): 79–87.

2. Brian Frost writes of Bradfield's story that it is "one of the least effective" of the 1980s. "The neurotic protagonist is so obsessed with wolves that he thinks about them all day and dreams of them at night. The tale is extremely vague and inconclusive, and leads the reader up a blind alley" (213).

3. See Corsini's dictionary and Otten (esp. sections 1 and 2). Contrast these with the tabloid-level book by Warren & Warren. I cover lycanthropy in more detail in chap. 11.

4. Among the scientists who have expressed dismay at this phenomenon is Richard Dawkins: "I noticed, the other day, an article by a literary critic called 'Theory: What Is It?'

Would you believe it? 'Theory' turned out to mean 'theory in literary criticism.' This wasn't in a journal of literary criticism; this was in some general publication, like a Sunday newspaper. The very word 'theory' has been hijacked for some extremely narrow parochial literary purpose." (Brockman, 23).

5. Andrew Ross's legitimization, including by some early ecocritics, is one point of proof itself. See Baudrillard's hyperbolic dismissal of "the whole of science" in *Simulacra and Simulation*. Eventually, for Baudrillard, *any* image "is its own pure simulacrum" (11) and a "murderer of reality" (12). See Joseph Carroll's rebuttal in *Evolution and Literary Theory* of Derrida's "White Mythology," particularly of Derrida's manipulation of metaphor's structure in the statement, "Each time that there is a metaphor, there is doubtless a sun somewhere." Stacy Alaimo, applying a Donna Haraway theme to ecofeminism, uses the phrase "discursive ecologies"—a bowdlerization of ecology diminishing it to environmentalist rhetoric (I strongly oppose any sexist model that essentially connects women and nature, but only as much as I oppose language being used to exploit ecology for the sake of a cultural program). Love's *Practical Ecocriticism* covers a list of poststructuralist biases against nature and hyperbole about it. See also Hirsch for a scathing indictment of the origins of theory as an obfuscating discipline to cover the tracks of complicity with fascism that employs the rhetoric of reversal to conflate collaboration with victimization. See Brian Boyd's article in *Philosophy and Literature*, which summarizes the current poststructuralist fashion of declaring itself "dead" but walking English Department hallways as a zombie. The "Sokal Hoax" and the ensuing self-service of Ross's edited *Science Wars* began a raft of sand kicking that includes Ross's own interviews offering "urban ecology" as a red herring argument subverting comprehension of the nonhuman world beyond an urban context. Despite its unfortunate ad hominem attacks, Gross & Levitt's *Higher Superstition* contains numerous examples (not simply assumptions) of egregious poststructuralist errors in both fact and logic.

6. See Jung, *Symbols of Transformation;* Eliade, *Myth and Reality;* and Propp, *Morphology of the Folktale.*

7. In *The Closing Circle* Commoner defines this motto as one of his "four laws of ecology" (14). In his defense, Commoner's practice is clearly more than mere *jouissance,* in which the play of the text is a game for the critic at everyone else's expense. His statement, however, is not defensible through an application of ecology. This kind of soft thinking in order to forward an environmentalist agenda has left a wake of damage. Everything connected to everything else conveniently leaves out the definition, distinction, and finally understanding necessary to our consideration of ecosystems and biospheric knowledge.

8. While I often cite Jung directly from the Princeton Bollingen Series, Jacobi's excellent synthesis is used here both because she has insights to offer on the material and because Jung's collected writings must be ordered and organized whenever a theme from them is addressed, and Jacobi has already done the herculean work.

9. See Pratt; Bodkin; Frye; Jung's *Archetypes and the Collective Unconscious* and *Memories, Dreams, Reflections.* Cf. Jacobi; Hall & Nordby; Leitch. The idea of the critic as artist

figure engaged in a cyclic solipsism of elevating criticism as art, eventually distancing art sufficiently so as to open the poststructuralist door to its "death," may be attributed to Frye, who launched the new hubris.

10. Frye's seasonal model is particularly pungent (see *Anatomy of Criticism*); see also Segal's summation of the in-house wrangling about myth's role, and its occidental bent.

11. See Jung, *Man and His Symbols*, 380, 385, and *The Earth Has a Soul*, 80, 139, 205; Raffa; Hannah.

Chapter Eleven ■ *The Loophole: Lycanthropy, Shape-Shifting, and the Werewolf Race*

1. See especially depictions of the Navajo skinwalker by Brady, Hillerman, Silko, and Kriss. Transformation tales are also covered in Jung's *Symbols of Transformation*, Campbell's Masks of God series, and Eliade's *Shamanism*. See also W. Morgan.

2. For representative examples of the latex werewolf and its slow and patchy progress before the advent of computer-generated imagery, see: *The Wolfman* (1941); *I Was a Teenage Werewolf* (1957); *I Married a Werewolf* (1962); *Moon of the Wolf* (1972); *An American Werewolf in London* and *The Howling* (1981); *Wolf* (1994); *An American Werewolf in Paris* (1997); and *Underworld* (2003).

3. *Buffy,* for instance, a darling of the academic cultural studies crowd, has perhaps the worst werewolf makeup in decades of TV and film. This could be a low budget metacamp gesture, but the choice of the decidedly nonlupine fuzzy-rug approach doesn't quite fit with the old teen-wolf low-budget choices. The show also had a few episodes containing a werewolf hunter named Caine and some rather fuzzy rules about how werewolves work (see the contradictory episodes *Buffy* "Phases" and, from the spin-off Buffyverse series *Angel,* the episode "Unleashed").

4. A corrective to assuming the shape-shifting myth to be "an Indian thing" is Andrew MacDonald et al. See also Edson (chaps. 7, 9), Eliade (*Shamanism*), and Bynum (esp. her first section, called "Wonder," and 79–80 on physical change) regarding shape-shifting particulars from various cultures.

5. Frost 89, 98–99, 101, 128 (see illustration), 129 (an American story of "hereditary lycanthropy," one of Frost's phrases that aligns with the Eckels rules), and 132 (C. L. Moore, whom Frost considers the best of the women contributing to *Weird Tales*).

6. Regarding wolf pogroms, Frost cites (the pages cited are from Frost; the sources he cites are included in my bibliography) Gregory, 293, 323; Wellman, 136–37; A. Campbell, 198, 248; and Hill, 226.

7. See especially G. R. Thompson's work on Poe, including *The Gothic Imagination;* "Romantic Arabesque, Contemporary Theory, and Postmodernism;" and *Circumscribed Eden of Dreams.*

8. The best delineation of this history of the werewolf I have found is actually a Web site, Ivan Schablotski's "Therianthropology 101": http://www.geocities.com/schablotski .geo/Therianthropology.htm. I am corroborating his timeline of therianthropy here for

credibility's sake, but his catalog work is thorough. He also wonderfully (and, we hope, facetiously) asserts that therianthropology is a "science," along with cryptozoology. See also Douglas; Summers; Harting.

9. See, for instance, Kennedy's juxtaposition of stories of the fée with stories of the Irish Fianna.

10. For the numerological motifs of seven and nine, see Tibbals (363) and Douglas (55, 135). For more thorough taxonomies of fable motifs and structures, see Kirby Smith's "Historical Study of the Werwolf in Literature" and Propp's *Morphology of the Folk Tale.*

11. See Otten; Tibbals; Douglas; Harting; McIntyre, *War;* Mather's *Magnalia Christi Americana* for the economics of spiritualizing wolf (and, through a metaphor of connection, Indian) destruction; and Slotkin.

12. For the moral relevance of wolf and werewolf texts as early as the *Physiologus,* see Wirtjes, lxxvii.

13. The Amala and Kamala hoax is explained in detail in Hutton and appeared in several psychological journals during the 1930s–1950s. It was proffered by the Reverend J. A. L. Singh, an orphanage rector, who beat Amala and Kamala into performing the behaviors he described as lycanthropy, then publicly exploited the "feral children" for financial gain. I mention it as well in chapters 2 and 14.

14. See Perrault; Zipes (on the Red Riding Hood tales); Bildauer & Mills; Ziolkowski. Ziolkowski is a good source to read for the historical roots of the tales and gives some indication of how and when they take on their multivalence.

15. Newstead provides a fine summary of works on Merlin and Arthur that corroborate this point, and Curley emphasizes Merlin's importance regarding beasts in Arthurian legend.

16. Harding cites Branwen, Pwyll, and Math as shape-changing stories influenced by Merlin as a legendary figure. Math contains the changing of two brothers into wolves (Harding, 18–19).

Chapter Twelve ■ *Wolf Channel: Ritual Masks as Visual Literature*

1. See Grumet on the Iroquois False Face ceremonies. Regarding Northwest Coast masks, see Malin; Layton (esp. 177). On the Yup'ik, see Fienup-Riordan.

2. See Lopez, *Of Wolves and Men,* 3. See as well the epigraph to John Murray's *Out among the Wolves,* which quotes Lopez on the imaginary wolf, and Lindquist, who examines the "imaginary wolf" in her work on the Saami.

3. See Ernst, 15 and passim; Bynum; Eliade, *Shamanism;* Riley.

4. I want to stress here the difference between this kind of participatory act and the tormenting of animals by musicians who somehow think they are "playing along," usually with captive animals and with no knowledge whatsoever of the acoustic effects of their contrived jam sessions. I saw such an example of a flautist at the Association for the Study of Literature and the Environment conference in Montana and am equally skeptical of the Paul Winter sessions with a wolf appearing on stage.

5. Panjabi-Trelease interview.

6. See Disaanayake; Edson; Ernst.

7. The term *ecological Indian* is Shepard Krech III's, based on an overstated thesis that the indigenous tribes of America were somehow just as abusive as white civilization in environmental management and sustainability. Under the veil of a corrective against romanticizing the noble savage, Krech slips into several non sequiturs and presentist arguments about "environmental standards" simply contradicted by the ecological conditions that persisted despite the tribes' apparent (even if comparable to colonizing populations') cultural shortcomings. *The Ecological Indian* contains a serviceable amount of useful information on cultural history, but that information is forced to serve a number of dubious conclusions about environmental history. Krech, like many of his reviewers, also misapplies the word *myth* to mean "delusion." And Krech's position as a contributing editor to *The Norton Anthology of American Literature* risks validating his thesis on a broad pedagogical scale.

Chapter Thirteen ▨ Raised by Wolves

1. For the Hemingway story, I again thank Robert Paul Lamb. Regarding Bowles: Frost (195) mentions Robin Schaeffer's "Night of the Wolf," which is a far less literary story but comparable to "The Frozen Fields."

2. The best biography of Bowles is by Christopher Sawyer-Lauçanno.

3. See, e.g., Grooms, 20; Dufresne and Spitzer's *Lonely Planet: Alaska;* D. Wood; and various paintings and illustrations titled *Misunderstood* by such artists as Craig Anthony Lomas.

4. See also Melson's *Why the Wild Things Are* on animal stories' effects on child psychology. Melson's study includes the pathological interactions, especially violent ones, that children may have with animals, and thoughtfully connects the behavior of children toward animals with such phenomena as truth-telling and disillusionment.

5. In a chart titled "Genre in Children's Literature," Lukens cross-indexes the genre "Animal Realism" with the category "Character" and incorrectly uses the term *personification* instead of *anthropomorphism,* a common error and an indication of the still-embryonic status of an interspecies lexicon (29). Oerlemans elucidates the distinctions made among various anthropomorphisms and between anthropomorphism and anthropocentrism, which are as far from synonymous as are personification and anthropomorphism.

6. One of the rules to which the Yellowstone wolf reintroduction program adhered was to number the wolves, both to more easily record them over time and to avoid anthropomorphic structures of identification. Early on, a wolf called "U-Black" for a marking on its fur (another variant of the wolf-naming pattern similar to calling a wolf "Oldtooth") slipped through the system. Otherwise, wolves are known, and indeed become famous among wolf-watchers, by such numbers as 42 or 10, sometimes with the sex designator following: 42F, 10M. Smith and Ferguson's *Decade of the Wolf* includes several chapters profiling Yellowstone's more famous wolves, interwoven with the story of the reintroduc-

tion program. There are also color-coded charts of the wolves kept by the Park Service and compiled through collected information on complex identification forms used by many radio telemetry trackings, flyovers in a Piper Super Cub, and wolf-watchers' reports.

7. The Nanabozho legends have their own complex history, various spellings, and cultural appropriations. Two issues of basic importance often surface in regard to this figure, who also has a wolf brother. First, Parkhill explains, Nanabozho is too often conflated with Kluskap, their relationship being at best narrative similarity. Parkhill explains this in greater detail in both his book and his article on Kluskap. Second, just as Leland popularized a bowdlerized legend of Kluskap, so did Henry Schoolcraft commit the same violation of the Ojibway Nanabozho stories. A fine article on Nanabozho is by Makarius. A less rigorous one, invoking Schoolcraft far too often, is by Clasby. The role of Schoolcraft in the legend's formation is found in his book *The Myth of Hiawatha and Other Oral Legends, Mythologic and Allegoric, of the North American Indians,* in which he incorrectly equates Hiawatha and Nanabozho, and which he dedicates to Henry Wadsworth Longfellow, an anthropological-literary connection adding greater significance to both the wolf's multidisciplinary iconicity and its selectively interpreted position.

Chapter Fourteen ■ *The Twins and the Timber Wolves: A Case Study*

1. Although Paul, Minnie, and their relations are all fictional, I have borrowed the grandparents' stories from Charles Eugene Johnson's "Recollections of the Mammals of Northwestern Minnesota." This use of documented tales provides, I hope, some added verisimilitude to the speculation—the strongest falsehoods, as it has been noted throughout this project, contain a few facts.

2. See Underwood, which appears also in Hogan, Metzger, & Peterson's *Intimate Nature,* 20–26, and McIntyre's *War against the Wolf,* 254–60.

3. See Ziolkowski, who traces the story all over medieval Europe prior to the advent of the fairy tale and whose article provides extensive citations covering the scope and history of the medieval story. See also Bettelheim's reading of the Three Pigs story in *The Uses of Enchantment* (41–50), which has since its publication been contested in psychological journals (see, for instance, Berman).

4. See Zipes, *Trials and Tribulations;* Róheim; Bettelheim; and Dundes, *Little Red Riding Hood,* x, 121, 159, 168.

5. The kineograph, which "animates" a series of sketches through the flipping of pages, was a contemporary to another early animation device called the "zootrope," later written "zoetrope." This is a small carousel with notches cut into the outside of the cylinder and a strip dropped into the inside; the zoetrope is then spun so that the notches appear to create a single "window" through which the viewer watches the sequential sketches on the strip. A children's toy, the zoetrope was named for its regular use of animals on the animation strips, such as a running horse or flying bird (though I have yet to find one depicting a wolf).

6. Movie renditions of the tale include Laurence Trimble's (1925), starring the famous German shepherd Strongheart (who also starred in the 1925 *Clash of the Wolves*); Frank Butler's (1936); Aleksandr Zguridi's Russian version (1946); the Ken Annakin 1974/1975 *Call of the Wild* and *White Fang* with Charlton Heston; a Tonino Ricci spin-off called *White Fang to the Rescue* (1974); Randal Kleiser's *White Fang* with Ethan Hawke (1991); and *White Fang 2*, an appropriative spin-off by Ken Olin (1994).

7. The biologist as a prominent character also appears in Barbara Kingsolver's *Prodigal Summer* and T. C. Boyle's "Dogology," found in his *Tooth and Claw*.

8. There is no explanation in the game for why the French loup-garou was mined for a tribal identity.

9. See Johnson & Aamodt; Turbak; and Mech, *Wolves of Minnesota*.

10. Again we have the sea connection common to Northwest mythology that links whale and wolf: the orca as the wolf of the sea and wolf as the orca of the land.

11. See Derounian-Stedola for the Penguin collection of captivity narratives, which corroborates this list of features. See also Strong; Calloway.

12. Linnaeus's work on this matter is the *Systema Naturae* of 1735. See Agassiz's *Principles of Zoölogy* as one of the proponents of craniometric measurements to justify organized racism, and Gould's *Mismeasure of Man* and *Ever Since Darwin* for a summation of Agassiz's contribution to the finally racist and ideological abuse of science to which craniometry was put.

Chapter Fifteen ■ *The Fall of the Wild: Jack London's Dog Stories*

1. On London's being the highest-paid author, see Dyer, 16 (and his "Answering the Call of the Wild" in *English Journal* 77, no. 4 [April 1988]: 57–62), and Tavernier-Courbin, 7. The cover blurbs for Harper's *Collected Stories* and Pine Street Books' *The Lost Face* make sure to include London's status as a figure in popular culture. Whenever possible, my references to London's short stories come from Teacher & Nicholls, *The Unabridged Jack London*. Of the many collections, including Earle Labor's excellent edition, *Unabridged* has most of the stories (with the exception of "Diable—A Dog") that I use. Dyer's annotated *Call of the Wild* is an invaluable resource. I cite it, a recent reprint of *White Fang*, and the reprinted stories because they are more accessible than the original texts (the dates for which are included in my bibliography).

2. See Haney; R. Morgan; and several of the essays in Hodson & Reesman.

3. This comes from a one-line rejection notice, famous among ecocritics, given to Norman Maclean for *A River Runs Through It*. The full rejection reads, "These stories have trees in them." Ironically, the Victorian gothic romance, which is chock full of dark forests and dangerous heaths, is a favorite genre among academics (especially postmodern theorists). That Ann Radcliffe is not a particularly adept writer seems to make less difference than the testosterone and pine-sap levels of a later work better written, because the romance provides the necessary symbolic and generic treatments that steer the Victorian narrative

inexorably inward toward the solipsistic terror of the human mind, rather than outward toward any kind of realizable world. This is, of course, Mark Twain's beef with the genre in his "Fenimore Cooper's Literary Offenses."

4. See James Oliver Curwood (*The Wolf Hunters; Baree: The Story of a Wolf-Dog; Kazan;* and *Kazan, Father of Baree*); and Walt Morey (*Kävik the Wolf-Dog; Hero;* and *Scrub Dog of Alaska*).

5. What I am referring to as a "pure" naturalism is the condition of the subject in an amoral world that precedes, consistently and overtly acts upon, and ultimately determines, that subject's resources, options, and circumstances. Pure naturalism has particular significance to our consideration of the nonhuman world's active agency in literature (crucial to any defensible ecocriticism). I am not saying that determinism is a critical tenet of ecocriticism, but that its position in naturalism invites especial ecocritical inquiry. For definitions and applications of naturalism, especially considerations of determinism, see Den Tandt; Fisher; Conder; Pizer (1982, 1984); and Howard.

6. Reynolds, *Young Hemingway* (49). Robert Paul Lamb also notes, "Reynolds did the inventory of books Hemingway owned, in which, whenever possible, he gives the date when the book first came into Hemingway's possession. He didn't own many books when he was a teenager, but one that he did was Jack London's *The Call of the Wild,* which he purchased in 1913, when he was only 14 years old." (Personal correspondence; see also Reynolds's *Hemingway,* 150.)

7. See esp. Kolodny (1975, 1984); Merchant; S. Griffin; Gaard & Murphy; also interesting on London and gender is Auerbach. The Kolodny material is dated now and is at times hyperbolic in its claims about symbolic thought and the natural world, but it established the basic premise for the argument against the conflation of land and woman. Gaard & Murphy likewise include several ecologically uninformed exaggerations regarding dualism and hierarchy, "boundary crossing," and body politics, which they assert as ecological concerns aside from their human symbolic uses, but without grounding in actual ecology. Ecofeminism is often as anthropocentric as the androcentric politics it critiques, and is at times (as in Donna Haraway's work) quite simply hostile to self/nature connections contesting urbanized and mechanized valuations of nature. Its foundation, especially in political activism (the work of Vandana Shiva and Wangari Matthai being two strong examples), is more than sound. Some of the best examinations into ecofeminism's possibilities are to be found in the works of Susan Griffin and Carolyn Merchant (when she is historicizing the movement and its approaches rather than placing the cause ahead of the analysis).

8. Elizabeth Hall uses the trope of the wolf pack adopting a dog in her 1997 *Child of the Wolves,* about a Siberian husky named Snowdrift who escapes the people who want to sell him as a sled dog. The pack leader has lost his pups to a wolf-hybrid breeder.

9. See Askins, esp. 143. Her notions about the wild and domestic are often examinations into what part human affinity, love, care, should play.

10. Of course, the eugenics project is the most egregious example of this mislogic. Regarding direct lineage and assumptions about accelerated generational passage, see Spencer's ten-volume *System of Synthetic Philosophy,* especially *First Principles.* Lamarck offers

a rich and recently reconsidered perspective on the connection of evolution and ecology (via environmental influence on adaptation); Darwin's supplanting of Lamarck is based largely on errors in Lamarck on morphological change over time that aim a hard eye toward breeding more than evolution. Lamarck's essays on zoological philosophy are the depth, but *Lamarck's Open Mind* (under "Lamarck" in my bibliography) contains the lectures and the basis for his position. See also Burkhardt's excellent examination of Lamarck's philosophy and his position in the history of evolutionary theory. Jung is tricky here; his interest in Lamarck never quite translated to his adherence to single-generational passage, and his work should in my view be read in the context of his departure from Freud's parental obsessions and the turn-of-the-century zeitgeist about inheritance (see esp. *Symbols of Transformation* and *Archetypes and the Collective Unconscious;* less so *Aion*).

11. See Bykov's work, especially *In the Steps of Jack London,* which is available in translation online at Centenary College, through the work of London scholar Earle Labor: http://www.jacklondons.net/index.html. See also Wasiolek.

12. In literary handbooks the plot structure called "Freytag's Pyramid" is not a pyramid but an angle. The mislabeling of it has always bothered me. Even when the model is drawn as a triangle, the lack of a base (let alone three-dimensionality) ruins the structure, forcing the angle of rising action, climax (the vertex), and falling action into a false symmetry (the denouement is always a shorter line). The structure should be called "Freytag's Angle."

13. My thanks again to Robert Paul Lamb, who has developed a brilliant pedagogical approach to this novel for college students that covers the range in criticism and student response from naive readings to sound, close analysis.

14. A distinction should be made here between the pit trap and pit fight. The first sets wolf against human (traditionally man); the second sets wolf against nonhuman animal. The first is imagined as a necessary means toward extirpating a pest but may include the torture of the wolf if the animal is captured alive, as in Audubon and Youmans. The pit fight is torture imagined as competition, abuse in the form of psychological scarring to the point of aberrant violence that is then projected as "natural" in the pit, as critiqued by McCarthy more than by London.

15. Mary Allen cites this example in a chapter called "The Wisdom of the Dogs" in her pioneering work *Animals in American Literature* (77).

Chapter Sixteen ■ *The Big North Draw*

1. One good corrective example is, again, the Oerlemans essay, which as part of its thesis challenges the generalization that Romantic poets were following the stereotypical male conquest model in constructing their works.

2. I have long been disturbed by this need on the part of modern America to sanctify the sacred-game idea simply because it was an integral part of many ancient (and native) societies. Many things we've happily denounced were parts of other tribal societies in days gone by. Our sacred pact is still with the king's vert and venison, the feudal gentry system of stock and take; the feed lot, hog stall, stacked and torturous chicken coop, as well as

with the delusion that human hunting is "good for the environment." And, ironically, we went on a rampage against those sacred pacts of native tribes over which we now get all misty.

3. A turn on this set-up is of course when the country mouse goes to the city. A strange version is Francis Walsh's "The Wolves of Manhattan," in which an Aussie's maladjustment to the big city is surreally represented as his being thrown to the wolves.

Chapter Seventeen ■ *She-Wolves: Wildness, Domesticity, and the Woman Warrior*

1. Consider especially the work of Vandana Shiva and the award of the Nobel Peace Prize to Wangari Matthai.

2. For the indictment of "science" as patriarchal, see Merchant 1980; Easlea; Harding & O'Barr; Christie; and esp. Haraway. A work that often more clearly distinguishes the profession of science from its fact-study relationship is Keller's *Reflections on Gender and Science.*

3. I do not recommend the work of Stephen Budiansky, which is a series of convenience arguments, thin and highly selective research, and rhetorical manipulation toward a thesis of human supremacy and nonhuman capitulation. I also do not mean "domestic animals"—that is, animals kept by humans. I refer instead to the nest, hole, web, aerie, lodge, hive, burrow. I refer to the fastidious pica making sure of the precise arrangement of its interior and doorway, to the cold trap dug in a wolf den, to the rough stucco of cliff swallow apartments. I refer to the grooming habits of animal families and colonies. There are books aplenty on these subjects. I refer the reader instead to the sources.

4. The phrase "woman warrior" was popularized by Maxine Hong Kingston, and in some ways my use of it is similar. However, the term here should be taken at face value, without the assumption that I am referring exactly to Kingston's application of it, which is certainly quite powerful. I will also refer again to Haraway, whose idea of the cyborg is apparently designed to empower a woman beyond or against the Earth Mother.

5. For an indicative example of the campfire myth, which I have mentioned in previous chapters and notes, see Budiansky. For early science writing on the myth, see Michael Fox's *Canine Behavior* and his "Man, Wolf, and Dog" in Hall and Sharp (25-30).

6. See, for instance, Feher-Elston's risky reference to "the evolution of wolf to dog" (191).

7. See "The Tapestry of Possibility—Author Diane di Prima—Interview" in *Whole Earth,* Fall 1999, online issue: http://www.findarticles.com/p/articles/mi_moGER/is_1999_Fall/ai_56457596.

8. A particularly jarring fallacy of bifurcation in Haraway is her comment, "I'd rather be a cyborg than a goddess," as if these were the choices. The page on which this appears (181) depends upon such suspect conflations as "organisms and organismic, holistic politics" and "birth and regeneration." Sadly, the book, especially the essay quoted, was greeted and anthologized with wide and enthusiastic acceptance among humanities scholars uncritically endorsing anthropocentric language ostensibly about "nature" that lacked

grounding in the natural sciences to which it gestured. The chapter titled "Animal Sociology," which I hoped would be about the abuse of Darwin by social evolutionists, unfortunately declares: "Nor must we accept lightly the damaging distinction between pure and applied science, between use and abuse of science, and even between nature and culture" (8). Surely, I thought, she couldn't mean that all use of science was abuse, and that nature was culture. I was hopelessly naive. "All," she continues, "are versions of the philosophy of science that exploits the rupture between subject and object to justify the double ideology of firm scientific objectivity and mere personal subjectivity." Suddenly penicillin becomes just a double ideology, and the extinction of species is unprovable, since proof is a matter of subjectivity (that is, a subjectivity besides the dodo's).

9. I turn again, surprisingly, to *Buffy the Vampire Slayer,* episode 7 of season 2, "Lie to Me," in which the vampire Angel ridicules a group of role-playing vampire wannabes and advises them to stop romanticizing a force that is ultimately, not just fashionably, indifferent to them.

Chapter Eighteen ■ *The Skull That Wakes the Spirits: Cormac McCarthy's The Crossing*

1. See Wayne, Lehman, Allard, & Honeycutt; Mech, *The Wolf.*
2. See Mech & Boitani (xv); Gipson et al.; Mech, *Arctic Wolf;* Busch, *Wolf Almanac.*
3. DNA sequencing is likely to change the taxonomy down to the grade-school level of pedagogy and has already effected interesting changes in lepidoptery. See Stoeckel; Hajibabaei et al.
4. Arnold includes several comparisons of McCarthy's style to other writers, including Faulkner (219), Jeffers (221), and Hemingway (228). McCarthy, especially in work on his southern novels, is often compared to Faulkner. Arnold's choices, especially with the inclusion of Jeffers, reflect his awareness of the environmental influences on McCarthy's vision.
5. Early in socialization experiments scientists used fear-reducing tranquilizers (Mech, *The Wolf,* 11).
6. This is hardly an egregious liberty and certainly has mythic implications. I give credit here to Leonard Neufeldt, who pointed this out to me during an early revision.
7. See Griffin, 37–39, for a good concise description of search images, with birds as the examples.
8. See Mech, *The Wolf,* chaps. 6–8, esp. pp. 262–63.
9. *Johnson's Universal Cyclopaedia* (1897), mentioned during the analysis of children's literature in chap. 14, is a particularly striking reference.
10. So far as I have been able to find, a direct connection between naturalism and the romance in McCarthy's work hasn't been made. For some treatments of the romance and brief mentions of naturalism, see Guillemin; Kiefer; and Sugg. For a fine article on McCarthy's work as ecocentric, see Lilley.
11. See Harrington & Asa in Mech & Boitani (86–87)
12. The poem also appears in Clarke's *Listen to the Night* and in Hogan, Metzger, &

Peterson's *Intimate Nature* (51–52). The poet renders both the human construct (e.g., "lighted elevators useless" and the "rubble of quiet blocks") and both the ("last") wolf and last poet as occupying the end of something—intensifying, rather than abating, the mythic vanishing.

13. Busch, *Wolf Almanac,* 26, makes the wolf/shepherd comparison. See Peterson & Ciucci in Mech & Boitani (112–13) for more detailed analysis of the wolf's jaws. A few books on wolves, including Lopez, Hall & Sharp, Mech (*The Wolf*), and Durward Allen have chapters on biology and morphology that include material on the canid jaw.

14. List compiled from Casey & Clark's *Wolf Tales,* McIntyre's *War against the Wolf,* Busch's *Wolf Almanac,* Lopez's *Of Wolves and Men,* Caras's *The Custer Wolf,* and Young's *Last of the Loners.*

15. See Coleman; McIntyre; Steinhart; Hampton.

16. I attended this town meeting on Mexican wolf reintroduction in Santa Fe, New Mexico, March 21, 1996.

17. Some of this work comes from my article "The Trapper Mystic," which Luce cites and from which her coverage of Brown and McBride ensues.

Bibliography

Abbey, Edward. *Desert Solitaire: A Season in the Wilderness.* New York: Ballantine, 1968.

Abram, David. *The Spell of the Sensuous: Perception and Language in a More-Than-Human World.* New York: Pantheon, 1996.

Abrams, Robert H., et al., eds. *Environmental Law and Policy: Nature, Law, and Society.* 3rd ed. New York: Aspen, 2004.

Agassiz, Louis. *Essay on Classification.* Edited by Edward Lurie. Cambridge, MA: Harvard University Press, 1962.

——. *Principles of Zoology: Touching the Structure, Development, Distribution, and Natural Arrangement of the Races of Animals, Living and Extinct.* Boston: Gould and Lincoln, 1873.

Alaimo, Stacy. "Cyborg and Ecofeminist Interventions: Challenges for Environmental Feminism." *Feminist Studies* 20, no. 1 (Spring 1994): 133–52.

Allard, Harry; James Marshall, illus. *It's So Nice to Have a Wolf around the House.* Garden City, NY: Doubleday, 1977.

Allen, Durward. *Wolves of Minong: Isle Royale's Wild Community.* Ann Arbor: University of Michigan Press, 1979.

Allen, Mary. *Animals in American Literature.* Carbondale: Southern Illinois University Press, 1983.

Allen, Paula Gunn. "The Feminine Landscape of Leslie Marmon Silko's *Ceremony.*" In *Studies in American Indian Literature: Critical Essays and Course Designs,* edited by Paula Gunn Allen, 127–33. New York: Modern Language Association of America, 1983.

Ammons, Elizabeth. *Conflicting Stories: American Women Writers at the Turn into the Twentieth Century.* New York: Oxford University Press, 1992.

Andersen, Hans Christian. *The Complete Hans Christian Andersen Fairy Tales.* Edited by Lilly Owens. New York: Gramercy, 1993.

Andrews, Ted. *Animal Speak: The Spiritual and Magical Powers of Creatures Great and Small.* St. Paul, MN: Llewellyn, 1993.

Applegate, K. A. *Animorphs: The Secret.* Animorphs. Vol. 9. New York: Scholastic, 1997.

Ardrey, Robert. *The Territorial Imperative.* New York: Delta, 1971.

Arensberg, Ann. *Sister Wolf.* New York: Knopf, 1980.

Armstrong, Kelley. *Bitten.* New York: Viking Penguin, 2001.

Arnold, Edwin T. "McCarthy and the Sacred: A Reading of *The Crossing.*" In *Cormac McCarthy: New Directions,* edited by James D. Lilley, 215–38. Albuquerque: University of New Mexico Press, 2002.

Asbjørnsen, Peter Christen, and Jorgen Moe. *Norwegian Folk Tales.* New York: Pantheon, 1982.

Ashwill, Gary. "Savagism and Its Discontents: James Fenimore Cooper and His Native American Contemporaries." *American Transcendental Quarterly* 8, no. 3 (1992): 211–27.

Askins, Renée. *Shadow Mountain: A Memoir of Wolves, a Woman, and the Wild.* New York: Doubleday, 2002.

———. "Shades of Gray." In *Intimate Nature: The Bond between Animals and Women,* edited by Linda Hogan, Deena Metzger, and Brenda Peterson, 375–79. New York: Fawcett Columbine, 1998.

Audubon, John J. *Selected Journals and Other Writings.* Edited by Ben Forkner. New York: Penguin, 1996.

Audubon, John J., and J. Bachman. *Audubon's Quadrupeds of North America.* Secaucus, NJ: Wellfleet Press, 1989.

Auel, Jean. *The Clan of the Cave Bear.* New York: Crown, 1980.

———. *The Mammoth Hunters.* New York: Crown, 1985.

———. *The Plains of Passage.* New York: Crown, 1990.

———. *The Shelters of Stone.* New York: Crown, 2002.

———. *The Valley of Horses.* New York: Crown, 1982.

Auerbach, Jonathan. *Male Call: Becoming Jack London.* Durham, NC: Duke University Press, 1996.

"Babbitt Gets Chewing Out over Wolves." From *Washington Post,* reprinted in *Santa Fe New Mexican,* January 27, 1994.

Bachelard, Gaston. *The Poetics of Space.* Translated by Maria Jolas. Boston: Beacon, 1964.

Baguley, David. "The 'Lure' of the Naturalist Text." *Canadian Review of Comparative Literature (Revue Canadienne de Littérature Comparée)* 19 (1992): 273–80.

Baring-Gould, Sabine. *The Book of Werewolves.* London: Studio Editions, 1995.

Baker, Carlos, ed. *Ernest Hemingway: Selected Letters, 1918–1961.* New York: Scribner's, 1981.

Ballard, W. B. "Brown Bear Kills Grey Wolf." *Canadian Field-Naturalist* 94, no. 1 (1986): 1–91.

Ballard, W. B., L. A. Ayres, C. L. Gardner, and J. W. Foster. "Den Site Activity Patterns of Gray Wolves, *Canis lupus,* in Southcentral Alaska." *Canadian Field-Naturalist* 105, no. 4 (1991): 497–504.

Ballard, W. B., and J. R. Dau. "Characteristics of Gray Wolf Den and Rendezvous Sites in Southcentral Alaska." *Canadian Field-Naturalist* 97, no. 3 (1983): 299–302.

Ballard, Warren B., and Paul R. Krausman. "Occurrence of Rabies in Wolves of Alaska." *Journal of Wildlife Diseases* 33, no. 2 (1997): 242–45.

Bamberger, Joan. "The Myth of Matriarchy: Why Men Rule in Primitive Society." In *Women, Culture, and Society,* edited by Michelle Zimbalist Rosaldo and Louise Lamphere, 263–80. Stanford, CA: Stanford University Press, 1974.

Banfield, A. W. F. "Notes on the Mammals of the Mackenzie District, Northwest Territories." *Arctic* 4, no. 2 (September 1951): 113–21.

——. "Review of F. Mowat's *Never Cry Wolf.*" *Canadian Field-Naturalist* 78 (1964): 52–54.

Barber, Richard. *Bestiary: Being an English Version of the Bodleian Library, Oxford, MS Bodley 764.* 1992. Reprint, Suffolk, UK: Boydell and Brewer, 2006.

Barnard, Mary. *Time and the White Tigress.* Portland, OR: Breitenbush, 1986.

Barthes, Roland. "The Death of the Author." *Aspen* 5–6 (1967): n.p.

Baym, Nina. "Again and Again, the Scribbling Women." In *Hawthorne and Women: Engendering and Expanding the Hawthorne Tradition,* edited by John L. Idol and Melinda M. Ponder, 20–35. Amherst: University of Massachusetts Press, 1999.

Bass, Rick. *The New Wolves.* New York: Lyons Press, 1998.

——. *The Ninemile Wolves.* New York: Ballantine, 1992.

——. "Swamp Boy," in *In the Loyal Mountains,* 19–34. Boston: Houghton Mifflin, 1995.

——. *Where the Sea Used to Be.* Boston: Houghton Mifflin, 1998.

——. "Why I Hunt." *Sierra Magazine Online,* July/August, 2001. http://www.sierraclub .org/sierra/200107/bass.asp.

——. "Wolf Palette." *Orion* 24, no. 4 (July/August 2005): 24–31.

Bateman, James A. *Animal Traps and Trapping.* Harrisburg, PA: Stackpole, 1988.

Bateson, Gregory. *Steps to an Ecology of Mind: Collected Essays in Anthropology, Psychiatry, Evolution, and Epistemology.* Chicago: University of Chicago Press, 2000.

——. *Mind and Nature.* New York: Dutton, 1979.

Baudrillard, Jean. *Simulacra and Simulation.* Ann Arbor: University of Michigan Press, 1995.

Beach-Balthis, Judy. *Yellowstone: A Children's Guide.* N.p.: Firehole Press, 1981.

Beck, Alan, and Aaron Katcher. *Between Pets and People: The Importance of Animal Companionship.* West Lafayette, IN: Purdue University Press, 1996.

Bekoff, Marc. "The Development of Social Interaction, Play, and Metacommunication in Mammals: An Ethological Perspective." *Quarterly Review of Biology* 47 (1972): 412–34.

——. *Minding Animals: Awareness, Emotions, and Heart.* New York: Oxford University Press, 2002.

——. "Social Play and Play-Soliciting by Infant Canids." *American Zoologist* 14 (1974): 323–40.

——. "Social Play in Coyotes, Wolves, and Dogs." *Bio-Science* 24, no. 4 (April 1974): 225–30.

Bell, Millicent. "Female Regional Writing: An American Tradition." *Revue Française d'Etudes Americaines* 1, no. 30 (November 1986): 469–80.

Belshaw, Michael. *All the Loving Wolves: Living and Learning with Wolf Hybrids*. Santa Fe, NM: Red Crane, 1990.

Bercovitch, Sacvan, ed. *The Cambridge History of American Literature*. Vol. 1 (1590–1820). New York: Cambridge University Press, 1994.

———. *The Puritan Origins of the American Self*. New Haven, CT: Yale University Press, 1975.

Berman, D. "Bettelheim's Three Pigs." *International Review of Psycho-Analysis* 14 (1987): 421–22.

Bernheimer, Richard. *Wild Men in the Middle Ages: A Study in Art, Sentiment, and Demonology*. New York: Octagon, 1970.

Berry, Thomas. *The Dream of the Earth*. San Francisco: Sierra Club Books, 1990.

———. *The Great Work: Our Way into the Future*. New York: Bell Tower, Random House, 1999.

Bettelheim, Bruno. *The Uses of Enchantment: The Meaning and Importance of Fairy Tales*. New York: Vintage, 1977.

Bierce, Ambrose. *The Devil's Dictionary*. 1911. Reprint, New York: Dell, 1991.

Bildauer, Bettina, and Robert Mills. *The Monstrous Middle Ages*. Toronto: University of Toronto Press, 2003.

Bishop, Norman. Interview. Bozeman, MT. August 5, 2002.

———. "The Ripple Effect." Yellowstone Association Institute course. Yellowstone National Park, February 2004.

Blackman, Margaret. "Facing the Future, Envisioning the Past: Visual Literature and Contemporary Northwest Coast Masks." *Arctic Anthropology* 27, no. 2 (1990): 27–40.

Blish, James. "There Shall Be No Darkness," in *A Work of Art and Other Stories*, 119–64. Sutton, Surrey, UK: Severn House, 1983. Originally published in *Thrilling Wonder Stories*, April 1950.

Boas, Franz. *Kwakiutl Culture as Reflected in Mythology*. Memoirs of the American Folk-lore Society, vol. 28. New York: American Folk-lore Society, 1935.

Bodkin, Maud. *Archetypal Patterns in Poetry: Psychological Studies of Imagination*. London: Oxford University Press, 1948.

Boitani, Luigi. "Wolf Conservation and Recovery." In *Wolves: Behavior, Ecology, and Conservation*, edited by L. David Mech and Luigi Boitani, 317–40. Chicago: University of Chicago Press, 2003.

Bonner, John T. *The Evolution of Culture in Animals*. Princeton, NJ: Princeton University Press, 1980.

Borchardt, Alice. *Night of the Wolf*. New York: Ballantine Del Rey, 1999.

———. *The Silver Wolf*. New York: Ballantine Del Rey, 1998.

———. *The Wolf King*. New York: Ballantine Del Rey, 2001.

Boudinot, Elias. *Cherokee Editor: The Writings of Elias Boudinot*. Knoxville: University of Tennessee Press, 1983.

Bowen, 'Asta. *Hungry for Home: A Wolf Odyssey*. New York: Simon and Schuster, 1998. Reprint as *Wolf: The Journey Home*. New York: Bloomsbury, 2005.

Bowen, Peter. *Wolf, No Wolf.* New York: St. Martin's Press, 1996.

Bowles, Paul. "The Frozen Fields." In *A Distant Episode: Collected Stories,* 139–56. New York: Ecco, 1988.

———. *The Sheltering Sky.* New York: Ecco Press, 1949.

———. *Without Stopping: An Autobiography.* New York: G. P. Putnam Sons, 1972.

Boy Scouts of America. *Wolf Cub Scout Handbook.* New Brunswick, NJ: BSA, 1969.

Boyd, Brian. "Theory Is Dead—Like a Zombie." *Philosophy and Literature* 30, no. 1 (April 2006): 289–98.

Boyd, Diane. Interview. Yellowstone Association Institute, Yellowstone National Park, March 2, 2002.

Boyd, D. K., and M. D. Jimenez. "Successful Rearing of Young by Wild Wolves without Mates." *Journal of Mammalogy* 75, no. 1 (1994): 14–17.

Boyd, D. K., D. H. Pletscher, and W. Brewster. "Evidence of Wolves, *Canis lupus,* Burying Dead Wolf Pups." *Canadian Field-Naturalist* 107, no. 2 (1993): 230–31.

Boyd-Heger, Diane. "Living with Wolves." In *Intimate Nature: The Bond between Women and Animals,* edited by Linda Hogan, Deena Metzger, and Brenda Peterson, 90–96. New York: Fawcett Columbine, 1998.

Boyle, T. C. "Dogology." In *Tooth and Claw, and Other Stories,* 32–56. New York: Viking, 2005.

Bradfield, Scott. *Animal Planet.* New York: Picador USA, 1996.

———. *Dream of the Wolf.* New York: Alfred A. Knopf, 1990.

Brady, Margaret K. *"Some Kind of Power": Navajo Children's Skinwalker Narratives.* Salt Lake City: University of Utah Press, 1984.

Branch, Michael. "Ecocriticism: The Nature of Nature in Literary Theory and Practice." *Weber Studies* 11, no. 1 (1994): 41–55.

Brand, Max. *The White Wolf.* New York: Leisure Books, 1995.

Briscoe, Brian, Mark A. Lewis, and Stephen E. Parrish. "Home Range Formation in Wolves Due to Scent Marking." *Bulletin of Mathematical Biology* 64, no. 2 (2002): 261–84.

Brockman, John. *Third Culture: Beyond the Scientific Revolution.* New York: Touchstone, 1996.

Brodhead, Richard. *Cultures of Letters: Scenes of Reading and Writing in Nineteenth-Century America.* University of Chicago Press, 1993.

Brown, Abbie Farwell; Fanny Y. Cory, illus. *The Book of Saints and Friendly Beasts.* 1900. Reprint, Great Neck, NY: Core Collection Books, 1976.

Brown, David E., ed. *The Wolf in the Southwest: The Making of an Endangered Species.* Tucson: University of Arizona Press, 1992.

Brown, James H. *Macroecology.* Chicago: University of Chicago Press, 1995.

Brown, W., et al. "Mexican Wolf Management Facility at Sevilleta National Wildlife Refuge." Washington, DC: U.S. Fish and Wildlife Service, August 19, 1996.

Browning, Robert. "Ivàn Ivànovitch," in *The Poems of Robert Browning,* 590–95. Ware, Hertfordshire, UK: Wordsworth Editions, 1994.

Brunel, Pierre, ed. *Companion to Literary Myths, Heroes, and Archetypes.* London: Routledge, 1996.

Bryant, William Cullen. "The Prairies." In *The Complete Poetical Works of William Cullen Bryant, Collected and Arranged by Himself,* 309–316. London: Knight and Son, 1854.

Buechner, Frederick. *Wishful Thinking: A Theological ABC.* New York: Harper and Row, 1973.

Budiansky, Stephen. *Covenant of the Wild: Why Animals Chose Domestication.* New York: William Morrow, 1992.

Burbank, James. *Vanishing Lobo: The Mexican Wolf and the Southwest.* Boulder, CO: Johnson Books, 1991.

Burgess, Steve. "Northern Exposure." Salon.com, May 11, 1999. http://www.salon.com/people/bc/1999/05/11/mowat/index.html.

Burke, Séan. *The Death and Return of the Author: Criticism and Subjectivity in Barthes, Foucault, and Derrida.* Edinburgh: Edinburgh University Press, 1998.

Burkert, Walter. *Homo Necans: The Anthropology of Ancient Greek Sacrificial Ritual and Myth.* Berkeley: University of California Press, 1983. Originally published Berlin: Walter de Gruyter, 1972.

Burkhardt, Richard. *The Spirit of System: Lamarck and Evolutionary Biology.* Cambridge, MA: Harvard University Press, 1995.

Burroughs, John. *Camping and Tramping with Roosevelt.* Boston: Houghton Mifflin, 1879.

Busch, Robert H., ed. *The Wolf Almanac.* New York: Lyons and Burford, 1995.

——. *Wolf Songs: A Classic Collection of Writing about Wolves.* San Francisco: Sierra Club, 1994.

Butler, Francelia, and Richard Rotert, eds. *Triumphs of the Spirit in Children's Literature.* Hamden, CT: Library Professional Publications, 1986.

Bykov, V. M. *In the Steps of Jack London.* Moscow: Moscow University, 1962. In Russian. Translated by Earle Labor for jacklondons.net. Full text: http://www.jacklondons.net/writings/Bykov/toc_InHissteps.html.

——. *Jack London.* Moscow: Moscow University, 1964. In Russian.

Bynum, Caroline Walker. *Metamorphosis and Identity.* Cambridge, MA: MIT University Press, 2001.

Callicott, J. Baird, and Michael P. Nelson, eds. *The Great New Wilderness Debate.* Athens: University of Georgia Press, 1998.

Calloway, Colin G. *North Country Captives: Selected Narratives of Indian Captivity from Vermont and New Hampshire.* Hanover, NH: University Press of New England, 1992.

Campbell, Angus [R. Chetwynd-Hayes]. "The Werewolf." In *Frights and Fancies,* edited by Stephen Jones, 235–48. London: Robert Hale, 2002.

Campbell, Donna M. "Realism and Regionalism." In *A Companion to the Regional Literatures of America,* edited by Charles L. Crow, 92–110. Blackwell Companions to Literature and Culture no. 21. Malden, MA: Blackwell, 2003.

——. *Resisting Regionalism: Gender and Naturalism in American Fiction, 1885–1915.* Athens: Ohio University Press, 1997.

Campbell, Janet, and David. G. Campbell. "The Wolf Clan." *Journal of Cherokee Studies* 7, no. 2 (1982): 85–91.

Campbell, Joseph. *The Historical Atlas of World Mythology. Volume 1: The Way of the Animal Powers.* New York: Harper and Row, 1983.

Camuto, Christopher. *Another Country: Journeying toward the Cherokee Mountains.* Athens: University of Georgia Press, 2000.

Caras, Roger. *The Custer Wolf: Biography of an American Renegade.* Boston: Little, Brown, 1966.

Carbyn, Ludwig (Lu) N. *The Buffalo Wolf: Predators, Prey, and the Politics of Nature.* Washington, DC: Smithsonian Books, 2003.

Carbyn, Ludwig N., S. H. Fritts, and D. R. Seip, eds. *Ecology and Conservation of the Wolf in a Changing World.* Occasional Publication No. 35. Edmonton: University of Alberta, Canadian Circumpolar Institute, 1995.

Carbyn, Ludwig N., S. Oosenbrug, and D. W. Anions. *Wolves, Bison: And the Dynamics Related to the Peace-Athabasca Delta in Canada's Wood Buffalo National Park.* Research Series No. 4. Edmonton: University of Alberta, Canadian Circumpolar Institute, 1993.

Carroll, Joseph. *Evolution and Literary Theory.* Columbia: University of Missouri Press, 1994.

———. *Literary Darwinism.* London: Routledge, 2004.

Carter, George F. "Man, Time, and Change in the Far Southwest." *Annals of the Association of American Geographers* 49, no. 3, pt. 2 of "Man, Time, and Space in Southern California: A Symposium" (September 1959): 8–30.

Cartmill, Matt. *A View to a Death in the Morning: Hunting and Nature through History.* Cambridge, MA: Harvard University Press, 1993.

Casey, Denise, and Tim W. Clark, eds. *Tales of the Wolf: Fifty-One Stories of Wolf Encounters in the Wild.* Moose, WY: Homestead, 1996.

Cather, Willa. *My Ántonia.* 1918. Reprint, New York: Vintage, 1994.

Cederstrom, Lorelei. "Myth and Ceremony in Contemporary North American Native Fiction." *Canadian Journal of Native Studies* 2, no. 20 (1982): 285–301.

Chabon, Michael. "Son of the Wolfman." In *Werewolves in Their Youth,* 3–31. New York: Picador, 2000.

Chaffin, James. *The Wolfer.* New York: Tower, 1968.

Charvat, William L., et al., eds. *Centenary Edition of the Works of Nathaniel Hawthorne.* 23 vols. Columbus: Ohio State University Press, 1962–1977.

Chase, Alston. *In a Dark Wood: The Fight Over Forests and the Myths of Nature.* Piscataway, NJ: Transaction, 2001.

———. *Playing God in Yellowstone: The Destruction of America's First National Park.* Boston: Atlantic Monthly Press, 1986.

———. "Purpose of Yellowstone's Wolf Return Circus." *Indianapolis Star,* February 11, 1996, D3.

Chatwin, Bruce. *The Songlines.* New York: Viking Penguin, 1987.

Christie, J. R. R. "Feminism and the History of Science." In *Companion to the History of Modern Science,* edited by R. C. Olby et al., 100–109. London: Routledge, 1990.

Ciucci, P., and L. D. Mech. "Selection of Wolf Dens in Relation to Winter Territories in Northeastern Minnesota." *Journal of Mammalogy* 73, no. 4 (1992): 899–905.

Clark, William, and Meriwether Lewis. *Original Journals of the Lewis and Clark Expedition, 1804–1806.* New York: Dodd, Mead, 1904. Reprinted in *Early Western Travels 1748–1846,* edited by Reuben Gold Thwaites. 32 vols. New York: Antiquarian Press, 1959.

Clarke, Ben, ed. *Listen to the Night: Poems to the Animal Spirits of Mother Earth.* San Francisco: Freedom Voices, 1995.

Clarkson, Ewan. *Wolf Country: A Wilderness Pilgrimage.* New York: E. P. Dutton, 1975.

Clasby, Nancy Tenfelde. "'Manabozho': A Native American Resurrection Myth." *Studies in Short Fiction* 30 (1993): 583–94.

Coe, Kathryn. "Art: The Replicable Unit—An Inquiry into the Possible Origin of Art as a Social Behavior." *Journal of Social and Evolutionary Systems* 15, no. 2 (1992): 217–34.

Cohen, Daniel; John Hamberger, illus. *Watchers in the Wild: The New Science of Ethology.* Boston: Little, Brown, 1971.

Cohen, Esther. "Law, Folklore, and Animal Lore." *Past and Present* 110 (February 1986): 6–37.

Cohen, Michael. *Reconnecting with Nature: Finding Wellness through Restoring Your Bond with the Earth.* Corvallis, OR: Ecopress, 1992.

———. *The Web of Life Imperative: Regenerative Ecopsychology Techniques That Help People Think in Balance with Natural Systems.* Friday Harbor, WA: Institute of Global Education, 2003.

Colby, C. B. *The First Book of Animal Signs.* New York: Franklin Watts, 1966.

Coleman, Jon T. *Vicious: Wolves and Men in America.* New Haven, CT: Yale University Press, 2004.

Commoner, Barry. *The Closing Circle: Nature, Man, and Technology.* New York: Random House, 1971.

Conder, John. *Naturalism in American Fiction: The Classic Phase.* Lexington: University of Kentucky Press, 1984.

Conley, Verena Andermatt. *Ecopolitics: The Environment in Poststructuralist Thought.* London: Routledge, 1997.

Cook, May Estelle. "Nature-Books for the Holidays." *Dial,* December 1, 1906, 380–90.

Cooke, Mark. *The Suburban Werewolf.* Cambridge, UK: Pegasus Elliot MacKenzie, 2007.

Cooper, J. C. *Symbolic and Mythological Animals.* New York: HarperCollins, 1992.

Cooper, James Fenimore. *The Last of the Mohicans.* New York: Penguin Classics, 1986.

———. *The Prairie.* New York: Penguin Classics, 1985.

Corcoran, Barbara; Richard L. Shell, illus. *Sasha, My Friend.* New York: Atheneum, 1972.

Cordingly, David. *Under the Black Flag: The Romance and the Reality of Life among the Pirates.* London: Little, Brown, 1995.

Corsini, Raymond, ed. *The Dictionary of Psychology.* New York: Psychology Press, 2002.

Cowan, Tom. *Fire in the Head: Shamanism and the Celtic Spirit.* San Francisco: HarperSan-Francisco, 1993.

Crane, Stephen. *The Red Badge of Courage, and Other Stories.* New York: Penguin Classics, 1991.

Crisler, Lois. *Arctic Wild.* New York: Harper and Brothers, 1958.

———. *Captive Wild: One Woman's Adventure Living with Wolves.* New York: Harper and Row, 1968.

Cronon, William. *Uncommon Ground: Rethinking the Human Place in Nature.* New York: W. W. Norton, 1996.

Curley, Michael J. "Animal Symbolism in the Prophecies of Merlin." In *Beasts and Birds of the Middle Ages: The Bestiary and Its Legacy,* edited by Willene B. Clark and Meradith T. McMunn, 151–63. Philadelphia: University of Pennsylvania Press, 1989.

Curtis, Edward. *The North American Indian.* 20 vols. New York: Johnson Reprint Corporation, 1906–1930.

Curwood, James Oliver. *Baree: The Story of a Wolf-Dog.* 1917. Reprint, New York: Newmarket Press, 2005.

———. *Kazan.* 1914. Reprint, Whitefish, MT: Kessinger, 2004.

———. *The Wolf Hunters: A Tale of Adventure in the Wilderness.* 1908. Reprint, Whitefish, MT: Kessinger, 2005.

Daniel, John. "The Impoverishment of Sightseeing." In *The Trail Home,* 35–46. New York: Pantheon, 1992.

Danvers, Dennis. *Wilderness.* New York: HarperCollins, 2000.

Darwin, Charles. *The Expression of the Emotions in Man and Animals.* 1872. Reprint, Chicago: University of Chicago Press, 1965.

Davis, S. "The Dog: Evidence for Its Domestication 12,000 Years Ago." *Israel Journal of Zoology* 26, no. 3/4 (1977): 252–53.

Dawkins, Richard. *Unweaving the Rainbow: Science, Delusion, and the Appetite for Wonder.* Boston: Houghton Mifflin, 1998.

DeBlieu, Jan. *Meant to Be Wild: The Struggle to Save Endangered Species through Captive Breeding.* Golden, CO: Fulcrum, 1991.

Deitering, Cynthia. "The Postnatural Novel: Toxic Consciousness in the Fiction of the 1980s." In *The Ecocriticism Reader: Landmarks in Literary Ecology,* edited by Cheryll Glotfelty and Harold Fromm, 196–203. Athens: University of Georgia Press, 1996.

Dekker, George, and John P. McWilliams, eds. *Fenimore Cooper: The Critical Heritage.* London: Routledge and Kegan Paul, 1973.

Deleuze, Gilles, and Félix Guattari. *A Thousand Plateaus: Capitalism and Schizophrenia.* Translated and with a foreword by Brian Massumi. Minneapolis: University of Minnesota Press, 1987.

DelGiudice, G. D., L. D. Mech, and U. S. Seal. "Gray Wolf Density and Its Association with Weights and Hematology of Pups from 1970 to 1988." *Journal of Wildlife Distribution* 27, no. 4 (1991): 630–36.

Deloria, Vine. *Custer Died for Your Sins: An Indian Manifesto*. Norman: University of Oklahoma Press, 1988.

———. *The Indian Reorganization Act: Congresses and Bills*. Norman: University of Oklahoma Press, 2002.

———. *Red Earth, White Lies: Native Americans and the Myth of Scientific Fact*. Golden, CO: Fulcrum, 1997.

Den Tandt, Christophe. "American Literary Naturalism." In *A Companion to American Fiction: 1865–1914*, edited by Robert Paul Lamb and G. R. Thompson, 96–118. Oxford, UK: Blackwell, 2005.

Derounian-Stedola, Kathryn Zabelle, ed. *Women's Indian Captivity Narratives*. New York: Penguin Classics, 1998.

Derrida, Jacques. "Hospitality." Translated by Forbes Morlock. *Angelaki* 5, no. 3 (2002): 3–18.

———. "White Mythology." In *Margins of Philosophy*, translated by Alan Bass. Chicago: University of Chicago Press, 1982.

———. *Writing and Difference*. Translated by Alan Bass. 1967. Reprint, London: Routledge, 2004.

DeVore, Lynn. "The Descent of White Fang." *Jack London Newsletter* 7, no. 3 (1974): 122–26.

DeVoto, Bernard. *The Year of Decision: 1846*. Boston: Little, Brown, 1942.

Dickey, James. Introduction to *The Call of the Wild, White Fang, and Other Stories by Jack London,* edited by Andrew Sinclair. New York: Penguin, 1981.

Dickson, Gordon. *Wolf and Iron*. New York: Tor, 1990.

Dillon, John B. *Oddities of Colonial Legislation in America*. Indianapolis: Robert Douglass, 1879.

Dingwall, Eric John. *Artificial Cranial Deformation: A Contribution to the Study of Ethnic Mutilations*. London: John Bale, Sons, 1931.

Dinzelbacher, Peter. "Animal Trials: A Multidisciplinary Approach." *Journal of Interdisciplinary History* 32, no. 3 (Winter 2002): 405–21.

di Prima, Diane. *Loba*. New York: Penguin, 1998.

Disaanayake, Ellen. *Homo Aestheticus: Where Art Comes from and Why*. Seattle: University of Washington Press, 1992.

Dodge, Richard Irving. *The Plains of North America and Their Inhabitants*. 1876. Reprint, edited by Wayne R. Kime, Newark: University of Delaware Press, 1989.

Dombrowski, Daniel A. *Babies and Beasts: The Argument from Marginal Cases*. Champaign: University of Illinois Press, 1997.

Doniger, Wendy, ed. *Mythologies*. Chicago: University of Chicago Press, 1991.

Donovan, Mortimer J. *The Breton Lay: A Guide to Varieties*. South Bend, IN: University of Notre Dame Press, 1969.

Dorsey, George A. *The Mythology of the Wichita*. Washington, DC: Carnegie Institution of Washington, 1904.

Dougherty, William H. "Crossing." *Verbatim* 21, no. 4 (1995): 5–7.

Douglas, Adam. *The Beast Within: A History of the Werewolf.* New York: Avon, 1992.

Dröscher, Vitus. *The Friendly Beast: Latest Discoveries in Animal Behavior.* New York: E. P. Dutton, 1971.

Duck, Leigh Anne. "'Go there tuh know there': Zora Neale Hurston and the Chronotype of the Folk." *American Literary History* 13, no. 2 (Summer 2001): 265–94.

Dufresne, Jim, and Aaron Spitzer, eds. *Lonely Planet: Alaska.* London: Lonely Planet, 2006.

Dundes, Alan, ed. "Earth-Diver: Creation of the Mythopoeic Male." In *Psychology and Myth,* edited by Robert A. Segal, 154–73. New York: Garland, 1996.

——. *Little Red Riding Hood: A Casebook.* Madison: University of Wisconsin Press, 1989.

Dunn, Charles W. *The Foundling and the Werwolf: A Literary-Historical Study of Guillaume de Palerne.* Toronto: University of Toronto Press, 1960.

Dusiak, M. A. "Record of a Timberwolf Attacking a Man." *Journal of Mammalogy* 28, no. 3 (1974): 294–95.

Dutcher, Jim, and Richard Ballantine. *The Sawtooth Wolves.* Bearsville, NY: Rufus, 1996.

Earle, Alice Morse. *Sabbath in Puritan New England.* Williamstown, MA: Corner House, 1974.

Earhart, H. Byron, ed. *Religious Traditions of the World: A Journey through Africa, Mesoamerica, North America, Judaism, Christianity, Islam, Hinduism, Buddhism, China, and Japan.* New York: HarperCollins, 1993.

Easlea, Brian. *Science and Sexual Oppression: Patriarchy's Confrontation with Women and Nature.* London: Weidenfield and Nicholson, 1981.

Easthouse, Keith. "Johnson: Wolf Could 'Devastate' Local Economies." *Santa Fe New Mexican,* November 15, 1996, A1, A2.

——. "Peers Blast Study Done on Wolves." *Santa Fe New Mexican,* December 7, 1995, A1+.

——. "US: Wolf Reintroduction Still Possible." *Santa Fe New Mexican,* January 14, 1996, B1+.

——. "Who's Afraid of the Mexican Wolf?" *Outside,* February 1996.

——. "Wolves Will Be Wild, but Not Popular." *Santa Fe New Mexican,* July 3, 1995, B1+.

Eckels, Richard Preston. "Greek Wolf-lore." PHD diss., University of Pennsylvania, 1937.

Edson, Gary. *Masks and Masking: Faces of Tradition and Belief Worldwide.* Jefferson, NC: McFarland, 2005.

Elder, John, ed. *The Return of the Wolf: Reflections on the Future of the Wolf in the Northeast.* Hanover, NH: University Press of New England, 2000.

Elhard, Jay Robert. *Wolf Tourist: One Summer in the West.* Logan: Utah State University Press: 1996.

Eliade, Mircea. *Myth and Reality.* New York: Harper and Row, 1963.

——. *The Myth of the Eternal Return; or, Cosmos and History.* Bollingen Series. Princeton, NJ: Princeton University Press, 1954.

——. *Shamanism: Archaic Techniques of Ecstasy.* New York: Pantheon, 1964.

Eliot, Alexander, Joseph Campbell, and Mircea Eliade. *The Universal Myths: Heroes, Gods, Tricksters, and Others.* New York: Penguin Putnam, 1990.

Elliott, Emory, ed. *The Columbia Literary History of the United States.* New York: Columbia University Press, 1988.

Elwood, Roger. *Wolf's Lair: A Novel.* Nashville, TN: Thomas Nelson, 1993.

Emel, Jody. "Are You Man Enough, Big and Bad Enough? Wolf Eradication in the U.S." In *Animal Geographies: Place, Politics, and Identity in the Nature-Culture Borderlands,* edited by Jennifer R. Wolch and Jody Emel, 91–117. New York: Verso Press, 1998.

Emerson, Ralph Waldo, and Henry David Thoreau. *Nature/Walking.* Boston: Beacon Press, 1994.

Ernst, Alice Herndon. *The Wolf Ritual of the Northwest Coast.* Eugene: University of Oregon Press, 1952.

Estés, Clarissa Pinkola. *Women Who Run with the Wolves: Myths and Stories of the Wild Woman Archetype.* New York: Ballantine, 1992.

Evans, Bergen. *The Natural History of Nonsense.* New York: Vintage, 1958.

Evans, E. P. *The Criminal Prosecution and Capital Punishment of Animals.* London: William Heinemann. 1906.

Evans, G. Blakemore, ed. *The Riverside Shakespeare.* Boston: Houghton Mifflin, 1974.

Evans, Howard E. *Miller's Anatomy of the Dog.* Philadelphia: W. B. Saunders, 1993.

Evans, Nicholas. *The Loop.* New York: Delacorte, 1998.

Farlow, James. "The Demythologized Lycanthrope." *Analog,* May 1977.

Feddersen-Petersen, D. "Observations on Social Play in Some Species of Canidae." *Zoologischer Anzeiger* 217, no. 1–2 (1986): 130–44.

Feher-Elston, Catherine. *Wolfsong: A Natural and Fabulous History of Wolves.* New York: Jeremy P. Tarcher/Penguin, 2004.

Fein, Judith. "Part of the Pack." *Santa Fe New Mexican,* May 28, 1995, E1+.

Fenton, James. "The Lobo Wolf: Beast of Waste and Desolation." *Panhandle-Plains Historical Review* 53 (1980): 57–70.

Ferguson, Gary. *The Yellowstone Wolves: The First Year.* Helena, MT: Falcon Press, 1996.

Ferling, John. "The New England Soldier: A Study in Changing Perceptions." *American Quarterly* 33, no. 1 (Spring 1981): 26–45.

Ferry, Georgina, ed. *The Understanding of Animals.* Oxford, UK: Blackwell, 1984.

Fetterley, Judith, and Marjorie Pryse. *Writing Out of Place: Regionalism, Women, and American Literary Culture.* Champaign: University of Illinois Press, 2003.

———, eds. *American Women Regionalists 1850–1910.* New York: Norton, 1992.

Field, Nancy, and Corliss Karasov; Cary Hunkel, illus. *Discovering Wolves: Journey into the Wild World.* Middleton, WI: Dog-Eared Publications and the Timber Wolf Alliance, 1991.

Fienup-Riordan, Ann, ed. *Agayuliyararput: Our Way of Making Prayer.* Anchorage, AK: Anchorage Museum of History and Art, 1996.

Fieser, James. "Moore, Spencer, and the Naturalistic Fallacy." *History of Philosophy Quarterly* 10 (1993): 271–77.

Filson, John. *The Discovery, Settlement, and Present State of Kentucke [sic].* 1784. Reprint, New York: Corinth, 1962.

Fischer, Hank. *Wolf Wars.* Helena, MT: Falcon Press, 1995.

———. Interview. Missoula, MT, November 22, 1995.

Fisher, Philip. *Hard Facts: Setting and Form in the American Novel.* New York: Oxford University Press, 1985.

Fitzgerald, F. Scott. "The Off-Shore Pirate." *Saturday Evening Post,* May 1920. Reprinted in *F. Scott Fitzgerald: Novels and Stories, 1920–1922,* edited by Jackson Bryer. New York: Library of America, 2000: 253–82.

Fitzpatrick, Tara. "The Figure of Captivity: The Cultural Work of the Puritan Captivity Narrative." *American Literary History* 3, no. 1. (Spring 1991): 1–26.

Flint, Valerie I. J. *The Rise of Magic in Early Medieval Europe.* Princeton, NJ: Princeton University Press, 1994.

Fogleman, Valerie M. "American Attitudes toward Wolves: A History of Misperception." *Environmental Review* 13, no. 1 (1989): 63–94.

Foreman, Dave. *The Lobo Outback Funeral Home.* Neenah, WI: Big Earth, 2004.

Foucault, Michel. *The Archaeology of Knowledge.* London: Tavistock, 1974.

———. *Power/Knowledge: Selected Interviews and Other Writings, 1972–1977.* New York: Pantheon, 1980.

Fox, Michael W. *Canine Behavior: A History of Domestication, Behavioral Development and Adult Behavior Patterns, Neurophysiology, Psychobiology, Training, Inheritance, Early Experience and Psycho-social Relationships, Experimental Neuroses and Spontaneous Behavioral Abnormalities, Congenital Anomalies and Differential Diagnosis of Neurologic Diseases.* Springfield, IL: Charles C. Thomas, 1965.

———. "Man, Wolf, and Dog." In *Wolf and Man: Evolution in Parallel,* edited by Roberta Hall and Henry S. Sharp, 25–30. New York: Academic Press, 1978.

Frank, H., and M. G. Frank. "On the Effects of Domestication on Canine Social Development and Behavior." *Applied Animal Ethology* 8 (1982): 507–25.

Freeman, Brad, and Christopher Howard. *Pentex Monkeywrench!* Stone Mountain, GA: White Wolf Games, 1994.

Freeman, R. C., and J. H. Shaw. "Hybridization in Canis (Canidae) in Oklahoma." *Southwestern Naturalist* 24, no. 3 (1979): 485–500.

Freud, Sigmund. *The Wolf-Man and Other Cases.* New York: Penguin Classics, 2003.

Fritts, Stephen H., William J. Paul, L. David Mech, and David P. Scott. "Trends and Management of Wolf-Livestock Conflicts in Minnesota." Washington, DC: U.S. Fish and Wildlife Service Resource Publication 181 (1992): 1–27.

Frost, Brian J. *The Essential Guide to Werewolf Literature.* Madison: University of Wisconsin Press, 2003.

Frye, Northrop. *Anatomy of Criticism: Four Essays.* Princeton, NJ: Princeton University Press, 2000.

Frye, Northrop, Sheridan Baker, and George Perkins, eds. *The Harper Handbook to Literature.* New York: HarperCollins, 1985.

Fujino, K. K., and K. M. Warren. "A Gray Wolf (*Canis lupus columbianus*) and Stone Sheep (*Ovis dalli stonei*) Fatal Predator-Prey Encounter." *Canadian Field-Naturalist* 92, no. 4 (1978): 399–401.

Fuller, T. K. "Denning Behavior of Wolves in North-Central Minnesota." *American Midland Naturalist* 121, no. 1 (1989): 184–88.

———. "Effect of Snow Depth on Wolf Activity and Prey Selection in North Central Minnesota." *Canadian Journal of Zoology* 69, no. 2 (1991): 283–87.

Gaard, Greta, and Patrick Murphy, eds. *Ecofeminist Literary Criticism: Theory, Interpretation, Pedagogy.* Champaign: University of Illinois Press, 1998.

Gardner, Muriel, ed. *The Wolf-Man, by the Wolf-Man, by Sigmund Freud.* New York: Basic Books, 1971.

Garfield, Viola E., and Linn A. Forrest. *The Wolf and the Raven: Totem Poles of Southeastern Alaska.* Seattle: University of Washington Press, 1961.

Garfinkle, Robert. *Star-Hopping: Your Visa to Viewing the Universe.* New York: Cambridge University Press, 1994.

Garreau, Joel. *The Nine Nations of North America.* Boston: Houghton Mifflin, 1981.

Gaston, Kevin J., and Tim M. Blackburn. *Pattern and Process in Macroecology.* Oxford, UK: Blackwell, 2000.

Geoffrey of Monmouth. *The History of the Kings of Britain.* Translated by Lewis Thorpe. New York: Penguin, 1966.

George, Jean Craighead. *Julie of the Wolves.* New York: HarperCollins, 1972.

———. *Julie's Wolf Pack.* New York: HarperCollins, 1997.

———; Lorence Bjorklund, illus. *The Moon of the Gray Wolves.* New York: Thomas Y. Crowell, 1969.

Gibson, Clare. *Signs and Symbols: An Illustrated Guide to Their Meaning and Origins.* Rowayton, CT: Saraband, 1996.

Giles, James R. "Thematic Significance of the Jim Hall Episode in *White Fang.*" *Jack London Newsletter* 2, no. 2 (1969): 49–50.

Gilman, Daniel Coit, Harry Thurston Peck, and Frank Moore Colby, eds. *The New International Encyclopedia.* Vol. 20. New York: Dodd, Mead, 1910.

Ginzburg, Carlo. *The Night Battles: Witchcraft and Agrarian Cults in the Sixteenth and Seventeenth Century.* 1966. Reprint, Baltimore: Johns Hopkins University Press, 1983.

Gipson, Philip. "Wolves and Wolf Literature: A Credibility Gap." In *War against the Wolf,* edited by Rick McIntyre, 345–53. Stillwater, MN: Voyageur Press, 1995.

———. Telephone interview. July 15, 1997.

Gipson, Philip S., Edward E. Bangs, Theodore N. Bailey, Diane K. Boyd, Dean H. Cluff, Douglas W. Smith, and Michael D. Jimenez. "Color Patterns among Wolves in Western North America." *Wildlife Society Bulletin* 30, no. 3 (2002): 821–30.

Girard, René. *The Scapegoat.* Translated by Yvonne Freccero. Baltimore: Johns Hopkins University Press, 1986.

——. *Violence and the Sacred.* Translated by Patrick Gregory. Baltimore: Johns Hopkins University Press, 1977.

Glazov, M. V., and S. V. Goryachkin. "Of Polar Deserts and Arctic Tundra: Noyaya Zemlya's Remarkable Terrestrial Ecosystems." *Russian Conservation News* 22 (2000): 14–15.

Glotfelty, Cheryll, and Harold Fromm, eds. *The Ecocriticism Reader: Landmarks in Literary Ecology.* Athens: University of Georgia Press, 1996.

Goddard, John. "A Real Whopper." *Saturday Night* III, no. 4 (1996): 47–54, 64.

Goldberg, Jim. *Raised by Wolves.* New York: Scalo, 1995.

Golani, I., and G. A. Moran. "Motility-Immobility Gradient in the Behavior of the Inferior Wolf during Ritualized Fighting." In *Advances in the Study of Mammalian Behavior,* edited by J. F. Eisenberg and D. G. Kleiman, 65–95. Special Publication No. 7. Shippensburg, PA: American Society of Mammalogists, 1983.

Golden, Joanne M. *The Narrative Symbol in Childhood Literature: Explorations in the Construction of Text.* Approaches to Semiotics Series no. 93. Berlin: Mouton de Gruyter, 1990.

Goodman, Patricia. Lecture. Wolf Park, IN. October 10, 1994.

Goodman, Patricia, and Erich Klinghammer. *Wolf Ethogram.* Ethology Series no. 3. Battle Ground, IN: North American Wildlife Park Foundation, 1985.

Goodwin, George C. "Wolf," in *The Encyclopedia Britannica.* Volume 29 of 29, 1989: 556–57.

Gottschall, Jonathan, and David Sloan Wilson, eds. *The Literary Animal: Evolution and the Nature of Narrative.* Evanston, IL: Northwestern University Press, 2005.

Goudey, Alice. *Here Come the Wild Dogs!* New York: Charles Scribner's Sons, 1958.

Gould, Stephen Jay. *Ever Since Darwin.* New York: Norton, 1977.

——. *The Mismeasure of Man.* New York: Norton, 1981.

Grambo, Rebecca L.; Daniel J. Cox, photog. *Wolf: Legend, Enemy, Icon.* Buffalo, NY: Firefly, 2005.

Gray, D. R. "The Killing of a Bull Muskox by a Single Wolf." *Arctic* 23, no. 3 (September 1970): 197–99.

Gray, Robert. *Gray Wolf: The Natural Life of North American Wolves.* New York: W. W. Norton, 1970.

"Gray Wolves in the Northern Rocky Mountains." U.S. Fish and Wildlife Service Report. April 10–23, 1999. Helena, Region 6.

Greenleaf, Sarah. "The Evolution of the Wolf in Children's Books." *Appraisal, Science Books for Young People* 22, no. 3 (1989): 1–6.

Gregory, Franklin. *The White Wolf.* New York: Random House, 1941.

Grey, Zane. "The Wolf Tracker." *Ladies' Home Journal,* February 1924. Reprint in Denise Casey and Tim W. Clark, eds., *Tales of the Wolf: Fifty-One Stories of Wolf Encounters in the Wild.* Moose, WY: Homestead, 1996. 179–99.

Griffin, Donald R. *Animal Minds.* Chicago: University of Chicago Press, 1992.

Griffin, Susan. *Woman and Nature: The Roaring inside Her.* San Francisco: Sierra Club Books, 2000.

Grimm, Jacob, and Wilhelm Grimm. *The Annotated Brothers Grimm.* Edited and translated by Maria Tatar, with a preface by Tatar and an introduction by A. S. Byatt. New York: W. W. Norton, 2004.

Grinnell, George Bird. *Blackfoot Lodge Tales: The Story of a Prairie People.* Lincoln, University of Nebraska Press, 1962.

———. *By Cheyenne Campfires.* New Haven, CT: Yale University Press, 1926.

Grooms, Steve. *Return of the Wolf: Successes and Threats in the U.S. and Canada.* Herentals, Belgium: Nova Vista, 2005.

Grumet, Robert Steven. *Voices from the Delaware Big House Ceremony.* Civilization of the American Indian Series no. 239. Norman: University of Oklahoma Press, 2001.

Guerber, H. A. *Myths of Northern Lands.* New York: American, 1895.

Guillemin, Georg. *The Pastoral Vision of Cormac McCarthy.* College Station: Texas A&M University Press, 2004.

Hajibabaei, Mehrdad, Daniel Janzen, John M. Burns, Winnie Hallwachs, and Paul D. N. Hebert. "From the Cover: DNA Barcodes Distinguish Species of Tropical Lepidoptera." *Proceedings of the National Academy of Sciences of the United States* 103 (2006): 968–71.

Haldane, Elizabeth S., and G. R. T. Ross, eds. and trans. *The Philosophical Works of Descartes.* 2 vols. 1911. Reprint, Cambridge, UK: Cambridge University Press, 1931.

Halfpenny, James C. *Yellowstone Wolves in the Wild.* Helena, MT: Riverbend, 2003.

Hall, Calvin S., and Vernon J. Nordby. *A Primer of Jungian Psychology.* New York: Signet, 1973.

Hall, Elizabeth. *Child of the Wolves.* New York: Houghton Mifflin, 1996.

Hall, Roberta, and Henry S. Sharp, eds. *Wolf and Man: Evolution in Parallel.* New York: Academic Press, 1978.

Hampton, Bruce. *The Great American Wolf.* New York: Henry Holt, 1997.

Haney, William. "Martin Eden: The Failure of Individualism." *Jack London Newsletter* 12 (1979): 38–41.

Hannah, Barbara. *The Archetypal Symbolism of Animals: Lectures Given at the C. G. Jung Institute, Zurich, 1954–1958.* Edited by David Eldred. Polarities of the Psyche series. New York: Chiron, 2005.

Hanning, Robert, and Joan Ferrante, eds. and trans. *The Lais of Marie de France.* Durham, NC: Labyrinth Press, 1978.

Haraway, Donna. *Simians, Cyborgs, and Women: The Reinvention of Nature.* New York: Routledge, 1991.

Harding, Carol E. *Merlin and Legendary Romance.* New York: Garland, 1988.

Harding, Susan, and Jean F. O'Barr, eds. *Sex and Scientific Inquiry.* Chicago: University of Chicago Press, 1987.

Harlow, Harry, and Stephen J. Suomi. "Depressive Behavior in Young Monkeys Subjected to Vertical Chamber Confinement." *Journal of Comparative and Physiological Psychology* 80 (1972): 11–18.

Harrington, F. H. "Chorus Howling by Wolves: Acoustic Structure, Pack Size, and the Beau Geste Effect." *Bioacoustics* 2, no. 2 (1989): 117–36.

——. "Ravens Attracted to Wolf Howling." *Condor* 80, no. 2 (1978): 236–37.

——. "Timber Wolf Howling Playback Studies: Discrimination of Pup from Adult Howls." *Animal Behavior* 34, no. 5 (1986): 1575–77.

Harrington, Fred H., and Cheryl S. Asa. "Wolf Communication." In *Wolves: Behavior, Conservation, and Ecology,* edited by L. David Mech and Luigi Boitani, 66–103. Chicago: University of Chicago Press, 2003.

Harris, Daniel. "Cuteness." In *The Best American Essays 1993,* edited by Joseph Epstein, 131–40. New York: Ticknor and Fields, 1993.

Harrison, Jim. *Wolf: A False Memoir.* New York: Delta/Seymour Lawrence, 1971.

Harrison, Robert Pogue. *Forests: The Shadow of Civilization.* Chicago: University of Chicago Press, 1993.

Hart, Mickey, and Jay Stevens. *Drumming at the Edge of Magic: A Journey into the Spirit of Percussion.* New York: HarperCollins, 1990.

Harting, James Edmund. *A Short History of the Wolf in Britain.* Whitstable, Kent, UK: Pryor Publications, 1994. Originally published in Harting, *British Animals Extinct within Historic Times . . .* London: Trübner, 1880.

Harvey, Lisa St. Clair. "Mr. Jefferson's Wolf: Slavery and the Suburban Robot." *Journal of American Culture* 17, no. 4 (1994): 79–89.

Hassig, Debra. *The Mark of the Beast: The Medieval Bestiary in Art, Life, and Literature.* London: Routledge, 1998.

Hauser, Marc D. *Wild Minds.* New York: Henry Holt, 2000.

Heard, D. C. "The Effect of Wolf Predation and Snow Cover on Musk-Ox Group Size." *American Naturalist* 139, no. 1 (January 1992): 190–204.

Hearne, Samuel. *A Journey from Prince of Wales's Fort in Hudson's Bay to the Northern Ocean, 1769, 1770, 1771, 1772.* Toronto: Macmillan of Canada, 1958.

Hearne, Vicki. "What's Wrong with Animal Rights: Of Hounds, Horses, and Jeffersonian Happiness." In *The Best American Essays 1992,* edited by Susan Sontag, 199–208. New York: Ticknor and Fields, 1992.

——. "Justice in Venice Beach." In *Intimate Nature: The Bond between Animals and Women,* edited by Linda Hogan, Deena Metzger, and Brenda Peterson, 187–88. New York: Fawcett Columbine, 1998.

Heimert, Alan. "Puritanism, the Wilderness, and the Frontier." *New England Quarterly* 26, no. 3 (September 1953): 361–82.

Hemingway, Ernest. "Judgment of Manitou." In *Ernest Hemingway's Apprenticeship: Oak Park, 1916–1917,* edited by Matthew J. Bruccoli, 96–97. Washington, DC: NCR Microcard Editions, 1971.

Heinrich, Bernd. *Mind of the Raven: Investigations and Adventures with Wolf-Birds.* New York: Cliff Street Books/HarperCollins, 1999.

Hendricks, George D. "Misconceptions concerning Western Wild Animals." *Western Folklore* 12, no. 2 (April 1953): 119–27.

Herndl, Carl G., and Stuart C. Brown, eds. *Green Culture: Environmental Rhetoric in Contemporary America*. Madison: University of Wisconsin Press, 1996.

Hickey, Joseph V., and Charles E. Webb. *The Lyons Serpent: Speculations on the Indian as Geographer*. Emporia State Research Studies 33, no. 4. Emporia, KS: School of Graduate and Professional Studies of Emporia State University, 1985.

Hill, Douglas, ed. *The Way of the Werewolf*. London: Panther, 1966.

Hillis, T. L., and F. F. Mallory. "Interrelationships of Snow Depth to Primary and Secondary Predator/Prey Systems in the Tundra/Boreal Ecotone of the Keewatin/Manitoba Region." *Musk-Ox* 37 (1989): 137–43.

Hirsch, David. *The Deconstruction of Literature: Criticism after Auschwitz*. Hanover, NH: Brown University Press/University Press of New England, 1991.

Hoagland, Edward. "Lament the Red Wolf." In *Red Wolves and Black Bears*. New York: Random House, 1995: 109–72.

Hodson, Sara S., and Jeanne Campbell Reesman, eds. *Jack London: One Hundred Years a Writer*. San Marino, CA: Huntington Library Press, 2002.

Hoffman, C. F. *A Winter in the Far West*. Vol. 1 of 2. London: Richard Bentley, 1835.

Hogan, Linda. "Deify the Wolf." In *Dwellings: A Spiritual History of the Living World*, 63–76. New York: Norton, 1998.

Hogan, Linda, Deena Metzger, and Brenda Peterson, eds. *Intimate Nature: The Bond between Women and Animals*. New York: Fawcett Columbine, 1998.

Holaday, Bobby. *The Return of the Mexican Wolf: Back to the Blue*. Tucson: University of Arizona Press, 2003.

Holman, Clarence Hugh, and William Harmon, eds. *A Handbook to Literature*. New York: Macmillan, 1992.

Holmes, Sue Major. "Wolf Hit by Car Tagged in Montana." *Albuquerque Journal*, April 19, 1995.

Horejsi, B. L., G. E. Hornbeck, and R. M. Raine. "Wolves, *Canis lupus*, Kill Female Black Bear, *Ursus americanus*, in Alberta." *Canadian Field-Naturalist* 98, no. 3 (1984): 368–69.

Hornblower, Simon, and Antony Spawforth, eds. *The Oxford Companion to Classical Civilization*. Oxford, UK: Oxford University Press, 2004.

Howard, June. *Form and History in American Literary Naturalism*. Chapel Hill: University of North Carolina Press, 1985.

Hoxie, Fredrick, ed. *Indians in American History*. Arlington Heights, IL: Harlan Davidson, 1988.

Huggard, D. J. "Effect of Snow Depth on Predation and Scavenging by Gray Wolves." *Journal of Wildlife Management* 57, no. 2 (1993): 382–88.

Hughes, Sandra, and Anita Hill; Seth Hughes, illus. *Yellowstone and Teton Kids' Field Book*. Bloomington, IN: One Feather, 1998.

Hughes, Ted. "Wolfwatching." In *Wolfwatching*, by Ted Hughes. London: Faber and Faber Ltd., 1991.

Hurston, Zora Neale. *Mules and Men*. New York: HarperPerennial, 1990.

———. *Their Eyes Were Watching God*. New York: HarperPerennial, 2006.

J. H. Hutton. "Wolf-Children." *Folk-Lore* 51, no. 1 (March 1940): 9–31.

Iljin, N. A. "Wolf-Dog Genetics." *Journal of Genetics* 42, no. 3 (1941): 359–441.

Iyer, Pico. "Leaning toward Myth." *Partisan Review* 62, no. 2 (1995): 309–14.

Jacobi, Jolande. *Complex, Archetype, Symbol in the Psychology of C. G. Jung*. Princeton, NJ: Princeton University Press, 1971.

Jacobs, Joseph. *English Fairy Tales, Collected by Joseph Jacobs*. Elibron Classics Series. London: Adamant Media, 2005.

Jacobs, Wilbur. "Francis Parkman—Naturalist—Environmental Savant." *Pacific Historical Review* 61, no. 3 (1992): 340–56.

Janovitz, Marilyn. *Is It Time?* New York: North-South, 1994.

Jenness, S. E. "Arctic Wolf Attacks Scientist: A Unique Canadian Incident." *Arctic* 38, no. 2 (1985): 129–32.

Johnson, Charles Eugene. "Recollections of the Mammals of Northwestern Minnesota." *Journal of Mammalogy* 11, no. 4 (1930): 443–44.

Johnson, Roger T. "On the Spoor of the 'Big Bad Wolf.'" *Journal of Environmental Education* 6, no. 2 (1974): 37–39.

Johnson, Sylvia A., and Alice Aamodt. *Wolf Pack: Tracking Wolves in the Wild*. Minneapolis: Lerner, 1985.

Johnson's Universal Cyclopaedia. Edited by Charles Kendall Adams. Vol. 8 of 8. New York: D. Appleton, 1897.

Jones, Karen. "'A Fierce Green Fire': Passionate Pleas and Wolf Ecology." *Ethics, Place, and Environment* 5, no. 1 (March 2002): 35–43.

Jones, Stephen, ed. *The Mammoth Book of Werewolves*. New York: Carroll and Graf, 1994.

Jung, Carl. *Aion: Researches into the Phenomenology of the Self*. Translated by R. F. C. Hull. Bollingen Series. Princeton, NJ: Princeton University Press, 1971.

———. *Archetypes and the Collective Unconscious*. Translated by R. F. C. Hull. Bollingen Series. Princeton, NJ: Princeton University Press, 1959.

———. *The Earth Has a Soul: The Nature Writings of C. G. Jung*. Edited by Meredith Sabini. Berkeley, CA: North Atlantic Books, 2002.

———. *Man and His Symbols*. New York: Dell, 1964.

———. *Memories, Dream, Reflections*. New York: Vintage, 1965.

———. *Symbols of Transformation*. Bollingen Series. Princeton, NJ: Princeton University Press, 1962.

Kaplan, Amy. "Nature, Region, and Empire." In *The Columbia History of the American Novel*, edited by Emory Elliott, 240–66. New York: Columbia University Press, 1988.

Keller, Evelyn Fox. *Reflections on Gender and Science*. Tenth Anniversary Edition. New Haven, CT: Yale University Press, 1995.

Kellert, Stephen R., and Edward O. Wilson, eds. *The Biophilia Hypothesis*. Washington, DC: Island Press, 1995.

Kennedy, George A. *Comparative Rhetoric: An Historical and Cross-Cultural Introduction*. Oxford University Press, 1998.

Kennedy, Patrick. *Legendary Fictions of the Irish Celts.* Detroit: Singing Tree Press, 1968.

Kermode, Frank. "Introduction to *Romeo and Juliet.*" In *The Riverside Shakespeare,* edited by G. Blakemore Evans, 1055–57. Boston: Houghton Mifflin, 1974.

Kerrigan, Michael. "Frontier Feelings." *Times Literary Supplement,* September 2, 1994.

Kiefer, Christian. "The Morality of Blood: Examining the Moral Code of *The Crossing.*" *Cormac McCarthy Journal* 1, no. 1 (Spring 2001): 26–37.

Kilham, Lawrence. *The American Crow and the Common Raven.* College Station: Texas A&M University Press, 1991.

Kimball, Rene. "Wolf Reintroduction Debated." *Albuquerque Journal,* May 21, 1992.

Kimberling, Clark. "David Dale Owen and Joseph Granville Norwood: Pioneer Geologists in Indiana and Illinois." *Indiana Magazine of History* 92 (March 1996): 2–25.

Kime, Wayne R. "Huck among the Indians: Mark Twain and Richard Irving Dodge's *The Plains of the North West and Their Inhabitants.*" *Western American Literature* 24, no. 4 (1990): 321–33.

King, Stephen. *Cycle of the Werewolf.* New York: Signet, 1983.

Kingman, Russ. "Introduction." In *The Call of the Wild: Complete Text with Introduction, Historical Contexts, Critical Essays,* edited by Earl J. Wilcox and Elizabeth H. Wilcox. New York: Houghton Mifflin, 2004: 1–10.

Kingsolver, Barbara. *Prodigal Summer.* New York: HarperCollins, 2001.

Kinsella, W. P. "Knocks at the Door a Stranger." In *Red Wolf, Red Wolf,* no pagination. Dallas: Southern Methodist University Press, 1987.

Kipling, Rudyard. *The Jungle Books.* 1894. Reprint, New York: Penguin, 1987.

Kittredge, G. L. *Arthur and Gorlagon: Versions of the Werewolf's Tale.* New York: Haskell House, 1966.

Klinghammer, Erich. "Woman Killed by Captive Wolf Pack." *Wolf!* 13:4 (1995): 3.

Kluckhohn, Clyde. *Navaho Witchcraft.* Boston: Beacon, 1944.

Koelsch, William A. "Antebellum Harvard Students and the Recreational Exploration of the New England Landscape." *Journal of Historical Geography* 8, no. 4 (1982): 362–72.

Koertge, Noretta, ed. *A House Built on Sand: Exposing Postmodern Myths about Science.* New York: Oxford University Press, 2000.

Kolb, Harold H., Jr. "Mark Twain and the Myth of the West." In *The Mythologizing of Mark Twain,* edited by Sara deSaussure Davis and Philip D. Beidler. Tuscaloosa: University of Alabama Press, 1984.

Kolodny, Annette. *The Land before Her: Fantasy and Experience of the American Frontiers, 1630–1860.* Chapel Hill: University of North Carolina Press, 1984.

———. *The Lay of the Land: Metaphor as Experience and History in American Life and Letters.* Chapel Hill: University of North Carolina Press, 1975.

Krech III, Shepard. *The Ecological Indian: Myth and History.* New York: Norton, 1999.

Kriss, Marika. *Werewolves, Shapeshifters, and Skinwalkers.* Los Angeles: Sherbourne Press, 1972.

Kurth, Willi. *The Complete Woodcuts of Albrecht Dürer.* New York: Crown, 1946.

Kyrouac, Gary. Wolf Park lectures. Battle Ground, IN, June 20, July 11, 1997.

Labor, Earle. "Jack London's Mondo Cane: 'Bâtard,' *The Call of the Wild,* and *White Fang.*" In *Critical Essays on Jack London,* edited by Jacqueline Tavernier-Courbin, 114–30. Boston: Hall, 1983.

Labor, Earle, Robert C. Leitz III, and I. Milo Shepard, eds. *The Letters of Jack London.* 3 vols. Stanford, CA: Stanford University Press, 1988.

Lackey, Kris. "Eighteenth-Century Aesthetic Theory and the Nineteenth-Century Traveler in Trans-Allegheny America: F. Trollope, Dickens, Irving, and Parkman." *American Studies* 32, no. 1 (Spring 1991): 33–48.

Lakoff, George, and Mark Johnson. *Metaphors We Live By.* Chicago: University of Chicago Press, 1990.

Lamarck, Jean-Baptiste. *Lamarck's Open Mind: The Lectures.* Gold Beach, OR: High Sierra Books, 2004.

Lamb, Robert Paul, and G. R. Thompson, eds. *A Companion to American Fiction: 1865–1914.* Oxford, UK: Blackwell, 2005.

Landis, Bob. Yellowstone Association Institute Presentation of Lamar Valley Wolves Film Footage. Yellowstone National Park, February 18, 2004.

Lane, Belden C. *The Solace of Fierce Landscapes: Exploring Desert and Mountain Spirituality.* New York: Oxford University Press, 1998.

Lang, Andrew. *12 Books in 1: Andrew Lang's Complete "Fairy Book" Series: The Blue, Red, Green, Yellow, Pink, Grey, Violet, Crimson, Brown, Orange, Olive, and Lilac Fairy . . . and Fairy Stories from around the World.* Unabridged. London: Shoes and Ships and Sealing Wax, 2006.

Larminie, William. *West Irish Folk-Tales and Romances.* Totowa, NJ: Rowman and Littlefield, 1973.

Latour, Bruno. *Politics of Nature: How to Bring the Sciences into Democracy.* Cambridge, MA: Harvard University Press, 2004.

Lawrence, B. "Antiquity of Large Dogs in North America." *Tebiwa* 11 (1968): 43–49.

Lawrence, B., and W. H. Bossert. "The Cranial Evidence for Hybridization in New England Canis." *Brevoria* 13 (1969): 330.

Lawrence, R. D. *Secret Go the Wolves.* New York: Ballantine, 1980.

Layton, Robert. *The Anthropology of Art.* Cambridge, UK: Cambridge University Press, 1991.

"Legislators Attack Wolves' Return." *Santa Fe New Mexican,* January 22, 1995, A1+.

Legler, Gretchen. "Wolf." In *Another Wilderness: Notes from the New Outdoorswoman,* edited by Susan Fox Rogers, 59–70. Seattle: Seal Press, 1997.

Le Guin, Ursula K. "The Wife's Story." In *Buffalo Gals and Other Animal Presences,* 67–74. New York: Roc, 1987.

Leitch, Vincent. *American Literary Criticism from the '30s to the '80s.* New York: Columbia University Press, 1988.

Leland, Charles Godfrey. *The Algonquin Legends of New England; or, Myths and Folk Lore of the Micmac, Passamaquoddy, and Penobscot Tribes.* Boston: Houghton Mifflin, 1884.

Lent, P. C. "Tolerance between Grizzlies and Wolves." *Journal of Mammalogy* 45, no. 2 (1964): 304–5.

Leopold, Aldo. *A Sand County Almanac: And Sketches Here and There.* 1949. Reprint, New York: Oxford University Press, 1987.

Leslie, Robert Franklin. *In the Shadow of a Rainbow.* New York: Norton, 1974.

Lévi-Strauss, Claude. *The Story of Lynx.* Translated by Catherine Tihanyi. Chicago: University of Chicago Press, 1895.

——. *Totemism.* London: Merlin, 1964.

Levitt, Norman, and Paul Gross. *Higher Superstition: The Academic Left and Its Quarrels with Science.* Baltimore: Johns Hopkins University Press, 1997.

Lilley, James J. "Of Whales and Men: The Dynamics of Cormac McCarthy's Environmental Imagination." *Southern Quarterly* 38, no. 2 (Winter 2000): 111–22.

Limerick, Patricia Nelson. "Insiders and Outsiders: The Borders of the USA and the Limits of the ASA: Presidential Address to the American Studies Association, 31 October 1996." *American Quarterly* 49, no. 3 (1997): 449–69.

Lindquist, Galina. "The Wolf, the Saami, and the Urban Shaman: Predator Symbolism in Sweden." In *Natural Enemies: People-Wildlife Conflicts in Anthropological Perspective,* edited by John Knight, 170–88. London: Routledge, 2000.

Link, Mike, and Kate Crowley. *Following the Pack: The World of Wolf Research.* Stillwater, MN: Voyageur Press, 1994.

Linnaeus, Carolus. *Systema Naturae, 1735.* Philadelphia: Coronet, 1964.

Livius, Titus. *The History of Rome.* Translated by George Baker. Boston: Wells & Lilly, 1823.

Loizos, C. "Play in Mammals." *Zoological Society of London Symposium* 18 (1966): 1–9.

London, Jack. "Bâtard." 1904. (Originally titled "Diable—A Dog" in 1902.) Reprinted in *The Unabridged Jack London,* edited by Lawrence Teacher and Richard E. Nicholls, 627–39. Philadelphia: Courage Books, 1997.

——. "Brown Wolf." 1906.

——. *The Call of the Wild.* 1903. Reprint, edited by Daniel Dyer (includes "Illustrated Reader's Companion"), Norman: University of Oklahoma Press, 1995.

——. "Diable—A Dog." 1902. (Renamed "Bâtard" in 1904.) Reprinted in *The Call of the Wild, and Selected Stories.* New York: New American Library, 1960: 82–96.

——. "The Law of Life." Reprinted in *The Unabridged Jack London,* edited by Lawrence Teacher and Richard E. Nicholls, 279–284. Philadelphia: Courage Books, 1997.

——. "The Other Animals." 1908. Reprinted in *No Mentor But Myself: A Collection of Articles, Essays, Reviews, and Letters on Writing and Writers.* Edited by Dale L. Walker. Port Washington, NY: Kennikat Press, 1979: 108–120.

——. *The Sea-Wolf.* New York: Macmillan, 1904.

——. "The Son of the Wolf." 1899. Reprinted in *The Unabridged Jack London,* edited by Lawrence Teacher and Richard E. Nicholls, 28–41. Philadelphia: Courage Books, 1997.

——. *White Fang.* 1906. Reprint, New York: Dover, 1991.

——. "The White Silence." 1900. Reprinted in *The Unabridged Jack London,* edited by Lawrence Teacher and Richard E. Nicholls, 19–27. Philadelphia: Courage Books, 1997.

Lopez, Barry Holstun. *Arctic Dreams.* New York: Vintage, 2001.

——. *Of Wolves and Men.* New York: Charles Scribner's Sons, 1978.

Lorenz, Konrad. *King Solomon's Ring.* New York: Thomas Y. Crowell, 1952.

Louv, Richard. *Last Child in the Woods: Saving Our Children from Nature-Deficit Disorder.* Chapel Hill, NC: Algonquin, 2005.

Love, Glen. *Practical Ecocriticism: Literature, Biology, and the Environment.* University of Virginia Press, 2003.

Luce, Dianne C. "The Vanishing World of Cormac McCarthy's Border Trilogy." In *A Cormac McCarthy Companion: The Border Trilogy,* edited by Edwin T. Arnold and Dianne C. Luce, 161–97. Jackson: University Press of Mississippi, 2001.

Lukens, Rebecca. *A Critical Handbook of Children's Literature.* 5th ed. New York: Harper-Collins College, 1995.

Lund, Thomas A. *American Wildlife Law.* Berkeley: University of California Press, 1980.

Lutts, Ralph H. *The Nature Fakers: Wildlife, Science, and Sentiment.* Golden, CO: Fulcrum, 1990.

——. "The Realistic Wild Animal Story." In *The Literature of Nature: An International Sourcebook,* edited by Patrick D. Murphy. Chicago: Fitzroy Dearborn, 1998.

MacDonald, Andrew, Gina MacDonald, and MaryAnn Sheridan. *Shape-Shifting: Images of Native Americans in Recent Popular Fiction.* Westport, CT: Greenwood, 2000.

Magoffin, Susan Shelby. In *Down the Santa Fe Trail and into Mexico: The Diary of Susan Shelby Magoffin, 1846–1847.* Edited by Stella M. Drumm. New Haven, CT: Yale University Press, 1926.

Makarius, Laura. "The Crime of Manabozo." *American Anthropologist* 75, no. 3 (June 1973): 663–75.

Malcolm, J. R. "Paternal Care in Canids." *American Zoologist* 25, no. 3 (1985): 853–56.

Malin, Edward. *A World of Faces: Masks of the Northwest Coast Indians.* Portland, OR: Timber Press, 1978.

Manfredo, Michael J., Peter J. Fix, and Jerry J. Vaske. "Project Report on Research Entitled Colorado Residents' Attitudes and Perceptions toward Reintroduction of the Gray Wolf (*Canis lupus*) into Colorado." Colorado State University and U.S Fish and Wildlife Service, HDNRU Report No. 21, December 1994.

Manley and Associates and Wolf Haven International. *Wolf.* CD-ROM. San Mateo, CA: I-Entertainment and Sanctuary Woods, 1994.

Marhenke, P. "An Observation of Four Wolves Killing Another Wolf." *Journal of Mammalogy* 52 (1971): 630–31.

Markey, Thomas. "The Celto-Germanic 'Dog/Wolf'-Champion and the Integration of Pre-/Non-IE Ideals." *North-Western European Language Evolution* 11 (1988): 3–30.

Martin, Lawrence T. "Animal Forms of Manidog in the Anishinabe Earth-Diver Story." In *Papers of the Twenty-sixth Algonquian Conference*. Edited and with an introduction by David H. Pentland, 240–50. Winnipeg: University of Manitoba Press, 1995.

Marx, Leo. *The Machine in the Garden: Technology and the Pastoral Ideal in America*. New York: Oxford University Press, 1964.

Masson, Jeffrey Moussaieff, and Susan McCarthy. *When Elephants Weep: The Emotional Lives of Animals*. New York: Dell, 1995.

Matthew, W. D. "The Phylogeny of Dogs." *Journal of Mammalogy* 11 (1930): 117–38.

Mather, Cotton. *Magnalia Christi Americana, 1701*. 2 vols. Edited by Thomas Robbins. Hartford, CT: Silas Andrus and Son, 1853.

——. "Nehemias Americanus." In *Magnalia Christi Americana, 1701*. Edited by Thomas Robbins, vol. 1, 118–31. Hartford, CT: Silas Andrus and Son, 1853.

Matthiessen, Peter. *Wildlife in America*. New York: Viking, 1987.

——. "The Wolves of Aguila." *Harper's Bazaar*, June 1958. Reprinted in *On the River Styx, and Other Stories*, 71–91. New York: Random House, 1989.

Maughan, Ralph. "Ralph Maughan's Wolf Report." March 1998. http://www.forwolves .org/ralph/wolfrpt.html.

McBride, Roy T. "The Mexican Wolf (*Canis lupus baileyi*): A Historical Review and Observations on Its Status and Distribution." Endangered Species Report no. 8. Albuquerque: U.S. Fish and Wildlife Service, 1980.

McCarthy, Cormac. *Cities of the Plain*. New York: Knopf, 1998.

——. *The Crossing*. New York: Vintage International, 1994.

McClellan, Doug. "Wolves Must Escape Their Negative Image." *Santa Fe New Mexican*, August 13, 1986, C3 +.

McDermott, Gerald R. "Jonathan Edwards and American Indians: The Devil Sucks Their Blood." *New England Quarterly* 72, no. 4 (December 1999): 539–57.

McElroy, Susan Chernak. *Heart in the Wild*. New York: Ballantine, 2002.

McLeod, P. J., and J. C. Fentress. "Patterns of Aggression within a Captive Timber Wolf Pack (Abstract)." *Aggressive Behavior* 17, no. 2 (1991): 84.

McIntyre, Rick. *A Society of Wolves: National Parks and the Battle over the Wolf*. Stillwater, MN: Voyageur Press, 1993.

——. Talk. Yellowstone Association Institute. Yellowstone National Park, February 20, 2004.

——, ed. *War against the Wolf: America's Campaign to Exterminate the Wolf*. Stillwater, MN: Voyageur Press, 1995.

McLuhan, Marshall. *The Medium Is the Massage*. New York: Bantam, 1967.

McNamee, Thomas. *The Return of the Wolf to Yellowstone*. New York: Henry Holt, 1997.

——. "The Wolves of Yellowstone: Year One." In *American Nature Writing 1997*, edited by John A. Murray. San Francisco: Sierra Club, 1997.

McRoberts, R. E., L. D. Mech, and R. O. Peterson. "The Cumulative Effect of Consecutive Winters' Snow Depth on Moose and Deer Populations: A Defence." *Journal of Animal Ecology* 64 (1995): 131–35.

Meadows, A. J. *The High Firmament: A Survey of Astronomy in English Literature.* Leicester, UK: Leicester University Press, 1969.

Mech, L. David. *The Arctic Wolf: Living with the Pack.* Stillwater, MN: Voyageur Press, 1988.

——. "Buffer Zones of Territories of Gray Wolves as Regions of Intraspecific Strife." *Journal of Mammalogy* 75, no. 1 (1994): 199–202.

——. "The Challenge and Opportunity of Recovering Wolf Populations." *Conservation Biology* 9, no. 2 (1995): 1–9.

——. "Neonatal Wolves More Resistant to Weather Than Previously Thought." Research Information Bulletin 18. Washington, DC: U.S. Fish and Wildlife Service, 1992.

——. "Regular and Homeward Speeds of Arctic Wolves." *Journal of Mammalogy* 75, no. 3 (August 1994): 741–42.

——. "Resistance of Young Wolf Pups to Inclement Weather." *Journal of Mammalogy* 74, no. 2 (1993): 485–86.

——. *The Way of the Wolf.* Stillwater, MN: Voyageur Press, 1991.

——. *The Wolf: The Ecology and Behavior of an Endangered Species.* Minneapolis: University of Minnesota Press, 1970.

——. "Wolf-Pack Buffer Zones as Prey Reservoirs." *Science,* October 21, 1977, 320–21.

——, ed. *The Wolves of Minnesota: Howl in the Heartland.* Stillwater, MN: Voyageur Press, 2000.

Mech, L. David, and Luigi Boitani, eds. *Wolves: Behavior, Ecology, and Conservation.* Chicago: University of Chicago Press, 2003.

Mech, L. David, R. C. Chapman, W. W. Cochran, L. Simmons, and U. S. Seal. "A Radio-Triggered Anesthetic-Dart Collar for Recapturing Large Mammals." *Wildlife Society Bulletin* 12, no. 1 (1984): 69–74.

Mech, L. David, S. H. Fritts, and W. J. Paul. "Relationship between Winter Severity and Wolf Depredations on Domestic Animals in Minnesota." *Wildlife Society Bulletin* 16, no. 3 (1988): 269–72.

Mech, L. David, and J. M. Packard. "Possible Use of Wolf (*Canis lupus*) Den over Several Centuries." *Canadian Field-Naturalist* 104, no. 3 (1990): 484–85.

Melson, Gail. *Why the Wild Things Are: Animals in the Lives of Children.* Cambridge, MA: Harvard University Press, 2001.

Melville, Herman. *Moby-Dick.* 1851. Reprint, Norton Critical Edition, edited by Harrison Hayford and Hershel Parker. New York: Norton, 1967.

Merchant, Carolyn. *Earthcare: Women and the Environment.* London: Routledge, 1996.

Meschutt, David. "'A Perfect Likeness': John H. I. Browere's Life Mask of Thomas Jefferson." *American Art Journal* 21, no. 4 (Winter 1989): 4–25.

Metzner, Ralph. *Green Psychology: Transforming Our Relationship to the Earth.* Rochester, VT: Park Street Press, 1999.

Michaels, Walter Benn. "The Vanishing American." *American Literary History* 2, no. 2 (Summer 1990), 220–41.

Miller, Jim Wayne. "Lambs and Wolves." *Thalia* 9, no. 1 (1986): 48–53.

Miller, Perry. *Errand into the Wilderness.* Cambridge, MA: Harvard University Press, 1956.

Milstein, Michael. *Wolf: Return to Yellowstone.* Billings, MT: Billings Gazette, 1995.

Milton, John. *Lycidas.* London: Ginn, 1897.

Mitchell, Stephen, trans. *Tao de Ching.* New York: HarperPerennial, 1992.

Mochanov, Yuri A. "The Most Ancient Paleolithic of the Diring and the Problem of a Nontropical Origin for Humanity." *Arctic Anthropology* 30, no. 1 (1993): 22–53.

Moore, Gregory. *Nietzsche, Biology, and Metaphor.* Cambridge, UK: Cambridge University Press, 2002.

Morey, Walt. *Hero.* 1980. Reprint, New York: Penguin, 1995.

———. *Kävik the Wolf Dog.* New York: E. P. Dutton, 1968.

———. *Scrub Dog of Alaska.* New York: Dutton, 1971.

Morgan, Richard. "Naturalism, Socialism, and Jack London's *Martin Eden*." *Jack London Newsletter* 10 (1977): 13–22.

Morgan, William. *Human-Wolves among the Navajo.* Monograph. *Yale University Publications in Anthropology* 11 (1936).

Morris, Edmund. *The Rise of Theodore Roosevelt.* New York: Modern Library, 2001.

Morris, John, ed. and trans. *Descartes Dictionary.* New York: Philosophical Library, 1971.

Mowat, Farley. *Never Cry Wolf.* 1963. Reprint, New York: Bantam, 1979.

———. *People of the Deer.* New York: Carroll and Graf, 2005.

Murie, Adolph. *The Wolves of Mount McKinley.* U.S National Parks Fauna Series No. 5. Washington, DC: Government Printing Office, 1944.

Murphy, Jim; Mark Alan Weatherby, illus. *The Call of the Wolves.* New York: Scholastic, 1989.

Murray, John A., ed. *Out among the Wolves.* Anchorage: Alaska Northwest Books, 1993.

Myerson, Joel, ed. *Selected Letters of Nathaniel Hawthorne.* Columbus: Ohio State University Press, 2002.

Nabhan, Gary Paul. *Songbirds, Truffles, and Wolves: An American Naturalist in Italy.* New York: Penguin, 1993.

Nash, Roderick. *Wilderness and the American Mind.* 3rd ed. New Haven, CT: Yale University Press, 1982.

———. "The Meaning of Wilderness and the Rights of Nature." Lecture. Purdue University, West Lafayette, IN, February 17, 1994.

Nelson, M. E., and L. D. Mech. "Observation of a Swimming Wolf Killing a Swimming Deer." *Journal of Mammalogy* 65, no. 1 (1984): 143–44.

———. "Observation of a Wolf Killed by a Deer." *Journal of Mammalogy* 66, no. 1 (1985): 187–88.

———. "Relationship between Snow Depth and Gray Wolf Predation on White-Tailed Deer." *Journal of Wildlife Management* 50, no. 3 (1986): 471–74.

———. "A Single Deer Stands Off Three Wolves." *American Midland Naturalist* 131, no. 1 (1994): 207–8.

Newstead, Helaine. "Arthurian Legends." In *A Manual of the Writings in Middle English,*

1050–1500, edited by J. Burke Severs. New Haven: Connecticut Academy of Arts and Sciences, 1967.

Nickl, Peter; Józef Wilkon, illus.; Marion Koenig, trans. *The Story of the Kind Wolf.* 1982. Reprint, New York: North-South, 1988.

Nida, William L. *Taming the Animals.* Story of Man Series, Book 3. New York: Laidlaw Brothers, 1930.

Nie, Martin E. "Wolf Recovery and Management as Value-based Political Conflict." *Ethics, Place, and Environment* 5, no. 1 (March 2002): 65–71.

Nietzsche, Friedrich. *Thus Spake Zarathustra.* Cambridge, UK: Cambridge University Press, 2006.

Nolan, Dennis. *Wolf Child.* New York: Macmillan, 1989.

North, Sterling. *Rascal.* New York: Puffin Books, 1963.

———. *The Wolfling: A Documentary Novel of the 1870s.* New York: Penguin, 1969.

Nowak, R. M. "Another Look at Wolf Taxonomy." In *Ecology and Conservation of the Wolf in a Changing World,* edited by Ludwig N. Carbyn, S. H. Fritts, and D. R. Seip, 375–97. Occasional Publication No. 35. Edmonton: University of Alberta, Canadian Circumpolar Institute, 1995.

———. "Wolf Evolution and Taxonomy." In *Wolves: Behavior, Ecology, and Conservation,* edited by L. David Mech and Luigi Boitani, 239–58. Chicago: University of Chicago Press, 2003.

———. "Wolves: The Great Travelers of Evolution." *International Wolf* 2, no. 4 (1992): 3–7.

Noyes, Deborah. *One Kingdom: Our Lives with Animals.* Boston: Houghton Mifflin, 2006.

O'Brien, Dan. *Spirit of the Hills.* New York: Crown, 1988.

Oelschlager, Max. *The Idea of Wilderness: From Prehistory to the Age of Ecology.* New Haven, CT: Yale University Press, 1993.

Oerlemans, Onno Dag. "'The Meanest Thing That Feels': Anthropormorphizing Animals in Romanticism." *Mosaic* 27 (March 1994): 1–32.

Offshe, Richard, and Ethan Watters. *Making Monsters: False Memories, Psychotherapy, and Sexual Hysteria.* Berkeley: University of California Press, 1994.

Olsen, S. J. *Origins of the Domestic Dog: The Fossil Record.* Tucson: University of Arizona Press, 1985.

Olsen, S. J., and J. W. Olsen. "The Chinese Wolf, Ancestor of New World Dogs." *Science* 196 (1977): 533–35.

———. "The Position of *Canis lupus variabilis,* from Zhoukoudian, in the Ancestral Lineage of the Domestic Dog, *Canis familiaris.*" *Vertegrata Palasiat* 20 (1982): 267.

Olson, Sigurd. *The Collected Works of Sigurd Olson.* Edited by Mike Link. Stillwater, MN: Voyageur Press, 1990.

———. "Organization and Range of the Pack." *Ecology* 19, no. 1 (January 1938): 168–70.

———. *The Singing Wilderness.* New York: Alfred A. Knopf, 1956.

———. *Songs of the North.* 1987. Reprint, New York: Penguin, 1995.

———. "A Study in Predatory Relationship with Particular Reference to the Wolf." *Scientific Monthly,* April 1938, 323–36.

Orr, David W. *Ecological Literacy: Education and the Transition to a Postmodern World.* Albany: State University of New York Press, 1993.

Otten, Charlotte F. *A Lycanthropy Reader: Werewolves in Western Culture.* Syracuse, NY: Syracuse University Press, 1986.

Owens, Louis. *Wolfsong.* Norman: University of Oklahoma Press, 1991.

Packard, Jane M. "Wolf Behavior: Reproductive, Social, and Intelligent." In *Wolves: Behavior, Ecology, and Conservation,* edited by L. David Mech and Luigi Boitani, 35–65. Chicago: University of Chicago Press, 2003.

Panjabi-Trelease, Tim. Interview. Canyon de Chelly, NM, June 28, 1997.

Paquet, P. C., and L. N. Carbyn. "Wolves, *Canis lupus,* Killing Denning Black Bears, *Ursus americanus,* in the Riding Mountain National Park Area." *Canadian Field-Naturalist* 100, no. 3 (1986): 371–72.

Paradiso, J. L., and R. M. Nowak. "Wolves." In *Wild Mammals of North America: Biology, Management, and Economics,* edited by J. A. Chapman and G. A. Feldhamer, 460–74. Baltimore: Johns Hopkins University Press.

Parents' Magazine Enterprises, Inc. *Wonders of Nature: A Child's Introduction to the World of Animals, Plants, Birds, Fish, and Insects.* New York: Parents' Magazine Press, 1974.

Parkhill, Thomas C. "'Of Glooskap's Birth, and of His Brother Malsum, the Wolf': The Story of Charles Godfrey Leland's 'Purely American Creation.'" *American Indian Culture and Research Journal* 16, no. 1 (1992): 45–69.

———. *Weaving Ourselves into the Land: Charles Godfrey Leland, "Indians," and the Study of Native American Religions.* Albany: State University of New York Press, 1997.

———. Phone interview. March 20, 2001.

Parkman, Francis. *The Journals of Francis Parkman.* Edited by Mason Wade. 2 vols. New York: Harper and Brothers, 1947.

———. *The Oregon Trail.* 1849. Reprint, New York: Penguin, 1985.

Parrish, Randall. *Wolves of the Sea: Being a Tale of the Colonies from the Manuscript of One Geoffry Carlyle, Seaman, Narrating Certain Strange Adventures Which Befell Him aboard the Pirate Craft "Namur."* Chicago: A. C. McClurg, 1918.

Parsons, David R. "The Bureaucratically Imperiled Wolf." *Conservation Biology* vol. 20, no. 4 (2006): 942–45.

———. "Case Study: The Mexican Wolf." In *New Mexico's Natural Heritage: Biological Diversity in the Land of Enchantment,* edited by E. A. Herrera and L. F. Huenneke, 101–23. *New Mexico Journal of Science* 36 (1996). Special edition.

Parsons, David R., comp. "A Critical Review of an Unpublished, Undated Paper by Dennis Parker (Biologist, Applied Ecosystem Management, Inc.) Titled 'Reintroduction of the Mexican Wolf: Instrument of Recovery or Instrument of Demise?'" U.S Fish and Wildlife Service, Albuquerque, November 10, 1995.

Pattee, Fred Lewis. *The Feminine Fifties.* New York: D. Appleton-Century, 1940.

Peirce, Charles Sanders. *Essays in the Philosophy of Science.* New York: Liberal Arts Press, 1957.
———. *Peirce on Signs: Writings on Semiotics.* Edited by James Hoopes. Chapel Hill: University of North Carolina Press, 1991.
Pells, Eddie. "Crasher Upsets Wolf Protest." *Albuquerque Journal,* September 22, 1995.
Penick, James L. *Progressive Politics and Conservation: The Ballinger-Pinchot Affair.* Chicago: University of Chicago Press, 1968.
Perrault, Charles. *The Complete Fairy Tales of Charles Perrault.* Translated by Neil Philip and Nicoletta Simborowski. New York: Houghton Mifflin/Clarion, 1993.
Peters, Roger. *Dance of the Wolves.* New York: Ballantine, 1985.
Petersen, David. *Yellowstone National Park.* True Books: National Parks series Danbury, CT: Children's Press, 2001.
Peterson, Merrill D. *Thomas Jefferson and the New Nation: A Biography.* New York: Oxford University Press, 1970.
Peterson, Rolf O. *The Wolves of Isle Royale: A Broken Balance.* Minocqua, WI: Willow Creek Press, 1995.
Peterson, Rolf O., and D. L. Allen. "Snow Conditions as a Parameter in Moose-Wolf Relationships." *Naturaliste Canadien* 101 (1974): 481–92.
Peterson, Rolf O., and Paolo Ciucci. "The Wolf as Carnivore." In *Wolves: Behavior, Ecology, and Conservation,* edited by L. David Mech and Luigi Boitani, 104–30. Chicago: University of Chicago Press, 2003.
Peterson, Rolf O., Amy K. Jacobs, Thomas D. Drummer, L. David Mech, and Douglas W. Smith. "Leadership Behavior in Relation to Dominance and Reproductive Status in Gray Wolves." *Canadian Journal of Zoology* 80, no. 8 (2002): 1405–12.
Phillips, Dana. *The Truth of Ecology: Nature, Culture, and Literature in America.* New York: Oxford University Press, 2003.
Phillips, Michael K., and Douglas W. Smith; Barry O'Neill and Teri O'Neill, photogs. *The Wolves of Yellowstone.* Stillwater, MN: Voyageur Press, 1998.
Phillips, Michael K., V. Gary Henry, and Brian T. Kelly. "Restoration of the Red Wolf." In *Wolves: Behavior, Ecology, and Conservation,* edited by L. David Mech and Luigi Boitani, 272–88. Chicago: University of Chicago Press, 2003.
Pilkington, William T. *Harvey Fergusson.* Boston: Twayne, 1975.
———. "Harvey Fergusson." In *A Literary History of the American West,* edited by J. Golden Taylor and Thomas J. Lyon, 546–58. Fort Worth: Texas Christian University Press, 1987.
Pimlott, D. H. "Review of F. Mowat's *Never Cry Wolf.*" *Journal of Wildlife Management* 30 (1966): 236–37.
Pinker, Steven. *The Blank Slate: The Modern Denial of Human Nature.* New York: Penguin, 2002.
———. *The Language Instinct: How the Mind Creates Language.* New York: HarperPerennial, 1995.
Pizer, Donald. *Realism and Naturalism in Nineteenth-Century American Literature.* Rev. ed. Carbondale: Southern Illinois University Press, 1984.

———. *Twentieth-Century American Literary Naturalism: An Interpretation.* Carbondale: Southern Illinois University Press, 1982.

Plato. *The Symposium.* New York: Penguin Classics, 1999.

Plotkin, Bill. *Soulcraft: Crossing into the Mysteries of Nature and Psyche.* Novato, CA: New World Library, 2003.

Powell, Constance B., and Roger A. Powell. "The Predator-Prey Concept in Elementary Education." *Wildlife Society Bulletin* 10, no. 3 (Autumn 1982): 238–44.

Pratt, Annis. *Archetypal Patterns in Women's Fiction.* Bloomington: Indiana University Press, 1981.

Preece, Rod, ed. *Awe for the Tiger, Love for the Lamb: A Chronicle of Sensibility to Animals.* London: Routledge, 2002.

Prince, Gerald. *A Dictionary of Narratology.* Lincoln: University of Nebraska Press, 1987.

Propp, Vladimir. *Morphology of the Folktale.* 2nd ed. Austin: University of Texas Press, 1998.

Pryse, Marjorie. "Literary Regionalism and Global Capital: Nineteenth-Century U.S. Women Writers." *Tulsa Studies in Women's Literature* 23, no. 1 (2004): 65–89.

Quammen, David. "The White Tigers of Cincinnati: A Strabismic View of Zookeeping," in *Wild Thoughts from Wild Places,* 81–89. New York: Scribner, 1999.

Raffa, Jean Benedict. *Dream Theatres of the Soul: Empowering the Feminine through Jungian Dream Work.* Philadelphia: Innisfree Press, 1994.

Raglon, Rebecca. "Voicing the World: Nature Writing as Critique of the Scientific Method." *Canadian Review of American Studies* 22, no. 1 (Summer 1991): 22–32.

Rausch, R. A. "Wolf and Wolverine-Wolf Summer Food Habits and Den Studies (July 1, 1968, to June 30, 1969)." Juneau: Alaska Department of Fish and Game, 1969. 3.

Ream, R. R., M. W. Fairchild, A. J. Blakesley, and D. K. Boyd. "First Wolf Den in Western U.S. in Recent History." *Northwestern Naturalist* 70 (1989): 39–40.

Rein-Hagen, Mark, Robert Hatch, and Bill Bridges, designers. *Werewolf: The Apocalypse.* 2nd ed. Stone Mountain, GA: White Wolf Game Studio, 1994.

Reynolds, Michael. *Hemingway's Reading, 1910–1940: An Inventory.* Princeton University Press, 1981.

———. *The Young Hemingway.* Oxford, UK: Basil Blackwell, 1986.

Riley, Carroll J. "The Makah Indians: A Study of Political and Economic Organization." *Ethnohistory* 15, no. 1 (Winter 1968): 57–95.

Robbins, Jim. "Hunting Habits of Yellowstone Wolves Change Ecological Balance." *New York Times,* October 18, 2005.

Roberts, Brian R. "Predators in the 'Glades: A Signifying Animal Tale in Zora Neale Hurston's *Their Eyes Were Watching God.*" *Southern Quarterly* 31, no. 1 (Fall 2002): 39–50.

Roberts, Catherine. *The Scientific Conscience: Reflections on the Modern Biologist and Humanism.* New York: George Braziller, 1967.

Robin, P. Ansell. *Animal Lore in English Literature.* London: Folcroft, 1970.

Robisch, S. K. "The Trapper Mystic: Werewolves in *The Crossing.*" In *Myth, Legend, Dust:*

Critical Responses to Cormac McCarthy, edited and with an introduction by Rick Wallach, 288–92. Manchester, UK: Manchester University Press, 2000.

Rogers, L. L., and L. D. Mech. "Interactions of Wolves and Black Bears in Northeastern Minnesota." *Journal of Mammalogy* 62, no. 2 (1981): 434–36.

Rogers, Pattiann. "Animals and People: The Human Heart in Conflict with Itself," in *Eating Bread and Honey,* 31–38. Minneapolis: Milkweed, 1997.

Rogers, Spencer L. *The Human Skull: Its Mechanics, Measurements, and Variations.* Springfield, IL: Charles C. Thomas, 1984.

Róheim, Géza. "Fairy Tale and Dream: 'Little Red Riding Hood.'" In *Little Red Riding Hood: A Casebook,* edited by Alan Dundes, 159–67. Madison: University of Wisconsin Press, 1989.

Roosevelt, Theodore. *Hunting the Grisly and Other Sketches.* New York: G.P. Putnam's Sons, 1900.

———. *"Hunting Trips of a Ranchman" and "The Wilderness Hunter."* With an introduction by Stephen E. Ambrose. New York: Modern Library, 1996.

Roper, Donna C., ed. *Protohistoric Pawnee Hunting in the Nebraska Sand Hills: Archeological Investigations at Two Sites in the Calamus Reservoir.* OMB No. 0704-0188. Washington, DC: U.S. Department of the Interior, Bureau of Reclamation, Great Plains Region, January 1989.

Roszak, Theodore, Mary E. Gomes, and Allen D. Kanner, eds. *Ecopsychology: Restoring the Earth, Healing the Mind.* San Francisco: Sierra Club, 1995.

Rugo, Mariève. "In the Season of Wolves and Names," in *Fields of Vision.* University: University of Alabama Press, 1983.

Sacks, Sheldon, ed. *On Metaphor.* Chicago: University of Chicago Press, 1979.

Sands, Donald B., ed. *The History of Reynard the Fox.* Cambridge, MA: Harvard University Press, 1960.

Savage, Candace. *Bird Brains: The Intelligence of Crows, Ravens, Magpies, and Jays.* San Francisco: Sierra Club, 1997.

———. *Wolves.* San Francisco: Sierra Club, 1988.

Sawyer-Lauçanno, Christopher. *An Invisible Spectator: A Biography of Paul Bowles.* London: Bloomsbury, 1989.

Scanlan, James J., trans. *Albert the Great: Man and the Beasts. De Animalibus, Books 22–26.* Binghamton, NY: Medieval and Renaissance Texts and Studies, 1987.

Schach, Paul. "Russian Wolves in Folktales and Literature of the Plains: A Question of Origins." *Great Plains Quarterly* 3, no. 2 (1983): 67–78.

Schama, Simon. *Landscape and Memory.* New York: Vintage, 1995.

Schoolcraft, Henry. *The Myth of Hiawatha and Other Oral Legends, Mythologic and Allegoric, of the North American Indians.* Philadelphia: Lippincott, 1856.

Schullery, Paul. *Searching for Yellowstone: Ecology and Wonder in the Last Wilderness.* Boston: Houghton Mifflin, 1997.

———. *The Yellowstone Wolf: A Guide and Sourcebook.* 1996. Reprint, Norman: University of Oklahoma Press, 2003.

———. Interview. Yellowstone National Park Headquarters, March 7, 2004.

Schultz, Ronald N., and Pamela C. Wilson. "Territorial Marking by Lone Male Gray Wolves." *Canadian Field-Naturalist* 116, no. 2 (2002): 311–13.

Scieszka, Jon; Lane Smith, illus. *The True Story of the 3 Little Pigs: By A. Wolf.* New York: Viking Kestrel, 1989.

Scigaj, Leonard M. *The Poetry of Ted Hughes: Form and Imagination.* Iowa City: University of Iowa Press, 1986.

Schwartz-Salant, Nathan. *Jung on Alchemy.* Encountering Jung series. Princeton, NJ: Princeton University Press, 1995.

Scully, Matthew. *Dominion: The Power of Man, the Suffering of Animals, and the Call to Mercy.* New York: St. Martin's, 2003.

Seal, U. S., and A. W. Erickson. "Phencyclidine Immobilization of the Carnivora and Other Mammals." *Federal Proceedings of the Symposium on Laboratory Animals and Anesthesia* 28 (1969): 1410–19.

Sebeok, Thomas A. *Essays in Zoosemiotics.* Monograph Series of the Toronto Semiotic Circle, no. 5. Toronto: Victoria College, University of Toronto, 1990.

———. *Perspectives on Zoosemiotics.* The Hague: Mouton, 1972.

———, ed. *Animal Communication: Techniques of Study and Results of Research.* Bloomington: Indiana University Press, 1968.

———. *How Animals Communicate.* Bloomington: Indiana University Press, 1977.

———. *The Tell-Tale Sign: A Survey of Semiotics.* Lisse, Netherlands: Peter de Ridder, 1975.

Sebeok, Thomas A., and Jean Umiker-Sebeok, eds. *Biosemiotics: The Semiotic Web 1991.* Berlin: Mouton de Gruyter, 1992.

Segal, Robert A. *Theorizing about Myth.* Amherst: University of Massachusetts Press, 1999.

Sendak, Maurice. *Where the Wild Things Are.* New York: HarperCollins, 1988.

Serpell, J., ed. *The Domestic Dog, Its Evolution, Behaviour, and Interactions with People.* Cambridge, UK: Cambridge University Press, 1995.

Servin, Jorge. "Duration and Frequency of Chorus Howling of the Mexican Wolf (*Canis lupus baileyi*)." *Acta Zoologica Mexicana,* n.s., 80 (2000): 223–31.

Seton, Ernest Thompson. "Lobo, King of the Currumpaw," in *Wild Animals I Have Known.* 1926. Reprint, New York: Dover, 2000. 13–44.

Setterburg, Fred. "Roughing the Truth with Mark Twain." *High Plains Literary Review* 8, no. 1 (1993): 35–62.

Shakespeare, William. *Macbeth.* In *The Riverside Shakespeare,* edited by G. Blakemore Evans, 1355–90. Boston: Houghton Mifflin, 1974.

Sharpe, Virginia Ashby, Brian G. Norton, and Strachan Donnelley, eds. *Wolves and Human Communities: Biology, Politics, and Ethics.* Washington, DC: Island Press, 2001.

Shelley, Mary. *Frankenstein.* Norton Critical Edition, edited by J. Paul Hunter. New York: W. W. Norton, 1996.

Shelley, Percy. *Adonais.* 1821. Reprinted as *Shelley's Adonais: A Critical Edition,* edited by Anthony D. Knerr. New York: Columbia University Press, 1984.

Shepherd, Allen. "The Way of the Road, Part II: Cormac McCarthy's *The Crossing*." *New England Review* 17, no. 2 (1995): 171–75.

Sherman, Stephen. "Was Your Dog Once a Wolf?" *Popular Science Monthly,* March, 1930, 13–16.

Shippey, Tom. *J. R. R. Tolkien: Author of the Century.* Boston: Houghton Mifflin, 2001.

Sidowski, J. B. "Psychopathological Consequences of Induced Social Helplessness during Infancy." In *Experimental Psychopathology: Recent Research and Theory,* edited by H. D. Kimmel, 231–48. New York: Academic Press, 1971.

Silko, Leslie Marmon. *Ceremony.* New York: Penguin, 1977.

Silverman, Kenneth, ed. *Selected Letters of Cotton Mather.* Baton Rouge: Louisiana State University Press, 1971.

Slotkin, Richard. *Regeneration through Violence: The Mythology of the American Frontier, 1600–1860.* 1973. Reprint, New York: HarperCollins, 1996.

Smith, Douglas W. Untitled talk. Yellowstone Association Institute, Yellowstone National Park, March 5, 2004.

Smith, Douglas W., and Gary Ferguson. *Decade of the Wolf: Returning the Wild to Yellowstone.* Guilford, CT: Lyons Press, 2005.

Smith, Henry Nash. *Virgin Land: The American West as Symbol and Myth.* Cambridge, MA: Harvard University Press, 1950.

Smith, Kirby F. "An Historical Study of the Werewolf in Literature." *Publications of the Modern Language Association* 9, no. 1 (1894): 1–42.

Smith, Roland. *Journey of the Red Wolf.* New York: Cobblehill, 1996.

Smith, Wayne. *Thor.* New York: Ballantine, 1992.

Snively, Susan. "Wolves." *Kenyon Review* 2, no. 3 (Summer 1980): 79–87.

Sokal, Alan. "A Physicist Experiments with Cultural Studies." *Lingua Franca* (May/June 1996): 62–64.

Sokal, Alan, and Jean Bricmont. *Fashionable Nonsense: Postmodern Intellectuals' Abuse of Science.* New York: Picador, 1999.

South, Malcolm. *Mystical and Fabulous Creatures: A Sourcebook and Research Guide.* Westport, CT: Greenwood Press, 1987.

Spears, James E. "Of Mules and Men." *Tennessee Folklore Society Bulletin* 58, no. 1 (1996): 1–48.

Spencer, Herbert. "The Data of Ethics." In *The Principles of Ethics.* Part 1 of 2, 1897. Revised and reprinted in *A System of Synthetic Philosophy,* vol. 9 of 10. 6th ed. London: Williams and Norgate, 1904.

———. *First Principles.* 1862. Revised and reprinted in *A System of Synthetic Philosophy,* vol. 1 of 10. 6th ed. London: Williams and Norgate, 1904.

Spiess, Arthur E. *Reindeer and Caribou Hunters: An Archaeological Study.* New York: Academic Press, 1979.

Spivak, Guayatri Chakravorty. "Can the Subaltern Speak?" In *The Post-Colonial Studies Reader,* edited by Bill Ashcroft, Gareth Griffiths, and Helen Tiffin, 24–28. London: Routledge, 1995.

Stegner, Wallace. "The Wolfer," in *Collected Stories of Wallace Stegner.* New York: Wings, 1994.

Steiger, Brad. *The Werewolf Book: The Encyclopedia of Shape-Shifting Beings.* Canton, MI: Visible Ink Press, 1999.

Steinbeck, John. *Of Mice and Men.* New York: Covici-Friede, 1937.

Steinhart, Peter. *The Company of Wolves.* New York: Vintage, 1995.

Stephenson, R. O. "Characteristics of Wolf Den Sites." Alaska Federal Aid to Wildlife Restoration. Juneau: Alaska Department of Fish and Game, 1974.

Stieber, Tamar. "Accord Could Help Save Mexican Wolf." *Albuquerque Journal* (May 22, 1993): 1, 3.

Stoeckel, Mark. "Taxonomy, DNA, and the Barcode of Life." *BioScience* 53, no. 9 (September 2003): 1–3.

Stone, Christopher. *Should Trees Have Standing? Toward Legal Rights for Natural Objects.* Los Altos, CA: W. Kaufmann, 1974.

Streiber, Whitley. *Wolf of Shadows.* New York: Knopf, 1985.

Strong, Pauline Turner. *Captive Selves, Captivating Others: The Politics and Poetics of Colonial American Captivity Narratives.* Boulder, CO: Westview Press, 1999.

Sturgis, Russell. *A Dictionary of Architecture and Building, Biographical, Historical, and Descriptive.* New York: Macmillan, 1901.

Sundquist, Eric. "Realism and Regionalism." In *The Columbia Literary History of the United States,* edited by Emory Elliott, 501–24. New York: Columbia University Press, 1988.

Sugg, Katherine. "Multicultural Masculinities and the Border Romance in John Sayles's *Lone Star* and Cormac McCarthy's Border Trilogy." *CR: New Centennial Review* 1, no. 3 (Winter 2001): 117–54.

Svee, Gary. *Spirit Wolf.* New York: Simon and Schuster, 1987.

Swan, Edith E. "Laguna Symbolic Geography and Silko's *Ceremony.*" *American Indian Quarterly* 12, no. 3 (Summer 1988): 229–49.

Swimme, Brian, and Thomas Berry. *The Universe Story: From the Primordial Flaring Forth to the Ecozoic Era—A Celebration of the Unfolding of the Cosmos.* New York: HarperCollins, 1994.

Swinburne, Stephen R.; Jim Brandenburg, photog. *Once a Wolf: How Wildlife Biologists Fought to Bring Back the Gray Wolf.* Boston: Houghton Mifflin, 2001.

Tafoya, Eduardo. "Group Wants to See Lobo Wandering Southern NM Again." *Santa Fe New Mexican,* February 1, 1987.

Tall Mountain, Mary. "The Last Wolf." In *Listen to the Night: Poems to the Animal Spirits of Mother Earth,* edited by Ben Clarke, 62–63. San Francisco: Freedom Voices, 1995.

Tatlock, J. S. P. "Geoffrey of Monmouth's *Vita Merlini.*" *Speculum* 43, no. 3 (1943): 265–87.

Taylor, Alan. "'Stopping the Progress of Rogues and Deceivers': A White Indian Recruiting Notice of 1808." *William and Mary Quarterly,* 3rd ser., 42, no. 1 (1985): 90–103.

Taylor, Graham. *The New Deal and American Indian Tribalism: The Administration of the Indian Reorganization Act, 1934–1945.* Lincoln: University of Nebraska Press, 1980.

Telfer, E. S., and J. P. Kelsall. "Adaptation of Some Large North American Mammals for Survival in Snow." *Ecology* 65 (1984): 1828–34.

Terrell, Stephen W. "The Wolf Monster." *Santa Fe Reporter,* March 21, 1984, 3, 7.

Thacker, Robert. "The Plains, Parkman, and the Oregon Trail." *Nevada Historical Quarterly* 28, no. 4 (1985): 262–70.

Theburge, John B. *Wolf Country: Eleven Years Tracking the Algonquin Wolves.* Toronto: McClelland and Stewart, 1998.

Thiel, Richard P. *The Timber Wolf in Wisconsin: The Death and Life of a Majestic Predator.* Madison: University of Wisconsin Press, 1993.

———. *Keepers of the Wolves: The Early Years of Wolf Recovery in Wisconsin.* Madison: University of Wisconsin Press, 2001.

Thomas, Elizabeth Marshall. *The Animal Wife.* New York: Random House, 1992.

———. *The Hidden Life of Dogs.* Boston: Houghton Mifflin, 1993.

———. *Reindeer Moon.* Boston: Houghton Mifflin, 1987.

Thomas, Lewis. "Crickets, Bats, Cats, and Chaos." 1992. Reprinted in *The Best American Essays 1993,* edited by Susan Sontag, 355–61. New York: Ticknor and Fields, 1993.

Thompkins, Jane. *West of Everything: The Inner Life of Westerns.* New York: Oxford University Press, 1992.

Thompson, Bruce. *Looking at the Wolf: Biology, Behavior, Biases.* Boulder, CO: Roberts Rinehart and the Teton Science School, 1987.

Thompson, G. R. *Poe's Fiction: Romantic Irony in the Gothic Tales.* Madison: University of Wisconsin Press, 1973.

———, ed. *The Gothic Imagination: Essays in Dark Romanticism.* Pullman: Washington State University Press, 1974.

———. *Circumscribed Eden of Dreams: Dreamvision and Nightmare in Poe's Early Poetry.* Baltimore: Edgar Allan Poe Society, 1984.

———. "Romantic Arabesque, Contemporary Theory, and Postmodernism: The Example of Poe's Narrative." *ESQ* 35 (1989): 163–271.

Thompson, G. R., and Eric Carl Link. *Neutral Ground: New Traditionalism and the American Romance Controversy.* Baton Rouge: Louisiana State University Press, 1999.

Tibbals, Kate Watkins. "Elements of Magic in the Romance of William of Palerne." *Modern Philology* 1, no. 3 (January 1904): 355–71.

Topsell, Edward. *The History of Four-Footed Beasts and Serpents and Insects* (1658). London: Routledge, 1967.

Torbenson, Michael, Odin Langsjoen, and Arthur Aufderheide. "Human Remains from McKinstry Mound Two." *Plains Anthropologist* 41, no. 155 (1996): 71–92.

Towery, Twyman L. *The Wisdom of Wolves: Nature's Way to Organizational Success.* Brentwood, TN: Wessex House, 2000.

Turbak, Gary; Lawrence Ormsby, illus. *Mountain Animals in Danger.* Flagstaff, AZ: Northland, 1994.

Turner, Mark. *The Literary Mind.* New York: Oxford University Press, 1996.

Twain, Mark. *Roughing It.* 1869. Reprinted in *The Unabridged Mark Twain,* edited by Law-rence Teacher, vol. 2, 551–900. 3 vols. Philadelphia: Running Press, 1979.

Underwood, Paula. *Who Speaks for Wolf: A Native American Learning Story.* 2nd. rev. ed. San Anselmo, CA: Learning Way, 1991.

U.S. Congress, House Committee on Resources. HR 2275: "A Bill to Reauthorize and Amend the Endangered Species Act of 1973." *Hearings.* 104th Congress, 1st sess. Serial No. 104–37. Washington, DC: Government Printing Office: September 20, 1995.

Van Ballenberghe, V., and A. W. Erickson. "A Wolf Pack Kills Another Wolf." *American Wildlife Natural Resources Conference Proceedings* 90, no. 2 (1973): 490–93.

Varley, J. D., and W. G. Brewster, eds. *Wolves for Yellowstone? A Report to the United States Congress.* 4 vols. Yellowstone National Park: National Park Service, 1992.

Victor, Frances Fuller. *The River of the West.* Hartford, CT: R. W. Bliss, 1870.

Viderman, S. "The Analytic Space: Meaning and Problems." *Psychoanalytic Quarterly* 48 (1979): 257–91.

Vilà, Carlos, Peter Savolainen, Jesus E. Maldonado, Isabel R. Amorim, John E. Rice, Rod-ney L. Honeycutt, Keith A. Crandall, Joakim Lundeberg, and Robert K. Wayne. "Mul-tiple and Ancient Origins of the Domestic Dog." *Science,* June 13, 1997, 1687–89.

Vinaver, Eugène. *The Works of Sir Thomas Malory.* 3 vols. 2nd ed. Oxford, UK: Clarendon Press, 1967.

Wade, Mason. *Francis Parkman: Heroic Historian.* New York: Viking, 1942.

Wallner, Astrid. "The Role of Fox, Lynx, and Wolf in Mythology." *KORA Bericht* 3 (April 1998): 31–33.

Warner, Marina. *Six Myths of Our Time: Little Angels, Little Monsters, Beautiful Beasts, and More.* New York: Vintage, 1994.

Warren, Ed, and Lorraine Warren. *Werewolf: A True Story of Demonic Possession.* New York: St. Martin's Press, 1993.

Warren, Karen J., and Nisvan Erkal, eds. *Ecofeminism: Women, Culture, Nature.* Blooming-ton: Indiana University Press, 1997.

Wasiolek, Edward. "Jack London." *American Literature* 37, no. 2 (May 1965): 219–20.

Wayne, R. K. "Molecular Evolution of the Dog Family." *Trends in Genetics* 9 (1993): 218–24.

——. "On the Use of Morphological and Molecular Genetic Characters to Investigate Species Status." *Conservation Biology* 6, no. 4 (1992): 590–92.

Wayne, R. K., N. Lehman, M. W. Allard, and R. L. Honeycutt. "Mitochondrial DNA Vari-ability of the Gray Wolf: Genetic Consequences of Population Decline and Habitat Fragmentation." *Conservation Biology* 6, no. 4 (1992): 559–69.

Weaver, J. L., C. Arvidson, and P. Wood. "Two Wolves, *Canis lupus,* Killed by a Moose, *Alces alces,* in Jasper National Park, Alberta." *Canadian Field-Naturalist* 106, no. 1 (1992): 126–27.

Webster, John. *The Duchess of Malfi.* Manchester, UK: Manchester University Press, 1997.

Weedon, Chris. *Feminist Practice and Poststructuralist Theory.* 2nd ed. Oxford, UK: Black-well, 1996.

Weinberg, Stephen. *The First Three Minutes: A Modern View of the Origin of the Universe.* 1977. Reprinted, New York: Basic Books, 1993.

Wellman, Manly Wade. "The Horror Undying." *Weird Tales,* May 1936, n.p. Reprinted as "The Undead Soldier" in *Sin's Doorway and Other Ominous Entrances,* vol. 4 of 5 in *The Selected Stories of Manly Wade Wellman,* 7–16. Portland, OR: Nightshade Books, 2003.

Welsh, James M. "Man and Nature, People and Other animals; Rawlings, Disney, Mowat, and Wolf: Environmental Memoirs into Film." *Philological Papers* (West Virginia University) 37 (1991): 209–15.

Westerkamp, Marilyn J. *Women and Religion in Early America, 1600–1850: The Puritan and Evangelical Traditions.* New York: Routledge, 2005.

Wetmore, A. "The Gray Fox Attracted by a Crow Call." *Journal of Mammalogy* 33, no. 2 (1952): 244–45.

White, David Gordon. *Myths of the Dog-Man.* Chicago: University of Chicago Press, 1991.

White, Richard. "The Current Weirdness in the West." *Western Historical Quarterly* 28 (1997): 5–16.

White, T. H., ed. and trans. *The Bestiary: A Book of Beasts.* New York: G. P. Putnam's Sons, 1960.

"White Sands Officials against Release on Missile Site." *Santa Fe New Mexican,* February 17, 1990.

Whole Earth. "The Tapestry of Possibility—Author Diane di Prima—Interview." Fall 1999. http://www.findarticles.com/p/articles/mi_moGER/is_1999_Fall/ai_56457596.

Wieck, Stewart, ed. *When Will You Rage? A Werewolf: The Apocalypse Anthology.* Stone Mountain, GA: White Wolf, 1994.

Wilcox, Earl. "'The Kipling of the Klondike': Naturalism in London's Early Fiction." *Jack London Newsletter* 6 (1973): 1–12.

Wilder, Laura Ingalls. *By the Shores of Silver Lake.* 1939. Reprint, New York: Penguin, 1968.

——. *Little House on the Prairie.* 1935. Reprint, New York: Penguin, 1964.

Wilhelmus, Tom. "Ranches of Isolation." *Hudson Review* 48, no. 1 (1995): 145–49.

Wilkinson, Charles F. *Crossing the Next Meridian: Land, Water, and the Future of the West.* Washington, DC: Island Press, 1992.

Willkomm, S. "Quantitative Analysis of the Ontogeny of Play Behaviour in Canid Hybrids." *Ethology* 86, no. 4 (1990): 287–302.

Willems, Robert A. "The Wolf-Dog Hybrid: Overview of a Controversial Animal." *Animal Welfare Information Center Newsletter* 5, no. 4 (Winter 1994/1995): 1.

Williams, Jeffery, and Michael Berube, eds. *Critics at Work: Interviews 1993–2003.* New York: New York University Press, 2004.

Wilson, Edward O. *Biophilia: The Human Bond with Other Species.* Cambridge, MA: Harvard University Press, 1984.

Wirtjes, Hanneke, ed. *The Middle English Physiologus.* Oxford, UK: Oxford University Press, 1991.

Wise, Steven M. *Rattling the Cage: Toward Legal Rights for Animals.* New York: Perseus, 2000.

Wolf, Tom. "Wild Things: Tracking the Lobo." *Santa Fe Reporter,* February 26, 1991, 17, 19.

Wolff, Patricia. "Wolf's Survival Depends on New Human Attitude." *Santa Fe New Mexican,* August 20, 1995.

Wolosky, Shira. "An 'Other' Negative Theology: On Derrida's 'How to Avoid Speaking: Denials.'" *Poetics Today* 19, no. 2 (Summer 1998): 261–80.

Wood, Daniel. *Wolves.* Wildlife Series. Vancouver: Whitecap Books, 1994.

Wood, Gordon S. "The Bigger the Beast the Better." *American History Illustrated* 17, no. 8 (1982): 30–37.

Wyman, Walker D.; Helen Wyman, illus. *Wisconsin and North Country Wolf and Bear Stories: Seventy-five Stories Told by Pioneer Settlers, Lumberjacks, and Other Yarn Spinners.* River Falls: University of Wisconsin–River Falls Press, 1984.

Youmans, Marly. *The Wolf Pit.* New York: Farrar, Straus and Giroux, 2001.

Young, Stanley P. *Last of the Loners.* New York: Macmillan, 1970.

Young, Stanley P., and Edward A. Goldman. *The Wolves of North America.* Part 1: *Their History, Habits, Economic Status, and Control.* Part 2: *Classification of Wolves.* 1944. Reprinted, New York: Dover, 1964.

Zimen, Erik. *The Wolf: A Species in Danger.* New York: Delacorte, 1978.

Ziolkowski, Jan M. "A Fairy Tale from before Fairy Tales: Egbert of Liège's 'De puella a lupellis seruata' and the Medieval Background of 'Little Red Riding Hood.'" *Speculum* 67 (1992): 549–75.

Zipes, Jack. *The Trials and Tribulations of Little Red Riding Hood.* 2nd ed. New York: Routledge, 1993.

——, ed. *The Oxford Companion to Fairy Tales: The Western Fairy Tale Tradition from Medieval to Modern.* Oxford, UK: Oxford University Press, 2000.

Senses, wolf, 98, 113, 115–16; represented in computer game, 276; werewolf, 367. *See also* Anatomy, wolf

Seton, Ernest Thompson, 30, 34, 61, 112, 281, 393–94, 404; his "Lobo, King of the Currumpaw," 398, 404; his *Wild Animals I Have Known,* 36

Sexton, Anne: her "Red Riding Hood," 265

Shadow, Jungian, 75, 257; ghost wolf as, 7, 17, 19, 21, 22, 181, 183, 187, 193, 198–201, 331, 361, 400; The Steppenwolf, 307; werewolves and, 211, 219

Shakespeare, William, 17, 231, 242

Shape-shifter, 8, 11, 12, 20, 142, 160, 205, 206, 209–12, 218–20, 225–27, 280, 366, 403; in Applegate, 248; cyber-, 279; and masks, 232, 237, 248. *See also* Twinning; Werewolf

Sharpe, Virginia Ashby, Brian G. Norton, and Strachan Donnelley: their *Wolves and Human Communities,* 65

Sheep, 45, 95, 232, 265, 267, 268, 269, 282; dall, 37, 39, 111; sheep's clothing, 169, 229

Shelley, Mary: her *Frankenstein,* 182–83, 345

Shelley, Percy: his *Adonais,* 106

She-wolf, 29–30, 102; in di Prima, 354–57; as gender construct, 8; harlot and, 10, 225, 286, 353; in McCarthy, 12, 375–97, 406, 408, 410–11; as mother, 9, 10, 12, 225, 282, 353, 382; in Seton, 404; were-wolf as, 215, 345, 366–67

Shippey, Tom, 128

Sierra Club, 51, 74, 274, 402–3

Silko, Leslie Marmon, 207; her *Ceremony,* 244–45; her "Story from Bear Country," 358

Singe, J. A. L., 281. *See also* Amala and Kamala

Sirius, 150–55; Alpha Canis Majoris, 151; Sereos, 150, 155; Skiritióhuts, 152; Dog star, 150; Wolf star, 152

Skidi Pawnee, 152–55, 165, 411. *See also* Pawnee; Myth

Skinwalkers, 207, 209, 244–46, 403, 408. *See also* Hillerman, Tony; Silko, Leslie Marmon; Werewolf

Skull/skeleton/bones, 95, 112, 237, 242, 245, 332, 371, 372, 374, 376, 414; craniometry, 372. *See also* Anatomy, wolf

sleigh/sledge chased by wolves, 21–23, 59, 97, 260, 267; as wolf transport to Yellowstone, 79

Slotkin, Richard, 157–58

Smith, Douglas, and Gary Ferguson, 66, 82, 362; their *Decade of the Wolf,* 77, 81

Smith, Kirby: his "An Historical Study of the Werewolf in Literature," 224–25

Smith, Wayne: his *Thor,* 215, 217

Snively, Susan: her "Wolves," 181

Snow, wolves in, 75, 95, 97–98, 106, 108, 115, 298, 377

Social constructivism, 200, 294 339–40. *See also* Academic humanities; Poststructuralism

Social Darwinism, 20, 103, 289–90, 312. *See also* London, Jack; Spencer, Herbert

Socialization, 38, 42, 49, 68, 99, 105, 116, 274, 311, 343, 349, 360, 380–81, 382, 411. *See also* Domestication; Habituation

Sontag, Susan, 33, 342

South, Malcolm: his *Mythical and Fabulous Creatures,* 277

South Dakota, 54; outlaw wolves in, 399

Species, 4, 7, 24, 49, 92–94, 114, 148, 170, 259, 269, 283, 327, 409; vs. individual behavior, 15–16, 21, 26, 35, 44, 75–76, 91, 100, 126, 197–98, 200, 250–51, 283, 288, 393, 400; interspecies exchange, 26, 55, 105, 112–13, 118–21, 160–61, 183, 189, 200, 209, 237, 272, 280, 281, 341–42, 388, 406; invasive, 54, 412; London and, 314, 322–23; Murie and, 37–39; Social Darwinism and, 103–4; subspecies, 78, 92–93, 107, 372–75. *See also Canis lupus;* Taxonomy

Spencer, Herbert, 20, 288, 290; in London, 302–7, 314–15. *See also* Social Darwinism

Spirit, 234, 240, 244, 255; of wilderness, 6, 317; of "Wolf" 133–35. *See also* Ghost wolf; Symbol, wolf as; Totem

Stableford, Brian: his *Werewolves of London,* 217

Stegner, Wallace: his "The Wolfer," 338, 398

Steinhart, Peter: his *The Company of Wolves,* 3, 33, 35, 127, 139, 391; in Evans, 330

Streiber, Whitley: his *Warday,* 274; his *The Wolfen,* 216: his *Wolf of Shadows,* 273–75, 347